C++
Effective Object-Oriented Software Construction

Concepts, Principles, Industrial Strategies, and Practices

Kayshav Dattatri

To join a Prentice Hall PTR internet mailing list, point to
http://www.prenhall.com/mail_lists/

Prentice Hall PTR
Upper Saddle River, New Jersey 07458
http://www.prenhall.com

Library of Congress Cataloging in Publication Data

Dattatri, Kayshav.
    C++: effective object-oriented software construction: concepts,
    principles, industrial strategies, and practices / by Kayshav
    Dattatri.
        p. cm
    Includes bibliographical references and index.
    ISBN 0-13-104118-5
    1. Object-oriented programming (Computer science) 2. C++
    (Computer program language) I. Title
    QA76.64.D37   1996
    005.13'3—dc20   96-41928
                                                CIP

Editorial/production supervision: *Nicholas Radhuber*
Manufacturing manager: *Alexis Heydt*
Acquisitions editor: *Paul Becker*
Marketing manager: *Dan Rush*
Editorial assistant: *Maureen Diana*
Cover design: *Rod Hernandez*
Cover design supervisor: *Jerry Votta*

© 1997 by Prentice Hall PTR
Prentice-Hall, Inc.
A Simon & Schuster Company
Upper Saddle River, New Jersey 07458

Prentice Hall books are widely used by corporations and government agencies
for training, marketing, and resale.

The Publisher offers discounts on this book when ordered in bulk quantities.
For more information, contact:
        Corporate Sales Department
        Phone: 800-382-3419 Fax: 201-236-7141
        E-mail: corpsales@prenhall.com
        Or write: Prentice Hall PTR
        Corporate Sales Department
        1 Lake St.
        Upper Saddle River, NJ 07458

All product names mentioned herein are the trademarks of their respective owners.

Printed in the United States of America
10 9 8 7 6 5 4 3 2 1

ISBN 0-13-104118-5

Prentice-Hall International (UK) Limited, *London*
Prentice-Hall of Australia Pty. Limited, *Sydney*
Prentice-Hall Canada Inc., *Toronto*
Prentice-Hall Hispanoamericana, S.A., *Mexico*
Prentice-Hall of India Private Limited, *New Delhi*
Prentice-Hall of Japan, Inc., *Tokyo*
Simon & Schuster Asia Pte. Ltd., *Singapore*
Editora Prentice-Hall do Brasil, Ltda., *Rio de Janeiro*

Contents

5   The Inheritance Concept   171

Part II: Using Object-Oriented Programming Effectively

11   Mastering Data Abstraction   575

Foreword

Object-oriented programming provides developers with powerful concepts to attack the growing complexity of today's systems. Unfortunately, it is also possible to write overly complex object-oriented programs. The feature richness of C++ makes that even easier. In fact, I've seen C++ programs that look more like compiler test suites than solutions to real problems. This is usually not a problem for smaller systems, but as your system grows, you can afford less and less extraneous complexity.

Yet, it would be unfair to blame C++ for this complexity problem. There are nice and elegant C++ programs. To be successful with C++, a developer must use its features judiciously. You have to understand not only the semantics and performance costs of each feature but also its costs in terms of "human understanding." You need to know its benefits, its shortcomings, and its perils.

Kayshav Dattatri has the experience to deliver these insights. I've known Kayshav from the early days of C++. We first met at the 1990 USENIX C++ conference, back when many papers presented at that conference were from AT&T-types, probably half of the participants were AT&T-types, and the program committee was packed with AT&T-types. Later we both found ourselves working for Taligent. People there were applying C++ on a huge scale, pushing it to its limits. It was an ideal environment in which to experience the issues of practical software construction with C++.

Those illuminating years really shine through this book. The practices suggested are well grounded in years of C++ experience. Kayshav isn't satisfied explaining object-oriented concepts in general and C++ language features in theory; he also covers important practices regarding effective use of inheritance, mix-in classes, template classes, and exceptions; issues in template instantiation, shared libraries, thread safety; and a host of others.

This book introduces C++ and object-oriented programming from the ground up. However, I'm sure that experienced C++ programmers will gain new and practical insights just as surely as newcomers will.

Erich Gamma
Head of Object Technology
IFA Consulting

Preface

Now that Object-Oriented Software Development is here to stay and is the preferred way to develop software, there is an increasing demand for good object-oriented software developers, designers, and system architects. To be successful in the world of object-oriented programming (OOP) one has to unlearn quite a few of the habits acquired from years of procedure-oriented programming and learn some new ways of looking at problems. Object-oriented technology (OOT) is the wave of today.

Object-Oriented Programming requires a thorough understanding of some fundamental paradigms, or concepts. Understanding these paradigms is essential to building a strong foundation in the OO software world. Any language that supports OOP must support these fundamental paradigms. In other words, learning effective OOP is simply learning a set of powerful paradigms that are supported by many languages like Eiffel, Smalltalk, C++, Java, etc.

Learning the syntax of a language that supports OOP is not the same as learning the concepts of OOP. One might be a *guru* of C++ or Java without any knowledge whatsoever of the basic OOP paradigms. On the other hand, anyone who imbibes the fundamental concepts of OOP will be able to use those concepts effectively with any language that supports OOP. Moreover, he or she would also know when to use a particular concept. As an analogy, anyone who has mastered the concept of a linked list will find it elementary to implement a linked list in Pascal, C, or Modula-2. If you know how to swim, you can swim in a lake, pond, or pool. The language is just a vehicle that helps in reaching the final goal.

The first goal of this book is to drive home the essential concepts and principles of Object-Oriented Programming. This is covered in Part I: Concepts, Practices, and Applications.

Since C++ is becoming increasingly popular (because of its rich feature set, strict static type checking, and strong support for writing industrial strength software) one ideally should be proficient in both C++ and OOP concepts. Well, just learning C++ syntax isn't much fun; we would like to pursue a much higher goal. In order to exploit the full potential of OOP with C++, there are a number of special patterns, techniques, and tricks that seasoned object-oriented software developers employ to *turbo charge* their programs. There are many such time-tested techniques currently being used in the C++ world. Also, at times it helps to know why certain features are the way they are in a language. It gives the programmer a better understanding of the language (and sometimes more respect for the designers of the language). It also helps in using the language more efficiently. The latter chapters in Part I cover those topics. Examples on many powerful C++ strategies and tactics are presented throughout the book.

Learning OOP concepts is just one milestone, but that's not the ultimate destination of any programmer/designer. One should be able to apply these concepts to problems in one's domain or area of expertise. A financial planner might want to develop an object framework to manage personal finances and a department store might build an application to manage its inventory. But it is not a straightforward task to apply OOP principles to all these diverse areas. Solving toy textbook examples might be trivial, but conquering domain-specific problems and building systems is no cakewalk. It helps to learn from specific examples from specialized domains (for example, file systems, car dealership management, desktop publishing, flight scheduling system, etc.) I'm definitely not knowledgeable in any of these areas and most readers may not find them very interesting because of their unfamiliarity with them. This is a classic problem authors face when writing about object-oriented design. However, there are certain rules of thumb that are useful to any software professional trying to solve complex problems, independent of the problem domain. One should know exactly when to use a butter knife or a chain saw. The second part of the book, Using Object-Oriented Programming Effectively, illustrates some advanced OOP techniques with simple examples. Powerful strategies for using OO designs effectively are presented in this section. Professional developers are not content with just learning tricks and tactics—they also would like to know the pros and cons of each technique, the alternatives, effect on portability and efficiency, and so on. All the necessary details of the various techniques have been described throughout. It is this overall knowledge that transforms a colt into a thoroughbred.

The emphasis throughout this book is on concepts and not on language syntax, although quite a few language issues are presented. Differences between C++ and other object-oriented languages are discussed for all major topics. Features from other OOP languages are compared to those in C++ to drive home concepts of OOP (and at times language design). This gives a deeper and broader picture of the OOP world. Just because the examples are coded in C++ does not mean that C++ is the only language to choose from. There are other equally good (if not better) OOP languages. It is good to gain an insight into the design goals of different languages. For readers already familiar with an OOP language other than C++, details of major concepts are first discussed from the C++ perspective, then followed by discussions of Eiffel and Smalltalk.

Beginners should read Part I first, which deals with paradigms, theories, and applications. Within Part I, chapters are organized based on relevance and the difficulty of the material. Chapter 1 is a preliminary introduction and is followed by a thorough discussion of data abstraction in Chapter 2. Brief overviews of the Unified Modeling Language and the Booch methodology can be found in Chapter 2 as well. Chapters 3 and 4 shed further light on the object model and good interface design. Inheritance is covered in all its glory in Chapters 5 and 6, followed by some simpler topics in Chapters 7 and 8. Generic programming is given its due share in Chapter 9. Finally, Chapter 10 deals with exception management. The first chapter in Part II, Chapter 11, tries to demonstrate strategies for building powerful abstractions, while Chapter 12 does the same with inheritance. Finally, Chapter 13 briefly delves into the C++ object model.

Any chapter can be read at random, but some continuity might be lost because some examples carry through from the first four chapters. Chapters in Part II stand on their own.

Throughout the book, I have avoided showing dry implementation code as much as possible to keep things focused and short. Most implementation code is quite uninteresting. Implementation code is only shown in places where it adds considerable value to the on-going discussion.

This book can be used as an introductory or advanced text on object-oriented programming and will be very useful for programmers and students who are new to OOP. The second part of the book is useful for programmers already familiar with OOP concepts. Programmers familiar with other OOP languages (other than C++) are better served reading Part I first and then concentrating on Part II. Part I of the book can serve as an introductory course on OOP for undergraduate students, and Part I and Part II together can be used for a graduate course on OOP and C++ topics.

This book assumes some rudimentary C++ syntax familiarity and some general programming experience (even classroom exposure is good enough). Some of the more complex parts of the C++ language (such as templates, exceptions, and inheritance) are covered in detail, with respect to language syntax.

Acknowledgments

This book grew from many years of teaching at the University of California Berkeley extension programs (and many companies). I am greatly indebted to hundreds of my students who participated in my courses, many of whom have become very good friends. These students allowed me to view things differently, and at times I realized that what I thought was simple was not. They have thrown many questions at me, the answers to which are in this book. They have made me aware of concepts, simple and complex, that students learning OOP/C++ often have difficulty understanding. I'm very grateful to Dr. Jack Grimes, who constantly reviewed the chapters in record time and provided many reference materials. He has been a source of inspiration for me throughout the writing of this book. Many thanks to Rajiv Maheshwari, Christine Lu, and Sumathi Kadur for reviewing the draft and their precious input. They helped eliminate many bugs and helped me to get the contents right. Thanks to Rampalli Narasimhan for his thoughtful comments. Special thanks to Dr. Erich Gamma for sharing some of his vast OO knowledge. His invaluable suggestions and insights into Smalltalk are priceless. Thanks to Dr. Brooks Applegate for introducing me to the Smalltalk world.

Special mention must be made of all my friends at Taligent, Inc. (my previous employer). They are a brilliant group of object technology experts and have given me a wealth of knowledge that is everlasting. Working with them was a pleasurable and enriching experience. In particular, thanks to David Goldsmith, the architect of the Taligent Design principles (this book follows many elements of the coding style used at Taligent).

My most sincere thanks to Narmada Iyer for her support and love. I couldn't have done it without her constant encouragement (and occasional impatience). She kept me going and guided me when I was losing track of time. Thanks for putting up with all my idiosyncrasies (and sorry for the missed vacations).

Thanks to the wonderful team at Prentice Hall, in particular, Paul Becker, for putting up with a never-ending schedule. Special thanks to Nicholas Radhuber for his patience despite my numerous revisions, additions and changes during the final phases. The final product wouldn't be what it is without his tireless efforts and dedication.

1

What Is Object-Oriented Programming?

Of late, almost everyone in the software industry seems to be attracted to the *Object-Oriented Programming* paradigm. Even managers, directors and marketing people love object technology. One gets the feeling that there is nothing better than *object-orientation*. It appears as though object-oriented software is the holy grail that everyone wants to capture. One might wonder as to what this new paradigm is and how it is different from what we have been doing for decades. Software developers might feel left out and get a feeling that their vast experience and hard-earned skills are no longer useful because of this object-oriented monster. Given all this, it might help to understand the following:

What is object-oriented software development all about?

What are its benefits?

How is it different from the traditional approach to software development?

What is its impact on our traditional software development skills?

How can one become object-oriented?

BACKGROUND

Programmers have been developing software for decades, and they have implemented very small programs to very large systems using a variety of programming languages like Algol, COBOL, Lisp, C, Pascal, etc. [A very *small program* refers to a small program,

such as the solution for towers of hanoi, the game of solitaire, a simple quicksort implementation, etc., that we write as part of some homework assignment in a course or just for
learning. These programs do not have any commercial value. They help us in learning a
new concept/language. In contrast, a *large system* refers to a software system that solves
big problems such as inventory control, word processing, hospital patient management,
weather forecasting, personal finance management, etc. Such systems involve teams of
programmers and designers working together to implement the system. And they are sold
by companies for profit. The lessons learned in designing and implementing small programs are helpful in solving big problems.] We use systems implemented using all these
languages in our daily life. We have also learned a lot from our experiences with these
languages and systems. So why should we switch to a different programming paradigm?
Well, read on. The answer should be evident after reading the next few paragraphs.

Procedure-Oriented Programming Example

Given a problem (i.e. given a verbal/written description of a problem), how would one go
about designing and implementing a solution to it using a language, such as C? The problem is split into more manageable chunks called modules. Then we design a number of
data structures that hold our data and we implement a number of functions (also called
procedures, or simply *routines*) to operate on this data. The functions would modify the
data structures, store them to file and also print them. All the knowledge about the system
is built into a set of functions. The main focus is on these functions because without them
nothing useful can be accomplished. This style of programming where the functions are
the prime focus is called **Procedure-Oriented Programming**. It is so called because of
its emphasis on procedures. It comes from thinking about the problem in terms of its functions and so is also known as the functional decomposition of the problem.

NOTE   The distinction among the terms procedure, function, subprogram, and routine
doesn't exist in C and C++. However, Pascal, Modula-2, and Eiffel use the term function
to indicate a routine that returns a computed value and the term procedure to indicate any
routine that accepts some arguments and performs an operation, but doesn't return any
value to the caller. In this book, the terms procedure, function, and routine are used interchangeably. They all have the same meaning. Programming languages like Algol, Fortran,
Pascal, and C are called procedural languages.

However, when we look at this implementation in more detail, we realize that information that is more important to us is in the data structures. What interests us most are the
values stored in those data structures that have been delegated to the back seat. The procedures that we implement are simple tools to modify these data structures. Without these
data structures, the procedures cannot do anything useful. We spend most of our time designing these procedures and pamper them with all our attention even though what's important is elsewhere. Moreover, the code in these procedures never changes in a running
program. It is the data in the different data structures that keeps changing during the lifetime of the program. In that sense, the procedures are quite uninteresting because they are
quite *static*. As a simple example, imagine a banking system where customers are allowed
to have different types of bank accounts (like savings account, checking account, and loan
account). Customers are allowed to make deposits, withdraw money, and make transfers

between accounts. If this system is implemented in C we would probably see a set of procedures like[1]

```
typedef unsigned long AccountNum;
typedef int bool;

bool MakeDeposit(AccountNum whichAccount, float amount);
float WithDraw(AccountNum whichAccount, float howmuch);
bool Transfer(AccountNum from, AccountNum to,
                       float howmuch);
```

and so on. AccountNum could just be a positive integer. We can have a simple data structure to manage our accounts:

```
// Just a plain bank account record

struct Account {
    char*      name;          /* name of account holder */
    AccountNum    accountId;
    float      balance;
    float      interestYTD;/* year to data interest */
    char       accountType;/* Savings, Checking, Loan etc */
    /* and many other details */
};
```

We could create an account for a customer by creating an instance of the Account structure by the function

```
AccountNum CreateNewAccount(const char name[], char typeOfAccount);
```

Representation of a Bank Account

This function returns the account number for the new account. When we look at this solution, it is very clear that customers are more interested in knowing how much money is in the account and how much interest it is earning than in the functions that allow them to make deposits and withdraw money. Customers view the account as a safe haven for their hard earned money. They don't really care how withdrawals are made or how the deposit is made; they only need an easy way to perform such mundane operations. But we, as programmers completely focused our attention on writing that uninteresting piece of code in the function MakeDeposit and the like and created a small data structure to manage the data. In other words, we are focusing our attention on something the customer hardly cares about. What's more, there is no special relation between customers and their bank accounts. The customer is just treated like a series of characters and numbers, and the account operations manipulate the data without any special consideration as to who owns the account and what it contains. The functions' idea of a bank account is just a number—the account number.

---

[1]Do not pay much attention to the syntax. What one needs to follow is the concept of procedures and arguments. Each language has its own syntax for declaring them.

Security for a Bank Account

We can further notice that anyone (or any other program or programmer) can create a bank account and operate on it. Because the account is maintained as a piece of data, anyone who gets access to a bank account record can modify it (even illegally) and make withdrawals. That's a consequence of the fact that the account is treated as a series of characters and integers. There is no protection for the different values kept in the bank account of a customer. There is no rule that says a bank account should be modified only by trusted bank employees and even if such a rule is implicit who will enforce it? The language (like C or Pascal) cannot do it because it doesn't know the difference between a bank account and a normal integer.

If we have to print all the accounts of a customer, then we would add a new function

```
PrintAccount(Account thisAccount);
```

which will do the printing. But the function should know what kind (checking, savings, etc.) of account it is printing. Well, that's easy—just look at the value in the **accountType** field. Let's say, to start with, we have the three account types (checking, savings, and loan) as mentioned earlier. The **PrintAccount()** function understands these types because it would be hard coded in the code for this function. So far so good. Now let's say we add a new type of account—**retirement_account**. What if we pass an account that happens to be a **retirement_account** to **PrintAccount**! It wouldn't work. We might see an error message that says

```
"Unknown account type - Cannot Print"
```

or even worse

```
"Illegal account type - Call Supervisor"
```

All this happened because the type of the account is a piece of information hard coded into the system and it cannot be changed unless the source code is changed, recompiled, and relinked. So if we add a new account type, we need to modify all functions that depend on this information and go through the compile-link-test phase. All these are tedious and error-prone. So, how did we get into this problem? The answer again lies in the fact that the functions and the data structures are treated as two disjoint entities having nothing in common. Hence, the change in the data structure is not something easily understood by the functions. We would like to build the system in such a way that each new account type added to the system doesn't affect any other account types and doesn't cause any major recompilation of code. In other words, making enhancements to the existing implementation are very difficult.

All these problems that we have been discovering can be attributed to our misguided focus in the original solution. We were more focused on the functions that we (wrongly) thought were important and completely lost focus of the data that is more important for the client (i.e., the bank customer). In other words, we were preoccupied with *how* to do it, even though it would have been more appropriate to focus on *what* to do.

This is where object-oriented programming differs from procedure-oriented programming.

Solving It with Object-Oriented Programming

If we were to solve this bank account problem using object-oriented programming techniques, our attention would have been on the bank account. We would first focus on what customers want to do with this account, what is important to them, and so on. **Stated simply, in object-oriented programming, the focus is on the data that is being operated upon and not the procedures that implement those operations.** We try to find out what a user (the bank customer in our case) would like to do with this data—the bank account—and then we go about providing those essential operations. **Furthermore, the data and the operations are not treated as separate entities as we did earlier**. It is seen as one integral entity. The data comes with a set of operations that allow the user to perform some meaningful operations on them. At the same time, the data itself is not directly accessible by any external program or procedure. The only way to modify the data in the bank account is by using the operation provided for that purpose. The operations provided with the bank account modify the data on behalf of the user. **We can now say that bank account is a *class* and we can create any number of bank account instances, each one of which is an *object* of the class bank account**. Therefore, *Object-Oriented Programming is a method of programming in which programs are made up of cooperating objects (which are instances of a class). Further, the classes themselves are probably related using inheritance relationships.*[2]

The key here is the concept of a *class* and *object*. A class is an entity that captures the common properties (or traits) of a group of objects. An object is an instance of a class. All objects of a class have the same structure and behavior as declared in the class to which they belong. One can view the class as the cookie cutter and the cookies as the instances that the cookie cutter creates. This analogy is very coarse but it still resembles the process of creating an object from a class. The cookie cutter determines the size and shape of the cookie (but not the taste). Similarly, a class determines the size and behavior of objects that are created. In a true object-oriented solution to a problem, everything is an object of a class.[3] Seeing this way, in object-oriented programming, we only think in terms of classes and objects and also the relationship between classes and the relationship between objects.[4] Shlaer-Mellor have a nice way to describe the difference between procedural-programming and OOP. *Functional decomposition addresses the three elements of system design (algorithms, control flow, data description) exactly in this order, and in the opposite order by OOP.*

Revisiting the bank account problem, now the bank account is the focus of our attention and it becomes a class. Here is a skeleton of the BankAccount class in C++. Again, don't worry too much about the syntax.

---

[2]Inheritance is covered in all its glory in a later chapter.

[3]This is *almost* possible in C++ if we assume that a main() program is like a root object where everything starts.

[4]There are some relatively unknown delegation languages where objects can create other objects.

```
class BankAccount {
    public:
        // Many details omitted for simplicity
        void MakeDeposit(float amount);
        float WithDraw();
        bool Transfer(BankAccount& to, float amount);
        float GetBalance() const;
    private:
        // Implementation data for the private use of the BankAccount class
        float     balance;
        float     interestYTD;
        char*     owner;
        int       account_number;
};
```

What is important to a client (i.e., anyone who wants to open a bank account and use it) are the public: operations available for this class (which are shown in **bold** typeface in Fig. 1-1). The declarations in the private: region are not accessible by these clients. It is for the exclusive internal use of the operations. For example, the MakeDeposit operation could be implemented as below. Again, don't worry about the C++ syntax.

```
// Implementation of an operation of class BankAccount
void BankAccount::MakeDeposit(float amount)
{
    if (amount > 0.0)
        balance = balance + amount;
}
```

The private member **balance** (and other private members) can only be accessed from within the operations declared in the class BankAccount. They are not available for normal use outside of the class. We refer to this private data as **encapsulated** data. This way of hiding something inside a class is called *Data Encapsulation*. More details on data encapsulation can be found in Chapter 2.

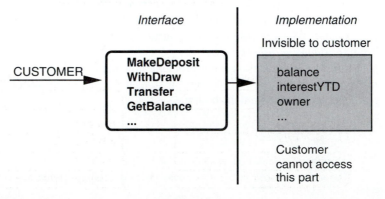

Fig. 1-1

UNDERSTANDING THE OBJECT MODEL

One of the difficulties in ramping up to the object-oriented programming (OOP) paradigm is the lack of understanding of the concept of class and objects. To be successful with OOP, one needs to have a very good grasp of these concepts.

The fundamental entity in OOP is the *class*. Continuing with the bank account example, every BankAccount object has the same structure and behavior. Therefore, all BankAccount objects have the operation MakeDeposit (and others declared in the class) available for use with them (i.e., we can use any of the operations on any object of the class). Further, all objects are guaranteed to have their own copy of the private data (balance, account_number, etc.). What is different among the objects is the values contained in the private data. For example, a BankAccount object alpha might have a value of 500 in the field balance and another object beta might have the value 10,000, as shown in Fig. 1-2.

Objects are instances (the "cookies") of a class. A class is visible only in the source code of the program, where as objects are live instances of the class that participate in a running program. Objects occupy memory locations. One can touch and feel an object. The process of creating an object of a class is also called *instantiating an object.*

In procedure-oriented programming, we always talk of calling procedures; we always talk in terms of "calling procedure X (or simply X) and calling Y" (where X and Y are procedures). But in OOP we never say "call X or call Y"; we instead say "invoke X on some object." If we have an object myAccount of the class BankAccount, we say "call the procedure MakeDeposit on the object myAccount." In other words, procedures are invoked (called) on objects. Without an object, we cannot simply call a procedure. We

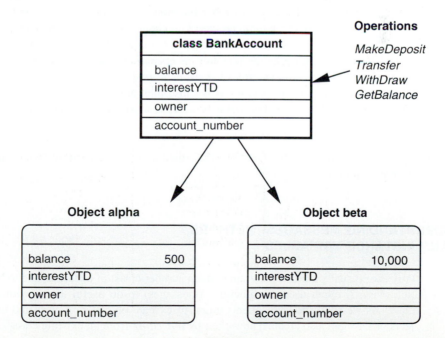

Fig. 1-2

never say "do this"; we have to say "do this to that object." Any operation is **applied** on an object and that operation will do something useful to that object (like making a deposit). The possibility of changing someone else's data is completely eliminated.

Under the procedure oriented programming model, when a programmer looks at a data structure, it is hard to get a feeling for what it is supposed to do and how it is supposed to be used. Further, it may not be clear as to who it is meant for. The purpose, usage, and restrictions of the data structure are hard to understand because the data structure is not an intelligent entity. All the intelligence required to use them correctly is buried deep in some collection of functions elsewhere. Object oriented programming does not suffer from this drawback because everything that anyone can do with a class is clearly stated in the class in terms of the public operations. There are no independent data structures lying around. In fact, there is no data structure separately visible to the client. All the client sees is a class and a set of clearly defined operations. The data structures (which are hidden inside the class) and the operations on them have become one integral entity. Stated differently, what a client can do with a class is clearly detailed in the class itself; the client does not have to look elsewhere.

TERMINOLOGY

Now, it is time we used the correct terminology for all these operations and data in a class (see also Fig. 1-3).

C++   Under C++, the functions inside the class are called *member functions* and the variables are called *data members*. The functions are almost like normal functions but they belong to a class and hence are member functions of that class. Along the same lines, the variables hold data that belong to an object and hence they are data members.

EIFFEL   Eiffel (and Ada) calls the functions as *operations* and the variables are called *attributes*. Eiffel distinguishes variables in classes as *attributes* but they are called *fields* inside objects. The functions are operations because they are used by clients to operate on the object. The variables are called fields because of an object's similarity to *records* in Pascal.

SMALLTALK   Under Smalltalk, the functions are called *messages* and the variables are called *instance variables*.

UNDERSTANDING MESSAGES, METHODS, AND INSTANCE VARIABLES

Any user (usually another program or even another class) of a class is said to be a *client* of that class. A client uses the functions (messages) to do useful things with objects of a class. As we shall see later, clients might just create objects of a class and use those objects or they can also create a new class by *inheriting* from an existing class.

SMALLTALK   Under Smalltalk, calling an interface function (member function) of an object is viewed as *sending a message to the object*. This seems appropriate. We send a message MakeDeposit to the BankAccount object asking it to accept a deposit. Sending a message (to an object) causes the execution of a *method* in that object. (i.e., the object executes a particular method (a function) when we send a message). In other words, the object *responds* to the message. The concept is that a message is just a name seen by the client and the name is bound (probably at run time) to the correct implementation of this message (the method) in the object receiving the message. Each and every instance of a class (i.e., every object) contains a separate copy of the instance variables, as shown in Fig. 1-2.

Terminology used in different languages

Definitions	C++ Term	Smalltalk Term	Eiffel
A description of a group of similar objects	Class	Class	Class
Grouping of private data and functions	Object	Object or Instance	Object or Instance
Higher level, generalized class	Base Class	Super Class	Parent Class
Lower level, specialized class	Derived class	Subclass	Child class
Way to reuse design and code	Inheritance	Inheritance	Inheritance
Type independent call	Polymorphism	Polymorphism	Polymorphism
A request for an object to carry out one of its operations	Member function call	Message invocation	Operation invocation
How to perform one of the operations	Member function implementation	Method	Routine (procedure or function)
Private Data	Data Member	Instance variable	Field, Attribute

Fig. 1-3

NOTE   The terms method (and message), operation, and member function are used interchangeably in this book. They all have virtually the same meaning.

What Is Contained in an Object?

Each and every object created (or *instantiated*) gets its own copy of the data members. Data members (except *static data members)* are not shared. As we will see later, only static data members (under C++) are shared among all the objects of a class in a running program. Smalltalk also supports shared data members.[5] What about the member functions? Does each object get its own copy of the code in each member function too? Definitely not. Each object is capable of responding to all the member functions declared in a class, but the object itself does not contain a copy of the implementation code. At the minimum, there is only one copy of the implementation code of the member functions in one running program (a process or task). No matter how many objects of a class are created in that process, the code for the member functions is not duplicated. The code is shared among all objects of the class. For simplicity, one can imagine that the implementation code of a class resides in a library. Many implementations might optimize this further and they may keep only one copy of all the implementation code for the entire system. This is usually done using dynamically shared libraries. All such details are very much operating system

[5]We will see more details of this when we discuss sharing among objects of a class.

specific. For example, we can use the class **Card** to represent a card in a deck of playing cards as follows:

```
enum Suit { Clubs, Diamond, Heart, Spade, Unknown};
enum Rank { Two, Three, Four, Five, Six, Seven, Eight,
            Nine, Ten, Jack, Queen, King, Ace, Invalid };
enum Color { Red, Black, White };

class Card {
    public:

        void FaceUp();          // Show card face up
        void FaceDown();        // Make it face down
            // And many other member functions
        Card(Rank r, Suit s); // Create a card with these specifications
    private:
            Rank      cardRank;
            Suit      cardSuit;
            Color     cardColor;
};
```

If we create a deck of 52 cards, there would be 52 objects of the class **Card** in the deck, each having its own copy of the data members **cardRank**, **cardSuit**, and **cardColor**.

```
Card    myDeck[52]; // Create a standard deck of 52 cards
```

Each card in the deck can be manipulated individually. We can also instantiate some card objects as follows and as demonstrated in Fig. 1-4:

```
Card spade_Ace(Spade, Ace); // Ace of Spades
Card clubs_2(Clubs, Two);    // Two of Clubs
Card diamond_Jack(Diamond, Jack);      // Jack of Diamonds
```

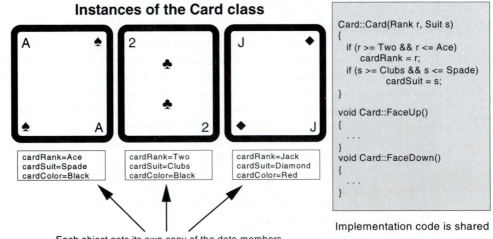

Fig. 1-4

Instantiating (or Creating) Objects

Once a class is designed and implemented, programmers who like to use objects of that class should *instantiate* them in their code. Languages differ in the way they support instantiation of objects. In C++, instantiation of an object looks like a simple declaration, as in

```
BankAccount myAccount;
```

With Smalltalk, the programmer has to send the predefined message **new** to the class to instantiate a new object of the class. This would look like

```
BankAccount new.
```

Under Eiffel, the predefined operation **make** has to be used to create a new object.

```
myAccount : BankAccount; — just a declaration, object is not created
myAccount.!!make; — Creates the object
```

WHAT CAN BE CATEGORIZED AS A CLASS?

It is easy to talk about classes and objects at length with simple examples but the ultimate goal is to discover the right set of classes for a given problem. One has to understand what a class represents and when something in a problem should be turned into a class and not just a piece of data (and vice-versa). As per our definition, a class should capture the common properties (or traits) of a group of objects. How *common* is common? When should we say something is a class and not an object of another class? These are all genuine concerns one encounters when learning OOP.

When we decide to make something a class, the first thing we should ask is, "Will there be a true need for more than one instance of this class?" If the answer to this question is a resounding "Yes," then we are probably correct in our approach—at least on the first cut. Furthermore, if there is absolutely no difference among instances of a class (i.e., every instance is equivalent to every other instance and they all behave exactly the same way) then we have probably created a class that should have been a value. For example, if we make **Color** as a class when dealing with flowers and all that color represents is a unique number, there is no point in making **Color** a class. However, if we are dealing with **Color** in graphics systems (involving complex color computations), definitely **Color** is a class because it has many components and shade variations based on the component colors (red, green, and blue). And **Color** would be controlled by controlling its components and so on. This shows that the **Color** in a graphics system is not just a value; it has a lot more behavior attached to it.

As another example, a person's home address (or just **Address**) might be treated as just an array of characters (or a value), but **Address** might be a class in an electronic mail system involving domain names, machine names, etc. and the address might indicate the nature of routing to be used for messages. Definitely, we cannot treat an address like an array of characters in such a system. It would be a true class.

Remember that it is almost impossible to get everything right in the first attempt. Things that were classes in the first round of design could become data in the next round and vice-versa. Problems to solutions evolve over time. It is highly unlikely that the final solution is the same as the first design.

All these bring out one important property of a class. A class is not just a container for some data that are modified by functions. A class is something that provides clients a simplified picture of a complex entity and allows them to operate on objects of the class to do useful things. Further, the class determines *how* things are done and it clearly states as to *what* can be done to objects of the class. That way, a class is much more than the sum of its parts. Revisiting the Color example, in a graphics system, just the red, green, and blue components don't mean much to the clients. It is how the Color class combines these components and projects them that adds value. On the same lines, a bank account is not something that just has characters and floating point numbers in it. The bank account class is seen as something that allows clients to manage their money easily and safely.

WHAT IS *NOT* A CLASS?

It is also very important to understand when something is not to be classified as a class. A class is not a bunch of functions just grouped together. This is the effect of converting a module (or a simple C header file) into a class. Just take all the functions exported by the module and make them public member functions and you have a class! Well, a class is not just a set of functions. It is much more than that.

For example, consider a module that implements a set of mathematical functions like square root (sqrt), power, inverse, etc. One might (wrongly) try to convert this module into a class called MathHelper.

```
class MathHelper {
        public:
                double Sqrt(double          aNumber);
                double Power(double          aNumber int raiseTo);
                double Inverse(double         aNumber);
        private:
                // any private data, probably none!
    };
```

The problem here is that there is nothing to manage inside the class MathHelper. The client calls one of the member functions and provides an argument. The member functions work with that argument to perform the necessary computation. But in carrying out the computation, the member functions need no help from the class. There is nothing stored in the class that could be of any use to the member functions. This is true for all member functions in the class. The functions are just grouped together (unnecessarily) without them having anything in common. All the class contains is a set of functions (code) and no data. A better approach would be to create a class Number and provide operations for the Number class.

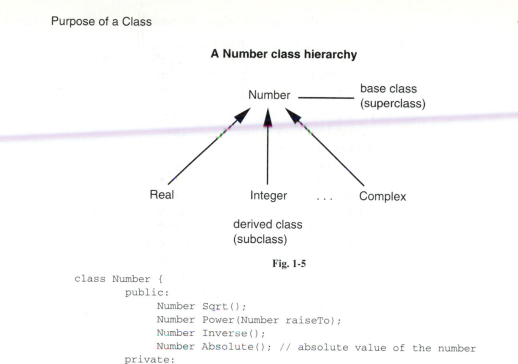

A Number class hierarchy

Number ——————— base class
(superclass)

Real   Integer   . . .   Complex

derived class
(subclass)

Fig. 1-5

```
class Number {
      public:
            Number Sqrt();
            Number Power(Number raiseTo);
            Number Inverse();
            Number Absolute(); // absolute value of the number
      private:
            // Use some internal representation to store the number
};
```

In this case, the class **Number** controls the internal representation of the number. Since clients do not have any knowledge of this internal representation, it is logical that the class provide the required operations.

Taking this design a step further, one could conceive an inheritance hierarchy that represents different types of numbers (real, integer, complex, etc.). These can become derived classes (or subtypes) of **Number** as shown above in Fig. 1-5.

Inheritance is discussed in Chapter 5 and Chapter 6.

Similarly, a C "struct" cannot become a class directly. One cannot change a struct to a class and make all the data private data members and then add a group of functions to get and set the data members. This is not a class either. A class is not just a group of functions that allows the clients to get and set the values in it. Data encapsulation hides the data in the class and provides a higher level of abstraction through the member functions. If you simply provide functions to read and write the data in a struct, then you haven't simplified anything. Classes with only "getter" and "setter" functions are usually examples of poor class design.[6]

PURPOSE OF A CLASS

A class is designed with one clear goal. It should never do anything more than that. A well designed class should be easy to understand and use. Its intent must be clear to the

---

[6]One function, GetXXX(), to retrieve the value and another, SetXXX(), to store the corresponding value.

clients. We cannot create a single **Color** class to represent colors of flowers and also colors in graphics systems. They have totally different requirements. Just to satisfy a group of clients, a designer should not add a function to a class that is totally unrelated to what the class is trying to achieve. In other words, every class is designed for one purpose in a specific domain. For example, consider the class **Person** shown below:

```
// Bad design
class Person {
        public:
                Person(/*some arguments */);
                ~Person();
                char* GetName();
                char* GetAddress();
                unsigned long
                    GetBankAccountNumber() const;
                //...
        };
```

The **GetBankAccountNumber** member function is unrelated to this abstraction. How do we know a person always has a bank account? For that we need a person who is also a customer of a bank.

Sometimes designers just throw in a member function because it doesn't fit anywhere else or they find a use for the member function in some restricted environment. But that breaks the abstraction and confuses the clients. The designer of this class is mixing the abstraction of a *Person* with that of a bank customer.

A good measure of a well designed class could be that the designer should be able to state the purpose of that class in one simple statement. If it takes a couple of paragraphs to describe a class, clearly there is too much (probably conflicting) functionality in the class and it is time to divide the class into a number of smaller classes. Another metric is the number of member functions in a class. A well designed class would not contain more than 15–25 member functions in it.

When clients look at a class, it should be possible for them to get a good feeling for what the class can do (and what it cannot do). The class should project a crisp and clear image of its capabilities and limitations. If after looking at the class, the client gets confused about its purpose, the design of the class is weak and probably wrong. And it is time to start all over again.

A class (actually objects of the class) has responsibilities to fulfill. When a class is designed, it (actually the designer of the class) is making a commitment to the clients about what it is capable of doing. In making the commitment, the class is responsible for managing certain details so that the clients need not have to worry about them. The **BankAccount** class is responsible for maintaining the correct balance while deposits and withdrawals are being made. The commitment from the class (to the client) is that when a client uses an object of the **BankAccount** class to manage a customer account, and the client sticks with the published methods of the class, the correctness and security of the bank account is guaranteed. In fulfilling its responsibilities, the **BankAccount** class might *collaborate* with other classes. This collaboration may or may not be of interest to clients but the designers of the class need to have a clear understanding of such issues. Collaboration among classes is described in a later chapter. We will learn more about good and bad classes further along in this chapter.

MORE ABOUT OBJECTS

As stated earlier, an object is an instance of a class. An object gives life to a class. In other words, what a class is capable of doing can be experienced by instantiating an object and operating on it. An object is intelligent; it knows what it can and cannot do. Further, an object has the knowledge (and resources) to modify and maintain its data members.

So what distinguishes a class from an object is the next logical question. Simply stated, an object is a live entity with **state** and **behavior**. The behavior of all objects of a class is defined in the class and state is maintained by individual objects. These two (state and behavior) are very simple words but with very profound meaning when applied to objects.

State of an Object

For this discussion, we revisit the bank account problem. Each **BankAccount** object has the data member **balance** in it. Assuming that we do not allow customers to overdraw on their accounts, we can probably state that the balance in an account may not be allowed to drop below zero (assuming no overdraft privileges). This would be a known property of any bank account object. We don't have to check the state of an object to verify this property. In other words, this would be a *static* property of every bank account object.

However, at any time during the life of a **BankAccount** object, the balance in the account is the value contained in the data member—**balance**. The value of this data member keeps changing as, and when, deposits/transfer/withdrawals are made from the account. So, we can say that the account balance is a dynamically changing value. In other words, it is a *dynamic* value of the **balance** data member. The state of an object is the sum of all the static properties and the dynamic values of these properties. A property is a unique feature or quality of an object. We could say that every car has a registration number as its property (with different values in them). Similarly, every person has a name (though not unique) as a feature.

The state of an object need not be (and usually is not) just primitive data types. Many objects contain other objects as a part of their state. For example, a **Car** object would contain an **Engine** object as a part of its state and a **Bank** object would have **BankAccount** objects and **Customer** objects as a part of its state (See Fig. 1-6).[7]

Why Is the State of an Object Important?

One might wonder why we are paying so much attention to pieces of data in an object that are encapsulated. How an object responds to our commands (operations) and what it does to other objects (and the client) directly depends on the state of the object. The outcome of the execution of a method directly depends on the state of the object. For example, when

---

[7]For a more complete discussion of state of an object, see [Booch94] and also Chapter 2.

State of an Object

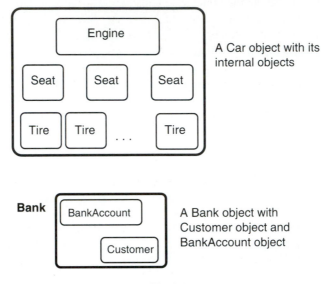

A Car object with its
internal objects

A Bank object with
Customer object and
BankAccount object

Fig. 1-6

the **Withdraw** message is sent to a **BankAccount** object, the following steps happen in sequence:

1. Check to verify that the account belongs to the person who invoked the operation

2. If the amount requested is greater than the current balance, print an error message and return to the caller.

3. Otherwise, reduce the balance by the amount being withdrawn and return.

All these steps need information about the state of the object. Every method depends on the state of the object. All the methods assume that the state is correct. If the state of an object is not correct (due to some unknown reason), the behavior of the object would be unpredictable.

Another good example of state is in a washing machine. When we push the "WASH" button, the machine checks to make sure that the door is closed (and probably clothes are loaded) using some data members in the object. The machine will not spin if the door is not closed. Most washing machines use a sensor (a simple switch) to check the condition of the door and the user is not expected to operate this switch directly (it would be an encapsulated data member). What if an overzealous user somehow gets access to this switch and operates it so that the washing machine is fooled to believe (incorrectly) that the door is closed. If the user now pushes the "WASH" button, sure enough the machine will spin the drum probably splashing detergent, clothes, and water all over. Such unpredictable (or predictable but unwanted) behavior is the direct outcome of uncontrolled change in the state of the object. A good implementation of a class should not allow direct access by clients to the state of the object. State should only be modified within the member functions and clients should only use those member functions to operate on objects. Along the same lines, consider what happens in a microwave oven if a user pushes the COOK button without closing the door. Nothing happens because the microwave oven implementation checks to ensure that the door is closed before turning on the magnetron (the device that generates microwaves). This is very similar to the sensor used in the washing machine. If a client finds access to this switch and closes it (without really closing the door), and then pushes the COOK button, the microwave oven will turn on the magnetron, even if the door is not closed, because it has been led to believe that the door is closed. This can cause irreparable damage to the person standing in the vicinity of the oven.

Who Controls the State of an Object?

From the previous paragraph, it is clear that the state of an object is modified within member functions. However, not all methods would modify the state of an object—some methods may just use the values in the state (as in the case of **GetBalance** in **BankAccount**). Any method in a class makes certain assumptions about the state of an object. Such assumptions might be documented and may also be implied in the code. Further, a class assumes that no one else modifies the state of an object from the outside—all changes to the state of an object take place within member functions. The member functions have that intimate knowledge of what they should do to/with the state values. *It is the member functions that control the state of an object.*[8] It is important to note that member functions execute on behalf of the client. A client invokes an operation (i.e., sends a request to the object) and the operation does something useful. Usually a method doesn't execute on its own; it is invoked by the client.[9]

Member functions also know about the constraints (or restrictions) on the state of an object. Again from the **BankAccount** example, the methods clearly know the restriction that the balance in any account cannot drop below zero. Every method enforces this constraint. If the state of an object is modified but not from within a member function, then the behavior of the object is no longer predictable. This is what happened with the washing machine example. As another example, if someone illegally taps into a bank account that does not belong to him and sets the **balance** to zero, the true owner of that account would not be able to withdraw any money from the account because the state indicates that the balance is zero. A language cannot prevent such intentional break-ins but it can prevent accidental errors. This protection is achieved by making the **balance** data member a part of the private implementation detail. In other words, anything that should not be accessed by normal clients would be *encapsulated* in the private region of the class. This is also called *Data Encapsulation*.

When classes are created, invariably something about the class is encapsulated. It is some house-keeping information that objects of the class need for correct behavior. A class without any data members is a sign of bad design because it signals an object without any state. We shall see more about data encapsulation in Chapter 2.

---

[8]A small exception is a C++ friend function; but one should view them, at least for the purpose of this discussion, as being part of the class.

[9]This may not be true in case of objects used as interrupt handlers and such.

Behavior of an Object

Clients use methods to do useful things with objects of the class. Objects *behave* in some fashion in response to the messages that clients invoke. *Behavior is how an object acts and reacts to messages.* The message might cause a change in state. It may also cause the sending of more messages to other objects or both. When a client sends a message to an object, it might send another message to a different object to complete the operation. For example, a BankAccount object, on receiving the Withdraw message, might send a message to an object (say tl) of a TransactionLogger class to log the current transaction. The object tl might in turn send a message to a database (probably in a different city) to store this transaction. So it is clearly evident that sending a message to an object might cause a chain of other messages to be sent to other objects. It is also possible that another message is sent to the original object (even recursively). Behavior captures the externally visible activity of an object in response to messages. It is what the client feels from the outside.

Some messages might cause a change in state and others may not. In C++ (and Eiffel), it is possible to clearly identify messages that do not cause any change in state.[10] What a message does (in terms of the clients view) should be clearly documented in a class for each method. Our intention as designers is to give the client as much information about the class as is practical without revealing implementation details of the class.

PHASES IN OBJECT-ORIENTED SOFTWARE DEVELOPMENT

Object-Oriented Analysis

Clearly, a software project does not begin with a set of classes or objects. We start off with a plain description (mostly incomplete) of the problem. This is the starting point. From here, we need to find our set of classes. Remember that most non-trivial problems require not one but a set of classes for a good solution. And the set of classes would have to *communicate, collaborate, and cooperate* with each other to achieve the end goal. How do we discover (or even invent) the classes that we need for our solution? This is probably the most difficult stage in object-oriented software development and takes up a good portion of the time. The reason finding classes is so hard is because the problem statements are usually incomplete, or are *implementation oriented* rather than problem oriented.

Object-Oriented Analysis (OOA) involves analyzing the problem from the perspective of classes and objects that are found in the problem domain. This is basically a modeling exercise, trying to build a model of the problem domain. These classes are not the ones that can be directly used in the final implementation. The problem is analyzed and the requirements clearly specified. A complete description of what the solution can (and can not) do is fully described in terms of classes and objects found in the customer's problem domain. In other words, the description of the problem uses classes and objects that the client can understand. These classes and objects are directly found in the problem domain.

---

[10]Such methods are called const member functions in C++. This is covered in more detail in a subsequent chapter.

The next question is: *What is the meaning of the term problem domain?* Any problem requiring a solution is related to one or more (usually known) areas. We need to rely on the knowledge and expertise of people familiar with that area to come up with a solution. For example, to design a solution for a bank management problem, we need help from those who use and manage banks in their day-to-day life. We say that the problem belongs to the banking (or financial) domain. Simply stated, a problem domain is the area or sector (or sectors) to which the problem belongs. Problem domains (or simply domains) can range from bathroom remodeling, bicycle manufacturing, mechanical design, accounts receivable, inventory management, FDA approval, geo-physical simulations, networking, user interface, animation, finance, office automation, distributed computing, mathematical analysis, computer communications, database management, etc. It is impossible for one person to have sufficient knowledge of all these areas to come up with a good design to solve problems in such diverse areas.

Even if one is an expert in the area of object-oriented software development, finding a solution to the bank management problem would require major assistance from people directly involved in the banking system. Those involved with the banking system know the requirements of their system and they would also know the drawbacks of their current system. They would be able to provide useful information about their future requirements too. They can be called *domain experts*. As it is not a requirement, these domain experts usually know nothing about programming.

Based on their input, a group of designers familiar with object-oriented software development might be able to come up with a solution for the problem. Without help from the domain experts, it would be impossible to come up with a good Object-Oriented (OO) design. Any real problem requires close cooperation and coordination between the domain experts and object-oriented software experts.

The outcome of the OOA phase is in no way complete. It is a skeleton solution that requires a lot of work before implementation can begin. But, it is a good starting point. Note that in the OOA phase, attention is paid to classes that are used in the problem domain, not in the implementation. Details of the implementation are covered during the Object-Oriented Design phase.

Given this discussion of OOA, it is interesting to note that finding classes is a natural thing for humans. In real life, we deal with different classes every day, such as a post office, mail box, pay check, manager, flower, newspaper, microwave oven, CD player, father, mother, car, etc. These are all objects that we interact with on a daily basis. We also know what they can do and what their purpose is. Software development involves modeling these objects that we know of in the problem domain. What we already know about real life objects is mapped into the logical view of the problem solution. For example, in a company management problem, the employees of the company are modeled as objects. Similarly, their pay is modeled in a payroll management system, again using classes and objects. This kind of *simulation* of the real world situation in a software solution makes problem solving easier because we already have a good understanding of the classes and objects involved. This also helps us in mastering (and managing) the complexity of the problem. We also know about the limitations of objects in real life. For example, I cannot ask the mailman to deliver flowers to my uncle; nor can I ask the microwave oven to play a CD. We clearly know the capabilities and limitations of objects that we interact with. This knowledge is mapped into our solutions. In some situations, this mapping is easy (as in the case of a company management system or the bank account management system), but in other cases, particularly with problems specific to computer software, finding these objects is much harder because we usually cannot identify the objects. For example, finding the correct set of classes for an interrupt management system is not very easy because there are no objects that we already know of. We need to analyze the problems thoroughly before any semblance of a solution can begin to develop. On the same lines, problems involving transaction processing would not be easy either.

Object-Oriented Design

This phase follows the OOA stage and it adds flesh to the skeleton that was developed previously. The problem is decomposed into classes and objects that will be used in the implementation. We define clear relationships among classes, describe how the objects might fit into the process model of the system, how objects should be partitioned across address spaces, how the system might behave dynamically, etc. The outcome of this phase is more clear and easier to follow. Still, it is not complete because the implementation of the design has not been done and hence nothing is known about the true behavior of the solution.

DISCOVERING THOSE ELUSIVE OBJECTS

Finding (actually inventing and discovering) a correct set of classes for implementing a solution is not a trivial task. In fact, this is one of the hardest things to do. There are many guidelines and proven methods used in this process. One would have to use all these guidelines and methods (and a good understanding of the problem) to generate an initial set of classes. In general, the following entities in a problem turn into classes:

> People, Places, and Things
> Events—Mouse input, Birth, Death, etc.
> Transactions—Loan Approval, Car Sale, etc.
> Roles played by people—Mother, Father, etc.

For simpler problems, designers might get a clue about classes by treating *nouns* as classes and *verbs* as methods on those classes. But, description of a problem in a language can be easily written such that the roles of nouns and verbs are completely reversed. *This is the reason why this approach might only give a clue to classes that might be of some use in the exploration.*

Both OOA and OOD may follow some existing design methodology. A methodology uses some notations for classes, objects, and their relations. It also provides support for depicting different models (logical, physical) of the system. They are basically tools that assist in the design process. The notation used also provides a common vocabulary for the design team; it is like a common language understood by the design team. Some of the popular methodologies in use are:

1. Booch Methodology[11]

2. Rumbaugh Methodology[12] (also called OMT—Object Modeling Tool)

3. Shlaer & Mellor methodology[13]
(1 & 2 are now unified into Unified Modeling Language, discussed in Chapter 2)

Note that just learning a design methodology doesn't make one an expert in OOD. The methodology is just a tool to express the design such that others can understand it. It helps in the design process but it cannot help in discovering and implementing classes. There is no substitute for the knowledge and experience of the design team.

OOA and OOD are not properties of the C++ language.[14] They are essential for solutions to any problem. In fact, OOA/OOD do not depend on any language. However, it might help if it is known beforehand what language will be used in the implementation. During the design phase, it is possible that a special relationship between some set of classes is used that is not available in a particular language. For example, multiple inheritance might have been used in the design. But, multiple inheritance is not supported by Smalltalk. So, how to implement this design using Smalltalk is a natural question. Though not impossible, it requires considerably more effort to implement. This is the reason why it is good to know (if possible) the language that will be used in the implementation. But, one should not use very fine syntactic details of a specific language in the design cycle. Design should be, as much as possible, independent of any language specific elements. Other than that, OOA and OOD are mostly independent of any language. One can implement a design in any *object-oriented language* of their choice.

OBJECT-ORIENTED PROGRAMMING

This is the last phase of the object-oriented software development cycle. The output from the OOD phase is the input to the OOP phase. In this stage, one writes real code in a language of choice (or as directed by the project requirements). As defined earlier, **Object-Oriented programming is a method of programming in which programs are made up of cooperating objects (which are instances of a class). Further, the classes themselves are probably related using inheritance relationships**.

KEY ELEMENTS OF THE OBJECT MODEL

The object model that we have discussed so far needs the following important elements in the problem solution:

Data Abstraction

Encapsulation

Hierarchy

---

[11]Refer *Object-Oriented Analysis and Design with Applications* by Grady Booch.

[12]Refer *Object-Oriented Modeling and Design* by Rumbaugh et al.

[13]*Object-Oriented Systems Analysis*, Modeling the world in Data—Shlaer, S. and Mellor, S.

[14]One could argue that the OOA&D notations constitute a visual language.

We will explore all of these elements in detail in subsequent chapters. However, here is a brief description:

Data Abstraction is the result of defining classes with emphasis on the similarities of its objects and ignoring their differences. Further, uninteresting and distracting elements are suppressed while the major features of the class (the *abstraction*) are projected. A class is an abstraction. Stated a bit differently, an abstraction focuses on the outside view of an object and clearly separates its essential behavior from the internal implementation details. We postpone further discussion of data abstraction until Chapter 2.

Encapsulation (or information hiding) is the result of hiding the internal implementation details of an abstraction. It clearly separates the external interface of an abstraction from the internal (mundane) implementation details. Encapsulation and abstraction are complementary to each other. A good abstraction encapsulates something and the encapsulated entity helps the abstraction to maintain its integrity. It is important to note that abstraction precedes encapsulation. Encapsulation is in focus only when implementation begins.

Hierarchy is the support for ordering abstractions. Abstractions are powerful and useful, but in most non-trivial problems, we may end up creating too many abstractions, which will hamper our understanding of the complete picture. Encapsulation and modules mitigate this problem to some extent, but still we may find ourselves in the midst of too many abstractions. A human mind can only comprehend a limited set of abstractions at a time. Projecting too many abstractions would be an information retentivity test for the reader. To avoid such detrimental effects, one would like to arrange abstractions in hierarchies so that a complete knowledge of all the abstractions in the hierarchy is not required to understand the major features. It is needless to point out that identifying such hierarchies is a non-trivial task and implementing them efficiently is even more daunting.

There are two kinds of hierarchies that are common in OOP. The inheritance concept supports class hierarchies (the "is-a" relation) (see Fig. 1-7). The aggregation relation (the "has-a") (see Fig. 1-8) supports the part-whole concept. Inheritance supports the generalization-specialization relation, whereas aggregation is useful for depicting relations involving containment and sharing.

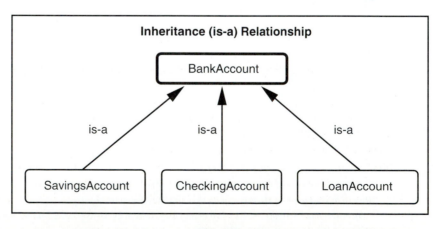

Fig. 1-7

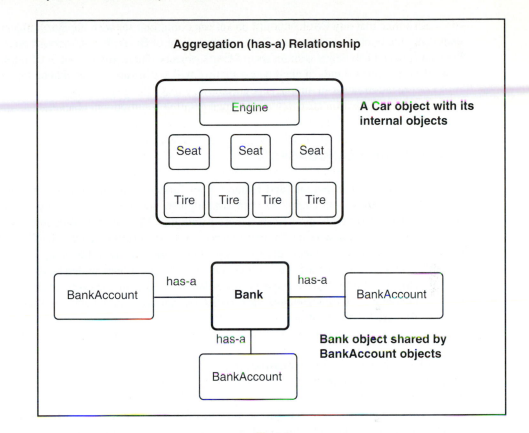

Aggregation (has-a) Relationship

Engine

Seat   Seat   Seat

Tire   Tire   Tire   Tire

A Car object with its internal objects

BankAccount   has-a   **Bank**   has-a   BankAccount

has-a

BankAccount

Bank object shared by BankAccount objects

Fig. 1-8

Inheritance (both single and multiple) is one of the most powerful paradigms of OOP. Much of the power of OOP and code reuse results from inheritance relations. As an example of inheritance, we could arrange different types of bank accounts in a hierarchy with BankAccount as the parent (or base) class and SavingsAccount, CheckingAccount, LoanAccount, etc. as the child (or derived) classes. A client can get the general picture of bank accounts by studying the interface of the parent class BankAccount without really worrying about the different kinds.

As an example of aggregation, a car is made up of engine, tires, seats, etc. We would say a Car *has* an Engine, a set of Wheels, a fixed number of Seats and such. For a normal user, a Car just appears as one single object, even though internally it is made up of many other objects. Further, how a Car object communicates and controls the internal objects is not of any concern to the clients of car objects. It is up to the Car member functions to manage the contained objects.

As a different kind of "has-a" relation, let's add another element to the BankAccount example, the association of a bank account with a Bank object. Clearly a BankAccount object does not own the Bank object. It just refers to it. In fact a BankAccount object shares the same Bank object with many other BankAccount objects. A "has-a" relation does not always imply that one object physically contains an instance of another; it just implies some kind of association between objects.

Also note that any BankAccount object can communicate with the Bank object by using only the public interface, just like any other client of Bank; BankAccount does not have any special privileges with respect to Bank objects. There are a number of implications of both of these kinds of aggregation that we will see in subsequent chapters.

Aggregation helps in simplifying an interface and also helps in object sharing. Inheritance and aggregation are discussed in great detail in a subsequent chapter.

OOP PARADIGMS AND LANGUAGES

Data abstraction, encapsulation, and hierarchy are fundamental concepts of the object-oriented programming paradigm; they are not language specific features. Any language that claims to support OOP must support these paradigms. Moreover, anyone interested in learning these concepts need not have to worry about specific languages. It is possible (and is even better) to understand these concepts in general instead of focusing on the language syntax that supports a feature. Once a designer/programmer understands the concept, it is much easier to learn the syntax of any language. It is like learning to drive a car; once you know the controls and how they work, you can drive anywhere—all that is new is the traffic rules and regulations.

REQUIREMENTS OF AN OBJECT-ORIENTED
PROGRAMMING LANGUAGE

Now it is time to look at programming languages from the point of support for object-oriented programming. Specifically, what makes a language an object-oriented programming language?

Any language that claims to support object-oriented programming must provide features that make it easy to design and implement.

Data Abstraction
Encapsulation
Inheritance

When we say "it should make it easy," we mean that abstraction and encapsulation should come naturally, without too much effort from the programmer. The language elements should make it very easy to implement elegant abstractions. Furthermore, it should be very easy to provide data encapsulation. The language should be designed with OOP support in mind.

Inheritance is another feature that is very critical for OOP. Without support for inheritance, a language cannot be called an object-oriented programming language. Some languages provide features for data abstraction and also encapsulation but they don't support any form of inheritance. Such languages are not object-oriented programming languages. They can be called *object based* languages because implementing objects would be possible but extending them through inheritance would not. Languages like Ada and Modula-2 belong to this category. Note that it is possible to do data abstraction and also

TABLE 1-1

Procedural Languages	Object-Based languages	Object-Oriented Languages	Rule based languages
PL/1, Algol, COBOL, Fortran, Pascal, C, etc.	Ada, Modula-2. etc.	Smalltalk, Eiffel, Objective-C, C++, Java, etc.	LISP, Prolog, etc.

some degree of encapsulation even under C. However, such abstractions and encapsulations require a lot of effort from the programmer; it does not come naturally from the language. Actually, one can do OOP in C, or even in an assembly language! It is a question of practicality. If you are going to use OOP concepts, it is more practical to use a language that supports those concepts directly and prevents careless errors. Remember that any object-oriented language is also an object-based language.

Languages like Smalltalk, C++, Eiffel, and Object Pascal are true object-oriented languages because of their elegant support for abstraction, encapsulation, and inheritance. Inheritance is the key feature that distinguishes an object-based language from an object-oriented language (See Table 1-1).

BENEFITS OF THE OBJECT MODEL

It is easy to talk and glorify object-oriented software development but in the end, what really matters, are the advantages of this approach. One should clearly understand the benefits of the object model to use it efficiently.

1. The object model encourages building of systems that evolve over time. This also ensures that systems are stable and extendible. Systems need not have to be thrown away (or redesigned from scratch) to provide new functionality. Inheritance exists to make this happen easily.[15] In other words, one can continue to use the existing software while extensions to it are being designed.

2. Thinking in terms of objects and classes is much easier for humans because of their familiarity with existing objects. In fact, even people who are not computer literate find this model easier to understand than traditional models.

3. The object model enforces disciplined programming by separating the client and implementor and prevents accidental damage. Such accidental damage is prevented through data encapsulation.

4. Reuse of simple classes such as date, time, point, etc. promotes a great degree of code reuse and avoids replication of code. Simple classes can also be used to build more complex classes, achieving an even higher degree of code reuse.

5. The object model encourages extensive reuse of software and design. Classes can be extended by inheritance to achieve reuse at the class level. But a much larger amount of reuse happens when an entire *framework* of classes is used to solve major prob-

---

[15]This is true only when the fundamental design of the system is robust.

lems. Stated simply, a framework is a group of cooperating classes designed to solve a particular problem. Clients would be able to refine, reuse, customize, and extend frameworks easily. A simple example is a mass storage device-framework that makes the process of writing new device drivers much easier. Another example is a framework for managing different transport protocols (like TCP/IP, X.25, and XNS). Furthermore, reuse of class hierarchies is quite common. Many of the data structures (like lists, queues, and hash tables) that we use regularly, usually come from a class hierarchy. This kind of reuse is very difficult to achieve in procedure-oriented programming.

CAUTION From all the discussion so far, one should not get a feeling that procedure-oriented programming is useless once we start using the object model. Contrary to that, the object model introduces new elements that build upon the vast experience that we have gained from using other programming models. The extensive knowledge that we have gained from decades of programming with other models should help us do things better. The object model provides new features that are not available in other models. On the other hand, the better you are at functional composition and C programming, the harder time you will have understanding and mastering object-oriented technology & C++! It is a paradigm shift of significant magnitude.

SUMMARY

The focus of the object model is on classes and objects.

We concentrate on what to do rather than how to do it in OOP.

Objects have state and behavior.

Objects communicate with each other to solve problems.

Data Abstraction, Encapsulation, and Inheritance are powerful paradigms of the object model and not features of any language.

A language that supports abstraction, encapsulation, and inheritance naturally is an object-oriented programming language.

Benefits of the object model can only be reaped through careful analysis of the problem, good design, and efficient implementation.

2

What Is Data Abstraction?

One of the fundamental tasks in object-oriented programming is creating classes with appropriate functionality, which hide the unnecessary details (i.e., *abstracting the data*). To illustrate the concept of data abstraction, let's walk through a simple, real life example.

Most of us have seen a laser disc player (or LD player). Here is a simple problem. Let's design a laser disc player that is easy to use and also easy to modify in the future in order to add more useful features.

NOTE   If a laser disc player is hard to understand one can substitute a CD player in place of the LD player without any loss of generality. In fact, a laser disc player's functions are a super set of a CD player's functions.

Some of the issues we need to tackle are:

1. What controls should be provided on the front panel?

2. What input and output facilities should be available to connect the player to different equipment (like an Amplifier, a TV, or a Computer)?

3. How many buttons should be available on the remote control?

The player should be able to:

Play a laser disc when requested

Search forwards/backwards to specified chapters (or songs if it is a CD player)

Allow the user to insert/eject a laser disc

Power-on and power-off at the request of the user

Pause at the request of a user while playing a disc

Completely stop at the request of a user

As a first cut, let's provide the following user controls (switches or buttons) on the front panel (See Fig. 2-1).

Let's analyze the function of one of the controls:

PLAY: When the **PLAY** button is pressed it's natural to expect the laser disc player to start *play*ing and display a picture on the TV screen to which it is connected. But what are the many other consequences of pressing the **PLAY** button?

a) The **PLAY** button responds only when the player is connected to a power source and the **POWER** switch is ON. Otherwise, there will be no response when the **PLAY** button is pressed.

b) The **PLAY** button will not respond if there is no disc inside the player.

c) If both (a) and (b) are satisfied, the laser beam inside the player is activated and the motor starts spinning the disc using the mechanical drive system of the player.

d) The laser beam is a pick-up mechanism reads the encoded information on the disc and converts it to a video signal (after numerous signal processing operations) and the video signal is then transferred to the TV, which displays the picture. The audio information encoded on the disc is treated similarly, both in CD and LD players.

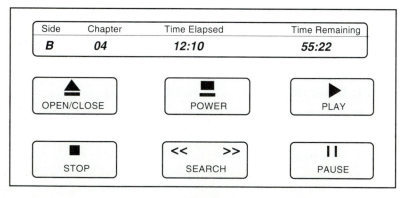

Fig. 2-1

e) If the disc loaded is not of the correct format (for example, if an NTSC disc is loaded in a PAL player), an error message will be displayed on the display panel of the player (or on the TV screen to which the player is connected).[1]

f) If all the pre-requisites are met, we give a visual (and/or audible) indication that the player is actually *playing.*

As is evident from this (grossly simplified) sequence, just pressing the PLAY button initiates a number of operations inside the player. But as far as the user of the player is concerned, all she is interested is in the picture that appears on the screen and the accompanying audio information.[2] She probably isn't aware of the fact that there is a laser beam being used in the player! She could care less for the spinning of the disc or the laser beam pick-up activation. She expects to see a picture on the TV screen and hear good sound when she pushes the PLAY button.

What does this tell us as the designers of the LD player?

The user sees the laser disc player as a magic box that accepts a laser disc and produces a picture on the TV screen when the PLAY button is pressed. This is an accepted property of any LD player (See Fig. 2-2).

Our design should satisfy this perspective of the user, but we have so many other things to worry about before a picture can be seen on the TV. The end user should not have to be bothered about those details.

We have designed a box, the LD player, that presents the notion of a gadget with many buttons, one of which is PLAY. When PLAY is pushed after loading a laser disc, a picture appears on the screen. Believe it or not, we have *abstracted* a piece of data (i.e., we have achieved Data Abstraction).

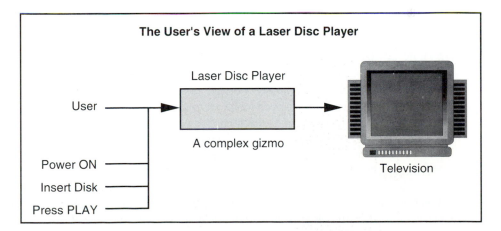

Fig. 2-2

---

[1]NTSC—*National Television Standards Committee*: (A system of color television, invented in USA). PAL—*Phase Alternation Line* (another system of color television, invented in Germany).

[2]Wherever there is a reference to a user I don't like to say he/she. Most of the time I use *she.*

Data Abstraction projects the *most important* features, from the user's perspective, of a class of objects, while ignoring or suppressing their differences. Further, the abstraction should hide those details that are useless for the end user of that object; out of context or diversionary details should be concealed.

Analysis of the LD player design

1. We did not bother the user about the laser beams, motor, etc. At the same time, we did not leave the user in the dark; we gave some clue as to what is happening inside the player by providing some visual (and/or audible) display of the status.

2. The user did not have to do anything other than pushing the PLAY button to view the picture recorded on the disc. She need not turn on the motor, power up the laser beam mechanism, or focus it on the disc, etc. Those are unnecessary, and sometimes highly dangerous, operations that a normal user should never be required to do. What if the user was required to handle the laser beam manually? The manufacturer would soon be the target of numerous lawsuits. (Uncontrolled exposure to laser beams is hazardous to living beings; be forewarned.)

3. If the user forgot to load a laser disc but pressed the PLAY button, the player would not turn on the laser beam nor would it run the motor. Our design is intelligent enough to detect that information; the player actually remembers its state and responds based on that information.

4. If the designer separates all the different parts of a LD player, lays them on a table, and tells a user that it is an LD player, they would surely suspect the designer's mental health. The design, or the *abstraction*, combines all the big and small parts and establishes a proper communication mechanism among them. Further, it projects a clean interface to the user that hides all these parts that make up the LD player (the implementation) and exposes only those controls that the user requires to operate the player.

SEPARATION OF INTERFACE AND IMPLEMENTATION

A careful reader might have already noticed the use of the terms *interface* and *implementation* in the last paragraph. Anyone with the traditional procedure-oriented programming mindset will not see much of a difference between an *interface* and an *implementation*. With OOP, the entire process of design revolves around interface.

Meaning of Interface

When we use any existing object, we pay attention to what we see up front. When you drive a car, all you look at is the different gauges (speed, fuel, temperature), the steering wheel, the gas pedal, etc. When you step on the gas pedal (also called throttle or accelerator), you expect the car to move (provided the gear is engaged and the parking break is released). But when you step on the gas pedal, numerous things happen inside the car:

1. Gasoline (*petrol*) is pumped from the fuel tank to the carburetor (or fuel injector).

2. Gas is delivered to the engine cylinders either by the carburetor or the fuel injector.

3. The distributor delivers electricity to the spark plugs, which ignites the fuel.

4. The pistons drive the crank shaft, which in turn rotates the wheels.

And so on. But for the driver of a car, all these unnecessary details are distractions from the goal. To the driver, a fuel injected engine doesn't make any more sense (if any) than a carburetted engine. All the driver expects is a smooth motion of the car. Further, the driving skill (or habit) of the driver is not affected by the way the internal fuel delivery mechanism works in the car.

When you look at the speedometer, you should be able to read the correct speed easily; how the speedometer senses speed is irrelevant to you. Speed may be measured by a mechanical coupling mechanism or an electro-mechanical (a combination electronics and mechanical systems) system.

In all these situations, what really matters is what the driver sees or feels from the outside and not how they operate inside. This outside view is supported by the *interface* of the object (class). The *interface* is the user's perception of what the object looks like and what she can do with it (and also what it does to her). Thus, the user's perception of the gas pedal is *something that controls the speed of the car* and the speedometer is *something that displays the current speed*. On the same lines, the user perceives the LD player as a device that accepts a laser disc and reproduces the encoded picture on the TV screen.

When we design a class interface, we try to satisfy most of the requirements of the users of that class and nothing else. These users are also called *clients* of that class. The client of a class is someone who just uses the class without knowing (or worrying) about its internal working. The client can create objects of the class and operate on them using the interface.

WHY THE INTERFACE TO THE OBJECT IS SO IMPORTANT

The goal of data abstraction is to provide a clean and sufficient interface that allows the user to access the underlying implementation in a controlled but convenient fashion. And the interface should satisfy the fundamental needs of a user of that object. Our only goal is to keep the clients in mind and always strive to make their life more comfortable. Therefore, the primary goal of an abstraction is to *simplify* things for its clients.

What Is a Sufficient Interface?

Just for the sake of discussion, assume that our LD player design did not provide the STOP button. Our player would play a disc forever! The only way to stop the player would be to turn off the power. The interface without the STOP button is not sufficient enough to satisfy the basic needs of the user. Most of the time, users tend to bypass all the protection and security when their needs are not satisfied by the existing interface. This is a major problem that a good interface tries to solve. An abstraction is a good abstraction, if, and only if, the interface provided by it satisfies the needs of its clients.

On the same lines, if we didn't provide the SEARCH button, our interface would be insufficient. A user of an LD player should have the choice to view any part of the disc she likes. She should not be required to start from the beginning just to view something at the end of the disc.

MEANING OF IMPLEMENTATION

This is much easier to understand if the concept of interface is understood. *Implementation* is where all the work is done. The interface tells the client what can be done and the implementation takes care of *how* it is done. A client does not need to know how an operation projected in the interface is implemented by the class. Therefore, the implementation exists to support the interface projected by the object. Continuing with the car example, the carburetor (or the fuel injector) exists to support the throttle mechanism, which is the interface; similarly, the speed sensing mechanism exists to support the speedometer, which is the interface that shows the speed.[3] The laser beam and the motor are parts of the implementation of the laser disc player and their purpose is to extract the encoded information from the laser disc. Knowledge of the implementation) is not required to use the interface. In fact, it is safer when the user of an interface knows nothing about the implementation. Partial (or even full) knowledge of implementation leads to hacking of code to overcome the interface/implementation barrier. Further, different implementations can be used to support one interface and a variety of interfaces can be supported by a single implementation.[4] More about this in later chapters.

NOTE   It is interesting to note that the world we live in is full of abstractions. The car mechanic knows how to fix a car and the customer knows how to communicate with the car mechanic, but the customer doesn't know how to fix the car. It is the responsibility of the mechanic to repair cars. The interface projected by the car mechanic to his customers is that of a person capable of repairing cars. Similarly, when we operate computers, we don't know much about them. If I hit a key on the keyboard while using a word processing program, I expect the corresponding character to appear on the connected display screen and in the document I am preparing. How the keyboard senses the key press, translates the information, and then relays it to the word processor are none of my responsibility. The keyboard, the auto mechanic, the computer, etc. are all abstractions in our world. Our life is mostly object-oriented!

PROTECTING THE IMPLEMENTATION

One of the caveats of traditional procedure-oriented programming is the lack of protection for the implementor. Any implementation is useless unless its integrity is maintained throughout its lifetime. Imagine what happens if someone tampers with the speedometer mechanism that senses the speed of your car? The speedometer will not show the correct

---

[3]In an electric car, the gas pedal (a misnomer) will control the speed of the motor that drives the wheels.

[4]This brings in the concept of a *View*.

speed of the car. What if an automated teller machine (ATM) allows the customer to manipulate accounts other than their own without any barriers? Or what happens if consumers are allowed to tap into electric power cables directly without using the power outlets that are provided?

All these situations have one thing in common. They can only be used in a specified way (the interface) and there is no way (hackers excepted!) to bypass this interface and get to the implementation directly. The driver cannot tamper with the speedometer, at least not very easily.[5] The ATM allows you to perform certain restricted operations on your own account. It doesn't allow customers to touch any account other than their own. On the same lines, it is illegal to tap electric power directly from the pole in front of your house (or from the distribution box). In all these cases, there is an interface (the speedometer, the ATM, and the power outlets) that is supported by an implementation and that implementation is protected by the interface (i.e., the interface provides a clean and well defined way of accessing the implementation). Further, the interface protects the implementation from devious access. In other words, the implementation works in a specific manner and it keeps track of its state. Moreover, the implementation assumes that its state can only be altered by the interface and not by anyone else. If this pre-condition is violated (i.e., somehow the state of the implementation is altered from outside without using the provided interface), there is no guarantee that the implementation operates correctly. Looking from the interface perspective, the implementation should be operated upon (or accessed via) the published interface to ensure the integrity of the implementation.

Revisiting the laser disc player, when we press PLAY, the LD player implementation checks to make sure that

a) a disc is loaded

b) the disc drawer (or tray) is closed

If these conditions are satisfied, it activates the laser beam mechanism and the motor drive, etc. and starts reading the disc. In order to sense conditions (a) and (b), the LD player probably uses some kind of micro switches. Further, the assumption is that nobody else will operate these switches directly; only the implementation has control over the switches. [This is somewhat similar to the *door closed* sensor on washers and dryers that we see so often. The instructions that come with these appliances clearly say that the washer will operate only when the door is closed. If you look carefully, there is a small sensor that is underneath (or behind) the door. When you close the door, the switch is depressed and this indicates to the washer that the door is closed. If you are curious, press the switch manually and sure enough the washer will run! But now you have by-passed the interface of the washer and this might cause some damage to you and/or the washer.] But if this assumption is violated, there is no guarantee that the player will operate as specified. If we somehow manipulate these switches manually and fool the player to believe that there is a disc loaded and that the drawer is closed, and then press PLAY button, the player will definitely activate the laser beam mechanism, probably causing irreparable damage to the player and its users (fortunately the construction of the player makes it al-

---

[5]It's against the law to tamper with a vehicle's speedometer.

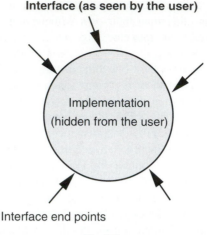

Interface (as seen by the user)

Implementation
(hidden from the user)

Interface end points

Fig. 2-3

most impossible to do so). This will not happen if a user abides by the published interface (i.e., the user plays by the rules).

Data abstraction brings in a related concept called *Data Encapsulation*. Whenever there is an object with an interface supported by an implementation, we invariably see *Implementation Hiding* (some call it information hiding). There is some information that is hidden in the implementation and this information, though very much important for the implementation, is of no value to the clients of the interface. The implementation is encapsulated by the interface and the only way to get to the implementation legally is through the interface (See Fig. 2-3).

This is like saying: *The only way to enter a room is through the doors provided for that purpose*. The LD player encapsulated its laser beam mechanism, motor, and the electronics. The encapsulated item could well be another object (or a set of objects). The motor and the laser beam are definitely objects of some other class. Note that the encapsulated data is critical for the implementation of the object. Further, it is mandatory that the integrity (or correct state) of the encapsulated information is maintained by the implementation.

WHAT IS THE BENEFIT OF DATA ENCAPSULATION?

When data is encapsulated, clients cannot directly access, let alone modify, the encapsulated data of the object. Only the interface functions can access/modify the encapsulated information. Further, users of the interface will not have any knowledge as to how the functions that describe the interface use the encapsulated information; and it is of no interest to the users of the object (or class). Because it is guaranteed by the postulates of OOP (and by the language used to implement the object) that the encapsulated information is accessible only through the published interface, the integrity of the object is assured. The LD player operates properly because the laser beam mechanism (and other electronics) is encapsulated and only the implementation has access to them (i.e., the implementation has exclusive access to the encapsulated information). And when the user operates on a LD player, the interface manipulates the encapsulated information on behalf of the user.

Another benefit of Data Encapsulation is *Implementation Independence*. Since the encapsulated data (or information) is not seen by the users of a class, they are not even aware of its existence (to some extent this depends on the language, as we will see in subsequent chapters). Therefore, the interface seen by the user is not affected (and should not be affected) by a change in the encapsulated data. To illustrate this aspect, let's revisit the LD player.

Let's assume that we used a set of 16 bit digital to analog (D/A) converters to convert the digital information on the disc to analog format in the first implementation and it is working fine. But our experiments show that a 20 bit D/A converter provides better audio and video resolution. So we change the implementation of the LD player electronics to use 20 bit D/A converters in place of the 16 bit D/A converters. After this change, will the user operate the player any differently? Definitely not. The user is probably not even aware of the fact that we are using any kind of D/A converters internally. And even if she is aware of this fact (probably by reading the technical specifications in the user's manual), she cannot directly access the D/A converters. Only the implementation has knowledge of the change from 16 bit D/A to 20 bit D/A converters. Since the interface has intimate knowledge of the implementation and the encapsulated data, it (the interface) knows how to work with the new implementation. Thus a change in the encapsulated information will only affect the way the interface operates on the encapsulated data (the implementation) but will not affect the client's interface to the object. A change in the implementation should not affect the interface seen by the clients of that object.

As an example of the benefit of abstraction and encapsulation, consider internet addresses. An internet address can be represented by a class TInternetAddress. This class would provide the necessary operations to extract the domain name, host name, etc. A client wouldn't have to know how an internet address is stored internally. When internet addresses were first introduced, they were represented using 32 bits. This was good enough to represent all domains and all nodes within a domain. But, with the growing popularity of the internet, thousands of new hosts are being put on the internet every month. At this rate, we will soon run out of internet addresses to handout. To overcome this limitation, very soon internet addresses will be represented using 128 bits. But, this is an internal implementation change and clients should not have to learn anything new to use the internet. This is easily accomplished by the class TInternetAddress. The representation of the internet address is encapsulated and switching to a 128 bit implementation would just cause a change in implementation and not the interface. Such are the benefits of abstraction and encapsulation.

RELATION BETWEEN INTERFACE, IMPLEMENTATION, AND DATA ENCAPSULATION

- The interface is the client's view of any class (and its objects).
- The interface is supported by the encapsulated implementation.
- A change in the implementation (that supports the interface) should not affect the interface seen by the clients of that class.

- An encapsulated implementation provides the implementor freedom to change it without affecting the interface; i.e., how the clients use the interface is independent of the implementation that supports the interface.
- Data abstraction and data encapsulation principles are not attributes of a language; they are the fundamental concepts of the *object-oriented programming* paradigm and any language that supports OOP must support Data Abstraction (and other concepts discussed in Chapter 1).

NOTE   A real world example (the laser disc player), which is easy to follow, has been used here. The goal here is to clearly understand the concepts. There are a plethora of other data abstraction examples in this and in subsequent chapters.

PRECAUTIONS WITH DATA ENCAPSULATION

It is a good idea to encapsulate information that is of no importance to the user. However, users might need to access the encapsulated information in order to use the object effectively. When some element is encapsulated, the implementor has to provide facilities in the interface to access or manipulate the encapsulated information. The access provided may be restricted or controlled. However, the interface must provide proper facilities to access/modify the encapsulated entity. If an abstraction encapsulates a piece of information that is very important for the user but fails to provide proper facilities to access the encapsulated information, the abstraction is not correct (i.e., the interface is not sufficient).

Going back to the LD player example, the mechanism to start and stop the motor is definitely encapsulated. The player should run the motor only when a disc is loaded and the disc tray is closed. Users would like to change discs as and when they like, which in turn requires that the motor be stopped. When the user pushes the OPEN/CLOSE button, the laser disc player turns off the motor and then releases the disc tray. Even though the motor control mechanism is encapsulated, the interface provides necessary and sufficient controls to manipulate the motor, albeit indirectly.

WHAT (AND WHEN) TO ENCAPSULATE

- If an item doesn't add any value to the user's perception of the class, encapsulate that item; i.e., removing that item from the interface doesn't reduce the usefulness of that class in any way.
- If an item is a piece of sensitive data (trade secrets, patented information, personal information, etc.) encapsulate it so that the users cannot access it directly.
- If some item is hazardous (laser beams, X-rays, microwaves, etc.) and requires special skills to handle (which normal users might not have), encapsulate it.
- If the class uses some elements for its own housekeeping and it doesn't add any value to the interface, it should be encapsulated.

- If some item is subject to change in the future (to use newer technology or to make it faster or safer) it should definitely be excluded from the interface of the class.

We will discuss many of these situations in the ensuing chapters with many clear examples.

ABSTRACT DATA TYPES

Sometimes people talk about *abstract data types* rather than *data abstraction*. This might be confusing for those venturing into OOP, but they are very closely related.

An abstract data type is a new type defined by the programmer, along with a set of operations to manipulate the new type. The definition of a new abstract type is a direct application of the data abstraction concept. Abstract data types are also called *Programmer Defined Types.*

Any language basically supports some built-in data types (like integers, floating point numbers, characters, etc.) and usually provides a set of operations to manipulate these built-in types.[6] But when we use these built-in (or language defined) types, we don't know how these data types are implemented nor do we care (data abstraction and encapsulation in use). But the language (more precisely, the implementor of the language compiler) has an intimate knowledge of the implementation. Further, users of the language defined types cannot access the internal representation of the type directly. One has to use the operations provided by the language to manipulate them.

For example, when we use floating point numbers provided by a language, we don't have any knowledge of the internal representation of the floating point type.[7] But we know for sure that operations like + and - are available to manipulate floating point numbers. When we use the floating point type, we indirectly use whatever representation the implementor of the language compiler provides and we can only use the operations defined by the language specification. This also provides independence from a particular compiler and a particular machine. We can use any language compiler that we like on any machine that the compiler runs on (i.e., we get implementation independence).

Languages that support structured programming (Pascal, Algol, C, etc.) also allow the user to define new types, called user defined types or programmer defined types. These user defined types in turn use the language defined types in their implementation. These languages also allow the programmer to define a set of operations (not to be confused with *operators* like + and −) on these user defined types. But the major problem is that the implementation of these user defined types is not encapsulated. Anyone using a programmer defined type has full knowledge of its implementation and the language does not protect the implementor of the new type from its users, i.e., data encapsulation is absent (some amount of encapsulation is possible in C using *static* data). The new type is generally defined as a combination of a data structure and a set of functions that manipu-

---

[6]These are *int, double or float, and char* in C++.

[7]A floating point number can be stored in a variety of different formats. IEEE defines a standard IEEE-754, that is usually followed by most compilers and processors.

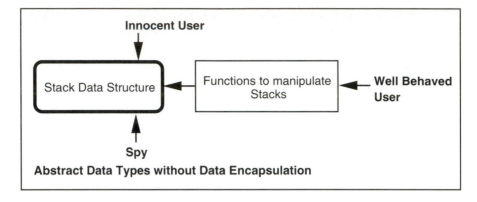

Fig. 2-4

late the data structure. The functions access the data structure in a specific manner. Any user of the new type is, in principle, required to use these functions to operate on the new type; i.e., the user should not access/modify the data structure directly. But the language has no way of enforcing this rule. Anyone can write a new function that operates on the data structure without any knowledge as to how the data structure is supposed to be used. In other words, the implementation is not protected from illegal access. In these languages (Pascal, Algol, C, etc.), data integrity is ensured only when users follow the implicit rules; the language cannot enforce these rules. In essence, the new type is nothing but a data structure supported by a set of functions (operations).

A simple example is a Stack with operations like Push() and Pop(). The data structure could be an array or a list (stack implemented using an array or a list). Operations Push() and Pop() modify the data structure as and when needed. We also need to worry about creation and destruction of multiple stacks. For the sake of simplicity let's restrict ourselves to a stack of integers (*int*s). The type of the elements stored on the stack doesn't make any difference to this discussion. In a subsequent chapter we will see how to implement generic stacks using template classes.

IMPLEMENTATION OF THE ABSTRACT DATA TYPE—STACK

The example below shows a simple Stack implementation in C.

File Stack.h—available to all users of the abstract data type, Stack.

```
typedef Stack* StackId;
typedef int bool;
struct Stack {
        int* data;              /* storage for elements on the stack */
        unsigned count;         /* number of elements on the stack */
        int* top;               /* pointer to top of stack */
        /* and more...*/
};
```

File Stack.c—Implementation of the functions provided to manipulate Stacks.

```
StackId CreateStack()
{
        /* code to create a new Stack.
            Returns the name (StackId) of the new stack*/
}

bool DestroyStack(StackId whichStack) // bool is a C++ data type
{
        /* code to destroy whichStack */
}

void Push(StackId whichStack, int thisElement)
{
        /* code to push thisElement onto whichStack */
}

int Pop(StackId whichStack)
{
        /* code to pop the top element from whichStack */
}
```

The file **Stack.c** is compiled with the **Stack.h** file and the object code is supplied to the user along with the **Stack.h** file. The users of **Stack** will not have access to the source code of the functions that manipulate Stacks.

The **Stack** data structure is just a piece of dumb data and the intelligence required to use the **Stack** properly is embedded in the functions **Push, Pop**, etc. that exist to support the data structure. But all the information that is important for the user is in the data structure **Stack**; the functions just provide a facility to manipulate the data. One can access and modify the **Stack** data structure without using the functions provided. The compiler cannot stop users from doing so. In other words, tight coupling between the data structure and the functions is lacking. However, with an OOP language, the functions and the data structure form an integral unit (the class **Stack**) and there is no way to directly access the data in the object without using the functions provided in the class. The object owns the data structure and only the interface is allowed to access it. It is easier to implement abstract data types in languages that support OOP.

Programmer defined types in procedure-oriented languages behave (almost) like new types that have been added to the language definition but they don't have much protection because anyone can modify them directly. Such programmer defined types are called *abstract data types*. The LD player that we designed earlier is an abstract data type. The advantage with OOP languages is that they offer data encapsulation that protects the implementation (and hence the implementor) and the programmer defined types are treated like language defined types. In other words, they have privileges and also responsibilities.

As an example, consider an integer data type that can hold very large numbers (often used in astronomy). Our requirement is not satisfied by a 32 bit integer (4 byte integer), so we want to create a new type, an abstract data type, **TInt**.

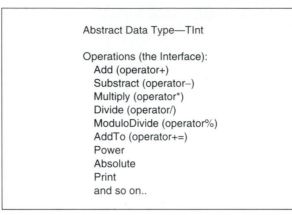

Abstract Data Type—TInt

Operations (the Interface):
   Add (operator+)
   Substract (operator–)
   Multiply (operator*)
   Divide (operator/)
   ModuloDivide (operator%)
   AddTo (operator+=)
   Power
   Absolute
   Print
   and so on..

Needless to point out that we will hide the implementation of the TInt type. We might use two 4 byte integers (or an array of 8 bytes) to implement this new type, but the clients of TInt will not have (and should not have) any knowledge of such details. In the future, if we use a processor that supports a 64 bit integer (which is very likely), then we might use that for our implementation instead of using our own representation, but again that decision is left to the implementor.

Using data abstraction, we have created a new type and provided a set of useful operations on this new type. Since the type is not supported directly by the language and the programmer implemented it using an abstraction, it is an abstract data type. It's for this reason that data abstraction is sometimes defined as the *process of defining an abstract data type along with a set of operations and hiding the implementation.*

NOTE   We would like to have all the privileges (and responsibilities) for our Abstract Data Type as is available for the language defined types (i.e., the clients of the new type should not see any difference whatsoever between the language defined types and the Abstract Data Types). This may not be possible with all object-oriented languages; it requires language support for operator overloading. More on this in subsequent chapters.

DATA ABSTRACTION WITH C++

The fundamental unit of data abstraction in C++ is the *class.*

STOP   You must have a rudimentary knowledge of C and C++ syntax to understand this section. You must be comfortable with function name overloading, C++ argument styles, const arguments and const member functions, references, etc.

The C++ notion of a **class** is an extension of the familiar **struct** concept of C (or the record in Pascal). Let's define the interface for the TInt class:

```
class TInt {
  public:
      // Constructor: Create a TInt from an int
```

```
    TInt(int value);
    TInt(long mostSignificant, unsigned long leastSignificant);
    // Create a TInt from a long integer
    TInt(long value);
    // Create a TInt from a short integer
    TInt(short value);
    // Default Constructor
    TInt();

    // Copy constructor
    TInt(const TInt& copy);
    // Assignment Operator
    TInt& operator=(const TInt& assign);

    // Destructor
    ~TInt();

    // Operators for the TInt type
    TInt    operator+(const TInt& operand) const;       // addition
    TInt    operator-(const TInt& operand) const;       // subtraction
    TInt    operator*(const TInt& multiplicand) const; // multiplication
    TInt    operator/(const TInt& divideBy) const;      // division
    TInt    operator%(const TInt& divideBy) const;      // modulo division
    // Add operand to this number
    TInt    operator+=(const TInt& operand);
    // many other operators omitted for simplicity

    // Raise this TInt number to the power 'to'
    TInt    Power(const TInt& to) const;
    void    Print() const;
    // Return the absolute value of this TInt
    TInt    Absolute() const;
    // Change sign of this number
    void    FlipSign();

    // Helper functions
    long GetMostSignificantPart() const;
    unsigned long GetLeastSignificantPart() const;

private:
    // Internal representation of the TInt type
    unsigned long    _leastSignificantPart;
    long             _mostSignificantPart;
    // and probably some private member functions too
};
```

ACCESS REGIONS IN A CLASS

Each class can have three distinct access regions. Of all the OOP languages that I have used, only C++ has this elaborate (and useful) scheme of three regions.

The **public** region is the most important region. It specifies the interface of the class to its clients. Anything listed under the **public** region can be accessed by all clients.

SOURCE CODE STYLE IN THIS BOOK

1. All class names begin with T. Classes behave like new *types* added to the language; Hence, the prefix T. However, the T is dropped from filenames in which these classes are implemented. For example, the file that contains the interface of TInt would be Int.h

2. All member functions begin with an upper case alphabet (Add(), FlipSign(), etc.).

3. All enumerations (*enum*s) begin with an E. Members in an enum begin with e.

4. All local (automatic) variables in functions begin with lower case alphabets.

5. All *constants* are coded with upper case alphabets and digits only. For example:

```
const unsigned DAYS_IN_WEEK = 7;
```

6. Underscore (_) is used in naming constants (as in DAYS_IN_WEEK above).

7. Comments in header files precede the declaration. Short comments may be on the same line as the code.

8. All data members (instance variables) begin with an _ (underscore).

9. Global variables/constants usually begin with g.
For example

```
// Change sign of this number
void FlipSign();
TInt operator+(...) const; // Addition
```

The **private** region is the other side of the class concept. It is the region used by the implementation. Anything that is listed under the **private** region cannot be accessed by anyone except the implementor of the class.

There can be more than one such region (**public , protected,** and **private**) declared in a single class; all of them are merged by the compiler.

The third region is the **protected** region. This is used for code extension and reusability (inheritance) and will be discussed in later chapters.

Understanding the code

1. Constructors: All member functions of a class that have the same name as the class (TInt in our example) are called *constructors*. They are used in creation and initialization of new objects. Why do we need constructors?

When we declare language defined types (say *int*), the language (or compiler) creates a variable of the type requested (*int* in our case). An initial value (if specified) is also stored in the *int* variable. For example:

```
int i; // No initial value
int j = 10; // create j with an initial value - 10
```

The compiler is responsible for allocating (or reserving) memory for i and j and initializing j to 10. Similarly, in case of objects, we need a facility to initialize any object that we create; we would like to store sensible values in the data members. The user might wish to provide some initial values for the TInt object. This is accomplished by the constructor(s). A class can provide a number of overloaded constructors. The only way to create (and initialize) an object in C++ is by calling one of the constructors provided by the class. In the class TInt,

```
TInt(int value);
TInt(long mostSignificant,
         unsigned long leastSignificant);
TInt(long value);
TInt(short value);
TInt();
TInt(const TInt& arg);
```

are all Constructors. They behave like overloaded functions (and are implemented by the compiler as overloaded functions but with a different name.

See Chapter 3 for more details on constructors.

2. Destructor: A member function of a class that has the same name as the class and is prepended with a ~ is called a *Destructor*. In C++, no other type (or declaration) can have a ~ in its name. It is used to do clean-up after an object of a class is no longer in the scope of a program segment. Unlike constructors, a class can have only one destructor. Destructors are very useful in garbage collection.

On exit from a function (or block), objects created in that function (or block) are destroyed by the compiler automatically. But an object might have accumulated resources (dynamic memory, disk blocks, network connections, etc.) during its lifetime (or at the time of its creation). These resources are stored in the object's data members and are manipulated by the member functions. When the object is destroyed (on exit from a function), it is necessary that the resources held by the object are released because the object is no longer accessible. Because the compiler isn't aware of the resources held by the object (they might have been dynamically allocated), it is the responsibility of the object to release such resources. To help an objects in doing so, on exit from a function (or block), the destructor is called on all objects created statically (i.e., created without using the new() operator) in that function (or block). The destructor should release all the resources held by the object. In other words, the destructor provides the mechanism by which objects can get rid of resources before their (object's) destruction. See the example below in copy constructors. More about destructors in Chapter 3.

Constructors and Destructors are special member functions; they don't have any return value types in their declarations (like ordinary functions), which imply that they cannot return any values.[8]

3. The Copy Constructor: This is a special constructor used to create a *new object from an existing object;* hence the name *copy constructor.* It is easy to identify a copy constructor because of its unique prototype (or signature).[9] When built-in data type variables (like int and char) are passed *by value* from one function to another, it is the responsibility of the compiler to make a copy of the variable and pass that copy to the called function. When objects are passed by value to a function, a copy of the object has to be made just as with the built-in types. However, objects are not simple variables. They are complex entities implemented by programmers. So, the compiler needs help in making a copy. Logically, the implementor of the object is responsible for making copies of the object (the implementor for the built-in types is the compiler). The copy constructor is provided for that purpose. Whenever a copy of an object is needed, the compiler calls on the copy constructor to make a copy of the object. Copy constructors are essential when a class uses dynamic memory in its implementation. If the implementor of a class doesn't provide a copy constructor, the compiler generates a copy constructor automatically. Whether the generated copy constructor satisfies the requirement of the class is another issue altogether. Note that the copy constructor is a constructor with special semantics. A normal constructor is invoked to create and initialize a new object (from scratch) where as a copy constructor is invoked to create a new object from an existing object. This is the major distinction between a copy constructor and any other constructor. The copy constructor is invoked when

- an object is passed *by value* from one function to another function
- an object is returned *by value* from a function
- a new object is instantiated from an existing object

```
void f()
{
    TInt x(100);    // create an object x of type TInt
    // g() is a function that accepts a TInt by value and
    // returns nothing
    void g(TInt); // prototype of function g()
    // ...

    g(x);
}

void g(TInt y)
{
    //.. code ..
}
```

[8]That might cause you to think 'How can we signal failures in constructors and destructors?' A discussion of the different solutions are presented in a subsequent chapter.

[9]In this book, the terms function signature and function prototype have the same meaning.

When function f() calls function g() with the argument x, a copy of x is made by the copy constructor and this copy is made available to g() as its actual argument y. On exit from g() the object y (its formal argument) is destroyed, i.e., the destructor is invoked on the object y. Needless to say that operations on the object y within g() have no effect on the object x within f() (as is expected in *pass by value* semantics).

See Chapter 3 and Chapter 4 for more details.

4. The Assignment Operator: A copy constructor is used to create a new object from an existing object, whereas an assignment operator is used when an existing object is assigned to another existing object explicitly. Assignment is an operation explicitly done by the user. For example:

```
TInt a;
TInt b(100);
// ...
a = b;    // Assign b to a; both a and b already exist.
```

Note that the source is the object b and the destination is the object a. Both objects already exist and are being used by the programmer. If an implementor of a class doesn't provide the assignment operator, the compiler generates an assignment operator for the class, if needed. Again, as with the copy constructor, whether the compiler generated assignment operator satisfies the requirements of the objects of the class is a different issue. The compiler generated operator is pretty simple and isn't normally useful. See Chapter 3 for more details.

5. All other functions are just ordinary member functions of this class. They can be used to operate on objects of the class TInt. A member function (more precisely a *non-static* member function) of a class can only be used with an existing object of its class.

6. Operator Functions: Since TInt is a new type that we have defined, we would like to provide operators (like + and −) to make it more useful. In other words, one should be able to use a TInt object just like an integer (int). For example:

```
TInt a(10);
TInt b(20);
TInt c;
int i = 100;
int j = 200;
int k;
// Add a and b and store the result in c
c = a + b;
// Add integers i and j and store result in k
k = i + j;
```

Adding i and j using the operator + is a simple operation. The operator + is provided by the language. In other words, the language *knows* how to add two integers because the implementation of int is provided by the language. If the language knows how to implement an int, it better know how to add them too.

Turning to TInt , the implementation of this abstract data type is provided by the implementor. How can I expect the language to know how to add two TInts? If we provide the implementation for the TInt type, it is also our responsibility to provide the implementation for the operator + (if we wish to). But not many languages allow this freedom to implement operators. Fortunately, C++ does. C++ allows the implementor of an abstract data type to provide sensible operators for it. What we are really doing is extending the meaning of the + operator to our TInt type. This is the concept of *operator overloading*. An operator function, a function that implements a specific operator, is defined just like any other member function but its name begins with the reserved keyword *operator* and is followed by the operator being overloaded. See Chapter 8 for more details.

Note that operator overloading is a very powerful mechanism that can be abused very easily. The class implementor must carefully choose the operators that are sensible for the class she is implementing. An operator cannot be used unless it is supported (i.e., implemented) by the class (except the assignment operator, operator =, which is generated by the compiler if the class implementor doesn't provide one).

NOTE   Strictly speaking, the operators like **+, -, *, /,** etc. should be implemented as non-member functions (or **friend** functions). The class interface above would look like

```
// Operations on the TInt type
 TInt operator+(const TInt& operand1, const TInt& operand2);
 TInt operator-(const TInt& operand1, const TInt& operand2);
// and so on
```

Many such details have been omitted just to keep the example as simple as possible. See Chapter 7 for details on the friend function concept.

7. Significance of const in Member Function Declarations: In the header file above, many of the functions have a trailing *const* keyword. For example:

```
void Print() const;
```

This **const** applies to the function and not to any arguments. Such functions are called **const** member functions. Only member functions (and not ordinary functions) can be declared **const**. Data members of a class, arguments to a function, objects, ordinary variables, etc. can also be declared **const**. A **const** member function guarantees that it will not alter the *state* of the object on which it is invoked. The Print() function assures that it will not modify the data members of the object on which it is invoked. Such functions are also called *Selectors*. It is a function that only reads from the object and doesn't write (modify) to any of the data members in that object. So

```
TInt aInt;
aInt.Print();
```

will not modify aInt in anyway. Compilers ensure this constantness by preventing assignment to data members of the object inside these **const** member functions. See Chapter 3 for more details.

Now with this knowledge of abstract data types, our laser disc player abstraction might be declared as follows (in C++):

```
typedef short ErrorCode;
class TLaserDiscPlayer {
        public:
                // Operations
                ErrorCode   Play(unsigned atChapter=0);
                ErrorCode   Stop(void);
                ErrorCode   SearchFor(unsigned chapter);
                ErrorCode   OpenTray();
                ErrorCode   CloseTray();
                void    PowerOn();
                void    PowerOff();
                ErrorCode   Pause();
                // Constructor
                TLaserDiscPlayer();
                // Destructor
                ~TLaserDiscPlayer();
                // and many more
        private:
                enum ETrayStatus { eClosed, eOpen };
                enum EPowerStatus { eOff, eOn };
                enum EPlayerMode { ePlay, eSearch,
                            ePause, eStop };
                ETrayStatus  _trayStatus;   // open or closed
                EPowerStatus _powerStatus;  // On or Off
                EPlayerMode  _playerMode;   // Playing, Searching etc.
                // and many more
};
```

The class declaration above does not reveal any details about how the interface functions (or simply the *interface*) are implemented. Such a class declaration is also called the **interface file** or, under C++, the **class header file** and is usually designated with a **.h** extension. The file above would be **Int.h**.

SOME TERMINOLOGY USED WITH CLASSES

The interface of a class is listed as functions inside the class. These are called *member functions* under C++. Smalltalk refers to them as *methods*. Ada refers to them as *operations* (not to be confused with *operators* provided in C++). They can also be called *interface functions* because they provide the interface to the class. These terms are used interchangeably throughout this book. The elements that are not functions are called *data members* in C++. A good abstraction (i.e., a well designed interface) never has any data members in the **public** region.[10]

Table 2-1 on p. 48 summarizes the different terms used in languages.

---

[10]There are some subtle differences between interface, type and class, that are discussed at the end of this chapter.

TABLE 2-1 Terminology used in different languages

Definitions	C++ Term	Smalltalk Term	Eiffel
A description of a group of similar objects	Class	Class	Class
Grouping of private data and functions	Object	Object or Instance	Object or Instance
Higher level, generalized class	Base Class	Super Class	Parent Class
Lower level, specialized class	Derived class	Subclass	Child class
Way to reuse design and code	Inheritance	Inheritance	Inheritance
Type independent call	Polymorphism		
A request for an object to carry out one of its operations	Member function call	Message invocation	Operation invocation
How to perform one of the operations	Member function implementation	Method	Routine (procedure or function)
Private Data	Data Member	Instance variable	Field, Attributes

SMALLTALK   Under Smalltalk, calling an interface function (member function) of an object is viewed as *sending a message to the object*. This seems appropriate. We send a message to the LD player asking it to PLAY the disc. Similarly, the message *Throttle_down* is interpreted by the car abstraction as a request to increase the speed of the car. Sending a message to an object causes the execution of a *method* in that object (i.e., the object executes a particular method (a function) when we send a message). In other words, the object *responds* to the message. The concept is that a message is just a name seen by the client and the name is bound (probably at run time) to the correct implementation of this message (the method) in the object receiving the message. Smalltalk refers to the data members as *instance variables*.

WHO IS THE IMPLEMENTOR OF A CLASS?

The programmer who writes the source code for implementing all the member functions is the implementor of the class. The implementor has all the code that implements the member functions and also has a very intimate knowledge of the data members and how they are used by the member functions. Finally, the implementor has the right and the liberty to change the implementation (but not the interface) when required. Changing the interface of a class is done very rarely. We will see the reasons behind this in later chapters.

The implementor compiles the source code (which results in object code) that implements all the member functions and gives it to clients along with the interface (header) file. The source code of the implementation is usually kept in a file with the same name as the class but with an extension like **.C**, **.cc**, **.cpp**, **.cp**, etc. (depending on the compiler and conventions used). This book uses the **.cc** extension whenever referring to implementation files. The implementor compiles the files **Int.h** and **Int.cc** to produce an object file (call it **Int.obj**). The clients of **TInt** never see the source code (the implementation of the member functions). The clients receive the interface file **Int.h** and the **Int.obj** file. The header file, **Int.h,** along with the **Int.obj** file, is all that is needed to use the class **TInt**. Note that both the implementor and the clients use the same interface (header) file, **Int.h.**

IMPLEMENTING THE MEMBER FUNCTIONS

Here is a part of the file **Int.cc:**

```
// Implementation of the Print member function
#include <iostream.h>
#include "Int.h"
void
TInt::Print() const
{
    // cout is an instance of ostream, a standard i/o stream library class.
    cout << "0x " <<_mostSignificantPart << ", 0x" << _leastSignificantPart;
    // any assignment to the data members in this function is illegal
}
```

Understanding the code. If we omit the class name TInt, the ::, and the trailing const keyword, the declaration looks like a plain function:

```
void Print()
{
    cout << "0x " <<_mostSignificantPart << ",0x", _leastSignificantPart;
}
```

This is just a normal function. How do we identify (or demarcate) functions that are member functions of a class? Simply add the name of the class and ::. Here, **::** is the **scope resolution operator**. TInt::Print declares that the function Print() is a member function of the class TInt (as declared in the header file). If function Print() is not declared in the header file, **Int.h,** trying to define it will cause a compile time error. The const qualifier is applicable to member functions only. Therefore, when we define member functions of a class, we use the classname::functionname syntax. It's that simple. Since the member functions belong to a class, two (or more) classes can have member functions with the same name. They don't conflict with each other. Inside a member function we can access any element (data member or member function) of the class.

IDENTIFYING THE TARGET OBJECT IN MEMBER FUNCTIONS

When writing code for the member functions (constructors, destructors, operators, etc.), how can we refer to the object on which this member function was invoked, explicitly? Or, if we want to how can we return the target object's value explicitly? How should one access a data member of the object on which the member function was invoked when inside the member function?

This is where the mystical **this** pointer steps in. Every member function of a class has access to a special pointer—this. The this pointer holds the address of the object on which the member function was invoked (i.e., the this pointer always points to the target object). The this pointer is valid only inside a member function and the name this is a reserved word in C++.

The type of the this pointer is 'pointer to the class to which the member function belongs'. We could also say 'the type of this is the class name'. Within the member function, the this pointer points to the instance of the class on which this member function was invoked.

There is nothing special about member functions as far as the compiler is concerned. In fact they are implemented by the compiler as normal functions but after some name mangling to make their names unique. The first argument received by every member function is the this pointer. Programmers never explicitly declare the this pointer but it is always there. The this pointer is usually the implicit first argument to every (non-static) member function. The compiler inserts this implicit argument into the declaration of every member function. For example, with the this pointer explicitly declared just to illustrate the concept, the Print() member function would look so:

```
void TInt::Print(const TInt* this )
{
    cout << "0x" <<_mostSignificantPart << ",0x" <<_leastSignificantPart;
}
```

In reality, the this pointer declaration is seen in the mangled function name. Therefore, TInt::Print would look like this:

```
void Print__3TIntFv(const TInt* this)
{
    cout << "0x" << this->_mostSignificantPart << ",0x" <<
    this->_leastSignificantPart;

}
```

Once we leave a member function, the name this is no longer valid.

☞ Should I always use the this pointer to reference members of my object?

Fortunately not. Whenever a member function uses an unqualified name of a member (data member or member function) of the class, it implies the use of the this pointer. The compiler inserts the this pointer in each and every expression inside a member function that references a member, if the user already didn't do so. Revisiting the Print() function, we can re-write it as

```
void TInt::Print()
{
    cout << "0x" << this->_mostSignificantPart << ",0x" <<
    _leastSignificantPart;
}
```

The expression this->_mostSignificantPart is the explicit way of accessing the data member _mostSignificantPart using the this pointer. The expression this->_mostSignificantPart means 'the member _mostSignificantPart in the object pointed by the pointer this'. The this pointer is just another argument to a member function that can be used like any other argument (but with some restrictions discussed elsewhere). Even in the previous implementations of Print(), the compiler automatically expands the expres-

sion _mostSignificantPart (without any reference to the this pointer) to
this->_mostSignificantPart.

In the code fragment

```
TInt aInt;
aInt.Print();
```

Print() is invoked on the object aInt (i.e., the message Print() is being sent to the object
aInt.). The this pointer will point to aInt inside Print().

Because this is a pointer to an object, to get the whole object using the this
pointer, we have to de-reference the this pointer (using the * operator) as *this. The this
is the address of the object and *this is the value of that object, just as with any other
pointer.

The concept of this pointer is not unique to C++ either. OOP languages use different names to refer to the object receiving the message. Smalltalk calls it **Self** and Eiffel
uses the name **Current**.

C++   Now, let's turn our attention to some operator functions of class TInt.

```
// Implementation of operator+
TInt TInt::operator+(const TInt& operand) const
// TInt is the return type of this operator function
{
    /*
    Code for computing the sum of operand and the TInt number on which the
    operator+ function is invoked which is pointed to by the this pointer.
    This function computes the sum of *this and operand and returns the
    sum as a new TInt number. It does not modify *this or operand (hence
    the const qualifier). The algorithm is
                1. Add the _leastSignificantPart parts and save the carry
                   bit.
                2. Add the _mostSignificantPart parts using the carry
                   bit.
                3. Store (1) and (2) in a temporary TInt number
                4. Return the temporary TInt number by value.
    */
        TInt           result = *this; // ❶ calls the Copy Constructor
        unsigned char carry = 0;

        // Add the leastSignificant parts and check for any carry
        result._leastSignificantPart += operand.GetLeastSignificantPart();
        if ( result._leastSignificantPart <
             operand.GetLeastSignificantPart() )
             carry = 1;

        // Add the mostSignificant parts with the carry
        result._mostSignificantPart += carry +
             operand.GetMostSignificantPart();

        return (result);
}
```

```
// Skeleton of a constructor
TInt::TInt(long msp, unsigned long lsp)
{
        // Copy the values passed to the constructor into the
        // corresponding data members
        _leastSignificantPart = lsp;
        _mostSignificantPart = msp;
}
```

❶ This way of creating and initializing an object in one step is more efficient than creating the object (using the default constructor in this case) and then assigning to it. More on this in a subsequent chapter.

A SAMPLE PROGRAM

A test program that uses the **TInt** class is shown below. It is here just for the sake of completeness and has no real significance otherwise.

```
#include "Int.h"

main()
{
        TInt hugeNumber(100, 2000); // create a TInt ❶
        TInt normalNumber(1000); // and another TInt ❷
        TInt sum;

        // Send message print to hugeNumber.
        // The this pointer will be setup to point to hugeNumber
        hugeNumber.Print(); // ❸
        // Change the sign of hugeNumber
        hugeNumber.FlipSign(); // ❹
        // Print it again
        hugeNumber.Print();

        // add hugeNumber and normalNumber and store
        // the result in sum. The statement sum = hugeNumber + normalNumber
        // is interpreted as
        // 1. Invoke operator+ function on hugeNumber and pass
        //    normalNumber as the argument.
        // 2. Invoke the assignment operator (operator=) on sum
        //    and pass the result from (1) as the argument.
        // sum.operator=( hugeNumber.operator+(normalNumber) );

        sum = hugeNumber + normalNumber; // ❺

        // Print the result i.e. invoke print() on sum.
        sum.Print();
}
```

❶ Here we create a **TInt** object specifying both the most significant part and the least significant part. Class **TInt** provides a matching constructor and we use it here.

❷ This creates another object with just a integer argument. There is a constructor in class TInt that accepts just an integer and it is used here.

❸ Here we invoke a member function on the hugeNumber object. The usual object.function syntax is used.

❹ Next we change the sign of the hugeNumber. This is done by the member function FlipSign.

❺ Here we compute the sum of hugeNumber and normalNumber, two TInt objects, and assign the result to sum—another TInt object. Note that neither hugeNumber nor normalNumber are affected by this addition operation. The member function operator+ is called on the first object (hugeNumber) and the second operand (normalNumber) is passed as the argument.

THE FOCUS IS ON THE OBJECT

In object-oriented programming, we always work with objects and nothing else. It is important to keep in mind that whenever we discuss *invoking a function* or *sending a message* it is imperative that there is an object involved. We invoke a function on an object (or we send a message to an object). Without an object to receive the message, one cannot send a message; you need a target to throw at and that target is the object. Hereafter, we always talk in terms of invoking a member function on an object and never simply calling a function. Moreover, you cannot send any arbitrary message to an object.[11] An object will only respond to messages that it implements (i.e. messages it supports and understands). And the methods implemented by an object are documented in the class interface file. If you keep these simple concepts in mind, OOP is fun and easy to learn.

An inquisitive reader might be wondering about the private region shown in the TInt class declaration above. It seems to be against the principles of data encapsulation. If something cannot be accessed (let alone modified), it should not be visible and should not be part of the class interface file. If you are thinking on these lines, you are not alone. Anyone new to C++ will be intrigued by this idiosyncrasy of C++, which is not evident in other OOP languages. This issue, which is connected with the implementation of the C++ compiler/language, will be discussed in a subsequent chapter.

STYLE   Since the **private** region has no significance in the interface of a class, list it at the bottom of a class declaration where it attracts the least attention. Put the **public** region on top and list the member functions. Use sensible names for the class and the member functions; avoid acronyms that only you can understand.

A SECOND LOOK AT INTERFACE

We already know the importance of interface in OOP. And we also have an understanding of the relationship between interface and implementation. Every object supports a set of

---

[11] Smalltalk is a little different in the area of messages.

operations (messages, member functions). These operations are declared by specifying the name of the operation, the objects it takes as parameters, and the operation's return value. This is what we refer to as the signature of the operation (or the prototype of the operation/function). The set of *all* signatures defined by an object's operations is called the interface of the object.

A *type* is a name used to denote a particular interface. This makes it easy to manage interfaces. Otherwise, how can one distinguish one interface from another. If an object supports all the operations defined in the interface TInt, then we say that the object is of type TInt. It is possible that an object may have many types. In other words, an object can support (or respond to) multiple interfaces. Two objects are of the same type if both of them support the same interface, but their implementations can be entirely different.

So, now you might be thinking that a class is nothing but an interface. It might appear so in some languages. but they are not really the same. It is necessary to understand the difference between an object's class and its type. An object's class defines how the object is implemented. It defines the object's internal representation and also the implementation of the operations. However, an object's type has nothing do with implementation—it only refers to the set of operations that the object can respond to. An object can have many types and different classes can have the same type. But, there is very close relationship between a class and a type. A class clearly defines the operations that an object of that class can perform. Therefore, the class also defines the object's type. Any object of a class supports the interface defined by its class.

In C++ (and also Eiffel), a class specifies both the object's type and also its implementation. Both in C++ and Eiffel it is not possible to define an interface without it being inside a class. In other words, interfaces are specified only through classes.[12] Languages like Java allow programmers to just define interfaces, without them being attached to classes. A class can then implement an interface (i.e., its objects support the interface). In Smalltalk, programmers don't have to specify the types of variables. At run-time, when a message is sent to an object, it must only be checked to ensure that the receiving object implements the message, but the object itself need not be an instance of a particular class.

There are some important lessons to be learned from this preceding discussion. It is a very good practice to write software that depends on interfaces, but not specific implementations. An interface can be supported by many different implementations and the software is not tied to any particular implementation. When new objects that support the interface become available, our software wouldn't have to change. This is exactly what we strive to achieve in software design. The more we are independent of implementations the better.

Sometimes, we might be aware of implementation details but we still like to pretend ignorance. If something changes in the implementation (even drastically) we don't need to worry about it because our interface remains the same. In many situations, programmers (knowingly or unknowingly) use knowledge of the implementation in their programs when dealing with objects, making the program highly dependent on a particular implementation. This causes major design and implementation changes sooner or later.

Coming from the other side (i.e., the interface design side), interfaces should not expose implementation details. And a carefully designed interface should not require the

---

[12]An abstract class (Chapter 5) without any implementation comes close to a pure interface.

client to know anything about the implementation. If some implementation detail (even very tiny) is exposed in the interface, some clients will count on that being available in all implementations, thereby making the software highly brittle.

NOTE   Please see Chapter 5 for some related discussion of the issues surrounding interface and implementation.

WHAT IS A MULTI-THREAD SAFE CLASS?

Traditionally, operating systems (OS) supported only processes (also called tasks). Every process has its own address space and it has a single thread of execution. A process executes a program, which is a sequence of instructions. But most modern operating systems support multiple threads in a single process. A task can contain as many threads as required. All threads in a single process share the address space of the process. The threads have access to all global data in the process.

There are a number of advantages to using threads. First of all, it is a lot cheaper (and faster) to create threads. Creating a new process involves quite a bit of work inside the operating system (setting up memory pages, registers, process context, etc.). Most of what a thread needs is already available in the process. Communication among processes (IPC) is not easy because they are in different address spaces. But communication among threads in a single process is very easy because they share the same address space. With multiple threads, operations that can block, can be handled in parallel. The operating system schedules each thread independently. For example, consider an application that copies files from one machine to another. The user might wish to stop the copy operation in the middle. Creating a separate process just to wait on the user input is an overkill. A separate thread that waits on the user input is more appropriate here. The main application carries out the copy operation and the helper thread waits on user input. If the user decides to terminate the copy operation, then the thread waiting on user input runs and it informs the main application about the user's intent to stop the operation. The main application thread can then abort the copy operation. It is very common to use many threads in a single application. As another example, a document processing application can use one thread to print the document while another thread carries out index generation. At the same time, yet another thread could be accepting summary information about the document from the user.

Any application that uses multiple threads can be called a multi-threaded application. But when multiple threads are involved, synchronization and mutual exclusion is critical. When one thread is accessing a piece of data (for example, the thread printing the document), other threads attempting to access the same data (for writing) must be prevented from doing so. Depending on the operating system, an implementation can use a mutex, semaphore, critical section, spin-lock, messages, events, etc. to achieve this goal. For example, every page in the document can be protected by a mutex that allows only one thread to access the page. No matter what scheme is used for access control, the implementation must ensure that deadlock situations do not occur.

An application (or system) that behaves correctly in an environment where multiple threads are running can be called *multi-thread safe*. Ensuring multi-thread safety is not easy. The implementation must use one of the synchronization schemes mentioned above to achieve mutual exclusion.

What we are discussing here is nothing new. Synchronization is an issue even when multiple processes are involved. But a process cannot access something inside the address space of another, making synchronization somewhat easier. But threads in a process share everything owned by the process. Therefore, it is very important to ensure proper synchronization. For example, in the document processing application, if the printing thread has acquired a lock on a page, the indexing thread must wait until the printing thread releases the lock before accessing the same page.

Multi-thread safety is even more critical in cases where *reference counting* (also called use counts) schemes are employed. Reference counting schemes are discussed in subsequent chapters. Modifying the reference count must be a thread safe operation.

When objects are being used in a multi-thread environment, it is even more important to pay attention to multi-thread safety. Things can be disastrous if multi-thread safety is not ensured. Two threads in a process can use the same object. Remember that member function code is shared among all objects. When a thread invokes a member function and before it completes the execution inside the member function, if another thread is scheduled (by the OS) to run, and it also invokes the same member function on the same object, the object must be able to maintain its integrity and function properly. If the object cannot do that, then the class is not thread-safe. It is possible that a class does not have anything (member function and data members) that requires anything special to achieve thread safety. Then, maintaining thread safety is not a problem at all.

When a new class is designed, it is very important to pay attention to multi-thread safety. If objects of the class are capable of maintaining their integrity even in multi-threaded situations, the class document must state that clearly. On the other hand, if objects of the class are not multi-thread safe, clearly state that limitation in the class header file and in the documentation. Don't be under the impression that every class needs to be multi-thread safe. That's not the case. Whether thread safety is required or not depends on the class and the intended clients of the class. Also remember that a class X might use other classes as part of its implementation. In order for the class X to be thread safe, it is essential that all other class that it uses are also thread safe. Or, at least X must be able to guarantee its thread safety even if the classes that it depends on are not thread safe (which is a lot more difficult). Here are some guidelines to achieve thread safety.

1. If your class claims to be thread safe, ensure that each and every member function implementation is thread safe.

2. If your class uses other classes (objects) in the implementation, ensure that you can still guarantee thread safety .

3. If you are using some class library to implement your class, ensure that the functions of the library that you are using are thread safe.

4. If you are using operating system calls, check to make sure that they are thread-safe.

5. When using libraries that are provided by your compiler, check if they are thread safe.

Many library vendors provide helper classes that assist in achieving thread safety. For example, it is very common to see classes that provide thread-safe reference counting. If your project needs thread safety, it might be helpful to implement a set of low level classes that ensure thread safety. Such classes might provide reference counting, thread safe pointers, thread safe printing utilities, etc. If the entire project team uses these classes in their implementation, then thread safety is assured for the entire project.

THREAD   In this book, a distinct sidebar highlights all situations where thread safety is an im-
SAFETY   portant issue. All such topics have the THREAD SAFETY sidebar, exactly like this paragraph, making it easier for the reader to locate them.

ENSURING RELIABILITY OF ABSTRACTIONS—CLASS INVARIANTS AND ASSERTIONS

Any abstraction must fulfill its contract with the clients. When a client uses a class she expects the object(s) of the class to behave correctly as published. The implementor of the class must do whatever it takes to ensure that the objects behave properly. But, a class can perform its duties correctly only when the client performs her part of the contract. For example, a member function of a class might require that the argument that is passed in be a non-zero pointer. If this pre-condition is satisfied then the member function guarantees its behavior. Therefore, there is some responsibility that the client must perform. In other words, if the client satisfies her part of the contract, the implementor of the object must honor her part of the contract and ensure proper behavior.

All this is well and good in documentation within classes and member functions. But, it will be even better to have these contract conditions as part of the class implementation code so that they are executed and contract conditions are checked. This is where assertions are invaluable.

An assertion is usually an expression that evaluates to true or false. The assertion is considered to have failed if the expression evaluates to false. For example, in the TLaserDiscPlayer class, the member function Play might have an assertion which requires that the tray be closed. We will see the syntax very soon.

Class Invariants

Looking deeper, just having an assertion in every member function (or even in multiple places inside a member function) may not be that convenient. Every class might have conditions that must *always* be true inside an object. These conditions must be true no matter what member function is being called. Such conditions are called *class invariants*. As the name indicates, these are conditions that are always true within an object. It would be really convenient if we could somehow add these conditions to a class and ensure that every member function code checks these conditions.

PreConditions and PostConditions

In addition to these class invariants, operations (C++ member functions) might want to express conditions that must be true before they execute their code. These conditions that

C++

> Assertions have been in use with C and C++ for a long time. The **assert** macro is supplied with all C and C++ compilers. This macro accepts an expression which must evaluate to true or false. If it evaluates to true, nothing happens and the execution continues. But, if the expression is false, then the program is stopped with an error message indicating the failure of the assertion. The filename and also the source code line number of the offending statement are displayed. This is the simplest (and the only available) form of assertions. Here is the code of the **Play** member function mentioned above.
>
> ```
> TLaserDiscPlayer ::Play(unsigned atChapter)
> {
>         assert(this->_trayStatus == eClosed);
>         // This is the assertion code
>         // rest of the code
> }
> ```
>
> The **Play** member function requires that the laser disc tray be closed before it is called, and this condition is expressed as an assertion.

must be true before the operation are called *preconditions*. Once the member function completes its operations, it might make certain assertions about conditions that must be true. In other words, if the member function completed successfully, then it will produce a result satisfying certain conditions. Such conditions are called *postconditions*.

EIFFEL   Both preconditions and postconditions are popular concepts very well supported in Eiffel. The Eiffel run-time system checks these conditions and ensures that they are true. Otherwise, the running program is stopped. Preconditions are expressed at the beginning of an operation in the **require** clause. The operation's postconditions are stated in the **ensure** clause at the end of the operation. This way, every operation has the freedom to use any preconditions and postconditions irrespective of what happens elsewhere.

Class invariants must be checked on entry and exit from each operation (member function). To make it convenient for the implementor, it would be nice if we could express all the invariants in one known place within a class. Class variants are statements about the state of an object that must always be guaranteed during the lifetime of an object. For example, a **Person** abstraction might have the invariant that the birth date of the person must always be a valid date and that the name is always correct. Similarly, a **BankAccount** abstraction without any overdraft facilities might have the invariant that balance should never drop below zero. These invariants are very powerful because they allow the implementor to clearly state certain properties of the class. Clients can count on these conditions being true with objects of the class.

Neither C++ nor Smalltalk have any built-in support for class invariants, but Eiffel does.

EIFFEL   Here class invariants are defined within a class in the **invariant** section and they are checked within every operation. Specifically, on entry and exit from every operation the class invariants are checked to be true. This ensures predictable behavior of objects of the class at all times. In effect, every precondtion and postcondition of an operation includes the evaluation of the class invariants.

Using Assertions for Implementing Invariants and Conditions

Since C++ does not have direct support for class invariants, we must somehow invent schemes to achieve a similar effect. The **assert** macro can be used for this facility. Here is a scheme that is simple to use.

One can simply define a pair of macros PRE_CONDITION and POST_CONDITION that simply uses the assert macro.

```
#define PRE_CONDITION(condition) assert(condition)
#define POST_CONDITION(condition) assert(condition)
```

If needed, a message can be added to these macros, that will be printed when the assertion fails.

```
#define PRE_CONDITION(message, condition) assert( (message, (condition)))
#define POST_CONDITION(message, condition) assert( (message, (condition)))
```

This is helpful when you want to include a message that must be printed when the assertion fails. For example, one could write

```
PRE_CONDITION("Laser disc tray is not closed", (_trayStatus==eClosed));
```

Such preconditions and postconditions are just simple assertions but they make programs more reliable and also more readable and easy to understand.

But, adding support for class invariants is not easy. Remember that class invariants must be true on entry and exit from every member function. One way of doing that would be to define a set of conditions in a function (call it **InvariantChecker**) and calling that function on entry and exit from every function. This is tedious and error prone because every member function must remember to make the call to this function. This is even more error-prone when new functions are added to the class. However, there is no other alternative available. It is better than having no such thing at all. If nothing else, at least clearly document class invariants so that your clients know exactly what your (implementor) part of the contract guarantees. Many class designers provide very clear documentation of their class invariants and follow some scheme to ensure that the invariants are enforced.

NOTE   When using any one of these schemes, also add support (an #ifdef pair) to turn them off or on as needed.

Using Assertions Effectively

Assertions can be used effectively to implement programs that are more reliable. Assertions at least guarantee that a program doesn't continue when a condition is violated. But, there is no recovery possible when an assertion failure occurs. The real answer to this problem is to use true exception management facility that is supported by C++ (See Chapter 10). But, exceptions are not that easy to understand and use—they require proper architecture and design to be effective. Programmers have been using assertions for many years because they are simple and easy to implement.

☞ **If you are not going to do anything elaborate, at least practice using simple assertions.**

Once you start using assertions, don't think you can't move to anything better. If in the future, you decide to use real exception management, just locate all points in the code that call assert and replace them with proper throw statements.

Like real C++ exceptions, using assert does not allow an error condition to be ignored. As discussed in Chapter 10, an exception can be caught and then taken care of but not an assertion failure—it always causes the stopping of the program. In other words, it is an uncatchable exception. In many cases, unnoticed errors wreak havoc on other parts of the program. For example, if one forgets to check if a pointer is zero (NULL), some other part of the function (or program) that tries to use the pointer will crash the application. Debugging such errors are much harder and highly time consuming, not to mention unbearably frustrating. A simple assertion would prevent all such undesirable consequences and would tell you the exact cause of the program crash. On some platforms (and/or compilers), accessing a member function using a zero pointer doesn't cause any problem and the application works. But, if this application is now ported to another platform where access through a zero pointer causes an immediate crash, your nightmares have just begun (which could have been avoided easily with an assertion).

A complete discussion of exception architecture and management issues can be found in Chapter 10.

NOTATIONS FOR REPRESENTING OO DESIGNS

Just as we need a language to express our thoughts, object-oriented design needs a vocabulary (or notation) to convey the ideas behind a problem solution. We need a notation to represent classes, objects, class relationships, state diagrams, process diagrams, object relationships, etc.

Originally, when I started writing this book, there were two object notations that were popular, namely the Booch notation (made popular by Grady Booch of Rational) and OMT (Object Modeling Tool, from James Rumbaugh and his team at General Electric). I followed the Booch notation because I liked it a lot. However, in 1994, Rumbaugh and Booch teamed up and started to work on a unified notation. Their work has now resulted in the **Universal Modeling Language** (UML).[13] In 1995, Ivar Jacobson (of Objec-

---

[13]For full details and updates on UML, checkout the rational web site at www.rational.com.

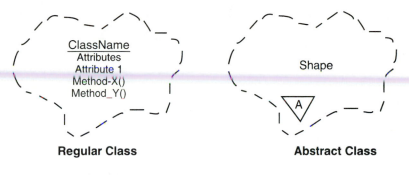

Regular Class   **Abstract Class**

Fig. 2-5

tory) and the proponent of the *use-case* approach became part of this effort (after Objectory was acquired by Rational). Some elements of the use-case approach can also be found in UML. At the time of this writing, the latest version of UML is 0.9 (July, 1996). Throughout this book, I had originally used the Booch notation. But, since the UML is gaining popularity and is soon going to be the standard OO notation, I have also included the UML diagrams (in addition to the Booch notation). If you are already familiar with the OMT notation, you will notice quite a few similarities between UML and OMT. Highlights of both UML and the Booch notation are described below.

THE BOOCH NOTATION

A class is denoted by an amorphous blob (an ameba) as shown in Fig 2-5.

Needless to say, only important attributes (C++ data members) are shown. Important operations (C++ member functions) may also be shown. An abstract class is denoted by an adornment as shown above. Abstract classes are discussed in Chapter 5.

An object is represented by a **solid** blob (Fig. 2-6). I rarely use object diagrams in this book. But, *object scenario diagrams* are very useful in depicting snapshots of problem solutions.

CLASS RELATIONSHIPS

The most important phase of analysis and design is discovering classes and establishing relationships among them.

The Booch methodology uses TWO main relationships between classes—the *is-a* and the *has-a* relationships. The complete list of relationships is:

Association
Inheritance (is-a)
Aggregation (has-a)
Using
Instantiation (Template)
Metaclass

Fig. 2-6

Association

This is used in early stages of analysis and it finally ends up being a has-a, is-a, or a using relationship.

This is a two way relationship. Clients of A can get to B and clients of B can also get to A (Fig. 2-7).

The numbers at the edges of the relation indicates the cardinality. Every bank can have 0..N customers and a Customer may have accounts in 0..N banks (Fig. 2-8).

Aggregation (has-a)

In this relation, instances of class A contain instances of class B (A *has-a* B). This does not imply physical containment. The containment could be through a pointer, reference, or even physical containment (by value). This relation is usually referred to as the **has-a** relationship. This relation is also called *aggregation*. It is used to denote the whole/part relationship (Fig. 2-9).

The relationship may be labeled to indicate the nature of the aggregation. The numbers at the ends of the relation denote cardinality.

A **Person** can have more than one driver's license (driving licenses of different countries, different types of vehicles, etc.). It is also possible that a **Person** does not have any driving license. This is indicated by the cardinality (0..N). In other words, **Person** can have 0 or more driving licenses. The • indicates the origin of the has-a relationship. Here, a **Person** has-a (one or more) **DrivingLicense**. Given a **Person** object, it would be possible to look at (or enumerate) the driving licenses of that **Person**. But, given a **DrivingLicense** object, it is not possible to find the **Person** that it belongs to. This is because has-a is a one way relationship. The • indicates where the relationship originates. The number 1 on **Person** indicates that any **DrivingLicense** object always belongs to

Class A is associated (in an yet undetermined way) with Class B.

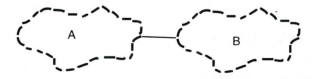

Fig. 2-7

Association

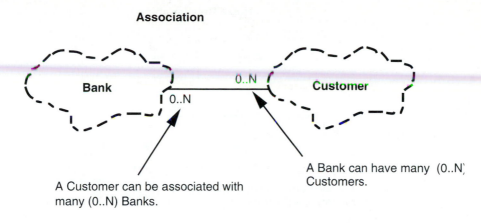

A Customer can be associated with
many (0..N) Banks.

A Bank can have many (0..N)
Customers.

Fig. 2-8

only one **Person**. The name of the relationship (Holds) can also be shown as is done in Fig. 2-9.

The has-a relationship can be implemented using a pointer, reference, or even by a contained object. In other words, has-a does not mean that every **Person** object physically contains many Person objects (although that is one possible implementation).

Choices for cardinality in a has-a relationship

1	Exactly 1
N	Unlimited Number
0..N	Zero Or more
1..N	One or more
3..9	Specified Range
1..4,7	Specified Range or exact number

The has-a and the is-a relationships are perhaps the most commonly used relationships between classes. The has-a relation is used in many places in this book to represent some kind of containment relationship between classes. Note that has-a is a general term that means many things. The fact that a person co-owns a vacation home is represented by a has-a relation between **Person** and **VacationHome**. Similarly, an employee is em-

Has-a Relationship

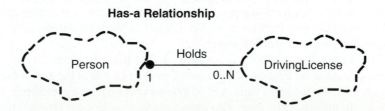

Fig. 2-9

Has-a Relationships

Person lives in a House

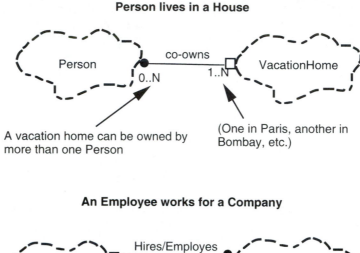

An Employee works for a Company

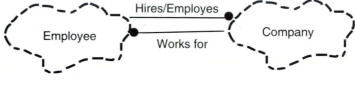

Fig. 2-10

ployed by a company. This is again represented as **Employee** has-a **Company** (see Fig. 2-10). The name of the relationship makes it easier to understand the nature of the relationship.

In the Employee-Company relation, the *Works for* relation shows the relation from the Employee perspective. Given an **Employee** object, one can find the Company (or companies) she works for. To find the **Employee** given a **Company** object, we need another relationship. This is shown above in the *Hires/Employs* relationship. This allows us to locate an **Employee** given a **Company** object. Such two way relationships are common. Continuing on these lines, note that it is not possible to find all the Persons associated with a specific **VacationHome** at any time because there exists no relationship between **VacationHome** and **Person**. There is a has-a relation from **Person** to **VacationHome** but not from **VacationHome** to **Person**. This is what we mean by the statement *Has-a is a one way relationship*. There is a cardinality number (0..N) on **Person** for the *co-owns* relationship. This only indicates that a **VacationHome** can be owned by more than one **Person** at a time. Clearly, a **VacationHome** object is not physically contained within a **Person** object.

Looking at another has-a relation, a **Car** has-a **Engine**. The fact that a **Car** physically contains an **Engine** is represented by the filled ■ at the end of the line, as shown in Fig. 2-11. On the other hand, a □ represents containment by reference.

In this example, every **Car** object has its own **Engine** object. This is a true physical containment relationship. Furthermore, every **Car** has exactly one **Engine** object, as indicated by the cardinality. Every Engine can have 4 or more cylinders as indicated in Fig. 2-11.

The has-a relation denotes a lifetime/control relationship. The lifetime of the object contained (**Engine**) is controlled by the object (**Car**) that contains it. When **Car** object is created, the **Engine** object is also created. When the **Car** object is destroyed, the **Engine** object (which is part of the **Car**) is also destroyed.

The Using Relationship

This is used to indicate mostly client/supplier relationship. If class **A** receives objects of class **B** as arguments to one of its member functions (or returns an object of class **B** from one of its member functions) but doesn't have any other kind of association with class **B**, then class **A** uses class **B**. The using relation also holds good if class **B** is used in the implementation of one of the methods of class **A**. The ○ (hollow circle) indicates a *using* relationship.

In Fig. 2-12 **MailGateway** is *using* **MessagePacket**. Remember that a *using* relationship does not imply has-a relationship. If **MailGateway** stores **MessagePacket** objects (in some form), then **MailGateway** has-a **MessagePacket**. Then there is no need for the *using* relationship. The has-a relation is a superset of a using relation and has-a is more powerful than the using relationship.

It is not very common to find *using* relationships in problem solutions.

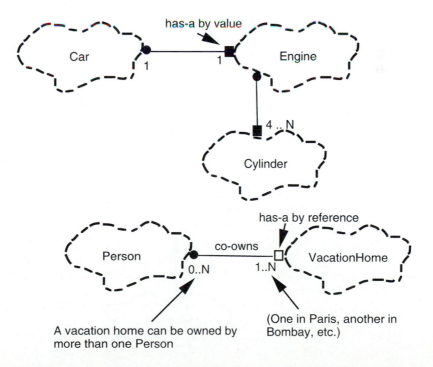

A vacation home can be owned by more than one Person

(One in Paris, another in Bombay, etc.)

Fig. 2-11

The Using Relationship

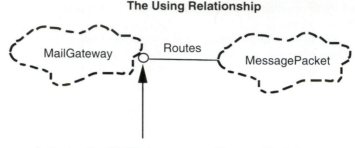

Indicates that MailGateway uses MessagePacket

Fig. 2-12

The Inheritance Relationship (is-a)

The is-a relationship is used to denote inheritance. It implies generalization-specialization from base class to derived class (Fig. 2-13).

A Manager *is-a* (kind-of) Employee. The arrow goes from the derived class (Manager) to the base class Employee. Detailed discussion of inheritance can be found in a subsequent chapter.

Most problem solutions use a combination of has-a and is-a relationships. Both is-a and has-a are very powerful relationships. They come with their own advantages and disadvantages. A designer must clearly understand when to use an is-a or a has-a. There are many examples in this book that clarify the differences between them.

Class Categories

In most projects, it is impossible to show all classes on a single page. To facilitate grouping (and modules) class categories are used. A class category provides services through the classes contained in it. A class category has its own unique name (just like classes).

The Inheritance (is-a) relationship

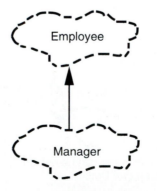

Fig. 2-13

SecurityControl is the name of the class category.

AcceesManager is a class within this class category.

Fig. 2-14

A high level description of a complete system might be shown using class categories only (See Fig. 2-14). The exploded diagram of a class category must show all the classes contained in the class category and their relationships.

THE UNIFIED MODELING LANGUAGE (UML)

The following paragraphs outline some features of the UML. Many of the examples come from the Version 1.0 UML specifications document.

A class is represented by a rectangle as shown in Fig. 2-15.

The classname is usually in bold typeface such as **Person** below. The second compartment (or box) contains attributes (with optional types and initial value). The third compartment contains a list of operations (with optional argument lists and return types). In a high level overview diagram of classes, the second and third compartment can be omitted, showing just the class name in a rectangle.

A *stereotype* might also be specified for a class just above the name of the class. The stereotype indicates what *kind* of class it is, such as an exception class, a controller class, an interface class, etc. This stereotype is enclosed in guillemots («»). Usually, these

Notation for a class

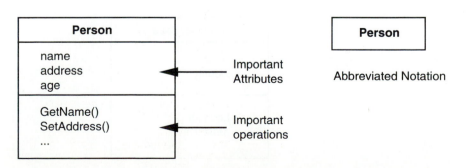

Fig. 2-15

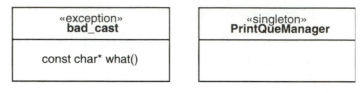

Fig. 2-16

characters are available in most character sets, but for convenience, a pair of (<< >>) can be used too (see Fig. 2-16).

This indicates that class bad_cast is class whose stereotype is exception. It implies that this class will be used in exception management (discussed in Chapter 10). Similarly, PrintQueManager is a singleton class (only one object of this class is ever created—details in Chapter 9). The intent here is to identify the nature of the class.

An abstract class (see Chapter 5) is represented by representing the name in *italics* (see Fig. 2-17). An abstract operation is also shown in italics.

An object is represented by a rectangle with the name of the object and its class being underlined (see Fig. 2-18).

The top compartment contains *objectName : className*. For anonymous objects, the objectName is omitted, but the : is dropped when the classname is not shown.

For both classes and objects, the figures can be as big (or as small) as you like.

CLASS RELATIONSHIPS

More than individual classes, we are interested in groups of classes. And these classes might exhibit relationships among them.

The Unified Modeling Language uses two main relationships between classes: association and the generalization.

Notation for an abstract class

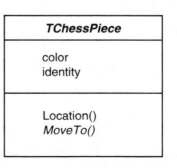

Fig. 2-17

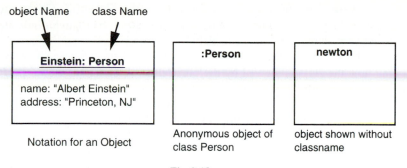

object Name   class Name

Einstein: Person

name: "Albert Einstein"
address: "Princeton, NJ"

Notation for an Object

:Person

Anonymous object of
class Person

newton

object shown without
classname

Fig. 2-18

Association
Inheritance (is-a)

ASSOCIATION

An association represents structural relationship between objects of different classes. Most associations are binary relations. Multiple associations between classes as well as self associations are valid too (see Fig. 2-19).

An association may have a name with an optional *directional triangle,* showing which way it is read. Note that the directional arrow is optional but not the name of the association. An association could have different names in each direction, but it is mostly not necessary (particularly when role names are used).

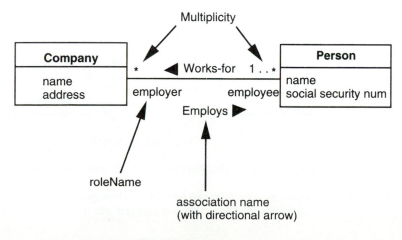

Fig. 2-19

Works-for is the name of the association from **Person** to **Company**. *Employs* is the name of the association from **Company** to **Person**. The triangles indicate the direction. It is not very common to find such elaborate naming.

Each end of an association is a *role*. Each role may have a name *(rolename)* indicating how the class is viewed by the other class. A *Company* views the *Person* as an *employee*. Similarly *Person* views the *Company* as an *employer*. The role names must be unique. A *rolename* is more important that an association name.

Each role indicates multiplicity of its class. For example, a **Person** may work for many companies (i.e., a person is associated with many companies). This indicates the multiplicity of the role (how many **Company** objects can be associated with one **Person** object?). The * indicates "many" (unlimited number of objects, actually 0..*). A **Person** can work for *many* Companies and a **Company** can employ many Persons. Therefore, the multiplicity of Company with Person is 1..* (many). Multiplicity can also be a number (1 or 5, etc.) or a range (1..5).

Navigability of an association is shown by an arrow at the appropriate end of the association. For example, if it is possible to navigate (traverse) the list of all **DrivingLicense** objects owned by a **Person**, it can be represented as follows in Fig. 2-20.

A **Person** can hold many driving licenses (different countries, different classifications, etc.). But a **DrivingLicense** always belongs to only one **Person**.

An association can be another class in itself, an *association class*. In the example below (Fig. 2–21), an automated teller machine (ATM) transaction has its own attributes and also operations on it. The association class can itself have other associations. The association class is shown as hanging from the association line, using a dashed line.

In this example (Fig. 2-21), the ATM class contains details such as **owner** (who operates the ATM, usually a bank), **address** (physical location), etc.

And of course, the **Job** held by a **Person** with a **Company** is a class by itself (see Fig. 2-22).

An association class might just contain attributes for the association, but no operations. In this case the name of the association class is not shown.

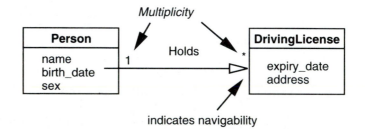

1 because a DrivingLicense belongs to only one Person

* because a Person can hold many DrivingLicenses (different countries, different classes, etc.)

Fig. 2-20

An association class example

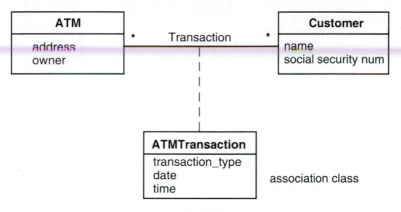

Fig. 2-21

Association as an Aggregation

In many cases, we like to show the whole-part relationship. Aggregation is a special form of association. Here the lifetime of the parts (what's contained) is dependent on the lifetime of the whole (see Fig. 2-24).[14]

A hollow diamond is attached to the class that is the aggregate. The diamond cannot be present on both ends of a line (Fig. 2-23). This is used to represent the familiar *aggregation by reference* when there are no lifetime dependencies between the classes. An Orchestra is an ensemble of Performers.[14] When the aggregation diamond is filled, it indicates a strong form of aggregation called *Composition*, which will be discussed soon.

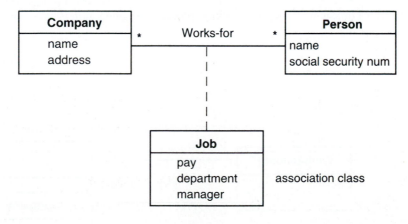

Fig. 2-22

[14]Aggregation is a form of containment relationship.

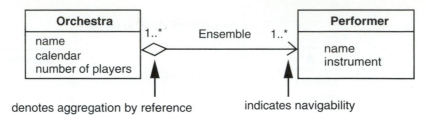

Fig. 2-23

The OR Association

In some cases, one class can participate in two associations, but each object can participate in only one of the associations at a time. This is the *this or that* scenario. A BankAccount can be held by one or more persons (joint accounts) or it can be held by a Company. This is indicated by the constraint {or}. Therefore, the multiplicity on Person is * and the multiplicity on Company is 1. A similar example is that of an Automobile; it can be owned by a Company or a Person.

COMPOSITION

This is a form of aggregation with strong lifetime and ownership dependencies between the part and the whole. The multiplicity of the aggregate (the container) cannot exceed one (no sharing). Composition can be represented in three different ways. One familiar notation is that of a filled diamond. For example, an AirPlane object has a CockPit, Engine, Seats, etc. An AirPlane object is created with a CockPit object (Fig. 2-25) and the CockPit object dies with the AirPlane object (the aggregation is unchangeable).

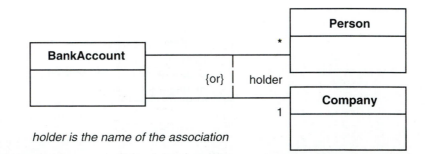

holder is the name of the association

Fig. 2-24

Composition Example

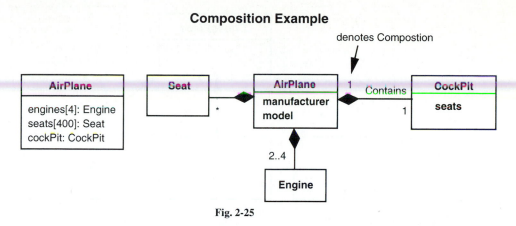

denotes Compostion
AirPlane
engines[4]: Engine
seats[400]: Seat
cockPit: CockPit
Seat
*
AirPlane
manufacturer
model
1
Contains
1
CockPit
seats
2..4
Engine

Fig. 2-25

AirPlane
Engine 4
CockPit 1
Seat *

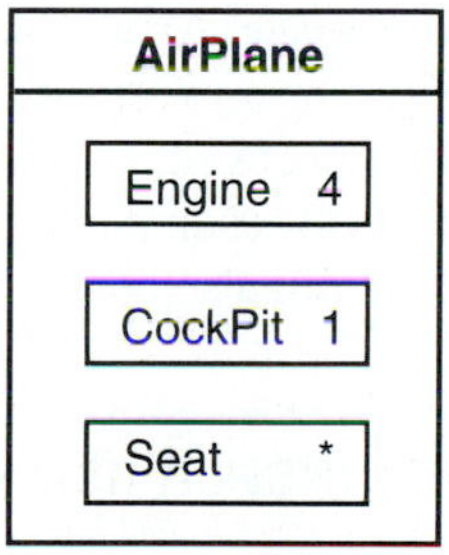

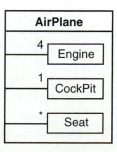

Fig. 2-26

AirPlane
4
Engine
1
CockPit
*
Seat

Fig. 2-27

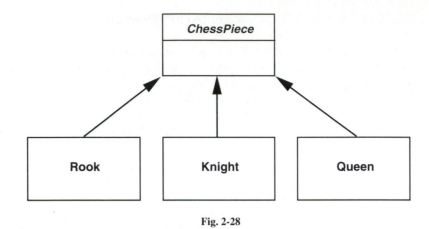

Fig. 2-28

When the multiplicity (cardinality) is greater than 1, parts may be created after the aggregate itself. Also, unless the parts are removed explicitly before the death of the aggregate, they die with the aggregate. An airplane can have multiple Engines, Seats, etc. Moreover, during the lifetime of an AirPlane object seats can be added and removed. When the AirPlane object is destroyed, all other objects contained in it are destroyed, unless they are removed from it (for example, the seats might be removed and reused in another AirPlane). Composition can also be represented as shown in Fig. 2-26 or Fig. 2-27.

THE GENERALIZATION RELATIONSHIIP (IS-A)

The generalization relationship is used to denote inheritance. It implies *generalization-specialization* from base class to derived class (see Fig. 2-28). The arrow heads must be *hollow*. An alternative representation is shown in Fig. 2-29. Multiple inheritance is represented as shown in Fig. 2-30. Inheritance is discussed in Chapter 5 and Chapter 6.

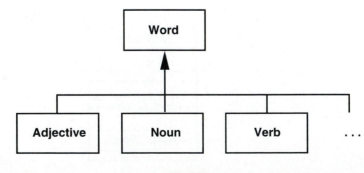

Fig. 2-29

THE IMPORTANCE OF THE HAS-A RELATIONSHIP

The has-a relationship (also called association, aggregation, containment, composition) is an important relationship very frequently used in OOD. But, many designers and programmers fail to understand its relevance and use leading to complicated, inflexible, designs and also unnecessary inheritance.

Reuse of software in OOD can be achieved primarily in two ways: inheritance and containment. Both have their advantages and disadvantages. A good designer knows their constrains, benefits, and costs and is able to apply them judiciously. Inheritance is discussed in detail in Chapter 5 and Chapter 6 (and also in Chapter 12, Part II).

Containment is a powerful design technique. It is easier to implement and manage than inheritance. Containment is a true application of programming to interfaces. Referring back to the example of a Car containing an Engine, a Car object has no special privilege with its contained Engine object. An object of Car operates (or uses) the Engine object only through its interface. There is absolutely no violation of encapsulation. Furthermore, clients of Car need not know anything about the contained Engine object because it is an implementation detail. The Car abstraction projects a well defined interface. Clients of Car only need to understand the interface and behavior of Car and nothing else. The implementor of Car also has the freedom to substitute a different object of type Engine (one that supports the Engine interface) at run-time. For example, if the Car ob-

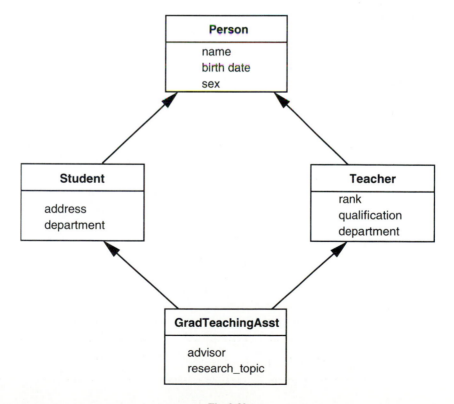

Fig. 2-30

ject holds a pointer (or reference) to an Engine object, at run-time it is possible to substitute some other object that supports the Engine interface. This change will in no way have any consequences to the clients of Car because it is an internal implementation detail (more details in Chapter 11, Part II).

Using aggregation, one can compose new behavior using different objects. It is possible to add new capabilities to existing objects by changing the internal implementation objects. This leads to software that is highly flexible, and enables the creation of software that adapts to changing requirements.

But, has-a relationships also have their share of disadvantages. Run-time inefficiencies are many times felt when using objects that use containment, because of the extra level of indirection. The behavior of objects that use aggregation is harder to understand and describe because, their behavior can easily change at run-time. Implementing reliable containment relationships also requires careful attention to resource management responsibilities (to avoid resource leaks).

In summary, when designing abstractions, pay careful attention to relationships between classes. Be extra careful when deciding between inheritance and containment. We revisit this topic again at the end of Chapter 6, after studying inheritance.

READ   Explore the message/method relationship in Smalltalk.

Investigate the interface/implementation separation in Eiffel.

Study the Modula-2 concept of *modules* and compare it with Objects.

Study *dynamic binding* and *static binding* issues in different languages.

Explore the *Package* concept in Ada.

Understand the class and interface model in Java.

SUMMARY

Data Abstraction projects the important features of a class while hiding the insignificant and irrelevant details.

A change in the implementation of an abstract data type will not change the interface to it in any way.

All details about the implementation is encapsulated and clients of a class have no knowledge of the encapsulated implementation.

Data Abstraction is not a specific feature of a language; it is a fundamental concept in OOP.

3

Data Abstraction with C++

The fundamental unit of abstraction in C++ is a **class.** A class is nothing but a very enhanced C struct. We will see how C++ supports data abstraction in this chapter.

FUNDAMENTALS OF THE CLASS CONCEPT

In C++, a **class** and **struct** are almost identical (except for a few minor differences that we will see very soon). The discussion of the class concept is equally applicable to a struct without any loss of information.

Some important features of a class are

1. A class has access regions **private, protected,** and **public**.

2. A class contains prototypes (or signatures) of static and non-static member functions, and declarations of data members.

3. A class can also contain the declaration of another class (a nested class) in it.

4. A class can also contain declarations of static data members and static member functions (to be discussed later) in it.

Here is an example of an integer Stack class, TIntStack.

```
const unsigned int DEFAULT_SIZE = 256;
/* TIntStack is a stack of integers. It provides the usual operations,
      Push and Pop.
 * For the purposes of this discussion, I'm using an Integer Stack. It is
      very easy to
 * implement a general Stack class (as we will see in Chapter-9)
 * This goes in the file IntStack.h
 */

class TIntStack {
    public:
        // Member Functions
        // Default Constructor
        TIntStack(unsigned int stackSize = DEFAULT_SIZE);
        TIntStack(const TIntStack& that); // Copy Constructor
        // Assignment Operator
        ~TIntStack(); // Destructor

        void Push(int thisValue);
        int Pop();
        unsigned int HowMany() const;
        // and many more member functions
    private:
        // Data Members
        int*      _sp;
        unsigned _count;
        unsigned _size;
};
```

DETAILS OF CLASS ELEMENTS

Access Regions

Anything declared under the public region of a class can be accessed by every client. One can imagine that it is the interface to the *general public*. This is the least restrictive region of a class, which also implies that it has no protection. A well designed class will never have data members in the public region; only member functions are seen in the public region. If there is a data member in the public region, the compiler controls access to such data members and not the class implementor. This is in violation of our data abstraction and encapsulation principle. This is why we almost always use private/protected data members.

SMALLTALK   Here, a class can never contain public instance variables. Only methods can be made public. The intention is that only the class implementation should have access to instance variables. And clients should invoke methods to get and set values of instance variables.

NOTE   A method that allows clients to *set* a value of a data member in an object is usually called a *Setter* and a method that returns the value of a data member, a *Getter*.

EIFFEL   Here, a class can *export* member functions as well as data members without any restrictions. But any exported data member is only *accessible* by clients; it cannot be modified by general clients. In other words, clients get *read-only* access for exported data members. The name of an exported member does not convey any information about whether it is a data member or a member function. This is like Pascal where the call to a function accepting no arguments looks like a reference to some variable.

Returning to C++, the other extreme is the **private** region. A member function implementation can access all members declared in the class (i.e., the members of a class are freely accessible within the scope of any member function of the class). Therefore, the programmer who writes the class member functions would be the implementor of the class. Normal clients of the class have nothing to do with the **private** region. The less they know about it the better. Needless to point out that any program that has access to members in the private region can access everything else that is in the class (including the **public** and **protected** regions). Actually, C++ is a little strange with respect to access control because it allows the general public to "see" the declarations of private data members, even though they can't be accessed by public clients.

The **protected** region is less restrictive than the private region but more restrictive than the public region. It is meant for the use of the derived classes (through inheritance) as we will see in later chapters. Clients who have access to the **protected** region also have access to the **public** region.

A class can have multiple **public**, **private**, and **protected** regions. There is absolutely no restriction on the number of such regions.

Any region can contain member functions as well as data members. Any member (data or function) declared in a class acquires the access rules of the region in which it is declared.

Constructors: A constructor is also a member function, albeit a little special. A class can contain any number of overloaded constructors. It cannot return a value. And it cannot be a **const** or a **static** member function either.

A constructor is always called when an object is created. Objects of a class can be created in many different ways. Here are some styles:

```
TIntStack myStack;                        // ❶
Tinstack s1(100);                         // ❷
TIntStack s2 = s1                         // ❸
TIntStack *dsp = new TIntStack(200); // ❹
TIntStack s3 = TIntStack(250);           // ❺
```

Analysis:

❶ **TIntStack myStack;**

Here, we would like to create a **TIntStack** object called **myStack**. This is similar to the declaration

```
int j; // Create an int called j
```

This declaration for **myStack** tries to call the default constructor, since **myStack** has no arguments. Remember (from Chapter 2) that a default constructor is a constructor that can be called without any arguments. We do have one in this class. It expects an unsigned int argument (**stackSize**), but this argument has a default value—DEFAULT_SIZE. Also remember that an object can only be created using a constructor.

CAUTION   If we did not declare any constructor in our **TIntStack** class, the compiler would generate a **default constructor** for our use. This generated default constructor does not accept any arguments and it just allows us to create an object. The object is not initialized. If we declare even one constructor in the class, the compiler will not generate a default constructor. Always remember this rule. One can imagine that the implementation of the compiler generated default constructor would look like:

```
TIntStack::TIntStack() { /* Empty */ }
```

Furthermore, it will be an inline function.

❷ `TIntStack s1(100); // Create an TIntStack object s1`

In this example, we are trying to create a **TIntStack** object called **s1** with a stack size of 100 elements. The syntax looks like a function call and it is a call to the constructor of **TIntStack** that can accept an integer (or unsigned int) argument. Our class has such a constructor and it is called.

In this implementation of **TIntStack**, let us use a pointer to an array of **int** as our implementation. We shall keep the size of the stack requested by the user in the data member _**size** and the count of the number of elements currently on the stack in the data member _**count**. We will allocate the memory for the elements of the stack in the constructor.

```
#include "IntStack.h"

TIntStack::TIntStack(unsigned int stackSize /* = DEFAULT_SIZE */)
{
    // Allocate memory only when stackSize is positive
    If (stackSize > 0) {
        _size = stackSize;
        _sp = new int[size]; // Allocate memory for stack elements
        // Initialize all elements to zero
        for (int i=0; i < size; i++)
            _sp[i] = 0;
    }
    else {
        _sp = 0; // set the pointer to the unique value
        _size = 0;
    }
    _count = 0; // no elements on the stack
}
```

When the constructor is called, just an empty object has been created and the data members contain garbage. They are just like uninitialized automatic variables. We need to initialize them properly. We check to verify that the requested stack size is a positive number and then allocate memory using the **new()** operator. We initialize *all* data members with appropriate values. This is all we need to do in the constructor.

CAUTION   If we declare a class **X** as

```
// X.h
class X {
        public:
                X(int size = 256); // ❽ Constructor
                X(); // ❾ Another constructor
        // and more..
};
```

we can immediately notice that there are two constructors and that they conflict with each other. For example:

```
#include "X.h" // Include the declaration of class X
main()
{
        X   alpha; // Create an object alpha of class X
        X   b(10); // and another object b
}
```

Which constructor should be called for the object **alpha**? We could say it calls ❾ above because there are no arguments passed. But ❽ can also be called without any arguments and there in lies the conflict. [A correct compiler should flag this conflict as soon as it encounters the declarations of the constructors in class **X**. So when **X.h** is compiled, the error would have been reported and the implementor of **X** would have been forced to fix it. This is called *error detection at the point of declaration,* and it helps in detecting errors as soon as they happen (i.e., at the compile time of **X.h** itself). However, some compilers don't detect this conflict until someone tries to use one of the constructors (i.e., the error would be detected while compiling the clients code). This is called *error detection at the point of use.* But the client cannot fix this error because she doesn't keep (or control) the code for class **X**. We can only hope that things improve as C++ compilers mature.

COPY CONSTRUCTOR

❸ TIntStack s2 = s1;

This is a bit tricky. We are trying to create another **TIntStack** object called **s2**. But we would like to initialize this object with **s1**. In other words, **s2** must be created from **s1**. Of course **s1** already exists. This is very similar to the declaration

```
int j;
int k = j; // Create a k and initialize it with j
```

In this case, the compiler knows how to initialize k from j because int is a language defined (built-in) type. Generalizing that notion, TIntStack is a programmer defined type
that implies that the programmer is responsible for initializing s2 from s1 (with some
help from the language). This is where the copy constructor (a special constructor) steps
in. Whenever we need to create a new object from an existing object, a copy constructor
provided for that class is used. Here we need a copy constructor in the class TIntStack
and we have declared one in the class. The copy constructor is declared as

```
TIntStack(TIntStack& source)
```

or

```
TIntStack(const TIntStack& source)
```

It takes an argument (a reference) of the class to which it belongs.

CAUTION   **If we did not provide a copy constructor in the class, the compiler again generates one for the class.**[1] This generated copy constructor may not be what we want. We
will learn more about copy constructors in Chapter 4. For this example, let's just implement our own copy constructor.

```
TIntStack::TIntStack(const TIntStack& source)
{
        // Code written here can access all regions of class TIntStack
        // since the copy constructor is a member function of the class.
        // The argument source is an object of TIntStack.
        _size = source._size;
        if (_size > 0) { // Allocate memory only when size is positive
            _sp = new int[_size]; // Allocate memory for stack elements

            _count = source._count; // # of elements on the stack

            // Next copy all the elements from " source" to our stack
            for (int i=0; i < _count; ++i)
                _sp[i] = source._sp[i];
        }
        else {
            _sp = 0; // set the pointer to the unique value
            _count = 0; // no elements on the stack
        }
}
```

This code requires some explanation. Just as in the other constructor, when the copy constructor is invoked, the data members in the new stack do not have any values (they all
contain garbage). We need to examine the values of data members in the object that is
passed in to the copy constructor (the source of the copy operation—the object *source*)

---

[1]Most compilers generate the default copy constructor only when it is used.

Before Copy Operation

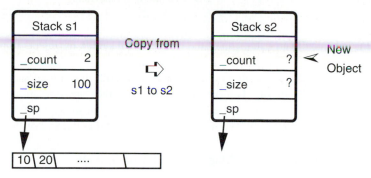

Fig. 3-1

and copy them correctly. First, we check to see if the source has any elements in it. If so, we allocate memory for it. Don't stop at that. Since we are copying one stack to another, a true *deep copy* operation requires copying the elements also (shallow copy and deep copy concepts are discussed in a subsequent chapter). Next, we walk through all the elements on the stack and copy them over to the destination stack.

In this copy operation, how do we map the objects in our problem to the arguments in the copy constructor? Well, a picture is worth a thousand words (see Fig. 3-1).

As we already know, member functions can only be called on existing objects. The compiler instantiates s2 (from the declaration TIntStack s2 =s1), and then on this s2, the copy constructor is invoked and is given the existing object s1 as the source of the copy operation. At this point, the data members of s2 have garbage. After the copy operation, the stack s2 is identical to the stack s1 as shown below in Fig. 3-2.

Now a user can operate on s1 and s2 independently. Operations on s1 doesn't affect s2 and vice-versa. In C++ we can also write

After Copy Operation

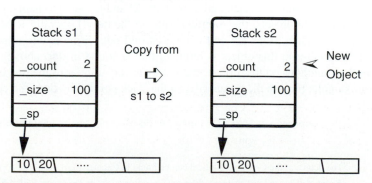

Fig. 3-2

```
int j;
int k(j); // This is as good as int k = j;
char *p("ABCD"); // as good as char *p = "ABCD";
```

This is basically an extension of the initialization syntax of objects to primitive types.

THINK   This copy operation would be expensive (both in terms of memory and CPU time) when the stacks are big. Is it possible to optimize the copy operation such that the storage and elements are not duplicated? You have to keep in mind that s1 and s2 can be operated upon independently. We will see a solution later at the end of this chapter.

❹ TIntStack   *dsp = new TIntStack(200)

In ❶ the memory for the stack object **myStack** (not the memory for the elements, which is dynamically allocated and stored in _sp by the constructors), was allocated by the compiler. The memory for the **TIntStack** object includes the memory for the data members (_size, _count, and _sp) and any other house keeping information that the compiler needs. The compiler controls the allocation and lifetime of such objects. In the declaration above using the **new()** operator we are specifying that the object pointed by **dsp** should be created by allocating memory dynamically on the heap. The lifetime of this dynamically allocated object would be controlled by the programmer and not by the compiler.
          Three steps happen when an object is created (no matter how it is created):

1. The compiler needs to acquire the required amount of memory for the object.

2. This acquired raw memory is converted to an object. This involves placing the data members at the correct positions and probably building a table of member function pointers, etc. (when **virtual** functions are involved). This is all internal to the compiler and programmers don't have to worry about it (see Chapter 13 for details).[2]

3. Finally, when (1) and (2) are done, the compiler invokes the constructor function (either supplied by the class implementor or the default constructor synthesized by the compiler) on this newly created object.

In case of statically created objects, the memory is already reserved in the process data area or on the run-time stack and only steps (2) and (3) need to happen. In case of dynamically allocated objects, the compiler calls on the **new()** operator to allocate memory for the object.[3] Then, steps (2) and (3) are carried out on the newly allocated memory. Finally, a pointer to this object is returned that is stored in **dsp** above. In order to invoke member functions on this object, the syntax is very similar to the one used with C structs. For example, to push the number 10 on the stack pointed by **dsp**, the code is:

```
dsp->Push(10); // Push 10 on to the stack pointed by dsp
```

---

[2]The details of the C++ object model can be found in Chapter 13.

[3]As we will see in later chapters, the new() operator might be the one provided by the compiler or a specialized new() operator supplied by the class implementor.

To do the same operation on the stack **s2**, the code is:

```
s2.Push(10);
```

Both are very similar. The **s2.Push(10)** is more straight forward. The object is directly referenced. In the case of **dsp->Push(10)**, we are again referring to an object but somewhat indirectly. We locate the object through the pointer and invoke **Push** on that object. The -> is the member access operator (which is available and widely used even in C). This -> operator is used with pointers to objects.

Accessing Data Members of an Object—the C++ Model

A careful reader, particularly one with an Eiffel and/or Smalltalk background, would find the copy constructor code above to be somewhat bizarre. Under Eiffel and Smalltalk, every member function can access the data members of the object on which it is invoked, just as in C++. In other words, a member function can access the **private** (and **protected** in case of C++) members of the current object, the object on which the method was invoked.[4] This is true in C++ also. But in the example of the copy constructor above, the code also tries to access the private data member _count of the argument **source**—a completely different object. In the C++ object model, *protection is applied at the class level and not at the object* level. On the other hand, Eiffel and Smalltalk enforce object level protection. What it means is that a member functions of a class can access the data members (and member functions) of any other object of the same class as long it has access to that object. An object **beta** of class **X** (with a member function **bar**) can access everything inside another object—**alpha**, of class **X** without any restrictions. Such access must use the dot syntax (or it must use the -> syntax). In Smalltalk and Eiffel, a member function can access private data of its own object (i.e., the current instance) but not any other object, even if they belong to the same class. In such languages, every access to private data in any other object (of the same class or a different class) must be through member functions. An object does not have any special privileges to access private data of another object; it has to use the methods provided for normal clients. This is one of the most confusing aspects of C++ for programmers migrating from Eiffel or Smalltalk.

NOTE   As mentioned earlier, every object gets its own copy of any non-static (i.e., the keyword **static** does not appear in the declaration) data member declared in its class. This is true in C++, Smalltalk, and Eiffel. However, Smalltalk and C++ support the notion of a shared member. There is only one copy of such a member in a running program, no matter how many objects of that class are created. Such members are called *Class Variables* in Smalltalk. A similar effect is achieved with C++ by using static data members. This concept is discussed in detail in Chapter 5.

❺   `TIntStack s3 = TIntStack(250);`

---

[4]Everyone can access public members. Always remember that.

This is actually identical to

```
TIntStack    s2 = s1;
```

but compiler optimizations might change the implementation of this declaration. Looking at the declaration, we are asking for a **TIntStack** object **s3** and we are specifying that a temporary **TIntStack** object for 250 elements should be created and used to initialize **s3**. The temporary object will go away soon after **s3** is created. The problem is, we unnecessarily created a temporary object and then copied it to **s3** and wasted time in doing so. Why not directly create the object **s3** with a size of 250? This is what most compilers do. They optimize the statement and build a **TIntStack** object **s3** of size 250 directly.

For the remaining parts, let us use an example. We shall write a function **PrintStack** that pops elements from the stack and prints them in order.

```
/*
 * Function to print all the elements of a Stack
 * We Pop() elements sequentially and print them in the same order.
 */
void PrintStack(TIntStack thisOne)
{
            // Find out the number of elements on the Stack
        unsigned i = thisOne.HowMany();
        for (unsigned j = 0; j < i; j++)
            cout << "[" << thisOne.Pop() << "]" << endl; // Print the
            popped element
}
```

And here is the main() program to exercise the **TIntStack**.

```
#include    "IntStack.h"
#include    <iostream.h>

main()
{
// Code written here can access anything in the public region of the class
    TIntStack and nothing else
// inside the class.
        TIntStack a(5); // auto object, destroyed on exit from main
        TIntStack  b(20); // auto object, destroyed on exit from main
        TIntStack *ip = new TIntStack; // dynamic object

        for (int i=1; i <= 5; i++) { // Push consecutive integers
            a.Push(i);
            b.Push(-i); // negative value pushed
        }
        // Continue Push operations on b
        for (int i=1; i < = 10; i++) { // Push consecutive integers
            b.Push(-i); // negative value pushed
        }

        PrintStack(a); // See what it contains

        a = b; // Assign one stack to another
```

```
        PrintStack(*ip);
        delete ip; // Why this? See below.

        return 0;
}
```

Let's see what happens. We created two TIntStack objects, a and b, statically on the run-time stack and another TIntStack object pointed by ip on the run-time heap. We pushed some numbers on these TIntStacks and then we called PrintStack with the object a.

But the function PrintStack accepts its argument by value (i.e., a is passed by value). This implies that a copy of a has to be made and this copy is to be passed to PrintStack. Who is responsible for making the copy and destroying it later? Here is how this process works.

If language defined types (like int and char) are passed by value, the compiler makes copies of them and passes them around and also destroys them on return from functions. But here we are passing a programmer defined object (TIntStack) by value. How can the compiler make a copy of it? It doesn't know anything about the object and definitely it doesn't know what is required to make a copy of the object. Notice that here again, a new object is created from an existing object.

As defined in C++ (and as explained earlier), whenever object copies are needed, the compiler invokes the copy constructor of the class to which the object belongs (TIntStack in our case). It is the responsibility of the copy constructor to make a meaningful (and safe) copy of the object. Hence, when PrintStack is called, the compiler invokes the copy constructor of TIntStack class to make a copy of the object a.

The source of the copy operation in this case is the argument of the call, the object a, and the destination is the formal argument of the function PrintStack, which is thisOne. When PrintStack is called from main(), the formal argument thisOne is initialized from the actual argument—a. The copy constructor is invoked for this operation. The copy constructor is invoked on the destination object as earlier and supplied with the object a as the source argument to it. We already know how the copy itself is done (see the code in copy instructor above). Now, function PrintStack gets its own copy of the original object and any changes it makes to thisOne will not affect the original object in main(). So everything is safe.

What happens to the object thisOne once we leave the function PrintStack? Anything allocated on the run-time stack (automatic variables) are cleaned up and their memory is recovered by the compiler. This is true for all language defined types. So on exit from PrintStack the local variables i and j go out of scope, (i.e., they are no longer available for use in the scope of main to where the program control returns). The compiler recovers the space occupied by them. Similarly, the local object thisOne goes out of scope and hence the memory occupied by it should also be recovered. The compiler definitely knows the size of the object itself but it is not aware of the fact that the pointer _sp in the object also points to some dynamically allocated memory that needs to be recovered. This is where the class destructor comes in handy.

Whenever an object goes out of scope, the destructor function (there is only one in the class) is invoked on the object before the compiler actually recovers the memory occupied by the object. The destructor should release any resource that the object has acquired. In our case, we need to deallocate the memory pointed by sp of the TIntStack object. Note that the destructor is like any other member function but it is invoked by the compiler when an object is no longer visible in a scope. [There are very few instances where a programmer needs to directly invoke the destructor.] Once the destructor finishes execution, the object is no longer accessible in that scope. Note that the destructor is invoked just before returning from the function (or just before leaving a block of code). The compiler invokes the destructors on objects created in that scope (function or block) just before exiting that scope. There is no chance of a programmer still using that object because the name of the object would not be visible on exit from that scope. The destructor–implementation to call other member functions of the object because the object to be destroyed is still alive and in good state.

Here is the implementation of the destructor:

```
TIntStack::~TIntStack()
{
        cout << "Executing the destructor for TIntStack\n";
        delete [] _sp;
}
```

The code for the destructor is quite simple. It just deallocates all the resources that were acquired by the object during its lifetime (the memory in _sp for **TIntStack**). Note that we don't have to worry about the space occupied by the other data members (_count and _size) because they are part of the object and their existence is known to the compiler. When an object of **TIntStack** is created, the size of the object includes the size of all the data members. The compiler doesn't know what _sp points to but it knows the size of the pointer _sp itself.

After the destructor function completes, the compiler does some internal house keeping operations to release the memory occupied by this object.

NOTE   Note that there is only one destructor per class. One might wonder why C++ doesn't allow more than one destructor. Why not have a destructor for every constructor (a constructor-destructor pair). The compiler should remember which constructor was called and match it with the corresponding destructor call. Providing this feature would require the storing of additional information in the object and also increase the responsibility of the implementor much more because now they also have to write a destructor for every constructor. If there is such a need, the class implementor can always keep some data members that keep track of which constructor was used and this information can be used in the destructor to do the right thing. Basically, the code of the different destructors (if it were allowed in the language) is moved into the only destructor allowed in the language and the implementor of the class executes the correct code based on the information stored in the object when it was created.

At the end of the **main** program, note that there is a **delete** call on the pointer **ip**. Why are we doing this? This is quite simple. Whenever we allocate something dynamically, we declare that we are responsible for controlling its lifetime. The compiler doesn't apply the destructor call on such dynamically allocated elements. The object pointed by **ip** is dynamically allocated using the **new** operator. It is not deallocated by the compiler automatically (i.e., no destructor is automatically called on this object). It is our responsibility to get rid of it when we no longer need it. The correct way to do that is to invoke the

delete operator on the pointer. When we want to get rid of a piece of dynamically allocated storage, we just invoke the **delete** operator on that pointer, as we have done for the data member _sp. When the delete operator is invoked on a pointer, two things happen.

1. If the pointer is a pointer to a class (as in **ip** above), then the destructor of the class (**TIntStack** in our case) is invoked on the object pointed by the pointer. This allows the programmer to clean up.

2. The memory referenced by the pointer is deallocated.

This sequence is basically the reversal of the steps that was done when we called operator **new()** in **main** for the pointer **ip**. The destructor call allows for releasing of all the resources acquired. Then the memory that was allocated by **new()** is released by the **delete** operator. This is the reason behind the call

```
delete ip;
```

in the **main()** program.

THE ASSIGNMENT OPERATION

Now let's analyze the statement

```
a = b; // Assign one stack to another
```

in the main program. Here we are assigning the object **b** to object **a**. Assignment is always done by the assignment operator. If **a** and **b** were simple integers, the compiler would overwrite whatever value that is in **a** with the value that is in **b**. It is as simple as that. But here, **a** and **b** are objects created by us. This implies that we are responsible for taking care of the assignment operation. We should know how assignment between **TIntStack** objects works and should be capable of implementing the assignment operator. For any assignment operator, we should pay attention to a couple of things.

1. Make sure that we are not assigning an object to itself (like **a** = **a**).

2. Reuse the resources in the object being assigned to or get rid of it.

3. Copy whatever needs to be copied from the source object to destination object.

4. Finally return a reference to the destination object.

The assignment operator has been declared in the class. An assignment operator for **TIntStack** has the signature

```
TIntStack& operator=(TIntStack& source) // ①
```

or

```
            TIntStack& operator=(const TIntStack& source) // ②
```

Here is the implementation:

```
TIntStack& TIntStack::operator=(const TIntStack& source)
{
        // Check for assignment to self (of the form a = a). 'this' is the
        // address of the object being assigned to and source is the object
        // being assigned. &source gives the address of the object.
        if (this == &source) {
                cout << "Warning: Assignment to self.\n";
                return *this;
        }

        /*
        If the count of elements on the stack of the source object is equal
        to or less than the size of the destination object, no sweat. All
        we have to do is copy the corresponding elements of the stacks and
        the count variable. On the other hand if the count of the number of
        elements on source object is bigger than the size of the
        destination object, we have to get rid of the memory in sp (of the
        destination object) and allocate a new piece of memory (equal to
        size in source) and then copy all elements.
        * /
        if (source._count > this->_size) {
                // The count of elements in source is more than the size of
                // destination
                // Throw away memory in sp and allocate a new one
                // See below for explanation.
                    delete [] _sp;
                    this->_size = source._size;
                    _sp = new int [ this->_size ];
        }
                // This code is common to both cases described above. Walk
                // through the stack and copy elements
                for (int i = 0; i < source._count; i++)
                     this->_sp[i] = source._sp[i]; // copy elements
                this->_count = source._count;

                return *this; // See below for explanation
}
```

Analysis: Assignment is an operation explicitly done by the programmer. It is never invoked by the system (compiler) directly. Assignment is an operation that is carried out between two **existing** objects. The statement

        a = b;

where **a** and **b** are objects, is interpreted as

        a.operator=(b);

In other words, the member function **operator=()** is invoked on the object on the left hand side (LHS) and is supplied with the operand that is on the right hand side (RHS) as the argument. The object on the RHS of the assignment operation (**b** in the example above) is not modified. As a side effect of this operation, a reference to the object on the LHS (**a**, in this example) is returned. Since the object on the RHS is not to be modified (we read from it and write into the object on the LHS), it is passed as a **const** argument to the **operator=()** function. However, if we use the assignment operator without the const argument shown in ① above, the object on the RHS can be modified. But doing so is not recommended because users of such classes wouldn't be very pleased when the object on the RHS changes in an assignment operation. Because **a** and **b** are both true existing objects, when we assign **b** to **a**, the values in **a** are overwritten by the corresponding values from **b**.

REMEMBER   If we don't provide an assignment operator in our class, the compiler generates a default assignment operator for the class (it never calls it automatically, but it does generate it). This default assignment operator may not do what we want to do. We will see more about this generated assignment operator in the next chapter.

In any assignment operation, what we would like to do is copy data from the source to the destination. That is easy in some cases and not so easy in others. In the **TIntStack** example, we need to copy values from the source stack to the destination stack. If the number of elements on the source stack is less than or equal to the space available in the destination stack, it is a straight forward operation. We just copy the corresponding stack elements. But what if the number of elements on the source stack are more than what the destination stack can hold. We could disallow such operations and return from the assignment operation after printing an error message. But, that would be too restrictive. Or we could change the destination stack to accommodate all the elements. When we accept the latter alternative, we need to allocate a new piece of memory for the stack elements that is of the same size as that in the source. Before that, we need to throw away the existing memory pointed by _sp in the destination. This is what is done by the **delete** call in the assignment operator above (there is no way we can extend this memory). Once this is done, we just copy the corresponding elements (see Fig. 3-3 and Fig. 3-4 on p. 93).

(extracted from the **main** program above)

```
TIntStack a(5); // auto object, destroyed on exit from main
TIntStack b(20); // another auto object
```

Finally, we return a reference to the destination object (i.e., stack **a**. One might wonder why this is done? Suppose we write a cascaded assignment operation like

```
c = a = b; // assign b to a and then the result of that to c
```

Assignment is an operation that proceeds right to left.[5] This turns the expression into

```
c = (a = b); // First assign b to a and then assign the result to c
```

---

[5]This has to do with operator overloading and associativity of operator which we will cover in Chapter 8. But for this discussion we only need to know that assignment associates right to left.

CAUTION | Just as we can write a = b we can also write

```
a = a; // Logically wrong but syntactically correct!
```

Such an expression might happen directly or indirectly through pointers and references (aliases). Our implementation has to check for such occurrences. All we have to do is verify that the address of the source and destination are different. **If assignment is being done on the same object, just don't do anything but return a reference to the destination object**. That is what is done in the implementation above.

If this *assignment to self* check is not done, it can cause major heartburn. Consider a class **TString** with a pointer data member:

```
class TString {
        public:
                TString (const char* sp) {
                    _data = new char[strlen(sp) + 1];
                    strcpy(_data, sp);
                }
                TString & operator=(const TString & assign);
        private:
                char* _data; // pointer to character string
};


TString&
TString::operator=(const TString& assign)
{
        // Wrong code. No check is done for assignment to self
        delete [] this->_data; // ❶
        _data = new char[strlen(assign._data) + 1]; // ❷
        strcpy(this->_data, assign._data);


        return *this;
}


TString      x1("Text string1");


x1 = x1;
```

With the above unsafe implementation of **operator=** in ❶, what is deleted is x1._data. But, in ❷ we try to use assign._data, which is the same as x1._data because the object on the left hand side (*this) is the same as the object on the right hand side (assign). So, we are shooting ourself in the foot. This program can crash when ❷ is executed or it can cause trouble elsewhere. Hence, the need to check for assignment to self.

Before assigment Operation

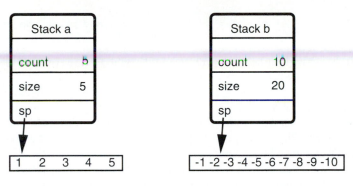

Fig. 3-3

After assigment Operation

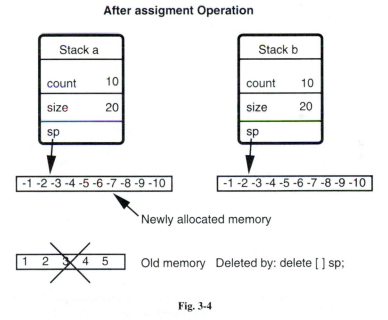

Fig. 3-4

Assigning b to a is straight forward and we have seen how it works. We would like to assign the result of this assignment (of b to a) to c. For this to work, the first assignment operation should return the value of (or a reference to) a. Otherwise, the second assignment of a to c wouldn't work. In general, in C and C++, we use the result of assignment operations without really knowing what happens internally. For example, the following code works because of this side effect of assignment.

```
int i = 10, j = 20; // No assignment here
int k;

cout << (i = j) << endl; // assign j to i and print the result of the
                         // assignment ❶

if ( k = j) { // Assign j to k and if the result is not zero do something ❷
      // code to do something
}
```

In ❶, the assignment returns the value of i after the assignment and that value is printed. Similarly, in ❷, j is assigned to k and the value of k, after the assignment, is returned, which is compared with zero.

For all this to work with assignment of objects, we need to make sure that our assignment operation returns a reference to the object a after the assignment is done.

PASCAL   In languages like Pascal, the assignment operation

$$a := b;$$

is an operation without the side effect of returning the value of a after the assignment. This is the reason why the statement

$$c := a := b;$$

will not work with Pascal (and similar languages like Modula 2).

THINK   If you look at the code in the copy constructor and the assignment operator, you see a lot of similarity. Both copy from an existing object to another object. But can you see the major difference between the two pieces of code? In other words, how is the assignment operator different from the copy constructor code? Can you make them share their implementations?

To complete our example of **TIntStack**, here is the implementation for the remaining member functions.

```
void TIntStack::Push(int what)
{
      if (_count < _size) { // If there is room for more elements
          _sp[_count] = what; // Store element
          _count++; // increment count
      }
      else {
          cout << "Stack is FULL. Cannot Push value << what << endl;
      }
}

int TIntStack::Pop()
{
      if (_count <= 0) { // Stack is empty
          cout << " Stack is EMPTY\n";
          exit (1); // How will we indicate failure otherwise?
```

```
                                // In production code we would throw an exception
                                // here
                }
                _count—;
                return _sp[_count];
}
unsigned TIntStack::HowMany() const
{
                return _count;
}
```

MORE ON THE this POINTER AND NAME MANGLING

In the implementation above, we access data members of an object sometimes using the **this** pointer. As mentioned in Chapter 2, the **this** pointer in a member function is the pointer to the object on which the member function was invoked. From the **main**() program above

```
                                a.Push(i);
```

invokes the **Push** member function on the object **a**. Inside the **Push** member function, the **this** pointer holds the address of the object **a**. This way, a member function can access any element (data members and member functions) of the object. As mentioned in Chapter 2, every member function is implemented by the compiler just like any other function but every member function should somehow get access to the object on which it was invoked. To achieve this goal, the **this** pointer is passed to every member function as a hidden argument and the **this** pointer is usually the first argument that the function receives (followed by the other arguments that were declared for it). Given that, the **Push** member function might look like

```
                void Push(TIntStack* this, int what)
                {
                        // implementation code above
                        // When Push is invoked on a i.e. a.Push(10)
                        // the "this" pointer points to the object a
                }
```

However, **Push** might be a function name already in use. Further, there could be a **Push** function in some other class too. How can the compiler (or linker) distinguish among them? And how do we represent overloaded constructor and the destructor? To do all this, the function name mangling concept is used.

NOTE   The ANSI C++ language standard doesn't mandate a particular style of name mangling discussed on the following page. Compiler implementors are free to follow their own (even proprietary) schemes. It is good to know that name mangling is taking place but it is not very essential to understand the exact mangling scheme used. The examples there just show the concept and it may not apply to your compiler.

Every member function of a class has the class name encoded in it (actually the type of the this pointer) along with some other information about arguments. The Push member function would probably become

```
void Push__9TIntStackFi()
```

There are two underscore (ASCII _, decimal 95) followed by a number. The number represents the number of characters in the class name (9 for TIntStack). This helps in parsing names. If a program has to search for the name of the class (to which this function belongs) then all it has to do is to look for this __ and the number (say N) following it. Then extract the next N characters and we have the name of the class to which this function belongs. The rest of the characters indicate the argument types and return value types. Note that only the type of the argument (and not its name) is used in name mangling. Everything after the __ sequence is an encoding of all the arguments that were declared for this function. In the mangled name above, Push is the original name, 9TIntStack indicates that the first argument is of type TIntStack (which is the this pointer), F[6] indicates that it is a global function and i indicates that it accepts one integer argument. **The return type is not part of the mangled name**.

A constructor doesn't have a unique name! It has the same name as the class name. To represent them the mangling process prepends

```
__ct__
```

in front of the mangled name. So the default constructor after mangling would be

```
    TIntStack();          // Normal unmangled name.
__ct__9TIntStackFv(); // Mangled name
```

Here again the 9TIntStack is for the this pointer and F is for the global function and v indicates that it doesn't accept any arguments (void).

Other constructors (if any) would have arguments and hence their exact name would be different. For example the copy constructor would be

```
TIntStack(const TIntStack&); //unmangled name
__ct__9TIntStackF9TIntStackRC();
// R - reference, C - const
```

The second 9TIntStack stands for the argument and the RC indicates that it is a reference to const. See the ARM for complete details of name mangling.

On the same lines, the destructor (only one per class) would be represented as

```
~TIntStack(); // unmangled
__dt__9TIntStackFv(); // mangled name
```

---

[6]Some compilers differentiate between near and far function by using N for a near function and F for a far function.

Similarly operator functions have special encoding. For example, the assignment operator is encoded as

```
__as__9TIntStack()
```

The global new() operator begins with __nw and the global delete operator begins with __dl.

All operators have a pre-defined encoding in the language.

Why you might ask, should I know all these gory details about name mangling?

Imagine that you implemented a class and forgot to implement some member functions. It would compile fine but the linker would spurt out some error message about undefined functions. But those functions may not look like what you had in your class header file[7]? And you are now thoroughly confused!

Because of name mangling, the linker never sees your original function names. It is given the equivalent mangled names by the compiler. The linker knows nothing about mangling (at least I haven't seen a linker which does, so far) and it just complains about the names that were undefined. This is where some knowledge of name mangling helps. If the name printed by the linker starts with __ct__ , you know it is some constructor and that should narrow your search for undefined member functions. As you write more and more C++ code, the mangled names would be something you would be able to decipher in your sleep! Trust me on this.

CAUTION   Continuing with the this pointer, remember that the this pointer is a very sacred pointer. One should not modify the this pointer; don't assign to it (ever)! There are some very rare situations where the this pointer might be modified within a member function. We will see this much later.

You might have also noticed that the this pointer is not used to access data members in each and every member function. For instance, in the function Pop, the data member _count is directly accessed without any qualifier. Whenever we use the name of a data member in a member function, the compiler prepends the "this" qualifier. Hence _count becomes this->_count. It is not necessary for us to explicitly use the this pointer unless we explicitly need a pointer to the object.

STYLE   In this book, whenever there is a chance of confusion, the explicit qualifier this is used. For example, in the assignment operator above, we have the statement

```
this->_count = source._count;
```

which could have also been written as

```
_count = source._count; // this is correct too!
```

---

[7]Linkers (and development environments) are getting more intelligent and it is not uncommon to find development environments where the unmangled name is presented to the user. But still it is good to have a cursory knowledge of name mangling.

But using the same name, _count, more than once in the same statement but on different objects might be confusing. Hence the explicit qualifier this.

When is it absolutely necessary to use the this pointer? When we would like to return a reference to the object on which the function was invoked, we have to say (*this). Otherwise, how else can we represent the concept *my object* explicitly? In other situations, which we have already seen in the assignment operator, we might want to get the address of our object. There again, we use the name this explicitly. *By far, these two are the most frequent situations where the name this is used explicitly.*

THE CONCEPT OF A const MEMBER FUNCTION

If you didn't already notice, the HowMany member function in the TIntStack class has the unique signature

```
unsigned HowMany() const;
```

As mentioned in Chapter 2, the const suffix declares that HowMany is a constant member function. It means that HowMany will not modify the object on which it is invoked. In other words, HowMany should not assign to any data members of the object on which it is called. And this restriction is enforced by the compiler. Here is the implementation:

```
unsigned TIntStack::HowMany() const
    {
        // What if we add the _sp = 0; statement (just as an example)
        // _sp = 0;
        return _count;
    }
```

☞ **Note that the const qualifier is specified both in the declaration and definition of a member function.**

The code above does not modify anything inside the object. It just reads the value of the data member _count. We can view a const member function as a *read-only* function. If one were to look at data in an object before the call to a const member function and if we examine the data in the same object again after returning from the const member function, there would not be any differences between the two sets of values. Nothing in an object should change because of the call to a const member function.[8]

If the code in the comments above were uncommented, the compiler would look at the assignment to the data member _sp and immediately flag it as an error because we are violating the constantness of the member function (i.e., we are changing a data member inside a const member function). Such errors are very easily caught by the compiler.

One might wonder as to the real benefit of const member functions. Recall the discussion about interfaces and clients in Chapter 2. A const member function assures its clients of its benign nature. It tells the clients that it is harmless to call a const member

---

[8]This is only true when the implementor follows bitwise constantness and not conceptual (or logical) constantness.

function. This instills a degree of confidence in the clients and they will develop more confidence in the software they are using.

In the discussion above, what we have seen is the concept of *bitwise* (or bit-pattern) constantness. The const member function did not change a single bit in the object. The bit pattern in the object before and after the call to the const member function is the same. Compilers only enforce this bitwise constantness.

However, there are instances when a member function changes the data in an object but the client's view of the object is not affected by this change. In other words, in spite of the change in data within the object, the object still looks unchanged to the client. Such a member function is said to enforce *conceptual* constantness (or virtual constantness). The object has remained conceptually constant even though some of the bits in the object changed. We will see some examples of this in Chapter 4. Compilers cannot enforce conceptual constantness, it has to be done by the implementor by cheating the compiler! We want to convey the view of a const member function to the clients and at the same time change some data in the object. We can easily convince the clients, but how can we change the data in an object within a const member function? The compiler would catch that error! Well, we can write code such that the compiler still feels that things are constant and achieve our goal (of modifying data). Think about how you can do it and we will see the solution in a later chapter.

THINK

HOW A COMPILER IMPLEMENTS A const MEMBER FUNCTION

It is interesting to see how the compiler enforces bit-wise constantness. Remember that a member function is nothing special. It is just a function with a weird name and the this pointer. So how can the compiler detect assignments to members?

It is quite simple. The only link between the data members and the function is the this pointer. A const member function has to treat the object as a const object. This can be easily done by declaring the this pointer to be a pointer to const. It is that simple. Now it is easy to look at the prototype of HowMany with the this pointer explicitly declared.

```
unsigned HowMany(const TIntStack* this);
```

With that declaration, any assignment to the data members within the object through the this pointer will be illegal because it is a pointer to something that is constant.

In the same class, we can have two identical functions, one being a non-const function and the other being a const function. This is perfectly correct and it is useful in some circumstances.

NOTE   A const member function cannot call another non-const member function in its implementation because the non-const member function will be called on the same object (same this pointer) and it would be free to modify the object. That would violate the constantness of the const member function that called it. This is (it should be) detected by the compiler.

EIFFEL   Eiffel supports a concept very similar to const member functions. Eiffel has two kinds of member functions—*procedures* and *functions*. Procedures are just like normal member functions but they don't have a return value. On the other hand, function is an operation that computes something based on the values contained in the object and returns the computed value. Such functions don't change the state of the object. Hence, they are like constant member functions. Smalltalk doesn't have anything similar.

DIFFERENCES BETWEEN CLASS AND STRUCT IN C++

There is no difference between a **class** and a **struct** except for one small feature. Here is that difference: Unless otherwise specified, everything in a **class** is **private**, whereas in a **struct** everything is **public**. For example:

```
class X {
    int     a; // This is a private data member
    void    f(); // This is private member function
};

struct Y {
    int     a; // This is a public data member
    void    f(); // This is a public member function
};
```

This is the only difference between a class and a struct in C++.

So far, we have seen some details about classes and objects under C++ and we have also seen some language specific details. This should enable (and encourage) you to write small C++ programs to hone your C++ skills. The rest of this chapter deals with OOP concepts of interface and clients perspective of classes. We also learn about finer elements of class design. This part, I believe, would be more interesting than what we have discussed so far.

WHAT CAN A CLASS CONTAIN?

Under C++, a class contains anything inside of it. A class can contain

data members that are primitive types (like **int** and **char**)

objects of another class

pointers and references to objects of another class (or the same class)

pointers and references to primitive types

static data members

member functions (both static and non-static)

pointers to member functions of another class

friend class/function declarations

declaration of another class (a nested class, a rarely used feature)

We will encounter examples of all these declarations (and their associated advantages and disadvantages) in chapters to follow. However, just to give the reader a flavor of these dif-

ferent declarations, here are some typical declarations. None of these are complete declarations—they are just pieces of code.

```
// A Person class
class TPerson {
        public:
                TPerson(const char theName[], const char theAddress[] = 0);
                const char* GetName() const;
        private:
                char* _name; // pointer to characters
                char*_address;
};


class TListNode; // a forward declaration - to be completed later
class TListIterator;
class TList {
        public:
                TList(); // Create a simple linked list
                unsigned HowMany() const;
        private:
                TListNode* _head; // first node on the list
                TListNode* _tail; // last node on the list
                friend class TListIterator;
}

class TListNode {

                // other declarations
        private:
                TListNode* _next; // pointer to next node
                TListNode* _previous; // pointer to previous node
};

class TStopWatch {
        public:
                TStopWatch ();
        private:
                static long& _systemClock; // a reference to the system clock
};
```

FOCUS IS ON THE INTERFACE OF A CLASS DURING DESIGN

We discussed the concept of *interface* and *implementation* in Chapter 2. Now it is time to
learn more about them. When a client (anyone who uses a class to create objects, or uses
it to create another class using inheritance) looks at a class, the most important thing that
catches her attention is what is declared in the class. More specifically, she pays attention
to the **public** region if she is just going to create objects of that class (as most clients do).
In addition, if she is trying to create (design) a new class by inheriting from this class, her
attention would be directed to the public as well as **protected** regions of the class. The
private region doesn't get much attention in these scenarios.

   Most of what a client can do with an object of a class is perceived by looking at the
public member functions in the class. These member functions are the only tools that the

client gets to perform any operations on the object. For example, going back to the laser disc player example from Chapter 2, most of what a user (client) can do with it is clear from the labeled buttons available on the front panel. The buttons are like member functions for the laser disc player abstraction. These buttons should fully capture the client's view of what the player is capable of doing. At the same time, we don't want to provide too many buttons (or controls) that would confuse the user. Further, the buttons should convey unambiguous information about their use. A button should have one and only one purpose so that the clients always get a unified picture of the player. But it might be hard to understand (and use) a particular button just by its name. This is where the user manual (or owners manual) comes in handy. The owners manual fully describes the functionality of each and every button and control. On the same lines, a well designed class also needs a document that describes the usage of each and every member function in the class. These are all critical for good interface design. Similarly, when you meet a person for the first time, you form an impression (friendly, hostile, superficial, etc.) about him/her. And the rest of the conversation would be directly influenced by this impression that you have in mind. A well designed class should be friendly to its clients. We will walk through some key elements of good interface design in the next few paragraphs.

CLASS NAMES, MEMBER FUNCTION NAMES, ARGUMENT TYPES, AND DOCUMENTATION

A class is mostly used by another programmer to create objects (or to create another class using inheritance) and methods are invoked on the object probably supplying arguments. We need to provide a meaningful name for a class and all the methods contained in it. We should also use sensible names for arguments of member functions such that a client clearly knows what a particular argument is being used for. Many programmers just specify the type of the argument that a function expects without giving it a name. This is a very bad habit that one should overcome. Sure, the compiler doesn't care what names you chose because it just matches types. But the name of the argument conveys a lot of information to the clients. Also, we should use the correct argument passing modes (value, references, or pointer).

The purpose of a class and its member functions is not clear in most cases by just looking at the name. One has to provide good documentation about the

purpose of that class

who it is intended for

what classes (if any) it depends on

what constraints the class brings with it

what it expects from its clients.[9]

In multi-threaded systems, it is very important that a class further declare whether it is usable in situations where there are multiple threads of execution. Most companies, projects, and architects require even more documentation from class designers and implementors. It is very important that one follows all those guidelines while designing and documenting classes.

---

[9]This might be surprising but many classes do depend on certain services from its clients.

It is also essential that the designer (and implementor) of a class very clearly state any restrictions on object creation. For example, some classes require that objects of the class be created only on the run-time stack (to ensure automatic destruction). And another class might restrict object creation to the dynamic heap only, (i.e., object must be created using the **new** operator only). Such restrictions on object creation are not very common, but don't be surprised if you see one. Documenting the restrictions on object creation is a good thing but it is not the best solution. It will be even better if the language can be used to enforce such restrictions. With C++, it is very easy to control where objects are created. Techniques for implementing them are described in Chapter 11.

For each and every method contained in a class, a similar documentation is required. The class documentation focuses attention of the client in one direction and the documentation (or description) for each method further clarifies what the method does in that class. This documentation should not be a big book. It could be simple comments inside the header file (for simple methods) and/or an auxiliary document that is supplied with the class. A big document will intimidate the client and they might hesitate to use it, fearing that the class is too complex to understand (and hence the need for a big document). A well designed and well documented class invites clients attention and encourages them to use it. It is like a well maintained park that entices you to walk in and take a stroll. It is always useful to put short, sensible comments in header files because most programmers look there first for information. Each method should also clearly specify the purpose of each argument that it expects. In case of references and pointers (mostly pointers), it is very important that storage ownership responsibility is clearly defined. Otherwise horrendous memory leaks or run-time crashes will plague the system. In fact, most resource related problems occur when the class implementor and the user do not understand their respective responsibilities clearly. When methods return values (reference, pointer, or value) to the caller, it is again required that storage ownership responsibility be clearly defined. It is a good practice to use **const** arguments and **const** member functions wherever possible because a **const** element is recognized by the compiler and it prevents accidental modifications. The language cannot prevent malicious users from casting things. The language only protects the user from accidental errors.

One might wonder, why all this fuss about documentation and argument passing, etc? Why can't we let the compiler handle all these things? The problem is that many things that programmers do cannot be checked by the compiler. The compiler cannot read our minds and figure out the intent of an argument in a function declaration. Each and every thing the compiler sees is just a name with a type and it doesn't care about function argument names. But they make sense to us. As designers of programs, we target specific issues in our design and we try to solve problems. The compiler cannot understand such issues because, for it, every program is just a set of instructions. It cannot get the "big picture." This is where our documentation, conventions, and guidelines help.

ARGUMENT PASSING MODES—THE CLIENT'S VIEW

When a class interface is designed, member functions of the class are declared and their arguments are also specified. Clients of the class supply the actual arguments (if any) when they invoke the member functions.

Each and every method should clearly specify the mode of argument passing. The argument could be passed by value, by reference, or by a pointer. They can be combined with const to make them more robust. The prototype of a function exists to convey this information to the clients.

The mode of each argument conveys a particular meaning to the client. Further, there are some time tested rules that are followed. Hence, it is important that we pick the right type for our arguments. In the next few paragraphs, we look at the different styles and their implications.

NOTE   In the ensuing examples, the term *caller* refers to a function f() (or main program) that makes a call to another function g(). In this scenario, g() would be the *callee*, the function called from f(). In other words, caller is the one initiating the transfer of control, and callee is the one receiving control.

In all these examples, two classes, T and X, and the member function f() of class X are used. It does not really matter what T and X contain as far as these examples are concerned.

1. void X::f (T arg) // First pass by value example

Callee can read and write from arg (it is a copy of the original). Any changes to arg within f() does not affect the caller of f() because it has been given a copy of the original object. This is perhaps the best and safest mode for passing arguments. The caller and callee are both protected from each other. The down side is that a copy constructor will be called to make a copy of the original object passed to f() and naturally a destructor will have to be called on arg on exit from f(). Always remember that every constructor call will require a destructor call to destroy the object sooner or later. The cost of this constructor/destructor pair could be high. Further, sometimes copying an object is restricted to privileged clients or it is completely forbidden. Under such situations, this style of arguments passing cannot be used; a reference argument may be better. Also, copying large objects is very time consuming and is usually not preferred. f() should not store the address of arg in one of the data members of its object (using the this pointer) because as soon as the function exits, arg will be destroyed.

2. void X::f (const T object) // Second pass by value example

This is very similar to the previous case. It is still pass by value and it has all the advantages and disadvantages of normal pass by value. But here, the callee can only read from arg and cannot write to it because it is declared to be a const object. One doesn't usually see this style of argument passing because the caller doesn't really care what the callee does to her copy of the object, since it is only a copy, not the real object. It is just an extra restriction that the callee imposes on its copy of the object.

3. void X::f (T& arg) // First pass by reference example

Unless otherwise documented, this could mean that callee should read from arg and then write to it, too. In other words, arg is an in-out parameter. The real object will be modified by the callee. That is, f() can read from arg any input parameter it needs and then write the result back into arg at the end. If this is the intent, clearly document that fact with comments. Note that arg is owned by the callee; f() should not destroy it.

On the other hand, the intent could be to use arg as an out parameter only. (i.e., the callee should write the result value(s) into arg but should not read from it). This cannot be enforced by the compiler. Usually, in this case, arg is an uninitialized object used for return value only (just an out parameter). The caller creates an empty object (probably using the default constructor) and passes it to f() and f() would write the return values into arg. Without more documentation the intent is not clear. If the intent is to use arg as an out parameter, it might be better if such functions follow a different naming convention (for example, a name beginning with *Copy*). Using references as an out parameter is a very popular scheme in cases where the caller picks the storage format she likes and the callee just fills it in without really knowing much about the original object. This is usually the case with inheritance hierarchies that we will discuss in later chapters. Remember that arg is owned by the callee. Passing an argument by reference also guarantees that the argument is really a live object; it cannot be something like a nil pointer. The object behind that reference is guaranteed to exist at least during the lifetime of the call to f(). Don't use a pointer to T in cases where you really need an object.

CAUTION   Whenever a reference argument is passed, it is usually accepted that the callee should not store the address of arg anywhere, because arg is not guaranteed to exist after the function exits. What is implied here is that f() should assume that the lifetime of arg is limited to the scope of f(). Imagine what happens if f() stores away the address of arg in one of its data members and then tries to use arg later through the stored address. By then, arg might have been very well destroyed in the callers scope. The caller didn't make any guarantees about the life time of arg! Doing anything like that is a sure way to crash programs (or cause unexpected behavior and potentially very hard bugs to track). We are not stating that f() should not take the address of arg; that is fine. We always do that in our assignment operators. But don't store away the address in one of your data members.

THREAD SAFETY   In multi-threaded environments, the caller has to guarantee that arg exists through the entire scope of the function f(). If a call to f() is made with some argument by one thread and before f() completes, if some other thread is scheduled for execution and it destroys the object that was passed to f(), things could get very ugly and debugging such code would be a nightmare.

☞ **Do not ever use pass by reference (without const qualifier) mode for in-only parameters.**

    4. void X::f (const T& arg)   // Second pass by reference example

This is much better than (3). Callee reads from arg but cannot write to arg because it is a reference to a **const** object. It is an in parameter only. This is an efficient way to pass large objects and is highly recommended. Use this style wherever possible (i.e., in cases where pass by value is not feasible). As in (3), this mode also implies that the callee should not store the address of arg anywhere because arg is not guaranteed to exist after the function returns. In both (3) and (4), function f() might want to make a copy of arg but that may not be what the caller had in mind. It is good to document the caller's intentions clearly.

     5. void X: : f (T* argp) // First Pass by pointer example

     C programmers love pointers. And they are justified in using them in C most of the time because C doesn't have the concept of a reference. However, under C++, pointers can be dangerous if their intent is not clearly understood. Whenever a pointer is used, one advantage is that a unique value—zero (also called NULL)—distinguishes an invalid pointer from a valid pointer. References do not have such distinction. One cannot distinguish between a valid reference and an invalid one. When references are used correctly, there will never be a reference that refers to an object that no longer exists.

     This case is a bit ambiguous and could be potentially dangerous. If the callee is only to write to what argp points to, then it is only an out parameter and the name of argp should be something that begins with *out;* even better, if such functions follow a different naming convention (for example, function name beginning with *Copy*). The caller must pass the address of an object that can be modified by f(). It is easy to pass a nil pointer (accidentally or intentionally). This means the callee cannot assume the existence of what argp points to. The pointer argp itself is passed by a value that implies that f() cannot create a new object and store its address in argp, such that the caller can retrieve this new address. If you really wanted f() to change the address contained in argp, you would want to pass a reference to the pointer argp.[10] It (argp) could also be used as an in-out parameter. In that case, the callee would read from what argp points to and then fill it in with the return values. This would not work if a nil pointer is passed in.

     If one really wants to use this mode, a better interface would be to have a default value for argp—say zero. If the interface is changed to

       void X::f (T* argp = 0)

we are clearly telling our clients that a zero pointer can be passed to this function without causing any unexpected behavior.

THE ADOPT SEMANTICS

Given all these restrictions, one might wonder where this method of argument passing could be useful. This mode is useful with the so called *adopt semantics*. What it really means is that the caller is passing on the responsibility for the storage (actually the life time of the resource) pointed by argp to the callee (i.e., the object to which f() belongs). The caller created a dynamic object (probably using new()) of type T; but the caller may not know when to **delete** this dynamic object (this situation arises in many circumstances) because the callee might be still using it (or the caller may not be around to delete it). It is also possible that the callee expects the caller to provide storage that will be used by the callee. Under these situations, the caller hands over the responsibility of the object pointed by argp to the callee. In other words, the callee *adopts* the storage pointed by

---

[10]For the incurably curious, the declaration would be f(T *& argp); If you are heading in that direction, be sure that you understand the syntax and the implications of such complex declarations.

argp. When the callee no longer needs the object pointed by argp it will delete it. A real life analogy would be a surrogate mother who gives birth to the baby (creates it) and then hands it over to the adopting parents. This situation may also be seen in an electronic-mail (e-mail) system where the user creates a message and then hands it over to the mail delivery system. The mail delivery system adopts the message that was created by the user.

CAUTION   The function (or object) that adopts the storage of the caller should know how to destroy the adopted entity. For example, if the caller used malloc() (a C library function for allocating dynamic memory) to create the object and the callee uses delete to destroy the same object, it would be disastrous. Further, the caller and callee must be within the same address space.[11] It is not trivial to make this work when ownership is being transferred across address space boundaries.

When using the adopt semantics, it is better to use a different naming convention for such functions (like names beginning with *Accept, Embrace, Own,* or *Adopt*). However, this naming convention cannot be used with constructors and operators. In such cases, the name of the argument should begin with one of these words. For example, in an e-mail system, the member function (in a class TEnvelope) taking over the responsibility of a user message could be called EmbraceMessage(), AdoptMessage(), OwnMessage(), or AcceptMessage().

6. void X::f (const T* argp) // Second pointer example

This mode cannot be used (at least not without casting) for *adopt* semantics because a pointer to const cannot be deleted. Of course, one can remove the const-ness by casting the pointer. But that is dangerous and is not recommended. Avoid such unsafe practices. However, if the protocol does not involve calling delete, it might still work. Here, the callee should only read from argp. Argument argp is read only (in parameter). The callee should check the incoming argument to ensure that pointer argp is not zero (0). Document if it is safe to pass a zero pointer. Or use the default value for argp (0) as mentioned in (5).

As is evident, both (5) and (6) are useful if the caller has an option to pass a real object or zero. It is also useful to implement adopt semantics. But if the callee always expects an object (and it is not adopt semantics), use a reference argument as in (3) or (4).

Pointers can also be incremented and decremented. If the callee needs to use the incoming argument (argp) to navigate what it points to, a reference is useless. Only a pointer can be used in such situations. But, none of the modes above mention anything about pointer arithmetic.[12] Unless otherwise stated, the client should assume that the callee will not increment or decrement the pointer argument that is passed in by the caller. If the callee needs to do arithmetic with the pointer, then the function signature should be

void X::f(T argp[])

---

[11]In this book, *same address space* implies the same process (or task) which controls an address space.

[12]By pointer arithmetic, I mean increment and decrement operations, and movement of the pointer to a different location using any other operation.

and not a simple pointer—*argp. This clearly states that an array is expected. In addition, the documentation for that function should clearly state such intentions (of pointer arithmetic). If the callee is not going to perform any arithmetic with the pointer argument, the callee can also assure the caller by declaring

> void X::f(T* const argp)

This clearly states that argp is a const pointer (not a pointer to const). In fact, any attempt to increment or decrement argp is detected by the compiler.

7. void X::f (T* const argp)

This is similar to (5). Callee can read and write what the pointer argp points to but the function cannot move the pointer (i.e., no arithmetic is allowed on argp). It also implies that the callee cannot access anything before or after the address pointed by argp. In other words, callee is assuring the caller about its intentions. Note that you can also delete argp. A pointer to const cannot be deleted (compile timer error) but a const pointer has no such restrictions.

8. void X::f (const T* const argp)

This is a combination of (6) and (7). The callee declares that it is not going to modify what argp points to and also that it will not perform any arithmetic on argp. This means argp is just an in-only argument. This scheme does not support *adopt* semantics as mentioned in (6).

SELECTING THE CORRECT MODE FOR ARGUMENTS

If possible, avoid passing large objects by value. Use pass by value only for primitive types and small objects. Copying objects is expensive, but if security is a major concern then stick with pass by value.

Don't pass pointers when you mean to pass objects.

```
void f (T* object);
```

a. A pointer doesn't guarantee that the pointer really points to an object. It could very well be a nil pointer.

b. If the callee expects a real object as the argument, then pass a reference not a pointer. It is guaranteed not to fail; the callee need not check for a nil reference (because there is no such thing).

c. If you want the callee to write into the object (out parameter), again, a reference is meaningful but it cannot be a reference to a const.

d. Passing a reference does not transfer the ownership of the object to the callee. The caller still owns (and is responsible for) the object and its associated storage. If the function expects the caller to give up ownership of the object, document that very clearly. Otherwise, the *double delete* problem will ruin your life. [Double delete occurs when a dynamic memory address pointed by a pointer is released (delete in C++, free in C) more than once. Any memory allocated using new() must be deleted exactly once using delete operator. But sometimes, due to programming errors, the same pointer is deleted more than once].

   e. A pointer might be useful when the callee needs to check if the pointer is nil. But such interfaces are very sneaky and hard to follow. If you need them, document them clearly so that there is no confusion.

When passing primitive type arguments, stick with value arguments. The cost of passing a pointer and an integer are the same. But pass-by-value is much safer.

   Use default value arguments where possible. They convey more meaning and also help in understanding the purpose of an argument. They reduce the burden on the clients because they have to pass in fewer arguments.

   Use const qualifiers for arguments and functions wherever possible. A const qualifier involves the compiler and hence makes the program more robust.

   If you want polymorphism to work with an argument (as we will see in later chapters), then pass by value cannot be used. One has to use a reference or a pointer argument. This applies to return values also (as described below).

FUNCTION RETURN VALUES

Many functions return some *thing* to the caller. The returned thing could be a value, a reference, or a pointer. One needs to understand their meaning before they can be used correctly and effectively.

   The possible modes are:

```
T X::f();              // return by value
T* X::f();             // return by pointer/address
const T* X::f();       // return by pointer to const
T& X::f();             // return a reference
const T& X::f();       // return a reference to const
```

   1. Never return a reference to a local variable. Once we leave the function, the local variable will be destroyed but the reference comes into existence soon after that and it will refer to something that is dead.

   2. If you are creating a new object inside a function and would like to transfer the ownership of the new object to the caller, then your function must return a pointer. The caller owns the memory pointed by the returned pointer. This usually happens when the called function creates a new object (or pointer to something) and the callee cannot control the lifetime of this new object. It is a good idea to have a naming convention for such functions (say CreateXXX()). Also, such functions must be clearly documented. This is the converse of the *adopt* semantics discussed earlier. We can also automate the deletion of pointers returned from such functions by using some reclaimer objects (C++ auto_ptr), discussed in a later chapter. For example, in a TPerson class we could have a member function

```
class TPerson {
  public:
    // ...
    char* CreateNameOfPerson() const; // member of class Person
};
```

Assume that **CreateNameOfPerson( )** allocates memory for the characters in the name and returns a pointer to it (which will be owned by the caller). The caller should deallocate it when it is no longer needed. Transfer of ownership for dynamic objects is only possible with pointer return values; it cannot be done (at least not easily) by returning a reference or value. If you don't like to return a pointer, then enclose the pointer in an object (like **string** object from C++ library) and return the object by value.

3. If the characters (or object) pointed by the returned pointer are not to be modified by the caller, then return a pointer to **const**. Again, in the **TPerson** class:

```
class TPerson {
  public:
  // ...
  const char* GetNameOfPerson() const;
};
```

This does not imply any transfer of ownership of memory. The caller can just read what the returned pointer is pointing to. Needless to say, the caller cannot delete it (that would be an error detected at compile time). If you are returning a pointer (for whatever reason) from a **const** function, you cannot return a non-const pointer to any of your data members. That would offset the benefit of the **const** function. Such errors are detected by the compiler. Returning a pointer to const (to one of the data members) is recommended in a case where returning by value is very expensive (or it is semantically not correct), but the caller should not modify what the pointer points to. The client has to respect the **const**-ness of the pointer and use it as such without casting.

CAUTION   *Remember: Don't ever return a non-const pointer to one of your data members. You are unnecessarily asking for trouble. Further, this weakens your abstraction by exposing your implementation data to clients. It breaks data encapsulation.*

Returning a pointer from a function is the only option if there is a possibility that the function fails to return the requested value. This is easily accomplished by returning a nil pointer. The nil pointer could indicate failure or non-existence of what the function was supposed to return (for example **GetNameOfPerson** above). This is one reason (in addition to the others mentioned above) why returning a pointer from a function is quite common.

4. If you are returning primitive types (**char**, **int**, **long**, etc.), then returning by value is as efficient as returning by reference or pointer. But returning by value is safer and much easier to understand.

5. In some situations (like **operator+**), you don't have any way of returning a reference because the outcome of the function is not known (and it cannot be pre-computed); a correct implementation would require returning by value (of a temporary variable created inside the function). This is the best and safest way to implement such functions. This is discussed in Chapter 8.

RETURNING REFERENCES FROM FUNCTIONS

As much as possible, avoid returning a reference from a function. This is due to a number of reasons discussed below:

1. When a reference to an object (say foo) is to be safely returned from a function, the function could not have created that object foo. Otherwise, who would be responsible for the storage of the newly created object? And because it cannot be a local object, this implies that the object foo must have existed before the call to foo() and it should be guaranteed that it will exist even after the function returns.

2. How will a function returning a reference to an object indicate failure to create the referenced object? There is no such thing as a nil reference. The only alternative is to *throw* an exception.[13]

There are some very special situations where returning a reference from a function makes sense (and is safe).

Some functions are called on existing objects. It is guaranteed that the object (on which the function was invoked) will exists at least for the duration of the function. In such cases, one can safely return a reference to the object (actually to *this). This is predominantly used in the assignment operator (operator =) and also in operators that have l-value semantics (like +=, *=, etc.). Please see Chapter 8 for details.

☞ **If you want to return something from a function polymorphically, the only option is a reference or a pointer (as we shall see in later chapters). It is impossible to use return by value in such situations.**

MEANING OF L-VALUE SEMANTICS

An l-value is something than can be used on the left hand side (LHS) of the assignment operator. For example, a = b implies that a is being modified and it is an l-value. Many C++ (and C) operators require l-values to operate correctly. All operators that combine assignment with some other operation, such as addition (+=), division (/=), etc. are l-value operators. Writing (a *= b) is the same as (a = a * b). The object a is being modified. Therefore, a must be an l-value. If a is a const, then (a *= b) wouldn't compile because a cannot be modified (it is not an l-value). Here b is an r-value. One can read from an r-value. Any object (or primitive type) that can be used as an l-value cannot be a const. The operators (=, +=, -=, *=, /=, etc.) all have l-value semantics. That is, the name on the LHS will be modified and therefore it must be an l-value.

---

[13]In fact the language (actually the compiler) itself throws an exception when it cannot create the reference (See the section on RTTI - run-time type identification in a subsequent chapter).

WRITING MEMORY SAFE CLASSES

A well implemented class manages the memory that it allocates correctly and does not cause any memory leakage, no matter how many objects are created (and how they are created) and used. Designing and implementing such classes is not easy. To understand the guidelines for memory safe classes we need to understand garbage collection, dangling reference, and initialization issues. We cover these topics in Chapter 4. That is a better place for the topic of memory safe classes.

Improving Performance

With all this discussion about values, pointers, and references, one might get worried about performance. Here are some guidelines that might help when performance of a class (or set of classes) needs improvement. It must be stressed (again and again) that performance is not something that one should be preoccupied with when writing the first version of the class. The first and foremost goal is to implement the classes correctly. After everything else is done, results of actual performance measurements should guide our quest for improvements.

REMEMBER   **1.** Avoid making copies of objects. Copying an object is expensive (both in terms of memory and CPU time).

Avoid creating new objects. Try to reuse existing objects. Creating (and hence destroying) an object is expensive.

Use **const** reference parameters when appropriate.

Use **const** member functions.

Use initialization semantics (and not assignment) wherever possible.

Use pointers instead of references as data members. Pointers allow for lazy *evaluation*; references do not. This is described in detail in Chapter 4 and also in Part II, Chapter 11.

Avoid storage allocation in the default constructor. Delay it until the member is accessed. This can be done easily with pointer data members (See Chapter 11).

Prefer pointer data members to reference and value members.

Use reference counting (discussed extensively elsewhere) wherever possible.

Eliminate temporary objects by reordering expressions and reusing objects.

2. Resist tricks in the initial stages.

Stick with safety first; make sure no memory leaks exist.

Don't worry about optimization in the early stages of development. They should be based on performance measurements that happen much later.

Don't get the impression that I'm advocating a *purist* approach here. It is agreed that in the real world, any piece of software is ultimately measured in terms of speed. Many times, customers don't care whether we used OO technology or *who-cares-what* technology. But, any piece of software has to be robust and reliable before it can be lightning fast. We can achieve improved performance with improvements in implementation and help from our performance tools. It is better not to worry too much about performance when a class is not even completely implemented.

CLIENT'S RESPONSIBILITIES WITH CLASSES AND FUNCTIONS

After all this discussion about satisfying clients' requirements and needs, it is time to understand their (client's) responsibilities. A well designed and documented class is only as useful as the client who uses it. Here are some points that the clients need to remember. Further, remember that most of us play both the roles of clients and implementors in the software world.

1. Understand the purpose of the class. Even if the name of a class indicates that it is what you need, the documentation may suggest otherwise. Very limited information is conveyed by the class name.

2. Clearly understand what the class implementor expects from you, the client. There is a contract between the client and the implementor.

3. Pay attention to every member function; in particular, const member functions—they are safer.

4. Understand the arguments being passed. Be careful when an argument is being *adopted* by the class. Never pass the address of a local object (stack object) to a function that adopts the object.

5. Understand what your responsibility is when pointers and references are returned from functions. In particular, understand storage responsibilities.

6. If the class documentation and the information in the header file differ, get clarification as to which is the correct one before using the class.

7. Prefer functions that accept arguments that are **pointers and references to const**. They are safer.

8. Even if the class implementor is your brother, don't rely on any undocumented class details that he might have told you. Stick to the class interface and documentation.

9. Be wary of classes that don't implement the minimum set of member functions (constructors, copy constructor, assignment operator, and destructor).

We will see more of such responsibilities in later chapters.

SUMMARY

Clearly understand the responsibilities and limitations of constructor, destructor, copy constructor, and assignment operator.

Understand what the compiler silently generates in case you don't provide it.

Use **const** member functions wherever possible. Clearly document cases where you are implementing conceptual constantness.

Choose class names and function names that convey their purpose. Avoid acronyms (unless they are very well known in the problem domain). Longer class names and function names convey more meaning without incurring any extra compile time or run-time cost.

Don't omit argument names in function declarations. Every argument name should very clearly convey its purpose to the client.

Understand the client's view of function argument modes and return values. Use the proper argument passing method and maintain a consistent style in all your code. Try to avoid returning non-**const** pointers from functions.

Document the purpose and intended audiences of every class. Provide meaningful documentation for every member function.

4

Initialization and Garbage Collection within OOP

In the preceding chapters, we focused on object creation and some aspects of interface design. But, when we look at the big picture of a system (or project), a number of objects are being created, copied, and destroyed any number of times. In a true object-oriented system, objects are the prime entities of computation. Almost everything is an object and every object needs to be created before it can be used. Once an object is created, it must be guaranteed to be destroyed sooner or later.

During the lifetime of an object it might be *copied* into another object (i.e. many copies of the object are made), it might be *assigned* to another object or another object might be assigned to it. It is essential that programmers and designers understand the implications of creation, copying, assignment, and destruction of objects. We focus on those issues in this chapter.

WHAT IS INITIALIZATION?

When a primitive data type is created (such as a char in C++) within a function or as a data member of a class what value does it contain?

Is it guaranteed to contain something pre-defined or is it some undefined garbage?

These are genuine concerns that one should have when learning a new language or a new paradigm (such as OOP). Consider a simple class, **TPerson** shown below. This class could be used in a motor vehicle registration system, employee database, etc.

```
class TPerson {
    public:
        TPerson(){/* no code */ }   // ❶ default constructor
        TPerson(const char name[], const char theAddress[],
            unsigned long theSSN, unsigned long theBirthDate);
        TPerson&     operator=(const TPerson& source);
        TPerson(const TPerson& source);
        ~TPerson();

        void SetName(const char theNewName[]);
        void Print() const;
        // details omitted for simplicity
    private:
        char*           _name;
        unsigned long   _ssn;  // social security number (here in the U.S)
        unsigned long   _birthDate;
        char*           _address;
};
```

And here is a typical usage:

```
    main()
    {
            int i;            // a local variable
            int j = 10;
            i = 20;
            TPerson alien;    // an object of the class TPerson
            alien.Print();
    }
```

Many questions arise.

    1. What is the value in the local variable i when it is defined?

    2. What value is contained in the data members _ssn, _name, and _birthDate in the object **alien** of class **TPerson**?

As defined in C++ (and C), the value in i is undefined. Its value is what was contained in the memory location (on the run-time stack) where it has been created. And no one knows what that value is. In other words, the variable i is *uninitialized*. On the other hand, the variable j contains the value 10; it has been created with the value 10. There is no instance of time in this program where the value contained in j is undefined. Variable j came into existence with an initial value of 10.

    Initialization is the process of storing a known value in a variable (or constant) during its creation. This means the variable being created (by any method) gets a value as soon as it is created. Furthermore, when the value is stored in it (which is the initial value—like 10 above) during initialization, we are not overwriting anything that is al-

ready contained in it. In other words, initialization does not obliterate any existing value of a variable. It just stores a known value in it as soon as it is created.

Looking at the code above, it is guaranteed that j will have the value 10 as soon as it is available for use. On the other hand, the variable i is available for use, but before the assignment of 20 to it, the value it contains is unknown. Moreover, when we assign 20 to i, we are obliterating any value (even though unknown) that is contained in it. This is where assignment differs from initialization.

Assignment always overwrites (or obliterates) any existing value in a variable. The original value of the variable is lost in this step. Initialization stores a value into a variable as soon as it is created. Nothing is lost because the variable being initialized did not exist before the initialization step. Initialization can happen only once for any variable, but assignment can be done any number of times. This is the fundamental difference between initialization and assignment.

If one were to use the value in i before the assignment (for example, to index into an array), the consequences are unpredictable. But using j is safe because we know its value. It is always safer to use an initialized variable because its behavior is predictable. Later in this chapter, we extend this principle to objects as well.

Initialization by Constructors

The preceding discussion focused on the local variables inside main(). But we are more interested in objects. So what is the value contained in the data members of the object alien? We don't know because they have not been initialized with proper values.

C++   **Unless the constructor of the class initializes it explicitly, the value in a data member of an object is undefined**. It is just like the variable i above. The only difference between i and the data member _height (or any other data member) is that the former is a local variable inside main() and the latter is a data member inside a class. *By default, a C++ compiler does not initialize any data member of an object. It is the responsibility of the implementor to take care of such things in a constructor. Even the generated default constructor of a class does not store any pre-defined values in the data members of an object.*

Why is it important to initialize data members?

Let's suppose we implement the code for Print() member function of class TPerson as follows:

```
TPerson::Print() const
{
        cout << "Name is " << _name << " SSN: " << _ssn <<;
        //... and more
}
```

Can you reliably guess the output of Print() when it is invoked on the object alien above? Definitely not. The character pointer _name (and also _ssn) is uninitialized. We don't know what memory address it contains. This might cause a variety of unpredictable output from the call to the insertion operator (<<) on cout. If we had known for sure that the pointer _name is always initialized properly, then the outcome of the call to the insertion operator above is always predictable. Not any more. Unless all data members of an object are properly initialized, it is impossible to predict the behavior of an object reliably and it is dangerous to use such objects. The designer and the implementor of a class should always guarantee the correct behavior of an object of a class no matter how it was created—it should never be unpredictable. If this guarantee cannot be fulfilled, then it is definitely a violation of the contract between the client and the implementor. Remember that a client can invoke any member function (of the class) on an object as soon as it is created. The implementor cannot enforce rules that restrict access to member functions. And an implementor cannot make assumptions about the sequence in which member functions are invoked by a client on an object. Therefore, the golden rule is:

☞ **Always remember to initialize all data members of an object with proper values.**

By *proper values* we mean values that can be interpreted clearly by every member function of the class. Any member function of the class must be capable of understanding the value in a data member and should be in a position to make decisions based on that value.

This topic may look very simple, but it's not. Initializing data members is not a straight forward issue. When executing inside a constructor, other member functions might be called. Those member functions might use data members that are not yet initialized. This can cause serious trouble. The constructor ensures that any member functions called from within the constructor can function properly. This implies that the constructor must store proper values in all data members before calling other member functions. In certain cases, the constructor must rely on the outcome of other member functions to complete the initialization of the object. But if those member functions try to use data members that are yet to be initialized, things get out of control. Implementors must pay serious attention to such tricky situations and might have to reorganize the code to overcome the problems. A solution might be to use non-member functions (static or global functions) to avoid accessing data members.

CAUTION   In some situations, when the constructor is called for an object, it (the constructor) can determine that some of its data members are not going to be used by the new *object* (based on the arguments passed to the constructor). Based on this knowledge, the constructor might choose not to initialize certain data members (because they are not going to be used within the object). This might be acceptable, but the implementor has to be very careful with this assumption. If, in the future, the class implementation is modified, extra care is needed to remember the assumption about the uninitialized data member. It is probably easier to just initialize all data members without worrying about whether it is going to be used within the object. Use your knowledge of the class and provide sufficient documentation and assertions about your assumptions.

SMALLTALK   Smalltalk is significantly different from C++ when it comes to initialization. Under Smalltalk, once an object is created, it is guaranteed that all instance members will be properly initialized. All instance members of an object created using the default creation method will have a predefined value nil. Note that nil is not an unknown value. It is a special condition that indicates that the instance member is uninitialized. There is no such initialization done under C++. The implementor has to take care of it explicitly. The creation of an object of a class in Smalltalk is controlled by its metaclass.

EIFFEL   In Eiffel, creation of an object is handled by the **make** operation, which is quite similar to a C++ constructor. This method initializes all primitive types (like integer and character) to well known values. All integer data members are set to 0 (zero), **boolean** types are set to **false** and all class references are set to **void**.[1] Since Eiffel does not support anything other than primitive types and references, this scheme takes care of all types of objects. If this default **make** is not suitable, implementors can define class specific **make** operation (with access protection) to handle initialization. Also note that just a declaration of an object does not create a new object. The method **make** must be invoked on the name of the object for it to be created at run time. Creation of a new object is indicated by the !! prefix (**!!objectname.make**). If **make** is invoked without the !! prefix, it resets the values in the existing object.

    With this background, let us complete the **TPerson** constructor. This constructor should replace the inline implementation (in ❶) on p. 116.

```
TPerson::TPerson ()
{
        // assignment style constructor, not recommended
        // but is still better than no code at all.
        _name = 0;
        _address = 0;
        _ssn = 0;
        _birthDate = 0;
}
```

That was quite easy. We just assign distinct values to data members. Note that the values chosen cannot exist in a normal **TPerson** object. A real person's name, ssn, etc. cannot be zero. This tells the member functions that the **TPerson** object does not represent a true person when some client tries to use it. With pointers, zero (0) is a distinguishing value because no valid pointer can contain the address zero. A distinct value must be selected carefully—there should never be a chance of the distinct value ever being present in the normal course. In some cases, (−1) might be a distinct value for an integer. This is particularly true if the integer happens to represent an index into an array. An array index cannot be negative (unless it is a user defined class) and therefore (−1) indicates an invalid index.

    But what if one of the data members is a constant. One cannot assign to a **const** data member; it can only be initialized when the object is created. For the sake of this example, let's assume we change the _birthDate data member to be a **const**. In other words, the birth date of a person should remain the same no matter what. Once a **TPerson** object is created, everything else in the object can change but not the birth date. Of course, now the constructor shown above is not correct and we shall fix it soon. The new class declaration is

---

[1] As mentioned in previous chapters, a reference is very similar to a pointer in Eiffel. An object can only contain references to other objects.

```
class TPerson {
      public:
            TPerson(unsigned long theBirthDate);
            TPerson(const char name[], const char theAddress[],
                        unsigned long theSSN, unsigned long theBirthDate);
            TPerson&    operator=(const TPerson& source);
            TPerson(const TPerson& source);
            ~TPerson();

            void SetName(const char NewName [])
            void Print() const;
            // details omitted for simplicity
      private:
            char*                 _name;    // as an array of character
            unsigned long         _ssn;
            const unsigned long   _birthDate;
            char*                 _address;// as an array of character
};
```

We can no longer assign to the _birthDate field because it is a const. We can only initialize it. To support this requirement, C++ provides the *initialization syntax* (for constructors) shown below:

```
TPerson::TPerson (unsigned long theBirthDate) : _birthDate(theBirthDate)
                                               ↑
                                        // initialization phase begins here
{ // Assignment phase of the constructor begins here
            _name = 0;
            _ssn = 0;
            _address = 0;
}
```

The **:** after the closing parenthesis of the constructor indicates the beginning of the initialization sequence. Anything done after this **:** but before the opening **{** of the constructor
(which is the beginning of the execution of the constructor—the body of the constructor)
is initialization. In fact, this phase of the constructor is called the **initialization phase**.
The opening **{** indicates the beginning of the **assignment phase** of the constructor. The
element to be initialized (which is _birthDate here) is followed by the value that initializes it in ( ). It looks like a function call. Just for the sake of understanding this syntax,
one can assume that the element inside the ( ) is being assigned to the element outside the
parentheses. Here, we are initializing the const data member _birthDate with the value
of the argument theBirthDate. If the class contains more than one const element, they
are initialized in sequence, in a comma separated list. If we forget to initialize a const
data member of a class in the constructor, the compiler will definitely flag the error if it is
not able to initialize the member correctly.

This initialization syntax has further implications too. If an object contains an object
of another class as a data member (i.e., an embedded object), how would one call the constructor for such an embedded object?[2] This again is accomplished by the initialization
syntax. For example, if TCar is a class (used in a car dealership):

----

[2]An embedded object is one that is a data member of another object (as in owner for TCar).

```
class TCar {
        private:
                unsigned _weight;      // weight of car, in pounds
                short    _driveType;  // four wheel or two wheel
                TPerson _owner;        // who owns this car?
                // other details not important
        public:
                TCar(const char name[], const char address[],
                        unsigned long ssn, unsigned long ownerBirthDate,
                        unsigned weight = 900, short driveType = 2 );
};
```

the constructor for **TCar** could be written as

```
TCar::TCar(const char name[], const char address[], unsigned long ssn,
                        unsigned long ownerBirthDate, unsigned weight /* =
                        900 */, short driveType /* =2 */)
     // Initializes the TPerson object, _owner, by calling an appropriate
     // constructor, supplying the owner's name, address, ssn, and birth
     // date.
: _owner(name, _ssn, address, ownerBirthDate)
        // Initializes the _owner data member
{
        // code for constructor not shown for brevity of example
}
```

In this example (Fig. 4-1), every **TCar** object has an embedded object **_owner** of class **TPerson**. See figure below.

```
                        (with its own data members)
                        _name, _ssn, _birthDate,
                        and _address)
```

CAUTION   Throughout the book, structure of objects are shown for ease of understanding. These diagrams provide a conceptual (or logical) layout of the objects involved. It does

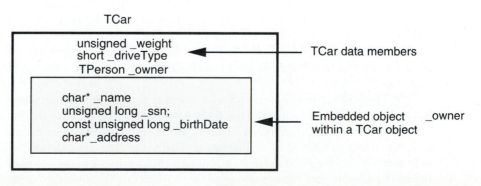

Fig. 4-1

not mean that compilers actually follow the exact layout shown. Details of such compiler implementation issues are discussed in Chapter 13. These diagrams are used to convey the overall effect of what might be going on under the implementation. Programmers do not have to know (mostly) anything about the actual byte layout of an object.

NOTE   A car can be owned by a person, a company, or a bank. This must be taken into account when designing a real application. However, in this example, the focus is on understanding the details of initialization, and not the **TCar** class. Therefore, let's just assume that a car is always owned by a person.

The initialization code states that the data member _owner should be initialized with the argument ownerBirthDate, name, ssn, etc. As we already know, initialization of an object is done by the constructor. In effect, we are calling the constructor for the _owner data member. A call to the constructor of **TPerson** is made because _owner is of type **TPerson**.

The initialization syntax is the only choice for data members that are **const**. Further, it is the only way to initialize embedded objects. We will see in a later chapter that it is the only syntax for initializing base classes. But this syntax is not limited to them. It can be used to initialize any data member. For example, we can rewrite the **TPerson** constructor as

```
TPerson::TPerson (unsigned long theBirthDate) :
        _ssn(0) ,
        _name(0),
        _birthDate(theBirthDate),
        _address(0)
        { /* empty constructor body */ }
```

Everything is done in the initialization phase and there is nothing left to do in the assignment phase. When dealing with primitive types, it is just a matter of style/preference to use one over the other. But in some cases, the initialization style is more efficient (with embedded objects) as will be shown in later chapters.

STYLE   Whenever there is a choice between initialization syntax and assignment, use initialization style. Your code will not have to be modified if the the member being initialized is a primitive data type in the first implementation but it is changed to an object of a class in a future implementation (see use of **TDate** on following page). If we use the assignment syntax for an object, remember that a constructor would have been already called on it before the assignment can happen and we could have probably made use of the constructor to initialize the object (thus eliminating the need for the assignment operation).

But it is not always possible to do everything in the initialization phase. In many classes, many operations must be carried out before every data member can be initialized completely. These might involve computing many different values or calling different functions (member as well as non-member). There might be a pre-defined sequence of steps that need to be carried out in the constructor. Such things can only be done in the assignment phase. It gets even more complicated when one data member depends on the initialized value of another. Therefore, it is better to use initialization style if possible, but one shouldn't be overly concerned with it. What ultimately matters is the integrity and correctness of the constructed object.

CAUTION   It is quite usual in procedure-oriented programming to rely on a special function, usually called Initialize (or Init), to initialize everything in an application (or module) just after the program starts running. That would be appropriate under procedure-oriented programming. But don't carry that same model into OOP. The correct (and only) way to fully initialize an object is to do it in the constructor. A class designer should not have a requirement that the client call a method Initialize() in order to initialize the object. This is highly error prone because it is very easy to forget to make that call to Initialize(). This type of initialization should be avoided like the plague. This style is required only when an object depends on another object for initialization and that other object is not created yet. This could happen in complex inheritance hierarchies with virtual basis.

Revisiting class **TPerson**, representing dates as numbers is very inconvenient. Sure, one can use julian dates but that is more suited for machines than humans. We would like to represent dates in an easier format (like 6/11/95). It would also be helpful if we could compare dates for equality and such. To make dates more user friendly, let's just represent date as another class—TDate. This is nothing but another simple abstraction. At this point, we are more interested in the interface of class **TDate**. Implementation issues are quite unimportant. Using a class such as **TDate** makes it easier to understand the interface and simplifies the implementation. Some design considerations of this class can be found in Chapter 11.

```
class TDate {
   public:
      enum EMonth { eJan=1, eFeb, eMar, eApr, eMay, eJun, eJul,
                               eAug, eSep, eOct, eNov, eDec };
      // Simple constructors
      TDate(unsigned day, EMonth mon, unsigned year);
      TDate(const char date[]); // date passed in as a string
      TDate();   // sets date from the operating system date

      unsigned GetYear() const;
      EMonth GetMonth() const;
      unsigned GetDay() const; // day of the month

      // Convenience functions.
      void AdddToYear(int increment);  // Increment can be negative
      void AddToMonth(int increment);  // Increment can be negative
      void AddToDay(int increment);    // Increment can be negative
      // Comparison operators
      bool operator==(const TDate& second) const;
      bool operator!=(const TDate& second) const;
      TString GetDate() const; // Returns a string representation
   private:
      short _year; // some implementation data
      short _day;
      EMonth _month;
};
```

Don't pay too much attention to the details of this class. We will discuss all the relevant issues in subsequent chapters. With this enhancement, our **TPerson** class is as follows:

```
class TPerson {
    public:
        TPerson(const char birthDate[]); // default constructor
        TPerson(const char name[],
                const char theAddress[],
                unsigned long theSSN,
                const char birthDate[]);
        TPerson&    operator=(const TPerson& source);
        TPerson(const TPerson& source);
        ~TPerson();

        void SetName(const char theNewName[]);
        void Print() const;
        // details omitted for simplicity
    private:
        char*               _name;
        unsigned long       _ssn;
        const TDate         _birthDate;
        char*               _address;
};
```

No change is required for the constructor implementation of **TPerson** (except changing the argument type of _birthDate to a const char[]).

Here, is the new conceptual object structure of **TPerson**:

A TPerson object

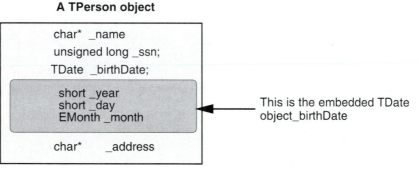

Fig. 4-2

Hereafter, this new **TPerson** class will be used in all the examples.

Rules to be Followed with Embedded Objects:

1. Every constructor of a class, which contains objects of other classes in it, must invoke an appropriate constructor for each of the embedded objects it uses during the initialization phase of the constructor.

2. If the implementor fails to make calls to the constructor of the embedded objects, the compiler will try to invoke the default constructor for them (if there is a default constructor available and is accessible).

3. If both (1) and (2) are unsuccessful, then the constructor implementation is in error (caused a compile-time error).

4. The destructor for every embedded object is automatically called by the destructor of the enclosing class. No programmer intervention is required.

GARBAGE COLLECTION ISSUES

Before we discuss garbage collection, let's see what is *garbage* and what is *dangling reference*.

Garbage

Garbage is a piece of storage (or resource) that is part of a program (or process) but there are no more references to it in the program. In terms of C++, we can say that it is some resource to which the program has no pointers. Here is an example.

```
main()
{
        // allocate a dynamic array of 1000 characters
        char* p = new char[1000];
        char *q = new char[1000]; // another piece of dynamic memory

        // Code that uses p and q for some operations
        p = q; // Assign q to p overwriting the address in p
        /* what happened to the 1000 characters of storage that p pointed
           to? p and q point to the same place and no one points to the old
           p storage! it is still there, taking up space, but it cannot be
           accessed (used) by the program anymore. This is called garbage.*/
}
```

Now the memory that was allocated in **main()** for **p** is garbage because it is still part of the running program, but all references to it have been destroyed.

Garbage does not do any damage to a program immediately but it will eat away memory gradually, and ultimately the program would run out of memory and the system would come to a halt. But in some situations, it might be impossible to stop the program due to a number of reasons.[3] As more and more garbage is created, the system will tend to run slower and slower. Periodic garbage collection would be a solution for recovering resources. Garbage collection involves running a program periodically that collects all garbage and returns it to the free pool. Garbage collection doesn't come for free because the garbage collector has to be run periodically (either automatically or manually). Besides, it may not always be possible to collect all pieces of garbage.

Dangling Reference

A dangling reference is created when memory pointed by a pointer is deleted but the programmer thinks that the address is still valid. For example:

---

[3]Imagine a piece of software running a life support system.

```
main()
{
        char *p;
        char *q;

        p = new char[1024]; // allocate a dynamic array of 1k characters
        //... Use it
        q = p; // pointer aliasing
        delete [] p;
        p = 0;
        // Now q is a dangling reference
        // If we attempt *q = 'A', it would be disastrous
}
```

One could try to access the memory pointed by q and get into major trouble. The pointer q is called a dangling reference. Dangling references are usually a result of *pointer aliasing* (i.e., more than one pointer holding the same address). Compared with garbage, a dangling reference is deadly because it is bound to cause havoc (most probably a run-time crash).

Remedies for Garbage Collection and Dangling References

Both these problems (garbage and dangling reference) are a direct result of pointer manipulations and pointer aliasing. They happen because addresses were copied but the semantics (and consequences) of copying addresses was not clearly understood by the programmer. These problems are not new to OOP but their effect is much more pronounced under OOP.

SMALLTALK   Some languages provide automatic garbage collection. Programmers working under the Smalltalk environment do not have to worry about garbage. Garbage collection is automatic under Smalltalk. The language keeps track of references to memory and it frees them when there are no more references to a piece of memory.

EIFFEL   Eiffel also provides automatic garbage collection in the form of an auxiliary program that runs in the background periodically collecting all items that are no longer accessible.

Note that dangling reference problem is mostly solved when programmers cannot create pointer types that hold addresses of memory locations. This is the situation in both Eiffel, Smalltalk and Java.

C++   C++ does not provide an automatic garbage collection mechanism. It supports all types of pointer variables. This leaves the programmer with the responsibility of garbage collection. In general, *storage management* is the issue here. Garbage collection in C++ is a research topic. Who knows, someday we might have automatic garbage collection in C++ also.

You might wonder why we are treating garbage collection and dangling reference as a special problem in OOP, even though this is a problem in any type of programming. Read on. In procedure-oriented programming systems, there is no concept of an object and memory allocation (and deallocation) does not happen as frequently. Under OOP, everything becomes an object and most non-trivial objects allocate resources. In any interesting system, it is very easy to see hundreds (or even thousands) of objects at any instance. Moreover, objects are created, copied, and destroyed continuously. Also, objects can be created in many different ways, even dynamically. Therefore, every class implementor must clearly understand garbage collection issues. Hence, this extra attention to storage management.

Garbage Collection and Language Design

The type of garbage collection supported by a language (automatic or programmer implemented) has much to do with the design philosophy of the language itself. Languages that provide automatic garbage collection (such as Eiffel and Smalltalk) are actually *reference* based languages. In a reference based language, every object is just a reference. When objects are created, all that is really created is a reference that holds the address of the real object, which is kept elsewhere. This makes copying and sharing of objects very easy and fast. But it also makes it less safe because one might end up modifying an object unintentionally by using a reference to the object.

On the other hand, C++ is a *value based* language (as is C). Here, everything (objects and primitive types) is a value. Each and every object is a real object. It is not a pointer to something stored elsewhere. C++ treats classes just like primitive types and this is a uniform model in the language.

EIFFEL   Eiffel follows a dual approach. Under Eiffel all objects are reference based but all primitive types are value based. A new object gets its own copies of all primitive instance variables but only a reference to any object contained within this new object. As mentioned elsewhere, a reference is either **void** or refers to a valid object.

SMALLTALK   On the other hand, Smalltalk is uniform in its treatment of objects and primitive types. Here, everything is an object. All primitive types are also objects. This makes the language much easier to understand because one need not have to worry about the distinction between objects and primitive types.

Here is an example that shows the difference between these languages. We revisit the **TCar** example.

```
class TCar {
      private:
            unsigned      _weight; // weight of car, in pounds
            short         _driveType; // four wheel or two wheel
            TPerson       _owner; // who owns this car?
            // other details not important
      public:
            TCar(const char name[], const char address[],
                  unsigned long ssn, unsigned long ownerBirthDate,
                  unsigned weight = 900, short driveType = 2 );
};
```

WHY GARBAGE CONTROL IS IMPORTANT

Garbage control is a serious issue in software design because of its effect on the overall behavior of an application. In case of non-critical applications that keep running for long periods of time (weeks or even months) without being stopped, memory leaks can be a serious problem. The performance of the application (and the overall system) is degraded as more and more memory is lost to garbage, causing more and more virtual memory paging activity. Ultimately, the entire system can come to a halt because even the paging file might become full.

In cases of mission critical applications that cannot be stopped easily (for example, a nuclear power station controller) this can be a disastrous thing. If the software that monitors and controls the reactor keeps leaking memory and finally stops the system, it can be a serious hazard for the neighboring community.

With embedded systems, where no big operating system is around for virtual memory management, such as a computer that controls a car's fuel delivery system, memory leaks can cause accidents. What if the software that drives the fuel injector leaks memory and after driving for a couple of hundred miles, it stops working? The car would abruptly stop in the middle of the road without a warning.

An automatic garbage collection scheme might look like a good solution for most of these problems, but it is not. When the garbage collector runs, the application must be halted from running for a short period of time. This could be as small as a couple of micro seconds or as large as hundreds of milli seconds. Imagine a camera focussed and ready to take an important picture. Just when it is clicked, the garbage collector runs and the software is halted (paused). By the time the garbage collector is finished, the moment of action has already passed, and the picture is lost.

Writing software that never leaks any resources (memory, file handles, network sockets, etc.) should be the goal of every software designer and developer.

Even though the class declaration is in C++, it is interesting to see the object structure in Eiffel, Smalltalk, and C++. Imagine a **TCar** object with the name **Jeep**, driveType=4 (i.e., four wheel drive) and weight of 800 pounds (see Fig. 4.3).

As can be seen, the three language models are quite different. Creating an object under C++ creates a true object. So the declaration

```
TCar       jeep ("6-22-66"); // C++ declaration. Birth date: 22 Jun 1966
```

creates a true object as shown above.

The declaration

```
             jeep : TCar; — Eiffel declaration
```

in Eiffel does not create any new object, it just creates a reference. The statement

```
             jeep.!!make; — Again, Eiffel code
```

Object Representation in Languages

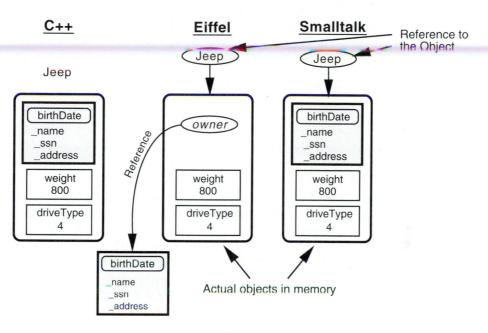

Fig. 4-3

causes the object to be created and initialized at run-time. Now the **jeep** reference is bound to an object somewhere in memory.

EIFFEL   In Eiffel, creation of an object is usually handled by the **make** operation. A class can have a number of such creation routines declared under the creation keyword. Access control can be applied to this routine just like any other routine. Creation of a new object is indicated by the !! prefix. If **make** is invoked without the !! prefix, it resets the values in the existing object.

Under Smalltalk, the declaration

```
jeep new TCar          "Smalltalk code"
```

creates a new **TCar** object with all the instance variables set to nil.

From these examples, it is quite clear that every language has a different way of creating objects. Further, the representation of an object is also different.

When Is Garbage Generated in C++?

Now let's see in detail what operations might generate garbage. Garbage is generated when a resource allocated by an object is not deallocated when it is no longer used and is no longer accessible. There are many situations under which something might become inaccessible, i.e., it is no longer usable (or is not going to be used) in the scope of the program, such as:

1. On exit from a function all local variables (including objects) created inside the function and all arguments passed by value are inaccessible.

2. On exit from a block all local variables (including objects) declared inside that block are inaccessible.[4]

3. Any temporary variables generated as part of a complex expression must be destroyed when they are no longer needed; otherwise it will become garbage.

4. Any dynamically allocated objects must be destroyed explicitly by the programmer when they are no longer used.

We are already familiar with these situations from our experience with procedure-oriented programming. But the scenario is much more complicated with objects because objects are not simple variables; they contain many other things, including other objects. When an object is no longer accessible, it is essential that resources (including other objects) allocated as a part of the object are also freed. This is a recursive process because an object can contain other objects that in turn might contain some more objects ad infinitum. It is essential that the resources allocated by all those objects inside an object get a chance to free whatever resources they allocated.

There is one more situation where garbage might be generated. This has to do with object copying and object assignment. We shall discuss this more, later in this chapter.

When Does an Object Acquire Resources?

When an object is created, it might acquire resources by dynamic allocation, passed by the client, etc. Further, resources might also be acquired during the lifetime of an object due to the different methods invoked on it. For example, in the **TPerson** class, memory might be allocated in the constructor for the characters in the name. Similarly the **TIntStack** objects from Chapter 3 will allocate memory for storing elements. It is also possible, particularly with classes that provide storage mechanisms (like Lists and Queues), that resources are allocated as and when they are needed during the lifetime of the object.

In other situations, an object might acquire resources because of the *Adopt* semantics discussed in Chapter 3. In such situations, some other object allocates the resources, but the ownership is transferred to a different object that would be responsible for releasing the resource when it is no longer needed (or accessible).

GARBAGE COLLECTION IN C++

The destructor of a class is provided exclusively for garbage collection. This does not mean that the destructor is the only place where garbage collection should happen. In fact, as we will see later in this chapter, there are some other member functions that also have to worry about garbage collection.

---

[4]In C++, a block is a sequence of instructions within a pair of { and }. It is almost like a mini function.

The destructor of a class gives the objects one last chance to free any resources that they have acquired. The destructor is invoked automatically by the language for every automatic (stack based) object created in a scope just before exit from that scope. At this time, the object is about to be destroyed (i.e., the memory occupied by the object is about to be reclaimed by the compiler). Once the destructor completes, the object completely disappears.

When a pointer to an object is deleted (using the **delete** operator), the destructor of the class to which this object belongs is invoked on the object.

```
TPerson *p;
p = new TPerson("12-25-95"); // creates a TPerson object on the heap
//...
delete p;    // causes the invocation of the destructor of class TPerson on
             // the object pointed by p.
```

After the destructor completes execution, the memory pointed by **p** is recovered. Here is an implementation for the constructor and destructor of the class **TPerson**.

```
// First Constructor
TPerson::TPerson (const char birthDate[])
:       _ssn(0), _name(0), _birthDate(theBirthDate), _address(0)
        { /* empty constructor body */ }

char* Strdup(const char* src)
{
    char* ptr = new char[strlen(src)+1];
    strcpy(ptr, src);           return ptr;
}
// Second Constructor
TPerson::TPerson(const char theName[], const char theAddres[],
        unsigned long theSSN, const char theBirthDate[])
      : _ssn (theSSN), _birthDate(theBirthDate)
{       // Initialize _name, _address, etc.
        _name = theName ? Strdup(theName) : 0;
        _address = theAddress ? Strdup(theAddress) : 0;
}
```

We have allocated memory on the heap to store the characters in the name of the person. It is the responsibility of the destructor to release this memory.

```
                // Destructor
                TPerson::~TPerson()
                {
                        delete [] _name;
                        delete [] _address;
                }
```

Now consider a piece of code like the one below:

```
        main()
        {
                TPerson john("11-23-45");
                //...
                john.SetName("John Wayne);
        }
```

The object **john** starts off with just the birth date but no name. Later in the code we set the name of **john** using the member function **SetName**. What should the member function **SetName** do? Here is the code.

```
void
TPerson::SetName(const char newName[])
{
    unsigned oldLength = _name ? strlen(_name) : 0;
    unsigned newLength = newName ? strlen(newName) : 0;

    if (oldLength < newLength) { // Not enough space in _name
        delete [] _name;  // Garbage Collection
        // Use Strdup function defined earlier
        _name = (newName ? Strdup(newName) : 0);
    }
    else {
        if (newName) strcpy(_name, newName);
        else _{delete [] name; name=0;}
    }
}
```

We check to see if the number of characters in **_name** are enough to hold **theNewName**. Otherwise the **name** is deleted and a new piece of memory is allocated. It is very important to remember to release the storage in **_name** before allocating a new piece of memory. This is what we mean by *acquiring resources during the lifetime*. The destructor for the **john** object would still work fine because **_name** is guaranteed to point to valid memory or it would be 0.

Revisiting the **TCar** example, what happens to the **_owner** object within a **TCar** object when it is destroyed? Fortunately, the language comes to our rescue. When a **TCar** object is about to be destroyed, the destructor for the enclosed object **_owner** (type **TPerson**) is invoked. This ensures that there is no resource leak. In general, when an object is about to be destroyed, the destructors for all objects contained within the object are invoked (recursively) until all enclosed objects are destroyed. This only applies to objects contained by value inside other objects. If an object contains pointers to other objects, it is the responsibility of the destructor to explicitly destroy them.

IDENTITY OF OBJECTS

Now it is time to analyze the concept of *naming* objects. Specifically, we need to clearly understand the differences among the name of an object, the identity of an object, and the semantics of sharing between objects.

For this example (Fig. 4-4), we revisit the **TPerson** class. Here is a piece of code that creates some **TPerson** objects.

```
main()
{
    TPerson  person0("Albert Einstein", 0, 0, "12-11-1879");
    TPerson  person1("12-11-1879");
```

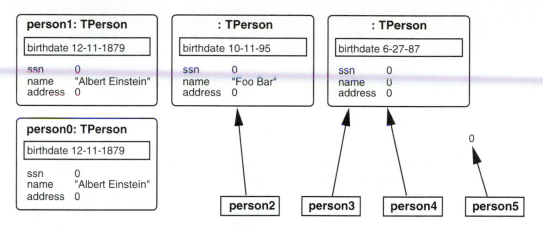

Note: The _ prefix in front of the data member names is not shown

Fig. 4-4

```
TPerson* person2 = new TPerson("10-11-95");   // dynamic object
TPerson* person3 = new TPerson("6-27-87"");
TPerson* person4 = 0;   // does not point to a person.
TPerson* person5 = 0;   // does not point to a person.

person1.SetName("Albert Einstein");
person2->SetName("Foo Bar");
person4 = person3;   // See Fig 4-3
}
```

The object **person1** is clearly an independent object with the name **person1**. But **person2** is not really the name of an object; it denotes an object without a name created somewhere in memory. Similarly, **person3** identifies another object in memory without a name. We may refer to the name of the object denoted by **person2** indirectly as *person2. In this example, it is easy to identify the objects but not their names. Strictly speaking, only **person1** is the name of an object. Others like **person2** and **person3** are pointers to anonymous objects in memory and **person4** denotes the same object that **person3** denotes. Here **person2** and **person3** identify distinct objects with different states. On the same lines, **person1** is the name of a distinct object with a distinct state.

The name of an object may not be unique over its lifetime but the identity of the object is always unique. The identity of an object does not change by changing the state of an object. According to [Booch94] *the identity of an object is the property of an object that distinguishes it from all other objects.* In the above program (and picture), an anonymous object created in memory acquires the names **person3** and also **person4** during the execution of the program. We can detach the name **person4** from the object to which it is attached but one cannot remove the identity of an object—every object has a unique identity which never changes in its lifetime.

Executing the **SetName** method on the object **person1** will change its state but not its identity. Similarly, executing **SetName** on the object denoted by **person2** does not change its identity either. Over its lifetime, an object may acquire different names and may go through many state changes but it has a unique identity. This is very similar to a train station having a unique identity; many trains may come and go (state changes) but the identity of the station remains the same. In other words, an object might be referenced using more than one name in its lifetime but the identity of the object is still unique.

Let us see what happens when the statement

```
person5 = person3;
```

is executed. Remember that **person3** designates a unique object. Now this object has acquired an alias in the form of **person5** (see Fig. 4-5).

Now if we operate on the object *denoted by* **person3** or on the object denoted by **person5**, we are in fact working on the same object. Even though the names (**person4**, **person5**, and **person3**) are different, the identity of the object is the same. In fact, we have now shared an object between three names, i.e., the structure (and hence the state) of the object is shared. As is evident from the picture, **person4** and **person5** are aliases to the object originally denoted by **person3**.

Note that the state of two objects might be identical (as in **person0** and **person1**) but they are not the same object because their identities are different. They consume different memory and are therefore located at different memory addresses.

One might wonder why the difference between identity and name is being given such importance. In order for proper object management without memory leaks, it is important that one clearly know the identity of the object that is being accessed. Dangling references are the direct result of multiple names (aliases) for an object. There is a possibility of memory leaks also.

If one were to execute the following code (see Fig. 4-6)

```
delete person4;
person4 = 0;
```

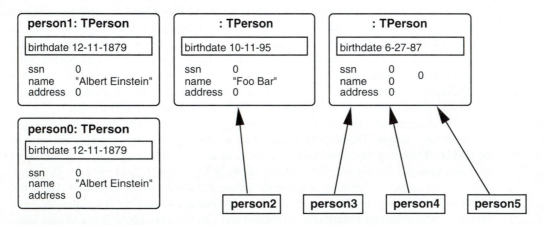

Note: The _ prefix in front of the data member names is not shown

Fig. 4-5

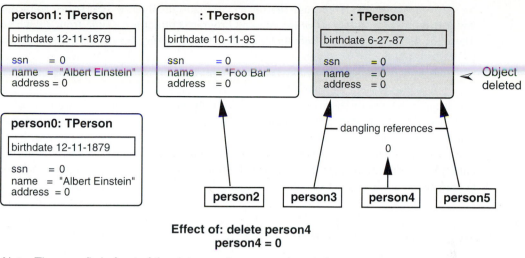
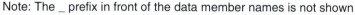

Effect of: delete person4
person4 = 0

Note: The _ prefix in front of the data member names is not shown

Fig. 4-6

definitely person3 and person5 become dangling references. On the other hand, without deleting person4, if we execute the statements (as shown in Fig. 4-7).

```
person4 = &person1;
person3 = person2;
person5 = 0;
```

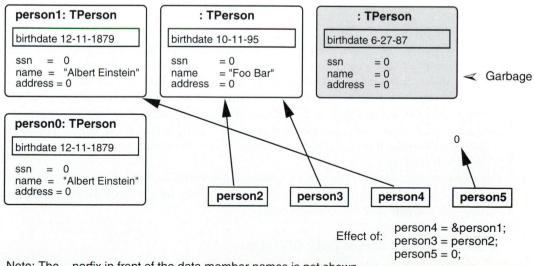

Effect of:
person4 = &person1;
person3 = person2;
person5 = 0;

Note: The _ perfix in front of the data member names is not shown

Fig. 4-7

we have created garbage because the object originally denoted by person3, person4, and person5 is lost. It is part of the running program but not accessible from anywhere. These are the consequences of not understanding the difference between a name of an object and the identity of an object.

So, is it *bad* to share objects? Definitely not. In many situations, sharing objects is the preferred approach. But while sharing objects, it is essential that one clearly understands and manages aliases to objects correctly. If object sharing is not followed correctly, the consequences are dangling references, memory leaks (garbage), and unexpected state changes to objects. A dangling reference would manifest itself as a serious run-time problem whereas memory leaks accumulate over time and cause problems. We will see different styles of sharing objects in this chapter. More techniques for object sharing are discussed elsewhere in this book.

SEMANTICS OF OBJECT COPYING

Making object copies is a natural operation in OOP. Since everything in our world is an object, we definitely come across situations where we need multiple copies of the same object.

As mentioned in Chapter 3, objects are copied in many different situations. A copy of an object is needed when arguments are passed by value (and returned by value) to functions. This is an implicit operation that happens when a function is called. In this case, the copy operation is initiated by the language (or compiler).

A copy of an object might be created explicitly by the programmer through declarations. One could write

```
TPerson p ("John Doe", "Anytown", 618552567, "12-22-78");
TPerson q = p;
```

Here q is a copy of p. In other words, q is created from p.

Copying an object is not a simple operation. Objects are not primitive types. They are complex entities with critical state information. Furthermore, an object might contain other objects inside of it and those objects might contain more objects and so on. How would one go about making copies of such objects? Sure, the language can carry out the copy operation, but that may not be what the implementor wants. The implementor might want to share some of the internal objects while making copies of the others. The compiler cannot make any such logical decisions. This is the reason why programmer intervention is required.

Copying objects is not a new problem in the world of OOP. Languages follow different schemes for copying objects. In the next few paragraphs, we explore the scenario in C++ and compare that with other languages.

Semantics of a Simple Copy Operation

One simple way of copying objects is to just copy the values of data members without regard to their types. Values contained in the data members of the source object are just copied into the corresponding data members in the destination object.[5] Here is an example, again using the **TPerson** class.

```
void foo(TPerson thePerson)
        // foo is some function accepting a TPerson argument by value
{
        // code not important
}

main()
{
        TPerson bar("Foo Bar", "Unknown", 4142325056, "6-6-99");
        //..
        foo( bar); // Call foo with the "bar" object
}
```

When **foo()** is called, a copy of the object **bar** is to be made. In C++, the copy constructor is used for such copying, i.e., making a copy of an object from an existing object. We have not implemented the copy constructor in our class **TPerson**, so the compiler generates the *default copy constructor*

<code>TPerson::TPerson(const TPerson& source)</code>

This copy constructor will perform a memberwise copy of the data members. The code in the copy constructor would look like Fig. 4–8.

```
TPerson::TPerson(const TPerson& source)
:       _birthDate(source._birthDate), // invokes copy constructor of TDate
        _name(source._name), _ssn (source._ssn), _address(source._address),
  { }
```

Every member is just blindly copied from the source object into the destination object. This is called a *shallow* copy. As can be seen (Fig. 4-8), the corresponding elements are copied. The address within the data member **name** (containing address **234876**) is also copied as though it was just an integer. There is no problem with this kind of copying except for the data members **_name** and **_address**. For the **TDate** object, the copy constructor of **TDate** is invoked to make the copy of the **_birthDate** object. When we leave the function **foo()**, the local object **thePerson** is going out of scope and hence the destructor will be called on it. This destructor deallocates the memory pointed by **_name** and **_address**. But when we return to **main()**, the original object **bar**, is still in use and its data member **_name** still holds the address of the memory that was deleted by the destructor. Now **_name** (and also **_address**) within **bar** has become a dangling reference. This is the problem with the default copy constructor (or shallow copy operation).

NOTE   The terms shallow copy and deep copy (discussed below) originated in Smalltalk and these terms are generally used to describe copy semantics. In general, a deep copy op-

---

[5]This is how *struct*s are copied in C.

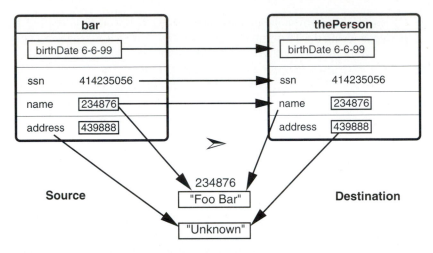

Note: The _ in front of the data member names is not shown

Fig. 4-8

eration indicates a true copy of the entire object recursively, whereas shallow copy indicates copying of the object but sharing of state between the original object and the copy.

Shallow copy is good enough if the object does not contain any pointers and references. For example, for a class **TPoint2D**, which represents a point in a two dimensional graphics system,

```
class TPoint2D {
      public:
            TPoint2D(double x = 0.0, double y 0.0 );
            DistanceTo(const TPoint2D& otherPoint);
            // Copy constructor and assignment operator omitted - will be
            // provided by the compiler
            //... other details omitted
      private:
            double _xcoordinate;
            double _ycoordinate;
};
```

the simple copy constructor synthesized by the compiler will be adequate. Objects of this class contain two double precision numbers and copying their values is all that is required.

Returning to our **TPerson** class, we don't want to copy the values of the **_name** and **_address** data members because they are pointers. We would like to allocate enough memory for their contents and then copy the contents. This way there is nothing shared between the source and destination object after the copy operation is completed. This is what is called as *deep copy*.

SMALLTALK   Smalltalk provides two methods—**shallowCopy** and **deepCopy** for any class for the purpose of copying objects. These methods are available for all objects in the

Smalltalk system. The method shallowCopy creates a new object but the new object shares its state with the original object. On the other hand, the method deepCopy copies the object as well as its state. Further, this copying is done recursively for all objects contained within the object. Hence deepCopy results in two identical but independent objects. The resulting objects don't share anything. Each class also gets the method copy and the default implementation of copy is shallowCopy. Classes that need a combination of shallowCopy and deepCopy (which is required in many situations) should implement their own copy method. The semantics of passing objects by value is very much equivalent to passing a reference under C++. However, note that some of the latest Smalltalk implementations (VisualWorks, for example) follow a slightly different scheme.

EIFFEL   Eiffel follows a combined reference-value semantics for object copying. The method for copying objects is called Clone(). It is available for all classes by default (just like Create). This member function makes true copies of primitive types like integer and character, i.e., their values are copied. However, if the original object contains a reference to another object, then only the reference is copied but not the object pointed by the reference. This is very similar to shallow copy. As mentioned elsewhere, Eiffel objects contain either primitive types or references to other objects. An object cannot contain another object by value—it can only contain a reference to the other objects (enabling easy sharing).[6] If the class implementor needs a different kind of copy semantics, then other member functions must be provided in the class. Eiffel doesn't really support call by value. Calling a function (or procedure) associates the formal arguments with the actual arguments, just like references in C++. But the called function cannot **directly** modify the actual arguments. In other words, for any argument arg the called function cannot change the value of arg. If arg is a primitive (simple) type argument the called function cannot change the value of arg (what it refers to). If arg is a class type, it cannot associate arg with a new object or make the reference void. But the function is allowed to invoke methods on arg that may modify arg. One should not confuse this scheme with the const member function of C++. A const member function cannot modify its object in any way, directly or indirectly. Given this property of Eiffel, the only way a function can return any result to the caller is through the predefined reserved name Result, which is available inside a function (but not in a procedure).

Another way to understand copying of objects is to imagine an object as the root node of a tree. This object (node) can contain references (and also pointers in C++) to any number of other objects (nodes). When we draw the picture of an object in the form of a tree, it could be a very big (and deep) tree. Deep copy starts at the root node of the tree and then recursively traverses the entire tree, copying each and every node. At the end of the copy operation, we get a new tree that is identical to the original. With shallow copy, only the root node is copied and all other nodes are shared between the original and the copy. This results in a tree with shared nodes (Fig. 4-9).

Now it is time to look at the implementation of the correct copy constructor with deep copy semantics.

[6]Unless the class explicitly specifies that it needs value based object and not a reference.

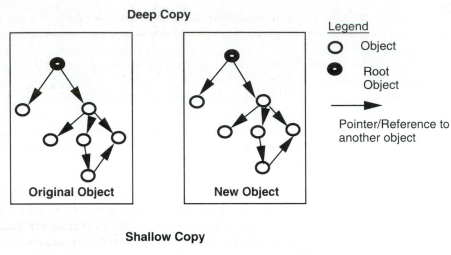

Deep Copy

Original Object

New Object

Legend

○ Object

◉ Root Object

⟶ Pointer/Reference to another object

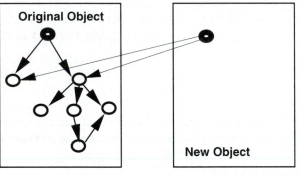

Shallow Copy

Original Object

New Object

Fig. 4-9

```
TPerson::TPerson(const TPerson& source)
    // Initialize appropriate data members
    : _ssn(source._ssn), // social security number
      _birthDate(source._birthDate) //❶   Refer Fig 4-9
{
    // Copy _name and _address if not NULL
    // We need to check if source contains non-zero pointers
    // and then allocate memory and copy the data.
    // We have already written Strdup() for this purpose (Page 131)
    // So, go ahead and use it.
    this->_name = source._name ? Strdup(source._name) : 0;

    // Next copy _address in a similar fashion
    this->_address = source._address ? Strdup(source._address ) : 0;
}
```

Since the destination objects' _name and _address data members don't point to any memory (because they were just created by the compiler), we allocate dynamic memory

COPY SEMANTICS AND LANGUAGE DESIGN

Object copy semantics in a language is very much tied to the design philosophy of the language. C++, which is a value based language, has a uniform treatment for objects as well as primitive types. When it comes to copying, it treats everything like a value and just copies the value. Furthermore, there is no way the language can make decisions about the semantics of pointer and reference usage. Such information is with the implementor and they should provide any additional functionality required for copying. The language makes it possible by allowing the implementor to provide the copy constructor. Further, the implementor can provide combined shallow copy and deep copy semantics.

Smalltalk is a reference based language and hence copying objects is easy. Here again, there is a uniform treatment of everything. Because everything in Smalltalk is an object, it is quite easy to follow a uniform approach. Smalltalk provides more functionality than C++ in terms of copying by providing both shallow copy and deep copy methods for every class. All this is possible because it is a reference based language and garbage collections is built into the Smalltalk system.

Eiffel treats primitive types and objects differently. Further, an object can only contain references to other objects. Like Smalltalk, garbage collection is part of the language itself. This is the reason why Eiffel only supports shallow copy. The only drawback is that defining deep copy semantics requires a method with a different name; Clone itself cannot be changed or overridden.

Effect of Deep Copy

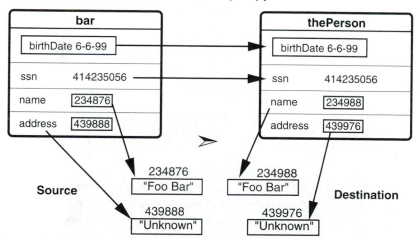

Note: The _ in front of the data member names is not shown

Fig. 4-10

for them and copy all the characters. Note that the copy constructor of **TDate** is invoked to copy the _birthDate object. Class **TPerson** doesn't know how to copy **TDate** objects. That should be the responsibility of **TDate**'s copy constructor. In the code above (p. 140) ❶ invokes the copy constructor on the _birthDate object (see Fig. 4-10).

REMEMBER   In summary, when a class contains any pointers, references, or other objects, the default copy operation is dangerous. Don't ever rely on this compiler generated copy constructor. Write your own copy constructor to provide the correct copy operation.

SEMANTICS OF OBJECT ASSIGNMENT

Assignment is an operation very similar to copying. Under C++, copying is an operation mostly invoked implicitly by the language (when objects are passed by value or returned by value). Copying also happens (but not very frequently) when a new object is created from an existing object. As opposed to copying, assignment is an operation always explicitly invoked by the programmer. With Eiffel and Smalltalk both assignment and copying are operations invoked by the programmer explicitly. This again is a result of the difference between value based languages and reference based languages.

Under C++, assignment has the same meaning for objects as well as primitive types. When a primitive type variable is assigned to another (compatible) primitive type variable, the values are copied. For example

```
int x = 10;
int y;

y = x;
```

copies the value of **x** to **y**. On the same lines, for objects

```
TPoint2D p1;
TPoint2D p2 (100, 200);

p1 = p2;
```

will copy the values in the data members from **p2** to **p1**. There is no special treatment of pointers and references; they are copied just like primitive data types. This is the **default assignment operation**. This method of assigning corresponding members is called **memberwise assignment**. It is implemented by the assignment operator,

```
TPoint2D::operator=(const TPoint2D& source);
```

Note that the keyword **operator** is a reserved word in C++. If a class does not declare and implement this assignment operator, the compiler automatically generates it. And this generated assignment operator (called the *default assignment operator*) performs memberwise assignment. The default implementation provided by the compiler would look like

```
TPoint2D::operator=(const TPoint2D& source)
{
        this->_xcoordinate = source._xcoordinate; // copy the x field
        this->_ycoordinate = source._ycoordinate; // copy the y field

        return *this;
}
```

This looks very similar to the shallow copy operation described above. We would not want this default assignment operator for our **TPerson** class because it contains pointers and we already know that copying pointers is dangerous. Hence, we will implement our own assignment operator for the **TPerson** class.

```
TPerson&
TPerson::operator=(const TPerson& source)
{
      if (this == &source)  // Assignment to Self; Do nothing
        return *this;

      // Copy (assign) all the primitive data
      this->_ssn = source._ssn;

      // Next we need to copy the characters in name
      // It is possible that there is enough room in name.
      // If so just copy the characters
      // Otherwise discard the existing memory pointed by
      // name, then allocate  a new piece of memory and
      // finally copy the characters

      if (source._name == 0) { // nothing to copy
        delete [] this->_name;
        this->_name = 0;
        return *this;
      }
      int nameLength = strlen(source._name);
      int thisNameLength = (this->_name) ?
                     strlen(this->_name) : 0;
      if (nameLength <= thisNameLength) // the easy case
        strcpy(this->_name, source._name);
      else { // The not-so-easy case
        delete [] this->_name;
        name = new char [nameLength + 1];
           // +1 for the terminating 0
        strcpy( this->_name, source._name);
      }

      // repeat the steps for address also
      if (source._address == 0) {
        delete [] this->_address;
        this->_address = 0;
        return *this;
      }
      int addressLength = strlen(source._address);
```

```
            int thisAddrLength = (this->_address) ?
                              strlen(this->_address) : 0;
        if (addressLength  <= thisAddrLength) {
          // the easy case
          strcpy(this->_address, source._address);
        }
        else { // The not-so-easy case
          delete [] this->_address;
          _address = new char [addressLength  + 1];
              // +1 for the terminating 0
          strcpy( this->_address, source._address);
        }
        return *this;
      }
```

This assignment operator that we just implemented is the one used whenever a **TPerson** object is assigned to another **TPerson** object explicitly. But we might encounter situations where there is a need to assign something else to a **TPerson** object. It is possible to implement overloaded assignment operator(s) in a class that accepts different arguments. We will see examples of such applications in later chapters. Also note that the data member _birthDate is not copied because it is a const and assignment to a const element is not allowed. Again the assumption here is that once a **TPerson** object is created, the birth date of that person cannot change during the lifetime of that person. This restriction on _birthDate might seem somewhat restrictive, but it serves to illustrate the purpose of a const data member with respect to copying and assignment. In applications where this restriction seems too rigid, _birthDate can be made a non-const member.

The rule to follow is

☞ **Always implement the assignment operator for every class. Don't rely on the default assignment operator generated by the language.**

It might be interesting to note that the generated default copy constructor and assignment operator are inline functions. Also, refer to Chapter 13 for the internal details of copy constructor in C++.

NOTE   Given this scenario, it is easy to control assignment and copying of objects in C++. If we want to disallow copying of objects by public clients and derived classes, all we have to do is to make the copy constructor **private**. The same is true for the assignment operator. It is interesting to note that it is possible to restrict (and not completely disallow) the number of copies than can be made. Later in this chapter, we will see why such copy control might be needed.

SMALLTALK   It is interesting to see the assignment semantics with Smalltalk. Assignment is denoted by the **<-** operator. For example, a <- b means assign b to a. For simple (or primitive) types, assignment just involves copying values as in C++. But when assignment is applied to objects, the behavior is quite different. Every object is a reference to some object in memory. Given that, object assignment is nothing but reference assignment. If a and b are objects and b is assigned to a by the operation a <- b, the object referenced by b acquires another reference through the name a. After the assignment, both a and b refer to the same object. Needless to say that whatever **a** referred to before the assignment is no longer accessible through **a**. Note that Smalltalk doesn't permit assignment to a formal argument inside a function body. This is a restriction in the language.

EIFFEL   Eiffel is identical to Smalltalk with respect to assignment. Assignment is done through the operator **:=** (as in Pascal). Again, assignment between simple types implies copying values, whereas assignment between objects (actually object references) means copying references. As in Smalltalk, Eiffel doesn't permit assignment to a formal argument.

Assignment as an l-value Operation

An l-value is something (usually the name on the left hand side of an assignment operator) that can be modified. See Chapter 3 for a description of l-value and r-value. The default assignment semantics in C and C++ produce an l-value. This means one can cascade assignment operations (i.e., a=b=c). This is also true in Smalltalk. In fact, every method in Smalltalk is guaranteed to return a value. This is a useful side effect of assignment and it helps in writing clear, concise expressions. But Eiffel does not allow cascaded assignment. It follows Pascal in this regard.

REMEMBER   C++ allows the implementor to define the semantics of copying objects.
C++ also allows the implementor to define the semantics of assignment.
The implementor can control copying and assignment semantics on a per class basis.

SEMANTICS OF OBJECT EQUALITY

Assignment and copying are definitely very important issues that class designers and implementors need to worry about. A related issue that is equally important is the concept of *object equality*.

When can we say two objects are equal and what does it mean to say an object is equal to another object? It is important to keep in mind the difference between the concept of two distinct objects being equal and two names representing the same object (i.e., the concept of *equivalence* between objects). Object equality has to do with structure and state of an object, whereas equivalence has to do with address of an object. Two distinct objects might be equal but they may not be the same object. Here is an example:

```
main()
{
        TPerson person1("Bugs Bunny", "Toon Town", 414235056, "12-30-56");
        TPerson* person2 =
        new TPerson bar("Daffy", "TV Land", 418325156,
                                        "6-6-55"); // dynamic object
        TPerson person3("Goofy", "Toon Town", 418235057, "11-30-60");
        TPerson* person4 = 0; // does not point to a person, yet.
        TPerson person5("Bugs Bunny", "Toon Town", 414235056, "12-30-56");
```

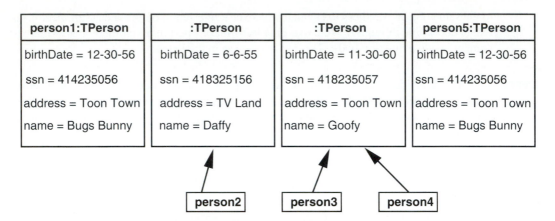

Note: 1. Objects are represented in UML notation
2. The _ prefix for data member names is not shown

Fig. 4-11

```
int i1 = 100; // ①
int i2 = 200; // ②

person4 = person3;
}
```

We can ask some simple questions about this picture (Fig. 4-11):

> Is person1 equal to person5?
>
> Is the object designated by person4 the same as the object designated by person3?

Surely, person1 and person5 are not the same object but they contain the same *state*. On the other hand, person4 and person3 are not separate objects but they designate the same object. Definitely, person3 and person4 are equivalent. Referring to ① & ② in the program above, if we ask the question: Is i1 equal to i2, the answer is quite simple—they are not. In this case, we just compare the values in i1 and i2 and immediately infer that they do not have the same value and hence are not equal. But we cannot make such easy decisions with objects because it is not easy to look at an object as a simple value. Definitely there are many interesting issues that we need to understand clearly.

Comparing objects is an important operation particularly with complex data structure objects like lists, queues, and trees.[7] Operations on such objects include searching for a specific object among those stored, sorting objects based on a key, etc. In all such opera-

---

[7]Also called Collections (or Containers) which will be discussed in Chapter 12.

tions, there is a need to compare objects to determine equality between objects. Further, determining equality of objects avoids accidental deleting of objects and also avoid duplicates. And the next interesting issue is the equality between two lists or two queues. Defining equality between an object that is an aggregate of other objects is even more complicated.

Object Equality and Object Equivalence

When dealing with objects, languages differ in the way equality of objects is defined. For example, C++ does not define any default meaning for object equivalence but Eiffel and Smalltalk do. Furthermore, the interpretation of equality between objects differs between programmers. Let us first look at reference based languages to see how object equality is represented.

SMALLTALK   Here, the language provides the == method for equivalence test. This method is available for all objects in the system. If this == method returns the value **true**, then the two objects being compared are the same object (they are equivalent). In other words, the two objects are distinct references to the same object. For testing object equality, the method = is provided. This method is implemented in terms of comparing corresponding instance variable values of the two objects involved. Any class that adds new instance variables is required to re-implement this method. For example, comparing a list object involves comparing the list sizes and then comparing each and every element on the list for their equality. This is very similar to the deep copy operation that navigates the entire object tree recursively. The counterpart of == is ~~, which determines if two objects are not equivalent. Similarly ~= is the counterpart of =, the *not equal* operator.

EIFFEL   Here again, the semantics are very similar to that of Smalltalk. The comparison operator for simple types is =. The comparison is based on the value contained in the simple type variable. For object references, the comparison operator uses the value of the reference itself. Two object references compare equal when they refer to the same object. For comparing objects (not references) the method *Equal* is available, which compares the current object with another object. But *Equal* is a shallow compare operation. It does not traverse the object references recursively to determine equality of objects. Programmers who need the deep compare semantics should write their own methods. The *not equal* operator is /=.

C++   C++ on the other hand is significantly different from Smalltalk and Eiffel, and understandably so. The comparison operator defined in C is ==, which is used for comparing values. (Comparing structures is not possible using == operator in C.) With C++, there is no default comparison mechanism defined. Designers who need the semantics of comparison for their classes should implement the operator ==. It is up to the implementor to provide the correct semantics of comparison in the overloaded operator == function. Comparing pointers is like comparing integers and it is part of the language. Two pointers, such as **person3** and **person4** above, will compare equal, implying that they contain the same address. Comparing references is no different from comparing variables (or objects if they are object references). For example

```
int i = 10;
int &ir = i;

int j = 100;
int &jr = j;

int k = 100;
int &kr = k;

if (kr == ir) { } // This will be false - Compares values of k and i
if (kr == jr) { } // This will be true - Compares values of k and j
```

Comparing the references kr and jr is nothing but comparing the values of j and k (because a reference is nothing but an alias to an existing entity). To compare TPerson objects, we need to implement the comparison operator.

```
class TPerson {
        public:
            // Other details as before
            bool operator ==(const TPerson& other) const;
            bool operator !=(const TPerson& other) const;

            void SetName(const char theNewName[]);
            void Print() const;
            // details omitted for simplicity
        private:
            // as before
};
```

```
bool
TPerson::operator==(const TPerson& other) const
{
        if (this == &other) { return true; } // Comparing aliases
        if (this->ssn == other._ssn && this->_birthDate ==
            other._birthDate) {
                // Now compare names
                if (strcmp(this->_name, other._name) == 0)
                // strcmp is a library function
                        return true;
        }

        return false; // they are not equal
}
```

The assumption here is that if the social security number, birth date, and the name are identical, the person must be the same. In fact, the social security number itself is unique and could have been used as the sole basis of comparison.

Another operator that is essential is the *not equal* operator, !=. When a class implements ==, it better implement !=. Doing so guarantees that only one of them (== or !=) is true for any pair of objects. If one of them is left out, the interface of the class looks incomplete and the client is forced to use the one provided, even when the other operator is more sensible.[8]

---

[8]This operator pair implementation is extendable to many other operators like <= and >=, < and > etc.

```
bool
TPerson::operator !=(const TPerson& other) const
{
    return ! (*this == other); // we can also write:
    // return! this -> operator == other);
}
```

REMEMBER   If your objects need comparison semantics, implement the operator==.
When you implement operator== remember to implement operator !=.
Also note that operator== can be a virtual function (discussed in Chapter 5) where as operator!= is usually non-virtual as shown above.

Looking back, comparing **TCar** objects would involve comparing details such as license plate number, vehicle identification number, etc. In this sense, a true comparison operation is quite similar to the deep copy operation. Any complex object might have to recursively invoke the comparison operator on all its internal objects, pointers, and references to determine equality. On the other hand, equivalence is much simpler in C++; it just involves comparing addresses.

NOTE   Smalltalk has a related concept of the hash value of an object. Every class supports the method **hash** as part of its fundamental operations. This method returns a unique integer for every object. Any two objects that are equal return the same hash value. But unequal objects may or may not return the same hash value. Usually, this method is used for quick look-up of objects in lists, queues, etc. Even though neither C++ nor Eiffel provide any such method as part of the language, many commercial software products provide the **hash** member function. And in many implementations, every class in the system is required to provide an implementation of the **hash** method. Language constructs are used to enforce such restrictions. A similar requirement is sometimes enforced for methods like **IsEqual()** and **Clone()**. All such decisions about intrinsic methods that need to be supported by all classes is a major design issue that any design team needs to tackle early in the design cycle.

WHY COPY CONTROL IS NEEDED

After discussing the issues surrounding copying and assignment of objects, it is time to understand why copy control might be needed. One might form the opinion that every class should provide **public** copy constructor and assignment operator functions.

Unfortunately, the situation is not that crystal clear. There are many situations where the semantics of an object prohibit copying. And in some other situations, copying would make sense only for a selected group of clients. And there might even be situations where a limited number of copies of an object might be allowed. All these requirements call for correct and efficient copy control. In the next few paragraphs we shall see some examples where copy control is essential. Once you review these examples, you will feel glad that C++ provides such flexible copy control mechanism on a per class basis. General techniques for controlling creation and copying of objects are discussed in later chapters.

A Semaphore Example

Imagine a TSemaphore class. Semaphores are used for synchronization between processes (and threads) to ensure safe resource sharing. When a process needs to use a shared resource, it needs to ensure mutual exclusion by acquiring the semaphore that guards the resource. This could be done by the method Acquire, provided by the TSemaphore class. If the resource is already acquired by some other task, then the Acquire call blocks and the calling task will be waiting until the other task relinquishes the resource. There could be more than one task waiting for the same resource.

Once a task acquires the resource, it has full ownership of the resource until it relinquishes the semaphore by calling the member function Release. Given this scenario, is it correct to copy the semaphore object. More precisely, what should the semantics be for copying a semaphore object? If we allow copying, does it mean there are now two independent semaphore objects that have acquired the same resource? This is not logically correct because a resource can only be acquired by one process at any time (or a limited number of processes in case of counted semaphores). Or does it mean that there are two semaphore objects that share the same state? Sharing state may be a better solution but it very much complicates the implementation and usage. Semaphores are seen as lightweight objects used quite often and complicating their implementation is not justified. These are some of the issues that need to be clarified before any kind of copy operation is supported. Perhaps a better solution would be to prohibit copying altogether. This implies that once a semaphore is created, it cannot be copied by anyone. Here is the class interface.

```
class TSemaphore {
      public:
            // Default constructor
            TSemaphore();
            // Called by clients to acquire the semaphore
            bool Acquire();
            // Call this when you no longer need exclusive access to the
                  resource
            void Release();
            // How many tasks are already waiting on this resource?
            unsigned GetWaiters() const;
      private:
            // TSemaphore objects cannot be copied or assigned
            TSemaphore(const TSemaphore& other);
            TSemaphore& operator=(const TSemaphore& other);
            // Details omitted
};
```

The implementation of such classes is highly operating system (and processor) specific. It might even require assembly language code.

A License Server Example

As another example, imagine a software package that allows site licensing. Instead of buying a number of separate copies of the same application, a company can buy a site li-

AUTOMATING ACQUISITION AND RELEASE OF SEMAPHORES (RESOURCES)

When using a class, such as **TSemaphore** above, programmers must remember to acquire the semaphore using the **Acquire** member function and, more importantly, release the semaphore (using **Release**) before leaving a function. Here is the typical code:

```
class X {
    public:
        // member functions
        void f();
    private:
        TSemaphore _sem;
};


void X::f() // Member function of X
{
    // Before anything, acquire the locking semaphore
    _sem.Acquire();
    // do whatever you have to do
    if (/* some condition*/) { /* do more stuff */ _sem.Release();
      return; }
    else { /* do some other stuff */ _sem.Release(); }
}
```

It is clear that one must remember to release the semaphore from every exit point in the function f(). This can be error prone. To avoid this burden, we can use a helper class to automate the acquisition and release of a semaphore by using a **TAutoSemaphore** class shown below.

```
class TAutoSemaphore {
    public:
        TAutoSemaphore(TSemaphore& sem)
            : _semaphore(sem)
        { _semaphore.Acquire(); }
        ~TAutoSemaphore() { _semaphore.Release(); }
    private:
        TSemaphore& _semaphore;
};
```

With this class, our code in f() would be simplified:

```
void X::f() // Member function of X
{
    // Before anything, create a TAutoSemaphore object
    // This also acquires the semaphore
    TAutoSemaphore autosem(_sem);
```

```
        // do whatever you have to do
        if (/* some condition*) { /* do more stuff */ return; }
        else { /* do some other stuff */ }
        // destructor of autosem automatically releases the semaphore _sem
           on exit from f()
}
```

Class **TAutoSemaphore** is trivial. The constructor expects a semaphore object to be passed and it acquires the semaphore as part of the constructor. The destructor of **TAutoSemaphore** releases the acquired semaphore. Therefore, once an object of **TAutoSemaphore** is created in some scope, its destructor will ensure the release of the acquired semaphore. Programmers don't need to do anything for this to happen. At least now we have one less thing to manage.

      Such classes are very common in C++ programs. Another one of such classes is a **TTracer**, which traces entry and exit to/from a function.

```
        class TTracer {
            public:
                    #ifdef DEBUG
                    TTracer(const char message[])
                        :_msg(message)
                    { cout << ">> Enter " << _msg << endl; }

                    ~TTracer() { cout << "<< Exit " << _msg << endl; }
            private:
                    const char* _msg;
                    #else
                    TTracer(const char message[]) {}
                    ~TTracer() {}
                    #endif
        };
```

More examples of this kind can be found in subsequent chapters.

cense for a fixed number of users. Now there is only one copy of the software (hence less storage requirement) that can be used by everyone in the company (subject to the number of licenses granted). A licensing server could be run on a server machine that grants *license tokens* to anyone who wishes to use the software. A license token is issued only when the number of outstanding tokens is less than the number of site licenses granted for that site. Here is the class **TLicenseServer**.

```
class TLicenseToken; // forward declaration

class TLicenseServer {
        public:
                // Constructor - creates a new license server with maxUsers
                // licenses
                TLicenseServer(unsigned maxUsers);
                ~TLicenseServer();
```

```
            // Grants a new license or returns 0 otherwise. Caller adopts
            // the returned object. The token should be destroyed when it
            // is no longer needed - see below
            TLicenseToken* CreateNewLicense();
      private:
            // Objects cannot be copied or assigned
            TLicenseServer(const TLicenseServer& other);
            TLicenseServer& operator=(const TLicenseServer& other);
            unsigned _numIssued;
            unsigned _maxTokens;
            // many details omitted
};

class TLicenseToken {
      public:
            TLicenseToken();
            ~TLicenseToken();
      private:
            TLicenseToken(const TLicenseToken& other);
            TLicenseToken& operator=(const TLicenseToken& other);
            // many details omitted
};
```

Since a **TLicenseToken** is issued by the server on a per user basis, it is essential to ensure that users do not copy the returned token. Otherwise, the license server has no way of controlling the number of users. Every time a new user wants to use the application controlled by the license server, she asks the server to generate a new **TLicenseToken** object. A pointer to a new **TLicenseToken** is returned if a new token can be generated. The caller owns this token. When the user no longer needs to use the application, she must destroy it. When the license token is destroyed, it communicates with the server to reduce the number of outstanding license tokens. Note that neither the server nor the token can be duplicated. No user can duplicate a token. The license token may contain information such as task id, machine name, user name, date of token generation, etc. Since the copy constructor and the assignment operator are private in both the server and the token, there is no chance for duplication of tokens, eliminating any possibility of fraud.

One thing that might be burdensome is the requirement on the part of the user to destroy the token. Implementation can be done such that the token keeps track of usage of the software and it automatically destroys the license token if the software hasn't been used for a predetermined period of time. In fact, such implementations are very common.

Another application of such an implementation is for billing purposes. Clients can be charged based on their usage of the service. This could be a common thing with *pay-per-view* programs on cable television.[9]

One might feel that the token should allow duplication but it should be considered a new token and the server should be informed of such duplication. Such an implementation is possible and it again requires copy control.

---

[9]The viewer is charged a fixed amount for watching (subscribing to) that program. The program could be a very recent movie, a popular sports event telecast live, or a concert.

A String Class Example

Programmers in all languages use character strings for error messages, user prompts, etc. We also use character arrays and manipulate the contents of such arrays often. The main problem with character arrays is that of storage management and lack of operations to manipulate them. Under C and C++, character arrays cannot be passed by value; only a pointer to the first character in the array can be passed around. This makes it hard to implement safe arrays. To overcome such hurdles, one would implement a **TString** class that provides all the necessary functionality. A **TString** object manages its own memory. We need not have to worry about it. Further, it takes care of allocating more memory when needed.

NOTE   The standard C++ library contains a powerful **string** class that also handles multi-byte characters. A string class is used here as an example because it is easy to understand and it illustrates the concepts clearly.
          Here is the declaration for class **TString**:

```
/*
 *A String class implementation. It is based on the ASCII character set.
 *TString objects can be copied and assigned. Class implements deep copy
 *Objects of this class can be created any where.
 *Use this class instead of " " strings of characters.
 */
class TString {

public:
            // Constructors
            // Create an empty string object
            TString();
            // Create a new string object which contains the characters pointed
            // by s. s must be NULL terminated. Characters are copied from s.
            TString(const char* s);
            // Create a string containing the single character aChar
            TString(char aChar);
            TString(const TStringarg);
            //copy constructor
            // Destructor
            ~TString();
            // Assignment operators
            TString& operator=(const TStringarg);
            TString& operator=(const char* s);
            TString& operator=(char s);

            // Member Functions
            // Returns the number of characters currently stored in the object
            int Size() const;
            // Returns a substring which represents the string starting at posn
            // of length len
            TString operator()(unsigned posn, unsigned len) const;
            // Returns the character at n
            char operator() (unsigned n) const;
            // Returns a reference to the character at n
```

```
        char& operator[](unsigned n);
        // Returns a new TString object which is a concatenation of one and
        // two
        friend TString operator+(const TString& one, const TString& two);

        // These methods modify the original object
        // Appends the character in other to this
        TString& operator+=(const TString& other);
        // Flips the case of all characters in this string
        TString& operator~();

        // Relational operators
        // Comparison is based on ASCII character set. Two string objects
        // are equal if they contain the same characters.
        friend bool operator==(const TString&, const TString&);
        bool operator!=(const TString&, const TString&);
        friend bool operator<(const TString&, const TString&);
        bool operator>(const TString&, const TString&);
        friend bool operator>=(const TString&, const TString&);
        bool operator<=(const TString&, const TString&);

        // Input/Output
        friend ostream& operator<<(ostream&, const TString&);
        friend istream& operator>>(istream&, TString&);
        // Prints the characters in the string to cout
        void Print() const;

private:
        // length is the number of characters stored in the object.
        // But the memory pointed by str is at least length+1 long.
        unsigned    _length;
        char*       _str; // pointer to characters
};
```

A simple implementation would allocate memory for the characters and would perform a deep copy of the object whenever needed. One such implementation is given below. It is easy to understand and implement.

```
TString::TString()
{
        _str = 0;
        _length = 0;
}

TString::TString(const char* arg)
{
        if (arg && *arg) { // pointer is not 0 and
                // also points to valid characters
                _length = strlen(arg);
                _str = new char[ _length + 1];
                strcpy(_str, arg);
        }
        else {
                _str = 0;
                _length = 0;
```

```
        }
}

TString::TString(char aChar)
{
        if (aChar) {
                _str = new char[2];
                _str[0] = aChar;
                _str[1] = '\0';
                _length = 1;
        }
        else {
                _str = 0;
                _length = 0;
        }
}


TString::~TString()
{
        if (_str != 0)
                delete [] _str;
}
// Copy Constructor
// Performs a deep copy. Allocates memory for
// characters and then copies
// the characters to this.

TString::TString(const TString& arg)
{
  if (arg._str != 0) {
                this->_str = new char[strlen(arg._str)+ 1];
                strcpy(this->_str, arg._str);
                _length = arg._length;
  }
  else {
                _str = 0;
                _length = 0;
  }
}

TString& TString::operator=(const TString& arg)
{
        if (this == &arg)
                return *this;

        if (this->_length >= arg._length) {
                // this is big enough
                if (arg._str != 0)
                        strcpy(this->_str, arg._str);
                else
                        this->_str = 0;
                this->_length = arg._length;
                return *this;
        }
        // Hmm, this doesn't have enough space _arg is bigger
                delete [] _str; // Safe
```

```
                this->_length = arg.Size();
                if (_length) {
                        _str = new char[_length + 1];
                        strcpy(_str, arg._str);
                }
                else
                        _str = 0;
                return *this; // Always do this
}
TString& TString::operator=(const char* s)
{
                if (s == 0 || *s == 0) {
                        // source array is empty. Make "this" empty too
                        delete [] _str;
                        _length = 0;
                        return *this;
                }

                int slength = strlen(s);

                if (this->_length >= slength) {
                        // this is big enough
                        strcpy(this->_str, s);
                        this->_length = slength;
                        return *this;
                }
                // Hmm, this doesn't have enough space _arg is bigger
                delete [] _str; // Safe
                this->_length = slength;
                _str = new char[_length + 1];
                strcpy(_str, s);

                return *this;
}
TString& TString::operator=(char charToAssign)
{
                char s[2];
                s[0] = charToAssign;
                s[1] = '\0';
                // Use the other assignment operator
                return (*this = s);
}

int
TString::Size() const
{
return _length;
}

TString& TString::operator+=(const TString& arg)
{
  if (arg.Size()) { / member functions can call each other
                _length = arg.Size() + this->Size();
                char *newstr = new char[ _length + 1];
                 if (this->Size()) // if the original is not a NULL string
                        strcpy(newstr, _str);
```

```
              else
                  *newstr = '\0';
              strcat(newstr, arg._str); // append the argument string
              delete [] _str; // discard the memory of the original
              _str = newstr;  // This is the new string created
        }
        return *this;
}

TString
operator+(const TString& first, const TString& second)
{
TString result = first;
result += second; // Call member function operator+=
return result;
}

int
operator==(const TString& first, const TString& second)
{
        return ( (strcmp(first._str, second._str)) == 0 );
        // strcmp is a library function
}

// Other comparison operators are implemented
// just like operator==. They are not shown here for the
// sake of brevity of code.
char TString::operator() (unsigned n) const
{
  if (n < this->Size())
            return this->_str[n]; // Return the character at n

  return 0;
}

const char& TString::operator[] (unsigned n)
{
  if (n < this->Size())
            return this->_str[n]; // Return the character at n

  cout << "Invalid subscript: " << n << endl;
        exit(-1); // Actually should throw an exception here
}

// Flip the case of each character
TString& TString::operator~()
{
    // Uses library functions isupper, toupper
    // islower and tolower
    if (_str && *_str) {
        char *p = _str;
        while (*p) {
            if (isupper(*p))
                *p = tolower(*p);
            else if (islower(*p))
                *p = tolower(*p);
```

```
                ++p;
            }
        }
        return *this;
}

TString
TString::operator()(unsigned posn, unsigned len) const
{
    int sz = Size(); // size of the source
    if (posn > sz) return ""; // an empty string
    if (posn + len > sz)
            len = sz - posn;

    TString result;
    if (len) {
            result._str = new char[len + 1];
            strncpy(result._str, _str + posn, len);
            result._length = len;
            result._str[len] = '\0';
    }
    return result;
}

ostream& operator<<(ostream& o, const TString& s)
{
        if (s._str)
                o << s._str;
        return o;
}

istream& operator>>(istream& stream, TString& s)
{
        char c;

        s = "";

        while (stream.get(c) && isspace(c))
            ; // do nothing
        if (stream) { // Stream is still OK
            // read characters till space is encountered
            do
                s += c;
        while ( stream.get(c) && !isspace(c));

        if (stream)
                // unget the extra character read
                stream.putback(c);
        }
        return stream;
}

void TString::Print() const
{
        cout << _str << endl;
}
```

ANALYSIS

A TString object is represented internally with a pointer and a _length data member. The default constructor sets the _length and the pointer _str to 0. The data member _length is a way of caching the number of characters in the string. Whenever the number of characters in a TString object is modified, _length is updated.

TString::TString(const char* arg) copies the characters from arg into the string object after allocating memory and then sets the _length correctly.

TString::TString(char c) makes a string object out of a single character.

TString::TString(const TString& arg) is the copy constructor. It performs a deep copy. First we allocate memory for the characters as indicated by arg then copy all the characters.

TString::operator=(const TString& arg) This is the assignment operator. It is somewhat optimized. If the _length of this is bigger than arg, then it is a simple copy operation. Otherwise, the memory pointed by _str is deleted (garbage collection) and a new piece of memory is allocated and then characters are copied.

TString::operator=(const char* s) This is another assignment operator. It allows clients to assign an array of characters to an existing TString object. Memory management is automatic.

TString::operator=(char charToAssign) This is another assignment operator. It allows clients to assign a single character to an existing TString object. Memory management is automatic.

TString::Size() returns the size (i.e., the number of characters stored) of the string.

TString::operator+=(const TString& arg) is the concatenation operator. Characters in arg are appended to this. It allocates memory for the combined string and then copies the characters. Note that arg is not modified. Also note that this implementation will work for cases like a += a.

operator+(const TString& first, const TString& second) The addition operator is implemented as a friend function for reasons discussed in the chapter on operator overloading (Chapter 8). For this discussion, it doesn't really matter whether it is a member function or friend function. This operator uses the operator += for its implementation.

EFFICIENCY   This code could have been written as

```
TString
operator+(const TString& first, const TString& second)¹⁰
{
  TString result;
  result = first;
  result += second; // Call member function operator+=
  return result;
}
```

but that would be inefficient. We create a new string object **result** using the default constructor. Next, we assign to it. Then, we append **second** to it. Note that the assignment

---

[10]Note that the operator+ can never return the result by reference or pointer. It should return the result by value. We will see the reason behind this condition in the chapter on operator overloading.

operation overwrites whatever was in result. Why can't we create the result object directly using the copy constructor? This is what is done in the implementation. The original code uses one copy constructor call and one operator+=. The implementation above uses one default constructor call, one assignment operator call, and one operator += call. Definitely, the original implementation is more efficient. This situation arises in many member functions. Whenever a new object is being created and is followed later by an assignment, check if the copy constructor can be used to directly create the object. This makes your implementation more efficient.

operator==(const TString& first, const TString& second) is the comparison operator. Here, comparison is based on the lexical comparison of characters in the string. Again, the operator == is implemented as a friend. All other operators will have a very similar implementation. The concept of a friend (or in general, non-member functions) is discussed in Chapter 7.

TString::operator() (unsigned n) is the sub-char operator that returns the character at the position n. Nothing fancy here.

TString::operator[] (unsigned n) is the subscript operator. This allows one to use the TString object like an array of characters. Note that it returns a reference to const character. This ensures that the characters in the string cannot be modified through the reference returned.

TString::operator~() is the flip case operator. It allows the user to flip the case of characters in any string.

TString::operator()(unsigned posn, unsigned len) is the substring operator. It returns a substring starting at posn of length len. Note that the new string object is returned by value. We will see a more sophisticated implementation of this operator in a later chapter.

The other member functions are self explanatory. Some of these member functions use the iostream library provided with every C++ compiler.

The goal of this detailed discussion of the TString class is not for learning C++ syntax. The focus is on something else that is explained below.

THINK   There is a small problem (or shall we say *bug*) in the code above. The _length data member keeps track of the number of characters in _str but not the original size of memory allocated. So if a TString object of 100 characters is created and then it is assigned with a string of 10 characters, the _length data member contains 10, even though _str points to a block of 100 characters. But, we can only use the first 10 characters of it. The rest is a waste. It would be nice if we know how much was allocated and how much has been used. Can you fix this problem? However, there is no memory leak.

THE COPY-ON-WRITE CONCEPT

This TString class is fairly easy to understand and implement. What happens when objects of this class are used heavily as function arguments and as return values using the pass-by-value scheme? Since the class uses deep copy semantics, if the number of characters in the TString object is not too small, significant time is spent in copying characters and in deleting the dynamically allocated memory. This also implies that object creation and destruction is expensive. The intention is that wherever character strings are needed,

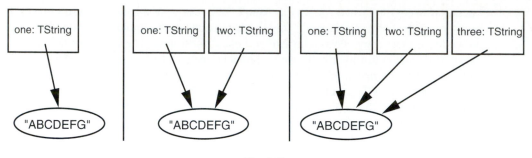

Fig. 4-12

TString objects should be used. But if the cost of creation, copying, assignment, and destruction of these **TString** objects is prohibitive, clients will refrain from using the class. Is there a way to optimize the implementation such that copying of objects can be made faster?

When **TString** objects are copied, all characters in the objects are also copied. But this might be a waste of time. We could change the implementation such that when a copy of a **TString** object is made, both the copies share the characters in the original string without actually copying them. We are all familiar with this kind of sharing. But when one of the copies tries to modify (or even destroy) the characters in the object, the sharing mechanism has to ensure that the **TString** object that attempted the modification gets its own copy of the characters without affecting the other objects that still share the characters. For example (see Fig. 4-12 for an illustration of the following code),

```
TString one ("ABCDEFG");
TString two(of one); // make a copy
TString three;

three = one;
```

Now if the object **three** tries to modify its characters using

```
~three; // three.operator~()
```

other objects (**one** and **two**) should not be affected. We should end up with the following scenario (Fig. 4-13).

If we can ensure this condition, we would have fulfilled our goal of making copying faster. This scheme of making a true copy when modification is attempted is called **copy-on-write.** This principle has been used for a long time in software design and more so in system software.[11] It basically means that the resource (in our case the characters) is shared till someone writes to it. When one of the objects sharing the resource tries to *write* to the resource, a *copy* is made.

---

[11]This is frequently used for page sharing between processes in operating systems. The mach micro kernel uses this for its virtual memory system. The UNIX system call vfork() does the same.

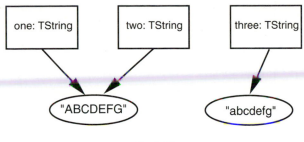

Fig. 4-13

This concept requires three fundamental conditions:

1. It should be possible to share the resource without incurring much extra cost (memory and CPU).

2. It should be possible to clearly identify and control all paths that might modify the resource.

3. The implementation must be able to keep track of the number objects sharing the resource under all circumstances.

First of these requirements implies that in order to share the characters in the string, we should not have to unduly increase the size of each object. Also, the implementation code required to make this happen should not be too complex. In other words, sharing should happen with minimal cost. Otherwise, the cost of sharing offsets the benefits.

The second condition implies that the objects sharing the resource should modify the shared resource only through well defined paths (or functions). Our implementation must be able to identify all those paths and do the right thing.

The third condition suggests that for correct operation, the implementation must correctly know, at any point, how many objects are sharing the resource. If this condition is not met, then problems of garbage and/or dangling reference are imminent. Needless to say, all these conditions must hold good even under multi-threaded environments.

The key to correct copy-on-write semantics is the separation of interface from the implementation. When a **TString** object is copied, it should not create a new set of characters but it must share the implementation that already exists in the original object. Furthermore, the implementation must remember the number of objects sharing the implementation (or resource). This is called the *reference count*. It is the number of references to the resource and it must be kept correct at all times. For this reason, sometimes this scheme is also called *reference counting* mechanism. But reference counting does not imply copy-on-write. In fact, we will see reference counting being used without copy-on-write in later chapters. Reference count is also called *use count*.

We will move the implementation (and storage) of the characters into a struct **StringRep**. This would be a nested struct within **TString**. Under C++, a nested class does not imply a nested object. Only the declaration is nested. Furthermore, the name **StringRep** is visible only within **TString** and not anywhere else. Here is the new class declaration.

```
class TString {
   public:
        // Constructors
        TString();                      // Default constructor
        TString(const char* s);
        TString(char);
        TString(const TString&other); // Copy constructor

        // Destructor
        ~TString();

        // Member Functions
        TString& operator=(const TString&other);
        TString& operator+=(const TString&other);
        int Size() const;
        TString operator()(unsigned posn, unsigned len) const;
        char operator() (unsigned n) const;
        TString& operator~();

        friend TString operator+(const TString&, const TString&);
        // Relational operators
        friend int operator==(const TString&, const TString&);
        // Other member function not shown

   private:
        struct StringRep {
            char* _str; // the actual characters
            unsigned _refCount; // # of references to it
            unsigned _length; // # of characters in the string
        };

        StringRep *_rp;
};
```

Every **TString** object contains a pointer to a **StringRep** object. When **TString** objects are copied, all that is copied is the pointer _rp. It is that simple. In fact, it is possible to make **StringRep** a truly independent class with constructors and destructors. In our situation, we don't need all that. We just need a place holder for a character pointer and a reference count (Fig. 4-14).

```
                TString one ("ABCDEFG");
                TString two(one); // make a copy
                TString three;

                three = one;
```

Now let us see how different the implementation would be.

```
TString::TString()
{
     _rp = new StringRep;
     _rp->_refCount = 1;
```

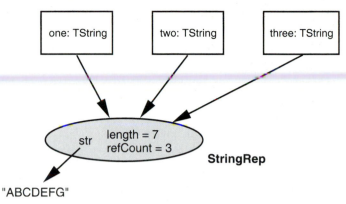

Fig. 4-14

```
     _rp->_length = 0;
     _rp->_str = 0;
}

TString::TString(const char* s)
{
     _rp = new StringRep;
     _rp->_refCount = 1;
     // This is the only object using the StringRep
     _rp ->_length = strlen(s);
     _rp->_str = new char [ _rp->_length + 1];
     strcpy(_rp->_str, s);
}

TString::TString(char aChar)
{
          _rp = new StringRep;
          _rp ->_length = 1;
          _rp->_str = new char [ _rp->_length + 1];
          _rp->_str[0] = aChar;
          _rp->_str[1] = 10;
          _rp->_refCount = 1; // This is the only object using the
                    StringRep
}

TString::TString(const TString& other)
{
     /* This is one of the most crucial operations. We need to increase
        the reference count on the object pointed by _rp within other.
      */
     // it acquires one more reference
     other._rp->_refCount++;
     // make them share the resource
     this->_rp = other._rp;
}
```

```
TString& TString::operator=(const TString& other)
{
    if (this == &other)
            return *this; // assignment to self
    /* This is another crucial operations. We need to increase the
    reference count on the object pointed by _rp within other. At
    the same time we need to decrement the reference count on what
    "this" points to. */

    // it acquires one more reference
    other._rp->_refCount++;
    / Decrement and test ; no one else using it?
    if (--this->_rp->_refCount == 0) { /
            delete [] this->_rp->_str;
            delete this->_rp;
    }
    // make them share the resource
    this->_rp = other._rp;

    return *this;
}

TString&
TString::operator~()
{
    // Optimization-1
    if (rp->length == 0)
            return *this; // no characters in the string

    char* p;
    if (rp->refCount > 1) {
            // Hmm. The hard part. Detach this TString object
            // and provide its own StringRep object. This is
            // the copy-on-write operation.
            unsigned len = this->rp->length; // save it
            p = new char [len + 1];
            strcpy(p, this->rp->str);

            this->rp->refCount--; // Since "this" is going away
                                  // from the pool
            this->rp = new StringRep;
            this->rp->refCount = 1;
            this->rp->length = len;
            this->rp->str = p; // Created above
    }

    // Optimization-2
    // If no one else using this string, then just go ahead
    // and change the characters.
    p = this->rp->str;
    if (p != 0) {
            while (*p) {
                if (isupper(*p))
                        *p = tolower(*p);
                else if (islower(*p))
                        *p = toupper(*p);
```

```
                        ++p;
                }
        }
        return *this;
}
TString:: TString()
{
        if (--_rp->_refCount == 0) {
                delete [] _rp->_str;
                delete _rp;
        }
}
```

Here is a small code fragment that shows how the assignment operator works (see Fig. 4-15).

```
TString x ("1234ABCDXYZ");
TString y (x); // copy construct y from x
TString a("PQRS");
TString b(a);

a = x;
```

These operations are by far the most crucial because they control object copying. Now for the sake of completeness, let us look at the flip case operator function (Fig. 4-16, p. 169).
Imagine a piece of code like

```
TString x("1234ABCXYZ");
TString y(x);
TString z = x;

~z;
```

Now let us look at the destructor for **TString**. When **TString** object goes out of scope, we need to get rid of the memory that _rp points to if no one else is using it. Otherwise, we just decrement the reference count and chug along.

CAUTION THREAD SAFETY   In all the cases above, where the _refCount data member is being modified, one needs to remember that it is not a multi-thread safe operation. In cases where multi-thread safety is required, such increment and decrement operations must be made multi-thread safe, using OS specific synchronization facilities (or even in assembly language routines); or such processor specific operations must be handled by a different class (to be seen in a later chapter) and one should use that class. What's important is to recognize thread safety; how it is implemented is just a detail.

THINK   The code above creates, deletes, and manipulates the **StringRep** object in many places. This is definitely not very elegant. Modify the implementation such that **StringRep** has its own constructor, destructor, and other member functions so that it is capable of managing itself. Further, complete the implementation of this class.

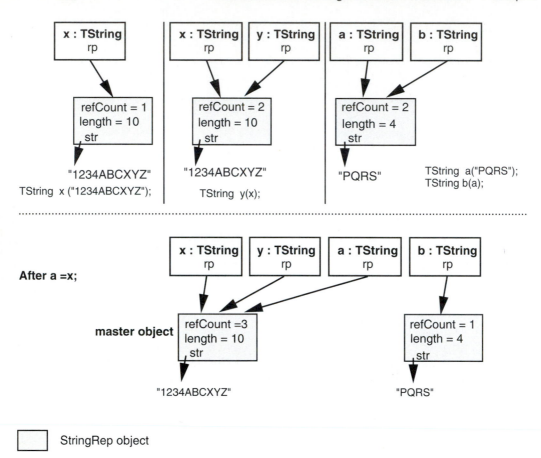

Fig. 4-15

When to Use Reference Counting

Reference counting is a neat scheme to use when resource sharing (with or without copy-on-write) is needed. Sharing resources is a very common feature of most applications. Reference counting facilitates more efficient and cleaner implementations and makes applications run faster. Reference counting takes the burden of resource management away from the client and makes it part of the implementation (which is the correct thing to do).

Summary of Copy-on-Write

The scheme of reference counting used above has some distinguishing characteristics.

A **TString** object acts as a handle to the **StringRep** object. The **StringRep** object can be considered the *master* object. It owns the storage and the reference count. The client doesn't really know how the whole thing works because the **copy-on-write** scheme does not affect her in anyway. She always gets the impression of having her own copy of

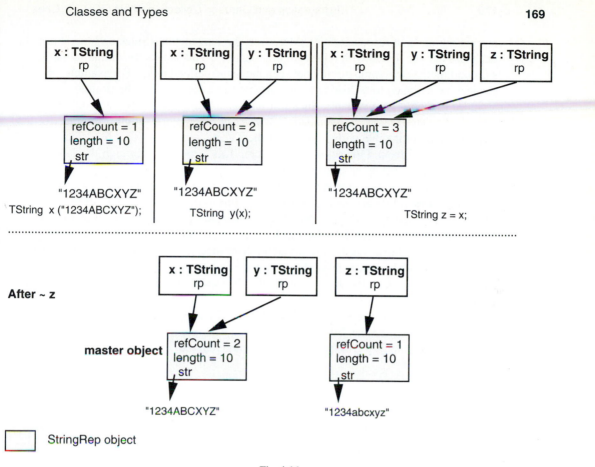

Fig. 4-16

the TString object, even though the implementation is more sophisticated than that. This concept is useful in places where copying cost is prohibitive and one needs a more efficient copying operation.

In cases where the **copy-on-write** scheme is not suitable (because the master object may not permit copying), but sharing is required, we use the reference counting semantics again but without the **copy-on-write**. Whether clients are allowed to modify the master object is always an issue to keep in mind in all these situations. We shall see some more examples of these concepts in later chapters.

CLASSES AND TYPES

So far, we have looked at class as the fundamental entity in OOP. But from the perspective of the language type mechanism, a class is almost like a new type added to the language.[12] And this is more so in C++ and Eiffel. A class represents a new type and objects are instances of the new type. Just like primitive types (or language defined types), a class

---

[12]This is true in most languages but there are some exceptions.

has restrictions and responsibilities. Moreover, the language has rules on how objects of one class may be mixed with objects of other classes. This is exactly similar to the issues surrounding the type compatibility between language defined types. For example, an integer may be assigned to a floating point variable but a variable of type **double** cannot be assigned to a **char** type variable. Such restrictions also apply to classes and objects. Only objects of related classes are compatible with each other. For example, an object of the class **TCar** is compatible with an object of the **TVehicle** class if **TCar** is a subclass (i.e., **TCar** is derived from **TVehicle**) of **TVehicle**. This is possible through the inheritance mechanism discussed in the next chapter.

Since a class acts like a new type designed by the programmer, she has to be aware of its properties, privileges, and responsibilities. Just as the language designer has to know about the language defined types, the class designer has to focus on the class. In general, objects of one class cannot be mixed with (assigned to) objects of another class except in cases where the classes are related through inheritance. The designer of the class hierarchy makes this inheritance possible. In other words, two objects are compatible only when the designer intended them to be. In all other situations, classes are distinct, incompatible types.

This *class-as-a-type* scheme helps in writing better software whose correctness can be verified at compile time. Since every class is a new type, very strict type checking can be enforced. This makes programs more robust and reliable.

SUMMARY

Always initialize objects completely. All constructors should ensure that all data members are initialized with proper values.

Always implement copy constructor, assignment operator and destructor for all classes. The compiler generated defaults are almost never useful in real, commercial grade programs.

Clearly understand garbage collection and dangling reference concepts. Ensure that your classes don't leak memory.

Understand identity of objects correctly. Don't confuse between pointers to objects and real objects.

Support copying and assignment for classes if they make sense. Disable (or control) copying and assignment where the semantics of the class does not allow for copying and assignment.

Make sure the reference counting mechanism is multi-thread safe if the implementation is to be used in multi-threaded systems.

For efficient implementations, use the copy-on-write scheme.

Don't use default constructor followed immediately by assignment. Instead, use a copy constructor for the operation.

5

The Inheritance Concept

Inheritance is one of the most powerful concepts in Object-Oriented software development. It can be used very effectively in a number of design scenarios if the concept is clearly understood. It is also subject to misuse by programmers new to OOP. Inheritance helps in solving some tough problems and makes the solution more elegant than one without it. It also simplifies the clients' view of the solution. Moreover, inheritance is one of the fundamental tools for code reusability, which is seen as one of the primary benefits of OOP. Even more important, inheritance is the key to interface and design reuse, which is essential for building robust, extensible software.

Using inheritance effectively requires a good understanding of the basic concepts. Once that is achieved, a good understanding of the problem is required to apply inheritance correctly. Inheritance is not the solution for all problems; it is the best medicine for many situations and at the same time it is not required in many others. This is where the design skills of the programmer come in handy. Inheritance should be used only when necessary. Many newcomers to OOP have a (wrong) feeling that without inheritance there is no OOP. Nothing is farther from the truth. Agreed, inheritance is a very powerful tool, but not every tool is useful in all situations. Many elegant (and simple) solutions don't need inheritance. Inheritance may look like a very "sexy" thing to use in all solutions. Abandon any such preconceived notions and have a clear mind when solving problems. In this chapter, we will see both good and bad uses of inheritance.

BASICS OF INHERITANCE

For this discussion, let us take up the problem of managing students, teachers, graduate students, graduate teaching assistants (GTA), research scholars, and employees in a university. The idea here is to understand the relationship among these people and manage them without much duplication of code.

We need to manage course names, student names, etc. These are basically character strings and we need to compare these strings for equality in many situations and we also need to manage their memory. We already have an elegant abstraction, TString (Chapter 4) to manage character strings that we can rely upon here (standard C++ library now supports an elaborate set of string classes). Similarly, to manage dates, we are going to reuse class TDate that was also shown in Chapter 4. Courses can be represented by another abstraction, class TCourse. Our interface and implementation would be much cleaner by using these simple abstractions, which are the building blocks for more useful (and bigger) abstractions. The tradeoffs to be considered when using TString objects over raw pointers is discussed in Chapter 11.

Class TCourse is shown below. Note that both TDate and TCourse support some essential overloaded operators. See Chapter 8 for a full discussion of operator overloading.

```
typedef long CourseId;

class TCourse {
    public:
        TCourse(const char name[], long id);
        TCourse(const TCourse& other); // Copy constructor
        TCourse& operator=(const TCourse& other); // Assignment operator
        ~TCourse(); // Destructor

        // Comparison operators
        bool operator==(const TCourse& other);
        bool operator!=(const TCourse& other);
        TString GetCourseName() const;
        void SetCourseName(const char name[]);
        CourseId GetCourseId() const;
        void SetCourseId(CourseId newId);
        // and probably others too
    private:
        TString     _courseName;
        CourseId    _courseId;
};
```

Implementing class TCourse is left as a trivial exercise to the reader. Implementation of the class is not required to understand the concepts that follow.

Let's first define some enumerations that are used throughout this example:

```
// A University caters to different types of students. This enum
// classifies them
enum EStudentStatus { eFullTime, ePartTime, eExchange };
```

```
enum EDepartment { eAccounting, eBusiness, eEngineering, eMathematics,
                   ePhysics eChemistry, eUnknown /* and more */};
// A student is allowed to enroll in this many courses per semester
const short MAX_COURSES_FOR_STUDENT = 5;

class TStudent{
    public:
        TStudent (const char theName[],
                  unsigned long theSSN,
                  const char theBirthDate[],
                  const char theAddress[],
                  EStudentStatus theStatus,
                  EDepartment theDepartment);
        // Copy Constructor
        TStudent (const TStudent& source);
        // Assignment operator
        TStudent& operator= (const TStudent& source);
        ~TStudent();

        void SetName(const char theName[]);
        TString GetName() const;

        void SetAddress(const char theAddress[]);
        void SetAddress(const TString& newAddress); // overloaded
                                                    // function;
        TString GetAddress() const;

        void SetDepartment(EDepartment dept);
        EDepartment GetDepartment() const;

        // Enroll the Student for aCourse
        bool EnrollForCourse(const TCourse& aCourse);

        bool DropFromCourse(const TCourse& theCourse);
        void ListCoursesRegisteredFor() const;
        void SetStudentIdentification(unsigned long newId);
        unsigned long GetStudentIdentification() const;

        // Display pertinent details of the Student
        void Print() const;
        // many other details omitted

    private:
        // The implementation is shown just for completeness. They are
        // not needed to understand the concepts.
        TString                 _name;
        TString                 _address;
        unsigned long           _ssn;
        const TDate             _birthDate;
        EStudentStatus          _status;
        EDepartment             _department;
        // an array of pointers to courses registered for
        TCourse*                _enrolled[MAX_COURSES_FOR_STUDENT];
        int                     _numCourses;// number of courses
                                            // registered for
};
```

This is a very simple class. It contains essential details of any student. Each student has a

> Name
>
> Address
>
> Associated Department
>
> List of Courses enrolled
>
> Social Security number (or student Identification number)

All these are shown in the class interface file. We have to write the code for all the member functions too. Let us look at some of the imporant member functions.

```
// Array of department names for easy printing. If you print an enum
// directly, what you see is an int. But we want to see the names of the
// departments. This array of strings is included for that purpose.
// Index this array using the EDepartment enum members to get the correct
// description.
static const char *departmentNames[] = {"Accounting", "Business",
                    "Engineering", "Mathematics", "Physics", "Arts",
                    "Chemistry", "Unknown" };

// The same reasoning, as with department names applies to this array also.
// We want to print the status of a student as a string. When this array is
// indexed with
// a member of the enum EStudentStatus we get the correct string.
static const char *statusLabels [] = { "Full time", "Part time",
                              "Exchange", "Unknown" };

TStudent::TStudent (const char theName[],
                    unsigned long theSSN,
                    const char
                    theBirthDate[],
                    const char theAddress[],
                    EStudentStatus theStatus,
                    EDepartment theDepartment)
            : _name(theName), // It is an object, hence the initialization
              _address(theAddress), // initialize address
              _birthDate(theBirthDate), // initialize birth date
              _ssn(theSSN),
              _status(theStatus),
              _department(theDepartment),
              _numCourses(0)
{
      // the list of courses would be empty to start with
  for(int i=0; i < MAX_COURSES_FOR_STUDENT; i++)
      _enrolled[i] = 0; // Note that these are pointers to objects
}

TStudent::TStudent(const TStudent& other)
    : _name(other._name),        // Copy name
      _address(other._address), // Copy address
      _birthDate(other._birthDate)   // Copy birthDate
      _ssn(other._ssn),
      _status(other._status),
```

```
        _department(other._department),
         _numCourses(other._numCourses)
{
      /* Simple data is copied as it is. Copy the courses correctly We only
         copy those course names that are not empty. Every student has place
         for MAX_COURSES_FOR_STUDENT courses But it is not guaranteed that
         all students would enroll for MAX_COURSES_FOR_STUDENT courses.
         Therefore, search the array of pointers "_enrolled", and allocate
         memory and copy only those courses that the student has enrolled
         in.*/
      for(int i=0; i < MAX_COURSES_FOR_STUDENT; i++) {
            if (other._enrolled[i] != 0) {
            // Student has enrolled in this course
                  // Allocate a TCourse object. Calls the copy constructor
                  // of TCourse
                  this->_enrolled[i] = new TCourse( *(other._enrolled[i]) );
            }
      }
}

void
TStudent::SetName(const char theName[])
{
    _name = theName; // Class TString takes care of the rest
}

void
TStudent::SetAddress(const char theAddress[])
{
    // Again calls the overloaded assignment operator of TString
    _address = theAddress;
}

bool
TStudent::EnrollForCourse(const TCourse& aCourse)
{
    if (_numCourses >= MAX_COURSES_FOR_STUDENT)
          return false; // Already enrolled in too many courses
    /*
     * _enrolled is an array of pointers to course objects. Every time a
       student enrolls in a new course, we allocate a new TCourse object
       and put it in the array enrolled. To start with, all entries in the
       array are 0.
     */
    for (int i=0; i < MAX_COURSES_FOR_STUDENT; i++) {
          if (_enrolled[i] == 0) { // Is this slot free?
                // Calls copy constructor of TCourse
                _enrolled[i] = new TCourse(aCourse);
                return true;
          }
    }
    return false;
    // student has already enrolled for the maximum number of courses
    // allowed
}
```

```
bool
TStudent::DropFromCourse(const TCourse& aCourse)
{
    /*
     * Search in the list of courses in _enrolled and find if the student
       has enrolled in this course. If found, delete it and decrement the
       number of courses enrolled in.
     */
    for (int i=0; i < MAX_COURSES_FOR_STUDENT; i++) {
            if (_enrolled[i] != 0) {
                    // Comparison operator call for two TCourse objects
                    if (*_enrolled[i] == aCourse) {
                            delete _enrolled[i]; // It was dynamically allocated
                            _enrolled[i] = 0;
                            _numCourses—;
                            return true;
                    }
            }
    }
    return false;
    // student has not enrolled for this course
}

void
TStudent::Print() const
{
    // Easy, just print the name of the student, status, his/her department
    cout << "Name: " << _name << endl;
    cout << "Address: " << _address << endl;
    cout << "This person is a " << statusLabels[(int)_status]
            << " student in the department of "
            << departmentNames[(int) _department] << endl;
}
```

This implementation is not very complicated and should be quite easy to understand. This is the direct result of using proper abstractions, **TString**, **TCourse**, etc.

Now let us look at the class **TTeacher**.

```
// The enum EDepartment declared in Student.h is also needed here

// Every teacher has an associated rank. This enum lists them
enum ERank { eInstructor, eAsstProfessor, eAssociateProfessor,
                                eResearchScientist, eDean };

// Maximum number of courses a teacher can teach per semester.
const short MAX_COURSES_FOR_TEACHER = 3;
const short MAX_GRADERS = 5;
class TTeacher {
    public:
            TTeacher (const char theName[], long theSSN,
                    const char theBirthDate[], const char theAddress[],
                    ERank theRank,
                    EDepartment theDepartment);
            TTeacher(const TTeacher& other);
```

```
              TTeacher& operator=(const TTeacher& other);
              ~TTeacher();

              void SetName(const char theName[]);
              TString GetName() const;

              void SetAddress(const char theAddress[]);
              TString GetAddress() const;

              void SetDepartment(EDepartment dept);
              EDepartment GetDepartment() const;

              // Change rank when the teacher is promoted
              void SetRank(ERank newRank);
              ERank GetRank() const;

              void ListCoursesTaught() const;
              // Offer this course
              bool OfferCourse(const TCourse& aCourse);
              // Cancel this course offered
              bool DropCourse(const TCourse& theCourse);

              void AssignGrader(const char newGrader[]);
              void DropGrader(const char grader[]);
              void ListGraders() const;

              // These functions probably don't belong here - not every client
              // should have access to this personal data. Better solutions are
              // presented in a later chapter.
              double GetSalary() const;
              bool SetSalary(double theSalary);
              void SetSupervisor(const char theName[]);

              void Print() const;

      private:
              // These implementation details are shown, just for completeness.
              // You do not need them in order to understand the concepts.
              TString           _name;
              TString           _address;
              long              _ssn;
              const TDate       _birthDate;
              ERank             _rank;
              double            _salary;
              EDepartment       _department;
              TString           _supervisor;
              int               _numCourses;// number of courses being taught
              // array of pointers to courses taught. Very similar to what is
              // found in the TStudent class.
              TCourse*          _coursesOffered[MAX_COURSES_FOR_TEACHER];
              // List of graders. This is an array of pointers to grader names.
              TString*          _graders[MAX_GRADERS];
};
```

That looks pretty simple too. Let us implement some member functions.

NOTE   There isn't much interesting information in the implementation code shown below. It is included here just for completeness. If you are quite familiar with C++ implementations (or you are not interested in the implementation details), you can safely skip this code without any loss of information and continuity.

```
// Array of rank names for easy printing. An enum, when printed prints as
// an integer. Just as with department names, we keep an array of string
// that correspond to the names of the departments.

static char *rankNames[] = { "Instructor", "Asst Professor",
                        "Associate Professor", "Research Scientist",
                        "Dean", "Unknown" };

TTeacher::TTeacher (const char theName[], long theSSN,
      const char theBirthDate[], const char theAddress[],
                    ERank theRank,
                    EDepartment theDepartment)
              : _name(theName),
               _address(theAddress),
               _birthDate(theBirthDate),
               _ssn(theSSN),
               _rank(theRank),
               _department(theDepartment),
               _numCourses(0),
               _salary(0.0)
{
   // To start with, the list of courses should be empty
   for(int i=0; i < MAX_COURSES_FOR_TEACHER; i++)
        _coursesOffered[i] = 0;

   // For proper state information, initialize other data members too
   for(int i = 0; i < MAX_GRADERS; i++)
        _graders[i] = 0;
}

void
TTeacher::SetName(const char theName[])
{_name = theName; /* Class TString takes care of the rest */ }

void
TTeacher::SetAddress(const char theAddress[])
{_address = theAddress; /* Class TString takes care of the rest */ }

bool
TTeacher::OfferCourse(const TCourse& aCourse)
{
     if (_numCourses >= MAX_COURSES_FOR_TEACHER)
           return false; // Teacher has already offered too many courses

     /* Walk through the array of pointers (coursesOffered) and find a slot
        which is unused. When found, allocate a new TCourse object and place
        it in the slot. If no free slots are found, it implies that the
        teacher has already offered the maximum number of courses*/
```

```
      for (int i=0; i < MAX_COURSES_FOR_TEACHER; i++) {
          if (_coursesOffered[i] == 0) {
                _coursesOffered[i] = new TCourse(aCourse); // Copy ctor is
                                                           // called
                _numCourses++;
                return true;
          }
      }
      return false;
      // this teacher has already offered too many courses

}

bool
TTeacher::DropCourse(const TCourse& thisCourse)
{
    /* Look for a course with this id number in the list of courses offered
       by this teacher. If found, drop (don't offer it!). If the course is
       not found, then the teacher never offered this course*/

    for (int i=0; i < MAX_COURSES_FOR_TEACHER; i++) {
          if (_coursesOffered[i] != 0) {
                if (*_coursesOffered[i] == thisCourse) {
                      delete _coursesOffered[i];
                      _coursesOffered[i] = 0;
                      _numCourses-;
                      return true;
                }
          }
    }
    return false;
    // teacher has not offered this course
    }

void
TTeacher::Print() const
{
    cout << "Name: " << _name << endl;
    cout << "Address: " << _address << endl;
    cout << "This person is a " << rankNames[ (int) _rank] << " in the" <<
          departmentNames[(int) _department] << " department " << endl;
}
```

We have implemented some member functions. For the sake of this discussion we don't really need all the member functions.

When we look at the interface files for **TStudent** and **TTeacher**, we notice some similarities. Both of them have the methods

SetName and GetName

SetAddress and GetAddress

SetDepartment and GetDepartment

Both classes also have data members for storing the corresponding information (name, address, and department). When we look at the implementation we further notice that the methods have identical code too. But still, these two are independent classes with nothing in common, as per our implementation. Let us see what happens when objects of these classes are created.

```
main()
{
    TStudent Einstein ("Albert Einstein" , 000, "1-1-1879", "Germany/USA",
                                        eFullTime, ePhysics);
    TTeacher Edison("Thomas Edison", 1111, "3-4-1847", "USA",
                                        eResearchScientist, ePhysics);
}
```

When this code is compiled and linked together, we will have two copies of the code for **SetName** and **GetName** (one each for **TStudent** and **TTeacher**), two copies for **SetAddress** and **GetAddress,** and two copies for **SetDepartment** and **GetDepartment.** Definitely, we would not like to duplicate code unnecessarily (see Fig. 5-1 below).

What if we find a bug in the **SetName** code for the **TStudent** class and fix it? Well, we should also change the code in **SetName** of the **TTeacher** class as well because it is doing the same operation. Will we always remember to make the second change? Doesn't it seem like a good idea to have the code in one place? How can we do it and yet have the code accessible from two separate classes? Read on.

There is one more problem. Imagine what we would have to do if we decided to change the way the address of students and teacher are managed. Let us say we would like to make address a separate class with attributes like street address, city, zip code, state, and country. For this change to take place, we need to change the header file for both **TTeacher** and **TStudent.** More than that, we need to completely rewrite the code that

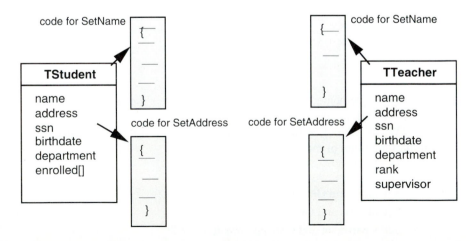

Fig. 5-1

manages the addresses, **SetAddress** and **GetAddress**. This code change has to happen in two different classes.

Any code changes to accommodate new features or to fix bugs are always dangerous and error prone. It is even more so if we have to modify multiple copies of the same code. Definitely, we don't want to get into this nasty code management problem. We somehow want to share the common code between the **TStudent** and **TTeacher** classes. When changes have to be made, we only have to do it once. But sharing methods is not that straight forward because we are dealing with objects that have state. The code in **SetName** (or any other method) is not independent of the state of the object. The methods use the state to provide the correct behavior. This implies that we cannot make these methods free floating procedures as we do in procedural programming.

The idea of code sharing is not something unique to OOP. Every procedure that we write under procedure-oriented programming facilitates code sharing. Every class that we implement facilitates code sharing. Objects are shared by various other schemes. But we need a way of sharing code that is in member functions of two different classes.

One should recognize the fact that both **TTeacher** and **TStudent** need the methods **SetName** and **GetName**, but we don't want to duplicate them in both classes. Furthermore, we would like to reuse the code in **SetName** and **GetName** in any other class(es) that we might implement for this university problem solution in the future.

Inheritance comes to our rescue in such scenarios. In its simplest form, *inheritance defines a relationship among classes wherein one class shares the structure and/or behavior defined in one or more classes.* When a class shares (*inherits*) the structure and behavior of just one class it is called *single inheritance.* And it is *multiple inheritance* when more than one class is involved.

In order for inheritance to be used in this example, we need to identify the behavior that is common to both **TStudent** and **TTeacher** and move that behavior (and the associated data members) into a different class. Recognizing this common behavior is the key to correct inheritance relationships.

Notice that the attributes like name, address, and age are not unique to teachers or students. They are common to all people, and definitely common to everyone in the university. Both teachers and students are persons. They have all the properties of a person and exhibit the behavior of a person. Given that, why can't we treat them as persons first and teachers and students second. All the common methods like **SetName** and **GetName** are methods applicable to any person and hence they belong in a class named, you guessed it, **TPerson**. With this knowledge, we can move the common structure and behavior of a person to the class **TPerson**.

```
class TPerson {
    public:
        TPerson (const char theName[], unsigned long theSSN,
        const char theBirthDate[],
                                        const char theAddress[]);
        // Copy Constructor
        TPerson (const TPerson& source);
        TPerson& operator=(const TPerson& source);
        ~TPerson();

        void SetName(const char theName[]);
        TString GetName() const;
```

```
            void SetAddress(const char theAddress[]);
            TString GetAddress() const;
            TDate GetBirthDate() const;
            unsigned long GetIdentification() const;
            void SetIdentification(unsigned long newId);

            void Print() const;

        private:
            TString _name;
            TString _address;
            unsigned long_ssn;
            TDate _birthDate;
    };
```

Here is the implementation of the member functions:

```
#include <iostream.h>

TPerson::TPerson (const char theName[], unsigned long theSSN, const char
                  theBirthDate[], const char theAddress[])
            : _name(theName), _address(theAddress),
              _birthDate(theBirthDate), _ssn(theSSN)
    { }

void
TPerson::SetName(const char theName[])
    { _name = theName; /* It's that easy. TString does the rest. */ }

void
TPerson::SetAddress(const char theAddress[])
    {_address = theAddress; /* class TString can handle this too. }

void
TPerson::Print() const
{
    cout << "— Printing details of a Person —" << endl;
    cout << "Name: " << _name << endl;
    cout << "Address: " << _address << endl;
    cout << "Birth Date: " << _birthDate << endl;
}

TPerson::~TPerson()
    { /* Nothing to do. Memory management is taken care of by embedded
      object. */ }

TPerson::TPerson(const TPerson& other)
    : _birthDate(other._birthDate), _name(other._name),
      _address(other._address), _ssn(other._ssn)
{ }

TPerson& TPerson::operator=(const TPerson& other)
{
    _birthDate = other._birthDate,
    _name = other._name;
```

```
    _address = other._address;
    _ssn = other._ssn;
}
```

We would like **TStudent** to inherit the structure and behavior of **TPerson**. The class **TPerson** is called the *base class* under C++, superclass in Smalltalk, and parent (or ancestor) class in Eiffel. But they all convey the same meaning. Along the same lines, **TStudent** is called the *derived class* in C++, the subclass in Smalltalk, and heir (or descendant) class under Eiffel. All these terms are used interchangeably in this book. The derived class **TStudent** can also be viewed as a *subtype* of the base type, **TPerson**.

The notation used in class diagrams to show inheritance relationship among classes is shown in Fig. 5-2.

The arrow goes from the derived class to the base class. Also note that the following relationship shown in Fig. 5-3 would be invalid because it creates a cycle (*who comes first?*). Is **TStudent** the base class of **TPerson** or is it the other way around? There is no definite answer to that question and hence it is invalid.

But we are not done yet! The figure shows that we want to share code and data between **TStudent** and **TTeacher**. How do we make this diagram work? How do we make the association between **TStudent** and **TPerson** and also between **TTeacher** and **TPerson**. We need a way to express the fact that students and teachers are persons first. Further, we need to ensure that a **TStudent** (and **TTeacher**) acquires the structure and behavior of **TPerson**. In other words, we have to express the fact that a student **is-a** person (or a kind-of person). This is done by the inheritance relationship. We basically state that students and teachers are subtypes of person. The syntax for doing so under C++ is shown below.

TStudent is a Derived Class of TPerson

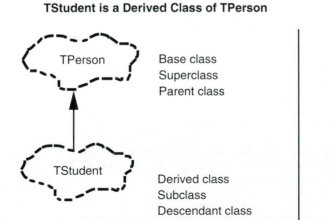

Base class
Superclass
Parent class

Derived class
Subclass
Descendant class

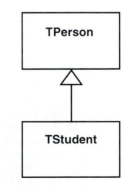

Fig. 5-2

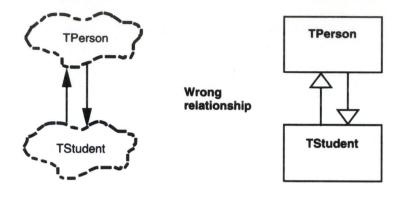

Fig. 5-3

```
// All the enums remain the same

class TStudent : public TPerson {
                // TPerson implements the left hand side part of
                // Figure 5.1 above
    public:
        TStudent(const char theName[],
                unsigned long theSSN,
                const char theBirthDate[],
                const char theAddress[],
                EStudentStatus theStatus,
                EDepartment theDepartment);
        // Copy Constructor
        TStudent(const TStudent& source);
        TStudent& operator= (const TStudent& source);
        ~TStudent();

        // The methods of TPerson are not duplicated here.
        void SetDepartment(EDepartment dept);
        EDepartment GetDepartment() const;

        bool EnrollForCourse(const TCourse& aCourse);
        bool DropFromCourse(const TCourse& theCourse);
        void ListCoursesRegisteredFor() const;

        void Print() const;
        // many other details omitted
    private:
        // same as in the earlier implementation
        // But the data that is already in TPerson is not
        // duplicated here anymore.
        EStudentStatus    _status;
        EDepartment       _department;
        // an array of pointers to courses registered for
        TCourse*          _enrolled[MAX_COURSES_FOR_STUDENT];
        int               _numCourses;// number of courses registered for
};
```

This piece of code deserves some detailed analysis.

The line **class TStudent : public TPerson** states that TStudent inherits from the TPerson class. The keyword public states that TPerson is a public base (as opposed to a private or protected) for the TStudent class. This implies that all public functionality of the TPerson class can be accessed from a TStudent object. Later in this chapter, we discuss the concept of private and protected base classes.

NOTE   C++ also supports the notion of private derivation (using a private base class). This is discussed in Chapter 6. But remember that private derivation is not considered true inheritance. The is-a relationship implies public inheritance.

The effect of this declaration is that TStudent inherits the complete structure and behavior of TPerson. Any method accessible by a client of TPerson is also available to a client of TStudent because of this inheritance relation between TStudent and TPerson. Every TStudent objects also inherits all the data members of the TPerson class. In other words, every TStudent object also contains the data members **name** and **address** that it inherits from the TPerson class. An object of the TStudent class has the following structure (Fig. 5-4).

```
TPerson      aPersonObject("ET", 123456789, "06-24-85", "Outer Space");
TStudent     aStudentObject ("Lassie", 423435063, "09-24-69", "Disney Land",
                                                           eFullTime, eArts);
```

Since every TStudent object inherits the complete behavior of a TPerson object we can write a simple program that exemplifies this feature.

```
main()
{
        TPerson aPersonObject("ET", 123456789, "06-24-75",
          "Outer Space");
        TStudent aStudentObject ("Lassie", 423435063, "09-24-69",
          "Disney Land", eFullTime, eArts);

        TDate personBD;
        TDate studentBD; // local birth date objects
```

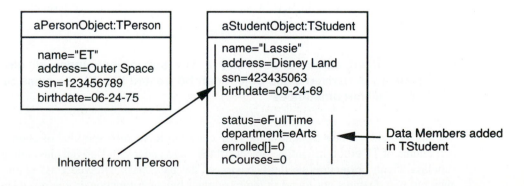

Fig. 5-4

```
        // Get the birth date of the person from aPersonObject
        personBD = aPersonObject.GetBirthDate();
        // Get the birth date of the student from aStudentObject
        studentBD = aStudentObject.GetBirthDate();
        // Next print the birth dates just retrieved
        cout << "Persons Birth Date: " << personBD << endl;
        cout << "Students Birth Date: " << studentBD << endl;
}
```

The output of this program is:

```
            Persons Birth Date: 06-24-75
            Students Birth Date: 09-24-69
```

Even though **TStudent** does not implement the **GetBirthDate** member function, it inherits it from **TPerson**. Hence, every **TStudent** object is capable of responding to the message **GetBirthDate** and produces the correct result. In other words, every **TStudent** objects **is-a** **TPerson** object. This is the reason why inheritance relationship is also called the is-a relationship.

Just for ease of understanding the relationship, one might imagine that there is a **TPerson** object within every **TStudent** object that can be accessed by clients.

MEANING OF THE IS-A RELATIONSHIP

One has to understand the meaning and implications of the inheritance (or the is-a) relationship to use it effectively. The is-a relationship implies *generalization/specialization* between the base class and the derived class. The base class is a general class whose behavior can be specialized in the derived class(es). The base class **TPerson** has the general behavior of any person and it is specialized by the **TStudent** derived class to suit the needs of a student. In realizing this specialization, none of the characteristics of **TPerson** are lost. Specialization in this context means more than one thing. A derived class could add to the functionality already provided by one or more base class method(s) (extension), or, it could re-implement some or all of the methods of the base class to suit the needs of the derived class (refinement).

> ☞ **A TStudent object is definitely a TPerson object under all circumstances. A derived class object can be treated like a base class object under all circumstances.**

The derived class is also a client of the base class but it is a different kind of client. Normal clients of **TPerson** instantiate objects of the class and use it. Derived class clients (or subclass clients) extend/refine the behavior of the base class. Derived class clients can also add new features not found in the base class but such functionality is not visible in the base class interface.

EFFECT OF INHERITANCE RELATIONSHIP

Let us turn to an example and see how the is-a relationship changes design. We would like to write a function PrintMailingLabel, which accepts a TPerson object and prints a correctly formatted mailing label. We could write this functions as

```
bool PrintMailingLabel (const TPerson& aPerson)
                  // Expects a reference to a TPerson object
{
        TString = aPerson.GetName();
        TString = aPerson.GetAddress();

        // code to print the mailing label
}
```

If we want to print a mailing label for a TStudent object, we would still like to use the same function above. We can write

```
TStudent aStudentObject ("Lassie", 423435063, "09-24-69", "Disney Land",
                                             eFullTime, eArts);
PrintMailingLabel(aStudentObject);
```

Even though the PrintMailingLabel function expects a TPerson object, we can pass an object of one of the derived classes of TPerson because any derived class of TPerson *is-a* TPerson. This is why we are able to pass a TStudent object where a TPerson object is required. This is the concept behind the *Polymorphic Substitution Principle* discussed below.

Direct and Indirect Base Classes

TPerson is the base class and TStudent is a derived class of TPerson. For TStudent, TPerson is a *direct base* class. Eiffel calls TStudent a *proper descendant* of TPerson. If we were to derive a class, say TGraduateStudent from the class TStudent as in Fig. 5-5

```
class TGraduateStudent : public TStudent { /* */ };
```

then TPerson is the *indirect base* of TGraduateStudent whereas TStudent is a direct base of TGraduateStudent. This terminology will be useful when we discuss constructors for base classes below.

POLYMORPHIC SUBSTITUTION PRINCIPLE

According to the Polymorphic Substitution Principle (PSP), Class D is a subtype of Class B if for each object Dderived of Class D there is an object Bbase of class B such that for any function F defined in terms of Class B, the behavior of function F is unchanged when the object Dderived is substituted in place of an object of Bbase.

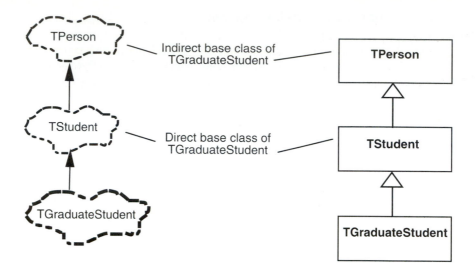

Fig. 5-5

Here (Fig. 5-6) class **B** is the base class and class **D** is the derived class. **D**derived is an object of the derived class **D**.

Even though the statement above seems complex, the principle itself is quite simple. Revisiting the example of PrintMailingLabel above, this function is defined in terms of the class TPerson. The function PrintMailingLabel assumes that any object that is passed in as the actual argument, returns the name and address through the functions Get-Name and GetAddress. When we call this function with the object aStudentObject, it

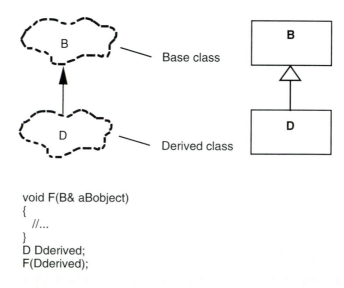

```
void F(B& aBobject)
{
    //...
}
D Dderived;
F(Dderived);
```

Fig. 5-6

still expects GetName and GetAddress to provide the same functionality. The behavior of PrintMailingLabel is unchanged when called with a TStudent object because every TStudent object is capable of behaving like a TPerson object. In fact, every TStudent object has everything that a TPerson object would contain. Just for the sake of understanding the polymorphic substitution principle, one can imagine that every TStudent object contains a TPerson object inside of it. When PrintMailingLabel looks at the actual argument (a TStudent) it sees a TPerson object that has been inherited by TStudent. Hence, the behavior of PrintMailingLabel is unchanged. Note that the correctness of the syntax is enforced by the compiler. The keyword in this discussion is *behavior*. The function PrintMailingLabel expects the behavior of GetName and GetAddress to be the same irrespective of where these methods come from. Any derived class that implements GetName and SetName should conform to the external published behavior of these methods as defined in TPerson. The internal implementation of the methods may be different but GetName should still return the name and GetAddress should provide the address.

In the previous example it was easy to enforce the polymorphic substitution principle because the derived class's behavior was no different from the base class's behavior for GetName and GetAddress. The methods GetName and GetAddress were not implemented in TStudent and hence the behavior of TStudent as seen by PrintMailingLabel was no different from that of a TPerson. Very soon we will see many examples where the derived class redefines the functions that it inherits from a base class and still conforms to the polymorphic substitution principle.

SMALLTALK

EIFFEL

C++

The polymorphic substitution principle is a common property of all OOP languages. It is not unique to C++. Without support for polymorphic substitution principle inheritance would be useless. However, there are some side effects in C++ that we shall see very soon.

Since every derived class object is-a base class object also, the following code is correct and is used quite often.

```
main()
{
        // Create a TStudent object
        TStudent aStudent("Lassie", 423435063, "09-24-69", "Disney Land",
                                                eFullTime, eArts);
        // Create a reference to a TPerson and initialize it with a TStudent
        TPerson& rp = aStudent;


        // Create a TStudent object on the heap and store its address in pp
        TPerson *pp = new TStudent ("Mickey", 423995063, "07-22-65",
          "Disney Land", eFullTime. eArts);
        TPerson aPerson("Phantom", 123555032, "1-1-1907", "Fantasy World");
        // Try to assign the student object to the person object
        aPerson = aStudent;
}
```

All this might look strange but a picture (Fig. 5-7) and a few sentences will clarify everything.

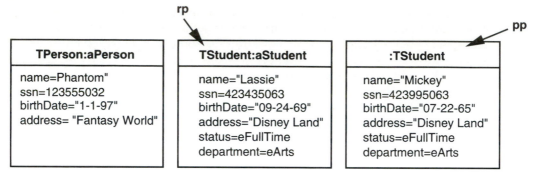

Fig. 5-7

The reference **rp** is associated with the **TPerson** part of the **TStudent** object—**aStudent**. Similarly, the pointer **pp** points to the **TPerson** part of the dynamically created **TStudent** object. All these initializations and assignment are legal. A base class pointer (reference) can always point (refer) to any derived class object. As we will see later, this is the basic requirement for polymorphism.

It is interesting to see the consequence of the assignment

```
aPerson = aStudent
```

Recall that **aStudent** object has its own data members in addition to those inherited from class **TPerson**. As a result, a **TPerson** object is definitely not big enough to hold all the data members contained in a **TStudent** object. But since a **TStudent** object is a **TPerson** object, the assignment should be legal—and it is. The effect of doing so is shown in Fig. 5-8:

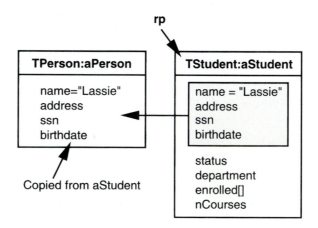

Effect of aPerson = aStudent;

Fig. 5-8

C++   The TPerson part of aStudent is copied into the aPerson object. The logical effect is as though the top portion of the aStudent object was sliced off and placed into the aPerson object. This is called *slicing*. This behavior is very rarely useful. Programmers have to be careful not to be bitten by the effect of slicing. Note that nothing happens to the aStudent object—it is still intact. For example

```
void g(TPerson thePerson)
{
    // Do something with the thePerson argument
}

main()
{
    // Create a student object with name Lassie (the dog). Just give it a
    // dummy department name and id.
    TStudent aStudent("Lassie", 423435063, "09-24-69", "Disney Land",
                                    eFullTime, eArts);

    g (aStudent);
}
```

The function g() accepts the TPerson argument by value. When a TStudent object is passed, it is syntactically correct because of the is-a relationship. But because it is *pass by value*, the TPerson part of aStudent should be copied into the argument thePerson. Here again, slicing happens; only the TPerson part of the aStudent object is seen by the function g(). Within g() there is no trace of the fact that a TStudent object was passed. This is highly undesirable when polymorphism is expected to work correctly, as seen later in this chapter.

        When argument passing is done by reference (as in PrintMailingLabel) or by pointer, there is no slicing involved. The original object is not copied (or sliced) but the called function can only access the TPerson part of the actual argument. Thus PrintMailingLabel can only access the public methods of TPerson because the argument thePerson is of type TPerson.

Initializing the Base Class Object

Every derived class should initialize its base class(es) when the derived class constructor is invoked. And this is done in the initialization phase of the constructor as shown below.

```
TStudent::TStudent(const char theName[], long theSSN,
                const char theBirthDate[], const char theAddress[],
                EStudentStatus theStatus,
                EDepartment theDepartment)
                // Initialize the base class object first
            : TPerson(theName, theSSN, theBirthDate, theAddress),
            _status(theStatus),
            _department(theDepartment),
            _numCourses(0)
{
    // Now perform the initialization for the student part only
```

```
                                // the list of courses would be empty
            for(int i=0; i < MAX_COURSES_FOR_STUDENT; i++)
                _enrolled[i] = 0;
}


// The Copy Constructor
TStudent::TStudent(const TStudent& copy)
    : TPerson(copy), // call base class copy constructor
    _status(copy._status),
    _department(copy._department),
    _numCourses (copy._numCourses)
{
    // Copy the courses correctly
            for(int i=0; i < MAX_COURSES_FOR_STUDENT; i++) {
            if (copy._enrolled[i] != 0)
            this->_enrolled[i] = new TCourse(*copy._enrolled[i]);
    }


}


// The Assignment Operator
TStudent& TStudent::operator=(const TStudent& other)
{
    if (this == &other) return *this;
    // Call the base class assignment operator
    TPerson::operator=(other);

    this->_status = other._status;
    this->_department = other._department;
    this->_numCourses = other._numCourses;

    // Copy the courses correctly

    for(int i=0; i < MAX_COURSES_FOR_STUDENT; i++) {
            if (this->_enrolled[i] != 0 && other._enrolled[i] == 0) {
                    // Get rid of the TCourse object
                    delete _enrolled[i];
            }
            else if (this->_enrolled[i] == 0 && other._enrolled[i] != 0) {
                    this->_enrolled[i] = new TCourse(*(other._enrolled[i]));
            }
            else if (this->_enrolled[i] != 0 && other._enrolled[i] != 0) {
                    *(this->_enrolled[i]) = *(other._enrolled[i]);
            }

    }

    return *this;
}

TStudent::~TStudent()
{
    for(int i=0; i < MAX_COURSES_FOR_STUDENT; i++) {
            if (this->_enrolled[i] != 0) {
                    delete _enrolled[i];
            }
```

```
        }
}

void
TStudent::Print() const
{
    cout << "Name: " << TPerson::GetName() << endl;
    cout << "Address: " << TPerson::GetAddress() << endl;
    cout << "This person is a " << statusLabels[(int)_status]
         << " student in the department of "
         << departmentNames[(int) _department] << endl;
}
```

Some important C++ features:
  The code

```
TStudent::TStudent(const char theName[],
                   long theSSN,
                   const char theBirthDate[],
                   const char theAddress[],
                   EStudentStatus theStatus,
                   EDepartment theDepartment)
                   // Initialize the base class object first
        : TPerson(theName, theSSN, theBirthDate, theAddress)
```

is for the constructor of the TStudent class. But before a TStudent object can come into existence, its TPerson part must be created and initialized. To accomplish that we need to call the constructor of the base class TPerson. The constructor of the base class initializes the base class part of the TStudent object. This is done during the initialization phase of the constructor as shown above. We directly use the name of the base class and pass the correct arguments to the constructor. This call actually looks identical to an object declaration. Once this initialization of the base class part is done, we can proceed with the derived class constructor. When a call to the base class constructor is made, the compiler searches for a matching constructor (based on the arguments) and if there is no such constructor, it would be a compile time error. If the call to the base class constructor is omitted from the code above, the compiler tries to insert a call to the base class (TPerson here) default constructor. But in our case, TPerson does not provide a default constructor and again a compile time error is generated.

NOTE This style of using the initialization phase to call the base class constructor is valid only with constructors (including copy constructor). Ordinary member functions cannot call the base class methods using this syntax.

C++ **Always remember to invoke a _direct_ base class constructor with the correct arguments as part of every derived class constructor.**

Note that a class can only invoke the constructor(s) of its direct base class(es). A class cannot invoke the constructor of an indirect base class. This restriction is relaxed only with virtual base classes, which will be discussed later.

Remember that the behavior and structure of the base class is inherited by the derived class. There is one exception to this rule. The constructor(s) of the base class are never inherited. A derived class must provide its own constructor(s). As in any class, when a class does not provide any constructors, a default constructor is generated for that class. This generated default constructor calls the base classes' default constructor (if one is available). Similarly, a derived class does not inherit the base class destructor.

Also note that the derived class constructor accepts all the arguments needed for its own use and also those needed for the base class. In the example above, theName, theSSN, theBirthDate, and theAddress are all arguments required for the base class but are passed to the derived class constructor. This implies that the derived class constructor is responsible for taking care of the needs of the base class. This is a mutual contract between the base class and derived class—the base class supplies its behavior and structure to the derived class and the derived class takes care of initializing the base class object correctly.

EIFFEL Here, the method make is used for object creation and initialization. Again, make is not inherited by a derived class. A derived class provides its own make or it gets the default make provided by the language.

Continuing with the TStudent example, let us analyze the copy constructor of TStudent. When a TStudent object needs to be copied, its TPerson part must also be copied. Copying the TPerson part can only be done by the TPerson class copy constructor. Hence the code

```
TStudent::TStudent(const TStudent& copy)
          : TPerson(copy)
```

Before copying its data members, the TStudent copy constructor calls the TPerson copy constructor. Since TPerson is the base class of TStudent, TPerson copy constructor can easily accept the argument other of type TStudent.

C++ **Always remember to call the base class copy constructor from the derived class copy constructor.**

Next in line is the assignment operator. The assignment operator goes through the usual steps. But before performing assignments of its own data, it calls the base class assignment operator. Note that the syntax is that of a normal member function call and not initialization. If we forget to make this call to the base class assignment operator, the name, address, and all other data members of the base class would still hold their old values and the TStudent data members nCourses, status, etc. would be updated. This leads to inconsistent state and all the related problems.

C++ **Always remember to call the base class assignment operator from within the derived class assignment operator. Otherwise your objects will have inconsistent state.**

Last but not the least, is the destructor. The TStudent destructor takes care of garbage collection for its data members. Unlike the copy constructor and assignment operator, it does not make an explicit call to the base class destructor (it should not). The compiler generates code to automatically call the base class destructor. The declaration of the destructor for **TPerson** is not really correct. We shall fix this as soon as we have some more knowledge about inheritance.

EXTENDING CLASS HIERARCHIES WITH INHERITANCE

With this basic knowledge of inheritance, we are ready to redesign the **TTeacher** class. Now **TTeacher** will descend from **TPerson** as shown in Fig. 5-9.

```
// Other details are as before

class TTeacher : public TPerson {
    public:
        TTeacher (const char theName[], long theSSN,
                    const char theBirthDate[], const char theAddress[],
                    ERank theRank, EDepartment theDepartment);
        TTeacher(const TTeacher& other);
        TTeacher& operator=(const TTeacher& other);
        ~TTeacher();

        void SetDepartment(EDepartment dept);
        EDepartment GetDepartment() const;

        // Change rank when the teacher is promoted
        void SetRank(ERank newRank);
        ERank GetRank() const;

        void ListCoursesTaught() const;
        // Offer this course
        bool OfferCourse(const TCourse& aCourse);
        // Cancel this course offered by name
        bool DropCourse(const TCourse& theCourse);

        void AssignGrader(const char newGrader[]);
        void DropGrader(const char grader[]);
        void ListGraders() const;

        /* These functions probably don't belong here - not every client
           should have access to this personal data. Better solutions are
           presented in a later chapter.*/
```

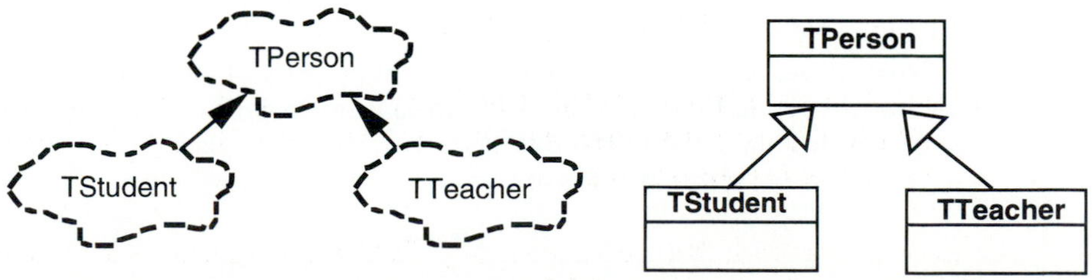

Fig. 5-9

```
        double GetSalary() const;
        bool SetSalary(double theSalary);
        void SetSupervisor(const char theName[]);

        void Print() const;

    private:
        // These implementation details are shown, just for completeness.
        // You do not need them in order to understand the concepts.
        ERank              _rank;
        double             _salary;
        EDepartment        _department;
        TString            _supervisor;
        int                _numCourses;// number of courses being
                                       taught
        // array of pointers to courses taught. Very similar to what is
        // found in the TStudent class.
        TCourse*           _coursesOffered[MAX_COURSES_FOR_TEACHER];
        // List of graders. This is an array of pointers to grader names.
        TString*           _graders[MAX_GRADERS];
};
```

And here is the implementation of the constructor.

```
TTeacher::TTeacher (const char theName[], long theSSN,
     const char theBirthDate[],
                const char theAddress[], ERank theRank,
     EDepartment theDepartment)
           : TPerson(theName, theSSN, theBirthDate, theAddress),
             _rank(theRank)
             _department(theDepartment),
             _salary (0.0),// not known yet
             _numCourses(0)
{
    // To start with, the list of courses should be empty
    for(int i=0; i < MAX_COURSES_FOR_TEACHER; i++)
         _coursesOffered[i] = 0;

    // To keep the state consistent, initialize other data members too
    for(int i = 0; i < MAX_GRADERS; i++)
         _graders[i] = 0;
}
```

Implementation of other member functions is trivial and is left as an exercise to the reader.

Now we are ready to explore one important property of inheritance. We have made **TTeacher** a new derived class of **TPerson** and implemented it. Can we now write a piece of code like this:

```
void f()
{
    // Create a local teacher object for the scientist, Albert Einstein
    // giving some dummy department, birth date, and id.
    TTeacherEinstein("Albert Einstein", 1111, "1-1-1879", "USA",
    eResearchScientist, ePhysics);
    PrintMailingLabel (Einstein);
}
```

Will the call to PrintMailingLabel work correctly? Or do we have to re-write PrintMailingLabel to accommodate the TTeacher class.

This code will work without any change to PrintMailingLabel. All we have to do is compile the file that contains the new TTeacher code and link it with the code of PrintMailingLabel. Everything will work like magic.

The code in PrintMailingLabel expects a TPerson argument and TTeacher is-a TPerson by virtue of public inheritance. Every TTeacher is capable of supporting all operations that a TPerson supports. Hence, no change to PrintMailingLabel is required because of PSP. In reality, PrintMailingLabel is not even aware of the fact that a TTeacher object has been passed as the actual argument. PrintMailingLabel always sees a TPerson argument.

SOME BASIC ADVANTAGES OF INHERITANCE

One might wonder why this feature is considered so important. Inheritance allows designers and programmers to extend and enhance software without any recompilation cost. All that is required is relinking. Imagine for a moment that we create a new class TResearchScholar in the university system. Without any doubt, this new class will also descend from TPerson. Should we have to rewrite PrintMailingLabel to accommodate this new class? Definitely not. As long as this new class descends from TPerson, PrintMailingLabel will still work with the new class. This allows us to add new classes to existing systems without modifying the existing code. The object code of the new code must be *linked* with the existing code. In many implementations, new classes can be added to running programs without stopping them (this requires some help from the operating system for dynamic linking and loading). This allows us to add new capabilities to systems that were not part of the original software without stopping them. Many programmers may not appreciate the benefit of this concept because they usually stop a program at will and don't see many problems with that. But in many critical applications, programmers don't have the luxury of stopping the program to upgrade the software. A satellite, for example, once launched cannot be stopped for a software upgrade. And many real time systems that monitor and control critical systems (such as patient monitoring) cannot be stopped. In all such cases inheritance allows us to add new features to running programs.

Another advantage is somewhat hidden. This has to do with implementation independence. When PrintMailingLabel was written to accept a TPerson argument, it is only dependent on the interface of TPerson. Thus, PrintMailingLabel would not be affected by any new derived classes of TPerson. Adding any number of derived classes to TPerson does not cause any problems for PrintMailingLabel. When we design and program with large class hierarchies, a client of the hierarchy should not have to worry about all classes at all levels.[1] Understanding the top level class (the root, for example, TPerson) gives the clients enough information to use the hierarchy effectively. At the same time, new classes can be added to the hierarchy without affecting any clients. This benefit is not that easy to understand (and much harder to realize), but further along in this chapter (and elsewhere) we will design and discuss such hierarchies to drive home this concept.

The aforementioned benefits are in addition to the code reuse benefit that we have already discussed.

NOTE   These are not the only benefits of inheritance. In fact, the major benefit of inheritance results from dynamic binding and polymorphism which are discussed in detail in the next section.

DYNAMIC BINDING, VIRTUAL FUNCTIONS, AND POLYMORPHISM

So far in our discussions, we have conveniently ignored the function Print. It is time to see what happens when we try to invoke Print. Here is an example:

```
main()
{
    TPerson foo("Alladdin", 618340063, "09-24-90", "Disney Land");
    TTeacher Einstein("Albert Einstein", 1111, "1-1-1879", "USA",
                        eResearchScientist, ePhysics);
    TStudent aStudent("Lassie", 423435063, "09-24-69", "Disney Land",
                        eFullTime, eArts);

    foo.Print(); // Print information about a TPerson
    cout << endl;
    Einstein.Print(); // Print information about the Einstein object
    cout << endl;
    aStudent.Print();
}
```

This produces the output

```
        — Printing details of a Person —
        Name: Alladdin
        Address: Disney Land
        Birth Date: 09-24-90

        Name: Albert Einstein
        Address: USA
        This person is a Research Scientist in the Physics department

        Name: Lassie
        Address: Disney Land
        This person is a Full Time student in the department of Arts
```

[1]A class hierarchy is a set of classes connected through inheritance and possibly other relationships. The TPerson-TStudent-TTeacher is a simple class hierarchy.

That seems to be correct. For every object, the printed information matches what we put in when the objects were created.

Let us create a new function—DisplayOutput(). The purpose of this function is to print the information about any **TPerson** in an appropriate window with the correct decorations (like borders and shadows etc.).

```
void DisplayOutput(const TPerson& aPerson)
{
    // Code to create a window conforming to the User Interface
    //...
    aPerson.Print();
}

main()
{
    TTeacherEinstein("Albert Einstein", 1111, "1-1-1879", "USA",
                          eResearch Scientist, ePhysics);
    TStudent aStudent("Lassie", 423435063, "09-24-69", "Disney Land",
                          eFullTime, eArts);
    TPerson foo("Alladdin", 618340063, "09-24-90", "Disney Land");

    cout << "Printing a Person object\n";
    DisplayOutput( foo);
    cout << "Printing a Student object\n";
    DisplayOutput (aStudent);
    cout << "Printing a Teacher object\n";
    DisplayOutput ( Einstein);
}
```

The output is

```
                    Printing a Person object
                    — Printing details of a Person —
                    Name: Aladdin
                    Address: Disney Land
                    Birth Date: 09-24-90

                    Printing a Student object
                    — Printing details of a Person —
                    Name: Lassie
                    Address: Disney Land
                    Birth Date: 09-24-69

                    Printing a Teacher object
                    — Printing details of a Person —
                    Name: Albert Einstein
                    Address: USA
                    Birth Date: 1-1-1879
```

This doesn't seem to be correct. When we passed the **TPerson** object to **DisplayOutput**, everything looks correct. The object is a **TPerson** object and the information printed is also for a **TPerson**.

Next we passed a **TStudent** object to **DisplayOutput**, but somehow **DisplayOutput** still thinks that the argument is just a **TPerson**. Similarly, when a **TTeacher** object is passed to **DisplayOutput**, the behavior is no different. **DisplayOutput** always thinks that it is getting a **TPerson** object. When a member function like **Print()** is invoked, we expect to get the correct data printed from the object. Therefore, when **DisplayOutput()** invokes **Print()** on a **TStudent** object, we expect to see the appropriate details of **TStudent** being printed, not just **TPerson**. In other words, an object should respond to a member function call correctly, producing the right output. Definitely, there is something going wrong.

A bit of analysis reveals that the behavior of **DisplayOutput** is correct but our understanding of the situation is wrong. Function **DisplayOutput** looks at the incoming object as a **TPerson** object. We could pass a **TStudent** and a **TTeacher** object because they are derived classes of **TPerson**. Within **DisplayOutput** the **Print** function is called with

```
aPerson.Print();
```

When this call is made, the compiler looks at the type of **aPerson**—which is **TPerson** as per the declaration

```
void DisplayOutput(const TPerson& aPerson);
```

Based on this knowledge, the compiler decides to call **TPerson::Print**. All this is done at compile time. In other words, the call to **Print** in **DisplayOutput** is bound to the member function **TPerson::Print** correctly. This is the normal behavior and we have seen this in all our examples. The C++ compiler's decision to call a particular function is made at compile time based on the *static* type of the reference, **aPerson**, used in the call. The declared type of **aPerson** is **TPerson** and hence the compiler *binds* the call to the method **TPerson::Print**. The behavior would be the same even if a pointer is used. For example

```
void DisplayOutput(const TPerson* personPtr)
{
    // Code to create a window conforming to the User Interface
    //...
    personPtr->Print();
}

main()
{
    TTeacherEinstein("Albert Einstein", 1111, "1-1-1879", "USA",
                        eResearch Scientist, ePhysics);
    TStudent aStudent("Lassie", 423435063, "09-24-69", "Disney Land",
                                    eFullTime, eArts);
    TPerson foo("Alladdin", 618340063, "09-24-90", "Disney Land");

    cout << "Printing a Person object\n";
    DisplayOutput( &foo );
    cout << "Printing a Student object\n";
    DisplayOutput( &aStudent );
    cout << "Printing a Teacher object\n";
```

```
        DisplayOutput( &Einstein );
}
```

will produce the same output. In this case, the compiler looks at the type of the pointer personPtr (which is TPerson) and decides to call TPerson::Print. Again, this decision is made when the code is compiled. This is actually called *static binding*. In other words, the binding (or the association) of a function name (Print in this case) to the appropriate method in a class is done by a static analysis of the code at compile time based on the static type (i.e., the declared type) of the object (reference or pointer) used in the call.[2] In the cases above, the reference type was TPerson (for aPerson) and the pointer type was also TPerson (for personPtr). This knowledge is available to the compiler during the compilation process. Unless otherwise specified, all calls to functions (member function or any other function) are *statically bound*.[3] This is true of all ***statically typed*** languages. The type information available at compile time (based on the declarations) is used in parsing expressions and function calls.

But in the examples above, static binding is not of much use to us. We would like to see the call to Print within DisplayOutput bound to the correct Print method based on the object passed in. When a TStudent is passed to DisplayOutput, the call to Print should end up calling TStudent::Print. On the same lines, for a TTeacher object, the call to Print must be bound to TTeacher::Print. But if TTeacher or TStudent does not implement the Print function, the call to Print should default to TPerson::Print.

This preceding paragraph implies that we don't like static binding for Print. The call should be decided based upon the true type of the object used in the call. This means that ***dynamic binding*** should be used for the function Print. Dynamic binding is also called *late binding*.

Meaning of Dynamic Binding

When a call to a member function is made using a pointer (or reference) to a base class, the actual member function invoked should be the one implemented in the object that the pointer or reference points (refers) to at the time of the call. The notion here is that the *dynamic form* of the object determines which method is called. One can view the Print method in TPerson, TStudent, and TTeacher as different versions of the same method. Dynamic binding picks the correct version of the method based on the real, dynamic type of the object. In the example above, within DisplayOutput the reference aPerson refers to a TStudent object when the call

```
        DisplayOutput (aStudent);
```

is made from main(). Within DisplayOutput the statement

```
        aPerson.Print();
```

---

[2]Compile time binding (static binding) is also called *early binding*.

[3]Languages like C, Pascal and Fortran all use static binding and static typing. And, by default, C++ also uses static binding.

should invoke TStudent::Print because at the time of this call, aPerson represents a TStudent object. To make this happen, the run-time implementation of the compiler needs to look at the object being used in the call and not just the static type of the reference (or pointer). Dynamic binding means that the binding of a function is done dynamically (i.e., when the program is running), rather than at compile time. In all the cases above, the static type of aPerson is still TPerson but aPerson may refer to any descendant of TPerson dynamically.

The idea here is that the object should respond to the message rather than the compiler making the decision to pick a method based on the static type information. When a *message* is sent to an object, the exact *method* executed depends on the object receiving the message. Even though the static type of the receiver of the message is TPerson, the real object that receives the message could be an object of TPerson or any of its derived classes. Hence the message Print is applicable to the TPerson class family (i.e., TPerson objects and also objects of any of its derived classes). It is guaranteed that any descendant of TPerson will respond to the message Print.

Support for Dynamic Binding—Virtual Functions

Now it is time to ask how C++ makes this dynamic binding possible. Dynamic binding is a concept applicable to an individual member function. Any member function that needs dynamic binding should be declared as a ***virtual function*** in the class declaration. For example, rewriting the TPerson class declaration, we would make Print a virtual function.

```
// TPerson class with Print() dynamically bound
class TPerson {
    public:
        TPerson (const char theName[], long theSSN,
        const char theBirthDate[], const char theAddress[]);
        // Rest of the details are as before, (not shown explicitly)
        // Print the essential public information.
        // Do not show unnecessary details.
        // Derived classes may override if necessary.
        virtual void Print() const;
    private:
        // same as before
};
```

The reserved word virtual is applied to any member function that needs dynamic binding. Only those functions prefixed with the virtual keyword are subject to dynamic binding; others (like GetName and SetName) are not dynamically bound. They are still statically bound. Once a member function is declared virtual in a class, it (the member function) retains its dynamic binding property in all the descendant classes. For example, Print would remain a virtual function in TStudent, TTeacher, and also in TGraduateStudent (which will be a descendant of TStudent). Moreover, any new classes that derive from TPerson in the future would also see Print as a virtual function. The virtual keyword is allowed only in the declaration and not in the definition of a member function. In fact, we did not change the implementation for TPerson or TStudent. Only the declaration of the member function Print has been changed.

STYLE   The **virtual** keyword is required only in the base class. The derived classes need not explicitly declare that a member function is virtual. In other words, an inherited virtual function remains virtual in all derived class(es). A derived class cannot turn an inherited virtual function into a non-virtual function either. Using the virtual qualifier improves the readability of the code, especially when someone is reading through the header file of a derived class. Hence, it is a good practice to explicitly use the virtual qualifier for all inherited virtual functions.

Here is the same example, now with virtual functions in place.

```
void DisplayOutput(const TPerson& aPerson)
{
    // Code to create a window conforming to the User Interface
    //...
    aPerson.Print();
}

main()
{
    TTeacher Einstein("Albert Einstein", 1111, "1-1-1879", "USA",
                            eResearchScientist, ePhysics);
    TStudent aStudent("Lassie", 423435063, "09-24-69", "Disney Land",
                            eFullTime, eArts);
    TPerson foo("Alladdin", 618340063, "09-24-90", "Disney Land");

    cout << "Printing a Person object\n";
    DisplayOutput( foo); // Pass the foo object to DisplayOutput and see
                         // if it works!
    cout << "Printing a Student object\n";
    DisplayOutput (aStudent); // Repeat the step with aStudent object
    cout << "Printing a Teacher object\n";
    DisplayOutput ( Einstein);
}
```

This produces the output

```
Printing a Person object
- Printing details of a Person -
Name: Aladdin
Address: Disney Land
Birth Date: 09-24-90

Printing a Student object
Name: Lassie
Address: Disney Land
This person is a Full Time student in the department of Arts

Printing a Teacher object
Name: Albert Einstein
Address: USA
This person is a Research Scientist in the Physics department
```

This is the expected behavior and it is possible only through dynamic binding.

NOTE   In C++, unless a member function is explicitly declared to be virtual, it remains a normal, non-virtual function. This is quite different from Smalltalk and Eiffel as described below. Making a member function virtual (or not) is a design decision. Also remember that only member functions of a class can be declared virtual.

EIFFEL   The Eiffel model is quite different with respect to dynamic binding. A derived class has to explicitly redefine an inherited function using the **redefine** keyword. Without the **redefine** keyword, declaration of the same function in a base class and also in the derived class is a compile-time error. The **redefine** keyword clearly states the intention of the derived class to *override* the inherited function. And all redefined functions are subject to dynamic binding. It is evident from this model that all methods redefined in the derived class are always dynamically bound. There is no other choice for inherited methods. This model is different from C++ because under C++, a derived class could implement its own version of an inherited non-virtual function. Implications of doing so are discussed below. In Eiffel a parent class can declare an operation to be **frozen**, making it non-overrideable.

SMALLTALK   The scheme under Smalltalk is quite similar to that of Eiffel. If a subclass adds a method with the same signature as the superclass, then the method in the subclass overrides the method of the superclass. But Smalltalk differs from C++ and Eiffel in the way the search for a method is performed in an object, as we will see soon.

EFFECT OF INHERITANCE ON DATA ENCAPSULATION

Inheritance is a very powerful mechanism that enables code sharing and also interface consistency, as we shall see soon. But one aspect of object-orientation, data encapsulation, is affected by inheritance. The interaction between inheritance and encapsulation is different in each language.

C++   Inheritance does not have any adverse effect on data encapsulation. Any private member (data or function) of a base class cannot be accessed by member functions of the derived class. Anything declared private in a base class is owned by the base class and only member functions (and also **friends**) of the class have exclusive access (and modification rights) to such members. Further, a derived class is free to add any member (data or function) even with the same name as the one in the base class without any conflict with the member in the base class.[4] Sharing between an object of the base class and its derived class is possible through **protected** members. Unless the base class specifies a member function as **virtual**, overriding and dynamic binding do not happen.

EIFFEL   Eiffel follows a dual approach with respect to encapsulation. Normal clients (those who *instantiate* objects), cannot access any encapsulated data. We have already discussed this elsewhere. However, a derived class is a different (privileged) kind of client. A derived class has access to the data members of the base class. A derived class is free to add

---

[4]As discussed later this may cause some problems depending on the accessability of the member.

THE COST OF DYNAMIC BINDING

A careful reader might already be wondering about the extra cost associated with using dynamically bound functions (virtual functions under C++). When we invoke a statically bound function, there is no extra overhead at run time to determine the correct function to invoke. The exact function to be invoked is clearly known at compile time. But what happens when a dynamically bound function needs to be invoked? How does the run time system determine the right function and what is the associated cost?

Under C++ and Eiffel, there is a fixed cost no matter which dynamically bound function is called. Both C++ and Eiffel keep a class specific table of methods and use this table to find the right function. It is important to remember that finding the right function does not involve any kind of searching through lists or tables. It is a one shot, direct look-up process. When a call to a dynamically bound function is made, the table that holds the address of all methods is located by using the object that receives the message. This usually needs only a couple of assembly language instructions. Next, the address of the correct function is picked up from this table (using an offset computed at compile time). Finally, the call to the function is made using the address just found. All these should require a few assembly language instructions. This cost of method lookup is constant no matter how complex the class (or class hierarchy). In other words, there is not a separate lookup for each level of derivation. There is a single lookup for all the levels in the class hierarchy (details of the C++ scheme is discussed later in this chapter).

Definitely, there is some extra cost per call for the dynamically bound functions. But in most situations, this cost is not too prohibitive as to avoid such functions altogether. In fact, there is no way to avoid them in Eiffel. But this should not (mis)lead one to believe that all functions in a class should be made virtual without any reservation. In some situations, we may like to avoid virtual functions for purely cost related reasons. But in most other situations, where we avoid virtual functions, it is because it does not make any logical sense to allow derived classes to override a particular function. This will be discussed very soon.

With respect to Smalltalk, the cost of dynamic binding is somewhat fuzzy. In the Smalltalk model, the search for a matching function is done at run time, traversing up in the hierarchy from the point of call. The search continues till a matching method is found or the top level class **Object**, which is the superclass (or root) for all classes in the system, is reached. If no method is found even after searching in the root class, the method **doesNotUnderStand** (implemented in the class **Object**) is invoked with the offending message as the argument. It is clear from this model that the cost of dynamic binding in Smalltalk is not fixed. It depends upon the complexity of the class tree and on the method invoked. It is definitely more expensive than C++ or Eiffel. It should be mentioned that modern Smalltalk systems don't employ this simple search-up-the-class-hierarchy principle anymore. They use elaborate caching techniques to minimize the cost of dynamic binding.

its own data members and functions, as in C++. But a derived class cannot add a new function with the same name as the one in the ancestor, unless it is a redefinition, as explained above. This form of inheritance is sometimes referred to as *Open Inheritance*. In this model, inheritance is a contract between a subclass and a superclass to fulfill the obligations of the superclass. To fulfill its part of the contract, the subclass is given access to the variables of the superclass. Eiffel also has the concept of a *selective export* whereby a class grants access to its implementation to another class(es). This is very similar to the friend function mechanism of C++ (discussed in Chapter 7). This means that an Eiffel class cannot encapsulate (hide) data or functions from its derived classes!

SMALLTALK   Here, a subclass object can access all the data members of the superclass as though they were its own. As in C++, a subclass is free to add its own variables (data members) but unlike C++ they cannot have the same name as those declared in the superclass. This restriction avoids ambiguities while accessing members. Note that a subclass can always override a method of the superclass.

From the preceding paragraphs, it is quite clear that C++ has the least restrictive environment for inheritance and also bullet proof data encapsulation. Both Eiffel and Smalltalk relax the rules of data encapsulation under inheritance.

THE MEANING OF POLYMORPHISM

One of the major benefits of dynamic binding is *polymorphism*. It is time we understood what polymorphism is all about. We revisit the DisplayOutput function.

```
void DisplayOutput(const TPerson& aPerson)
{
        // Code to create a window conforming to the User Interface
        //...
        aPerson.Print();
}

main()
{
        TTeacher Einstein("Albert Einstein", 1111, "1-1-1879", "USA",
                            eResearchScientist, ePhysics);
        TStudent aStudent("Lassie", 423435063, "09-24-69",
                            "Disney Land", eFullTime, eArts);
        TPerson foo("Alladdin", 618340063, "09-24-90", "Disney Land");

        cout << "Printing a Person object\n";
        DisplayOutput(foo);
        cout << "Printing a Student object\n";
        DisplayOutput (aStudent);
        cout << "Printing a Teacher object\n";
        DisplayOutput (Einstein);
}
```

The function DisplayOutput() accepts a TPerson object reference as the argument. But on every call to DisplayOutput() in main(), we pass different types of objects. When DisplayOutput() is called with the foo object it is truly a TPerson object. However, when called with the aStudent, object aPerson behaves like a TStudent object and when called with the object Einstein, aPerson behaves like a TTeacher object. The be-havior of aPerson depends on the actual argument passed in. In other words, aPerson takes on the *shape* of the actual object that was received in the call. This is what is called as *polymorphism*. Polymorphism is a combination of two words; *poly* means multiple and *morphos* means shape. Polymorphism means (taking on) multiple shapes. The formal ar-gument aPerson above exhibits polymorphism because it takes on the shape (behavior) of the actual argument. Within the function DisplayOutput(), sometimes aPerson looks like a TStudent object and at other times like a TTeacher object or even a TPerson ob-ject. And the actual shape (or behavior) of aPerson is not known at compile time. Be-cause of polymorphism, an object of a class (actually a reference or pointer) behaves like an object of one of the derived classes. Polymorphism is possible only with inheritance and virtual functions under C++. With Eiffel and Smalltalk, inheritance implies dynamic binding and hence it is not easy to separate the concepts of inheritance and polymor-phism. The aPerson argument is a reference (pointer) and hence it refers (points) to the original object and exhibits its behavior rather than that of TPerson.

Polymorphism allows us to write programs that behave correctly even when used with objects of derived classes. The derived class implementor is free to refine the behav-ior of a virtual function without affecting the polymorphic interface. By using the TPerson reference above, the clients of DisplayOutput() get the specialized behavior of the derived classes, but the implementor of DisplayOutput does not have to worry about any of the derived classes. Furthermore, any new derived classes that are added in the fu-ture would also work correctly because of this polymorphic interface. Any designer who wishes to be insulated from changes in the underlying classes of the TPerson hierarchy would design to the interface of TPerson. But, due to polymorphism, the behavior of the correct derived class is selected automatically. This is one of the guiding principles of programming with hierarchies that we shall see quite often in the rest of this book.

The converse of polymorphism is *monomorphism,* which is the normal (predictable) behavior with statically bound function calls.

C++ CAUTION   For polymorphic behavior, it is essential that the element used in a call be a refer-ence or a pointer to a base class; it should not be a value argument. If an object is passed by value, the effect of polymorphism is completely lost because of object slicing dis-cussed earlier. In the example above, if aPerson is passed by value, then within DisplayOutput, aPerson would always be a TPerson object, regardless of the actual ar-gument passed in. For example, when object Einstein is passed by value, slicing takes place and only the TPerson part of Einstein is actually copied and hence DisplayOutput has no trace of the fact that aPerson actually refers to the TPerson part of a TTeacher object. This causes monomorphic behavior, (i.e., the object always has the same behavior (that of TPerson here) even when virtual functions are called).

USING VIRTUAL FUNCTIONS (DYNAMIC BINDING) EFFECTIVELY

Dynamic binding is a very useful feature when used correctly. It is a powerful tool when used by a skilled craftsmen. Designers and implementors need to understand the implica-tions of using (and not using) virtual functions clearly to realize the full potential of OOP. We shall discuss some of these issues in the following paragraphs.

The Concept of Overriding

When a class is designed as a derived class of another class, the derived class inherits the structure and behavior of the base class. But if the derived class is not able to refine the inherited behavior, then inheritance would not serve any useful purpose. A base class provides a well defined interface and also an implementation. The implementation in the base class reflects the behavior of the base class objects. However, the implementation in the base class may not be adequate for the derived class. In such situations, the derived class would like to *override* (or redefine) the inherited behavior such that its objects exhibit their own behavior rather than the one inherited. For example, the default behavior of the method Print() in TPerson is good enough for objects of TPerson but definitely not for TTeacher and TStudent. We definitely expect TTeacher and TStudent to respond to the message Print() but in their own specific way. In other words, Print() is a common message and you want its behavior to be the same, except that objects are different, and so the implementation of Print() must be changed such that its behavior can be the same on these different objects. Designer of the TPerson class should realize this requirement and allow the derived classes the freedom to override Print() and customize it for their clients. If this requirement is to be satisfied, Print() should be a virtual function in TPerson. Only member functions that are declared virtual in the base class are overridable in the derived classes. Overriding is impossible without the base class declaring the function to be virtual.[5] Derived class implementors should always pay careful attention to this rule. On the other hand, the base class designer should make only pertinent functions virtual and hence overridable. If the derived class should not change the behavior of a particular method implemented in the base class, then it should not be a virtual method. Overriding is also called redefinition because the derived classes can re-implement the method to have the same behavior on objects of the derived classes.

The base class TPerson implements a simple Print method that is applicable to all TPerson objects. The member function Print should display the values of important details of any TPerson object. This is the expected behavior of Print. For a TPerson object, the essential details are name, address, etc. TPerson class implements Print accordingly. The essential details of a TStudent are the department and status, in addition to the name, address, etc. Hence, it is correct to redefine Print in TStudent and the base class grants permission to redefine the function by making Print a virtual function and explicitly stating so. *Just the virtual keyword for a method in a base class should not be construed by derived classes as the permission to override that function.* The base class designer might be intending it to be a truly overridable function in the future but not at the present time. The virtual keyword informs the compiler of the dynamic nature of the method. But the actual overridability of the method should be clearly documented. Designers of the base class should make the function virtual and also explicitly state that derived classes can override it. This is the best way to unambiguously publish the intentions of the base class. Mandatory overrides can also be explicitly stated. More on these *pure virtual* functions later.

When a derived class redefines a base class function, what is different in the derived class (from that in the base class) is the implementation of the method. The essential *se-*

---

[5]This is not the case in Eiffel and Smalltalk. Here almost all methods are dynamically bound.

mantics of the method should not be drastically different. The base class publishes a certain behavior to its clients and this behavior is expected to be similar in all derived classes. That is what polymorphism is supposed to accomplish. When a derived class implementor decides to override a virtual method, it is very important that the semantics of the overriding implementation not deviate from that published in the base class. When TStudent overrides Print, it is still displaying essential information about the TPerson but only as applied to a TStudent; there is no change in the behavior. This is the most important rule to be followed when overriding methods from inherited classes. By *semantics*, we mean the expected outcome of invoking that method. One would expect Print to show essential information of a person. This property (or trait) of Print should not change when Print is redefined in the derived classes. For example, Print should not be a method that does something completely different. Overriding is for specializing behavior and not for changing the semantics of the behavior. Unfortunately, this principle cannot be enforced by the language or the compiler. It is one of many programming conventions that good programmers and designers follow. There is no syntactic element that a compiler (or any other tool) can check to ensure correct behavior.

☞ **When overriding a base class virtual method, the semantics of the behavior of the method in the derived class has to be the same as that in the base class.**

This rule might seem quite trivial and easy to follow, but many implementors forget about it in the midst of all their deadlines and code crunching, leading to non-uniform behavior (of a method) across a class hierarchy. Remember that the base class declares the behavior of all of its derived classes to its clients. This published behavior must be honored by the derived classes. As mentioned earlier, inheritance is a form of contract between the base class and its derived classes. The base class allows the derived classes to override a method with the good faith that the derived classes will stick to the semantics of the base class method. Derived classes should not break this faith. In most languages, it is almost impossible to ensure that semantics of the base class method are preserved in the derived classes. Eiffel makes it possible to enforce some of the semantics by assertions that are inherited by the derived classes. Base class designers should clearly and precisely define the semantics of the behavior of overridable methods such that derived classes know what to do in their implementation. From this discussion, it should be clear that a language only provides syntactic hooks to allow overriding. But preserving the semantics of the base class method in the derived classes is still left to the designers and implementors. The language compiler is mostly useless in this regard.

SMALLTALK   Smalltalk is somewhat different from C++ with respect to virtual functions. In C++, the base class designer can specify whether a method is overridable or not. But in Smalltalk, every base class method is overridable in the derived classes. Hence under C++, the base class implementor has more control (and more responsibility) over the methods. The base class designer in C++ can selectively make methods overridable, but not in Smalltalk.

EIFFEL   Eiffel is quite similar to C++ with respect to virtual functions. In C++, the base class designer can specify whether a method is overridable or not by using the virtual keyword. By default, in Eiffel, every base class method is overridable in the derived classes. But if a base class method is declared to be **frozen**, then a derived class cannot redefine the method. This way, a base class implementor can selectively make methods overridable.

NEED FOR A VIRTUAL DESTRUCTOR

C++ Continuing with the **Person/Student** hierarchy, here is an interesting piece of code:

```
main()
{
        TPerson* p;
        // Create a person object and store it's address in pointer p
```

OVERRIDING VS OVERLOADING

All this discussion about dynamic binding, overriding, and virtual functions might easily confuse a beginner, particularly with respect to overloading. We already have a good understanding of overloading and in this chapter we have seen overriding. It is very important that one understand the difference between overloading and overriding.

Overloading is a completely compile time (or static) concept. It is a tool that distinguishes between functions of the same name but with different arguments (type, number, order). When functions with same names are declared, the compiler resolves calls to such functions at compile time and determines the exact function to call. Hence, at runtime there is absolutely no extra overhead or decision making involved in calling the overloaded function. In reality, once the program is compiled, there is no trace left of the overloaded function—everything is just a normal function. Overloading does not involve any change in behavior. Overloading is a useful tool that allows programmers to use the same name for functions that do similar things but with different inputs. Moreover, overloading has nothing to do with classes; it is only used with functions. It so happens that most of the functions we use in C++ are member functions.

Overriding, on the other hand, allows a derived class implementor to use the same interface that is published in its base class but with a different implementation. The overriding mechanism is only possible with dynamic binding. Overriding makes it possible to use the correct method implemented by an object, irrespective of the call interface used. Overriding is on a per function basis. A method of a derived class overrides the same method declared in the base class. Overriding is applicable only to methods in classes and not to free functions. Overriding implies the inheritance relationship. Without inheritance, overriding does not exist. The decision to pick a function among the set of overrided functions is done at run time dynamically. It is not a compile time concept (even though the syntactic validity of overriding is verified at compile time).

```
p = new TPerson("Bill Clinton", 1234567, "07-24-50", "White House");
//..
// Deallocate the object pointed by p
delete p; // p points to a TPerson object
// Using the is-a relationship, make p point to a student object
p = new TStudent("Bart Simpson", 456, "06-23-80", "Fox TV",,
                                          ePartTime, eArts );

// Declare a course object and set up fields
TCourse astronomy("Advanced astronomy", 503);
// Now enroll the student in the astronomy course
p->EnrollForCourse(astronomy); // See ❶ and ❷ in Figure 5-10
p->ListCoursesRegisteredFor();
// Deallocate the object pointed by p
delete p; // Which object is deleted (TPerson or TStudent)?
}
```

When **delete** is called on **p**, the compiler determines that the destructor of **TPerson** needs to be called based on the static type of **p** (which is **TPerson**). Because of this static binding, even though **p** points to a **TStudent** object, the destructor of **TPerson** (within **TStudent**) is called. This causes only a partial destruction of the **TStudent** object. The destructor for the **TPerson** object part of **TStudent** is called. So whatever resources were allocated by the **TPerson** object are deallocated. But the destructor of **TStudent** is never called because the static type of **p** indicates that it is a **TPerson** object (Fig. 5-10).

The **TStudent** object pointed by **p** is destroyed completely. However, the memory allocated by **TStudent** constructor (and other member functions) is not recovered because the destructor of **TStudent** was never called. When the **TStudent** object pointed by **p** was allocated, the compiler knows the size of a **TStudent** object and allocated enough memory (say xx bytes) for it. Furthermore, it remembers the amount of memory allocated for **p**. Later on, when **p** is deleted, it deallocates the xx bytes of memory pointed **p**. But the compiler does not have any knowledge of the resources allocated by the object pointed by **p**. The destructor is implemented for every class just to get rid of any resources

Problems with a non-virtual destructor

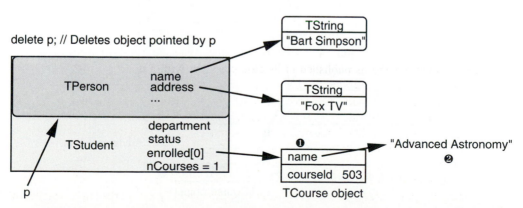

Fig. 5-10

allocated by the object in the member functions. But since we deleted a pointer to TPer-son, the compiler only called the destructor of TPerson but not that of TStudent. The entire TStudent object pointed by p is destroyed but since the destructor of TStudent was not called, any memory allocated by TStudent member functions is not deallocated (a TStudent object would allocate memory for the list of courses, course names, etc). This causes serious memory leaks.

Referring to the figure above, the TStudent object pointed by p has enrolled in one course (Advanced Astronomy). When the member function EnrollForCourse is called, a new TCourse object (❶) is created and the name of the course is stored in another piece of dynamic memory (❷). When the destructor of TStudent is called, it deallocates all the resources (❶, ❷). But, since the destructor TStudent is never called, these resources were not deallocated. After delete p; we end up with the following situation (Fig. 5-11).

Note that we did the correct operation—that of deleting the pointer to the object. But the destructor is called for the base part only based on the static type of the pointer. The derived class destructor never gets called and hence whatever resource was allocated in the derived class object is never recovered. Also note that the TStudent object is no longer usable.

To solve this problem, we need a destructor that is dynamically bound—just like a virtual function. If we have a virtual destructor, then the delete call on p will be bound based on the type of what p points to at that instance of time (which is TStudent in our case). So we add the keyword virtual in front of the destructor in class TPerson.

**Problems with a non-virtual destructor
Causes Memory Leaks**

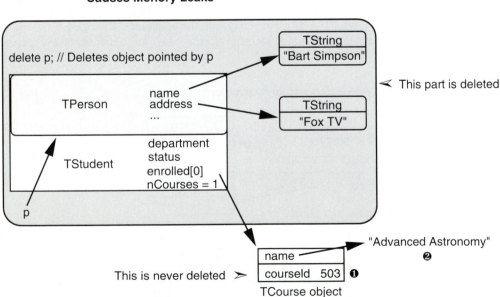

Fig. 5-11

```
class TPerson {
    public:
    //.. other details not shown
        virtual ~TPerson();
};
```

It is the responsibility of the base class to designate the destructor to be virtual (just like a normal virtual function). It cannot be done in any derived class. With this change, when delete is called on p, the destructor of the TStudent is called (because of dynamic binding). The TStudent destructor automatically invokes the TPerson destructor. This is done by the compiler and needs no help from the programmer.

CAUTION   When using a class B as a base class, pay careful attention to the destructor of the class B. If the destructor of the class B is not declared virtual, then there is cause for concern. If the person who designed class B never wants anyone to derive from it, then not declaring the destructor virtual is the right thing to do. *This is a hint to others that class B was never designed to be a base class* (for whatever reason). In such situations, be wary of inheriting from B. There is no way one can implement a memory safe class (one that doesn't leak any memory) derived from B.[6] The problem is that any object of the derived class of B would never be able to get rid of resources it allocated when it is destroyed because its destructor never gets called when a pointer to the base class object is deleted. If the derived classes never allocate any resources that need to be deallocated in the destructor, then it is still possible to inherit from the base class and provide correct behavior. In other words, the derived class must not contain resources that require deallocation. This severely limits the functionality of the derived class. Further, note that this problem exists only in situations where objects are deleted polymorphically. In the case of statically created objects, the type of the object is known at compile time and hence the compiler invokes the correct destructor.

For objects whose type is known at the time of creation, the absence of a virtual destructor does not cause any memory leak problems. Here is an example

```
void fx()
{
    TStudent superMan("Super Man", 789, "06-23-80", "Silver Screen",
                        ePartTime, eArts );

    // Declare a course object and set up fields
    TCourse astronomy("Advanced astronomy", 503);
    // Now enroll the student in the astronomy course
    superMan.EnrollForCourse(astronomy);
    // destructor of TStudent will be called on superMan automatically
}
```

When function fx() completes, all local objects are destroyed. Since superMan is a local object, the destructor (of TStudent) is invoked on it. This destructor takes care of deallocating all dynamically allocated resources (TCourse and others) inside the object. There is no memory leak caused in this scenario. The problem arises only in situations where an

---

[6]Another possibility, which is less likely, is that the designer of B does not know C++ very well.

object is polymorphically used with a base class pointer, and the base class pointer is deleted but it points to a derived class object. Having a virtual destructor in the base class takes care of the polymorphic usage also.

CONSTRUCTORS AND VIRTUAL FUNCTIONS

In C++, behavior of virtual functions during the execution of constructors can lead to unexpected results, if the programmer is not careful. When an object has been fully constructed and a virtual function is invoked on it, the dynamic binding mechanism binds the call based on the true type of the object. But, what happens if a vitual function is invoked during the exectution of a base class constructor? Here is an interesting example:

```
class B {
    public:
        // calls the virtual function f() in the constructor!
        B() { this->f(); /* and more code */ }
        virtual void f() { cout << "Executing B::f()" << endl; }
};

 class D : public B { // D is a derived class of B
    public:
        D() { } // automatically calls B::B()
        virtual void f() { cout << "Executing D::f()" << endl; }
};

main()
{
    D d;
    cout << "Object d was created successfully" << endl;
    d.f(); // Call virtual function
}
```

The output of this program is:

```
Executing B::f()                    ❶
Object d was created successfully
Executing D::f()                    ❷
```

The output line ❶ might seem incorrect. This output came from the call to the virtual function inside B's constructor. The object being created is of type D. But. how come the call ended up calling B::f instead of D::f? One would seem to think that since the object involved is of type D, the function D::f would get called.

There is nothing wrong here. When executing the constructor of B as part of D's constructor, the D object is not fully created. When the base class constructor is called, the derived class part (D) doesn't exist yet. Once the B part of the D object is created, the D part is created. Therefore, in B::B(), the real type of the object being created is still B. Hence the dynamic binding mechanism appropriately binds the call this->f() to B::f. The output line ❷ is as expected because at this point the D object has been fully created and the dynamic binding mechanism works as expected.

CAUTION   Why is this important? Well, if you are a base class implementor relying on some derived class virtual function implementation inside a base class constructor, things are not going to work correctly.

☞ **Do not rely on the virtual function mechanism during the execution of a constructor.**

THE GENERALIZATION-SPECIALIZATION CONCEPT

Inheritance combined with dynamic binding is very useful in implementing the generalization-specialization relationship. In this model, a base class is a *general* class that provides an interface and probably a default implementation. The subclasses inherit from the general class (the interface and implementation) and may add more methods and data members. Further, the derived classes *specialize* the behavior by overriding the necessary methods. The base class clearly publishes the methods that are overridable and grants permission for overriding (by making the methods *virtual*). If the implementation of a method in the base class is not suitable for a derived class, then the derived class would redefine the method and provide its own implementation. This is a very common application of inheritance in software design.

Revisiting the Print method of the TPerson hierarchy, the base class TPerson implements the Print method and also provides a default implementation. It has also been made virtual and permission to override has been granted. The Print method is applicable to the derived classes (TStudent and TTeacher) also but the default behavior provided in TPerson is not quite sufficient. So TStudent and TTeacher re-implement Print to satisfy their needs. The re-implemented Print method does not change the semantics of the behavior in any way; it still prints pertinent information. Here, TPerson is a general class and TStudent and TTeacher are both specializations of the general class. The specialized derived class is still a client of the base class and hence it gets to use all the methods of the base class; the derived class need not duplicate all the methods of the base class. This is one form of reusability. The code and interface of the base class is reused in the derived class.

THE ABSTRACT (DEFERRED) CLASS CONCEPT

Inheritance has been very effectively used to specify the behavior of a family of classes in many applications and projects. Consider the problem of representing ones personal assets. The intention here is to find the net worth of a person to plan for future needs and expenses. Automobiles, jewelry, real estate, stocks & bonds, bank deposits, and cash are all different types of personal assets. All forms of assets have a net worth. The net worth is the current cashable value (in the local currency) of the asset. The method of computing the net worth of each asset type is different. For example, the net worth of a home is the appraised value of the home in the local market, less what is owed. And the net worth of stock of a company is the current trading price of that company's stock. Similarly, the net worth of an automobile is its fair market value based on its maintenance, mileage, and age (less what is owed). The net worth of some assets might increase over time (such as jewelry and stocks) and many others constantly decrease (such as with automobiles) over time. A person's total worth is the sum of the net worth of all his/her assets. This total worth is used by many financial institutions in approving loans. How can we go about representing these different types of assets as a class hierarchy and still capture the common properties of all kinds of assets?

We could start off with a simple base class **TPersonalAsset**, as follows

```
class TPersonalAsset {
    public:
        TPersonalAsset(const char purchaseDate[]);
        // Copy ctor, assignment operator, etc. not shown but they must
        // be implemented too.
        virtual ~TPersonalAsset();

        // What's the current worth of this asset?
        virtual float ComputeNetWorth() const;
        // Can this asset be insured?
        virtual bool IsInsurable() const;

        void SetPurchaseDate( const char date[]);

        // and many more...
    private:
        TDate _purchaseDate;
};
```

This looks like a simple class and we can happily proceed with the implementation.

```
        float
        TPersonalAsset::ComputeNetWorth() const
            {   /* How do we compute the net worth? */ }

        void
        TPersonalAsset::SetPurchaseDate(const char date[])
            {   _purchaseDate = TDate(date); }

        TPersonalAsset::~TPersonalAsset() { }
```

When we try to implement the method **ComputeNetWorth**, we find ourselves in a dilemma. How can we compute the net worth of any tangible asset without knowing what that asset really is? If this asset is a piece of gold jewelry, then we have to determine the current market price of gold and then compute the net worth based on its weight. On the other hand, if this asset is a bank account, we have to perform some simple calculations (based on interest rate and term of deposit) to determine the net worth. One size does not fit all! But on the other hand, it is guaranteed that every asset has a net worth that can be computed. So it is logically correct to provide the method **ComputeNetWorth()** in the class **TPersonalAsset** but we cannot provide any implementation that works for all types of assets.

Using our knowledge of inheritance, we can represent the different types of assets as derived classes (Fig. 5-12).

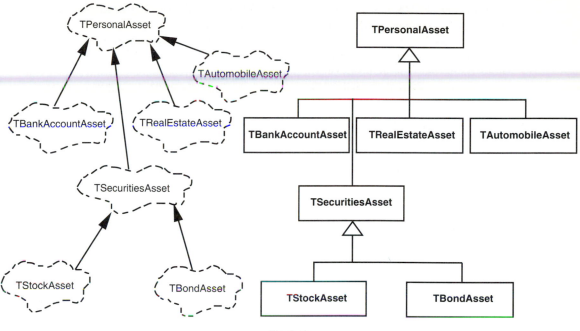

Fig. 5-12

Every asset that a person owns is a TPersonalAsset guaranteed to have some net worth (might even be zero or negative). Stocks and bonds (and even mutual funds) are grouped together as securities. Apartments, land, and houses would be subclasses of the class TRealEstateAsset. Different types of bank accounts would be subclasses of TBankAccountAsset.[7]

Given this scenario, one can implement the TBankAccountAsset class as follows:

```
class TBankAccountAsset : public TPersonalAsset {
    public:
        TBankAccountAsset(float openingDeposit = 0.0);
        // Copy ctor, assignment operator, etc. not shown but they must
        // be implemented too.

        virtual float ComputeNetWorth() const { return _balanceOnHand; }
        // and many more methods
    private:
        float _balanceOnHand; // includes _interestYTD
        float _interestYTD; // interest earned year-to-date
};
```

In this class, we do have the knowledge to implement the method ComputeNetWorth. In fact, in all the derived classes we have enough information to implement the

---

[7]Banks in different countries have different types of accounts. For example in U.S. checking account and savings account are very common. Deposits in savings account (and also some special checking accounts) earn interest.

ComputeNetWorth method without much difficulty. It is the class TPersonalAsset that causes all the problems with respect to ComputeNetWorth.

We are in a situation where a specific method (or methods) is appropriate and very useful in the interface of the base class (and derived classes) but it cannot be implemented there (in the base class) due to lack of information. The derived classes should implement the method in their classes based on the information they have. We would like to guarantee the availability of ComputeNetWorth for all derived classes of TPersonalAsset. Further, we want to ensure that no one is able to create an object (*instantiate*) of the class TPersonalAsset (because the method ComputeNetWorth is not implemented). All these goals are easily met by making TPersonalAsset an **Abstract Class**.

Abstract Class: Any class that contains (even by inheritance) at least one *pure virtual* function.

We just defined one unknown (abstract class) in terms of another unknown because we haven't defined *a pure virtual* function yet.

Pure Virtual Function: A virtual function equated to zero in the class declaration.

Here is the class TPersonalAsset after making ComputeNetWorth a pure virtual function

NOTE   The code in italics below is just boiler plate code for any C++ class and is not important for understanding the example but, is shown here just for completeness. It can be safely skipped without any loss of information.

```
class TPersonalAsset {
    public:
            TPersonalAsset(const char date[]);
        // Copy ctor, assignment operator, etc. not shown but they must
          be implemented too.
        virtual ~TPersonalAsset();

        virtual float ComputeNetWorth() const = 0;

        virtual bool IsInsurable() const;
        void SetPurchaseDate(const char date[]);

        // and many more...
    private:
        TDate _purchaseDate;
};
```

As per the definition of *Abstract classes* above, TPersonalAsset is now an abstract class. An abstract class has many unique properties.

1. No objects of an abstract class can be created, but pointers and references to an abstract class are still legal.

2. An abstract class can only be used as a base class. In other words, the only clients of an abstract class are derived classes.

3. Every derived class of an abstract class must implement the inherited pure virtual functions if objects are to be created from it (otherwise the derived class would be an abstract class too).

Now our problem is simple and easy to conquer. **TPersonalAsset** is an abstract base class and the different types of assets are implemented as derived classes of this abstract base class. Every derived class will implement the pure virtual function **ComputeNet-Worth**. Clients can only create objects of the derived classes and it makes sense to do so. For example, for my car, I will create a **TAutomobileAsset** object to represent this asset. A client would never have a need to create objects of the abstract base class directly because, as the name implies, it represents an abstract concept—not a tangible entity.

NOTE   You might be wondering why **IsInsurable** member function is virtual? Yes, one might consider that it is an inherent property of any asset that never changes during its lifetime. But, here the idea is that over time an asset might become uninsurable (too old, no market value, etc.). To account for that behavior change, every asset can override this member function and determine their individual insurability dynamically.

PURPOSE OF AN ABSTRACT CLASS

Given this discussion, one might wonder as to the usefulness of an abstract base class **TPersonalAsset**. First of all, it unifies all the different types of assets with one interface. Any client dealing with different types of assets but only interested in their net worth and nothing else would just have to treat all the different types of assets as **TPersonalAsset**s and she would never have to know the differences among the different types of assets. Base classes contain common things—code and interfaces. If you have several items that show up in every class, consider putting them in the base class (at least the interface for the common items). If only the interface is common, then we have an abstract class.

☞ **The abstract base class provides a uniform interface to deal with a number of different derived classes.**

This is a very useful feature frequently used when designing class hierarchies. A client can use the asset hierarchy correctly by just understanding the interface of the base class **TPersonalAsset**. She does not have to know any details of the derived classes. The entire asset hierarchy can be easily understood by just understanding the base class **TPersonalAsset**. Stated somewhat differently, the interface of the base class is repeatedly reused in the derived classes. This is called *interface reuse*. Code reuse is one benefit of inheritance that has been discussed earlier. Interface reuse is even more powerful because it lends itself to the creating of large and powerful class hierarchies in which the abstract interface of the base class is reused (in many cases with further specialization in the derived classes) again and again. This repeated interface reuse is very useful in writing client code that deals with a large number of different classes with one uniform interface at a very high level. This gives the hierarchy designer a great deal of flexibility in refining their implementations over time without affecting the clients.

☞ **An abstract class delegates implementation responsibility to the derived classes.**

Looking at an abstract class from a different angle, it gives class designers a tool to delegate implementation responsibility to derived classes while still enforcing a uniform interface. When designing TPersonalAsset, one cannot implement ComputeNetWorth but definitely it is an important method that can be applied to any asset. We also know that derived classes have the necessary (and correct) information to implement this method. By making a method pure virtual (and hence the class abstract), derived classes are forced to implement the inherited pure virtual function—i.e., they provide the correct behavior. The base class knows that the method ComputeNetWorth is essential but does not have the necessary information to implement it. In fact, there is nothing to implement in the method ComputeNetWorth in the base class. One might argue that we could have left the function empty (no implementation code) but that would change the semantics of the behavior of ComputeNetWorth. No matter where it is used, ComputeNetWorth should return the current worth of that asset. It cannot be empty.

To understand why the uniform interface concept (described above) is important, let us look at an example. We would like to compute the total worth of a person in the function ComputeTotalWorth. This function accepts as argument a pointer to a TPersonalAsset array, as shown below.

```
float
ComputeTotalWorth(const TPersonalAsset *assets[], unsigned size)
{
    // assets - array of pointers to TPersonalAsset objects
    // size - number of elements in the array

    float totalWorth = 0.0;

    /* Every location of the assets array points to a TPersonalAsset object
       of some kind. We want to invoke the ComputeNetWorth method on this
       object. The dynamic binding mechanism picks up the correct method for
       the object.*/

    for (int i=0; i < size; i++)
        /* Invoke the virtual method on the asset object at this location
           assets[i] is a pointer to a TPersonalAsset object. Add the
           returned value of worth to totalWorth. Repeat this for all
           objects in the array*/
    if (assets [i] ! = 0)
        totalWorth += assets[i]->ComputeNetWorth();

    return totalWorth;
}
```

Looking at this function, it is very clear that ComputeTotalWorth does not know anything about any derived classes of TPersonalAsset. It only knows (and cares) about the interface in TPersonalAsset and treats every asset (polymorphically) as a TPersonalAsset. But a normal client managing her assets would have to know about the different asset types. Clients not interested in the differences among different types of assets do not have to know anything more than the interface projected by TPersonalAsset. At the same time, the implementor of TPersonalAsset need not be concerned about providing a suitable implementation for the pure virtual method. Thus, an abstract base class is a very powerful design tool that allows designers to enforce an interface without worrying about the implementation details.

A simple test program might look like this.

```cpp
#include <icstream.h>
class TAutomobileAsset : public TPersonalAsset {
    public:
            TAutomobileAsset(float originalPrice, const char license[],
                const char date[], float loanAmount);
            // Copy ctor, assignment operator, etc. not shown but they must
            // be implemented too.
            virtual bool IsInsurable() const;
            // This class overrides ComputeNetWorth because the steps
            // involved in computing the net worth of an auto is different
            virtual float ComputeNetWorth() const;
    private:
            float   _purchasePrice;
            TString _licensePlate;
            float   _amountOwed; // remaining loan on this automobile, if any
};

TAutomobileAsset::TAutomobileAsset(float originalPrice,
                                   const char license[],
        const char date[], float loanAmount)
    : TPersonalAsset(date), _licensePlate(license),
      _amountOwed(loanAmount) _purchasePrice (originalPrice)
{ }

float TAutomobileAsset::ComputeNetWorth() const
{
        /* Code to compute current value based on original price, time
            elapsed and current mileage, less any amount of loan etc, owed on
            the automobile - Left as an exercise to the reader*/

        return _purchasePrice; // just as an example
}

class TBankAccountAsset : public TPersonalAsset {
    public:
            TBankAccountAsset(const char* owner, long acNum,
                float initialDeposit, float intRate, const char date[]);
            // many other details omitted for simplicity
            virtual void IsInsurable() const { return true; }
            virtual float ComputeNetWorth() const;
    private:
            float       _balance;
            float       _rateOfInterest;
            TString     _name;
            long        _accountNum;
            float       _interestYTD;
};

TBankAccountAsset::TBankAccountAsset(const char* owner, long acNum,
                float initialDeposit, float intRate, const char date[])
```

```
  :   TPersonalAsset(date),_balance(initialDeposit), _rateOfInterest(intRate),
      _accountNum(acNum),
      _interestYTD(0.0), _name(owner)
{ }

float
TBankAccountAsset::ComputeNetWorth() const
{  return _balance; }

main()
{
    // This declaration will not compile because TPersonalAsset is
    // abstract.
    // TPersonalAsset someAsset;

    TBankAccountAsset    myAccount("John Wayne", 4555, 2500, 5.0,
                         "01-01-95");
    TAutomobileAsset Ford_Taurus(16000, "2MED410", "03-22-94", 17000);
    TAutomobileAsset Mercedes_S400(10500.0, "3XMZ20", "06-20-89", 45000);

    // Initialize the array of pointers myAssets with addresses of objects
    // created above
    TPersonalAsset* myAssets[] = { &Ford_Taurus, &Mercedes_S400, &myAccount
                                 };

    float myTotalWorth;
    myTotalWorth = ComputeTotalWorth(myAssets, 3);
    cout << "My total worth is: $" << myTotalWorth << endl;

    return 0;
}
```

Figure 5-13 shows the layout of the array of pointers. Each location of the array can store the address of any derived class object of **TPersonalAsset** because of inheritance (is-a relationship). To the function **ComputeTotalWorth**, every asset appears as a **TPerson-**

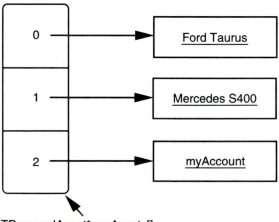

TPersonalAsset* myAssets[];

Fig. 5-13

alAsset. But since the method ComputeNetWorth is virtual, the correct method from the object is called.

As stated earlier, one can create pointers and references to TPersonalAsset. So we can write

```
TAutomobileAsset Truck_1959(300.0, "XYZ410", "03-23-59", 35000);
TPersonalAsset& pr = Truck_1959;
```

Similarly one can write

```
TPersonalAsset* ap = new TAutomobileAsset(3000.0, "XY422", "03-23-77",
                                          22000);
```

C++   Before C++ Version 2.1 a pure virtual function could not have any implementation in the base class.[8] This restriction was relaxed in C++ 3.0. In C++ 3.0 and later, a pure virtual function (one that is equated to zero inside the class declaration) can have an implementation but the function still remains pure virtual. The only way to invoke such functions is by using the classname::functionname syntax from a derived class. For example, if ComputeNetWorth had an implementation in the base class TPersonalAsset, then it can be invoked from within a derived class method using the call TPersonalAsset:: ComputeNetWorth. The intention here is to allow class implementors the freedom to provide some default implementation but still enforce the abstract class rules. A derived class can make use of the available (base class) implementation of the pure virtual method. But the derived class must still implement the pure virtual function. Even though objects of an abstract class cannot be created, the implementor must still implement all other methods (including constructors and destructors) that are not pure virtual. Note that any method in the base class can invoke any other method (including pure virtual methods) through the this pointer. The actual function invoked would be the one in the derived class because the object (the this pointer) used in the call would be an object of a derived class.

EIFFEL   Under Eiffel, an abstract class is called a *Deferred Class*. It implies that the implementation of some method(s) in the class is deferred. The keyword *deferred* is placed in the body of the method making it a deferred function. Eiffel goes a step further in terms of enforcing semantics of behavior of the deferred method. The base class is allowed to place preconditions and postconditions in the body. This way, the deferred method can still enforce correct behavior while still making the class abstract. Any deferred class declaration must begin with the two keywords *class deferred*. This makes it easy to identify such classes.

SMALLTALK   In Smalltalk there is no syntactic element that clearly projects the abstractness of a class but the concept is still supported (and used) in the language. If a message used in one of the methods of the class is not implemented in that class, then the class is considered an abstract class. Just as in Eiffel and C++, it doesn't make any sense to create objects of an abstract class. Smalltalk provides a special message, subclassResponsibility,

---

[8]The C++ version number are based on the draft ANSI C++ standard.

in the superclass **Object**. This message should be used in all methods that cannot be implemented in a class. This message produces an error report, indicating to the programmer the correct way to fix the problem.

NOTE   In all the examples in this chapter, you might have noticed, that when we are dealing with dates, a character string is used as the input argument type even though the date is internally stored in objects as **TDate**. Why not directly use **TDate** as the argument type? Well, that's a perfectly correct approach. If class **TDate** provides a constructor that accepts a character string (which it does), we can use **TDate** directly in the interface of classes such as **TPersonalAsset** and **TPerson**. The language would automatically do the conversion from **const char[]** to a **TDate** object. I have just used character string representation of dates to keep things simple (the focus is on inheritance and not conversion issues). Please see Chapter 8 and also the Annotated C++ Reference Manual (ARM) for more details on conversions.

A More Complete Example of Abstract Classes—
The Game of Chess

After understanding the rudimentary features of an abstract class, let us look at a more complete and fun example and see how an abstract class becomes a very powerful tool in object-oriented design.

Let's design and implement a chess game that can be played by two players.[9] Each piece involved in the game should know their valid moves and must refuse to move when a player makes an invalid move. The player instructs a piece to move from one square to another and it is the responsibility of the piece to ensure that the move is valid. The overall game strategy is still left to the individual player. This way the implementation can be used as a *chess tutor* also. The design skills that we learn in this example are invaluable.

Let's do a preliminary design. Since there are six different kinds of pieces (rook, bishop, knight, pawn, queen, and king) each having its own movement logic (different *behavior*) one might decide that we need six unrelated classes to represent these six types of pieces. However, a more closer look reveals that the only feature important for any piece is its movement. The only thing any player can do to a piece is to ask it to move from one square to another. Hence, movement is a common behavior of any piece. The only thing different about one piece from any other is the semantics of the movement. A knight's movement is completely different from that of a bishop, but they all *move*! Given this common behavior, we can create a single base class called **TPiece** that represents any piece involved in the game. There would be six different subclasses of **TPiece** that implement the correct movement semantics. For the sake of simplicity, let us restrict ourselves to simple ASCII display terminals as the output device. Each piece is represented on the screen by a two character code. For example, the code for white queen is **wQ** and the code for a black bishop is **bB**. The color is represented by a lower case alphabet and the

---

[9]For those not familiar with chess, it is played by two players and each player controls the movements of 16 pieces. The game has 32 pieces—16 black and 16 white. Each player has 8 soldiers (also called pawns), 2 rooks (elephants), 2 knights (horses), 2 bishops (camels), a queen (also called minister in some parts of the world) and a king. The game is played on an 8X8 board with alternate black and white squares. Each piece has well defined moves. The game ends when the white or black king is trapped and has no place to move further.

piece name by an upper case alphabet. Each piece supports two important methods, MoveTo and GetIdentity.

```
typedef unsigned short Square;
enum EColor { eBlack, eWhite };
enum EIdentity { eKing, eQueen, eRook, eBishop, eKnight, ePawn };

/* Any move that is attempted is
 1. A correct move (eValid)
 2. A move that causes an attack (check) on the king (eCheck)
 3. an invalid move
 4. A castle operation between an unmoved rook and king
The move could be invalid because there is already a piece of the same
color at the destination square. Or there are other pieces obstructing the
route to the destination square. Or the piece is not allowed to make such
irregular moves
*/

enum EMoveType { eCheck, eValid, eCastle, eInvalid };

enum EMoveType { eCheck, eValid, eInvalid };

struct Point {
    short row;      // Row number
    short column;   // column number
};
class TPiece {
      public:
            TPiece(EIdentity id, EColor pieceColor);
            TPiece(const TPiece& copy);
            TPiece& operator=(const TPiece& assign);
            virtual ~TPiece();

            /* Move piece from current location to "toWhere". Returns
               eValid if successful, eInvalid (or eCheck) otherwise. If
               movement fails, the current location of the piece remains
               the same and nothing about the piece changes*/
      virtual EMoveType MoveTo(Square toWhere,
                    const TPiece* const chessBoard[8][8]) = 0;

            // Returns the identity of this piece
            EIdentity GetIdentity() const;

            EColor GetColor() const;

            // Returns the current location of the piece on the game
            // board
            virtual Point GetCurrentLocation() const = 0;

            // This method is not for general consumption. It is provided
            // for the exclusive use of the derived classes (in
            // particular TQueen).
            // There are no checks performed in this method
            // Returns the old position of the piece
            virtual Point SetCurrentLocation(Point newLocation) = 0;
```

```
        private:
              EIdentity    _identity;
              EColor       _colorOfPiece;
};
```

Class **TPiece** is our all important base class. The constructor accepts the name of the piece and stores it internally.

    The GetIdentity method: The most important thing to note is that it is not a virtual function. Once a piece is created, its identity is not going to change—ever. The information about the identity of the piece is available at object creation time and never changes thereafter during the lifetime of any piece. Identity of a piece is just a *value*. Hence the **GetIdentity** method should not be (and cannot be) overridden in the derived classes. For example, the only thing different between the identity of a knight and the identity of the bishop are the enum values that represent them. In contrast, the **MoveTo** method represents a behavioral change—each piece exhibits a different kind of movement subject to a different set of rules. The golden rule to remember is:

☞ **Use virtual functions (dynamic binding) only when there is a change in the implementation, but no change in the semantics of the behavior in the subclass(es).**

A change in value can be represented by a data member(s). This avoids complexity and also reduces the burden on the subclasses because the subclasses do not have to worry about providing their own implementation. Identifying change in behavior as opposed to change in value (and vice-versa) is a very important skill that any designer has to develop.

    The same logic applies to the **GetColor** method. The color of any piece is just a value and never changes during the lifetime of a piece.

    The MoveTo method: This is an important method for every piece. It contains the crucial logic that controls the movement of a piece on the board. The first argument specifies the destination square. The second argument (**chessBoard**) is a bit confusing. Why should one pass the chess board as an argument to the piece? The problem here is that every piece needs to check certain conditions to verify that the move is valid. For example, a piece cannot be moved to another square already occupied by a piece of the same color as the one we are moving. Further (except for knights), a piece cannot skip over any other piece that might exist in the squares between the current square and the destination square. To check such conditions, a piece needs to know the current status of the board. Hence the chess board is passed as an argument to the **MoveTo** method. The chess board itself is just an array of pointers to 64 pieces. Note that the argument **chessBoard** is declared to be an array of 64 constant pointers to constant objects. The intention here is to allow each piece to look at (*read-only*) the board but they cannot modify the state of the board.

    The GetCurrentLocation method: This is a tricky method. Applying the same logic as in **GetIdentity**, location of any piece is a value. It is not a change in behavior. But still **GetCurrentLocation** has been made pure virtual. This is definitely confusing. The problem here is that of communication between the base class and the derived class. At the beginning of the game the location of every piece is known.[10] When a piece is moved

---

[10]Each piece has a predefined location on the game board at the start of a game.

by calling the **MoveTo** method (which is a pure virtual function), the method executed will be the one in a derived class. It is the derived class that knows the new position of the piece. Hence, keeping track of the location is delegated to the derived classes. One could argue that the location can be kept in the base class **TPiece** and every time a piece moves it should (the derived class **MoveTo** method) update the location stored in the base class. This can be done by using a protected data member in the **TPiece** base class and the **MoveTo** method in every derived class should remember to update this data member on every move. This can lead to errors if one of the derived classes forgets to update the location. Another way to achieve this effect would be to use a combination of a virtual function and a protected (or even private) non-virtual function. This technique will be demonstrated in Chapter 12 using a more complex example. For our chess program we don't like to complicate it any more than is necessary.

THINK   If we were to implement this same chess program in a graphical display system where every piece paints its representation (as is done in commercially available chess programs), we would add the method **Paint()** to the **TPiece** base class. Considering the discussion of value versus behavior above, would this method **Paint** be virtual or not?

Next, we need a class that controls the game—sort of a game manager or referee. Let us call the class **TGameManager**. This class is responsible for setting up the game board with the pieces, giving the players turns, and monitoring the game. The game manager drives a game from start to finish.

```
class TGameManager {
    public:
        // Requires names of players (or use a TPlayer class)
        TGameManager(const char playerWhite[], const char playerBlack[]);
        TGameManager(const TGameManager& copy);
        TGameManager& operator=(const TGameManager& assign);
        ~TGameManager();

        void StartGame();

        // Returns the name of the winner (if any), NULL otherwise.
        const char* GetWinner() const;

    private:
        TString      _name1;
        TString      _name2;
        int          _winner;
        Color        _currentPlayer;
        // This is the game board. Each location is a pointer to a piece.
        // A location will have the value NULL when there is no piece at
        // that location.
        TPiece* _board[8][8];
        TPiece* _capturedW[15]; // pieces captured by black player
        TPiece* _capturedB[15]; // pieces captured by white player
};
```

Note that there is nothing fancy about the game manager. The game manager is given the names of the two players. It is assumed that the first player controls the white pieces and the second player controls the black pieces. Once the game is started with a call to **StartGame**, the method stops only when the game ends. When **GetWinner** is called, it returns the name of the winner of this game. The game manager is responsible for setting up all the pieces correctly and keeping track of pieces in existence on the game board. The game manager prompts the players in turn for the next move. For the sake of simplicity, a player is required to enter the from and to coordinates of the piece being moved in any of the following formats:

    10,50

    10 50

    10   50

where (10) is the current location and (50) is the destination.[11] The board coordinate system (in our example) is shown in Fig. 5-14. All pieces follow this coordinate system. We could have used the (x, y) coordinate system, forcing the user to enter the (x, y) coordinates of both the to and from squares. The intention here is to minimize the amount of input the user needs to enter. The layout of the chess board, along with the square numbers, is on the following page in Fig. 5-14.

Based on the move entered, the game manager selects the correct piece and asks it to move to the destination square. Now it is up to the piece to determine if it is a valid move. If it is a valid move then the piece moves and the game manager draws the representation of the piece at its new location. The strategy for making moves still exists with the players themselves. The game manager is responsible for coordination and control only.

Here is a part of the implementation of the derived class of **TRook**:

```
class TRook : public TPiece {
    public:
        TRook(Point startAt, EColor color);
        // Copy ctor, assignment operator, etc. not shown but they must
        // be implemented too.
        ~TRook();

        virtual Point GetCurrentLocation() const;
        virtual EMoveType MoveTo(Square toWhere,
                        const TPiece* const chessBoard[8][8]) ;

        // Sets the position of the piece to newLocation
        // without performing any checks.
        // Returns the old position of the piece
        // Not to be used by general clients
        virtual Point SetCurrentLocation(Point newLocation);
    private:
        Point _current;
        bool _notMoved; // used in a castle operation.
};

// Array of 64 squares.
// This array is used for ease of computations while verifying moves.
```

[11]Commercially available chess games use a graphical *drag and drop* interface where players drag and place pieces on the board using the mouse (or keyboard). In such systems, the movements must be translated to appropriate square numbers.

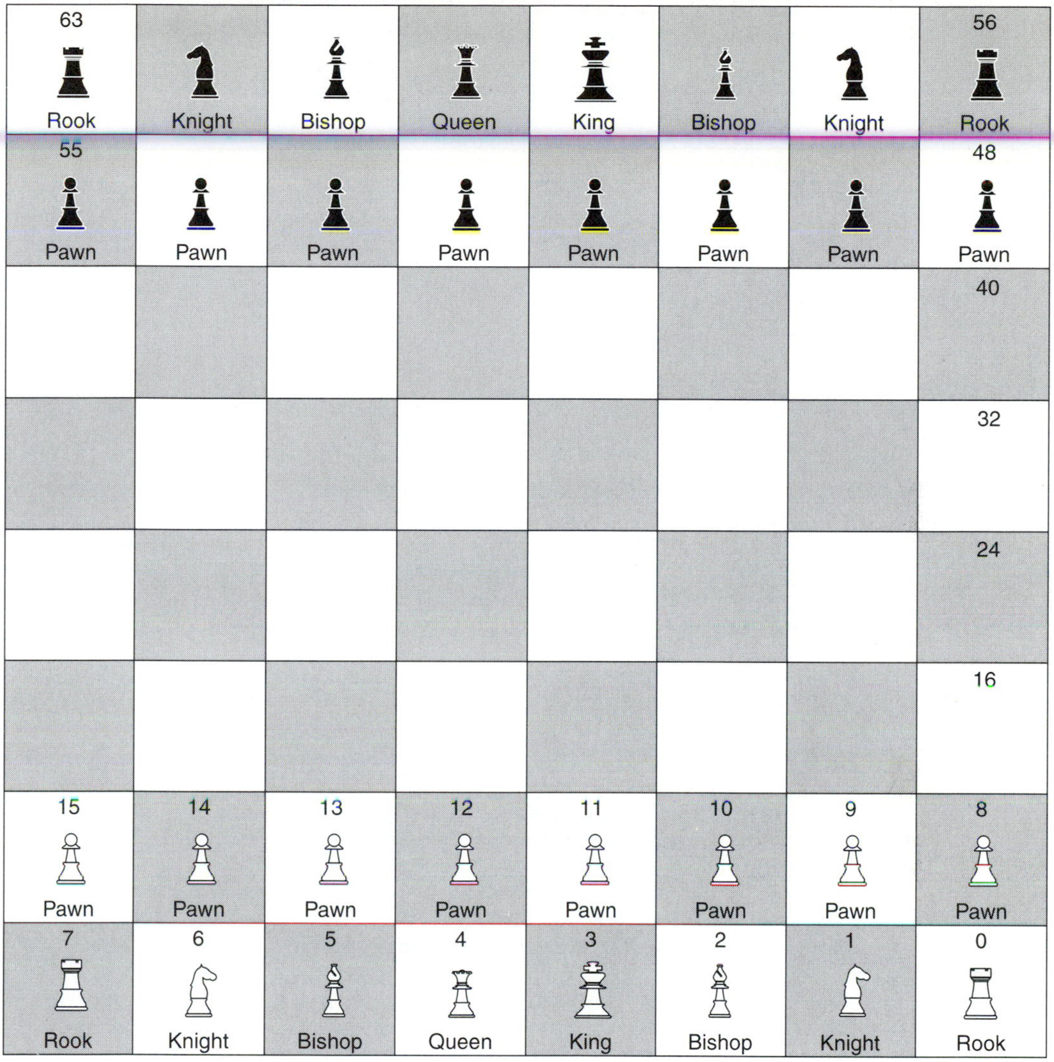

Fig. 5-14

```
// The user has to enter only the square number, and each piece internally
// uses this table for translations.

Point Board[64] = {
{1, 1}, {1, 2}, {1, 3}, {1, 4}, {1, 5}, {1, 6}, {1, 7}, {1, 8}, // Row 1
{2, 1}, {2, 2}, {2, 3}, {2, 4}, {2, 5}, {2, 6}, {2, 7}, {2, 8}, // Row 2
{3, 1}, {3, 2}, {3, 3}, {3, 4}, {3, 5}, {3, 6}, {3, 7}, {3, 8}, // Row 3
{4, 1}, {4, 2}, {4, 3}, {4, 4}, {4, 5}, {4, 6}, {4, 7}, {4, 8}, // Row 4
{5, 1}, {5, 2}, {5, 3}, {5, 4}, {5, 5}, {5, 6}, {5, 7}, {5, 8}, // Row 5
{6, 1}, {6, 2}, {6, 3}, {6, 4}, {6, 5}, {6, 6}, {6, 7}, {6, 8}, // Row 6
{7, 1}, {7, 2}, {7, 3}, {7, 4}, {7, 5}, {7, 6}, {7, 7}, {7, 8}, // Row 7
{8, 1}, {8, 2}, {8, 3}, {8, 4}, {8, 5}, {8, 6}, {8, 7}, {8, 8} // Row 8
    };
```

```
// Utility function to compare locations.
short inline min(short a, short b) { return (a < b) ? a : b; }

short inline max(short a, short b) { return (a > b) ? a : b; }

TRook::TRook(Point startAt, EColor color)
   : TPiece(eRook, color), // Call base class ctor
   _current(startAt)
{ }


Point
TRook::GetCurrentLocation() const
{ return _current; }


EMoveType
TRook::MoveTo(Square whereTo, const TPiece* const chessBoard[8][8])
{
    EMoveType move;
    // Call the internal implementation of the base class to check if this
    // is a valid move for this piece
    move = TPiece::MoveTo(whereTo, chessBoard); // See discussion
                                                // below

    if (move == eInvalid || move==eCheck)
        return move; // No need to continue

    Point to = Board[whereTo]; // find the coordinates of the destination
     point
    if (to.row == _current.row && to.column == _current.column)
          return eInvalid; // No move required

    // A rook moves from one column to another in the same row
    // OR it moves from one row to another in the same column
    if (to.row == _current.row) { // moving in the same row
       // Verify that there are no pieces in between the to and from
           points
        short start = min(to.column, _current.column); // Decide where to
                                                       // start
        short end = max(to.column, _current.column); // Decide where to end
        for(; start < end; start++)
            if (chessBoard[to.row][start] != 0 )
                        // There is already a piece at this location
                return eInvalid;

    }
    else if (to.column == _current.column) { // moving in the same column
          short start = min(to.row, _current.row); // Decide where to start
          short end = max(to.row, _current.row); // Decide where to end
          for(; start < end; start++)
              if (chessBoard[start][to.column] != 0 )
                      // There is already a piece at this location
                return eInvalid;
    }

    // Exercise: See if this is a CASTLE operation with King?
    // Check if this move causes a threat (check) on the opponents king.
    // Finally, it is a valid move
    _current= to; // update location of the piece
```

```
    return eValid;
}


Point
TRook::SetCurrentLocation(Point newLocation)
{
    Point oldLocation = _current; // save for return value

    _current= newLocation;
    return oldLocation;
}
```

Analysis of the implementation: In the MoveTo method, for each piece there are some common checks done to ensure that the move is valid. These checks are the same no matter what piece is being moved. Every piece checks to ensure that the destination isn't already occupied by a piece of the same color and also that the destination square specified is a valid square. This code has to be repeated in all derived classes. This is unnecessary code repetition. How can we avoid this code repetition but still retain the abstractness of the TPiece class?

Fortunately, C++ provides a clean solution for this situation. Even though MoveTo is pure virtual, the language does not stop us from providing an implementation for this function. We can provide an implementation while still retaining its pure virtualness. However, the only way to invoke this internal implementation is through an explicit qualified call from a derived class. So we can move the common code for MoveTo to the TPiece class and specify that any derived class that needs this functionality (all classes except TKnight) should invoke this internal implementation explicitly. Here is the code snippet to do this.

```
EMoveType
TPiece::MoveTo(Square whereTo , const TPiece* const chessBoard[8][8])
{
    if (whereTo < 0 || whereTo > 63)
      return eInvalid;        // Invalid location number
    Point to = Board[whereTo];
    // Also cannot move to the specified square if it contains a
    // piece of the same color as the one being moved (this piece)

    const TPiece* piece =  chessBoard[to.row][to.column]; // What's there?
    if (piece == 0) return eValid; // the target square is unoccupied
    if ( (piece->GetColor() == this->GetColor()) &&
                    piece->GetIdentity() != eKing) {
      return eInvalid; // a piece of the same color exists at the location
    } else {
      // There is a possibility that it is a castle operation.
      // This must be checked in the TRook derived class
      // Left as an exercise to the reader.
    }
    if (piece->GetIdentity() == eKing)
      return eInvalid;   // The king cannot be òtakenó
    return eValid;
}
```

This way, it is guaranteed that class **TPiece** remains abstract but still provides some service to the derived classes. The derived classes have to focus only on their specialized behavior. For this scheme to work effectively, it is mandatory that the base class clearly document what it does in the implementation of the pure virtual function so that the derived classes have enough information to decide whether they want to call the base class function. Note that the base class is not imposing its implementation on the derived classes. Instead, the base class makes a judicious decision to provide an optional service (to the derived classes). Any derived class is free to ignore this service (as would happen in the **TKnight** class).

The **MoveTo** member function of the derived class **TRook** (seen earlier) makes an explicit call to the base class **MoveTo** member function like

```
TPiece::MoveTo(whereTo, chessBoard);
```

before executing its own code. This style of calling a base class member function is very common in C++. In general, a derived class member function can call an inherited member function from the base class explicitly. Note that this call is explicit and it is not dynamically bound. The function being called is clearly known at compile time.

SMALLTALK   This flexibility to make a class abstract and still be able to provide some useful im-
EIFFEL plementation in the deferred method is unique to C++. It is not available with Eiffel or Smalltalk. In Eiffel, a deferred operation cannot have any implementation.[12]

Analysis of the TGameManager class: The game manager class is also quite simple and easy to implement. It gets the next move from the user and passes it on to the piece (if any) at the specified square. The game manager doesn't even know the exact identity of the piece at any square. All it needs to know is that there is a piece at a square or not. If there is no piece at the specified square it issues an error (a beep). The game manager also takes care of pieces that get *taken* (or captured) by a player during the game.

THE POWER OF INHERITANCE

It is amazing that a game like chess could be designed and implemented this easily (and without much code). This is possible because of inheritance and the abstract base class—**TPiece**. Imagine what would have happened if we had not used inheritance and implemented one independent class for each piece (six different classes). The game manager would have to understand the interface of six different classes compared to just one in our design. And the problems don't end there. How would the game manager know what piece is in any given square? And further, how can we ensure that each piece provides an implementation for its movement strategy? The task of writing six different (unrelated) piece classes is by itself an imposing task. Add to that these other problems mentioned above and we have our plate full. This is where inheritance helps us immensely. Anyone manipulating different pieces needs to understand just one class—**TPiece**. At the same

---

[12]In C++ 2.0 (and earlier versions). a pure virtual member function could not have an implementation. This restriction was removed in C++ 2.1

time, implementors of different types of pieces have the freedom (and responsibility) to provide an implementation for the method **MoveTo**. And a client of a piece is assured of correct movements by all pieces because of dynamic binding. Isn't inheritance a wonderful tool?

EFFECTIVE CODE REUSE

There are a number of techniques employed by professional programmers to achieve a great degree of code reuse. We shall see many such techniques in this book. We are about to use one right now.

Let us continue with the chess game and see how the piece **TQueen** can be implemented. Movements made by a queen are a combination of moves made by the rook and the bishop. The rook moves in unobstructed horizontal and vertical directions only, whereas the bishop moves only in unobstructed diagonals. The queen can move in horizontal and vertical directions, as well as diagonals. The behavior of the queen is a combination of the behaviors of the rook and the bishop. We have already implemented the **TRook** and **TBishop** classes. Definitely, there is no gain (or extra knowledge) in reimplementing the same code again for the **TQueen** class. Any repetitive work is always boring and error prone. We would somehow like to reuse the implementation of **TRook** and **TBishop** in the implementation of **TQueen** *without duplication of code*. To achieve this, we are going to use the composition (has-a) *has-a* relationship (see Fig. 5-15).[13]

The **TQueen** class will contain a **TBishop** and a **TRook** object in its implementation. For every move made by the **TQueen**, the **MoveTo** (in **TQueen**) method in turn uses the **MoveTo** methods in **TBishop** and **TRook**. If both the **TRook** and **TBishop** fail to make the move, then it is an invalid move. Here is the implementation:

```
// A Queen is also a kind of TPiece
// But, it exhibits the moves of both TRook and TBishop
// To make use of the existing implementation of TRook and TBishop,
// a composition (aggregation)
// relationship is used.
class TQueen : public TPiece {
    public:
            TQueen(Point startAt, EColor color);
            TQueen(const TQueen& copy); // copy constructor
            TQueen& operator=(const TQueen& assign);
            ~TQueen();

            virtual Point GetCurrentLocation() const;
            virtual EMoveType MoveTo(Square toWhere,
                            const TPiece* const chessBoard[8][8]) ;
```

[13]A careful reader might be thinking in terms of multiple inheritance. **TQueen** could inherit from **TRook** and **TBishop**. First of all we haven't discussed multiple inheritance techniques. Further, using multiple inheritance in this scenario violates the substitution principle as we shall see later. Further, a **TQueen** is not a **TBishop** or a **TRook**; it is a piece that moves like a rook and also a bishop. If we polymorphically substitute a **TQueen** in place of a **TBishop** or a **TRook**, it will be disastrous.

Class Hierarchy for the Chess Game

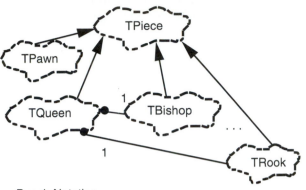

Booch Notation

Class Hierarchy for the Chess Game

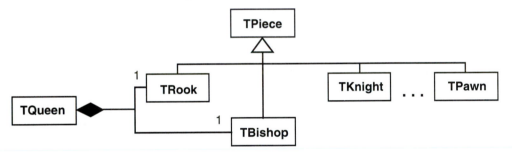

UML Notation

Fig. 5-15

```
        // Sets the position of the piece to newLocation without
           performing any checks. Returns the old position of the piece
           Not to be used by general clients
        virtual Point SetCurrentLocation(Point newLocation);
    private:
        Point   _current;
        TRook   _rookProxy;
        TBishop _bishopProxy;
};
extern Point Board[/*64*/]; // No need to show the dimensions

TQueen::TQueen(Point startAt, EColor color)
    : TPiece(eQueen, color), _current(startAt), _rookProxy(startAt, color),
      _bishopProxy(startAt, color)
{
    /*
     * The proxies are at the same position as the queen. The client does
       not know anything about these proxies - it is our internal
       implementation.
     */
}
```

```
TQueen::TQueen(const TQueen& copy)
    : TPiece(copy), _current(copy._current), _rookProxy(copy._rookProxy),
      _bishopProxy(copy._bishopProxy)
{ }

TQueen& TQueen::operator=(const TQueen& assign)
{
    if (this != &assign) {
        _current = assign._current;
        _rookProxy = assign._rookProxy;
        _bishopProxy = assign._bishopProxy;
    }
    return *this;
}

Point
TQueen::GetCurrentLocation() const
{   return _current; }

Point
TQueen::SetCurrentLocation(Point newLocation)
{
    Point oldLocation = _current; // save for return value

    _current = newLocation;
    _bishopProxy.SetCurrentLocation(newLocation);
    _rookProxy.SetCurrentLocation(newLocation);

    return oldLocation;
}

EMoveType
TQueen::MoveTo(Square whereTo, const TPiece* const chessBoard[8][8])
{
    Point to = Board[whereTo];

    if (to.row == _current.row && to.column == _current.column)
        return eInvalid; // No move required
    /*
     * This is the tricky part. For any move, the queen asks whether the rook
     * proxy can make this move. If the answer is yes, then this move can be made
     * by the queen. Otherwise, next we ask the bishop proxy if it is capable
       of making this move. If yes, then it is a valid move and the move happens.
     * If both of these attempts fail, then we return an error indicating that
     * it is an invalid move.
     * HERE STATE MANAGEMENT IS VERY, VERY IMPORTANT.
     * The queen is relying on two other
     * pieces for its moves. It needs to ensure that the two proxies are always
       in sync (in terms of position, color etc). Otherwise the queen will
       end up making invalid
     * moves. This is the price an implementation has to pay to achieve code
       reuse.
     */

    EMoveType move = _rookProxy.MoveTo(whereTo, chessBoard);
    if ( move == eValid // move == e Check) {
        // This is a good move. Set location for the bishop proxy
        // such that the entire implementation is in sync.
```

```
            _bishopProxy.SetCurrentLocation(to);
            _current= to; // Modify queen's internal location
            return move;
    }
    if (move == eValid || move == eCheck) {

        // Repeat the steps for the bishop proxy
        move = _bishopProxy.MoveTo(whereTo, chessBoard);
        if (move == eValid // move == eCheck) {
            // This is a good move. Set location for the rook proxy
            // such that the entire implementation is in sync.
            _rookProxy.SetCurrentLocation(to);
            _current= to; // Modify queen's internal location
            return move;
        }


        // Otherwise it is an invalid move.
        return eInvalid;
}
```

This implementation requires careful state management within TQueen but not much code. The logic required for MoveTo is already available in TBishop and TRook, which are reused. This type of implementation reuse is quite common in OOD. Moreover, note that this type of design is not specific to C++. It can be easily done in other OO languages as well. We shall see more examples of this kind in later chapters.

Validity of the SetLocation Member Function: This method is somewhat out of place. The original design goal was to move pieces and let the piece decide if the move was correct. In other words, the piece would internally set the location when a valid move was made. A player (or the game manager) could never directly set the location of a piece. We have changed this condition by making the SetLocation method public but we clearly state that the method is not meant for public consumption. This does not prevent anyone from changing the position of piece accidentally or even intentionally. A better solution is to hide this method in the protected or private region of all classes and then create some kind of a relation between TQueen, TBishop, and TRook. This could be done using a friend function concept. We haven't really used friend functions so far. But suffice to say that we have made SetLocation a public method just for simplicity. We shall see better designs in later chapters.

CLIENTS OF AN ABSTRACT BASE CLASS

A normal class (non-abstract class) has two types of clients. The more common clients are those who just create objects of the class and use it. The second type of clients are more sophisticated. These clients subclass (or derive) from the class and create a new class. These are usually called *subclass clients* (or derived class clients). Subclass clients can also create normal objects of the base class.

For an abstract class, the scenario is a bit different. An abstract class has only derived class clients because an abstract class can never be instantiated. This might project the (wrong) view that designing an abstract class is much easier than designing a non-abstract class because the abstract class has far fewer clients. But that is not the case. In fact, designing an abstract base class is a lot harder than designing a normal class.

The most important part of an abstract class is its interface. Clients of a hierarchy (such as the chess piece hierarchy discussed earlier) use the abstract base class interface to interact with all the underlying classes of the hierarchy. This places a tremendous amount of responsibility on the designers of the interface. Given below are some important characteristics of an abstract class interface.

1. It must be complete.

2. It must be concise and easy to understand.

3. It should be possible to use the entire hierarchy effectively with this (base class) interface without ever understanding how the derived classes are implemented.

4. It must be easy to provide the required functionality in the derived classes. Otherwise, the derived classes would never be able to provide the implementation for the pure virtual functions. This leads to a situation in which there are very few derived class clients of this base class, rendering the hierarchy almost useless.

5. The base class must not keep too much state information (base class that is too smart). Otherwise, the derived classes would have to rely too much on the base class to get this state information. And this precludes the derived classes from providing more efficient implementations. Furthermore, if there is too much interaction between the base and the derived class, it will be hard to understand the semantics of the communication and hence it would be much harder to implement the derived classes.

6. The base class must clearly define what information is stored within its state so that the derived classes do not duplicate any such information. It is ideal if the base class has no state information (pure interface only class).

7. The interface of the base class must be as general as possible. It should be possible to create a wide variety of derived classes using this base class. This aids in a great degree of interface reuse. But this feature also has a down side. If the interface becomes too general, there may not be anything useful about it. It requires careful design to arrive at a delicate balance. This also implies that the base class has a decent understanding of the possible derived class clients.

8. The abstract class must allow for overriding of the essential methods so that the subclasses can specialize them.

9. With C++, the base class might provide some default implementations that are useful to all subclass clients, even in pure virtual functions.

Some of these issues are applicable to any class (abstract or not) but they are more important with abstract classes because the primary focus of abstract classes is interface reuse.

SUMMARY OF BENEFITS OF INHERITANCE

We have already seen many benefits of inheritance and polymorphism. Here is a summary and some more benefits of inheritance:

1. Inheritance supports code sharing at many levels. The code in one base class can be shared by many derived classes. This not only reduces program size but also increases reliability and maintainability.

2. When a member function implementation is inherited from a base class without any changes (no overriding), the code in that method is being reused in the derived class. This way, code for repeated tasks (like inserting elements into a list or sorting an array, etc.) need not be written again and again. This kind of reuse is also done in procedural programming, but classes and objects make it much easier to do. This kind of reuse also increases the reliability of software. The more situations in which the code has been reused, the better the reliability of that piece of code because most of the problems would have already been detected and fixed. This reuse benefits whole projects and hence reduces software development costs, which in turn makes software cheaper to produce and market, which ultimately benefits the end user.

3. Abstract classes promote consistency of interface across big class hierarchies performing complex things.

4. When class libraries using abstract classes and class hierarchies are created, rapid prototyping becomes much easier. When it is possible to create new software almost out of existing software components, development time is reduced considerably and this time saved can be better used in understanding/testing the behavior of the new piece of software. This kind of programming is very helpful in areas where implementation goals and behavior are vaguely understood by the project team (during the initial stages).

5. Inheritance is the essential ingredient for creating large, reusable object frameworks.[14] The power of frameworks is mostly due to very effective (and careful) use of inheritance. Frameworks promote a much greater degree of software reuse and help in solving very complex problem areas, such as file systems, multi-media, international text, etc.

6. Inheritance also promotes a much higher degree of responsibility in software design. Designing hierarchies (especially base classes) places a tremendous amount of responsibility on the designer (or team). Because the base class acts as a representative of the entire hierarchy, designers will spend more time and energy in designing them correctly. This benefits the entire software industry.

PERILS OF INHERITANCE AND DYNAMIC BINDING

All this discussion about inheritance and polymorphism might make one feel that there is no object-orientation without inheritance. And it is likely that programmers and designers get carried away and start using inheritance and dynamic binding unnecessarily. Of course, inheritance is a powerful tool but it comes with an associated cost.

1. Inheritance increases the coupling between classes. We strive to reduce the degree of coupling between modules and functions under procedural programming. Simi-

---

[14]A framework is a collection of tightly coupled, cooperating classes, designed and implemented to solve a particular problem.

larly, we would like to keep the dependency between classes as small as possible. This makes classes more robust and makes class maintenance much easier. It is always good to have a set of classes that are as independent as possible (at least in theory). But inheritance goes the opposite way. Every derived class relies heavily on its base class(classes[15]). If there is a change in the base class interface, then all derived classes would have to change to take care of the changes in the base class. This is the reason why we always strive to design base classes that almost never change. But until every one of us is an expert designer of classes, it is good to keep in mind the cost of increased coupling between classes due to inheritance.

2. The second problem is the cost of dynamic binding. A non-virtual method is bound at compile time (i.e., the function to be called is known at compile time). Hence, there is no run-time cost associated with a method call. This is not true with dynamically bound methods. There is a fixed cost (in C++ and Eiffel) associated with a call to a dynamically bound method—usually in the order of four or five assembly language instructions. With Smalltalk, the cost depends on where the method is implemented. Hence, the cost is not fixed. Because of this extra cost, programs using a number of dynamically bound method calls would run slower compared to a program that doesn't use dynamically bound methods. But the advantages of using dynamic binding far outweigh the cost of these methods. But it is good to keep in mind the cost involved so that virtual functions are used only when absolutely necessary. Again, the knowledge required to make such judicious decisions comes only with experience.[16] When too many dynamically bound methods are used (and are invoked too many times), the cost really adds up and programs exhibit a degradation in performance. There are design scenarios presented throughout this book that should help in using virtual functions correctly.

The other cost of dynamic binding has to do with object size. Every object of a class that declares a virtual function has an associated size overhead. It is usually one extra pointer (the **vptr** in C++ discussed later in this chapter). Depending on the implementation (and the processor), a pointer usually requires four bytes on a 32 bit machine. Hence, the size of an object increases by four bytes. This increase in size might look trivial but it is still there. This cost is more visible when a very large number (thousands) of objects are in use. This might cause virtual memory paging thereby hampering the performance of the program. With large objects (those that have large implementation data), this cost of an extra pointer is almost negligible. But when the object size is relatively small, this extra pointer is a major part of the size of an object. For example, a class **TPoint**, which represents a point in a two dimensional coordinate system, might contain two long numbers (usually four bytes). The size of the implementation data for such a class is eight bytes (four bytes each for x and y coordinates). If any method in such a class is virtual (including the destructor), the size of the object increases by 50 percent. If a graphics system uses objects of the class **TPoint**, definitely a very large number of objects would be created (even millions of objects). It is very critical that designers pay attention to classes such as **TPoint** and ensure that they don't hog memory. A good design

---

[15]When using multiple inheritance, which is discussed in the next chapter.

[16]With C++, the programmer has explicit control over a member function being virtual or not (as discussed earlier). It is not that simple with other languages.

will not have any virtual functions in such classes and it would also not allow subclassing (because once we have subclasses the destructor needs to be virtual).

3. Software Complexity: Use of class hierarchies and frameworks definitely increases the complexity of the system. It requires a thorough understanding to use them correctly. In other words, it increases the learning curve for beginners. Designing these hierarchies correctly is not easy either. And extending existing hierarchies to add more value is by no means a trivial task. Any design (and implementation) using inheritance and polymorphic usage is going to be quite complex. But at least the drudgery of repeated code writing, code modification, and debugging are eliminated. Viewed this way, increase in complexity because of inheritance is not such a big issue. Also the cost (in time and money) of producing new (and improved) software is much less when inheritance is used correctly.

How Dynamic Binding (Virtual Function) Is Implemented in C++?

For the curious reader, here is how most C++ compilers implement dynamic binding.[17] There is a per class and also per object cost in most situations (Fig. 5-16).

Every object of a class with at least one virtual function contains a pointer, **vptr**, to a table called the virtual function table (denoted as **vtbl** above—pronounced *v-table*). This table contains the addresses of all virtual functions that are available (inherited or implemented) in the class. There is only one **vtbl** per class. The pointer **vptr** always resides at a known byte offset (decided by the compiler) within every object. When a call to a virtual function is made through an object, the following steps are needed to invoke the correct function:

a. Get the value of **vptr**

b. Index into the address of the function in the table.

c. Call the function using the address stored in the **vtbl** slot.

NOTE   Most compilers implement virtual functions as shown in Fig. 5-16 above. But there is absolutely no implementation specified by the ANSI C++ standard. Compiler implementors are free to follow their own schemes.

Cost of Virtual Functions

To look-up and then call the correct function requires access through the **vtbl** using **vptr** and then a call through a function pointer. This might require (depending on the compiler architecture) about 4 or 5 extra assembly language instructions. Note that a call to a virtual function need not always be bound dynamically. Compilers can detect and optimize calls to virtual functions and make the calls statically bound if the type of the object is known at compile time. Further details of virtual function implementation can be found in Chapter 13.

---

[17]More details of this scheme and other implementation details can be found in Chapter 13.

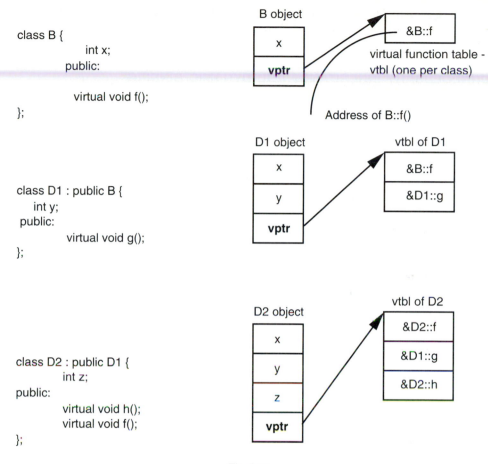

```
class B {
            int x;
        public:

            virtual void f();
};
```

```
class D1 : public B {
    int y;
public:
        virtual void g();
};
```

```
class D2 : public D1 {
        int z;
public:
        virtual void h();
        virtual void f();
};
```

Fig. 5-16

Dynamic Binding and Type Checking

At this point, a careful reader might be wondering about the type safety of this dynamic binding mechanism. In particular, one might feel that the benefits of static type checking are lost due to dynamic binding. What happens if a derived class does not implement a virtual function? Well, the situation is still under control. Remember that it is the base class that declares a function as a virtual function. And the base class also provides an implementation. A derived class object will at least have this base class function when it does not implement its own. This guarantees the existence of the function called in any object that is a derived class object. In terms of type checking, the compiler still verifies everything just as with any other member function. The only decision that is postponed is the actual function that is invoked. Everything else is done at compile time. Dynamically bound functions are as safe as statically bound functions. There is no possibility of a program calling a non-existent function. The virtual function called is guaranteed to exist, at least in the base class.[18] Therefore, the **vtbl** entry for the function will definitely contain a valid function address.

UNNECESSARY INHERITANCE AND DYNAMIC BINDING

In many situations, programmers end up using inheritance and virtual functions unnecessarily, making the problem solution more complex.[19] This is because beginners (and sometimes even experienced designers) might feel that programming using inheritance and virtual functions is the only way of doing powerful object-oriented programming. Nothing is farther from truth. Inheritance is one of the tools available to a good designer. Just as a good craftsman uses the right tool for the appropriate job, inheritance is meant to be used only where it makes the problems easier to solve. Many problems use inheritance without any virtual functions. Inheritance makes it easier to manage information. This next example clearly depicts the unnecessary use of virtual functions.

The Library Checkout System

Our goal here is to design and implement a simple library media management system. Members are allowed to check-out all types of media (books, periodicals, CDs, video cassettes, art prints, etc.) from the library. Each type of media is checked out for a fixed number of days. If media is not returned (checked back in) within the stipulated period, a late fee is charged to the customer. Every media type has a name given to it. For example, a video has a title and so does a CD; a periodical also has a name as does a book. Here is the first cut (Fig. 5-17).

TLibrary: This class provides two methods, **Checkin** and **Checkout**. The class is very simple. It puts a date stamp when a media is checked out and compares this date stamp when the media is returned (checked in).

We have different types of media, but all media can be checked out. So we recognize that inheritance is appropriate to unify all types of media. The base class is **TMedia**. The subclasses are **TPeriodical**, **TCompactDisc**, **TAudioTape**, **TVideoTape**, **TBook**, and **TArtPrint**. Since every media has a different check-out period, we need a virtual function **GetCheckoutPeriod**, which is pure virtual and implemented in each derived class. We also need another virtual method, **GetLateFeeRate**, which returns the per day rate for the media when returned late. Assume that check out period is always specified in terms of number of days.

```
class TMedia; // forward declaration
typedef long CustomerId;
class TLibrary {
    public:
        TLibrary();
```

---

[18]There is a very remote possibility of calling a pure virtual function from within an abstract base class constructor.

[19]The C++ term virtual function is used interchangeably with dynamic binding. But the discussion applies to all OO languages.

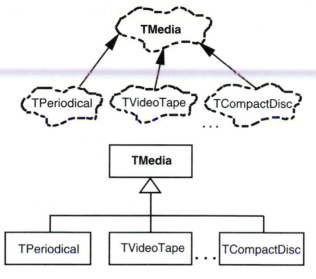

Fig 5-17

```
        // Copy ctor, assignment operator, etc. not shown but they must
        // be implemented too.

        // Puts a date stamp on the media and checks it out
        virtual void CheckOut(TMedia& thisMedia, CustomerId toWho);

        // Verifies the checkout period based on the date stamp and
        // todays date. Returns 0 if the media is returned within the due
        // date. Otherwise returns the late fee.
        virtual float CheckIn(const TMedia& thisMedia);
    private:
        unsigned long _total; // # of media checked out
        TDate              _date; // todays date. Assume that the
                                  // library gets this from some
                                  // clock/calendar
};

// First version of class TMedia
class TMedia {
    public:
        TMedia(const char mediaDescription[]);
        // Copy ctor, assignment operator, etc. not shown but they must
        // be implemented too.
        virtual ~TMedia();

        virtual unsigned short GetCheckoutPeriod() const = 0;
        virtual float GetLateFeeRate() const = 0;
        TDate GetCheckoutDate() const { return _checkoutDate; }
    private:
        void SetCheckoutDate(ConstTDate and date){ _checkoutDate = date;}
        // Media is owned by the library - no copying
        // and no assignment
        TMedia(const TMedia& copy);
```

```
            TMedia& operator=(const TMedia& assign);
            TDate       _checkoutDate; // date checked out
            TString     _mediaTitle;
            friend class TLibrary;  // discussed in chapter 7
    };

    TMedia::TMedia(const char mediaDescription[])
       : _mediaTitle (mediaDescription)
       // date will be set to today's date automatically
    {
    }

    class TPeriodical : public TMedia {
        public:
        TPeriodical(const char description[],
                    unsigned short period, float rate)
            : TMedia(description), _checkoutPeriod(period), _feeRate(rate)
            {}
        ~TPeriodical() {}

            virtual unsigned short GetCheckoutPeriod() const
                { return _checkoutPeriod; }
            virtual float GetLateFeeRate() const
                { return _feeRate; }
        private:
            unsigned short _checkoutPeriod;
            float _feeRate; // rate per day
    };

    class TVideoTape : public TMedia {
        public:
            TVideoTape(const char description[],
                    unsigned short period, float rate)
                : TMedia(description), _checkoutPeriod(period),
                  _feeRate(rate)
                {}
            ~TVideoTape();

            virtual unsigned short GetCheckoutPeriod() const
                { return _checkoutPeriod; }
            virtual float GetLateFeeRate() const
                { return _feeRate; }
        private:
            unsigned short _checkoutPeriod;
            float _feeRate;
    };


    class TCompactDisc : public TMedia {
        public:
            TCompactDisc(const char description[],
                    unsigned short period, float rate)
                : TMedia(description), _checkoutPeriod(period), _feeRate(rate)
                {}
            ~TCompactDisc() {}
```

```
            virtual unsigned short GetCheckoutPeriod() const
                { return _checkoutPeriod; }
            virtual float GetLateFeeRate() const
                { return _feeRate; }
    private:
            unsigned short  _checkoutPeriod;
            float _feeRate;
};
// Implementation for TLibrary

TLibrary::TLibrary() : _total(0) // No media checkout out yet.
{    /* code to set date */ }

void
TLibrary::CheckOut(TMedia& thisMedia, CustomerId toWho)
{
    thisMedia.SetCheckoutDate(_date);
    _total++; // one more media checked out
    // any other house keeping code goes here
}

float
TLibrary::CheckIn(const TMedia& thisMedia)
{
    TDate checkoutDate = thisMedia.GetCheckoutDate();
    float latefee = 0;
    // code to compare checkoutDate with today's date and calculate late
    // fee (if any)

    return latefee;
}
```

There are some interesting things that are worth analyzing in this code.

Class **TMedia**: The only pieces of information that **TMedia** supplies is the check-out period, check-out date, and the late fee rate for any media. It is correct to store the check-out date within the media object because each media is checked out on a specific date and there is no way of sharing this information with other **TMedia** objects.

However, the late fee rate does not change from one object to another nor does the check out period. Also, every type of media (**TCompactDisc**, **TPeriodical** etc.) has a preset check-out period. It is not going to change from one object to another object of the same class. In other words, the check-out period is common across all objects of a class and is different from one **TMedia** subclass to another. There is no need to keep this information in every object. It should somehow be made available from within the class without duplicating it. This is where static data members and static member functions become handy (see box on next page).

By using static data members, we can simplify our **TMedia** hierarchy. Every **TMedia** subclass will have a private static data member _checkoutPeriod. This static data member would be initialized when the library checkout system is started up. A similar scheme is followed for the _feeRate data member.

Using static data member, we have simplified the **TMedia** subclasses. Since static member functions cannot be virtual (no this pointer), how would the **TLibrary** class ac-

STATIC DATA MEMBERS

When a piece of information needs to be shared among all objects of a class, static data members can be used. A static data member belongs to a class and can be accessed by every object of the class. This is very convenient because it provides a way of communication among all objects of a class. Further, static data members are very handy to keep track of statistics about class objects. For example, if one needs to know how many objects of a class have been created, a static data member can be used.

```
class TResource {
        public:
            TResource(const char name[]) : _resourceName(name)
            // Constructor
                    { _howMany++; /* do whatever else is required */}
            int HowManyInUse() { return _howMany; }
            //.more functions...
            ~TResource() { _howMany—; }
            TResource(const TResource&  copy) { _howMany++; }
    private:
            // Keep track of the # of instances of this resource
            static int     _howMany;
            TString        _resourceName;
};

void f(TResource rc)
{
    cout << "Number of TResource Objects: "
       << rc.HowManyInUse() << endl;
}

int TResource::_howMany = 0; // definition of static data member
main()
{
    TResource alpha("Alpha"), gamma("Gamma");

    cout << "Number of Resource Objects: "
       << alpha.HowManyInUse() << endl;
    f(gamma);
    cout << "Number of Resource Objects: "
       << gamma.HowManyInUse() << endl;
}
```

The statement

```
int TResource::_howMany = 0; // definition
```

is the definition for the static data member. The declaration within the header file is not the definition. Before a static data member is used, it should be defined and initialized as shown above. Note that this initialization is valid even if the static data member is private. Initialization is different from accessing and hence, initializing a private static data member by clients who do not have access to the private member of the class is allowed even when they are private. The static data member is shared within a single process (or in a single task). If one creates two independent running programs—say foo and bar both foo and bar have their own individual copies of the shared static data member howMany, as shown in Fig 5-18 below.

Static data members acquire the accessibility of the region in which they are declared.

Another convenient feature that goes hand in hand with static data members is a static member function. Any function that is prefixed with the keyword *static* is a static member function. One can call a static member function without ever creating an object of the class. We can modify the class above to include a static member function.

```cpp
class TResource {
    public:
        // Constructor
        TResource(const char name[]) : _resourceName(name)
            { _howMany++; /* do whatever else is required */}
        static int HowManyInUse() { return _howMany; }
        //.more functions...
        ~TResource() { _howMany-; }
        TResource(const TResource&  copy) { _howMany++; }
    private:
        // Keep track of the # of instances of this resource
        static int    _howMany;
        TString       _resourceName;
};
```

With this change, our test program is

```cpp
int TResource::_howMany = 0; // definition
main()
{
        cout << TResource::HowManyInUse() << endl;:
        TResource alpha("Alpha"), gamma("Gamma");
```

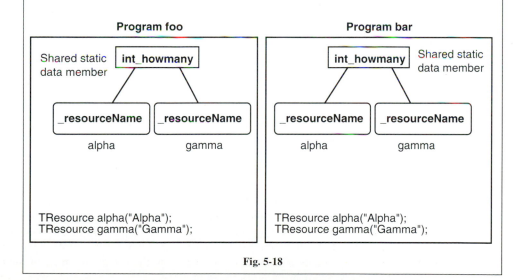

Program foo

Shared static data member — int_howmany

_resourceName (alpha)   _resourceName (gamma)

TResource alpha("Alpha");
TResource gamma("Gamma");

Program bar

int_howmany — Shared static data member

_resourceName (alpha)   _resourceName (gamma)

TResource alpha("Alpha");
TResource gamma("Gamma");

Fig. 5-18

```
              cout << "Number of Resource Objects: "
                   << alpha.HowManyInUse() << endl;
              f(gamma);
              cout << "Number of Resource Objects: "
                   << TResource::HowManyInUse() << endl;
        }
```

We can use the **classname::staticfunctionname** syntax. And a static member function can be called even before a single object of the class has been created. Note that a static member function does not receive the **this** pointer as the first argument. Hence, a static member function can only access static data members and other static member functions of the class. One might feel that this scheme can be implemented by using global data, but the problem is that global data does not have any access control and the notion that it belongs to a class is lost. Also note that unless explicitly specified, a static data member is not a constant. It can be modified by any object.

In multi-threaded environments, be careful when modifying static data members. Mutual exclusion might have to be enforced when accessing static data members.

Static data members are useful when there is a need for sharing data among objects of a class. Without this feature, one would have to resort to global variables without any access control. Static objects and static data members are a clean and convenient replacement for global variables and constants. A static data member makes it easier and more elegant to share data among objects of a class. For example, to share a group physics constants, one can create a simple class, **TPhysicsConstants**.

```
class TPhysicsConstants {
   public:
       static const double _LightSpeed;  // speed of light in
                                          // kilometers/sec
       static const double _SoundSpeed; // speed of sound in meters/sec
       //...
};
```

Once these static constants are initialized, they can be accessed by all programs using the **TPhysicsConstants::_LightSpeed** syntax. This is much better than using global constants and variables. It can still be accessed by any program that needs it. And there is no extra run-time cost either. A reference to **TPhysicsConstants::_Light Speed** is translated at compile time into a reference to some const data within the process. This scheme also avoids name conflicts because the data members within **TPhysicsConstants** do not conflict with any other members of the same name somewhere else. In fact static data members are more powerful than global variables because we can enforce access control for static data members but not for globals.

SMALLTALK   Smalltalk also supports this feature through *class variables*. Any instance member that begins with an upper-case character is shared among all the objects of that class; it is not duplicated per object. A class variable belongs to a class and can be used by every object of the class to which it (the class variable) belongs. By convention, class variable initialization is usually done in the unary method **initialize**. This makes it convenient to perform all such initializations in one method. Further, when a class is created (by a meta class), all class variables have the value nil.

EIFFEL   Even though Eiffel does not support a true class variable concept, it is possible to produce a similar effect using once functions. These functions execute their body the first time they are called and on subsequent calls they just return the value created in the first execution.

cess the check out period and late fee information? Do we still need the virtual method GetLateFeeRate and GetCheckoutPeriod? No, definitely not.

Notice that once an object of TMedia subclass is created, the information about late fee rates and check-out period never changes during the lifetime of the object. If a piece of information never changes after the object has been created, we can use constructors to pass the information to the TMedia class. This is what we did in the chess program too. So, every subclass of TMedia would pass the check-out period and late fee information to the TMedia class using the constructor of TMedia. This is the first simplification we can do. Once this is done, the pure virtual methods GetCheckoutPeriod and GetLateFee-Rate can become non-virtual methods (they can even be inline). This type of specialization by a subclass, wherein the subclass constructor provides a specific piece of data to the base class constructor during object creation, is called *Constructor Specialization*. The constructor specializes the contents of the object by using its call to the base constructor. In other words, the specialization in the derived class occurs in the form of a *change in value*. Constructor specialization is a very useful tool that can replace dynamic binding in many situations.

Here is the new TMedia class. The class hierarchy is repeated here in Fig. 5-19 for easy reference.

```
// Other declarations are as in the previous implementation
class TLibrary {
    public:
        TLibrary();
        // Copy ctor, assignment operator, etc. not shown but they must
        // be implemented too.

        // Puts a date stamp on the media and checks it out
        virtual void CheckOut(TMedia& thisMedia, CustomerId toWho);
```

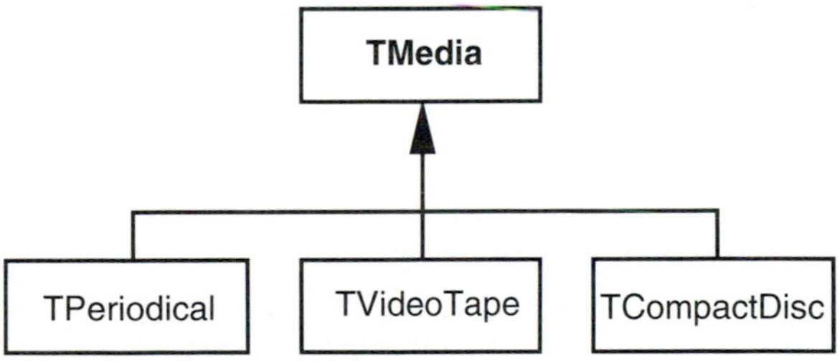

Fig. 5-19

```
                // Verifies the checkout period based on the date stamp and
                // todays date. Returns 0 if the media is returned within the due
                // date. Otherwise returns the late fee.
                virtual float CheckIn(const TMedia& thisMedia);
                private:
                unsigned long _total; // # of media checked out
                TDate _date; // todays date. Assume that the library gets this
                                    // from the operating system
                };


// Second version: TMedia class without virtual functions. The destructor is
// not virtual in this class. This class is subclassable but derived
// classes should not allocate resources that need cleanup in the
// destructor. Objects of this class can created anywhere (stack or heap).

class TMedia {
    public:
            TMedia(const char mediaDescription[], unsigned short period,
                float lateRate);
            ~TMedia(); // Not virtual intentionally, see discussion below

            unsigned short GetCheckoutPeriod()const{ return _checkoutPeriod; }
            float GetLateFeeRate() const { return _feeRate; }
            TDate GetCheckoutDate() const { return _checkoutDate; }
    private:
            void SetCheckoutDate(TConst TDated date){ _checkoutDate = date; }
            // Media is owned by the library - no copying
            // and no assignment, so we make these functions private
            TMedia(const TMedia& copy);
            TMedia& operator=(const TMedia& assign);

            TDate          _checkoutDate; // date checked out
            TString        _mediaTitle;
            float          _feeRate;
            unsigned short _checkoutPeriod;
            friend class TLibrary; // friend classes are discussed in
                                    // Chapter 7
};

TMedia::TMedia(const char mediaDescription[], unsigned short period, float
    lateRate)
    : _feeRate(lateRate),
      _checkoutPeriod(period),
      _mediaTitle(mediaDescription)

{
}

class TPeriodical : public TMedia {
    public:
            /* Each periodical has a description s such as (Time weekly,
                National Geographic Monthly, etc.) The duration of checkout
                (days, weeks, etc.) is a static maintained in the class. This
                value is being passed to the base class constructor. The late
                fee rate in case a customer fails to return a media on the due
                date. This is also a static data member in the class.*/
```

```
            TPeriodical(const char description[])
                    // Call the base class constructor with the proper arguments
                    : TMedia(description, TPeriodical::_checkoutPeriod, // ❶
                                         TPeriodical::_feeRate)

                    {}
            ~TPeriodical() {}
    private:
            // # of days the customer can keep the media
            static unsigned short      _checkoutPeriod;
            // late fee/day if periodical is not returned on time
            static float               _feeRate; // rate per day
};

class TVideoTape : public TMedia {
    public:
            TVideoTape(const char description[])
                    // Call the base class constructor with the proper arguments
                    : TMedia(description, TVideoTape::_checkoutPeriod, // ❷
                                         TVideoTape::_feeRate)

                    {}
            ~TVideoTape() {}
    private:
            // # of days the customer can keep the media
            static unsigned short      _checkoutPeriod;
            static float               _feeRate; // rate per day
};

class TCompactDisc : public TMedia {
    public:
            TCompactDisc(const char* description)
                    // Call the base class constructor with the proper arguments
                    : TMedia(description, TCompactDisc::_checkoutPeriod, // ❸
                                     TCompactDisc::_feeRate)

                    {}
            ~TCompactDisc() {}
    private:
            // # of days the customer can keep the media
            static unsigned short      _checkoutPeriod;
            static float               _feeRate; // rate per day
};
// Other classes (TArtPrint, TBook etc) are identical
```

This code is quite simple. Every subclass of **TMedia** just passes the relevant information (late fee rate and checkout period) to the base class when the constructor is called. This can be seen in ❶ ❷ ❸ above. All the necessary information is available at object construction time in all the **TMedia** subclasses and, hence, there is no need for virtual functions. The only precaution required is to ensure that all the static data members of all the **TMedia** subclasses are initialized with proper values.

```
// Implementation for TLibrary

TLibrary::TLibrary() : _total(0) // No media checked out yet.
{ }
```

```
void
TLibrary::CheckOut(TMedia& thisMedia, CustomerId toWho)
{
    thisMedia.SetCheckoutDate(_date);
    _total++; // one more media checked out
    // any other house keeping to be done goes here
}

float
TLibrary::CheckIn(const TMedia& thisMedia)
{
    TDate today = thisMedia.GetCheckoutDate();
    float latefee = 0;
    // code to compare dates and calculate late fee (if any)
    return latefee;
}
```

The information about any particular media object is different. Every compact disc has a different name and so does every periodical. This is a per object information. Hence, it is supplied by the subclasses of **TMedia** and stored inside each **TMedia** object. Again, this information is not going to change during the lifetime of an object.

Now it is time to compare the first version of **TMedia** with the refined second version. The first version had two virtual (pure) functions. In comparison, the second version has none. That is something we have to be proud of. We have eliminated unnecessary virtual functions. We have also eliminated data duplication in the subclass objects by making late fee and check out period static data members. This isn't much of a savings because the same data is now in the base class **TMedia**. But once a **TMedia** subclass object is created, there is no communication between the base and the derived class. With static data members, it is also very easy to administer any changes in the fee rates and check-out periods. All that is needed is a change in the initialization values of the static data members.

One might be tempted to avoid keeping late fee and check-out information even in base class objects. But the base class would not know where to get the information from when it is needed because it does not know the name of the correct derived class. This could probably be eliminated if some type identification code is passed from the derived class to the base class at object creation time. But that would prevent future extensions to the hierarchy because the code in **TMedia** would depend on static information. Another solution would be to pass a pointer to the static data members to the base class. But then **TMedia** would have to store these pointers, thus completely eliminating any savings in object size.

In both versions of **TMedia**, the media title and the check-out date are stored in **TMedia** objects. In the second version, we have added two more fields—_feeRate and _checkoutPeriod—to **TMedia**. In reality, this does not change the size of any **TMedia** object in comparison with the first version of **TMedia**. In the first version, this information (_feeRate and _checkoutPeriod) were kept in the derived classes of **TMedia**. In the second version, they have been moved to the base class. So, there is no change in any **TMedia** (actually **TMedia** subclass) object size. But we are ignoring the implications of virtual functions (and the associated **vtbl** and **vptr** cost). First of all, there are no virtual methods in **TMedia**. Hence, there is no dynamic binding cost associated with any member function call. This improves speed of execution significantly. Also, notice that the destructor of **TMedia** is no longer virtual. This is done intentionally. The derived classes don't need to allocate any resources because all the necessary information is kept in the base class. With this change (i.e., no virtual destructor) there is no need for the pointer to the virtual function table (**vptr**) because there are no virtual functions in **TMedia**. This saves us four bytes per object of **TMedia** in comparison with the first version.[20] This is the kind of analysis and design that a good programmer needs to cultivate to achieve both speed and space savings. In most situations, we have to consider the trade-off between speed/size versus flexibility and dynamic binding. Making the destructor non-virtual is a hint to the derived classes not to allocate any dynamic resources. If a class has any virtual functions (even just the destructor being virtual), then there is the cost of **vptr**, which adds a minimum of four bytes per object. Adding more virtual functions does not change the size of the object. The advantage of virtual functions has already been explored. But execution of a virtual function also costs some extra instructions. If behavioral specialization is crucial, then one has to go with dynamic binding. But only those methods that really need dynamic binding need to be declared virtual. If there is no significant change in behavior but only some change in value(s), then don't use virtual functions. Constructor specialization is a powerful tool that can solve many *change-in-value* problems (such as the library problem above). So always remember:

☞ **If possible, use Constructor Specialization instead of dynamic binding to reduce complexity and improve performance.**

We have retained inheritance but eliminated virtual functions.

With the new design, one might wonder if it is possible to eliminate all the derived classes and just keep the **TMedia** class? We could do that but it makes the interface less clear. Because of the derived classes, the client (library employee at the check-out stand) does not have to make any decision about late fee rate and check-out period. The client specifies that a particular type of media has to be checked-out. The class takes care of the rest. If we eliminate the derived classes, then the client would have to provide the required information (late-fee rate and check-out period) to the **TMedia** object. This blurs the distinction among different types of media. There is always scope for errors in such situations. Hence, eliminating the derived classes is not a good design decision. Keeping the subclasses around also lends itself to future extensions of the hierarchy. Any new media type (for example, video game cartridges) can be easily added without affecting the **TMedia** class and the integrity of the check-out system in any way.

DIFFERENT MODES FOR USING VIRTUAL FUNCTIONS

You might have noticed the different ways that virtual functions were used in the preceding examples. In general, a derived class overrides a base class virtual function if needed. There are really two modes of overriding virtual functions in a derived class.

1. Derived class defines a new implementation

---

[20]I'm assuming that the compiler uses virtual function tables and such. If not, this logic may not apply.

Here, the derived class implementation is completely different from that in the base class; there's nothing in common (derived class implementation replaces base class implementation). Therefore, the derived class provides its own implementation and it does not use the base class implementation at all. When pure virtual functions are used, this is usually the case because every derived class is expected to provide its own behavior. But, if pure virtual functions are not involved, extreme caution is required in the derived class implementation to ensure that it preserves the semantics of the base class. Otherwise, there is every chance for the violation of contract between the base class and derived class. Hence the need for extra care with this mode.

2. Derived class overrides buts adds to the base class virtual function

Here again, the derived class overrides the base class function. But, the behavior of the derived class function is something more than what the base class provides. Therefore, the derived class virtual function uses the base class function (by calling it explicitly) and then adds its own code. This was the case in the MoveTo function of TPiece. Every derived class of TPiece needed the base class implementation of the virtual function but they also needed to do more. The base class function is called explicitly by the derived class function at some point in its code. A similar situation is seen in the TGraduateStudent's member function EnrollForCourse in the next chapter.

This second mode is sometimes called *incremental overriding* because the derived class incrementally adds to the base class virtual function's behavior. Since the base class function is called at some point during the execution of the derived class virtual function, there is some guarantee that the semantics of the virtual function is preserved. Hence this mode is much safer than the previous mode and is to be preferred. Usually, the derived class first calls the base class function and then executes its own code.

As another example of this mode, consider a class TList that implements a general list abstraction for void pointers. This class is not thread safe.

```
class TListNode; // forward declaration

class TList {
        public:
                TList(void* storeThisElement);
                TList(const TList& copy);
                TList& operator=(const TList& assign);
                virtual ~TList();
                // Append a new node to the list (at the tail)
                // Return true if successful
                virtual bool Append (void* newElementToAdd);
                virtual void* Remove(void* elementToRemove);
                // and many more methods
        private:
                // details not important
};
```

This is a very simple class. We are not too much worried about its details. In fact, more details of this class are shown in subsequent chapters.

If we need a list that is usable under multi-threaded conditions, then TList is not the one to use. But, TList definitely has all the capabilities we need except thread safe operations. To solve this problem, we can create a derived class TThreadSafeList.

```
class TThreadSafeList : public TList {
        public:
                TThreadSafeList (void* storeThisElement);
                TThreadSafeList (const TThreadSafeList & copy);
                TThreadSafeList& operator=(const TThreadSafeList & assign);
                virtual TThreadSafeList ();
                // Append a new node to the list (at the tail)
                // Return true if successful
                bool Append (void* newElementToAdd);
                void* Remove(void* elementToRemove);
                // and many more methods
            private:
                // details not important
};
```

Class TThreadSafeList would override all relevant member functions from TList. For example, the member function Append() can be implemented as follows:

```
bool TThreadSafeList ::Append(void* newElementToAdd)
{
        // Perform steps to lock this object for thread safety
        // A critical section would do the trick.
        // Then invoke the base class function to append the new element
        bool result = TList::Append(newElementToAdd);
        // Now release the lock on the object

        return result;
}
```

Here the derived class member function uses the base class function after performing some extra operations. This is a clear case of code reuse with enhancements.

NOTE   Private derivation is discussed in Chapter 6.

SUMMARY

Inheritance is a very powerful tool in OO design and programming.

Dynamic binding is very essential to model change in semantics of behavior.

Inheritance is a form of contract between a base class and its derived classes.

Designing elegant inheritance hierarchies is crucial for software reuse.

Inheritance is not required to solve all problems. It is another tool that is very useful in many design scenarios.

When using polymorphism with C++, remember not to cause object slicing.

Even when using inheritance, avoid needless use of virtual functions.

Be careful when inheriting from a base class with a non-virtual destructor.

Remember that the litmus test for correct polymorphism is the polymorphic substitution principle.

Abstract base classes are mostly used for interface inheritance.

When inheriting from a base class, understand your rights and responsibilities as a sub-class—play by the rules.

Objects of classes with virtual function(s) incur a fixed size cost as well some execution speed penalties.

6

The Concept of Multiple Inheritance

Multiple Inheritance (MI) is a controversial topic in the object-oriented software domain. Many seasoned OO designers use MI as a way to simplify the class hierarchies in their design. In addition, MI allows more direct modeling of real world situations. For example, you are a result of MI! On the other hand, many designers completely avoid any use of MI in their designs and they argue that MI unnecessarily complicates the design. Further, they emphasize that any design that uses MI can be converted to one that only uses single inheritance. Controversy aside, it is good to know the concept of MI and problem scenarios where it might be applicable. It is essential for the reader to clearly understand that most solutions don't need MI. Single inheritance is one of the more powerful tools very frequently used in good design. Most design solutions don't need MI in their solutions. Many design solutions use MI incorrectly—they use MI where multiple *has-a* relationships would have been more appropriate. Just as with single inheritance, this chapter demonstrates both good and bad usage of MI.

Among the languages discussed in this book, only C++ and Eiffel support multiple inheritance. Smalltalk only supports single inheritance. Hence, the discussions in this chapter exclude Smalltalk.

SIMPLE DEFINITION OF MULTIPLE INHERITANCE

Multiple inheritance is a form of inheritance where a class inherits the structure and be-
havior of more than one base class. In other words, there are multiple (more than one)
parent classes for the child (or derived) class.

Under single inheritance, a derived class inherits from exactly one base class (it has
a single parent). The scenario is quite simple, both in terms of implementation and concept. Multiple inheritance, on the other hand, involves multiple base classes. The language (C++ or Eiffel) does not impose any limit on the number of base classes that can be
used.[1] If the designer is capable of imbibing the complexity of the MI relationship, the
language compiler should not have any problems in processing the code. MI can also be
treated as a combination of multiple single inheritance relations, all used at once. The best
way to understand the complexity and usage of MI is to use it in an example. And we already have one ready for us from the chapter on single inheritance.

THE UNIVERSITY EXAMPLE

Let's revisit the solution we implemented in the previous chapter. The hierarchy we created is reproduced below in Fig. 6-1.

The class **TGraduateStudent** was mentioned in the discussions but it was not implemented in the previous chapter. Here is the implementation of the class **TGraduate-**
Student. It is quite simple because a **TGraduateStudent** has more restrictions on the
courses she can enroll for and also more responsibilities (like research and seminars).

```
/ *
  * Need to include the header file for TPerson, TStudent, and TTeacher
    Just for the clarity of this example, here are the enums used earlier
  enum EStudentStatus { eFullTime, ePartTime, eExchange };
```

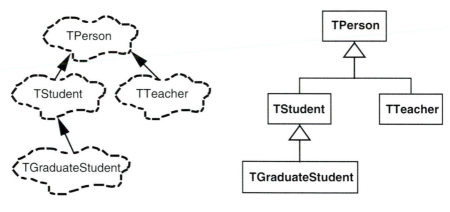

Fig. 6-1

```
    enum EDepartment { eAccounting, eBusiness, eEngineering, eMathematics,
        ePhysics,
                        eChemistry, eUnknown };
And courses are represented by:
    class TCourse {
    public:
        TCourse(const char name[], long id);
        other details not shown
    };
 Array of department names for easy printing
 If you print an enum directly, what you see is an int. But we want to see
 the names of the departments. This array of strings is included for that
    purpose.
static const char *departmentNames[] = {"Accounting", "Business",
    "Engineering","Physics", "Arts", "Chemistry", "Unknown" };
static const char *statusLabels [] = { "Full time", "Part Time",
    "Exchange", "Unknown" };
*/


/*
 The Graduate student class.
 Very similar to the student class but cannot enroll for low level
 courses (less than GRAD_COURSE_LEVEL). A graduate student always has an
 advisor who guides/controls the academic duties of the graduate student.
*/

// Number of courses a graduate student can enroll for in a semester
const unsigned MAX_COURSES_FOR_GRAD_STUDENT = 5;
const unsigned MAX_COURSES_FOR_GRAD_STUDENT = 5;

 // Cut off course number. A graduate student cannot enroll
 // in courses below this level (the course number).
 const unsigned GRAD_COURSE_LEVEL = 400;

class TGraduateStudent : public TStudent {
    public:
        TGraduateStudent (const char theName[],
                    unsigned long theSSN, // of the graduate student
                    const char theBirthDate[],
                    const char theAddress[],
                    EStudentStatus theStatus,
                    EDepartment theDepartment,
                    const TTeacher& advisorInCharge);

        // Copy Constructor
        TGraduateStudent(const TGraduateStudent& source);
        TGraduateStudent& operator=(const TGraduateStudent& source);
        ~TGraduateStudent();

        // Need to override this method because a graduate student is
        // only allowed enrollment in some predefined courses whereas an
        // undergraduate student can enroll in any course
        bool EnrollForCourse(const TCourse& aCourse);

        void ChangeAdvisor(const TTeacher& newAdvisor);
        TTeacher GetAdvisor() const;
```

```
                // Information relevant to a graduate student is printed by
                // this method
                virtual void Print() const;
                // All other methods are inherited without change
                // because a TGraduateStudent is no different from TStudent
                // with respect to name, address, dropping from a course etc.
                // That's the power of inheritance.
            private:
                // The advisor (a faculty member) for this graduate student
                TTeacher            _advisor;
                // number of courses already enrolled for
                unsigned short      _numCourses;
};

#include <iostream.h>

/* All the arguments for TGraduateStudent are the same as those for
   TStudent except for the advisorInCharge argument. Hence we just call the
   base class (TStudent) constructor and then we initialize the advisor
   object in TGraduateStudent using the copy constructor of TTeacher. We
   receive a fully constructed TTeacher object(advisorInCharge) and we need
   to construct the TTeacher object inside TGraduateStudent using this
   argument. This is the scenario where a new object is being created from
   an existing object. The copy constructor of TTeacher is tailor-made for
   this situation */

TGraduateStudent::TGraduateStudent(const char theName[],
                    unsigned long theSSN,
                    const char theBirthDate[],
                    const char theAddress[],
                    EStudentStatus theStatus,
                    EDepartment theDepartment,
                    const TTeacher& advisorInCharge)
                    // Initialize the base class object first
                : TStudent(theName, theSSN, theBirthDate, theAddress,
                            theStatus, theDepartment),
                // Next initialize the advisor object (uses copy
                // constructor) of TTeacher
                    _advisor(advisorInCharge)
{
        // Now perform the setup for the GraduateStudent part, if any
        _numCourses = 0;
}
// Usual boiler plate code
// The Copy Constructor
TGraduateStudent::TGraduateStudent(const TGraduateStudent& other)
    : TStudent (other), // call base class copy constructor
        _advisor(other._advisor),
        _numCourses(other._numCourses)
{
 // Nothing to do here
}

// The Assignment Operator
TGraduateStudent&
TGraduateStudent::operator=(const TGraduateStudent& other)
{
```

```
      // Check assignment to self
      if (this == &other)
            return *this;

      // Call the base class assignment operator
      TStudent::operator=(other);

      this->_advisor = other._advisor;
      this->_numCourses = other._numCourses;

      return *this;
}


TGraduateStudent::~TGraduateStudent()
{
 // Nothing to do here
}


// Most of the information to be printed resides in the TStudent class. We
// retrieve relevant information from TStudent (and TPerson) and print them
// in the right order. In addition, the name of the advisor is printed
void
TGraduateStudent::Print() const
{
    cout << "Name: " << GetName() << endl;
    cout << "Address: " << GetAddress() << endl;
    EStudentStatus status = GetStatus();
    EDepartment dept = GetDepartment();
    cout << "This person is a " << statusLabels[(int)status]
         << " Graduate Student in the department of "
         << departments[(int) dept] << endl;
    cout << "The Advisor is: " << _advisor.GetName() << endl;
}


bool
TGraduateStudent::EnrollForCourse(const TCourse& aCourse)
{
    // Verify that this grad student hasn't already exceeded the limit
    // for number of courses
    if (_numCourses >= MAX_COURSES_FOR_GRAD_STUDENT) {
            cout << "Graduate Student cannot enroll for more than " <<
                  MAX_COURSES_FOR_GRAD_STUDENT << "courses<<endl;
            return false;
    }

    // Verify that the course level isn't below the set limit for grad
      students
    if (aCourse.GetCourseId() < GRAD_COURSE_LEVEL) {
        cout << "Sorry, Graduate students cannot enroll for courses below "
            << GRAD_COURSE_LEVEL << "level <<endl;
            return false;
    }

    // Otherwise, ask the TStudent base class to do all the mundane work of
    // enrollment. If enrollment succeeds then increment the # of courses
    // enrolled for.
    bool result = TStudent::EnrollForCourse(aCourse);
```

```
    if (result == true)
        _numCourses++;

    return result;

}
// Return the advisor (a TTeacher) object by value
TTeacher
TGraduateStudent::GetAdvisor() const
{
    return _advisor;
}

// Assign the newAdvisor object to the existing advisor object
void
TGraduateStudent::ChangeAdvisor(const TTeacher& newAdvisor)
{
    _advisor = newAdvisor;
}
```

Code Reuse with Refinement

Pay attention to the simplicity of the TGraduateStudent class. The class interface and implementation appear very simple—don't be fooled by this simplicity; there are some major design features to be understood. Even though a TGraduateStudent also enrolls for courses, most of the work is done in the TStudent class. The TGraduateStudent class does re-implement the EnrollForCourse method but it only checks for certain restrictions that are imposed on graduate students. This is a clear example of a situation where a derived class method accepts most of the behavior of its base class but needs some refinement (or preprocessing/post-processing). To achieve this goal, the derived class method overrides the inherited base class method (EnrollForCourse from TStudent). The implementation of EnrollForCourse in TGraduateStudent does some checks and then invokes the base class method. And after the base class method (TStudent::EnrollForCourse) finishes its part, the TGraduateStudent::EnrollForCourse method does some post-processing based on the outcome of the TStudent::EnrollForCourse. This is another major benefit of inheritance. In the previous chapter, we studied the various benefits of inheritance. This capability to enhance/refine a base class method is one of them. Note that TGraduateStudent does not change the semantics of the behavior of EnrollForCourse—the method is still used for enrolling a student, but more restrictions are enforced. This example illustrates the benefit of code reuse made possible by using inheritance. Definitely, we don't want to rewrite all the uninteresting code for managing the enrollment of a student in several different courses—it has been already done in TStudent. We would like to (re)use it again. But the TGraduateStudent class has more restrictions on enrollments, so we want to enhance (or extend) the code inherited from the TStudent class. And we have successfully done that in TGraduateStudent. This is classic example of code reuse (Fig. 6-2). Many commercial inheritance hierarchies are built this way. One can imagine that each level of inheritance adds a new layer to the system with more capabilities.[2]

---

[2]Don't be of the impression that code reuse is this easy in all situations—it is not. This example has been chosen to exemplify the concept. Designing a base class for reuse in different scenarios is quite a demanding task.

Inheritance viewed as Layers

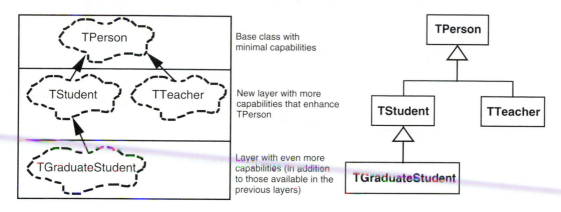

Fig. 6-2

We also want to manage graduate teaching assistants (GTA) in the university. A GTA is a) a graduate student enrolled in the university, and b) teaches some restricted (usually low level undergraduate) courses. Thus, a GTA has a dual role in the university system: Most of the time a GTA is a (graduate) student but at times she behaves like a teacher. We already have students and teachers in our system but not a combination of both. Moreover, the behavior of a GTA is a combination of the behavior of a student and a teacher—and we have already implemented them in our system. There is no fun in implementing the same thing again. We should be able to pull the behavior of TStudent and TTeacher into the class TGradTeachingAsst. Applying our knowledge of single inheritance, this is an extension of the is-a relationship with more than one parent. And that leads us to MI. The new hierarchy is shown in Fig. 6-3.

Class TGradTeachingAsst inherits from both TTeacher and TGraduate-Student. In other words, a TGradTeachingAsst **is-a** TTeacher and **is-a** TGraduate-Student at the same time. A TGradTeachingAsst exhibits the behavior of both TTeacher and TStudent at all times. In the case of single inheritance, we stated that TStudent is-a TPerson always and also that TGraduateStudent is-a TStudent at all times. Now we have extended that definition with TGradTeachingAsst to include two base classes.

One might wonder why this design scenario is considered complex and hard to understand. It seems to be quite simple because we have only scratched the surface of MI. Wait till you see the big picture in the ensuing paragraphs.

The class diagrams show the class relationship among the different classes involved. It is also called a class lattice. (The annotated C++ reference manual uses a slightly different diagram called *directed acyclic graph* (or simply DAG). More precisely a DAG shows the relation between objects under MI. With single inheritance, a DAG would be identical to a class diagram that we have been using. But under MI, the DAG is really the sub-object relationship diagram.)

Now let's see what the syntax looks like in C++.

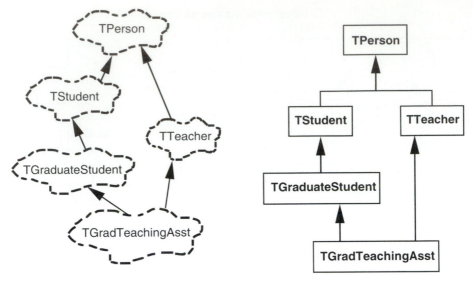

Fig. 6-3

```
class TGradTeachingAsst : public TGraduateStudent, public TTeacher {
    // class member functions and data members
};
```

This code syntax is also an extension of the single inheritance syntax that we are already familiar with. The declaration above says that **TGradTeachingAsst** has two public base classes. The order of the base class names does not change the effect or meaning of the hierarchy. (The order of base class declarations might be important if you are trying to maintain release to release binary compatibility; see Chapter 13 for details.) We could have also written

```
class TGradTeachingAsst : public TTeacher, public TGraduateStudent  {
    // class member functions/data
};
```

CAUTION The comma (,) character separates the base class names. And don't forget the **public** keyword—it should appear in front of every base class name. If the **public** keyword is omitted from one or more base class names, those base classes become **private** base classes (discussed later in this chapter). Be careful.

THE MEANING OF MULTIPLE INHERITANCE RELATIONSHIPS

Again, let me use the student-teacher hierarchy. Just as single inheritance, MI also asserts the is-a relationship among the derived class and its base classes. In this case, the is-a relationship must be valid between **TGradTeachingAsst** and **TGraduateStudent**, as well as between **TGradTeachingAsst** and **TTeacher**, at all times. Even though in real life this student behaves as a teacher at some fixed periods of time and as a graduate student during most other times, that is not the case with MI implementation code. Any **TGradTeachingAsst** object must be capable of being substituted in place of a **TGraduateStudent** and **TTeacher** at all times. There is no relaxation of this rule at any time during the lifetime of a **TGradTeachingAsst** object. In other words, the *polymorphic substitution principle* must be applicable between **TGradTeachingAsst** and all other direct and indirect base classes. So we should be able to substitute a **TGradTeachingAsst** object in place of **TPerson**, **TStudent**, **TGraduateStudent**, and **TTeacher** without any change in behavior. At any time, a **TGradTeachingAsst** object is-a **TPerson**, **TStudent**, **TGraduateStudent**, and **TTeacher**. Furthermore, it has the necessary intelligence to take on the behavior of any of these classes. If the **TGradTeachingAsst** class (object) is not capable of taking on the behavior of any one of these classes, then rules of MI have been violated and the MI relationship no longer holds. Stated a little differently, MI signals that a derived class has (at least) the behavior of all of its base classes (and probably more) combined together. This should happen naturally in a well designed MI relationship because the derived class automatically inherits the behavior of all of its base classes. The problem is in ensuring the validity of the polymorphic substitution principle under all circumstances.

THE MI SCENARIO

Now let's look at the implementation of the class **TGradTeachingAsst**.

```
// Need the class header file for TGraduateStudent here
// GraduateTeachingAsst has been added to teacher ranks
enum ERank { eInstructor, eGraduateTeachingAssistant, eAsstProfessor,
                    eAssociateProfessor, eProfessor, eDean };

class TGradTeachingAsst : public TTeacher, public TGraduateStudent {
    public:
        TGradTeachingAsst(const char theName[],
                unsigned long theSSN, // of the graduate student
                const char theBirthDate[],
                const char theAddress[],
                EStudentStatus theStatus,
                EDepartment studentDepartment,
                const TTeacher& advisorInCharge,
                EDepartment teachingDept);

        TGradTeachingAsst(const TGradTeachingAsst& copy);
        TGradTeachingAsst& operator=(const TGradTeachingAsst& assign);
        ~TGradTeachingAsst();

        // This method intentionally omitted - See text below
        // void Print()const; ❶

        void SetStudentsDepartment(EDepartment dept);
        EDepartment GetStudentsDepartment() const;

        void SetTeachingDepartment(EDepartment dept);
```

```
        EDepartment GetTeachingDepartment() const;
        // and probably other functions
};
```

There are a number of interesting issues to deal with in the class TGradTeachingAsst.
Some of the issues are specific to C++ and MI, and some are general complications aris-
ing out of the use of MI.

    Methods inherited more than once—Name Conflicts: The virtual method Print
is inherited by TGradTeachingAsst from TTeacher and from TGraduateStudent.
That leads to complications. Here is a piece of code to clarify things.

```
    main()
    {
        // This is the advisor for the teaching assistant
        TTeacher        Einstein ("Albert Einstein" , 000, "1-1-1879",
                        "Germany/USA", eFullTime, ePhysics);
        // This is the graduate teaching assistant
        TGradTeachingAsst Curie("Marie Curie", 999887777, "06-29-1867",
                    "Anytown, France", eFullTime, eChemistry, Einstein,
                    eMatheMatics);
        Curie.Print();
    }
```

In this piece of code, when Print() is invoked on the TGradTeachingAsst object Curie,
which Print() method should be called? Since Print() is (intentionally) not implemented
in TGradTeachingAsst, an inherited Print() method should be called. But
TGradTeachingAsst inherits two Print() methods, one from TGraduateStudent and
another from TTeacher because of MI. In effect, we are on a road that forks two ways
and there is no one at the intersection to guide us correctly.

    There is a *name clash* (or name collision) in TGradTeachingAsst with respect to
the method Print(). How should one resolve this conflict? Or a better question is: What
does the language do to prevent such name clashes?

Resolving Name Conflicts in C++

Under C++, the name conflict would be a compile-time error, and the class
TGradTeachingAsst must re-implement the method Print(). Doing so will make the invocation of Print() unambiguous. So when the TGradTeachingAsst class header file is
created, it must have the declaration of member function Print() in it.

    There is an interesting situation here. When the header file for TGradTeaching-
Asst is created without the declaration of the method Print() in it (as shown on p. 265),
should the compiler detect the missing Print() problem (that we might encounter soon)
and flag the missing declaration (of Print) as an error when we try to compile the header
file? Or is it better if the compiler detects the error if and when Print() is invoked on an
object of TGradTeachingAsst later?

    It is better if the compiler detects the name collision as soon as we try to compile
the header file of TGradTeachingAsst class. This would be early error detection—the
problem is detected at the first possible opportunity and the implementor should fix it immediately. This would prevent more serious problems in the future. Let's call this *conflict
detection at the point of declaration* (or early conflict detection). The name collision can

Ambiguity of Print() in TGradTeachingAsst

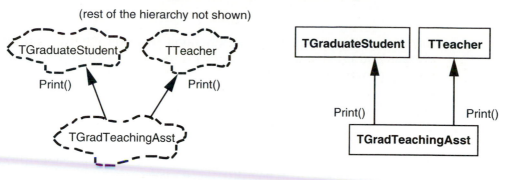

Fig. 6-4

only be detected when the TGradTeachingAsst class declaration file is compiled. This is the earliest time to detect such errors. Once this error is fixed, clients of TGradTeaching-Asst will not have to worry about name collisions when using the TGradTeachingAsst class.

But if the compiler fails to detect the error until some programmer invokes Print() on an object of TGradTeachingAsst it creates new problems for the client. Moreover, the problem is not in the client's code—the error is caused by the missing Print() method in TGradTeachingAsst, and the fix for the problem is in the class TGradTeachingAsst, not in the client's code.[3] Imagine what happens if the TGradTeachingAsst class is implemented and shipped in a library to clients without any testing done on the member function Print(). As soon as some client tries to invoke the Print() method on an object of TGradTeachingAsst class, the compiler should generate an error message (about the ambiguity of Print). And the client cannot fix the error because she does not have source code for the TGradTeachingAsst class. I call this *conflict detection at the point of call* (or late conflict detection) because the error is not detected until someone uses the method. It should be noted that neither TGraduateStudent nor TTeacher can be blamed for the name clash. After all, they are just like any other class. It is the way these two classes are combined by TGradTeachingAsst that causes trouble, and the solution is also to be found there (in TGradTeachingAsst).

Of these two possible error detection schemes, the former (conflict detection at the point of declaration) is much superior because it detects errors at the earliest preventing future problems. But, none of the compilers that I have used provide this level of service. They report the missing Print method as an error only when it is called on a TGradTeachingAsst object. Hopefully, in the years to come better tools (and compilers) would be available that detect these problems (at least report them as a warning).

REMEMBER   This demonstrates the need for thorough testing of classes. In particular, each and every method implemented and inherited by the class must be tested for correct behavior. If this is done diligently, then there wouldn't be any problems for the clients of the class. Also, designers should pay close attention to methods that they inherit from base classes. The proper design in the discussion above is for TGradTteachingAsst to provide an im-

---

[3]As we shall see later, there is a remedy for such situations (using explicit name qualification) in C++ but it is only a work-around. The real solution is to fix TGradTeachingAsst.

plementation of Print because only TGradTteachingAsst knows what relevant information it should display.

☞ **Pay close attention to member functions that you inherit from base classes and provide an implementation for every method that you inherit from more than one base class.**

C++   Under C++, combining classes that contain members (functions and data members) with the same name (and prototype in case of functions) is not an error. The trouble arises when a programmer tries to the ambiguous name. both of which contain a function f(), then invoking f() on an object of Z is ambiguous. The programmer must clarify as to which f() is being invoked (X::f() or Y::f()). But, if a programmer just creates an object of Z and never invokes f() on Z, then there is no problem. However, if f() were to be a virtual function, then class Z would not compile (as seen with Print above). Note that these problems are detected at compile time. One need not have to worry about run-time crashes.

EIFFEL   The scenario is much safer under Eiffel. Here, name conflicts are completely prohibited, and the principle of early conflict detection is applied here. When a child class inherits the same method from two or more of its parents, then at least one of the inherited methods should be *renamed* to something more appropriate. Of course, both the inherited methods (in our example of TGradTeachingAsst) could be renamed. This scheme ensures that, in a class, any name is always unambiguous. Here is the Eiffel code fragment that shows the renaming concept:

```
class TGradTeachingAsst export
    — all exported features are listed here
  inherit
    TGraduateStudent — name of the inherited class
      rename Print as GSPrint;
    TTeacher   — name of the other inherited class
```

This Eiffel scheme prevents name clash propagation. The disadvantage is that a programmer is forced to invent new names for all clashing feature names. For example, renaming Print inherited from TGraduateStudent as GSPrint is not the best way of doing it because we have to find a new name that clearly reflects the purpose of the method. But finding reasonable names that convey their intent is not an easy task. Note that a renaming in one level of the hierarchy may cause a name clash in a subsequent layer of the hierarchy. Note that the renaming facility is not limited to methods—it is applicable to any feature (data members as well as methods). However, it is more frequently used with methods than with data members.

It is important to remember that name clashes are not limited to member functions. They are possible with data members also, but it is less probable because it is very rare for a derived class to have access to the data members of its base classes. It is very likely that classes have data members with the same name but those data members aren't usually shared with other classes.

Here is the (partially) correct version of TGradTeachingAsst:

```
class TGradTeachingAsst : public TTeacher, public TGraduateStudent {
    public:
        // other details as before

        // This method must be overridden for proper behavior
        virtual void Print()const;

        void SetStudentsDepartment(EDepartment dept);
        EDepartment GetStudentsDepartment() const;

        void SetTeachingDepartment(EDepartment dept);
        EDepartment GetTeachingDepartment() const;

};
```

And here is a simple implementation of the member function **Print.**:

```
void TGradTeachingAsst::Print() const
{
    // We get the appropriate pieces of data and print them
    EStudentStatus studentStats = GetStatus(); // no ambiguity here
    EDepartment  studentDepartment = TGraduateStudent::GetDepartment();
    EDepartment  teachingDepartment = TTeacher::GetDepartment();

    // Explicit qualification needed for GetName and
    GetIdentificationNumber
    // Otherwise, it is ambiguous (there are two TPerson objects) in GTA
    cout << "Name: " << TGraduateStudent::GetName() << endl;
    cout << "Id Number: " << TGraduateStudent::GetIdentificationNumber()
                                            << endl;
    cout << "This person is a Graduate Student" << endl;
    cout << " in the department of: " <<
                    departments[(int) studentDepartment] << endl;
    cout << "The graduate teaching assistantship is in the department: "
                << departments[(int) teachingDepartment] << endl;
}
```

Here is a simple implementation of the constructor:

```
    TGradTeachingAsst::TGradTeachingAsst(const char theName[],
            unsigned long theSSN, // of the graduate student
            const char theBirthDate[],
            const char theAddress[],
            EStudentStatus theStatus,
            EDepartment studentDepartment,
            const TTeacher& advisorInCharge,
            EDepartment teachingDept)
            // Initialize direct base class TGraduateStudent
        : TGraduateStudent(theName, theSSN, theBirthDate, theAddress,
                    theStatus, studentDepartment, advisorInCharge),
            // Initialize direct base class TTeacher
        TTeacher(theName, theSSN, theBirthDate, theAddress,
                    GraduateTeachingAssistant, teachingDept)
    {
```

```
                    // Implementation code for TGradTeachingAsst
    }
```

Problem of Ambiguous Base Classes

Another problem with MI is that of ambiguity in implicitly derived base class conversion
(as described in Chapter 5). With single inheritance hierarchies, there are no problems because there is always one base class for any derived class and the implicit conversion happens automatically. But the scenario isn't that simple under MI. Consider this example (in
relation to the Teacher-Student hierarchy).

```
// This is an ordinary overloaded function expecting a
// TTeacher argument polymorphically
void foo(const TTeacher& teacher) // ❶
{
    // some code to do processing - not important for this example
}

// This is an overloaded function foo() expecting a
// TGraduateStudent argument polymorphically
void foo(const TGraduateStudent& gradStudent) // ❷
{
    // some code to do processing - not important for this example
}

main()
{
    // This is the advisor for the gta object below
    TTeacher  Super_Smart_Alien("Super_Smart_Alien", 1112223333,
                        "1-1-1900", "Planet Venus", eDean, ePhysics);

    TGradTeachingAsst  gta("Smart_Alien", 777665555, "1-1-2000",
                    "Planet Mars",
                    eFullTime, // Student Status
                    ePhysics,  // Student department
                    Super_Smart_Alien, // Advisor
                    eBusiness // TA department
                    );
    // try calling one of the foo() functions with a TGradTeachingAsst
    // object
    foo(gta); // Which function foo() can be called?
    // Convert gta to TGraduateStudent and call ❷
    // OR convert gta to TTeacher and call ❶
}
```

When we try to invoke **foo()** with the **gta** object, there is an ambiguity. Any
TGradTeachingAsst class object can be implicitly converted to a **TGraduateStudent**
object or a **TTeacher** object because **TGradTeachingAsst** inherits from both of these
classes. In other words, **TGradTeachingAsst** *is-a* **TGraduateStudent** as well as
TTeacher at all times. Both of the **foo()** functions above are equally good candidates for
the call **foo(gta)**. The compiler cannot pick one between the two overloaded **foo()** functions. Hence, the call is ambiguous. This error is again detected at compile time. This is

another potential problem with MI hierarchies. This kind of problem is encountered when programmers add new overloaded functions to existing programs. For example, if one of the foo() functions above were not present, the example above would work without ambiguity. If someone were to add another foo() function later (probably to overcome some other problem), this code (that used to work) will not even compile anymore. Note that foo() could have been a constructor of a class foo, or a set of overloaded member functions in a class.

This problem is very much like the ambiguity of the Print member function discussed earlier. In the case of Print(), the compiler could not resolve between the same member function in two different base classes. In the case of the call to foo(), a TGradTeachingAsst object can be converted to a TTeacher or to a TGraduateStudent. But the compiler cannot pick one conversion over another. Both conversions are valid and equally correct. Here, the ambiguity is because of conversions to accessible base classes.

CAUTION   This problem (of ambiguities) also arises when an existing single inheritance hierarchy is *enhanced* by adding MI. Code that used to compile and run wouldn't even compile. Refrain from using MI until you are aware of the consequences and the caveats.

PRELIMINARY BENEFITS OF MULTIPLE INHERITANCE

It's about time we discussed some of the benefits of using MI. From the example of TGradTeachingAsst above, some benefits are easy to see.

1. We can fully reuse the implementation found in two (or more) different classes and create a new class without much code. This is the case with TGradTeachingAsst. This class gets most of its behavior from the base classes. At the same time, TGradTeachingAsst still upholds the is-a relationship. Stated in a different way, MI allows us to combine classes to create new abstractions, and these new abstractions add more value than the individual abstractions by themselves.

2. MI also helps in modeling relationships that go more than one way. Without MI, a designer is forced to choose among the many possible relationships, even though all of them are valid. When a class exhibits behavior found in more than one (base) class, MI might be appropriate.

3. Multiple inheritance lends itself to a great degree of code reuse. Every additional base class enhances code reuse. Without MI, one would be forced to use the has-a relationship, thereby reducing code reuse (and increasing implementation and testing time).

ALTERNATIVES TO MULTIPLE INHERITANCE

If, for some reason, a project design team decides not to use MI, there are some alternative design scenarios that have been used quite well. The scheme that we are about to explore supports better encapsulation but reduced code reuse. Here is an example.

First Alternative

If we were to implement the **TGradTeachingAsst** class using *has-a* (aggregation) instead of MI we could write it as follows (just for clarity I am using a different name for this class).[4]

```
// Name of class is different just to avoid confusion

class TGTA {
    private:
        TTeacher _teacherProxy;
        TGraduateStudent _studentProxy;
    public:
        TGTA(const char theName[],
                unsigned long theSSN, // of the graduate student
                const char theBirthDate[],
                const char theAddress[],
                EStudentStatus theStatus,
                EDepartment studentDepartment,
                const TTeacher& advisorInCharge,
                EDepartment teachingDept);

        TGTA(const TGTA & copy);
        TGTA& operator=(const TGTA & assign);
        TGTA();

        void Print()const;

        void SetStudentsDepartment(EDepartment dept);
        EDepartment GetStudentsDepartment() const;

        void SetTeachingDepartment(EDepartment dept);
        EDepartment GetTeachingDepartment() const;
            // and many more methods
};
```

The member functions in the implementation of **TGTA** have to invoke the corresponding function from one of the proxies (**_teacherProxy** or **_studentProxy**) (see Fig. 6-5). For example

```
        void
        TGTA::SetStudentsDepartment(EDepartment dept)
                {_studentProxy.SetDepartment(dept); }
```

This needs to be done for every member function implemented in **TGTA** because there is no inheritance. Moreover, none of the member functions in **TTeacher** and **TGraduate-Student** can be overridden in **TGTA**, again because there is no inheritance relation. This increases the implementation responsibility for the class **TGTA**. Class **TGTA** must provide the member functions needed to interact with **TPerson, TStudent, TGraduateStu-**

---

[4]Has-a relationship (aggregation and composition) has been discussed in Chapter 2.

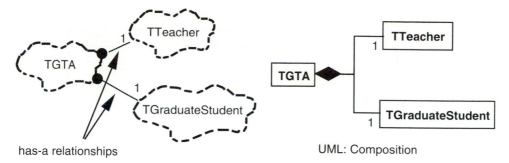

has-a relationships   UML: Composition

Note: TGraduateStudent still inherits from TStudent which inherits from TPerson.
TTeacher also inherits from TPerson. This part of the hierarchy is not shown here.

Fig. 6-5

dent, and TTeacher because clients of TGTA would definitely want access to name, address, courses, etc. of a TGTA. We also have the problem of a duplicated TPerson object—one from TTeacher and another from TGraduateStudent. This problem exists
both in the has-a case and also in the MI scenario that we discussed earlier. We shall see a
solution for the MI case soon but in the has-a situation there is no easy solution. All these
requirements can be satisfied easily with simple implementations, but the implementor
must write code for all the required member functions (using the exported methods of
TGraduateStudent and TTeacher). In case of inheritance, all the methods were inherited automatically and TGradTeachingAsst class had to override only those methods
that did not fit its needs. In other words, class TGradTeachingAsst did a selective re-
implementation of methods. But in TGTA, almost all the methods that are already implemented in TTeacher and TGraduateStudent that are needed must be re-implemented
(using the methods in TTeacher and TGraduateStudent). All this is totally uninteresting code and one would not enjoy doing this implementation of TGTA. Lack of inheritance causes all these problems. This discussion should convince the reader about the
power of inheritance.

It might help to look at the conceptual layout of a TGTA object that clearly shows
duplication of TPerson objects (Fig. 6-6). In this picture, even though TTeacher inherits
from TPerson, we can imagine that TTeacher internally contains a TPerson object.[5]
The same argument applies to TGraduateStudent. Every TTeacher object contains all
the data members of TPerson, in addition to those it adds. The data members are still private—there is no violation of access rules.

Because of this duplication of TPerson objects, TGTA needs to ensure correct state
management when the details of TPerson change due to methods invoked on TGTA. For
example, if the address of TGTA needs to be changed, should we change the address
stored inside of TPerson within the TTeacher object or the TPerson inside the TStu-

---

[5]In reality, this is what most C++ compilers do. A derived class object internally contains a base class
object. See chapter 13 for details of the C++ object model.

Structure of a TGTA object

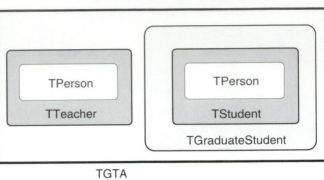

Fig. 6-6

dent object (which is inside TGraduateStudent). If the TGTA implementation completely ignores the TPerson object inside TTeacher and always uses the one inside of TStudent, it might appear that the problem goes away because we never use any data stored in the TPerson object within TTeacher. But what if one of the methods of TTeacher uses the data in its TPerson object through one of the methods in TPerson? There is no way the implementor of TGTA can modify that method in TTeacher to stop this usage. This is one of the problems with duplicated objects. In such an implementation, TGTA object will exhibit different behavior depending on whether TGTA internally invokes the methods in TTeacher or those in TGraduateStudent. Such inconsistent behavior from the same object will confuse the clients and they in turn avoid using such classes. But, there are some benefits in this *has-a* implementation. It provides better encapsulation. A client of TGradTeachingAsst could access the TStudent, TTeacher, TGraduateStudent, and TPerson objects inside of a TGradTeachingAsst object without any restrictions because they are all public base classes of TGradTeachingAsst. There is no such freedom available to client of TGTA. A client of TGTA can only use the public methods of TGTA and nothing else. The fact that TGTA has an object of TTeacher and TGraduateStudent inside of it is an implementation issue—it is of no use to the client. This provides more flexibility to the implementor of TGTA because she has the freedom to export only those methods that are useful to clients. And she has the freedom to change the internal implementation (for example, using a TStudent object instead of a TGraduateStudent object). Such flexibility is not available with TGradTeachingAsst using MI. This is an important advantage of using has-a relationships and we shall see more advantages of this scheme later in this chapter.

Second Scenario

Let's see if we can use a combination of single inheritance and has-a relationship to our advantage. One approach is to use TGraduateStudent as the base class of TGTA with a has-a relationship with the class TTeacher (Fig. 6-7).

Second Alternative to MI: **Combination of is-a and has-a relationships**

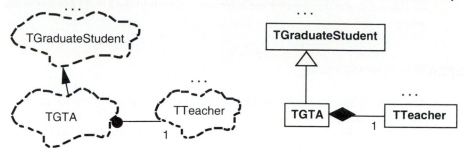

Note: TGraduateStudent still inherits from TStudent which inherits from TPerson.
TTeacher also inherits from TPerson. This part of the hierarchy is not shown here.

Fig. 6-7

The code for **TGTA** is shown below:

```
class TGTA : public TGraduateStudent {
    private:
        TTeacher  _teacherProxy;
        // Details about the student are in the base class,
        // TGraduateStudent
    public:
        TGTA(const char theName[],
                unsigned long theSSN, // of the graduate student
                const char theBirthDate[],
                const char theAddress[],
                EStudentStatus theStatus,
                EDepartment studentDepartment,
                const TTeacher& advisorInCharge,
                EDepartment teachingDept);

        TGTA(const TGTA& copy);
        TGTA& operator=(const TGTA & assign);
        TGTA();

        virtual void Print()const;

        void SetTeachingDepartment(EDepartment dept);
        EDepartment GetTeachingDepartment() const;
           // and many more methods
};
```

The situation is less complex now because **TGTA** inherits all the features of **TGraduate-Student** (indirectly those of **TStudent** and **TPerson** also). Therefore, **TGTA** does not have to re-implement all the methods that treat **TGTA** as a graduate student. But **TGTA** must implement (using the corresponding member functions of **TTeacher**) those methods that add the capability of a teacher to **TGTA**. But this is much easier than the first scenario, which uses pure has-a relationships. We still have the problem of duplicated **TPerson** objects—**TGTA** inherits a **TPerson** object indirectly from **TGraduateStudent** and **TTeacher** inherits from **TPerson**, but controlling the duplicated object is somewhat easier in this scheme. It is better to use the **TPerson** inherited through **TGraduateStudent** (ignoring the one in TTeacher). Since TGTA controls all access to TTeacher, it might be able to ensure that (with some effort) the TPerson data in TTeacher is not used anywhere.

REPEATED INHERITANCE

The original inheritance hierarchy of TGradTeachingAsst is reproduced here in Fig. 6-8 for easy reference.

So far, we have conveniently ignored the problem of duplicated objects inside of a derived class object (inside TGradTeachingAsst in our example). This is a major problem with multiple inheritance. When the same class X appears as the base class of more than one parent class (i.e., indirect base class), then the completed object of the derived class will have more than one object of X. In Eiffel, it is legal for a class to inherit *directly* from the same base class more than once, but C++ does not allow it. The situation where a class appears as the (direct or indirect) base class more than once in a hierarchy is called *repeated inheritance*. In our example, TPerson is the base class for both TTeacher and TStudent. When TGradTeachingAsst inherits from both TTeacher and TGraduateStudent, it is indirectly inheriting TPerson twice. We end up with a TGradTeachingAsst object with two TPerson objects inside it. What is really duplicated are the data members of the class TPerson. Every TGradTeachingAsst object ends up with two instances of TPerson and each of those TPerson objects have their own data members—_name, _address, _ssn, and _birthDate. Any TGradTeachingAsst is a unique person with a name, address, and such. We don't need two copies of such data. But that's what we get by this default style of MI.

NOTE   C++ does not allow *direct repeated inheritance*. For example, the following piece of code is incorrect.

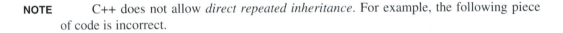

```
class TTeacher : public TPerson, public TPerson { /* ... */ }; // Wrong
```

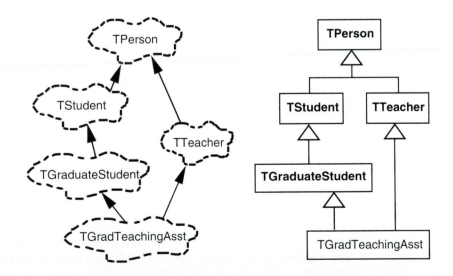

Fig. 6-8

Here, TTeacher inherits directly from TPerson twice. It is impossible to distinguish between the two TPerson objects within TTeacher. But, indirect repeated inheritance (as in TGradTeachingAsst) is perfectly correct.[6]

The problem with TGradTeachingAsst is that TTeacher and TStudent share the structure and behavior of the same class, TPerson, but they don't share the same TPerson object. When a TGradTeachingAsst object is created, it in turn instantiates (calls the constructor of) its base class, TGraduateStudent, which in turn instantiates TStudent, which in turn instantiates a TPerson object with same name, address, etc. In the same TGradTeachingAsst object, when TTeacher is instantiated, it in turn instantiates TPerson with the same name, address, etc. This creates a TGradTeachingAsst object with two TPerson objects (see Fig. 6-9 and code below).

Structure of a TGradTeachingAsst object

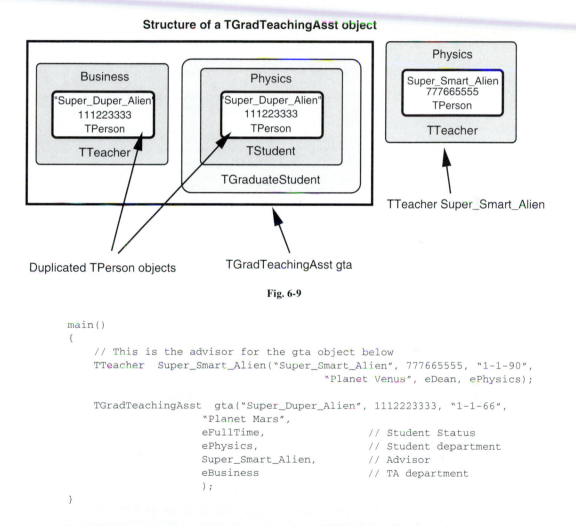

Fig. 6-9

```
main()
{
    // This is the advisor for the gta object below
    TTeacher  Super_Smart_Alien("Super_Smart_Alien", 777665555, "1-1-90",
                                "Planet Venus", eDean, ePhysics);

    TGradTeachingAsst  gta("Super_Duper_Alien", 1112223333, "1-1-66",
                    "Planet Mars",
                    eFullTime,                    // Student Status
                    ePhysics,                     // Student department
                    Super_Smart_Alien,            // Advisor
                    eBusiness                     // TA department
                    );
}
```

In addition to wasting space, this duplication of TPerson objects causes inconsistent behavior also. For example, if the name of a TGradTeachingAsst is to be changed and if

[6]In Eiffel, direct repeated inheritance is allowed.

the implementation of TGradTeachingAsst ends up changing the _name data member in the TPerson within TGraduateStudent (and not that in TTeacher) then anyone accessing the TPerson object through the TTeacher path would get the old name and clients accessing the TPerson through the TGraduateStudent path will get the new name. Here is a code snippet that demonstrates this situation.

```
main()
{
    // This is the advisor for the gta object below
    TTeacher   mickey("Mickey Mouse", 1112223333, "1-1-1928", "Disney Land",
                                                          eDean, eArts);

    TGradTeachingAsst  bugs("Bugs Bunny", 777665555, "12-1-1940",
                        "Looney Tunes", // address
                        eFullTime,      // Student Status
                        ePhysics,       // Student department
                        mickey,         // Advisor
                        eArts           // TA department
                   );
    // Make a TGraduateStudent pointer point to a TGradTeachingAsst object
    // This is fine because a TGradTeachingAsst is a TGraduateStudent
    TGraduateStudent*  gsp = &bugs
    /*
     Now change the name of the TGradTeachingAsst using the TGraduateStudent
     interface. When we call SetName() using gsp, we are invoking
     SetName as seen in the interface of TGraduateStudent. This will
     access the TPerson which TGraduateStudent inherits from
     TStudent. But nothing has changed in the TPerson inherited by
     TTeacher. It still has the old name "Bug Bunny"
    */
    gsp->SetName("Daffy Duck");
    gsp->Print(); // Print invoked through the TGraduateStudent interface

    /*
      Next create a pointer to TTeacher and access the TGradTeachingAsst
      object through the TTeacher interface. Now we get the old name that
      was stored in TPerson
     */
    TTeacher*  tp = &bugs;
    // The line below will print the old information: "Bugs Bunny"
    cout << "Name through Teacher is: " << tp->GetName() << endl;
    // The next line will print the new information: "Daffy Duck"
    cout << "Name through TGraduateStudent is: " << gsp->GetName() << endl;

}
```

In this scenario, for the same object, the result of GetName() is different based on the calling interface. This kind of behavior is highly misleading to clients and they cannot fix the problem easily. The correct solution is to fix the hierarchy such that TPerson is not duplicated. Another problem is that of ambiguity; when a TGradTeachingAsst object needs to be used polymorphically where a TPerson is expected, there is no direct conversion to TPerson possible because there is more than one TPerson object in TGradTeachingAsst. Here is an example:

```
// This is just a simple function accepting a TPerson object
// polymorphically Can be called with any derived class object of TPerson
void foo(const TPerson& aPerson)
{
    // some code - not important for this example
}

main()
{
    // This is the advisor for the gta object below
    TTeacher  mickey("Mickey Mouse", 1112223333, "1-1-1928",
       "Disney Land", eDean, eArts);

    TGradTeachingAsst  bugs("Bugs Bunny" 777665555, "12-1-1940,
                       "Looney Tunes",
                       eFullTime, // Student Status
                       ePhysics,  // Student department
                       mickey, // Advisor
                       eArts // TA department
                       );

        // Call foo() polymorphically using the TTeacher object
        foo(mickey); // Works fine because TTeacher is a TPerson

        // Try to do the same thing with TGradTeachingAsst object
        // Call foo() with the object
        foo(bugs); // Ambiguous conversion to TPerson - fails
}
```

The call to foo() using the bugs object is ambiguous because there isn't a unique TPerson object within a TGradTeachingAsst object (as shown in Fig. 6-9). Hence, the implicit conversion to TPerson is not possible.

What we really need is a facility by which we can share specified data members of the class TPerson in a TGradTeachingAsst object, while at the same time duplicating those that need to be duplicated in hierarchies where there is more than one object of TPerson. In other words, it will be very nice to have control over the sharing of individual data members of the class TPerson. If we could retain only one copy of the data members _name, _age, _ssn, and _birthDate inside of TGradTeachingAsst objects, our problem would be solved. But, remember that private data members are not accessible (nor shareable) outside the class under C++. So it is not possible to have control over the individual data members of the class TPerson. The next best thing we can expect is to keep only one copy of the TPerson object inside of TGradTeachingAsst objects. This is made possible by *virtual base classes*.

SOLUTION TO REPEATED INHERITANCE

Sharing objects with Virtual Base classes in C++

By making the base class TPerson a virtual base within TGradTeachingAsst, we get only one TPerson object within a TGradTeachingAsst. But notice that the TPerson class is a direct base of TTeacher and TStudent and not of TGradTeachingAsst.

Therefore, TTeacher and TStudent should share the TPerson object when they (TTeacher and TStudent) are combined as part of TGradTeachingAsst objects. Hence, the TTeacher and TStudent class should declare their intentions of sharing the TPerson object. This is done by the following declaration:

```
class TTeacher : virtual public TPerson {
      // all the rest of the code
};

class TStudent : public virtual TPerson {
      // all the rest of the code
};
```

Notice that the ordering of the keywords virtual and public is not important. In the above declaration, TPerson is a **virtual** base for both TTeacher and TStudent. It implies that in any hierarchy where a TTeacher and TStudent are direct or indirect base classes, then the TPerson object would be shared by them (TTeacher and TStudent). In other words, TPerson is not an absolute (or real) base class, as we have seen so far in other inheritance hierarchies. With this change, the real class hierarchy is as shown in Fig. 6-10.

Objects of the class TGradTeachingAsst will have a single object of TPerson inside them (as opposed to two in the previous case). Now, TPerson is referred to as a **virtual base class**. Needless to say, this scenario is not easy to understand without some good explanation of the different possibilities and responsibilities.

1. The TPerson object is shared only within objects of TGradTeachingAsst. If we create a stand alone TTeacher, TStudent, or a TGraduateStudent object, they all get their own TPerson object—nothing is shared among them. This is perfectly sensible. Any TTeacher object has nothing in common with any other TStudent object (unless

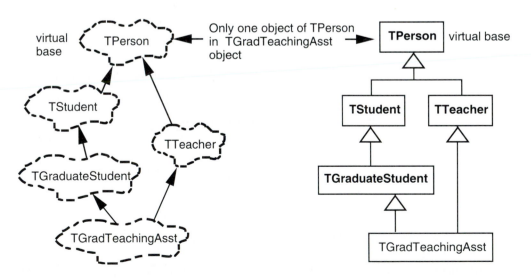

Fig. 6-10

they are part of the same TGradTeachingAsst object).

2. When a TGradTeachingAsst object is instantiated, the compiler recognizes the virtual base TPerson and only one object of TPerson is created. This ensures that a TGradTeachingAsst has a unique name, address, etc.

3. Even though the TPerson object is shared only when a TGradTeachingAsst object is created, the responsibility and forethought to ensure this lies with the TTeacher and TStudent classes—they have to declare the base class TPerson to be a virtual base. Making such decisions is not a trivial task.

Fig. 6-11 clearly demonstrates the presence of TPerson objects in various scenarios.

In effect, classes TTeacher and TStudent, by making TPerson a virtual base, state that they will share a single TPerson object between them when they are combined in a derived class, by virtue of multiple inheritance. Thus, a virtual base class signals sharing of object(s). In TGradTeachingAsst, all the objects (TGradTeachingAsst, TStudent, TTeacher, TGraduateStudent) share the same TPerson object. This sharing of the TPerson object is within the TGradTeachingAsst object. No other class needs to know anything about the sharing.

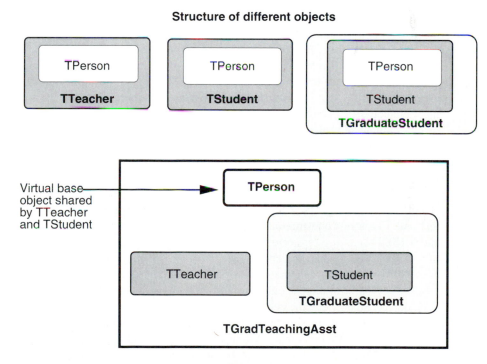

Fig. 6-11

Benefits of Virtual Base Classes

The advantage of this scheme is that clients of TGradTeachingAsst will always get the same behavior no matter how they access the TPerson object. Remember that TPerson, within a TGradTeachingAsst, can be reached from TGraduateStudent or from TTeacher. If the name or address within a graduate teaching assistant (TGradTeaching-Asst object) is changed, then anyone using this TGradTeachingAsst object will see the new name (address). The old name (address) no longer exists in the object. This makes state management much simpler.

Virtual base classes also help in sharing information. Any data that should not be duplicated inside a complete object can be placed inside a virtual base class. The virtual base ensures that there is only one copy of its object in any complete object such as TGradTeachingAsst.

Virtual base classes help immensely in solving design problems where sharing information is essential. In many situations, the same class is inherited more than once indirectly. One cannot stop this from happening because such relationships are quite natural in inheritance hierarchies. Virtual base classes ensure sharing without the individual class designers having to worry about it (only the classes that directly inherit from the virtual base need to know about the sharing). This scenario is visible in C++ iostreams library implementations. Class ios (which holds the state of the stream) is a virtual base class for istream, ostream, and iostream, classes.

New Problems Due to Virtual Base Classes

NOTE Much of the following discussion is very specific to C++. A reader not interested in language details may skip this section without any loss of continuity. But it is interesting to read this section from the viewpoint of language complexity and language design.

Virtual base classes are definitely useful when the designer uses it carefully. But a virtual base class also brings with it some new problems that never existed until now. The C++ language has solutions to these problems, but remembering the rules and implementing them correctly is not easy.

Problem of multiple constructor calls: In the original TGradTeachingAsst hierarchy, each derived class invokes the constructor of its direct base classes. So TStudent invokes TPerson constructor—the direct base of TStudent. Similarly, TTeacher also invokes TPerson constructor. On the other hand, TGraduateStudent invokes TStudent constructor (which in turn invokes the TPerson constructor). Finally, TGradTeaching-Asst invokes TGraduateStudent constructor (which in turn invokes TStudent constructor) and TTeacher constructor (which in turn invokes TPerson constructor) (Fig. 6-12 and 6-13).

When we traverse the constructor call paths, it is easy to notice two calls to the TPerson constructor. And that is really confusing because in this hierarchy with virtual base class TPerson, there is only one TPerson object in any complete TGradTeaching-Asst object. So how can the constructor execute *twice* for one object of TPerson?

Remember that we have not changed any implementation code in the TGradTeachingAsst hierarchy. We just added the virtual keyword to the base class declaration of TStudent and TTeacher. In the original hierarchy, without virtual base class TPerson, we really did create two TPerson objects (hence two calls to TPerson con-

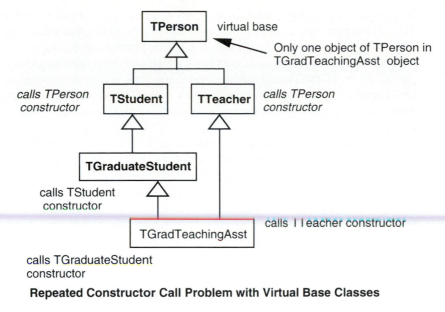

Repeated Constructor Call Problem with Virtual Base Classes

Fig. 6-12

structor). But that is no longer true in the new hierarchy with virtual base classes. The language must have some way of avoiding this duplicated constructor call.

As defined in the C++ language standard, it is the responsibility of the *most derived class* constructor to invoke the constructor for the virtual base class. In the above hierarchy, Fig. 6-12 or 6-13, **TGradTeachingAsst** is the final object or the *complete object*. In other words, **TGradTeachingAsst** is not created as part of another derived class—it is a

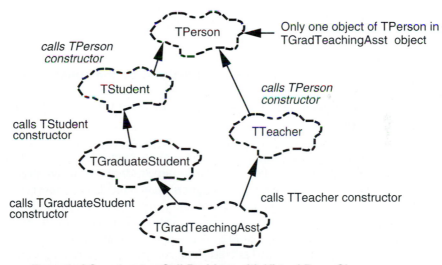

Repeated Constructor Call Problem with Virtual Base Classes

Fig. 6-13

stand-alone object. The TGraduateStudent object is a sub-object created as part of the TGradTeachingAsst object. In fact, four sub-objects (TGraduateStudent, TTeacher, TStudent, TPerson) are created within a TGradTeachingAsst object. The class of the completed object is the most derived class which is TGradTeachingAsst in this example. So every TGradTeachingAsst constructor must invoke an appropriate constructor for TPerson. In our implementation, we have a single constructor in the TGradTeaching-Asst class that must invoke the constructor of the virtual base class TPerson as part of its initialization phase.

A careful reader would have already noticed a major problem with this scheme. It is easy to understand the rule about the most derived class being responsible for invoking the virtual base class constructor. But the other classes in the hierarchy were written before TGradTeachingAsst class and those classes invoke the constructor of TPerson as part of their initialization. For example, TTeacher class invokes the constructor of TPerson and so does TStudent. The code to do this is already written. We cannot go back and change that code just because the TGradTeachingAsst class needs to call the TPerson constructor. One should not have to change an existing class when a new derived class is added—that is contrary to the principles of software reusability and encapsulation. Here is a code fragment from the TTeacher class that clearly depicts the situation.

```
TTeacher::TTeacher(const char theName[],
                   unsigned long theSSN,
                   const char theBirthDate[],
                   const char theAddress[],
                   Rank theRank,
                   EDepartment theDepartment)
             : TPerson(theName, theSSN, theBirthDate, theAddress)
{
   // and the rest of the implementation code
}
```

Does the virtual base class create more problems than it solves? The next few paragraphs will answer that question.

☞ **All virtual base classes are initialized by the constructor of the most derived class. When a complete object is being created, existing calls to the virtual base class constructor from the sub-object constructors are ignored.**

In our example, when an object of TGradTeachingAsst is created, it is the complete object, and TStudent, TTeacher, and TGraduateStudent are all sub-objects (Fig. 6–14). The most derived class, TGradTeachingAsst should invoke the constructor of TPerson. In addition to that, TGradTeachingAsst also invokes the constructors for TTeacher and TGraduateStudent. With normal object creation, TTeacher's constructor would call TPerson's constructor and TStudent's constructor would also invoke TPerson's constructor. But when the TGradTeachingAsst constructor executes (remember that it is the most derived class), existing calls to the TPerson constructor from TStudent and TTeacher are ignored and only the call from TGradTeachingAsst constructor to TPerson constructor is used. In effect, when a TGradTeachingAsst object is created,

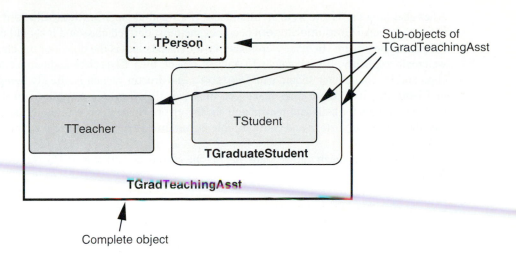

Fig. 6-14

the compiler knows that it is the complete object and constructor calls to the virtual base class object from other sub-objects are ignored. At least, the programmer need not worry about the issue. Note that in all these situations we never have to know the ordering of constructor calls. Programmers just need to make all the constructor calls and leave the responsibility of ordering the calls to the compiler. The compiler knows the correct order in which to invoke the constructors.

NOTE   If the most derived class constructor fails to invoke a constructor of the virtual base class(es) explicitly, then the compiler will try to invoke the default constructor of the virtual base class(es), if there is an accessible default constructor in the virtual base class(es). Otherwise, a compile-time error is generated.

Anyone using virtual base classes must remember the above rule about virtual base class constructors. It would be easier to write code if the virtual base class(es) has a default constructor (one which can be called without any arguments) because then the compiler will make the right constructor calls; we don't have to remember all the details. This does not imply that every virtual base class must provide a default constructor. The decision to provide a default constructor (for that matter any other constructor) in a class is an interface design issue that cannot be compromised. A default constructor is logical only if the object of the class can be properly initialized, even without any arguments to the constructor. Programming with virtual base classes is a little easier when they (virtual base classes) have default constructors. But if adding a default constructor to a class compromises the interface of the class, then one should not provide it. In our **TPerson** example, it does not make any sense to provide a default constructor because there are no default values for a person's name, age, etc.—they must all be specified when a **TPerson** object is created.

☞ **Don't provide some member function just to make compiling code easier. It is more important to have abstraction integrity.**

After changing the TPerson to a virtual base, if a stand-alone TGraduateStudent object is created, then TGraduateStudent becomes the most derived class and it should call the TPerson constructor. In other words, the most derived class is the object of the class that we create explicitly. If we create a TTeacher object, then TTeacher is the most derived class and its constructor should call TPerson's constructor, which is already being done in TTeacher. If all these rules make you dizzy, don't worry, the compiler will flag the missing constructor calls and makes you fix the error. There is no way the error can get past the compilation stage and cause trouble at run time (unless of course the compiler itself has bugs in it).

With all this taken into account, here is the correct constructor of TGradTeaching-Asst:

```
TGradTeachingAsst::TGradTeachingAsst(const char theName[],
        unsigned long theSSN, // of the graduate student
        const char theBirthDate[],
        const char theAddress[],
        EStudentStatus theStatus,
        EDepartment studentDepartment,
        const Teacher& advisorInCharge,
        EDepartment teachingDept)
    // Initialize direct base class TGraduateStudent
  : TGraduateStudent(theName, theSSN, theBirthDate, theAddress,
                theStatus, studentDepartment, advisorInCharge),
        // Initialize direct base class TTeacher
    TTeacher(theName, theSSN, theBirthDate, theAddress,
          eGraduateTeachingAssistant, teachingDept),
        // Initialize the virtual base class TPerson
  TPerson(theName, theSSN, theBirthDate, theAddress)
  {
      // Implementation code for TGradTeachingAsst
  }
```

By now, one must be thoroughly convinced about the complexity and rules of MI, and more so with virtual base classes. It is clearly evident that MI is not for the faint hearted. Using MI correctly and effectively requires very good knowledge of the language and design principles.

EIFFEL   Under Eiffel, the solution to avoid duplication of features (method or instance variable) is a little different. It is not an error for a class to inherit repeatedly (even directly) from a single class. A feature (not an object) from the common parent class is considered shared in the final object if the feature has not been renamed along any of the inheritance paths. (Renaming was discussed earlier in this chapter.) This rule is quite powerful and easy to understand. When a class inherits from another class, it has to rename any feature that encounters a name clash. If a feature has not been renamed in the hierarchy, it guarantees that the feature has no name conflict anywhere in the hierarchy (otherwise it would have been renamed.) Any such feature would be shared in the object of the final class—it is not duplicated. In the example above, none of the features of TPerson (name, age, address, ssn, birthDate) would be renamed (there is no need to) in TStudent, TTeacher, and TGraduateStudent and, hence, would not be duplicated in TGradTeachingAsst. Hence, in Eiffel, TGradTeachingAsst need not do anything extra to retain only a single copy of name, age, ssn, address, and birthDate. At first glance, this rule in Eiffel may not appear to be very different from the C++ virtual base classes in this particular example. But it is a little different and more powerful. For example, let's assume that a graduate teaching assistant would like to have two different mailing addresses—one for student related correspondence and another for graduate teaching assistant related correspondence. With this requirement, the declaration of TGradTeachingAsst in Eiffel would be:

```
                    — Eiffel Code
            class TGradTeachingAsst
                inherit
                        TTeacher
                        rename
                                address as teaching_address

                        TGraduateStudent
                        rename
                                address as student_address
                — Other details of class not shown
```

With this declaration, objects of TGradTeachingAsst will automatically get two copies of the feature address but one of them is referred as teaching_address and the other one as student_address. Other duplicated features (name, age, etc.) inherited by TGradTeachingAsst from TTeacher and TGraduateStudent are automatically shared because they have not been renamed anywhere along the paths leading to TGradTeachingAsst class. The advantage is that neither TTeacher not TGraduateStudent need to know anything about this duplicated feature—address. This is not done so easily under C++ without changing the classes TTeacher and TStudent.

Because of this renaming of features, Eiffel can easily handle directed repeated inheritance. For example , assume that class A has a feature X and class C inherits from A as follows:

```
            class C
                    inherit
                            A — first inheritance from A
                            rename
                                X as X_1

                            A — second inheritance from A
                            rename
                                X as X_2
```

Because of renaming, when C refers to the feature X in A, it will use the name X_1 or X_2. Hence, there is no ambiguity as to which A within C is being accessed.

Comparing MI in Eiffel and C++

The solution for duplicated objects is somewhat more elegant under Eiffel. Here, needless duplication of individual features (data members or methods) are eliminated automatically, whereas in C++, duplication of objects is eliminated by the programmer by using virtual base classes. With C++, if we really want to retain multiple copies some data members of a class (but not all of them), then there is no easy solution except to redesign the hierarchy such that only those that never have to be duplicated reside in the virtual base class. Duplication of features under Eiffel can be controlled at the feature level, whereas with C++, granularity of duplication control is limited to a class. In the above example, with Eiffel one can control the sharing (or replication) of each feature (data member) in TPerson, but in C++, we only have the option to share or replicate TPerson within TGradTeachingAsst objects.

Here is the corrected TGradTeachingAsst class, which initializes the virtual base class TPerson:

```cpp
class TGradTeachingAsst : public TTeacher, public TGraduateStudent {
    public:
        TGradTeachingAsst(const char theName[],
                unsigned long theSSN, // of the graduate student
                const char theBirthDate[],
                const char theAddress[],
                EStudentStatus theStatus,
                EDepartment studentDepartment,
                const TTeacher& advisorInCharge,
                EDepartment teachingDept);

        TGradTeachingAsst(const TGradTeachingAsst& copy);
        TGradTeachingAsst& operator=(const TGradTeachingAsst& assign);
        ~TGradTeachingAsst();

        // This method must be overridden
        virtual void Print() const;

        void SetStudentsDepartment(EDepartment dept);
        EDepartment GetStudentsDepartment() const;

        // This method must be overridden because
        // for a GTA the rank cannot be changed
        bool SetRank(ERank newRank);

        void SetTeachingDepartment(EDepartment dept);
        EDepartment GetTeachingDepartment() const;

};
```

And for completeness, here is part of the implementation:

```cpp
#include <iostream.h>

TGradTeachingAsst::TGradTeachingAsst(const char theName[],
            unsigned long theSSN, // of the graduate student
            const char theBirthDate[],
            const char theAddress[],
            EStudentStatus theStatus,
            EDepartment studentDepartment,
```

```
                 const TTeacher& advisorInCharge,
                 EDepartment teachingDept)
          // Initialize direct base class TGraduateStudent
     : TGraduateStudent(theName, theSSN, theBirthDate, theAddress,
                 theStatus, studentDepartment, advisorInCharge),
          // Initialize direct base class TTeacher
       TTeacher(theName, theSSN, theBirthDate, theAddress,
              GraduateTeachingAssistant, teachingDept),
          // Initialize the virtual base class TPerson
       TPerson(theName, theSSN, theBirthDate, theAddress)
     {
          // Implementation code for TGradTeachingAsst
     }

void
TGradTeachingAsst::Print() const
{
     // We get the appropriate pieces of data and print them
     EStudentStatus studentStats = GetStatus();
     EDepartment studentDepartment = TGraduateStudent::GetDepartment();
     EDepartment teachingDepartment = TTeacher::GetDepartment();

     cout << "Name: " << TPerson::GetName() << endl;
     cout << "This person is a Graduate Student" << endl;
     cout << " in the department of: " <<
          departments[(int) studentDepartment] << endl;
     cout << "The graduate teaching assistantship is in the department: "
          << departments[(int) teachingDepartment] << endl;
}

void
TGradTeachingAsst::SetStudentsDepartment(EDepartment dept)
{ TStudent::SetDepartment(dept); }

EDepartment
TGradTeachingAsst::GetStudentsDepartment() const
{    return TStudent:GetDepartment(); }

void
TGradTeachingAsst::SetTeachingDepartment(EDepartment dept)
{    TTeacher::SetDepartment(dept); }

EDepartment
TGradTeachingAsst::GetTeachingDepartment() const
{    return TTeacher::GetDepartment(); }

bool
TGradTeachingAsst::SetRank(ERank newRank)
{
     // Do nothing because the rank of a TGradTeachingAsst cannot be changed
     // It is always eGraduateTeachingAssistant which is already set in
     // the constructor call to TTeacher
     cout << "Error: Cannot change the rank of TGradTeachingAsst\n";

     return false;
}
```

GENERAL PROBLEMS WITH INHERITANCE

We have discussed inheritance in all its glory and usefulness in this chapter and also in Chapter 5. If you haven't already noticed, inheritance is a static relationship, meaning it is a relationship that does not lend itself to changes easily—it lacks flexibility. Furthermore, changing the relationships in a MI hierarchy is even more difficult. Inheritance is a great tool for modeling relationships found during domain analysis. But inheritance is not the best tool for situations where changes in relationships among classes need to be considered. The relationships in an inheritance hierarchy are decided and coded based on static relationships among classes. But making changes/additions to these relationships later is a difficult task. And this difficulty is felt even more with MI hierarchies. It is impossible to model dynamically changing relationships using MI. For example, TGradTeachingAsst is both a **TGraduateStudent** and a **TTeacher** at all times. This is a very rigid relationship. In reality, a person plays the role of a **TTeacher** when she is teaching some course and she behaves as a **TGraduateStudent** while attending graduate school. Strictly speaking, she exhibits the characteristics of a **TTeacher** at times and **TGraduateStudent** some other time but she is not both at the same time. This property of a TGradTeachingAsst is not reflected in the hierarchy that we have seen so far.

Taking a different approach, enrolling for courses is a capability that a **TPerson** can acquire. Similarly, teaching courses is also a capability a **TPerson** can acquire after going through some certification process. And a **TGradTeachingAsst** acquires both. This looks correct until we consider adding a new capability to any **TPerson**. For example, consider what happens if we want to add a research assistant capability to a **TPerson**. A research assistant need not be a student. One could extend the hierarchy as follows in Fig. 6-15:

New class TResearchAsst added to the existing hierarchy

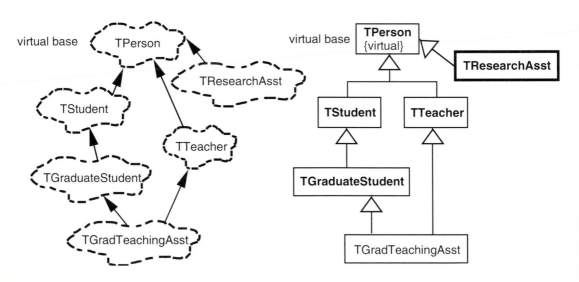

Fig. 6-15

That looks like a reasonable design—any **TResearchAsst** is also a **TPerson**. What if a **TGraduateStudent** also takes on the job of a **TResearchAsst**, probably in a different (or even in the same) department. With all our experience with inheritance, can we say that **TGraduateStudent** is also a **TResearchAsst**? Definitely not because *not all* **TGraduateStudents** are **TResearchAssts**. The problem is that performing research duties is a capability that some **TPerson** can acquire without being a student or a teacher. A student (or even a teacher) can also be a research assistant but that is not always true. Inheritance is suitable for modeling relationships among classes that are always true. Definitely a **TGraduateStudent** is always a **TStudent** - nothing wrong with that. But how can we model the situation of a **TGraduateStudent** who is also a **TResearchAsst**? And can we add another class **TEmployee** to this hierarchy to model employees in the university. Teachers and research assistants are employees, and a student could also be employed in the university. But not all students are employees. We encounter conflicting requirements, and inheritance relationships are no longer suitable to model such complex relationships. We need to look elsewhere for more meaningful solutions.

The scenario depicted in the previous paragraph is a common situation in commercial software development. We encounter the necessity to add different capabilities to different classes. There can be many such capabilities and it should be possible to pick one or more of them. We discuss two possible solutions for adding capabilities to classes. One of them is a more static relation and the other one is more suited for dynamically changing environments.

USING MIXIN CLASSES FOR ADDING STATIC CAPABILITIES

In our university example, we can easily notice the fact that teaching a course, qualifying to register for a course, performing research duties, etc. are capabilities a **TPerson** can acquire. Moreover, a person can acquire any combination of these capabilities. For example, a person could be a student in the Electrical engineering department with research work in Aerospace Engineering. Similarly, a person could be a student in the Computer Science Department with a graduate assistantship in the Mathematics Department and research duties in the Physics Department. These situations show different combinations of capabilities (or roles). A mixin class is very handy to model such scenarios.

Definition of a Mixin Class

A mixin class adds new capabilities to other classes. One never creates an instance of a mixin class. It does not make any sense to create an instance of the mixin class because the mixin class adds *flavor* to some other class—it is to be mixed in with another class. In this book we shall use a unique notation to represent mixin classes—they always start with the letter 'M'.[7] By using mixin classes, one can combine different capabilities (flavors) to form new capabilities. This is very similar to adding toppings to ice cream. At an ice cream parlor, the customer can choose any combination of toppings. I might pick

---

[7]As you already know, normal classes begin with 'T'.

cherries, nuts, and cookies. Someone else might opt for berries and chocolate syrup. One has the freedom to make ice creams with any combination of toppings. There is no restriction on the combination of toppings. Each topping can be viewed as a mixin class that adds a new flavor. Mixin classes afford this freedom to application designers. We are going to make use of mixin classes to solve our university problem.

NOTE Mixin classes represent static relationships. They allow us to add capabilities when designing hierarchies. We cannot add capabilities to an object dynamically (at run time) using mixin classes. A scheme for adding capabilities dynamically is discussed later in this chapter.

The ability to become a student in the university system can be captured in the mixin class MCanBecomeStudent. This mixin adds methods to register for courses, set student identification, etc. Most of these methods would be pure virtual, making the mixin an abstract base class.

```
enum EQualification { eNoSchooling, eHighSchool, eUnderGraduate, eGraduate,
                                      eDoctorate };

class MCanBecomeStudent {
     public:
             // Constructors and other usual functions not shown
             void SetDepartment(EDepartment dept);
             EDepartment GetDepartment() const;

             virtual bool EnrollForCourse(const TCourse& aCourse) = 0;
             virtual bool DropFromCourse(const TCourse& course) = 0;
             virtual void ListCoursesRegisteredFor() const = 0;
             virtual EQualification GetStudentQualification() const;
             // and many more
};
```

Given this new class, we can change our student-teacher hierarchy as follows (see Fig. 6-16).

New hierarchy using mixin classes

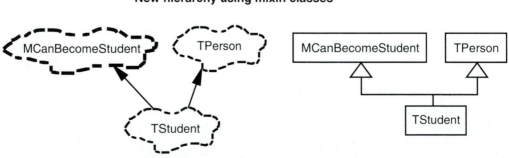

Fig. 6-16

Now, a student is any person who acquires the capabilities to become a student. Class **TStudent** must implement all the pure virtual methods inherited from **MCanBecomeStudent**. It is also possible to provide all the (default) implementation in **MCanBecomeStudent** and make it optional for **TStudent** to override them. The decision to make a method pure virtual in a mixin class is entirely dependent on the services provided by the mixin class.

The next step is to add a mixin class that captures the capability to teach a course in the university. A person can teach a course if she is qualified to do so. The ability to teach is captured in a new mixin class **MQualifiedToTeach**. This class will provide methods to manipulate courses taught, supervisor, department, etc.

```
class MQualifiedToTeach {
    public:
        // Usual constructors, etc. not shown for simplicity
        virtual void SetDepartment(EDepartment dept);
        virtual EDepartment GetDepartment() const;
        virtual void ListCoursesQualifiedToTeach() const = 0;
        virtual double GetYearsOfExperience() const;

        // What degree (master, Phd, etc) does the Teacher have?
        virtual EQualification GetHighestDegree() const = 0;
        virtual TPerson GetSupervisor() const = 0;
        virtual double GetSalary() const;
        // and many more
};
```

Method **ListCoursesQualifiedToTeach** shows all the courses the person has been certified to teach. This list of courses might be setup during object creation and might also be updated later through other methods. It is also possible that the university keeps a database of people with their certification history. Salary is the compensation paid to the person for teaching the course(s).

The new hierarchy is shown in Fig. 6-17.

On the same lines, we can add another mixin class to account for people who are involved in research. Let's call this mixin class **MQualifiedToDoResearch**. This class captures the essential features of a person doing research.

```
class MQualifiedToDoResearch {
    public:
        // number of years of research experience
        virtual double GetResearchExperience() const;
        // number of papers published
        virtual int GetNumberOfPublications() const;
        virtual EDepartment GetDepartment() const;
        virtual EQualification GetHighestDegree() const;
        // and other methods
};
```

With this new class, it is easy to model a **TResearchAsst**. This class inherits from the mixin **MQualifiedToDoResearch** and **TPerson**. A graduate research assistant will be another class inheriting from **TGraduateStudent** and **TResearchAsst** (see Fig. 6-18 and 6-19).

New hierarchy using mixin classes

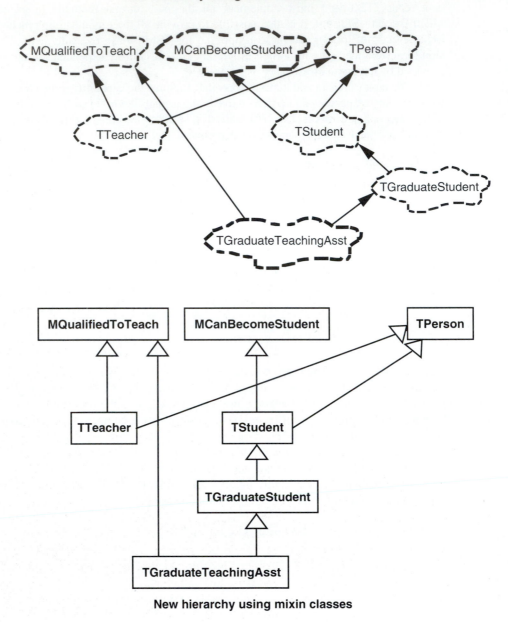

New hierarchy using mixin classes

Fig. 6-17

New hierarchy using mixin classes

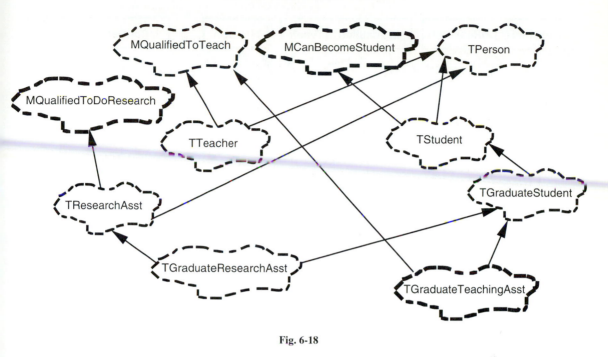

Fig. 6-18

NOTE   In this example of mixin classes (Fig. 6-19), the reader might have noticed that no implementation code is shown. It is more important to understand the concept of mixin classes. The implementation code is not very hard to write once the design concepts are clear. Hence, the emphasis is on concepts rather than code.

This new hierarchy exemplifies the power of mixin classes. They allow the designer to provide orthogonal capabilities that can be mixed together in any combination desired. One does not have to pick a compromise solution (which is often the case with simple MI). This design gets rid of the virtual base class **TPerson**. We ran into a number of complex design issues and code management issues because of the virtual base class **TPerson**. Mixin classes help in eliminating virtual base classes. The original MI hierarchy with the **TGradTeachingAsst** looks like a diamond. These diamonds are a potential source of many problems when designing for flexibility. Mixin classes provide an alternative in such situations. The flexibility and simplicity of design is achieved because the capabilities of a person are now decoupled. In the original design, a teacher was a person and the teaching capability was embedded in the class **TTeacher**. Another problem with the original design was that of rigidity. It is almost impossible to add new classes to the hierarchy to allow for new capabilities. Moreover, adding a new class will affect every class in the hierarchy. The mixin class hierarchy takes care of that problem. We can add new capabilities without affecting other classes in the hierarchy (as was done with **MQualifiedToDoResearch**).

New hierarchy using mixin classes

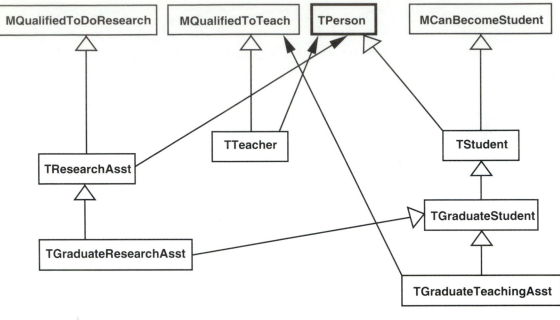

Fig. 6-19

When to Use Mixin Classes?

1. When there are a number of independent characteristics that any class can acquire, it makes sense to represent the characteristics as mixin classes. See MQualifiedToDoResearch and others above.

2. When a new capability needs to be added selectively to some classes in an existing hierarchy, mixin classes may be the only alternative. Existing classes that need the capability would inherit from the new mixin class but other classes that don't require this capability don't have to worry about the new mixin class.

NOTE   Mixin classes need not always be used with public inheritance. As illustrated later in this chapter, a mixin class can be useful even under private derivation. For further discussion of this concept please refer to the section on private derivation later in this chapter.

DESIGNING FOR DYNAMICALLY CHANGING SITUATIONS

The mixin design presented above is definitely better than our original design using virtual base classes. But it is still not flexible enough. To understand the drawbacks of the new design, let's review a typical run-time scenario.

We want to minimize duplication of data at all times. That's why we used virtual base classes. Duplication of data not only causes wastage of resources but also causes data management headaches. So avoiding duplication of data is a noble goal. We also want to copy minimum data when objects are copied or when they need to change. For example, if a normal student in the university becomes a graduate student, we want to be able to modify (add) information that only affects the student related data. Definitely, there is no need to tinker with the data in TPerson. In other words, when a TStudent becomes a TGraduateStudent we should be able to just add the TGraduateStudent part of the data to TStudent. On the same lines, when a TGraduateStudent becomes a TTeacher, we would like to throw away the TGraduateStudent part and add the TTeacher capabilities, without modifying the TPerson part. These seem like easy goals to achieve but one careful look at the object management scenario reveals the underlying problems.

When we have a TStudent object, how do we convert that object to a TGraduate-Student object? We have to create a new TGraduateStudent object using the data in the TStudent object. There is no simple way of doing this. We have to extract each and every field from the TStudent object and use that information (and the information provided by the client for the TGraduateStudent object) to create a new TGraduate Student object. Then we have to discard the TStudent object. The code fragment might look like this:

```
// This function creates a new TGraduateStudent object from an existing
// TStudent object. It deletes the original TStudent object after the new
// TGraduateStudent object is created.
TGraduateStudent*
CreateNewGraduateStudentFromStudent(TStudent* adoptStudent,
                    EDepartment newDepartment,
                    TTeacher& theAdvisor)
{
    // We extract the necessary information from the existing TStudent
    // object (pointed by adoptStudent), and pass that information to
    // TGraduateStudent constructor.
    TGraduateStudent *gp
        = new TGraduateStudent(adoptStudent->GetName() // get name part
            adoptStudent->GetIdentificationNumber(), // Student ID
            adoptStudent->GetBirthDate(), // birth date from TPerson
            adoptStudent->GetAddress(), // address from TPerson
            adoptStudent->GetStudentStatus(), // status from TStudent
            newDepartment,             // department for the grad student
            theAdvisor);

    // Next delete the TStudent object
    delete adoptStudent;

    return gp;
}
```

It is interesting to note that even though the TPerson part of the TStudent remains the same in the TGraduateStudent, we still couldn't reuse the data directly. We had to create a new TGraduateStudent (which created a new TStudent and a new TPerson) and then throw away all the existing useful pieces of information in the original **TStudent** object.

NOTE   There is another solution possible for this scenario. Class **TGraduateStudent** could provide a constructor that accepts a **TPerson** object. This constructor would create a new **TGraduateStudent** object using the information provided in the **TPerson** argument. This principle can also be applied to **TTeacher** class. This solution doesn't prevent the duplication of data because the new object created would copy the information from the **TPerson** object. The user must delete the **TPerson** object if it is no longer needed. Needless to point out that a **TStudent** can be substituted in place of the **TPerson** argument to the constructor. Generalizing, any derived class of **TPerson** can be passed to this special constructor. This scheme is used quite often in the industry. In general, a derived class must provide constructors to accept base class objects, if there is a requirement to create derived class objects from existing base class objects. This can be further extended to assignment operators also (derived class assignment operator accepting a base class object as the argument).

Another approach could be to create an empty **TGraduateStudent** object and then copy in the information from **TStudent**, as follows in Fig. 6-20.

```
// This function creates a new TGraduateStudent object from an existing
// TStudent object. It deletes the original
// TStudent object after the new TGraduateStudent object is created.
TGraduateStudent*
CreateNewGraduateStudentFromStudent(TStudent* adoptStudent,
                 EDepartment newDepartment,
                 TTeacher& theAdvisor)
{
    // Create an empty TGraduateStudent object
    TGraduateStudent *gp
        = new TGraduateStudent(0 // no name specified
               0, // Student ID not specified
               0, // birth date not specified
               0, // address not specified
```

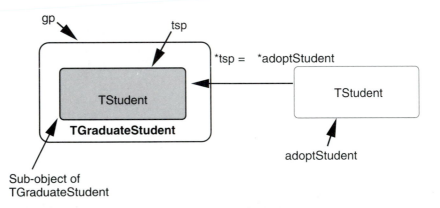

Fig. 6-20

```
               eUnknown,              // status not specified
               newDepartment,         // department for the grad student
               theAdvisor);

     // Valid Initialization because TGraduateStudent is a TStudent
     TStudent* tsp = gp;

     // Next copy all the essential information from TStudent. Dereferencing
     // tsp (which is a TStudent pointer) gives access to a TStudent object.
     // But since tsp actually points to a TGraduateStudent object, we are
     // assigning to the TStudent part of a TGraduateStudent
     *tsp = *adoptStudent;
     // Assignment from old TStudent to new TGraduateStudent. After this
     // assignment, the department part of the TGraduateStudent needs to
     // reset.
     gp->SetDepartment(newDepartment);
     // The advisor part is not accessed by TStudent, so it is fine.
     // Next delete the TStudent object
     delete adoptStudent;

     return gp;
}
```

This scheme still doesn't avoid the copying of data from old **TStudent** to the new **TGraduateStudent** object. It would have been perfect if we could somehow add the extra information about **TGraduateStudent** (like advisor) to the existing **TStudent** and convert it to a **TGraduateStudent**. We can only hope for that but it is not possible with any of our MI hierarchies discussed earlier (no matter whether it is C++ or Eiffel).

CAUTION   If the existing **TStudent** object should not be deleted by the function **CreateNewGraduateStudentFromStudent**, then do not use this function. If the intention is to create a **TGraduateStudent** from a **TStudent** but without destroying the **TStudent** object, one could write an overloaded function **CreateNewGraduateStudentFromStudent** that accepts a reference to **TStudent** or we can add a **bool** argument (with a default value) to the existing function that indicates the client's intention. Whatever implementation is chosen, ensure that the client understands the consequences with clear documentation and argument types.

This scenario shows the inflexibility of MI for dynamically changing scenarios. What we just discussed is a very common situation in databases.

When a **TGraduateStudent** becomes a **TTeacher**, the scenario is even worse. The only common piece of information here is the **TPerson** part. But we still have to copy it into a new **TTeacher** object as follows.

```
// This function creates a new TTeacher object from an existing
// TGraduateStudent object. It deletes the original TGraduateStudent object
// after the new TTeacher object is created. Follows the same scheme as the
// one shown above for creating a TGraduateStudent from TStudent

TTeacher*
CreateNewTeacherFromGradStudent(TGraduateStudent* adoptStudent, EDepartment
                                newDepartment, ERank theRank)
```

```
{
    TTeacher *tp = new TTeacher( 0, // name
             0,                 // Id
             0,                 // Birth date
             0,                 // address
             theRank,
             newDepartment     // department for the grad student
             );

    // Next copy all the essential information from TGraduateStudent
    TPerson* p = tp; // again valid because a TTeacher is a TPerson
    *p = *adoptStudent; // This will copy the TPerson information

    delete adoptStudent;
    return tp;
}
```

Here again, there is quite a bit of data copying and deletion of useful information. This is a problem for which there might be a better solution.

Another problem is with multiple capabilities. Imagine what happens if a person is a graduate student in one department but a research assistant in another department. To manage these situations we have to create two independent objects—one for the graduate student and another for the research assistant in the other department. There is quite a bit of information (about the **TPerson**) duplicated here. And what if the same person is a student in two different departments (which is a very normal situation)? The scenario gets worse as we add more capabilities to the hierarchy.

We are assuming that every person has only one *role* in the university system, which is completely wrong. A person is a student in only one department or a teacher in some other department but not both. In reality, we play many different roles. There is nothing unusual about a teacher of biochemistry wanting to become a student in computer science. And a student of finance could be an instructor in the athletics department. MI with virtual base classes is definitely not suitable for this situation. And the mixin hierarchy also fails because one needs to identify all possible combinations of leaf classes (such as **TStudent, TStudent+TTeacher, TStudent+TStudent**), which will cause a combinatorial explosion of classes leading to a very complex (and yet very fragile) hierarchy.

We need to recognize the fact that a person plays many roles, but only one role is active at any time. Even though a person could be a teacher and student in the same university, she will be performing only one of the roles at a given time and not both. This is a normal trait of human beings. We play roles of father, manager, gardener, church choir singer, etc. in our daily life but not more than one at a time. The common feature of teacher, student, research assistant, graduate student, etc. is the fact that they are all roles played by a person. Once we recognize this key characteristic, it is easy to organize the hierarchy as follows in Fig. 6-21.

In this figure, every person has 'n' **TUniversityMember** roles. Each role belongs to only one person, as implied by the *for whom* relation. We can ask each **TUniversityMember** object as to whom this role belongs. Since a **TPerson** maintains a list of roles played, it is possible to enumerate all the roles played by a person.

What we have done is to decouple the roles from the person playing them. In that sense, it is similar to the mixin classes. However, it is very different from the mixin

A person plays many roles

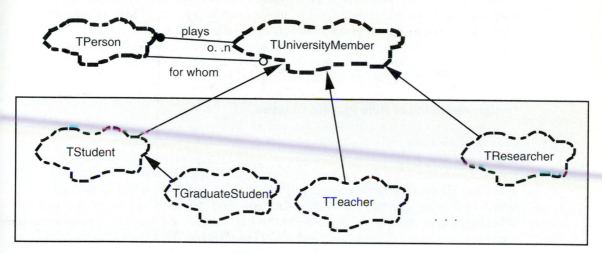

Different roles played by a person

A Person plays many roles

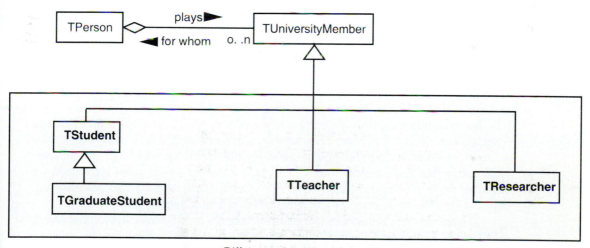

Different roles played by a person

Fig. 6-21

classes because the roles form a separate hierarchy. One can add any number of roles to a person, even the same role twice, such as student in more than one department. At any time, only one of the many roles played by the person is active. The TPerson class maintains a list of all roles played by the person. The individual roles maintain information relevant to that role only. So a TTeacher only keeps the information related to the teaching assignment (just as with mixin classes). Since all roles are attached to a person, there is no duplication of data about the person (such as name, address, etc.).

Design Flexibility of Role Playing Classes

Does this new hierarchy solve the problem of dynamically changing scenarios? Yes, it does it very well. For example if a person maintains three roles, say a teacher in one department, a student in another, and a researcher in yet another, we have a TPerson object with three TUniversityMember objects. If this person stops doing research, we need to reflect this change in the roles played. All we have to do is to discard the role TResearchAsst. Nothing else about the person has changed. Similarly, if a student role needs to be converted to a graduate student, we create a new TGraduateStudent object and assign the existing TStudent to the new TGraduateStudent (as we did earlier), but now the information to be assigned is highly diminished because there is no information about the TPerson in TUniversityMember. It also takes less time to create (and copy) any of the TUniversityMember subclass objects because the information that needs to be put into these objects is quite less. Compared to the previous designs, there is no extra memory consumed by this design because the information that is stored in any of the TUniversityMember objects is the same (all relevant information is in the derived classes of TUniversityMember). In fact, when one looks at the complete picture of managing changing roles, this new design requires somewhat less memory because it avoids data duplication completely.

How to Use Role Playing Classes?

It is time we understand how this new design works in reality. Class TPerson needs to support a new method AddRole. This methods adds a new role to the existing set of roles (if any) for the person. We need another method SetActiveRole, which specifies the currently active role. For example, when dealing with a student who is also a researcher, we would set the active role to be the student role when manipulating the students attributes. Even though a person has many roles, only one of them is active at a given time.

The next problem is that of invoking specific methods on a TUniversityMember object. A TStudent, TTeacher, TResearchAsst, etc. have different methods but they have a common base class TUniversityMember. When we ask a TPerson object for the current active role, it will return a TUniversityMember object. We cannot apply methods from TTeacher on a TUniversityMember object because TUniversityMember is not a TTeacher (but a TTeacher is a TUniversityMember). So how do we overcome this problem?

This is a classic problem of type matching. Given a TUniversityMember object, how can we check if it is really an object of one of the derived classes. Furthermore, is it possible to convert (safely) a TUniversityMember object to the correct derived class object? All these problems have been encountered by object-oriented software developers time and again and fortunately there is a solution to this problem.

RUN-TIME TYPE IDENTIFICATION (RTTI)

RTTI is a comparatively new feature of C++. It allows programmers to safely (and in a portable manner) convert pointers and references to objects from one type to another. RTTI is clearly defined and is part of the language specification.

One of the most important features of RTTI is the **Dynamic Cast Operator.** This new operator allows the programmer to convert (if possible) a pointer of one type to a pointer of another type, at run-time. If the conversion fails, the result is 0. For example, if we have a pointer to **TUniversityMember** object and we would like to convert this pointer to a **TTeacher** pointer (if the **TUniversityMember** is really a **TTeacher** object), the following code would be appropriate:

```
void f(TUniversityMember* rp)
{

    // Is this pointer (rp) to TUniversityMember, really a pointer to
    // TTeacher?
    TTeacher* = dynamic_cast<TTeacher*> (rp);
    if (tp != 0) {
        // Yes, the object pointed by rp is a TTeacher object.
        // Perform any operations on the object using tp
    }
    else {
        // No. The object pointed by rp is NOT a TTeacher object
        // It is something else. Now tp is 0
    }
}
```

This conversion (or casting) of a pointer to a base class object to a pointer to a derived class object has been traditionally called *down casting*. Going from a base class to a derived class is seen as going *down* the class hierarchy and hence the name. Such down casts were done by using ad-hoc schemes (by keeping home grown type information in objects) and was very dangerous. RTTI makes it safe. Performing an unchecked cast from a base class to a derived class is similar to leaping off a cliff with the hope of finding a soft landing platform below; you are either successful or you end up breaking many bones! RTTI doesn't allow you to jump unless there is a well formed platform below. Here is the syntax for the dynamic_cast operator.

```
dynamic_cast<Typename> (pointer)
```

The name within < and > is the type name to which you want to convert the pointer to. If the pointer really points to an object of the requested type, then the conversion takes place. Otherwise, the dynamic cast operator returns a 0 pointer. The name inside the ( ) is the pointer undergoing the test and conversion. In the sample code above, we wanted to cast the pointer **rp** to the type **TTeacher**.

The dynamic cast operator executes some implementation code to verify the validity of the conversion. In other words, there is some run-time cost associated with this operation—it is not a compile-time operation. It is also called a safe cast because the dynamic cast operator verifies the validity of the conversion and will return 0 if the attempted conversion is not possible. Hence, invalid implicit cast operations are not possible. Any cast operation will only succeed if the object is of the correct type. There is no guess work or blind leap of faith. Hence, it is safe to use.

Dynamic cast also works for object references, but the usage is a little different.

```
void f(TUniversityMember& refRole)

    // Is this reference to TUniversityMember really a reference to
    // TTeacher
        try {
        TTeacher& teacherRef = dynamic_cast<TTeacher&> (refRole);
        // Yes, the object referred by rp is a TTeacher object.
        // Perform any operations on the object using teacherRef
        }

    catch (bad_cast& b) {
        // No. The object referred by refRole is NOT a TTeacher object
        // It is something else. bad_cast is a pre-defined class used
        // by the language
    }
}
```

A pointer that is valid can never be zero. It is easy for the dynamic cast operator to return 0 when the cast fails. But for a reference to an object, there is no such distinguishing value to indicate an invalid reference. References are aliases to existing objects and a reference is always valid. Therefore the dynamic cast operator indicates failure by raising the **bad_cast** exception.[8] In anticipation of this situation we *catch* the exception. If the catch block is entered, then it is clear that the checked cast failed.

Dynamic casts work for *polymorphic* types only (i.e., for classes with virtual functions). The RTTI information is available for objects of classes with at least one virtual function. Dynamic cast will not work for objects that do not have any virtual functions. This is not really a problem because in most classes, if not any other method, the destructor is a virtual function making the class a polymorphic type. A polymorphic type is any type that can exhibit polymorphism. Dynamic casts work for virtual base classes and void pointers also. One can attempt to cast a void pointer to a pointer to some other class.

The typeid() operator

Dynamic cast internally uses a more powerful and general operator called **typeid**(). This operator returns type information about a specific type. It can also return the type information about an object whose type is not known exactly.

---

[8]Exception management is discussed in chapter 10. For now, it is enough to understand that it is an error condition that must be handled immediately or else the program will abort.

For example,

```
void f(TUniversityMember& roleRef)
{
    if (typeid(roleRef) == typeid(TTeacher) {
        // The object is really a TTeacher
    }
    else {/* It is not a reference to a TTeacher object */ }
}
```

typeid() returns a **type_info** object (described below) for the actual object. If two objects are the same type, then their typeids will compare equal. **typeid()** operator can be used for polymorphic types as well as non-polymorphic types. It works for language defined types as well as programmer defined types. Also note that **typeid** works for type names as well as object names.

```
// Built-in types
double di = 22.33;

double& dr = di;
if (typeid(dr) == typeid(double)) // NOT typeid(double&)
{     /* Do something */ }
```

typeid() operator is based on the class **type_info**.

```
class type_info {
    private:
        type_info(const type_info& );
        // cannot be copied by users
        type_info& operator=(const type_info&);
        // implementation dependent representation
    public:
        virtual ~type_info();
        bool operator==(const type_info&) const;
        bool operator!=(const type_info&) const;
        bool before(const type_info& rhs) const;9

        // Returns a pointer to the name of the type
        const char* name() const;
};
```

Objects of this class cannot be copied because the run-time system maintains these objects and uses them as needed.

CAUTION   RTTI is not a solution for all problems. It is useful (mostly) in situations where a down cast operation is needed. Such down cast operations are not very frequent. Most type dependent operations can be easily handled by using virtual functions. One should not write code that explicitly depends on the RTTI information. Not only is it expensive, but RTTI also makes your code less extensible.

9bool is language defined type in C++, which can be either "true" or "false."

> The C++ RTTI mechanism also provides a static_cast mechanism for performing casts. static_cast<T>(e) converts the value e to type T, provided an implicit conversion exists from the type of e to type T. But, static_cast cannot cast away const. There is also a const_cast<T>(e) operation to convert a const or volatile. Here T differs from the type of e only in the presence or absence of const//volatile. The reinterpret_cast can be used for implementation-defined casts. It is identical to the old style (T)(e) casts. But reinterpret_cast cannot cast away const. Use these casts instead of the old style (T)(e) casts. These are safer, easy to locate in code if modifications are required, and they clearly convey the intention of the programmer. Refer to the C++ language reference manual for details.

The solution is based on the concept of run-time type determination. What we need is a way to query (and probably convert) the exact type of a given object. Given a TUniversityMember object, we should be able to determine its exact type (TTeacher, TStudent, etc.). All this is made possible by *Run-time Type Identification*.

EIFFEL   Support for querying the *real* type of an object (and an objects internal structure) is supported in Eiffel by the predefined class INTERNAL. Any class that requires such facilities should inherit from the class INTERNAL.

SMALLTALK   Facilities are available in Smalltalk to query the type of an object (class), checking if an object responds to a message (respondsTo), etc.

Now we are ready to continue with the university management problem and analysis of role playing classes. Once we get the current role, we can use RTTI to determine if it is of the required type (TTeacher, TStudent, etc.). If the TUniversityMember object is what we want, then we can use checked cast operator to down cast it (the TUniversityMember object) and safely perform all operations required. We can also provide methods in TUniversityMember to query if it is of a given type (one of TTeacher, TStudent, etc.). This can be done using type_info objects. With these modifications, the TPerson class would look like this:

```
/* The new TPerson class. All details are not shown. Only the new additions
   related to the role playing concept are shown. All TUniversityMember
   objects are owned by TPerson. Whenever a new role is created and added
   to a TPerson object (using the AdoptNewRole method), it will be adopted
   by the TPerson object. When a TPerson object is destroyed, the
   associated role objects are also destroyed.
*/
const short MAX_ROLES = 6; // Just an arbitrary limit

class TPerson {
    public:
        TPerson (const char theName[], unsigned long theSSN,
            unsigned long theBirthDate, const char theAddress[]);
        TPerson (const TPerson& source);
```

```
        TPerson& operator= (const TPerson& source);
        ~TPerson();

        // Add one more role to this person. Return true if successful,
        // false if it is not possible to add a new role
        bool AdoptNewRole(TUniversityMember* newRole);
        // Change the active role of this person
        TUniversityMember* SetActiveRole(TUniversityMember* thisOne);
        // Is this one of the roles being played by this person?
        // Returns true if successful, false otherwise
        bool IsRoleValid(const TUniversityMember* thisOne) const;
        // Return the active role of this person
        TUniversityMember* GetActiveRole() const { return _activeRole;}
        // Count of the number of roles played by this person
        unsigned short GetRoleCount() const;
        // This person no longer has this role. So remove it from the
        // list of roles available. Returns true if successful.
        bool DeActivateRole(TUniversityMember* thisOne);
    private:
        char*                   _name;
        char*                   _address;
        unsigned long           _ssn;
        unsigned long           _birthDate;
        // Any person cannot have more than MAX_ROLES roles
        // If this is a problem, a dynamic data structure such as a list
        // can be used. _allRoles is an array of pointers to
        // TUniversityMember objects. As and when new TUniversityMembers
        // are added, their addresses are placed in this array.
        TUniversityMember*      _allRoles[MAX_ROLES];
        unsigned short          _roleCount;
        TUniversityMember*      _activeRole;
};
```

Here is a part of the constructor that will initialize all the **TUniversityMember** slots to 0.

```
TPerson::TPerson(const char theName[], unsigned long theSSN, unsigned long
                          theBirthDate, const char theAddress[])
{
    // other details not shown
    // To start with, there are no roles for the person
    for (int i=0; i < MAX_ROLES; i++)
          _allRoles[i] = 0; // no role set
    _roleCount = 0;
    _activeRole -= 0;

}
```

Let's look at some other methods.

```
bool
TPerson::IsRoleValid(const TUniversityMember* thisOne) const
{
    /* We walk through the role array and compare (addresses) of the role
       pointers in the slot with the argument "thisOne". If they compare
```

```
       equal, then return true. One might feel that address comparison
       isn't adequate. If so, this TUniversityMember can implement
       comparison operators to do more elaborate comparison. It is more
       important to understand what needs to be done. How it is done is up
       to the implementor.
     */
    for (int i =0; i < MAX_ROLES; i++)
        if (_allRoles[i] != 0 && (allRoles[i] == thisOne)
                return true;

    return false; // there is no such role for this person
}


bool
TPerson::AdoptNewRole(TUniversityMember* newRole)
{
    /* Add a new role to the list of all roles available
     * Walk through the array of roles and look for a free slot
     * A free slot will have a 0. Store address in that slot
     */
    for(int i=0; i < MAX_ROLES; i++)
        if (_allRoles[i] == 0) {
                _allRoles[i] = newRole;
                _roleCount++;
                return true;
        }
    return false; // failed because this person already has too many roles.
}


// Change the active role of this person
TUniversityMember*
TPerson::SetActiveRole(TUniversityMember* thisOne)
{
    // Set the active role to the argument passed in.
    // Return the old active role.
    if (thisOne != 0) {
            TUniversityMember* oldRole = _activeRole;
            _activeRole = thisOne;
            return oldRole;
    }
    // An exception would be more appropriate than returning 0
    return 0;
}


bool
TPerson::DeActivateRole(TUniversityMember* thisOne)
{
    /* Remove a role from the list of roles
     * Walk through the array of roles and look for thisOne
     * Set it to 0
     */
    for(int i=0; i < MAX_ROLES; i++)
        if (_allRoles[i] == thisOne) {
                _allRoles[i] = 0;
                _roleCount--; // One less role played
                return true;
        }
```

```
        return false; // failed because thisOne is not a role played by this
                      // person
}
```

It is important to understand the significance of the **SetActiveRole** and **GetActiveRole** methods. At any time, a **TPerson** is capable of playing only one role. Any client of **TPerson** depends on these methods to access the current role. Without these methods, a client will not be able to access any **TUniversityMember** object contained in a **TPerson** because the role objects are private implementation data inside **TPerson**. For proper functioning of the system, every client must use the **SetActiveRole** and **GetActiveRole** methods. Access to **SetActiveRole** might also be controlled to ensure that only authorized clients can modify roles of a **TPerson**.

Here is a skeleton of the **TUniversityMember** class.

```
class TUniversityMember {
    public:
            // Create a role object for the person thisPerson
            // roleName is the name of the derived class that created it.
            // This would be TTeacher, TStudent, etc.
            TUniversityMember(const char role[], const TPerson* thisPerson);
            TUniversityMember(const TUniversityMember& copy);
            TUniversityMember& operator=(const TUniversityMember& assign);
            virtual ~TUniversityMember();

            // Return the person associated with this role object.
            TPerson* RoleFor() const { return_ownerOfRole; }

            // Associate this role with a different person. Returns the
            // existing TPerson associated with this role.
            TPerson* ChangeOwnerTo(TPerson* newPerson);
            EDepartment GetDepartment() const;
            void SetDepartment(EDepartment newDept);
    private:
            // roleName is the name of the derived class that created it.
            char* _roleName;
            TPerson* _ownerOfRole;
            // Information common to all roles
            EDepartment _department;
};
```

Just to show what this class does, here is the constructor.

```
TUniversityMember::TUniversityMember(const char role[], const
    TPerson* thisPerson)
{
    if (_roleName != 0) {
            _roleName = new char [strlen(role) + 1];
            strcpy(_roleName, role);
    }
    else _roleName = 0;
    _ownerOfRole = thisPerson;
}
```

The way we use TTeacher, TStudent, etc. hasn't changed. We still instantiate these classes when needed. But now, they are roles, and so every object (of TTeacher, TStudent, etc.) must be associated with the correct person. A role belongs to a person. We need to setup the association between any TUniversityMember (the role) object and the corresponding TPerson object (the person who plays the role). This could be done in two different ways. We could pass the TPerson object to the constructor of TTeacher (TStudent, TGraduateStudent, etc.), which in turn passes it to TUniversityMember constructor. Another approach is to leave this responsibility to the university management system. TUniversityMember would have a method (SetRoleFor) that accepts a TPerson object and sets up the association of the role with that person. With the latter approach, implementation of the existing classes (TTeacher, TStudent, etc.) would mostly remain as it is. But the caveat is that a role could remain unattached to any person. With the former approach, the implementation of the class TTeacher (TStudent, TGraduate-Student, etc.) must be changed but it ensures that TUniversityMember objects are always bound to persons.

Let's look at a simple function that illustrates how RTTI is useful in this example (Fig. 6-22 and code below). Here, the function EnrollStudentInCourse takes care of the steps necessary in enrolling a student in a course. This function would exist in our earlier implementations also. It would probably be a method of some other class in the university system.

```
void EnrollStudentInCourse(const TCourse& newCourse, TPerson* aStudent)
{
    TUniversityMember* role = aStudent.GetActiveRole();
    // Now we have the active role. But we aren't sure if this role
    // is really a TStudent. We can use RTTI to verify that.

    TStudent* studentPtr = dynamic_cast <TStudent*> (role);
    if (studentPtr != 0) {
        // Wonderful, the role is really a TStudent. Invoke the
        // EnrollForCourse member function on the TStudent object
        // pointed by studentPtr ...
```

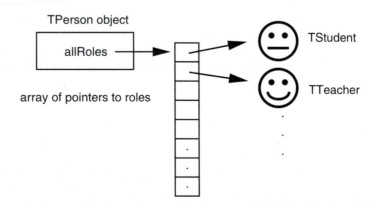

Fig. 6-22

```
                studentPtr ->EnrollForCourse(newCourse);
    }
    else {
        // This role is not a TStudent. Cannot enroll person.
        // throw an exception to indicate failure
    }
    // More uninteresting code to update other information
}
```

This function could also be written as

```
    void EnrollStudentInCourse(const TCourse& newCourse,
                                    TUniversityMember* aStudent);
```

in which case the call to **GetActiveRole** is not needed. The caller of **EnrollStudentIn-Course** would do the preprocessing required to access (and pass) the correct **TUniversityMember** object.

When we use a **TUniversityMember** object, we can not do many useful things with it because it doesn't have many useful methods. A **TUniversityMember** is really just a unifying base class. We are more interested in determining the exact subclass of the **TUniversityMember** object—TStudent, TTeacher, etc. We need RTTI for such operations. Note that once we determine the exact subclass of a **TUniversityMember** object, the procedure to perform different chores is identical to what it is under the earlier design scenarios. The use of RTTI is only needed when using a **TUniversityMember** object.

Another Alternative for Managing Roles

In some situations, maintaining the notion of an active role may not be feasible because the relevance of the applicable role is based on state information stored inside the **TPerson** object. From an abstraction perspective it also makes more sense to ask the **TPerson** object if it is capable of playing the role, say by using a member function **TPerson::GetRoleFor**. This function would return a pointer to the correct role object if the person is currently capable of playing that role. Otherwise a nil pointer is returned. This way, the person determines the validity of a role. It is possible to implement this scheme using RTTI.

```
    class TPerson {
        // all other details as before
        TUniversityMember GetRoleFor(const type_info& whichRole) const;
    };
```

Member function **GetRoleFor** () needs to know what role the caller is interested in. One way of doing this would be to use some character string description for every role ("Student", "Teacher", etc.). Then we can use a member function to get the role description. The problem with using character strings to identify roles is that a central registry (or some such) of role names must be used to ensure uniqueness of role names. This can be tedious and can become an unnecessary bottleneck. A more portable and language supported scheme would be to use the **type_info** information available with every class. The caller of **GetRoleFor()** would pass the **type_info** object of the role she is looking for.

The code in GetRoleFor() sequentially compares the type_info of the different TUniversityMember objects that are stored inside the TPerson object with the one passed to it, returning the TUniversityMember object that matches. If the person does not have any TUniversityMember object that matches the type_info argument (whichRole), then a nil pointer is returned indicating the absence of any such role. Here is the skeleton code.

```
TUniversityMember*
TPerson:::GetRoleFor(const type_info& whichRole) const
{
    // Walk through the role array and compare type_info of each role with
    // whichRole.
    for(int i=0; i < MAX_ROLES; i++)
        // Compare the type_info objects
        if (typeid(*_allRoles[i]) == whichRole) // matching role found
            return _allRoles[i]; // return its address
    return 0; // role not found
}
```

A typical usage might be:

```
void EnrollStudentInCourse(const TCourse& newCourse, TPerson* person)
{
        // see if the person currently plays the role of a student?
        TUniversityMember* ptr = person->GetRoleFor(typeid(TStudent));
        if (ptr != 0) { // Yes, the person does play this role
            // apply dynamic cast to convert to TStudent
            TStudent* studentPtr = dynamic_cast <TStudent*> (ptr);
            if (studentPtr != 0) {
                // Wonderful, the role is really a TStudent. Invoke
                // the EnrollForCourse member function on the
                // TStudent object pointed by studentPtr ..
                studentPtr ->EnrollForCourse(newCourse);
            }
            else {
            // This role is not a TStudent. Cannot enroll .throw an
            // exception to indicate failure
            }
        }
}
```

With this scheme, the responsibility to determine if the person plays a role rests (appropriately) with the TPerson class. As with the earlier scheme, if the person plays more than one role of the same type (say two student roles), then locating and distinguishing between them is not an easy task.

Polymorphic Usage of TUniversityMember Objects

When a TUniversityMember object (a TUniversityMember reference or pointer) is an argument of a function, any object of the derived classes of TUniversityMember can be substituted. But the function wouldn't be able to do anything useful with the TUniversityMember object because it lacks any useful interface. Again, we need to use RTTI to determine the exact subtype of the **TUniversityMember** object and perform necessary operations. In other words, polymorphic usage of **TUniversityMember** objects doesn't help much because we still need to know the exact type of the object passed in as the actual argument. True polymorphism, which we discussed elsewhere, insulated the user from the exact type of the object by allowing us to use the common interface. But in case of **TUniversityMember**, there is hardly any common interface. **TUniversityMember** just cannot capture all the interface of the derived classes (it will be futile to even attempt such a task). But since **TTeacher**, **TStudent**, etc. are no longer derived classes of **TPerson**, there is no need for polymorphism with **TPerson**. A person is just a person—nothing else (unless of course if we create new subclasses of **TPerson**). And one can get to the roles played by a person using the interface in the **TPerson** object. In essence, we have not lost any of the advantages we had in the earlier designs, but this new solution is a little more complicated because we must use RTTI with **TUniversityMember** objects. We have gained more flexibility at the cost of a little complexity. Now changing roles of a person is very easy.

Changes Required to the Existing Classes

To use this new design, many of the classes that we built earlier must be modified. Classes **TStudent**, **TTeacher**, **TGraduateStudent**, and, **TGradTeachingAsst** no longer inherit from **TPerson** (but they inherit from **TUniversityMember**). Moreover, **TPerson** is not a virtual base class anymore. That's a big relief because it eliminates all the complicated rules about most derived class, constructor calls, and name conflicts. All the methods in any class other than **TPerson** that need access to the name, address, etc. of **TPerson** must get them indirectly using the **RoleFor** method of **TUniversityMember**. For example, here is the code for **TStudent::Print** with this change:

```
void
TStudent::Print() const
{
    // Get the person object associated with this TStudent role object.
    // RoleFor is a method in the base class TUniversityMember.
    TPerson* person = RoleFor();
    //Ensure that the TPerson is not zero
    if (person != 0) {
        cout << "Name: " << person->GetName() << endl;
        cout << "Address: " << person->GetAddress() << endl;
    }
    cout << "This person is a " << statusLabels[(int)status]
        << " student in the department of "
        << departments[(int) department] << endl;
}
```

This new design also eliminates the need for a separate **TGradTeachingAsst** class. A person (a graduate student) plays the role of a teacher in the department where she works as a graduate teaching assistant. She also plays the role of a graduate student, but not both at the same time. When she is performing the role of a graduate teaching assistant, the active role would be set to the **TTeacher** role, and when she is performing the role of a normal graduate student, the active role (set by **SetActiveRole**) is **TGraduateStudent**. This simplicity of multiple roles makes this design more elegant than any of our previous designs.

Creating, copying, and deleting of the role objects can be minimized very easily. Every TUniversityMember object is decoupled from the person performing that role. A TUniversityMember object contains information specific to that role. If two people are enrolled in same set of courses and do exactly identical duties, then these TPerson objects do not differ in their roles but only in the TPerson information. The TUniversityMember objects associated with the two TPerson objects would look identical. This facilitates sharing of TUniversityMember objects. An implementation could create a single TUniversityMember (for example, TResearchAsst) object and attach it to different TPerson objects without really keeping multiple copies of them around. For example, a set of people (TPerson) might be performing research in the same area under the same professor. All these people are performing the same role but they have different name, address, etc. A single TResearchAsst object can be used to represent the roles of all these people, and this object can be attached to all TPerson objects. [*There is one problem here. As stated earlier, every role belongs to a person. When the method RoleFor is applied on a TUniversityMember object, it returns the associated TPerson object. This is a one-to-one relationship. Every TUniversityMember object is owned by exactly one TPerson object. But if we allow the sharing of role objects (i.e., TUniversityMember objects), then our assumption about every role belonging to only one person collapses. If minimization of objects created is the goal, then we can make a group of TPerson objects share a single TUniversityMember object, but the TUniversityMember object would belong to only one TPerson at a time. The RoleFor member function returns the associated TPerson. The association can be changed dynamically by using the ChangeOwnerTo method.*] And when this group of people are no longer involved in the research project, it might be beneficial to just keep the TResearchAsst object around for future use because another group of researchers might take the place of those who left. This avoids repeated object creation and deletion of TResearchAsst objects. The salient point here is that different people take on the same role(s). The duties (or characteristics) of a role remain the same but different people are associated with them. The roles essentially stay the same but the people playing the roles come and go. As another example, if a teacher assigned to a course is replaced by another teacher, only the TPerson associated with the TTeacher role must change. The TTeacher role object remains the same. If two teachers are assigned to the same class, there needs to be only one TTeacher role object but two TPerson objects associated with this TTeacher object. Such sharing is almost impossible with the previous designs because the person and the role are the same object. In summary, the role objects are transferable. The role is like a rental car. The car can be rented out to different customers (even jointly, where possible). The characteristics of the car never change, but the customers renting it come and go, and a same person can rent multiple vehicles (car, boat, cycle, etc.).

Most of the code implemented in our classes are still usable with minor modifications. The complete implementation of the hierarchy is left as an exercise to the reader.

Mixin Classes vs Role Objects—Applicability

At this point, one might be wondering as to where mixin classes are more appropriate, compared with role playing objects (or vice-versa). Both mixin classes and role objects seem attractive. In particular, one should understand where one is preferred over the other. If you are thinking along these lines, you are not alone.

Mixin classes add *static* capabilities. The decision to use (or not use) a mixin needs to be made when designing the class lattice (i.e., hierarchy). An object cannot acquire any new capabilities at run-time because the inheritance hierarchy of a class (object) cannot be changed. Once an object is created, it can only respond to messages that its class contains, including those inherited from other classes. No new feature can be added to the object at run-time. Therefore, mixin classes are useful only in situations where the decisions can be made at class hierarchy design time. Once the hierarchy is created and objects are instantiated, nothing can be changed. But mixin classes are very easy to understand and implement. Mixin classes are not very useful when many different combinations of classes are possible. Also note that the mixin class hierarchy cannot model the situation where a person plays the same role more than once. For example, it is not possible to model a person performing research in more than one department in the same semester.

Creating many mixin classes might seem like a good solution. But mixing these mixin classes in various combinations could lead to a proliferation of classes (also known as *combinatorial explosion*). For example, one can easily visualize different combinations of a person (student+teacher, student+researcher, graduate student+researcher, etc.). Such a complex hierarchy is shown in Fig. 6-23 and 6-24.

Multiple inheritance hierarchies are difficult to understand (compared with single inheritance hierarchies). The solution is even more difficult to understand when virtual base classes are added. When we add more roles (such as **TEmployee**, **TLaboratoryAssistant**, etc.) the hierarchy gets more and more complex and very soon it becomes unmanageable. Any hierarchy with too many classes is hard to understand and different combinations of mixin classes don't make it any easier for the designers, implementors, and clients.

Role playing objects (such as the **TUniversityMember** with **TPerson** objects) are more suited for dynamically changing situations. One of the major advantages with role playing objects is the elimination of combinatorial explosion of classes encountered with mixins. One might create a **TPerson** object without any roles, but we are free to assign new roles to this person as and when needed. The only restriction is that the **TUniversity-Member** derived classes be known when the program is compiled. The **TUniversity-Member** hierarchy itself is fixed, but a **TPerson** can acquire (and release) any role at any time. In reality, this design is more suited for dynamically changing situations, and commercial software definitely needs such flexibility. There is absolutely no constraint on the roles a person can acquire (and relinquish). It is only limited by the available derived classes of **TUniversityMember**. Moreover, this design permits duplication of roles, which is required in many situations. As seen earlier, there is nothing wrong in a person being a research assistant in more than one department. And it is quite natural for a student to hold many teaching assistantships. This is very easy to model with role objects but not mixin classes (at least not without data duplication). When using role objects, it is very easy to add new roles because there is no change required in **TPerson**. The disadvantage with role objects is its dependency on RTTI (or some such mechanism) and the need for some extra code to retrieve and convert **TUniversityMember** objects. The design concept is quite easy to understand but implementation isn't that easy. But the run-time flexibility achieved justifies the extra code and complexity.

Cominatorial Explosion of classes with mixin classes

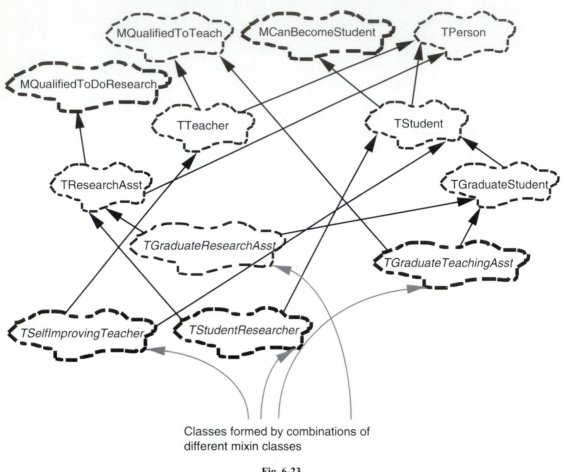

Classes formed by combinations of
different mixin classes

Fig. 6-23

☞ **Use role playing objects if there are too many possible combinations
of the roles and/or if role combinations can change dynamically.**

☞ **Use mixin classes if the number of combinations is limited and duplication of roles is not allowed.**

PRIVATE DERIVATION IN C++

Until now, we focused our attention on public inheritance, which is the most common
type of class derivation. In fact, public inheritance is the only style of class derivation supported in Eiffel and Smalltalk. Under C++ we say

Cominatorial Explosion of classes with mixin classes

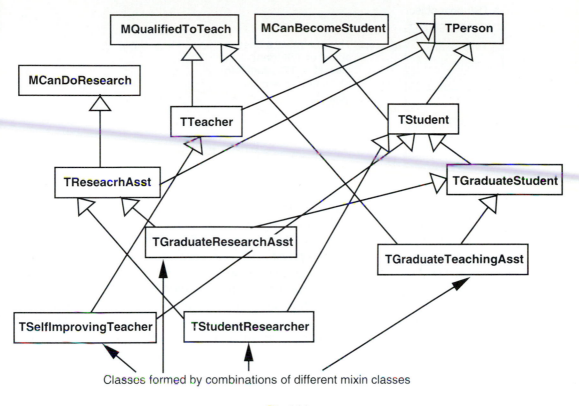

Classes formed by combinations of different mixin classes

Fig. 6-24

```
class TStudent : public TPerson {
    // all the details
};
```

The public keyword indicates the normal style of inheritance, which supports polymorphism. We can also write

```
class TStudent : private TPerson {
    // all the details
};
```

This indicates private derivation in C++. Let's use the phrase *private derivation* to indicate a private base class.[10] The term *inheritance* has already been used to indicate normal public inheritance, the *is-a* relationship.

---

[10]C++ also supports *protected* derivation wherein the base class is a protected base.

Private Base Class

A TStudent object

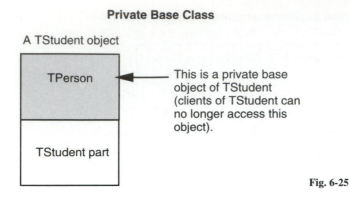

This is a private base object of TStudent (clients of TStudent can no longer access this object).

Fig. 6-25

With this declaration, class **TPerson** is a private base class of the derived class **TStudent**. A normal client of **TStudent** (anyone who instantiates an object of **TStudent**) cannot access the **TPerson** base class object within the **TStudent** object because within **TStudent** the base class **TPerson** is private. All members of the base class (private, protected, and public) **TPerson** become private members of the derived class **TStudent** and these private members cannot be accessed by clients of **TStudent**. Private derivation also voids the polymorphic conversion of a **TStudent** object to a **TPerson** object. One can convert from a derived class to a base class only when the base class is accessible. But with private derivation the base class object within the derived class object is no longer accessible by clients of the derived class. Hence, a **TStudent** object cannot be passed as the actual argument where a **TPerson** is expected because the called function is not allowed access to the private base class object within **TStudent**.

With this implementation, polymorphism of **TPerson** with **TStudent** is no longer applicable and polymorphic substitution principle is also violated. It is natural to wonder as to what new benefits are achieved by this style of derivation. We will look at the benefits very soon.

With normal (public) inheritance, a derived class inherits the interface and implementation of its base class. The interface (any member function) of the base class can be used with an object of the derived class. Moreover, every derived class also contains the complete structure (implementation) of the base class. With private derivation, the interface of the base is no longer applicable to a derived class object. But the derived class object still inherits the structure and implementation of the base class object. Hence, this style of derivation is also called *Implementation Inheritance*. The figure above (Fig. 6-25) clearly shows the structure of the derived class object. *Any member function of the derived class can still access the available methods of the base class.*[11] Polymorphism also works *within* the member functions of the derived class. Any member function of the derived class can still pass a derived class object to a base class method polymorphically. For example, if one of the member functions of **TPerson** expects a **TPerson** object (reference or pointer), any member function of **TStudent** can pass a **TStudent** object as the actual argument. Polymorphic substitution principle still works within the derived class

---

[11]Needless to point out that the derived class cannot access the private members of the base class.

implementation but not outside, (i.e., clients who create objects of the derived classs cannot use the derived class object in place of a base class object polymorphically because the base class is not **public**). The derived class implementation is free to use the implementation of the base class, but clients of the derived class have no access to the member functions of the base class using objects of the derived class. Don't get confused about this access restriction with **TPerson**. Access to the **TPerson** object within a **TStudent** is restricted because **TPerson** is a private base. Anyone can still create independent **TPerson** objects and use them as they like. Stated differently, for normal clients, **TStudent** is no longer a **TPerson**.

The code below illustrates the scenario. Assume that **TStudent** has been implemented using **TPerson** as a private base class.

```
void f(TPerson&     nomad) // Accepts any TPerson object, polymorphically
{
        // do something with nomad object
}
main()
{
    // Michale Faraday, famous for inventions in eletro-magnetism
    TPerson faraday("Michael Faraday", 123456789, "9-22-1791",
                                        "London, United Kingdom" );
    TStudent bugs ("Bugs Bunny", 423435063, "12-1-1940", "Looney Tunes",
                                        eArts, eFullTime);

    f(faraday); // This line compiles
    f(bugs); // Generates a compile error
    // bugs (type TStudent) cannot be converted to TPerson object because
    // TPerson is a private base class of TStudent. An ordinary client
    // cannot access the private base class object of TStudent
}
```

The implementation of **Print** within **TStudent** can still invoke **Print** in **TPerson**.

```
void
TStudent::Print() const
{
    // Ask base class to print information about the person
    TPerson::Print(); // TStudent can still access all public and protected
    // members (functions and data) of TPerson
    // print the student information
}
```

If you are still confused about the private derivation concept, read on. The next example clearly illustrates the concept.

When to Use Private Derivation

Private derivation is useful in some design scenarios. This example illustrates the concept clearly. Assume that we already have a class **TList** with the following interface. Just to keep it simple, only important member functions are shown. Class **TListElement** represents nodes on a **TList**.

```
class TListElement;
class TList {
    public:
        TList ();
        // Returns true if successful
        virtual bool Prepend(TListElement* item);
        // Returns true if successful
        virtual bool Append(TListElement* item);
        virtual oid InsertAt(TListElement* what, int Where);
        virtual TListElement* DeleteItem(TListElement* which);
        virtual TListElement* RemoveFirst();
        virtual unsigned HowMany() const;
        virtual ~TList ();
        // and many more methods
    private:
        // private members used in the implementation
        TListElement* _firstElement;
};

class TListElement {
    public:
        TListElement(void* data);
        void* GetData() const { return _element;}
        // and many other methods
    private:
        void* _element
        // and many more
};
```

When we need to implement a stack abstraction, class **TStack**, it would be a waste of time to write the entire implementation from scratch. A stack can be implemented using a list. But definitely stack is not a *kind of* list. Therefore, public inheritance should not be used. Class **TStack** can use **TList** as a private base class. Private derivation clearly indicates the lack of polymorphism.

```
// This is a heterogeneous stack
class TStack : private TList {
    public:
        TStack (unsigned theSize=100);
        TStack (const TStack & source);
        virtual bool Push(void* what);
        virtual void* Pop() ;
        // re-exported from TStack
        TList::HowMany;
        virtual ~TStack ();
        // and many more
    private:
        // private data members
};
```

There are some interesting facts here. A stack has limited operations. The important member functions are **Push** (which pushes a new element onto the stack), **Pop** (which removes the top element from the stack and returns it), and **HowMany()** (which returns the count of the number of elements on the stack—depth of stack). But class TList exports many other member functions too. Definitely, we don't want clients of TStack to be able to access all the methods of TList. As is evident from the preceding paragraphs, private derivation comes to the rescue. Because TList is a private base class, clients of TStack cannot access the public member functions of TList through objects of TStack. That's really very advantageous. Unlike true inheritance, clients of TStack are limited to what TStack exports explicitly.

The member function Push in TStack is nothing but a Prepend operation on TList. So we can implement TStack::Push in terms of TListElement::Prepend. Here is the code for Push:

```
bool TStack::Push(void* theElement) {
        TList::Prepend( new TListElement(theElement) );
}
```

When Push is invoked on a TStack object, it internally invokes Prepend on its private base class TList. Nothing more to do. Applying the same logic, TStack::Pop is nothing but removal of the first element of TList, which is already supported in TList by TList::RemoveFirst.

```
void* TStack::Pop() {
        TListElement* pElem = TList::RemoveFirst();
        void* elem = pElem->GetData();
        delete pElem; // remember that we created it in Push
        return elem;
}
```

Hardly any extra code but all the functionality we need.

Re-exporting Members of the Private Base Class

The member function HowMany of TStack is a bit tricky. For the member functions Push and Pop, we had to implement them in TStack (even though they in turn call a member function of TList) because we want the appropriate names for member functions of TStack. The member function of TStack that returns the count of the number of elements on TStack is HowMany. Class TList already supports HowMany. So it would be beneficial if clients of TStack get to TList::HowMany directly, without any intervention from TStack. In other words, the TList::HowMany must be made available to clients of TList but without any implementation in TStack. This can be done by re-exporting TList::HowMany from within TStack. The line

```
TList::HowMany; // re-export HowMany of TList to clients
```

in the class TStack above does just that. The member function HowMany which TStack inherits from TList, is exported by TStack to its client directly. A client of TStack can now invoke HowMany on any object of TStack. This re-exporting of TList::HowMany does not need any extra code in TStack (other than the statement above). When clients of TStack invoke HowMany, the member function TList::HowMany is executed. In the declaration above, TStack should not specify any return type nor the argument list for the member HowMany because the declaration of HowMany in TList is used. If TList contains a set of overloaded HowMany member functions, then the declaration above makes all such overloaded functions public members of class TStack (if possible).[12] Class TStack just wants to re-export the member HowMany that it inherits from TList. The declaration of HowMany in TList is used to validate all calls to HowMany. This selective re-exporting of features from a private base is very useful in many situations.

When implementing a new class, one might find that an existing class already supports all the features we need. So there is no fun in re-implementing something already in existence. But it is likely that the existing class supports many other member functions that are not applicable to our new class. For example, TList::Append is not applicable to TStack. In such situations, we want to limit the set of methods that are available to clients of the new class. Normal public inheritance does not allow the derived class to restrict access to inherited methods. Therefore, public inheritance is not applicable in such situations. This is where private derivation comes to the rescue. The derived class inherits the complete implementation of the private base class and is free to selectively re-export only those member functions (and even data members) that it needs. All those members of the private base class that are not re-exported by the derived class are not accessible by clients of the derived class. For example, clients of TStack do not have access to methods Append, InsertAt, etc., which are not re-exported by TStack. Class TStack only re-exports the method TList::HowMany. This is a way of reusing an implementation of an existing class but with a diminished interface. Re-exporting of members is not limited to member functions; even data members can be re-exported. But a derived class can only re-export those members of the private base class that it can access. Class TStack cannot re-export the private member TList::firstElement because TStack is not allowed access to any private member of the base class TList.

NOTE   With the namespace facility available in C++, re-exporting of members from a derived class can be done more elegantly. Please refer to the ANSI C++ reference manual for details.

Restrictions on Re-exporting Members

Re-exporting members of a private base class is a simple concept but with some restrictions. While re-exporting a member of the private base class, the derived class cannot change the access level already specified in the base class for that member. For example, when TStack re-exports HowMany, it is re-exporting it as a public member because HowMany is declared to be a public member function of TList. Class TStack does not have the freedom to re-export HowMany as a **private** (or **protected**) member of TStack. In other words, *when re-exporting members of a private base class, a derived class cannot increase nor decrease the access level of that member in the derived class.* The derived class must re-export members with the same level of access already specified in the private base class. The following piece of code should generate a compile time error.

---

[12]It is not possible to selectively re-export some overloaded functions among a set of overloaded functions. It is an all or nothing situation. Further, if the specified access control is not applicable to one of the overloaded functions, then the re-export fails.

```
class TStack : private TList {
    public:
        TStack (unsigned theSize=100);
        TStack (const TStack & source);
        virtual bool Push(void* what);
        virtual void* Pop() ;
        virtual ~TStack ();
        // and many more
    private:
        TList::HowMany;
        // Attempt to re-export as a private member within TStack
        // Should cause an error
};
```

☞ **When re-exporting members of a private base class, the derived class can neither increase nor decrease the level of access specified in the base class.**

It should be clear from the preceding paragraphs that private derivation is almost always contrary to the generalization-specialization concept of public inheritance. Public inheritance is the common mode of inheritance and private derivation is useful only in some special situations. Eiffel and Smalltalk support public inheritance only.

☞ **Private derivation is not true inheritance. The is-a relation is not applicable with private derivation.**

Alternative to Private Derivation—Containment

Revisiting TStack, it is easy to argue that TStack can be implemented by using an object of TList internally (TStack *has-a* TList in the implementation). The code would be:

```
class TStack {
    public:
        TStack(unsigned theSize=100);
        TStack(const TStack & source); // copy ctor
        virtual bool Push(void* what);
        virtual void* Pop() ;
        virtual unsigned HowMany() const;
        ~TStack();
        // and many more
    private:
        TList _list; // TList object used in the implementation
};
```

The method Pop is

```
void*
TStack::Pop()
{
    TListElement* pElem = _list.RemoveFirst();
    void* elem = pElem->GetData();
```

```
            delete pElem; // remember that we created it in Push
            return elem;
        }
```

and Push is

```
        bool
        TStack::Push(void* element)
        { return _list.Prepend(new TListElement(element) ); }
```

This implementation using *containment* (aggregation) is very similar to what was done with private derivation. The difference is that every method of TStack internally invokes corresponding methods on the internal object _list. But unlike private derivation, we cannot re-export TList::HowMany. It should be implemented in TStack as follows:

```
            unsigned
            TStack::HowMany() const { return _list.HowMany(); }
```

This is one benefit that is lost when using an object of TList internally. Private derivation allows for easy re-export of members. When using internal implementation objects, the enclosing class (TStack) must implement the member function using the enclosed object (_list). This is not a big drawback because we can make the call to _list.HowMany in TStack is an inline function and thus eliminate the extra function call. With this modification, there is no perceivable difference between the implementation using private derivation and that using an encapsulated object. But still the advantage of overriding member functions and access to protected members can be useful with private derivation. Class TStack can override virtual member functions of TList even in private derivation (even if it is not very useful for clients of TStack), which is not possible with the has-a implementation. If you have to choose between private derivation and has-a relation, definitely has-a relation is preferable. The has-a relation is much easier to understand and implement. Private derivation in most situations does not offer any extra advantages (see below). Deciding between private derivation and has-a is a pure implementation issue. Choosing one over the other does not change the behavior nor the interface of the class.

☞ **Try to use aggregation (has-a relation) instead of private derivation.**

The Need for Private Derivation

There are some implementation scenarios where private derivation is a better choice. A simple example illustrates the concept. Consider the problem of implementing a simple list class, which must be a derived class of the abstract class TAbstractList, which defines the general interface of any type of list and also allows the derived class implementors the freedom to use various implementation strategies.

```
    class TListElement;
    class TAbstractList {
        public:
            TAbstractList ();
            virtual bool Prepend(TListElement* item) = 0;
            virtual bool Append(TListElement* item) = 0;
```

```
                    virtual void InsertAt(TListElement* what, int Where) = 0;
                    virtual TListElement* DeleteItem(TListElement* which) = 0;
                    virtual unsigned HowMany() const = 0;
                    virtual ~TAbstractList ();
                    // and many more methods
        };

    class TListElement {
         public:
                    TListElement(void* data);
                    // and many other methods
                    void* GetData() { return _element; }
         private:
                    void* _element
                    // and many more
        };
```

A fast, fixed size linked list can be implemented using simple arrays. Assume that we already have a class **TFixedSizeArray**.

```
class TFixedSizeArray {
    public:
    // Allocates space for "size" elements. Each element is a pointer to
    // a void allowing us to store anything we want.
    TFixedSizeArray(unsigned size);
    // Store an element into the array
    virtual void Put(void* what, unsigned where);
    // Get an element from the array
    virtual void* Get(unsigned fromWhere);
    // Sets all elements in the array to 0.
    virtual void Clear();
    virtual unsigned HowMany() const;
    // and many more
    protected:
    unsigned _count; // # elements in the array
    // Copying and assignment of objects is not allowed for general
    // clients
    TFixedSizeArray(const TFixedSizeArray& );
    TFixedSizeArray& operator=(const TFixedSizeArray& );
    private:
     // more implementation details
};
```

Our class **TFixedSizeList** can be implemented as follows:

```
// Multiple inheritance: TAbstractList is a public base but TFixedSizeArray
// is a private base
class TFixedSizeList : public TAbstractList, private TFixedSizeArray {
    public:
            TFixedSizeList (unsigned numElement = 100);
            // Copying and assignment of list objects is allowed
            TFixedSizeList(const TFixedSizeList& copy);
            TFixedSizeList& operator=(const TFixedSizeList& assign);
```

```
        bool Prepend(TListElement* item);
        bool Append(TListElement* item);
        void InsertAt(TListElement* what, int Where);
        TListElement* DeleteItem(TListElement* which);
        unsigned HowMany() const;
        virtual TFixedSizeList ();
        // and many more methods
    private:
        // whatever needed
};
```

By any stretch of imagination, a list is not an array but a list could be implemented using an array. Definitely, public inheritance of TFixedSizeList from TFixedSizeArray is not valid. But we cannot use has-a relation because TFixedSizeList needs access to the protected members of TFixedSizeArray. And only derived classes can access protected members of a base class. This leaves us with no other option but private derivation. Class TFixedSizeList wants to allow copying and assignment between objects but TFixedSizeArray does not (it has made the copy constructor and assignment operator protected!). But copying of TFixedSizeList objects is only possible when TFixedSizeArray objects can be copied. So we need to gain access to the protected members of TFixedSizeArray. Hence, the use of private derivation.

Another scenario that might lead to private derivation involves overriding virtual functions. If the derived class needs to override a virtual function of a base class but without public inheritance, the only alternative is private derivation because only derived classes (private or public) can override inherited virtual member functions. This situation may not be very clear because clients can never call a function of the private base class directly anyway (they always call the derived class function). Carefully analyze the situation below.

```
class X {
    public:
        virtual void f() = 0;
};

class Y {
    public:
        virtual void fY() { this->gY();} // virtual call of gY
        virtual void gY();
};

class Z : public X, private Y {
    public:
        virtual void f(); // override pure virtual function, X::f()
        virtual void gY(); // Overrides the privately inherited Y::gY
        virtual void fY() { Y::fY(); }
};

main()
{
    Z az;
    az.fY();
}
```

In this example, class Z derives privately from Y and publicly from X. Class Z wants to override Y::gY because the behavior of Y::gY is not suitable for Z. So it does override the virtual function with Z::gY. When a client invokes az.fY(), the call ends up in Y::fY because Z::fY in turn calls the private base class function Y::fY. But Y::fY internally calls gY.[13] For proper behavior, the gY() that is executed must be the one in Z because the message was originally sent to a Z object, aZ (in the main program). If Z did not override gY then the call this->gY would end up calling Y::gY which is not appropriate for Z. So Z appropriately overrides Y::gY to provide the correct implementation. The call this->gY ends up calling Z::gY because the original object is an object of the class Z.

This flexibility is not possible if we use an embedded object of Y (instead of private derivation) in Z. Here is the example with embedded Y object.

```
class X {
    public:
        virtual void f() = 0;
};

class Y {
    public:
        virtual void fY() { this->gY();} // virtual call of gY
        virtual void gY();
};

class Z : public X {
    public:
        virtual void f(); // override pure virtual
        virtual void gY(); // new method -has no relation with Y::gY
        virtual void fY() { _embeddedY.fY(); } // new method
    private:
        Y _embeddedY;
};

main()
{
    Z az;
    az.fY();
}
```

The call az.fY will invoke Z::fY which forwards the call to Y::fY. Next Y::fY calls this->gY(), but it ends up executing Y::gY because it has not been overridden. There is no way Z can override any member functions of Y. This leads to incorrect behavior. Moreover, Y::gY cannot access any data in Z because it is not even aware that it is part of a Z object. This problem cannot be solved with embedded objects. Private derivation is the correct solution. The situation is still the same even if Y had a pure virtual function. Class Z must override the inherited pure virtual function to make Z a concrete (not abstract) class. The point here is that even though external polymorphism is not possible with ob-

---

[13]It is very common for one method to call another (virtual) method. This might result in the execution of a method in the derived class that originally issued the call to the base class. In fact, we shall discuss a very powerful design technique that uses this scheme in a later chapter.

jects of Z (because of the private base class), internal implementation can still use dynamic binding and overriding (between derived class and private base class).

A VERY USEFUL EXAMPLE OF MIXIN CLASSES AND PRIVATE DERIVATION

Reference counting is a very useful feature that is very frequently used in commercial software. It is necessary to understand the principle of reference counting. One type of reference counting scheme has been already shown in Chapter 4 (with reference counted TString class). In this example, we look at another scheme of reference counting.

In many situations, we would like to keep track of the number of clients using a particular resource. For example, a shared library might be loaded in memory and the operating system (OS) needs to keep track of the number of processes using that shared library.[14] Here, the OS would like to keep only one copy of the shared library in memory (Fig 6-26).

Process (or task) P1 makes a call to a function in a shared library SL and that causes the loading of SL by the OS into memory. As long as P1 is using the shared library it will remain in memory.

Now imagine what happens when another process, P2 makes a call to a function in the same shared library SL. Since the shared library SL is already loaded into the OS memory, there is no need to load another copy of SL into memory. That would be a waste of memory. The OS should remember that more than one process is using the library SL. This is what is called as the reference count or the **use-count**. At this instance, when P1 and P2 are using SL, the use count is 2 (Fig. 6-27).

When P1 exits (or indicates to the OS that it will no longer use SL), the OS will decrement the reference count by 1 but will still keep the shared library in memory because the process P2 is still using it. The decision to keep SL in memory is based on the reference count, which is still not zero (Fig. 6-28).

It is the reference count that tells the OS when the shared library needs to be removed from memory. When the reference count on SL reaches zero (0) then it is clear that there is no other process using SL and, hence, it is safe to remove it from memory.

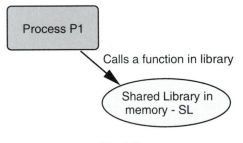

Fig. 6-26

[14]For those familiar with the MS-Windows (or Windows-NT) world, a shared library is a dynamic link library (DLL).

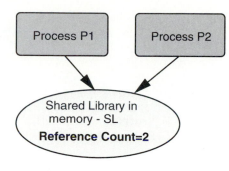

Fig. 6-27

When P2 also stops using SL, the reference count on SL will be decremented by the OS (Fig. 6-29). At this time, the reference count on SL is zero and hence it is safe to remove SL from memory, freeing up the space occupied by it.

In this entire scenario, the key feature was the reference count. Every time a new process starts using SL, the reference count needs to be incremented and as soon as a process dies, the reference count on SL should be decremented. In reality, this is done by the OS for all shared libraries used by a process. This reference counting semantics is also needed by many other resources. Moreover, the increment and decrement operations on a reference count must be *thread-safe*. Thread safety implies that even if multiple threads are trying to access the same reference count variable, it must be guaranteed that only one thread is granted access to the variable. Further, no other thread should be able to get access to the same variable until the original thread that was granted access to the variable relinquishes control of the variable. This can be implemented in many different ways (semaphores, mutex, critical sections, etc.). The simplest method is to increment (or decrement) the variable using atomic assembly language instructions. These instructions guarantee that the operation cannot be interrupted before it completes.

Thus, the essence of reference counting lies in providing an integer that can be incremented and decremented safely. Any class (or resource) that requires reference counting semantics can use the reference counted variable. Is it possible to create an open scheme where any class is free to add reference counting when required? The answer is a mixin class—MReferenceCounter.

This class provides all the necessary implementation needed for reference counting. Any class requiring reference counting semantics, just mixes it in (i.e., derives from it).

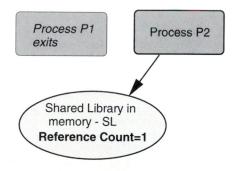

Fig. 6-28

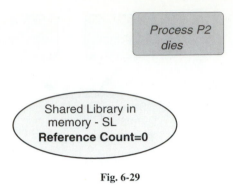

Fig. 6-29

```
/*
 * A thread safe reference counting mechanism.
   Methods Increment() and Decrement() guarantee thread safety. These
   methods must be implemented by the user on their platform (using
   assembly language instructions, if needed). Most clients will override
   GoingAway() to do whatever they need to do when the reference count
   drops to zero. The default implementation attempts a suicide with
   "delete this" which will cause all kinds of trouble for objects created
   on the stack - BEWARE. This class must be subclassed (inherited from).
   It cannot be instantiated.
 */
class MReferenceCounter {
    protected:
        // Constructor sets the initial count to 1
        MReferenceCounter(unsigned initialCount=1) {}

        // Increment the count by 1 and return the new count
        unsigned Increment();
        // Decrement the count by 1 and return the new count
        // If count drops to zero after the decrement operation,
        // the overridable method GoingAway() is called
        unsigned Decrement();

        // Derived classes must override this member function
        // to perform any clean-up in their implementation
        virtual void GoingAway()
        {
            // default behavior -CAREFUL
            delete this;
        }
        virtual ~MReferenceCounter() {}
    private:
        // Whatever data needed to implement the reference counting
        // mechanism. This could just be an integer with some assembly
        // language functions for the thread safe (atomic) operations. Or
        // it can use critical sections, mutex, etc. (provided by the OS)
        // to ensure thread safety.
};
```

There are some interesting things happening here.

1. This class, **MReferenceCounter,** is to be used only as a mixin—no direct instantiation.

2. Both **Increment** and **Decrement** methods must guarantee thread safety.

3. The most important method is **GoingAway.** When the reference count drops to zero after the **Decrement** operation, the resource (the shared library in this example) must do whatever is necessary as part of the clean-up. In the case of the shared library, the OS must reclaim the space occupied by the shared library and update any other data structures to indicate that SL is no longer available. All such operations must be done in **GoingAway.** For example, if the loading of shared libraries is done by the class **TSharedLibraryLoader,** here is how it might look. The code below is not complete by any means. It just shows some of the steps involved in managing such an operation. The emphasis is on the reference counting mechanism. Commercial implementations are much more complex.

Here is a skeleton of the shared library loader class.

```cpp
class TSharedLibraryLoader : private MReferenceCounter {
    public:
        TSharedLibraryLoader(const char loadThisLibarary[]);

        // Actually loads the library into memory
        // If the library has been already loaded into memory
        // the use-count (reference count) is incremented
        bool LoadLibrary();

        // Converse of LoadLibrary.
        // Decrements the reference count. If the reference count
        // drops to zero, GoingAway is automatically called
        // which will reclaim the memory used by this library
        void UnLoadLibrary();

        // Overrides the inherited function of MReferenceCounter
        virtual void GoingAway();

    private:
        char* _libName;
        bool _isLoaded;
        // Indicates if the library is already loaded into memory
};

void
TSharedLibraryLoader::TSharedLibraryLoader(const char loadThisLibrary[])
        : MReferenceCounter(0)
        // No one is using the library yet
{
    // Just remember the name of the library
    // The actual code will not be this simple but we
    // are more interested in the reference counting semantics
    _libName = new char[strlen(loadThisLibrary)+1];
    strcpy(_libName, loadThisLibrary);
    _isLoaded = false;

}
```

```
void
TSharedLibraryLoader::LoadLibrary()
{
    if (_isLoaded)
            Increment(); // ask MReferenceCounter to add
                    // one more reference
    else {
            // Code to actually load the library into memory
            Increment(); // ask MReferenceCounter to add
                    // the first reference
    }
    return true;
}
void
TSharedLibraryLoader::UnLoadLibrary()
{
    // Very easy
    Decrement(); // Ask MReferenceCounter to remove one existing reference.
                 // This might cause the
                 // invocation of GoingAway which ends up
                 // calling the GoingAway in our class
                 // because we have overrided the inherited
                 // member function
}

void
TSharedLibraryLoader::GoingAway()
{
    // Code to remove the library from memory
    // 1. Free the memory occupied by the library
    // 2. Update internal data structures to reflect the non-availability
    // of this shared library
    _isLoaded = false;
}
```

Clients of **MReferenceCounter** never have to worry about the intricate details involved in managing reference counts. They only worry about calling the base class methods as needed (**Increment** and **Decrement**). If everyone uses this class in their implementation, then all classes will have the same reference counting behavior.

Private derivation has been used because a **TSharedLibraryLoader** is *not* a **MReferenceCounter**. But, **TSharedLibraryLoader** wants to use reference counting. But at the same time, for proper behavior, the **GoingAway** virtual member function must be overridden in **TSharedLibraryLoader**. Therefore, the best alternative is **private** derivation.

NOTE   Normal clients of **TSharedLibraryLoader** should not be able to access the public member functions of **MReferenceCounter** directly. Managing reference counts should be left to **TSharedLibraryLoader** class member functions. Moreover, the use of reference counting is an internal implementation issue. Therefore, even if **MReferenceCounter** supported some public member functions, it should not be possible to access them through **TSharedLibraryLoader** class. Hence, the use of private derivation.

PORTABILITY
THREAD
SAFETY

Moreover, this scheme makes our code highly portable also. Imagine what needs to be done if we need to implement this reference counting scheme on a different system (OS or processor). All that needs to be reimplemented is the mixin **MReferenceCounter** class that hides all the details of thread safety and other related operations.

NOTE   The reference counting scheme discussed above is useful where one needs to keep track of the usage of a resource. No copying of objects is involved. We only need to know how many clients are using the resource. This scheme is very heavily used in operating system to keep track of memory pages, shared libraries, etc. There is no master-slave object scenario as discussed in the reference counting scheme presented in Chapter 4 (with the TString class). In many situations, we cannot copy an object but we can use it. In such cases, the owner of the object needs to know the number of clients using the object. This reference counting scheme is very handy in such situations.

NOTE   More useful applications of private derivation can be found in subsequent chapters.

☞ **Embedded objects do not allow overriding and access to protected members. Private derivation allows overriding of member functions of the private base by the derived class and also provides access to protected members of the private base class in the derived class.**

INHERITANCE VERSUS CONTAINMENT

Now that we understand interfaces, classes, types, inheritance and also containment (aggregation), it is time understand their implications and differences.

As mentioned elsewhere, inheritance is a static relationship. But, containment can be implemented as either a static relation (containment by value) or as a dynamic relation (containment by reference). For reuse of functionality, one has to choose between inheritance and containment.

Inheritance is straightforward to use and also to understand. It is directly supported by OO languages and is a fundamental paradigm of OO programming. It makes it easy for derived classes to tailor their behavior when needed by overriding member functions of the base class. And it has the benefit of polymorphism.

But inheritance brings in a permanent binding between the base class and the derived class. As seen earlier, a derived class (using public inheritance) is always a base class. There is no way to change this relationship. In other words, it is a rigid relationship determined at compile time. A child class cannot pick some other class as its parent class at run-time (this was the kind of problem we tried to solve using the role playing classes). Another problem is that with base classes that also define their representation (usually data members). The derived classes must be prepared to accept the representation of the base class as it is. Or, the base class would have to expose its representation to the derived classes (happens by default in Eiffel). Exposing the representation of a base class weakens the encapsulation of the base class. Moreover, once the representation of the base class is exposed, derived classes use it directly and their implementation is tightly coupled to the implementation of the base class. This forces the derived classes to change their implementation whenever the base class representation is changed. This is highly unfortunate. This problem can be overcome by using abstract base classes without any implementation in them.

Another reuse problem with inheritance is the suitability of the base class. When inheriting from a base class, if some part of the implementation of the base class is not suitable for the derived class, then the base class must be reimplemented or the derived class must look for a more appropriate base class. This is common problem faced by designers trying to implement derived classes in new problem domains. This kind of dependency hinders true reusability and the benefit of OOP. This can be solved by using true abstract base classes that provide little or no implementation.

Containment (has-a), on other hand, affords more flexibility. This was briefly discussed towards the end of Chapter-2 and we elaborate on that here in comparison with inheritance. With containment relationship, there is flexibility to change contained objects at run-time. This was seen in the example of role playing classes where the roles played by a TPerson could be changed dynamically. Another advantage is that encapsulation boundaries are not compromised. The class (say class A) that contains objects of another class (say class B) must use the published interface of the contained class to manipulate it. There is no other liberty available to class A with respect to class B. This truly enforces the fundamental paradigm of OOP—honoring interfaces. Using containment allows designers to combine objects in various ways to achieve end goals. Again, we could see this with role playing classes.

Designs that use containment are usually quite shallow (no deep hierarchies). With inheritance hierarchies, controlling growth is a difficult task (recall the complexity with the Teacher-Student hierarchy). And once a hierarchy keeps growing in different directions uncontrollably, it becomes a management nightmare. In designs that favor containment, there are more objects and usually fewer classes. The problem with this is that the behavior of the application depends on the relationships among many objects, where as with inheritance the behavior is defined in one class. For example, the behavior of TPerson depends on all the role objects contained in it at any instance. In contrast, with inheritance, a TGradTeachingAsst object's behavior is always well known.

There is a well known principle behind containment. Containment favors the *buy-and-assemble* approach rather than *implement-your-own* approach. But, it is easier said than done because all the components that are required to complete the task are usually not available. With inheritance, we can create new components by extending existing ones. When containment and inheritance are combined, very difficult problems can be solved elegantly.

In any system, neither containment nor inheritance, by itself will achieve the end goal of good design with reuse. It is a combination of these two techniques that is usually more powerful. This is what we did with the role playing classes. To complete any task, different tools are required. Any tool by itself wouldn't be sufficient to solve the problem. But, when different tools are used together, even very difficult problems can be solved easily.

SUMMARY

Multiple inheritance hierarchies are more complex, harder to design, implement, and understand than single inheritance hierarchies.

As with single inheritance, MI is a static relationship among classes. It cannot be changed at run-time.

Many difficult design problems can be easily solved by using MI hierarchies but MI is not the answer for all complex problems.

It is very hard to achieve dynamic flexibility in MI hierarchies.

Beware of virtual base classes. It is not for the weak hearted.

Many MI hierarchies can be easily reduced to single inheritance (or no inheritance) hierarchies with containment.

7

Selective Exports from Classes (Friend Functions)

So far, we have learned that the only way to do anything useful with an object is by using the exported public member functions. It is not possible for a client to access anything inside an object directly because of the protection mechanism inherent in the object paradigm. This is a great fire wall that really protects the implementors and clients very well.

But there are some problems with this rigid access control. Revisiting our university example from previous chapters, consider the member function **GetSalary** and **SetSalary** in **TTeacher**. In a correct design, it should not be possible for everyone (any class) to access these methods. Access to such personal information should be restricted. But how can we restrict access to these methods? Some employees of the university (such as the Dean of a department and some members of the payroll department) need access to these member functions so that they can change the salary of a **TTeacher** as and when needed. But most other classes in the system should not have any access to these methods. And therein lies the problem. How can we allow certain classes access to some set of member functions in a class while keeping out other classes. If we make these methods public, any class in the system can use those methods without any reservations. But if we make them private, no client can access these methods. This all or nothing decision doesn't fit the real world. This is a big dilemma that faces many designers in some crucial design scenarios.

WHAT WE NEED

It would be wonderful if the language (C++, Eiffel, Smalltalk, etc.) allows us to selectively export specified members (member functions or data members) to specific classes. And designing object-oriented software would be really fun if we could specify such access restrictions for every member of the class. But in reality, only Eiffel provides such fine grain control.

Taking a different view, one might question the usefulness of exporting methods to specific classes. For example, **SetSalary** might be a method that is only accessed by one or two other classes. No other class should be allowed to access them. In such a situation, is it really worthwhile to spend all the time and effort to implement a method that is going to be used only by a couple of other classes. One might consider allowing the selected class(es) direct access to the data member, say **_salary** and dropping the methods **GetSalary** and **SetSalary** altogether. That sounds like a good design decision. If no other class can access the member and it is only used by a specified set of classes, we might as well trust those classes and allow them direct access. This is another possible alternative.

THE C++ SCENARIO

C++ is a little weak in this area. In C++, we cannot export a specific member (data member or member function) of a class to another class (or a set of classes). As we have already seen, there are only three different access regions—**private**, **protected**, and **public**. Anything declared in these regions obey the access rules specified in the language. Once a member of a class such as **_salary** is private, no one outside of the class can access the member **_Salary**. When the data member **_salary** is private or protected in **TTeacher**, an unrelated class of **TTeacher** cannot access it. But, class **TTeacher** cannot permit a specified class to access the data member **_salary** while prohibiting access to other members declared in the same region. If class **TTeacher** allows another class, such as **TPayrollDept**, to access the private data member **_salary**, all member functions of class **TPayrollDept** can also access other data members (such as **_birthDate**) declared in class **TTeacher**. It is an all or nothing situation. But that is a real benefit in some situations that will be discussed very soon.

This selective export in C++ is achieved through the concept of a *friend function* (or friend class). A class can designate another function as a friend function. It can also designate another class as a friend class. In other words, a class can *grant* friendship to another function or class. When a class grants friendship to another class, all methods of that class become friend functions of the class granting the friendship. It is an easy way of declaring all member functions of a class to be friend functions. Here is the syntactic detail (See code below and Fig. 7-1).

```
class TPayrollDept; //forward declaration
class TTeacher {
    public: // all other details not shown
    private:
        float _salary;
        friend class TPayrollDept; // ❶
        // other declarations
};
```

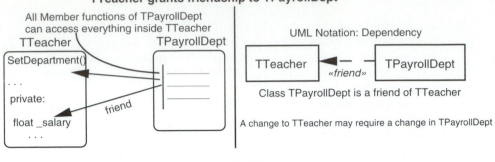

Fig. 7-1

   With this declaration (❶ above), every member function of the class **TPayrollDept** can access everything inside a **TTeacher** object. Note that it does not matter where the friend declaration is placed. The friend declaration above can be moved to the public region of the class but it does not alter the friendship between **TTeacher** and **TPayrollDept**. Let's look at a usage scenario. Here is a very small part of the class **TPayrollDept**.[1]

```
class TPayrollDept{
    public:
        void PerformAnnualSalaryReview(TTeacher&  thisTeacher);
        // many other methods
};

void TPayrollDept::PerformAnnualSalaryReview(TTeacher& thisTeacher)
{
    float raiseInSalary = 0.0; // Default is no increase in salary!
    // Do whatever is necessary to compute the raise based on performance
    // and other related issues. Update tax withholding records and
    // retirement contributions etc. Finally change the salary
    thisTeacher._salary += raiseInSalary;
    salary
}
```

The method **PerformAnnualSalaryReview** can access the data member **_Salary** inside the object **thisTeacher** because class **TPayrollDept** has been granted friendship by **TTeacher**. Every member function of **TPayrollDept** can access any data member or member function of **thisTeacher** because the entire class **TPayrollDept** is a friend of **TTeacher**.

   Here, class **TPayrollDept** can access **all** the members of the class **TTeacher**, regardless of whether they are private, protected, or public because of the friendship granted by **TTeacher**. It is not possible for **TTeacher** to grant **TPayrollDept** access only to the data member **_Salary**. This is one drawback of the friend relationship. However, **TTeacher** can grant friendship to a specific member function of **TPayrollDept**.

---

[1]I'm using this **TPayrollDept** class just to illustrate the preliminary details of this concept. Better examples will follow soon.

**TTeacher grants friendship to the member function
TPayrollDept::PerformAnnualSalaryReview only**

UML Notation: Dependency

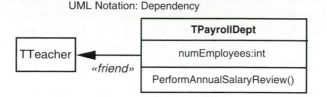

*Other Member functions of TPayrollDept cannot access any
private/protected members of TTeacher*

Fig. 7-2

If PerformAnnualSalaryReview is the only method of TPayrollDept that needs to modify _salary and no other method needs access to the private members of the class TTeacher, a better solution is to grant friendship to the method PerformAnnual-SalaryReview only. But to do so, class TPayrollDept must have been declared before class TTeacher.

```
class TPayrollDept {
    public:
        void PerformAnnualSalaryReview(TTeacher& thisTeacher);
        // many other methods not shown for simplicity
};

class TTeacher {
    public: // all other details not shown
    private:
        float _salary;
        friend void TPayrollDept::PerformAnnualSalaryReview(TTeacher&
                                    thisTeacher); // ❷
        // other declarations
};
```

The declaration inside TTeacher (❷ above) says that the member function PerformAnnualSalaryReview of TPayrollDept has been granted friendship by TTeacher. The declaration inside the class must provide the complete prototype of the function being granted friendship (to take care of overloaded function ambiguity). The keyword friend must not be used in the definition of PerformAnnualSalaryReview (inside TPayrollDept). Other member functions of TPayrollDept do not have any extra privileges with TTeacher; they can only access public members of TTeacher (see Fig. 7-2).

This scheme allows the method PerformAnnualSalaryReview of TPayrollDept access to the internal details of TTeacher. Other methods of TPayrollDept have no extra privileges with TTeacher—they must follow normal public protocol.[2] This scheme is more controlled and less dangerous. It is only useful if TTeacher is certain that no other method of TPayrollDept needs access to _salary.

[2]They can only use public methods of the class TTeacher.

NOTE   Whenever you see the keyword friend inside a class, immediately recognize the fact that you are looking at the declaration of a non-member function. A friend function is not implemented inside the class granting friendship (unless it is an inline declaration and definition of the friend function, which is rare). A friend function lives in another class or it could be a free function not attached to any class. But one should view the friend function as being part of the class interface even though it is not part of the class implementation. A friend function can change the behavior of an object of the class.

CAUTION   Just as in real life, one has to pick friends carefully. When you grant friendship to a function (or class), that function can do whatever it wishes with objects of the class to which it is a friend. It can also do very bad things to the object. Ensure that the function (or class) that you are granting friendship to is trustworthy. The situation is even more dangerous when an entire class is granted friendship because you need to trust *all* the methods in the class that you are granting friendship to. In many situations, the class granting the friendship and the function receiving the friendship are implemented by the same person (or team) and the friend mechanism is just used for convenience—which makes the scheme quite safe.

☞ **A class grants friendship to specific classes and functions as and when needed by placing the friend declaration inside the class header file. A function (or another class) cannot proclaim itself to be a friend of another class.**

IMPLICATIONS OF THE FRIEND RELATIONSHIP

Until now, it was easy to predict the behavior of objects because their behavior was affected only by member functions declared in their class. But now, that picture has somewhat changed. We need to keep in mind the friend functions of the class when trying to understand the complete behavior of objects. These friend functions may not do anything harmful to an object but their presence is very much felt.

Granting friendship to many different functions by a class complicates the interface of the class and confuses the clients. When only member functions are involved, there is a clear interface and implementation separation and the behavior is well defined (and controlled). But when friend functions are part of the picture, it is not very easy to predict the behavior of an object because the state of an object can be modified without invoking any member function. This is one good reason to keep friend functions to a minimum—use them only when necessary.[3]

If a function f() is granted friendship to a class X, then f() can access each and every member (data members and member functions) of any object of X that is accessible by f(). There is absolutely no restriction on what f() can do with an object of X. In that sense, a friend function is subject to the same access control as a member function. It is not possible to expose only some parts of the class to a friend function while keeping others hidden.

---

[3]This, again, mimics our real life. Don't use your friends for things that you can do yourself easily.

Here is an example of a class granting friendship to a specific function.

```
class X {
    public:
        X() { xMember = -1; } // Simple constructor
        friend void f(); // class grants friendship to function f()
        int GetMember() const { return xMember; }
    private:
        int xMember;
};

X gX; // global object of X

class Y {
    public:
        Y() {}
        int GetValue() const { return yMember.GetMember(); }
    private:
        X yMember;
};

Y gY; // a global object of Y

void f() // This is the implementation of the friend function
{
    // Try to set the data member in gX to 0
    gX.xMember = 0; // Valid, because f() is friend of X
    cout << gX.GetMember() << endl; // This is fine too.
    gY.yMember = 100; // Invalid because f() cannot access private members
                      // of Y
}
```

In the next example, class **X** grants friendship to class **Y**.

```
class X {
    public:
        X() { xMember = -1; } // Simple constructor
        friend void f(); // class grants friendship to function f()
        friend class Y; // ❶
        int GetMember() const { return xMember; }
    private:
        int xMember;
};

X gX; // global object of X

class Y {
    public:
        Y() { yMember.xMember = 100; } // ❷
        int GetValue() const { return yMember.GetMember(); }
    private:
        X yMember;
        int yInt;
};

Y gY; // a global object of Y
```

```
void f() // This is the implementation of the friend function
{
      // Try to set the data member in gX to 0
      gX.xMember = 0; // Valid, because f() is friend of X
      cout << gX.GetMember() << endl; // This is fine too.
      gY.yInt = 100; // Invalid because f() cannot access private members
                     // of Y
}
```

In ❷ above, any member function of Y can access any data member or member function of the X object **xMember** because Y is declared to be a friend of X in ❶.

But the preceding paragraphs (and examples) shouldn't lead you to believe that the friend mechanism is a very bad thing that one must never use—far from it. Friend functions can solve some tricky design problems that cannot be solved by using member functions. And a friend function is a godsend in situations where the complexity of access through member functions becomes unmanageable. We shall see such examples soon.

EIFFEL   Among all the major OO languages, the Eiffel approach is perhaps the most elegant (and clean). It provides very fine grain export/access control over members of a class. In Eiffel, a class can export its members to specified class(es). For every feature (function or data), an export list can be specified. The most common scheme is to export the most useful features to all clients. This is the unrestricted export clause (the **public** region of C++). But if a feature should only be accessible by a specified set of classes, an export list can be specified with that feature. There can be an export list for every feature. This export list can contain more than one class. For example, the **TTeacher** class in Eiffel would be

```
− A piece of Eiffel code
class TTeacher
export
     SetDepartment,
     GetDepartment
     SetRank,
     GetRank,
     salary { TPayrollDept }
feature
     − description of each feature as functions and procedures
end − class TTeacher
```

Class **TTeacher** declares that its features **SetDepartment, GetDepartment**, etc. are available to every client. This is specified by the general export clause above. But the feature **salary** is exported to the class **TPayrollDept** only. The selective export recipients are listed inside the {...} following the feature name. This ensures that only class **TPayrollDept** can access the **salary** feature of a **TTeacher** object—no other class can.

A careful reader might be wondering as to how this is different from the **friend** concept in C++. Well, in general, both schemes try to achieve the same goal, but the side effects are different. With selective exports of Eiffel, the class that is listed in the selective export list can only access the specified feature of the class; it cannot access other non-exported members of the class. But in C++, once a function is granted friendship, it can access all the members declared in the class—there is no protection for other member of the class. The Eiffel scheme is more secure. If class **TPayrollDept** does something wrong, the damage in TTeacher is limited to the **salary** feature and not others. But with C++, member functions of class TPayrollDept can wreak havoc on the data in TTeacher because they can access each and every data member and member function of an accessible TTeacher object.

But there is an advantage with the C++ approach also. In C++, one can grant friendship to a specific function. But in Eiffel, the selective export is to an entire class. One cannot selectively export a feature to a specific function. This has some very good benefits (particularly when implementing stream operators, which we shall see soon).

We can summarize the difference between the two schemes as follows. In C++, the invited guest (a friend function) is allowed to live in the house of the host and is given access to all rooms and amenities. In Eiffel, the guest is asked to live in a small portion of the owner's house. The guest cannot use any other part of the house. In C++, we can invite individual guests and/or their families to come and live with us but in Eiffel we have to invite entire families (class).

SMALLTALK   Smalltalk does not support selective exports of any kind. It sticks to true object-orientation and provides methods and instance variables only. A class requiring services from other classes must use the public methods. There are no short cuts.

APPLICATIONS OF FRIEND FUNCTIONS

Case I : Minimizing Heavy Interactions Between Classes

There are other situations where friend functions (and friend classes) are quite useful. Imagine a pair of classes, A and B, where A depends on B quite heavily. We can implement all the methods required and enforce the OO paradigm by requiring A to use the correct methods of B to perform all the operations. But this might lead to a large number of member function calls leading to a performance bottleneck. It might be beneficial to make A a friend of B. With this friend relationship in place, there is no need for A to invoke methods of B. Member functions of class A can directly access the implementation of B eliminating the member function calls altogether. This definitely reduces the complex interactions between A and B and improves performance dramatically. This friendship definitely violates strict OO design principles (the *purist* approach).[4] But when striving for performance improvement, we must use all tricks in our bag. If there is strong coupling and dependency between A and B it might be easier to create a friend relation between them.

☞ **If there is strong coupling and communication between a pair of unrelated classes and performance is affected by this communication, try to use a friend mechanism between the classes.**

But this shouldn't lead you to think that friendship between classes (and functions) is the best thing to do under all circumstances. Stick with normal member functions. They offer

---

[4]Purists feel that the only way of doing anything with an object must be through its public member functions—there should be no other way to communicate with objects.

protection and a clean interface. Resort to friendship when interactions between a pair (or a group of) classes is very high and the communication between (among) them is getting out of control. Note that this could also be an indication of poor OO design.

There is another benefit with this approach of using friend functions. Without the friend mechanism, class A must implement many more member functions in addition to those used by general clients. Minimally, class A will have to provide a pair of methods for each data member—one to *set* its value and another to *get* its value. This complicates the interface of class A. Moreover, we don't want clients to access these Get and Set methods. They are to be used only by class B. So class A makes all these methods private. But how will class B get to them unless class A grants friendship to B? Once B is a friend of A, there is no need for these private member functions because class B can directly access the data members in A. Class A doesn't have to implement all those extra private member functions. If the implementor of class A recognizes the close relationship with class B and uses the friend class mechanism, she can save a lot of time (by not implementing the extra member functions). This situation arises in cases where class B provides extra services to clients of class A. For example, a TList class (class A) can depend on another class TListNavigator (class B) to provide different navigation (traversing the list) schemes. Here, TListNavigator must be fast and efficient. And TListNavigator could be a hierarchy of classes providing different navigation styles (unordered, ordered, etc.). Definitely, class TList cannot implement all the different navigation schemes that clients expect—that would make class TList a very fat and ugly class. Class TList provides storage management and list integrity whereas navigation (different ways to traverse) is implemented by TListNavigator. Class TList must declare class TListNavigator to be a friend so that TListNavigator can directly access the list data structure inside the class TList. This seems logical because any implementor of a TListNavigator must know all the implementation details of the TList. Otherwise, there is no way she can implement the TListNavigator class. And the interaction between TList and TListNavigator is quite complex. Imagine how complex TList would be if it has to implement all the methods needed for all styles of navigation. Furthermore, separating the navigation from storage mechanisms keeps the abstractions boundaries crisp and clear—there is no overlap of functionality. And with this scheme, the same TList object can simultaneously support multiple TListNavigator objects that use different navigation schemes.[5]

This brings us to the object-oriented implementation of a TList class. A TList is separated from what it contains. A list is a collection of nodes. Each node holds one object. A node on the list is represented by the class TListNode (see Fig. 7-3).

Class TList manages the TListNodes in it. Each TListNode contains a pointer to the next element and the previous element on the list. The client supplied data is stored in TListNode. The shaded box does not change, no matter what is stored on the list, because the list class provides a general storage mechanism. Shown below is the skeleton code for these classes.

---

[5]This is the concept of separating Containers from Iterators which is discussed at length in Part II, Chapter 12.

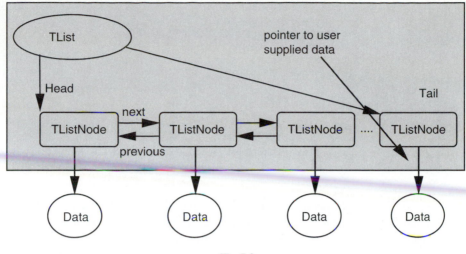

Fig. 7-3

```cpp
class TListNode; // forward declaration

class TList {
        public:
               TList(void* storeThisElement);
               TList(const TList& copy);
               TList& operator=(const TList& assign);
               virtual ~TList();

               // How many elements are stored on the list?
               unsigned int HowMany() const;
               // Append a new node to the list (at the tail)
               // Return true if successful
               bool Append (void* newElementToAdd);
               // Prepend a new node to the list (at the head)
               // Return true if successful
               bool Prepend (void* newElementToAdd);
               // Does this element exist in one of the list nodes?
               bool Exists(void* thisElement);
               // Remove this element (if it exists) from the list
               void* Remove(void* elementToRemove);
               // and many more methods
        private:
               TListNode* _head;
               TListNode* _tail;
               unsigned int _count;
               friend class TListNavigator; // See discussion below
};

class TListNode {
      public:
               // Constructor to create a new TListNode given user's data
               TListNode(void* userDataPointer=0);
               // Copy constructor etc.
```

```
            // Remove the user's data and return it and make the node empty
            void* RemoveContent();
            void ReplaceContent(void* newElement);
            // Return the pointer to data of this node
            void* GetContent() const;
            // and others..
    private:
            TListNode* _next;
            TListNode* _previous;
            void*      _userData; // pointer to user supplied data
            friend class TList;
            friend class TListNavigator; // See discussion below
};
```

Class **TListNode** declares **TList** to be friend because, when a new **TListNode** is appended (or prepended) to the **TList**, the existing pointers to next and previous **TListNode** data members will have to be changed. And this is an operation that happens very frequently and needs to be fast. Only **TList** can change the internal pointers in **TListNode**. This is ensured by making **TList** a friend class of **TListNode**. Note that clients don't directly deal with **TListNodes**—they only provide data (pointers to void). It is up to **TList** to create **TListNode** objects and to store them on the list. If there were no friendship between **TList** and **TListNode**, then **TListNode** must implement all the methods required for manipulating the **_next** and **_previous** pointer (which is dangerous). Normal clients should not be allowed to manipulate these pointers. Because these pointer manipulations must be fast, it is much more convenient to use the friend relationship. If the friendship is not used, class **TListNode** would be

```
// Class declared without friendship with TListNode

class TListNode {
    public:
            // Constructor to create a new ListNode given user's data
            TListNode(void* userDataPointer=0);
            // Copy constructor etc.

            // Remove the user's data and return it and make the node empty
            void* RemoveContent();
            void ReplaceContent(void* newElement);
            // Return the pointer to data of this node
            void* GetContent() const;

            TListNode* GetNext() const;// ①
            TListNode* GetPrevious() const;// ②
            void SetNext(TListNode* toThis) ;// ③
            void SetPrevious(TListNode* toThis) ; // ④

            // and others..
    private:
            TListNode* _next;
            TListNode* _previous;
            void*      _userData; // pointer to user supplied data
};
```

This would put more burden on the clients because now they must know how to manipulate pointers safely. It also increases the complexity of **TListNode**. Suffice to say that the friendship between **TList** and **TListNode** really simplifies the implementation. Class **TListNavigator** might have the following interface.

```
class TListNavigator {
    public:
            // Create a navigator for the specified TList
            TListNavigator(TList* forThisList);
            //other important mandatory member functions
            // Return the value in the current TListNode element
            void* Current();
            // Move to the next node on the list and return its value
            void* Next();
            // Move to the previous node on the list and return its value
            void* Previous();
            // Move to the last node on the list and return its value
            void* Last();
            // Move to the first node on the list and return its value
            void* First();
            // Move to the Nth node on the list and return its value
            void* MoveTo(unsigned whichNode);
            // operators for comparing navigator objects also required
                bool operator==(const TListNavigator& other) const;
                bool operator!=(const TListNavigator& other) const;
    private:
            // Implementation data
};
```

An object of the **TListNavigator** allows the client to traverse a list without really knowing the implementation details of **TList** and **TListNode**. Moreover, a client is free to create more than one instance of **TListNavigator** for the same **TList** object. One **TListNavigator** object could start at the end of the **TList** and another at the beginning of the **TList**. The two list navigator objects could be part of separate threads. This would be almost impossible to do if the navigation protocol was part of **TList**. It is conceivable that **TList** and **TListNavigator** are implemented by the same person (or team). But the friendship between them makes their interactions hidden and also makes their interfaces very crisp. Class **TList** only provides list creation and management facilities whereas **TListNavigator** adds list navigation capabilities. Class **TListNavigator** must be a friend of **TListNode** because a **TListNavigator** object must be able access the **TListNode** objects on a **TList** directly, again for speed (see Fig. 7-4). Here is an example usage.

```
main()
{
    TList  aList;
    // code to add elements to the list
    //...
    // Create a TListNavigator object for aList
    TListNavigator listnv1(&aList);
    // Move this navigator to the first element on the list
    listnv1.First();
```

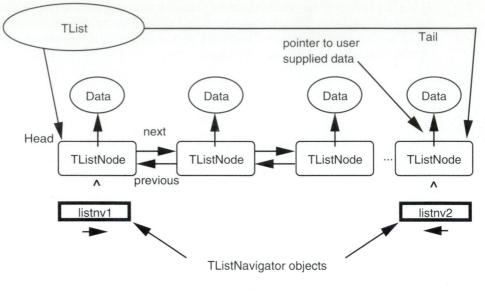

Fig. 7-4

```
// Create another TListNavigator object for aList
TListNavigator listnv2(&aList);
// Move this navigator to the last element on the list
listnv2.Last();
// Next keep doing operations on the list elements while moving the
// listvn2 towards the first element and listnv2 towards the last
// element. Stop when listnv2 and listnv1 are at the same element. It
// would be even more beneficial if listnv1 and listnv2 have their own
// threads of execution.
for(int n=aList.HowMany()/2; n >= 0; n--) {
    // Do some operation using the iterators (for example, a
    // palindrome search). Rest of the code is not shown
    listnv1.Next();       // go the next element (forward move)
    listnv2().Previous(); // go the previous element (backward move)
}
```

NOTE   The list example shown here uses **void** pointers to hold data in the **TListNode** objects. In reality, this will be done using other classes (or template classes). Real implementation of such classes will be shown in a later chapter. Using **void** pointers does not change the intrinsic operations of **TList** or **TListNode**—it relaxes type checking and requires type conversions by the user.

EIFFEL   This list implementation in Eiffel would include the italicized member functions (①② ③ ④) of **TListNode** shown on page 346. But **TListNode** would selectively export them to **TList**.

In the **TList** example, the manipulation of pointers inside **TListNode** is not a very complex operation and, hence, **TList** was declared a **friend**. But if manipulating the pointers is a complex operation involving many steps (such as thread safety issues), it would still make sense to retain the friend relation. But in such a situation, **TListNode** would implement the member functions to manipulate the pointers and keep them private. With that change, only **TList** still gets access to the private region of **TListNode** and it can rely on the private member functions to complete its operations. This approach keeps the knowledge required for the operation within the **TListNode** class but still controls access by using friend classes. Needless to say, such implicit assumptions must be documented clearly so that both classes' implementors know exactly what they have to do.

Case II: Overcoming Syntax Problems

This section describes another application of the friend function concept. It involves the **iostream** classes and stream operators. Even though this discussion involves operator overloading, which we haven't studied yet, the topic is very much related to friend functions. Therefore, it is included here rather than waiting until we get to operator overloading (Chapter 8).

C++   As you already know, printing of language defined types (built-in types) is usually done using the **insertion (<<) and extraction (>>)** operators.[6] These operators get their name based on what they do. The **operator<<** stores the representation of an object (or whatever is given to it) in the stream—it *inserts* the object into the stream. Similarly, **operator>>** reads data from a stream and stores the data into the object—it *extracts* from the stream and stores into the object. These operators are implemented in the **iostream** library classes.[7] These operators work with all types of streams (files, memory streams, etc.).

ABOUT THE INPUT/OUTPUT STREAM LIBRARY

Classes **istream, ostream, ios,** and **streambuf** are the most basic classes of the **iostream** class hierarchy. They contain the basic protocol for all language defined types. Classes **ostream** and **istream** deal with the default screen output and keyboard input. For input and output from files, class **ifstream, ofstream,** and **fstream** are provided. Class **fstream** allows input and output at the same time on a file. Class **ofstream** is derived from class **ostream** and class **ifstream** derives from class **istream**. Class **fstream** inherits from **iostream**. The protocol for streaming to/from a file is the same as that for **ostream** and **istream**. A client need not know whether she is reading from a keyboard or a file. Similarly, clients do not have to know whether they are writing to the display or a file. Class **ostream, istream,** and **iostream** can be used polymorphically to deal with different types of streams.

---

[6]These operators still retain their C language interpretation—left shift and right shift. They are called insertion and extraction operators when used with **iostreams**.

[7]These iostream library classes are template classes as per the latest ANSI C++ draft (they used to be simple, non-template classes). But the discussion here is still relevant despite this change.

For in-memory formatting, classes istrstream, ostrstream, and strstream are provided.[8] These classes allow the client to treat a block of memory as a stream. These classes again inherit from istream, ostream, and iostream, respectively. The protocol is the same for all types of streams.

Given these classes, a client can write a function that uses ostream in the interface and can deal with files (fstream) and memory (strstream) polymorphically. The function would never have to know what kind of stream it is writing to. That is the power of inheritance.

Given this framework, clients can implement their own stream classes. For example, one can write a netstream class that manages streaming to/from a network connection (a *socket*). Needless to say, the protocol remains the same and any existing users of iostream do not have to know anything about this new netstream class, again because of inheritance. This is the extensibility principle that results from well designed inheritance hierarchies.

This brings out one important aspect of programming with streams. When you are using istream (or ostream) in your interface, don't assume that the actual stream that is passed in is an istream(ostream) object—it could very well be an object of one of the derived classes of istream. Stick to the published protocol of istream (ostream) and the behavior of your program will be correct no matter what stream object is used.

Insertion operator is implemented in the class ostream (the output stream). Class ostream provides a simple interface for output to the screen. Similarly, class istream (input stream) provides a simple interface for input. Every C++ development system provides two predefined objects cout and cin for iostream operations. Object cout is an instance of class ostream and object cin is an instance of class istream.[9] Typical usage of ostream is shown below.

```
#include <iostream.h> // For the classes istream, ostream and such

main()
{
    int myInteger= 1997;
    cout << "Integer myInteger is: " ;
    cout << myInteger << endl;
    // endl is a predefined manipulator that sends a newline to the stream
}
```

The statement

```
                    cout << myInteger
```

is interpreted as *send the object* myInteger *to the* ostream *object* cout.

---

[8]For those familiar with C, it is similar to the sprintf and sscanf facility.

[9]These are similar to stdout and stdin of the C i/o library but they are not the same. In fact, mixing output between cout and printf does not guarantee sequential ordering of output because cout and printf are handled by completely different code and protocols. Beware.

The compiler tries to parse this statement as a call to a member function of the class **ostream** with the argument **myInteger**.

```
cout.operator<<(myInteger);
```

As we already know, << is an operator (just like + and −). A statement of the form

```
a + b
```

can be parsed as

```
a.operator+(b)
```

if **a** and **b** are objects of some class. Here, + is an infix operator—it appears in the middle of its operands **a** and **b**.

The compiler is trying to invoke the insertion operator (<<) function on the **cout** object passing **myInteger** (of type **int**) as an argument to it. This will work only if class **ostream** (of which **cout** is an object) supports a public **operator<<**. When you look in the header file **iostream.h** it is easy to find this operator.

```
ostream&          operator<<(int a);
```

So the parsing of the expression succeeds and the member function **operator<<(int)** from the class **ostream** is invoked. In fact, class **ostream** implements one such member function for every language defined type and pointers (**void*** and **char***). This is the reason why stream operators work beautifully with language defined types.

Now let us extend the scenario further to our classes. Let's say we implement a new class **TRangeInt**, which provides range checked integers. Objects of this class have limits on their maximum value and minimum value. We can create a **TRangeInt** object with a value of 25 and a lower limit of 0 and a higher limit of 50. Here is a skeleton of this class. Implementating this class is left as an exercise to the reader.

```
class TRangeInt {
    public:
        enum ELimits { eLow=0, eHigh = 255 };
        // Create a TRangeInt object with these limits and value
        TRangeInt (int vlow, int vhigh, int val);
        // Create a TRangeInt object with default limits (in Elimits)
        // and this value
        TRangeInt (int val=0);
        // What is the value contained?
        int GetValue() const { return _value; };
        // Methods to get limits
        int Low() const { return _low; }
        int High() const { return _high;}
        // and many more not shown
    private:
        int _value; // actual integer value
        int _low;
```

```
        int _high; // range limits
};
```

This looks like a simple class. Clients can use this just like integers. When we want to print **TRangeInt** objects, we would like to treat them as an integer defined in the language. It would be convenient if we can still use the stream operators. Let's see if the following code compiles and runs!

```
#include "RangeInt.h"
#include <iostream.h>
main()
{
        // Create a TRangeInt with a lower limit of 0, high limit of 99
        // and value 10
        TRangeInt rangeInt(0, 99, 10);
        int xx = 100;
        cout << "The int xx is: " << xx << endl;
        cout << " And TRangeInt rangeInt is: ":
        cout << rangeInt << endl;
}
```

This will not compile because **ostream** does not know how to print a **TRangeInt** object. Class **ostream** understands how to print **int**, **char**, etc. When the statement

```
                cout << rangeInt;
```

is compiled, the compiler tries to parse it as

```
                cout.operator<<(rangeInt);
```

For this to work, there should be an **operator<<** in **ostream** declared as

```
        ostream& operator<<(TRangeInt x);
                // OR ostream& operator<<(const TRangeInt& x);
```

But there is no such declaration in class **ostream** and hence the line fails to compile. So the compiler puts out an error message and understandably so.

The implementor of class **ostream** knows about all the language defined types in C++ (**int**, **char**, **float**, etc.) and, hence, an **operator<<** for each one of them is explicitly implemented as a member function in class **ostream**. Hence, all language defined types can be streamed to **cout** directly and the results are as expected. The set of all language defined types in C++ is a finite set (the members of the set are clearly known). But how can the implementor of the **ostream** class (in general the **iostream** library) expect that some program will stream a **TRangeInt** object to it (to **cout**). We might insert (using the insertion **operator <<**) a **TRangeInt** object in this program and we might later try to insert a **TPerson** object to the **cout** (any object of **ostrteam**). How can **ostream** possibly implement insertion operators for all such classes, **TRangeInt**, **TPerson**, etc. Any programmer can create a new class that she wants and can try to stream it to **cout**. The number of classes that C++ programmers can create is infinite. There is no way class ostream can provide an ostream operator for all classes.

But printing using the insertion operator seems to be a very logical thing to do. This is even more so with TRangeInt because TRangeInt is almost an integer. Therefore, it must be possible to print it just like an integer. But just printing the value of an TRangeInt isn't good enough. We also want to print the range limits of TRangeInt objects. What is contained in the implementation of a TRangeInt object (and how to use the private data) is only known to the member functions of class TRangeInt. Therefore, it seems logical to add the insertion operator to the class TRangeInt so that it can print itself correctly. This operator would print the correct representation of TRangeInt on the specified ostream. So the insertion operator must take an ostream object as the only argument. Let's add the insertion operator as a member function to TRangeInt and see what happens.

```cpp
class TRangeInt {
    public:
        enum Elimits { eLow=0, eHigh=255 };
        // Create a TRangeInt object with these limits and value
        TRangeInt (int vlow, int vhigh, int val) ;
        // Create a TRangeInt object with default limits (in Elimits)
        // and this value
        TRangeInt (int val=0);
        // What is the value contained?
        int GetValue() const { return _value; };
        // Methods to get limits
        int Low() const { return _low; }
        int High() const { return _high;}
        // Print it as (lowL, value, highH)
        ostream& operator<<(ostream& stream){
            stream << '(' << _low << "L, " << _value << ", " << _high
            <<"H"; return stream; }
        // and many more not shown
    private:
        int _value; // actual integer value
        int _low;
        int _high; // range limits
};

#include "TRangeInt.h"
#include <iostream.h>
main()
{
    // Create a TRangeInt with a lower limit of 0, high limit of 99 and
    // value 10
    TRangeInt rangeInt(0, 99, 10);
    int xx = 100;

    cout << "The int xx is: " << xx << endl;
    cout << " And TRangeInt rangeInt is: ";
    cout << rangeInt << endl;
}
```

Trying to compile this doesn't get you any further than the previous case. The problem is with the statement

```
cout << rangeInt << endl;
```

We added the insertion operator to the class **TRangeInt**, but this statement does not make any attempt to invoke it. If our intention is to use the **operator<<** in the class **TRangeInt**, we should have written

```
rangeInt << cout;
```

which would translate to

```
rangeInt.operator<<(cout)
```

and this matches the signature of member function **operator<<** in class **TRangeInt**. Our **main()** program still has the same code from the previous example and there is no call to a member function **operator<<** of class **TRangeInt**. If our main program is rewritten as below, it would work.

```
#include "RangeInt.h"
#include <iostream.h>
main()
{
    // Create a TRangeInt with a lower limit of 0, high limit of 99 and
    // value 10
    TRangeInt rangeInt(0, 99, 10);
    int xx = 100;

    cout << "The int xx is: " << xx << endl;
    cout << " And TRangeInt rangeInt is: ";
    rangeInt << cout << endl;
}
```

Sure enough, that compiles and runs correctly. But before you think our problem has been solved, look at the statement

```
rangeInt << cout << endl;
```

This seems to indicate that we are inserting the **ostream** object **cout** into the **TRangeInt** object **rangeInt**. But we are attempting the opposite. Anyone even vaguely familiar with C++ would not agree with this usage of the insertion **operator <<** in this example. The accepted style is to put the **ostream** type object in front followed by objects (or variables) to be *inserted* into the stream. The statement above is completely in violation of that style. The problem is with the member function implementation of **operator<<** in class **TRangeInt**. If we prefer to implement **operator<<** as a member function in **TRangeInt**, there is no way we can use the (correct) style

```
cout << rangeInt;
```

But if we use this correct style, the program doesn't compile because it fails to locate the correct operator<<. Well, what a wonderful predicament we are in?

☞ **If the accepted style of streaming objects to/from** ostream **and** istream **is required, then** operator<< **and** operator>> **cannot be implemented as a member function of the class whose object is being streamed.**

This is where non-member functions (and friend functions) come to the rescue.

How C++ Looks for the Correct Operator << and >> When C++ (the compiler) looks for matching functions, it follows certain well defined rules. Given the statement

```
cout << rangeInt;
```

the compiler goes through the following steps.

1. Parse it as cout.operator(rangeInt). Look for a matching member function operator<< as part of the class ostream

2. If (1) fails to find a matching member function, look for a function operator<< that can accept two arguments. Here, the expression

```
cout << rangeInt;
```

is converted to a prefix expression

```
operator<<(cout, rangeInt);
```

If there exists a normal non-member function operator<<(ostream, TRangeInt) then the call is resolved.

3. If (2) also fails to locate a matching function, then look for a template function for operator<< from which the correct function operator<<(ostream, TRangeInt) can be generated.[10]

4. If after steps (1) through (3) there still is no matching function, then the call is in error (unresolved).

When the compiler applied these steps to our call

```
cout << rangeInt;
```

it comes out empty because

a) there is no member function operator<< in class ostream accepting a TRangeInt object;

---

[10]This will be dicussed in detail later in the chapter on Generic Types. (Chapter 9)

b) there is no non-member function operator<<(ostream, TRangeInt);

c) and we definitely haven't created any template operator<< function anywhere.

To resolve the call to the operator<<, we need to provide a function, operator<<, with the appropriate arguments. This cannot be a member function of TRangeInt for reasons mentioned above. So let us create a new function operator<< as follows.

```
// A normal function to stream (insert) an TRangeInt object to a specified
// stream. theStream is the ostream to which the TRangeInt object anObject
// is streamed. The stream theStream is returned from the function to make
// cascading work. We use the methods GetValue, Low and High from class
// TRangeInt.
ostream& operator<<(ostream& theStream, const TRangeInt& anObject)
{
        theStream << anObject.Low() << "L, ", << anObject.GetValue()
        << ", " << anObject.High() << "H ";

        return  theStream;
}
```

Add this function to our main() program file (or the TRangeInt class file) and try to compile the program. Sure enough, everything works like a charm. So we have at least one solution to the streaming problem. Now you might wonder why this topic is being discussed under friend functions because the operator<< function above is not a friend of any class—it is a free function (like so many others that you might have written in C and C++).

The operator<< function above uses the methods GetValue(), Low(), and High() from the class TRangeInt to stream the TRangeInt object into the ostream object theStream. That looks simple and correct. This TRangeInt is a simple class and it provides methods to get all the required details (range limits and value) because these methods are useful for many clients—not just the insertion operator. So the operator<< function just used these public member functions in the implementation. But not all classes are this simple and definitely all classes don't (cannot) provide member functions to get the values of all data members (that would be considered poor design). Furthermore, not all classes have simple data members that can be printed directly. For example, printing an object of the TList class discussed earlier requires navigation of the list using the pointers to head and tail. In such cases, the operator<< cannot be implemented using only member functions because access to data members in the class is required. So in cases where access to data members of the class is required for the implementation of the insertion operator (and extraction operator), friendship between the class and the corresponding operator<< and operator>> function is required. Even if the class provides member functions to access the necessary data in the class, for efficiency reasons, it may not be feasible to go through the member function interface. Again, in such cases, it is necessary to have a friendship between the class and the insertion and extraction operators.

☞ **The insertion operator must be implemented as a non-member function to reflect the correct syntax. If access to private data members is required for the implementation of the insertion operator, then it is declared to be a friend of the class.**

Implementing the insertion and extraction operator this way allows the programmer to extend the familiar syntax that is used with language defined types (cout << j) to programmer defined types very easily. Classes that follow this scheme get the same behavior as the language defined types. The same syntax can be used uniformly with programmer defined types as well as language defined types.

So far we have been bestowing all our attention on the insertion operator. Isn't it time we also looked at the extraction operator? Insertion operator writes the object to the stream whereas the extraction operator reads data from the stream into the object. In the simplest case, a user might type in the range limits and the value for the TRangeInt object, which will be stored into the object. Usually classes allow clients to get the values of important fields (data members) of an object but they may not allow the client to set the values of fields (to maintain class integrity). No harm is done (in most cases) to an object when the client reads values of data members.[11] But allowing the clients to set values of data members is quite dangerous, particularly in cases where pointers to other objects are involved. For example, what if the class TList allowed clients to set the value of the head data member? How can TList ensure that the value of the pointer head is valid. And if TList cannot ensure that the pointer head is valid, there is no way it can fulfill its responsibilities to clients. Under no circumstance, a client should be allowed to compromise the integrity of an object (class). That is the first rule in object-orientation. The extraction operator for a class definitely sets values of the data members of the object, which may require access to the private data members of the object. Therefore, usually extraction operator functions are friends of the corresponding class. For a class, even if the insertion operator is not a friend function of the class, the extraction operator is usually a friend function.

☞ **The extraction operator is usually implemented as a friend function of a class because it needs to set the data members of the class and also must reflect the accepted syntax. If access to data members is not required then make it a global non-member function.**

NOTE   This is not a very rigid rule. There are many classes for which even the extraction operator does not need friendship. Member functions provided by the class allow the extraction operator to set the corresponding data members. In such cases, there is absolutely no reason why the extraction operator must be granted friendship.

Let us implement the extraction operator for the class TRangeInt. Before we jump into the code, we need to specify the input format. A user can enter the details of a TRangeInt object in one of the following formats:

---

[11]When an object contains pointers to other entities, it is equally dangerous to allow clients to get the values of the pointers because once the client gets the pointer she can do whatever she likes with it without the knowledge of the object holding the pointer. If it is really essential to provide access (read) to a pointer, provide a member function that returns a pointer to const. This is discussed in Chapter 3.

1. only the value of the **TRangeInt** specified (no range limits);

2. only the range limits specified (value should be set to 0); or

3. both value and range limits are specified.

Next, we need to specify the exact interpretation of the input.

a. If just a number is entered, it is the value of the **TRangeInt** object.

b. If data is in the format (l, h) then just the range limits have been provided and value is set to l (the low limit) because we don't know what the user wants it to be.

c. If data is entered as (l, v, h) then both the value and the range limits are specified.

Here is one simple implementation of the extraction operator. Note that it expects the input in the exact format. No scanning for extra spaces and tabs is done. If you want it to be real fancy, then you are on your own. The implementation below shows the basic protocol.

```
/*
        Input formats for TRangeInt numbers are:
        num
        value
        (low,high)
        (low, value, high)
        This is a very simple implementation. No error checking is done
        for invalid input. It is here just to illustrate the implementation
        scheme.
*/
istream& operator>>(istream& is, TRangeInt& ri)
{
        int value = 0, low = 0, high = 0;
        char c; // For reading from stream

        is >> c;// Read first character
        if (c == '(') {
                // The user is typing in only the ranges or both range and value
                // We need to scan further and see what it is.
                is >> low >> c; // read (possibly) lower limit and the next
                character
                if (c == ',')
                        is >> value >> c; // read value (possibly) and next
                                          // character
                if (c == ')' ) {
                        // User is specifying only range limits and not the value
                        // of the TRangeInt
                        high = value;
                        value = low; // Set value to the low limit
                            // because we don't know what it should be
                }
                else if (c == ',') {
                        // User is specifying all three
```

```
                    is >> high >> c;
                    if (c != ')') {
                        // Bad input format. Set stream to bad state
                        is.clear(ios::badbit);
                    }
                }
        }
        else {
            // User is typing in the value only. First put the last character
            // read back into the stream because it is part of the value
            is.putback(c);
            is >> value;
        }
        if (is) { // If stream is still in good state (no errors)
            if (low >= high)
                    return is; // We could throw an exception (details in
                            // Chapter 10)
            if (value >= low && (value <= high)
                    ri._value = value; // value is within the range limits
            else return is; // bad range limits
            ri._low = low;
            ri._high = high;
        }
        return is;
}
```

And here is the corresponding class header file.

```
#include <iostream.h>
class TRangeInt {
    public:
            // other details as before The operator<< is not a friend - it is
            // just a free function (declared below)
            friend istream& operator>>(istream& is, TRangeInt& ri);
            // other details as before
};
// Non-member insertion operator function for TRangeInt objects
ostream& operator<<(ostream& theStream, const TRangeInt& anObject)
```

Shown below is a test program for the **TRangeInt** class extraction operator.

```
main()
{
    // Create an TRangeInt with a lower limit of 0, high limit of 99 and
    // value 10
    TRangeInt rangeInt(0, 99, 10);
    int xx = 100;

    cout << "The int xx is: " << xx << endl;
    cout << " And TRangeInt rangeInt is: " << rangeInt << endl;

    cout << "Changing the values of the TRangeInt object\n";
    cout << "Enter the new contents for the TRangeInt object\n";
    cout << "Format is : value\n";
```

```
cout << "                        (low,high)" << endl;
cout <<"                         (low, value, high)" << endl;
cin >> rangeInt;
cout << "Printing the new contents of the TRangeInt object:" << endl;
cout << rangeInt;

}
```

REMEMBER   One should not infer that << and >> can no longer be used as right shift and left shift operators in C++ (which is their original meaning in C). These operators still retain their original meaning even in C++—they are very much bitwise shift operators. When they are used with classes that support overloaded << and >> operators, the new meaning of extraction and insertion comes into play. There is no rule in the language that forces an implementor to use << and >> as insertion and extraction operators. It is just an accepted practice in the C++ domain to treat them as operators for reading and writing. The C++ user community is familiar with the usage of << and >> with **ostream** and **istream**, and implementors and designers try to follow this accepted normal usage.

Also remember that both << and >> associate left to right (just like + and −). A programmer cannot change that. Both << and >> are binary operators, (i.e., an operator requiring two operands). Here is a simple example.

```
int someInteger = 16;
int y;
y = someInteger << 2;
```

The value of the integer **someInteger** is being shifted left by 2 bits and the result is assigned to **y**. For the operator << above, **someInteger** is the first operand and 2 is the second operand. The number of operands required for any operator is clearly defined by the language and it cannot be changed. Note that the value of **someInteger** above does not change because of the shift operation.

A normal member function receives the implicit **this** pointer. But a friend function is not a member function and hence it does not have the **this** pointer associated with it. Any arguments that a friend function needs must be explicitly passed to it—there are no implicit arguments.

☞ **A friend function does not have a** *this* **pointer**

Case III: Functions that Need to Communicate with More than One Class

In some situations, a function acts as a communication channel between two (or more) classes. In other words, the operation of the function depends on more than one class. The function needs access to the implementation of both classes to work efficiently. Ideally, the function should be a member function of both classes. But we already know that the same function cannot be a member of more than one class. This causes a dilemma—which class should this function belong to? It could be a member function of any one of them and both classes seem to be good candidates. One can overcome this dilemma by making the function a common friend of both classes. We have already seen such a case in the TList example. The class TListNavigator is a friend of both TList and TListNode because it needs to communicate with both TList and TListNode. Every method in TListNavigator needs access to both TList and TListNode. Commercial software is full of such examples.

Another common example is that of a multiplication operation between a vector and a matrix.[12] TMatrix is a common matrix implementation. One can create an (m*n) matrix by using the constructor of this class. Class TVector is another simple class that represents a one dimensional vector (very similar to an array). Multiplying a matrix by a vector is a common operation that results in a new vector object. Which class should contain the Multiply method: TMatrix or TVector? Both are good candidates but making it a member of either one of them requires that the other class grant friendship to it. It is probably more convenient to make it a normal function having friendship with both classes.

```
class TVector {
    public:
        friend TVector Multiply (const TMatrix& mx, const TVector& ve);
        // Other details not important
};

class TMatrix {
    public:
        friend TVector Multiply (const TMatrix& mx, const TVector& ve);
    // Other details not important
};

TVector Multiply (const TMatrix& mx, const TVector& ve)
{
    // Multiply each element of the matrix mx by the vector ve
    // and generate a new TVector object.
}
```

This way, Multiply has equal access to both classes. It can access the implementation of both TMatrix and TVector directly and produce the resulting vector efficiently. Here the function Multiply is a common channel for communication between TMatrix and TVector.

THE ADVANTAGE OF NON-MEMBER FUNCTIONS

C++ is a multi-paradigm language. It allows one to write a wide variety of programs. One can just use it to construct classes and objects without any non-member functions. Others might use it to create classes as well as non-member functions. And yet another community might use it like a procedural language. C++ is a good language for all such situations.

One might wonder if there are some advantages to using a non-member function interface as opposed to a member function interface. The answer to this question is some-

---

[12]This example is discussed in Bjarne Stroustrups' C++ Programming Language (Second Edition).

what interesting. When a class is implemented, only the implementor of the class has full control of the class and what the member functions can do. When clients start using the class, they might find that the class interface is insufficient as far as their needs are concerned. The class is not wrong, but the facilities provided by it do not fulfill all the needs of the client. This is a situation encountered in many situations. In such situations, should the clients implement their own classes from scratch or should they inherit from the existing class and add the needed functionality (if inheritance and overriding is possible)?

With traditional object-oriented languages, the only alternative is to extend the class, if possible, by using inheritance or by aggregation, if possible. But, again, there is no guarantee that inheritance would solve the problem. It depends very much on the class and what the client needs. In such languages, one cannot write normal non-member functions—they only support member functions. Moreover, creating a new class (through aggregation or inheritance) might be an overkill.

Turning to C++, adding a friend functions requires modifications to the header file and recompilation of all other classes that depend on the class. This can be a big cost that most projects try to avoid. Moreover, using friend functions is not something acceptable to all designers. It is considered a violation of object-oriented programming principles. A friend function is tied to the implementation details of the class to which it is a friend. When the class implementation is changed (but not the interface), the friend functions must be modified to conform to the new implementation. This dependency is something not to be taken lightly.

In some situations, the class does not provide the required operation directly but it provides enough interface for the client to extract the information and implement the necessary operation. In such a scenario, a normal client can extend the class by writing some ordinary non-member functions that utilize the existing public interface of the class. This way, no modifications to the class header file are required. And, it also avoids uncontrolled access of private data members because these functions are non even friend functions. This facility allows a client to extend the usability of a class by adding many useful operations. It does not suffer from the drawbacks of a friend function (implementation dependency) because a non-member function uses the interface of the class and knows nothing about the implementation. Such functions must change only when the class interface changes. But, a class interface does not (should not) change every day. Moreover, when the class interface changes, anything and everything that depends on the class must change anyway.

☞ **A non-member function can add operations that are missing from a class without any implementation knowledge.**

But, don't assume that you should use a non-member function only when what's needed is missing from the class. Class designers might themselves provide a class with a minimal implementation (only essential member functions) while implementing all other operations as non-member functions utilizing the interface of the class. This way, the designers don't have to change everything when the class implementation is modified. This makes the class implementation code easier to manage because there is not much code to be managed. This is a very powerful scheme that has been used successfully in many projects.

☞ A class can provide a minimal interface/implementation but it can add more functionality by using non-member functions.

We have already seen an application of this principle with the **TRangeInt** class above. The insertion operator is implemented as non-member functions utilizing other member functions of the class. If class **TRangeInt** is changed (let's say to provide more error checking), the insertion operator need not be changed. It still uses the same interface of the class. As another example, class **TDate** (already used many times in Chapters 4, 5 and 6) with a set of non-member functions is shown below.

```
// A date class that uses the Gregorian calendar
class TDate {
    public:
        enum EMonth { eJan=1, eFeb, eMar, eApr, eMay, eJun, eJul, eAug,
                                       eSep, eOct, eNov, eDec };

        TDate( short day, EMonth month, short year);
        TDate(); // sets date from the operating system date

        unsigned short GetYear() const;
        EMonth GetMonth() const;
        unsigned short GetDayOfMonth() const; // day of the month

        // Convenience function.
        void AddToYear(int increment); // Increment can be negative
        void AddToMonth(int increment); // Increment can be negative
        void AddToDay(int increment); // Increment can be negative

        // Returns a character representation of the date
        TString GetDate() const;

        // utility functions
        bool IsLeapYear() const;
        unsigned short HowManyDaysInYear() const;
        bool IsDayInMonth(unsigned day) const;
        unsigned short DayNumberInWeek() const;
        unsigned short DayNumberOfYear() const;

        // Returns a character representation of the day
        TString DayName() const;
        TString MonthName() const;
    private:
        // Not shown
};
```

Shown below are a set of helper functions for **TDate** class. These function do not depend on the implementation details of the class. They use the same public interface as everyone else and add more useful functionality.

```
// Increments the day (same as AddToDate). Prefix version
TDate& operator++(TDate& date) { date.AddToDay(1); return date; }
TDate& operator++(TDate& date, int notUsed) // Postfix version
{ date.AddToDay(1); return date; }

// Decrements the day - Prefix version
TDate& operator--(TDate& date) { date.AddToDay(-1); return date; }

TDate&
operator--(TDate& date, int notUsed) // Postfix version
{ date.AddToDay(-1); return date; }

// Add n days to this date object
TDate&
operator+=(TDate& date, int n) { date.AddToDay(n); return date; }

// Comparison functions
bool
operator==(const TDate& first, const TDate& second)
{
    return ( (first.GetYear() == second.GetYear())
        && (first.GetMonth() == second.GetMonth())
        && (first.GetDayOfMonth() == second.GetDayOfMonth()) );
}

bool
operator !=(const TDate& first, const TDate& second)
    { return !(first == second); }
```

CAUTION   However, this discussion should not lead you into believing that this scheme is the best way to design/implement classes. That's not the point here. When you have so many functions floating around, naturally a coherent picture of the usefulness of the class is lost. Too many functions scattered in many different files is not a good way to design software. This scheme of adding non-member functions shows the multi-paradigm focus of C++ and it also shows how a client can make a class more useful.

There is another bigger benefit from this approach. When these non-member functions are implemented using the public interface of the class, it tests the usability of the class. These functions use the class in many different scenarios and therefore act as a test bed for the class. Also, it is another degree of code reuse. Code in the class implementation is being reused in many non-member functions. When all these non-member functions work correctly, it adds a degree of confidence in the implementation of the class.

CHOOSING FRIEND FUNCTIONS VS MEMBER FUNCTIONS

One needs to understand the distinction between a friend function and a member function clearly to use the appropriate one when implementing classes. Here are some guidelines

- In general, prefer a member function over everything else. Member functions follow the simple **object.memberfunction** syntax and are natural when programming with classes and objects. Member functions have an implicit **this** pointer, making it very convenient to access data inside the object on which they are invoked. But one must pass all arguments explicitly to a friend function.

- A friend/non-member function that is not a member function of another class is in the global name space and hence pollutes the global name space (can be controlled using **namespace**s).

- A friend/non-member function (that is not a member function of another class) can be called by anyone—it does not need an object. Access control can be applied only to member functions. Friend functions that are not member functions of another class do not have any access control.

- Even when there is a need to use a friend function, try to use friend functions that are member functions of another class.

- Use friend/non-member functions when implementing stream insertion and extraction operators.

- Some operators that need conversions (discussed in Chapter 8) may require friend/non-member function implementation.

- Even when using friend functions, it is better if the implementor of the class and the implementor of the friend function is the same person (or team). In such cases, friend functions are used for syntactic convenience and still the integrity of the class is maintained.

- If interactions between two classes gets very complex and unmanageable, try to use friendship between them.

- If the efficiency of the implementation is degraded because of member function calls and object boundaries, try to use friend functions if it improves performance dramatically. In this, as well as the previous case, one must be able to justify the need for friend functions (performance, cleaner implementation, smaller code, etc.).

Shown below is a general algorithm for deciding whether one should use a member function, friend function, or non-member function.

For any function **F** and class **C**:

```
If (F needs to be a virtual function)
     make F a member function of C;
else if (F is operator >> or operator <<) {
     make F a global function;
     If (F needs access to non-public members of C)
          make F a friend of C;
}
else if (F needs type conversions on its leftmost (first) argument) {
     make F a global function;
     If (F needs access to non-public members of C)
     make F a friend of C;
}
else
     make F a member function of C
```

REMEMBER   Friend mechanism is a one to one relationship between a class and a function (or a class and another class). It cannot be a transitive relation. For example, if class **A** grants friendship to class **B** and class **B** grants friendship to class **C**, there is absolutely no relationship between class A and class C. In other words, friend of a friend is NOT a friend. Also, friendship is not inherited. If class B grants friendship to a function f(), and class D is derived from class B (i.e., B is the base class), the function f() is NOT a friend of class D.

SUMMARY

Friend functions support a form of selective exports. Use them cautiously.

Eiffel supports selective export of individual members from a class to other classes—C++ does not.

Smalltalk does not support any kind of selective exports from a class.

A friend function of a class can access public, protected, and private regions of the class—there are no restrictions.

A friend function of a class can be a member function of another class.

Classes that support stream insertion and extraction operators should try to implement them as non-member functions. If access to private data members is required in the implementation of these functions, then the friend mechanism must be used.

8

The Concept of Operator Overloading

DIFFERENCE BETWEEN LANGUAGE TYPES AND PROGRAMMER DEFINED TYPES

When programming in a language, many times programmers feel betrayed by the language in certain areas. Usually the language allows a wide variety of operations on integers, characters, floating point numbers, etc. But when programmers try to implement the same operations for their own types (programmer defined types), the language doesn't allow the programmer to do so. In such situations, the language is more of a hindrance than help. The language seems to treat the language defined types as first class citizens and the programmer defined types as aliens without many rights.

For example, a simple language defined type such as int has many useful operations associated with it. One can perform addition (+), subtraction (−), etc. on a pair of integers. Given two integer variables x and y, we always write

```
x + y
```

without even thinking about what + would do because the implicit meaning of + is already known to everyone (not just to programmers). The programming community is also very much accustomed to that ease. The symbol + is called an *operator* in any language. Every programming language provides a host of such operators for the convenience of programmers.

Now consider the TRangeInt class that was discussed in Chapter 7. A TRangeInt object is almost an integer except for the restriction on its values—it has an upper and a lower limit. Definitely, we would like to compute the sum of (and subtract, multiply, etc.) a pair of TRangeInt objects. These seem like very common operations. Class TRangeInt is an abstract data type defined by us programmers. We have the responsibility to define the necessary operations for such abstract data types. While it is obvious to us that a TRangeInt is almost an int, the compiler doesn't know that. Therefore, we have to clearly tell the compiler what all the different operations mean for our abstract data type. For example, can we write the following piece of code?

```
TRangeInt i1, i2, i3;
i1 = i2 + i3; // Compute the sum of i2 and i3 and assign the result to i1
```

This is a very simple piece of code. The expression (i2+i3) will not compile because the + operation cannot be applied to TRangeInt objects. That is because the language does not know how to compute the sum of TRangeInt objects. The language knows how to compute the sum of two integers so why can't it compute the sum of two TRangeInt objects? The answer is quite simple. The type int is implemented (and well supported) by the language. The language knows how the bits and bytes of an integer are stored and it defines all the operations possible for the type int (the interface of the type int). Based on that implementation knowledge it can perform the operation of computing the sum of two integers. The type int is well known to the language—int is its own baby. On the other hand, TRangeInt is our baby—the language doesn't know much about the semantics of usage and the implementation of the programmer defined type TRangeInt. We (the programmer) know what TRangeInt represents and also how to use it. But since the language does not have this crucial knowledge it is not able to carry out the operation + for TRangeInt objects. This has been the case with many popular languages like Pascal, Fortran, Modula-2, C, etc.

Let us consider a possible solution to this problem. Type int is implemented and controlled by the language compiler. It knows best how to perform an operation on the type int. For the TRangeInt class, the programmer is the implementor and has full control and knowledge of the implementation. Therefore, the programmer must be able to define the meaning of the operation + (and −, *, etc.). This is a simple division of rights and responsibilities. The language gives us the type int and provides the necessary operations to use integers effectively. One can imagine (just for understanding this discussion) that int is a class that is implemented by the language compiler with a well defined interface. On the same lines, TRangeInt is a class defined by the programmer with a clear interface. Therefore, the programmer must have the freedom to define whatever operations are appropriate for the class TRangeInt. So if operation + is sensible for the class TRangeInt, the programmer should be able to provide it. That seems like a fair argument, doesn't it?

The argument fails for many popular languages. For example, if this same TRangeInt class is defined as a record in Pascal (or a new type in Modula-2) the programmer still cannot define the operation + for TRangeInt. This restriction leads to the definition of a function such as Sum shown below.

```
TRangeInt Sum(TRangeInt operand1, TRangeInt operand2)
{
    This is a piece of pseudo code
    Code to compute the sum of operand1 and operand2
    Returns the sum computed
    Does not modify operand1 or operand2
}
```

With a function like that, programmers can write

```
TRangeInt  i1, i2, i3;
i1 = Sum (i2, i3);
// Compute the sum of i2 and i3 and assign the result to i1
```

That definitely works but it has lost the simplicity and elegance that we are used to in normal programming. Definitely (i2+i3) is much simpler and easier to read and understand. Moreover, one can use the name **Add** for the function instead of **Sum**—the language does not control the naming of functions. And yet another programmer might call this function **Plus**. In other words, there is no common vocabulary for naming such functions.

Fortunately, there is a solution to this problem in C++. In C++, the class implementor has the freedom to define (actually overload) operators for objects of a class. For example, class **TRangeInt** is free to provide an **operator+** as follows:

```
class TRangeInt {
    public:
        enum ELimits { eLow=0, eHigh = 255 };
        // Create a TRangeInt object with these limits and value
        TRangeInt (int low, int high, int val) ;

        // Create a TRangeInt object with default limits and this value -
        // val
        TRangeInt (int val=0);
        // What is the value contained?
        int GetValue() const;
        // Methods to get limits
        int Low() const { return_low; }
        int High() const { return_high;}
        // The operator<< is a not a friend function. It is free function
        // (declared below) This is the extraction operator that reads
        // from the stream into the object
        friend istream& operator>>(istream& stream, TRangeInt& ri);
        // The this pointer represents the first operand
        TRangeInt operator+ (const TRangeInt& operand2);
        // and many more methods not shown
    private:
        int _value; // actual integer value
        int _low, _high; // range limits
};

// Insertion operator for objects of TRangeInt
ostream& operator<<(ostream& stream, const TRangeInt& printThis);
```

The declaration of operator+ inside the class TRangeInt above is a typical overloaded operator declaration. The keyword operator is a reserved word in C++. The operator being overloaded is +. The keyword operator is followed by the actual operator symbol (could be more than one character, like +=) being overloaded and then by the function declaration of that operator. The declaration specifies that it will accept one operand of type TRangeInt (a reference to an object) and it returns a TRangeInt object by value (which should be the sum of this and operand2).

WHAT IS AN OVERLOADED OPERATOR?

In the previous paragraph, the phrase *overloaded operator* was cautiously used. It is important to remember that + is an overloaded operator and not a new operator defined by TRangeInt. It is very important to understand the significance of this statement. C++ language supports a well defined set of operators such as +, −, ++, − −, etc. These operators have well defined meaning and behavior when used with a language defined type such as int. The language compiler follows strict rules when parsing expressions containing these operators. Most importantly, the associativity (whether an operator is evaluated left to right or right to left) and precedence (which operator is evaluated first in an expression which contains more than one operator) of these operators is clearly defined when used with language defined types. The class TRangeInt above declares that it will provide an implementation of the + operator. Class TRangeInt is defining the meaning of + when it is applied to objects of TRangeInt. The operator + can be used with types int, float, long, double, etc. There is a well defined meaning (and implementation) when + is applied to integers. Similarly, there is a well defined interpretation and behavior when + is applied to a pair of double numbers.

```
void SomeFunction()
{
    double  d1, d2, d3;
    // Compute the sum of d2 and d3 and assign the result to d1
    d1 = d2 + d3;

    int  i, j, k;
    i = j + k; // Compute the sum of j and k and assign the result to i
}
```

In the code fragment above, the operator + is used with different arguments, once with double numbers and with int later. The same operator + is being used in both cases. However, the exact code for computing the sum of two integers (which is provided by the compiler) is different from the code required to compute the sum of two double numbers. So if operator + is like a function, we have a set of + functions each with a different set of arguments. Just for the sake of understanding the concept, one could imagine that the compiler internally has a pair of functions:

```
double operator+(double operand1, double operand2);
int operator+(int operand1, int operand2);
```

Aren't these a set of overloaded functions? We say operator + is now overloaded. Our class TRangeInt also has the operator + defined for a pair of TRangeInt objects. In other words, operator + has been further overloaded by TRangeInt. The operator + in TRangeInt will be used only when computing the sum of two TRangeInt objects. All that has been done in class TRangeInt is to overload the operator +, which (operator +) is already supported by the language. This is the reason why the process is called **operator overloading**. *We are not defining a new operator—we are only defining a new meaning for + when the operands are of type TRangeInt* .

Operators are implemented just like any other (member) function; the same over-loading resolution rules apply.[1] The only difference is that the name of the function be-gins with the reserved word operator and is followed by the operator being overloaded.

This preceding discussion also implies that a programmer cannot define new opera-tors. *We can only overload existing operators in the language.* We cannot invent new op-erators and implement them in our classes. Since we are *overloading* an existing operator, the precedence and associativity of the operator already defined by the language cannot be changed by the programmer either.

When an operator is used in an expression (such as x+y), the determination of the exact operator+ function to be used is done at compile time based on the types of the operands (x and y). There is no run-time overhead involved in this call; everything is type checked at compile time. If x and y are int variables, the built-in + defined for int type is used. On the other hand, if x and y are objects of the class TRangeInt, then the opera-tor+ defined (if any) in the class is used. If there is no matching definition of operator+ in that scope for the types of x and y, then the call to operator+ is an error.

NOTE In the class TRangeInt above, operator+ is declared with only one operand (which is operand2). Since operator+ is being defined as a member function, it must be in-voked on an object of TRangeInt and that object is implicitly passed to the operator+ function via the this pointer, which is the first operand to operator+. This is true for all operators implemented as member functions. So, a binary operator (an operator that re-quires two operands), when implemented as a member function, will only declare one ar-gument explicitly—the other operand comes via the this pointer implicitly. Similarly, a unary operator (an operator that requires a single operand) when implemented as a mem-ber function, will not have any explicit argument declaration because the only operand re-quired is received via the this pointer. An operator can also be implemented as a friend function. More on this later.

WHY (NOT) OPERATOR OVERLOADING—PROS AND CONS

One might ponder about the benefit of an overloaded operator. In particular, what extra benefits does it offer to a designer? If you are thinking on these lines, you are not alone. Operator overloading just looks like a syntactic feature of C++ that programmers can use if they like it (or need it). But it also has implications on software design. The rest of the chapter will try to bring out some of the issues.

---

[1]Except that an operator function cannot have default value arguments.

C++   By default, the only operator automatically available to a class is the assignment operator, operator =. All other operators must be explicitly implemented by the class when required. If an operator is not overloaded by a class, then it is not available for use by the clients of that class. Not implementing an overloaded operator is one way of indicating that the operator is not applicable to the class.

More Elegant Abstract Data Types

If you recall the discussion of *abstract data types* in Chapter 2, a class is nothing but an abstract data type. An abstract data type is a programmer defined type with a set of operations defined on it. Every member function defined in a class is an operation on the abstract data type. But many operations are represented (and used) using symbols such as +, −, etc. It would be more convenient if the language allows the designer to provide operators as member functions in the class. This would make the abstract data type interface more elegant and less confusing. A majority of the operators have a well defined meaning in the language and if this meaning is preserved in the abstract data type, clients can just use these operators without any reservations.

As mentioned earlier, operators provide a well known vocabulary for the designer of a class and the clients. It is easier to understand + and − symbols than a set of functions with different names (such as Plus, Minus, etc.), and the elegance of terse expressions (such as x+y) is augmented when appropriate operators are supported by a class.

Most operators have a well defined meaning and behavior in the language and a well designed overloaded operator must mimic this meaning and behavior for objects of its class. But there are other operators (such as -> and the function call operator, operator()) that don't have a well defined meaning when they are used with classes. Such operators can be used by classes to provide some powerful new features that are not possible to implement with normal functions. We shall see such examples later.

Convoluted Operator Overloading

But operators can also be misused very easily. Most operators have a predefined meaning in the language. But the language does not prevent an implementor of an overloaded operator from changing this predefined meaning drastically. For example, what if someone implements an operator + such that (x + y) adds y to x, thereby modifying the original value of x.[2] This is a convoluted implementation of the operator +. Unsuspecting clients suffer due to this bad implementation. Just like any other tool, operators can be used effectively to add more value and simplicity to a class interface or it can be misused by bad designers and implementors to create an interface and implementation that is more confusing and misleading. There is nothing the language can do to prevent misuse by programmers. This is one argument against operator overloading. If operator overloading is not allowed, then designers and implementors must use ordinary (member/non-member) functions (such as Plus, Minus, Add, Subtract, etc.) and there is no predefined meaning for any of these functions. The meaning (or behavior) of any function is what the implementor specifies it to be. Clients using a function must read the documentation to under-

---

[2] It will be even worse if + means subtraction instead of addition.

stand what a specific function does. There is no short cut around that. A client knows exactly what the behavior of the function is going to be when she uses it. The language cannot enforce what a function can (or can not) do. This makes the contract between designers and clients quite clear and straight forward. But once operator overloading is introduced, the scenario is a bit more complex. The language clearly defines what an operator does with language defined types and most clients expect a similar behavior (for objects) from an overloaded operator implemented in a class. If the implementation of the operator does not honor the expected behavior of the operator, there is a mismatch between what the client expects and what the implementation provides. When a clients' expectation about a class is violated, she no longer trusts the implementation of the class and will try to avoid using the class. This is one major reason why most languages do not allow overloaded operators.

☞ **Do not use tricks when implementing operators. Stick with the accepted usage and meaning of the operator in the language.**

Following this important rule will save you and your clients from many frustrating problems.

Failure to Understand Precedence and Associativity Rules

Another major issue with operator overloading involves precedence and associativity rules. Languages clearly define the precedence and associativity of each operator. An overloaded operator is subject to the same precedence and associativity rules. There is no way a programmer can change those rules. When a class implementor provides a new operator as part of the class interface, it is important that she understands the precedence and associativity rules of that operator. If not, the clients of the class will be surprised by unusual (and even incorrect) behavior.

For example, C++ does not support an exponentiation operator (such as **, which is supported in some languages). One might try to use the operator^ to provide this functionality.[3] Let us see what happens if we add the **operator^** as the exponentiation operator for the **TRangeInt** class.

```
class TRangeInt {
    public:
        // Other details omitted for brevity
        TRangeInt operator^ (long toPower);
        TRangeInt operator+ (const TRangeInt& operand2);
    private:
        // details as before
};
```

The **operator^** raises the value of the **TRangeInt** object on which it is applied to the power specified (which is a long integer argument). Let us try a simple expression:

---

[3]In some languages, ^ is an exponentiation operator. But in C++ (and C) it is the bitwise exclusive OR operator.

```
TRangeInt  x(10), y; // create two objects

y = x^10; // This should work — y should be 100
```

Definitely, this statement will produce the correct result. How about something a bit more complex.

```
y = x^2+15; // Raise x to power 2 and then add 15 to the result
```

With languages that support an exponentiation operator, the precedence of the exponentiation operator is higher than that of operator +. But in C++ (where ^ is the bitwise exclusive OR operator) + has a higher precedence than ^. So our expression translates to

```
y = x^(2+15); // Oops — not really what we want
```

To overcome this problem, the client of **TRangeInt** must write

```
y = (x^2) + 15; // Parenthesize to overcome precedence problem
```

Note that it is the client who must remember to use parentheses correctly—the class **TRangeInt** cannot enforce any such rules. This places an undue burden on clients because the implementor of class **TRangeInt** chose to implement ^ as the exponentiation operator without realizing the consequences. If the client forgets to place parentheses around (x^2), the expression still works but produces the wrong result.[4]

☞ **Do not ever attempt to implement an overloaded operator without understanding the precedence and associativity rules, and accepted usage clearly.**

The importance of this rule cannot be stressed enough.

Operators also interact with each other and in many situations the same operation can be done in many different ways. For example

```
int  i;

i = i + 1;
i++;
i += 1;
```

All three expressions above increment the value of the integer i by 1 (one). If a class overloads all these operators, it should ensure that the outcome is the same no matter which operator is used. If k++ (where k is an object of a class) produces a different result than (k = k + 1), then definitely there is something wrong in the implementation.

Another caveat is that of incomplete interfaces. Many operators belong in families. For example, (+, −, *, /, %) is a family of frequently used operators. If your class implements one of them, it is necessary that you implement the full family. Otherwise, the class

---

[4]Imagine a situation where this exponentiation is used in a bank to manage accounts!

interface is not complete. If a client can perform addition, she must be able to do subtraction also (unless of course subtraction makes no sense for that class). And if you overload binary - (minus), you should overload unary - (minus) also for completeness. Similarly, (>, <, >=, <=) are also a family of operators. Also, if you implement equality (operator ==), you better implement operator != also.

☞   **Many operators belong to a family of operators. If you implement one of them, implement the others too.**

And last but not the least, remember to check for assignments of the form x=x for any class that implements the assignment operator operator= (as described in Chapters 3 and 4).

NOTE   It is quite common to implement operator== as a virtual member function. However, its counterpart, operator!= need not be a virtual function because it is implemented in terms of operator==. Here is a skeleton.

```
class X {
    public:
        virtual bool operator==(const X& rhs) const { /* code */ }
        // For operator!=, reuse operator ==
        bool operator!= (const X& rhs) const { return ! (*this == rhs); }
};
```

Operator overloading requires that the programmer understand the operator algebra and the precedence, associativity, and properties of C++ operators. Programmers must also understand the different usage styles of operators. Any overloaded operator must behave the same way that a normal programmer with good C++ operator knowledge would expect it to behave. There should not be any surprises when an overloaded operator is used by clients. For example, imagine a program that uses integers (type int) and many different operators with them. If this program is changed to use TRangeInt instead of integers, one would expect that there would be no change in behavior (assuming that TRangeInt implements all operators). Unless the class TRangeInt follows all the rules and guidelines described so far, there is no guarantee that the program will behave properly.

It is because of these problems that many languages do not support operator overloading. Operator overloading, when used incorrectly increases the burden on the programmer and the client. But when correctly implemented and used, programs look really neat and concise.

EIFFEL   There is no support for operator overloading in Eiffel. Any operation required must be implemented as a member function. There are no complex rules to remember and the Eiffel community seems to like it. It keeps the language rules simple.

SMALLTALK   Smalltalk also does not support true operator overloading as C++ does. But in Smalltalk, the supplied base class Number has methods for general operations such as +, – etc., that can be overridden by subclasses (such as LargePositiveInteger). Unless a class is a subclass of **Number**, it is not allowed to override these operators. Other than that, there is no true support for operator overloading.

ADA   Ada also supports operator overloading. The declaration of an operator function is very similar to a normal function except that the name of the function is replaced by the operator being overloaded.

OVERLOADED OPERATORS IN C++

C++ allows the overloading of the operators (shown in Table 8-1):

All the operators allowed in the language have been shown just for your reference. But you are not going to see an example for each one of them. Some of the operators above are very rarely overloaded. For example, an overloaded comma (,) operator is very rarely used.

NOTE   ANSI-C introduced some special tokens to substitute for symbols that are not present in some international character sets. The C++ standardization committee followed the ISO recommendations and has included some additional representations for standard C++ tokens. Table 8-2 shows the original token and the new alternative.

Most of these operators are used by classes that implement mathematical classes such as **TRangeInt** above. Another example is a **TComplex** class, which implements complex numbers. The most frequently overloaded operator is of course assignment (=).

We shall now see an implementation of the unary ++ operator. This operator can be used in two flavors—prefix and postfix. And C++ allows us to overload both of them. The typical usage is shown below.

```
int  i = 10;
int  j;

j = ++i; // Prefix flavor
```

Variable i is incremented first and then its value is assigned to j. After this statement, both j and i contain the value 11. The prefix ++ increments the variable and returns the value of the variable.

```
int  i = 10;
int  j;

j = i++; // Postfix flavor
```

Here the value of i is assigned to j and then i is incremented. The effect is as though the value of i is saved in a temporary somewhere, then i is incremented and the saved value is finally returned.

```
Effect of i++
1. Save value of i in a temporary variable
2. Increment i
3. Return the saved value of i
```

Table 8-1

Operator	Function of the operator
new	dynamic memory allocation operator
delete	release the memory allocated by new
new[]	dynamic allocation of arrays
delete[]	delete a dynamically allocated array
+	binary addition or unary plus
−	binary subtraction or unary minus
*	binary multiplication or unary dereferencing (of pointer)
/	binary division
%	binary modulo division
^	bitwise exclusive OR
&	bitwise AND or unary address of
|	bitwise inclusive OR
~	bitwise complement
!	logical NOT (negation)
=	assignment
<	less than
>	greater than
+=	add and assign
-=	subtract and assign
*=	multiply and assign
/=	divide and assign
%=	modulo divide and assign
^=	bitwise exclusive OR and assign
&=	bitwise AND and assign
|=	bitwise inclusive OR and assign
<<	left shift
>>	right shift
>>=	right shift and assign
<<=	left shift and assign
==	logical equality
!=	logical NOT equal
<=	less than or equal
>=	greater than or equal
&&	logical AND
||	logical OR
++	increment (prefix and postfix)
——	decrement (prefix and postfix)
,	comma
->*	pointer to member
->	member access
()	function call
[ ]	subscript

Table 8-2

Standard	&&	&=	&	|	~	!
Alternate	and	and_eq	bitand	bitor	compl	not
Standard	!=	||	|=	^	^=	
Alternate	not_eq	or	or_eq	xor	xor_eq	
Standard	}	{	[	]	#	##
Alternate	%>	<%	<:	:>	%:	%:%:

After the statement above, the value of j is 10 and the value of i is 11.

What if we add the ++ and — operators to the **TRangeInt** class? Class **TRangeInt** is almost an integer and it makes sense to provide this operator because programmers would like to treat **TRangeInt** just like an integer. Here is the class declaration:

```
class TRangeInt {
    public:
        enum Elimits { eLow=0, eHigh = 255 };
        // Create an TRangeInt object with these limits and value
        TRangeInt (int low, int high, int val);
        // Create a TRangeInt object with default limits and this value
        TRangeInt (int val=0);

        // Other details have been omitted for brevity
        TRangeInt& operator++(); // Unary prefix increment operator
        TRangeInt operator++(int notUsed); // Unary postfix increment
                                            // operator
        // and many more not shown
    private:
        int _value; // actual integer value
        int _low, _high; // range limits
};
```

If the **operator++** member function is declared with an **int** argument, then it is the postfix version of the operator. The **notUsed** integer argument is guaranteed to be zero with normal usage (i.e., when used in an expression like **x++**). The **operator++** without any arguments is the prefix version of **operator++**. Here is a simple implementation:

```
//Prefix version of operator++
TRangeInt& TRangeInt::operator++()
{
    // Check to make sure that the value is still less than the limits
    // If so, increment the "value" and return the object

    if (_value < _high) { // it is within limits
        _value++;
        return *this;
    }
    else {
        // An exception must be thrown here because the "value" cannot be
        // incremented. And we cannot return anything invalid because we
        // must return an object. So the best solution is to throw an
        // exception indicating the cause of failure. See Chapter 10
        // for details on exceptions
    }
}
```

That was easy. The implementation shown above works just like the built-in operator ++ for integers. Here is a typical expression that uses the prefix ++ operator:

```
            TRangeInt x, y;

            x = ++y; // Translates to x = y.operator++()
```

And here is the implementation for the postfix version:

```
// Postfix version of operator++
TRangeInt TRangeInt::operator++(int notUsed /* NOT USED */)
{
    // First we must save the current value of *this. Then we modify *this.
    // And finally return the saved value

    TRangeInt temp(*this); // Uses the copy constructor
    // Check to make sure that the value is still less than the limits
    // If so, increment the "value" and return the object

    if (_value < _high) { // it is within limits
        _value++;
        return temp; // return by value
    }
    else {
        // An exception must be thrown here because the "value" cannot be
        // incremented. And we cannot return anything invalid because we
        // must return an object. The best solution is to throw an
        // exception indicating the cause of failure.
    }
    /* Alternate solution: Reuse the prefix implementation
        TRangeInt temp(*this);
        ++(*this);
        return temp;
    */
}
```

NOTE   A compiler might generate a warning about notUsed being not used inside the postfix **operator++** function above. An easy way to get rid of the warning is by omitting the name of the int argument [**operator++**(int /* argument not used */)].

NOTE   Even though it is good to follow the behavior of the operators as they are implemented for built-in types, for efficiency reasons, sometime we change the return types. In the overloaded prefix ++ operator above, we return a reference to *this instead of returning an object by value. This is definitely more efficient. For most operators, C++ does not enforce any restrictions on return value types. There is nothing wrong in making prefix operators return by reference.

When the operator++ is used like:

```
            TRangeInt x; // Create an object

            x++;
```

the value of the **notUsed** argument within the postfix **operator++** function is guaranteed to be 0 (zero). However, the following explicit call is also possible.

```
        TRangeInt x;

        x.operator++(4); // Explicit call of the postfix ++ function
```

When such an explicit call is made, the argument 4 is being passed as the actual argument and the value of notUsed within the operator++ function will be 4. This could be used as a sneaky way to increment the object by some value other than 1. For example, the operator++ above can check the value of notUsed. If it is zero, then the value is incremented by 1 (unity). But if the argument notUsed is not zero, then the data member _value could be incremented by the amount specified by notUsed. This would happen when a programmer makes an explicit call using the syntax shown above. But as described earlier, one should avoid tricks when providing operators. So stay away from using the argument notUsed within the operator++ function—just ignore it. The implementation of operator– – , which is identical to operator++, is left as an exercise to the reader.

ANOTHER APPLICATION FOR THE ++ AND – – OPERATORS

Let us revisit the TListNavigator class that we discussed in the chapter on selective exports (Chapter 7). It is reproduced below for convenience.

```
class TListNavigator {
    public:
        // Create a navigator for the specified TList
        TListNavigator(TList* forThisList);
        //other important mandatory member functions

        // Return the value in the current TListNode element
        void* Current();
        // Move to the next node on the list and return its value
        void* Next();
        /*
         * Operator ++ is identical to the method Next. It moves the
           navigator object to the next TListNode object on the TList and
           returns its value. It does not do anything extra. It is
           provided just for syntactic convenience only.
         */
        void* operator++();
        void* operator++(int notUsed);
        // Move to the previous node on the list and return its value
        void* Previous();
        /*
         * Operator -- is identical to the method Previous. It moves the
           navigator object to the previous TListNode object on the TList
           and returns its value. It does not do anything extra. It is
           provided just for syntactic convenience only.
         */
        void* operator--();
        void* operator--(int notUsed);

        // Move to the last node on the list and return its value
        void* Last();
        // Move to the first node on the list and return its value
        void* First();
```

```
          // Move to the Nth node on the list and return its value
          void* MoveTo(unsigned whichNode);
          // operator for comparing navigator objects also required
          // bool operator==(const TListNavigator& other) const;
          // bool operator!=(const TListNavigator& other) const;

   private:
          // Implementation data
};
```

When using indexes (or pointers) with arrays, programmers use ++ (move forward) and −
− − (move backward) to increment and decrement the index. Similarly, when navigating a
TList, we might like to use ++ and − − with **TListNavigator** objects to move forward and
backward on the list.

```
   // Using indexes on simple arrays
   int   ia [10];
   for (int i=0; i < 10; i++)
         ia[i] = 0;

   // Using navigator objects on TList.
   TList list;
   TListNavigator  lv(&list); // Create a navigator object for the list
   void*  element;
   for(element = lv.Current(); element != 0; (element-lv++) {
         // Do some operations on the element in the list
   }
```

The **for** loop using the **TListNavigator** object ends when the end of the list is reached.
When the **TListNavigator** object reaches the end of list, the **operator++** returns 0. Similarly, **operator − −** returns 0 (zero) when it is applied on the first element of the list. We
already have functions **Next()** and **Previous()** to do these operations, but ++ and − − reflect the natural style of operations that programmers are already used to, so we might as
well provide the operators ++ and − − also. The class implementor must clearly document
the correct usage of such tricky operators. There is no mandatory requirement for such
operators. If you feel that you don't like to add unnecessary methods, you are justified in
omitting these operators. The intention here is to familiarize the reader with different applications for such operators.

We have already seen **operator− −** and **operator++** with **TDate** class in Chapter 7.
It is shown below just to refresh your memory.

```
      // Increments the day (same as AddToDate). Prefix version
      TDate&
      operator++(TDate& date)       { date.AddToDay(1); return date; }

      TDate&
      operator++(TDate& date, int notUsed) // Postfix version
      { date.AddToDay(1); return date; }
      // and others...
```

The Subscript Operator: operator [ ]

One of the trickier operators is the familiar [ ] operator, which is normally used for subscripting arrays. C++ allows us to override this operator also, but one needs to understand the usage of this operator before attempting to overload it.

Unlike most other operators, operator [] can be used on both sides of the assignment operation. Here is an example:

```
int  myArray[10];

myArray[5] = 22; // Store the value 22 at the index 5 of myArray ❶
int  j;
j = myArray[3]; // Copy into j whatever is contained at index 3 of myArray
```

When operator [] is used on the left hand side (LHS), we are writing into the location indexed by the value within the []. So in the statement ❶ above, the location **myArray[5]** is being modified. For this to happen correctly, the subscript operation (**myArray[5]**) must return the address of (or a pointer or reference to) the sixth (remember that subscripts start at zero in C++ and C) location of the array. But when the operator [] is used on the RHS of the assignment operation (as in **myArray[3]** above), it only needs to return the value contained in the fourth location of **myArray**.

☞ **When operator [] is on the left hand side of =, it must return an** *address* **(l-value) and when it is on the right hand side it must return a** *value* **(r-value).**

So what is the problem with that, you say. Well, the operator [] is implemented by a function, just like any other operator. How can the function tell whether it is being used on the LHS or on the RHS? And even if it could somehow find out on which side of the assignment operator it (operator []) is being used, how can the same function return an address once and a value another time. A function can have only one return type, and we cannot overload a pair of functions that only differ in their return types. So how can we ever implement this operator correctly?

When the compiler implements the [] operator for arrays of language defined types, it has the necessary knowledge to determine where the operator [] is being used. Based on that information, it can adjust the outcome of operator [] correctly. But we (the programmer) don't have any clue as to where the operator [] is being used.

Whenever we are in such a dilemma, references come to our rescue. A reference can be treated as a value or as an address. Depending on the context of usage, the compiler will do the right thing with a reference. The programmer need not do anything extra for that behavior. Here is an example.

```
int  j = 10,  i;
int&  rj = j; // Bind the reference rj to variable j

rj = 20; // Store 20 at whatever rj refers to    ❸
i = rj; // Store the value of rj in i ❹
```

In ❸, storing the value 20 in whatever rj refers to involves writing into the location occupied by integer j. This operation requires that rj somehow access the address of j and modify its contents. In ❹, where rj is being assigned to i, the value of j is assigned to i. Here, rj (being on the RHS of =) just returns the value of whatever it is bound to. So the outcome of using a reference on the RHS of = results in a value and when the same reference is used on the LHS of =, the result is an l-value.[5] This is all we need to know in order to implement operator [] correctly in most situations. To further illustrate this concept, here is an implementation of a **TSafeArray** class. The implementation here is for storing int variables (an array of integers). But it is very easy to modify this class to make it a template class (a generic array class) that can be used with any type. We will do that when we discuss generic classes in Chapter 9.

But why are we implementing a class for array of integers when the language already supports arrays of integers, you might wonder? The answer is quite simple. The built-in array type does not have any kind of subscript range checking. When we create an array of 10 elements and try to access the twelfth (**index 11**) element accidentally, unexpected things will happen—the program might crash or even worse, some other piece of data might be overwritten. We need arrays that are safe. An array implementation that automatically checks every access for a valid subscript value will be useful because it avoids unexpected behavior and helps us to find bugs and fix them, leading to more robust and reliable software. Another advantage of implementing array classes is that we can copy (and assign) entire arrays. In C++ (and C), a programmer cannot copy arrays directly—it must be an element by element copy operation. It would be nice if we could assign one array to another directly. This can also be supported by the **TSafeArray** class. It is also possible to implement arrays that grow (and shrink) as needed. None of these features are available with built-in arrays.[6] Hence, the attempt to implement the abstract data type **TSafeArray**.

```cpp
// An array of ARRAY_SIZE is created if the user does not specify the size
#include <iostream.h>
const unsigned int ARRAY_SIZE = 256;

class TSafeArray{
    public:
        TSafeArray(unsigned int arraySize = ARRAY_SIZE);
        // Copy Constructor
        TSafeArray(const TSafeArray& copy);
        virtual ~TSafeArray(); // Destructor
        // Assignment operator
        TSafeArray& operator=(const TSafeArray& assign);

        // What is the size of this Array?
        unsigned int GetSize() const { return _size; }
        // The subscript operator
        int& operator[](int index);
        // Print the array object using stream operators
```

---

[5]It will not be an l-value if it is a reference to a const (as in const int& ir = 10;) Now we cannot write ir = 20.

[6]Can you think of other benefits resulting from an array class?

```
        friend ostream& operator<<(ostream& stream,
         const TSafeArray& object);
        // This next one is for those clients who prefer calling methods
        // directly. It prints to cout
        void Print() const;
        // and many more functions
    private:
        int _size;
        int* _ip;
};


// The implementation of member functions

#include <stdlib.h> // all C library functions

TSafeArray::TSafeArray(unsigned int arraySize )
{
    // If _size is correct, then we allocate memory for the array
    // and initialize it with zeroes. Otherwise the pointer is set to 0.
    if (arraySize > 0) {
        _size = arraySize;
        _ip = new int[_size];
        for(int i=0; i < _size; i++)
            *(_ip+i) = 0;
        }
    else {
        _ip = 0;
        _size = 0;
    }
}


TSafeArray::~TSafeArray()
{
    // Just discard the memory allocated in the constructor.
    if (_ip != 0)
        delete [] _ip;
}


// This is the copy constructor Called by the system for copying objects
TSafeArray::TSafeArray(const TSafeArray& copy)
{
    // If the _size of the source array object is positive, allocate
    // memory for the new array object and copy elements
    if ( copy._size > 0) {
        _size = copy._size;
        _ip = new int [_size];
        for(int i=0; i < _size; i++)
            *(_ip+i) = copy._ip[i]; // element by element copy
    }
    else {
        _size = 0;
        _ip = 0;
    }
}
```

```
// The actual assignment operator (for a=b etc.)
TSafeArray&
TSafeArray::operator=(const TSafeArray& assign)
{
    if (this == &assign) { // Check assignment to self
        cout << "Warning: Trying to assign object to itself\n";
        return *this;
    }
    // It is possible that the _size of the array object on the RHS is not
    // the same as that on the LHS

    // LHS is bigger than RHS - No problem, just copy elements
    if (this->_size >= assign._size) {
        // The easy case - Just copy elements
        for (int i=0; i < assign._size; i++)
            _ip[i] = assign._ip[i];
        _size = assign._size;
    }
    else {
        // LHS is smaller - Need to allocate enough memory
        // First discard existing memory and then allocate a new array
        if (_ip != 0)
            delete [] _ip; // discard existing memory
        this->_ip = new int[assign._size];
        this->_size = assign._size; // Copy _size also
        // Copy elements
        for(int i=0; i < _size; i++)
            _ip[i] = assign._ip[i];
    }

    return *this;
}


// This is the important operator. Users definitely like to use TSafeArray
// just like any simple array
// The [] operator facilitates that very easily. The most important feature
// is the return by reference

int& TSafeArray::operator[](int index)
{
    // If index is beyond the end of the array (or is negative), the
    // operation cannot complete. The best thing would be to throw an
    // exception indicating "Subscript out of range". Since we have not
    // covered exceptions yet, just call exit. exit is a library function
    // that stops the running program
    if (index < 0 || index >= _size) {
        cerr << "Fatal: Index out of range\n";
        cerr << "Size=" << _size << "  Index=" << index << endl;
        exit(1); // Should really "throw" an exception here
    }
    // Index is valid - just return a reference to the element specified
    return _ip[index];
}

ostream&
```

```
operator<<(ostream& stream, const TSafeArray& array)
{
      // Print elements sequentially to stream
      stream << endl;
      for (int i =0; i < array._size; i++)
            stream << array._ip[i] << " " ;
      stream << endl;
}

void
TSafeArray::Print() const
{
      // Print elements sequentially
      cout << *this; // Reuse the implementation of operator<< above
                     // This is interpreted as: operator<<(cout, *this)
}
```

Here is a small test program.

```
main()
{
      TSafeArray sa1(24), sa2(10);

      sa1[10] = 100; // Sets the eleventh element using the operator [] on
                     // the LHS
      int i;
      i = sa1[1]; // Copies the value in the second element to i
                  // operator[] on the RHS

      sa2 = sa1; // Assign one array to another. Works correctly because of
                 // overloaded operator= in the class

      // Here the same operator [] is used on both sides in the same
      // statement. But it still works like a charm
      sa1[1] = sa1[2]; // The most complex operation

      sa2[25] = 0; // Causes subscript checking to fail
}
```

This example shows the power of the overloaded subscript operator. No matter in what combination it is used, it works correctly. This is one operator that is very helpful when implementing arrays. Without operator overloading, a class such as **TSafeArray** would have to provide a pair of functions **Get()** and **Put()** to read/write elements of the array. This would work, but the style isn't natural. An array, no matter who implements it (programmer or language), should support natural usage. The most fundamental operation on an array is subscripting. Without the subscript operator overloading, **TSafeArray** would be unattractive. One of our primary goals is to make classes look and feel as natural as possible. The subscript operator is a godsend in achieving that goal.

    Also note that for an overloaded operator, the index argument can be of any type that the implementor wants—it is not limited to integers. One can implement associative arrays that are indexed by character strings. For example. a simple lookup table indexed by character strings can be built using the subscript operator. Such implementations can be found in [Stroustrup92].

THINK   If you analyze the implementation of TSafeArray carefully, you can find a bug in the code and it is in the assignment operator. When the array object on the LHS is bigger than the one on the RHS, elements are just copied and then the _size data member is also copied. Once this happens, the array object on the LHS looks like a smaller array than it really is. If the object on the LHS is a 100 element array and the object on the RHS is a 50 element array, after the assignment, the array on the LHS also becomes a 50 element array, even though it still has space for 100 elements. A client would not be able to use the array as a 100 element array anymore because the _size data member is set to 50. This does not cause any memory leaks because when the destructor executes, it deletes the pointer _ip, which points to whatever was originally allocated. Is there a way to fix this anomaly? You need an additional data member to distinguish between the allocated size of the array and the number of elements contained in the array. Try this enhancement of TSafeArray as an exercise.

NOTE   Once you see the one dimensional array, you might get curious about two (or n) dimensional arrays. But don't go looking for operator [][]. There is no such operator. C++ only supports (as do most other languages) the subscript operator []. A two dimensional array is nothing but an array of arrays. The language allows one to create multi-dimensional arrays but subscripting is still done by the operator []. The third element in the second row of a two dimensional array X is accessed using the expression X[2][3]. But the element at X[2] is an array. This array at X[2] is further indexed by X[3] to get the element at X[2][3]. If you implement a class T2DArray, you might be tempted to implement the subscript operator that works for expressions of the type X[2][3]. But that is not easy—it requires some complicated code and I really don't feel it is worth that much effort. One might as well provide an overloaded function call operator, operator() to do subscripting. Just implement operator() (int rowIndex, int columnIndex) to do the operation. With this operator, we must write X(2, 3) instead of X[2][3]. Clients would not be able to use the [] operator on T2DArray, but that is not a big loss.

A MORE SOPHISTICATED OPERATOR—THE MEMBER ACCESS OPERATOR: OPERATOR ->

Of all the overloaded operators in the C++ language, the most difficult operator to understand is the member access operator -> (the *arrow* operator). This operator is used with pointers to structs and classes as follows.

```
void f()
{
    struct 2DPoint {
        long x, y;
    };

    2DPoint aPoint;         // Create a 2DPoint object
    2DPoint *ap = &aPoint;  // Make ap point to the above object

    TSafeArray x;
    TSafeArray *p = &x; // Make p point to the array x
```

```
      p->Print(); // Invoke Print on the object pointed by p ❶
      ap->x = 0;  // Set the x coordinate (to zero) of whatever ap points to
      ap->y = 10; // Set the y coordinate to 10
}
```

These are typical usages of a member access operator ->. The -> operator can only be used with a pointer variable on the left hand side. Contrary to what the expressions above may indicate, -> is a postfix unary operator. Just like other operators in C++, this -> operator can also be overloaded by a class, but the overloading scheme and the semantics are very different. Here is an example:

```
class Foo {
    public:
          int m; // just for convenience of access, it is public
};

class Z {
    public:
          Foo* operator->() { return &f; }
    private:
          Foo f;
};

void g()
{
    Z zb;

    zb->m = 0; // Invoke the -> operator on the object zb and set m to
               // zero using the pointer returned
}
```

Class Foo above has a public data member m (just for convenience). Class Z overloads the -> operator. This operator returns the address of its data member f, which is an object of class Foo (again just as an example). All the magic happens in the statement

$$zb->m = 0;$$

Because zb is not a pointer to a struct or class, the normal interpretation of a pointer to an object (as in ❶) will not work. Therefore, the statement is interpreted as

$$(\textbf{zb}.operator->())->m = 0;$$

The overloaded operator-> is first invoked on the object zb. Class Z does overload the operator-> and, hence, there is nothing magical about it. But the processing doesn't end there. Next, the compiler uses the return value of the operator-> and tries to access the member m. We already know that -> operator is used with pointers to classes and structs. When the compiler uses the return value of operator-> as a pointer and then tries to access the member m using that return value, it implies that the operator-> (within Z) must return a pointer to a class or struct. Moreover, the class (to which the operator-> returns a pointer) must contain an accessible member m. In this example, operator-> in Z returns a pointer to the class Foo. And objects of Foo contain a public data member m. So the expression

```
zb->m = 0;
```

sets the data member m of the object returned by the operator-> of class Z to zero. Any overloaded operator-> of a class must return a pointer to a class or struct (or another object that has an -> operator defined for it). That is the first rule. Next, when we try to access a member (such as m above) using the pointer returned from the operator->, the member must be accessible within the scope from which the call to operator-> is made. In our case, member m within class Foo is a public data member and, hence, there is no problem in accessing it. Even though operator-> is a unary operator, the following expression is syntactically incorrect:

```
zb->; // Is not interpreted as zb.operator->()
```

This does not work because the compiler will look for an accessible member after the ->.

From this example, it is quite clear that operator-> goes through a two step process when used with objects.

1. Invoke the operator-> member function if the object supports an overloaded -> operator (class Z above).

2. Next, apply the -> operator on the return value from (1) to access the element on the other side of -> (-> m above).

This operator is very useful in some situations. Until now, we used -> operator just as a convenience to access members through pointers to objects. But now, we can do something more. When a class implements an overloaded -> operator, the member on the RHS of the -> operator is not evaluated (accessed) until the overloaded operator-> function returns. The overloaded operator-> gives us a chance to do some interesting things before the member on the RHS of -> is accessed. For example, the overloaded operator-> above can do whatever it likes before returning a pointer to a Foo object. Speaking in the C++ parlance, the overloaded operator-> provides one more level of *indirection*. This added indirection can really do wonders. Here is an example to illustrate the point.

We use remote files in software development quite frequently. A remote file is one that resides on a machine other than the one on which the program that needs access to the file is running. Accessing a remote file usually involves going across a network. It might involve opening a network connection to another machine and then performing the usual checks (file exists, it can be opened by this program, etc.) on the file. This requires considerable amount of code and is not a trivial operation. So we might create a class TRemoteFile to support such files and implement all the operations in it. As soon as a TRemoteFile object is created (by the constructor), we can open the network connection to the other machine and perform all the usual operations to open the file and keep it ready for subsequent operations. But a program might create a TRemoteFile object but may never do anything with it (no read, write, etc.). If that happens, we would have wasted time in locating the file and opening it when the TRemoteFile object was created.

We would like to defer the opening of the remote file until it is absolutely necessary. This can be done by the operator->. Instead of using the class TRemoteFile directly, let us use class a TRemoteFilePtr. The intention is that clients are better off using TRemote-FilePtr instead of TRemoteFile. They can use all the member functions in TRemoteFile on objects of TRemoteFilePtr. Here is a skeleton interface:

```cpp
#include <stddef.h>
#include <string.h>
#include <iostream.h>

/*
 * TRemoteFile represents a file that is (possibly) on a remote machine.
   Clients specify the name of the machine and the file name when object is
   created. Clients should not use this class directly. It is recommended
   that class TRemoteFilePtr be used to work with remote files. See main()
   program below for an example. The machine name is separated from the
   file name by ::. For example, Atlas::TestFile represents the file
   TestFile on the machine Atlas. If there is no :: in the name it
   represents a local file. This is just a convention.
 */
class TRemoteFile {
    public:
        // How should the file be opened?
        enum EOpenMode { eRead, eWrite, eReadWrite };
        // Read specified number of bytes into buffer
        void Read(char* inputBuffer, size_t howMuch);
        // Write specified number of bytes to file from buffer
        void Write(const char* outputBuffer, size_t howMuch);
        // and more methods relevant to a file
    private:
        // Cannot create objects directly - Use TRemoteFilePtr
        TRemoteFile(const char* completeName);
        bool Open(EOpenMode openMode);
        bool Close();
        friend class TRemoteFilePtr;
        // Some other data members to hold a handle to the real file
};


class TRemoteFilePtr {
        public:
            TRemoteFilePtr(const char completeName[],
                            TRemoteFile::EOpenMode openMode);
            ~TRemoteFilePtr();
            TRemoteFile* operator->();
        private:
            TRemoteFile* _realFilePtr;
            char* _name;
            EOpenMode _mode;
};

TRemoteFilePtr::TRemoteFilePtr(const char completeName[],
                            TRemoteFile::EOpenMode openMode)
        : _realFilePtr(0), _mode(openMode)
{
    // Store the name and mode for later use
```

```
    // The remote file is not open yet.
    _name = new char [ strlen(completeName + 1)]; // No error checks
    strcpy(_name, completeName); // strcpy is a library function
    // nothing else to do here
}

TRemoteFile*
TRemoteFilePtr::operator->()
{
    if (_realFilePtr == 0) {
        // Create a new TRemoteFile object
        _realFilePtr = new TRemoteFile(_name); // ❶
        // Next open the file in the correct mode
        bool result = _realFilePtr->Open(_mode);
        if (result == false) {
            // Something went wrong - open failed
            // Should really throw an exception here
            cout << "Open failed for file: " << _name << endl;
            exit(-1);
        }
    }
    // File is already open (or was opened successfully now)
    // Just return the pointer
    return _realFilePtr;
}

TRemoteFilePtr::~TRemoteFilePtr()
{
        _realFilePtr->Close();
}

// A Test program that illustrates how an object of class TRemoteFilePtr is
// used with class TRemoteFile

main()
{
        // Open the file MyTestFile on machine Hercules
        TRemoteFilePtr testFile("Hercules:MyTestFile",
                                TRemoteFile::eRead);
        char buf[256];

        // Read 100 characters from file
        // The next statement causes the creation of the TRemoteFile
        // object inside
        // TRemoteFilePtr class::operator-> member function (see ❶ above)
        testFile->Read(buf, 100);
        cout << buf << endl; // print the contents
}
```

Let us analyze this implementation. Class **TRemoteFile** provides operations natural to a file. It does not matter that it is a remote file. The operations on a file are the same irrespective of whether it is local or remote, but the implementation of the operations is different. A user is not able to instantiate **TRemoteFile** objects directly because the constructor is **private**. The intention is that clients use **TRemoteFilePtr** instead. Class

TRemoteFilePtr only has a constructor, destructor, and the overloaded operator-> , and nothing special in it. But this class still performs all the magic.

When an object of TRemoteFilePtr is created, it just stores the details of the file. Nothing else is done with the file.[7] For example, in the main program an object testFile is created but it does not open the file. The internal pointer to the TRemoteFile object is set to zero to indicate that the file has not been opened yet. Any operation on the TRemote-FilePtr object must use the pointer syntax (it must behave like a pointer) using the over-loaded operator ->. The first time an operation is attempted on the TRemoteFilePtr object, the operator-> function is invoked.

```
testFile->Read(buf, 100); // (testFile.operator->() )->Read(buf, 100);
```

The TRemoteFilePtr::operator-> function checks to see if the _realFilePtr is zero. If so, it opens the file (doing whatever is necessary to locate the file on the remote machine). The actual code required to open the file is not shown—it is very much operating system dependent and is not required to understand the concept behind overloading operator->. The operator -> of class TRemoteFilePtr is invoked before any operation is done on the file. Once the file is successfully opened, subsequent operations on a TRemoteFilePtr object just return the TRemoteFile pointer (_realFilePtr) directly. In effect, the member function Read above is invoked on the _realFilePtr returned by the operator->. Ulti-mately, when the TRemoteFilePtr object goes out of scope, the class destructor is in-voked, which closes the actual TRemoteFile—clients don't have to do anything.

Class TRemoteFilePtr allows the client to use its objects just like any other pointer. But TRemoteFilePtr is an intelligent (*smart*) pointer. It gets notified through the operator-> whenever an operation is attempted. Furthermore, TRemoteFilePtr isolates the clients from the mundane steps of opening and closing the file. Such operations are transparently managed by TRemoteFilePtr. All this is possible because the operator-> in TRemoteFilePtr is invoked first. No other operation is possible with TRemoteFilePtr objects because there are no other member functions supported. For a casual reader the code

```
testFile->Read(buf, 100);
```

might appear to be wrong because TRemoteFilePtr does not support the member func-tion Read. But testFile is not a normal pointer—it is an object that behaves like a pointer. So the operator-> function of class TRemoteFilePtr is being invoked. It is im-portant to see what the operator-> in class TRemoteFilePtr returns to understand this piece of code. The Read call (if possible) is on the return value of operator->. The oper-ator-> in TRemoteFilePtr returns a pointer to TRemoteFile object. So the Read call is on an object of class TRemoteFile, which does support a Read member function. If there is an error here, the compiler would detect it immediately. There is no chance for any run-time mishap.

---

[7]This is basically *lazy evaluation* discussed in Chapter 4 & Chapter 11.

There is one little thing missing from class **TRemoteFilePtr**. When programmers use pointers, they use both the -> notation and the * notation. Here is an example:

```
void h()
{
    struct 2DPoint {
        long x, y;
    };

    2DPoint a;
    2DPoint *p = &a; // make p point to a

    // Pointer style access with pointers to objects
    // Using the pointer p, I want to set x to 0 in whatever object p
    // points to. I already know that p is pointer to 2DPoint with member
    // x and y
    // p->x: access member x in the pointed by p. set it to 0.
    p->x = 0;

    // Another style uses pointer dereferencing. Dereference the pointer p
    // and set x in the dereferenced object to 10. In this case I am using
    // true object style for accessing members. With an object in hand, we
    // use the object.member syntax. When we have a pointer to an object,
    // we can use the dereferencing operator * to access the object
    // denoted by the pointer. Therefore (*p) gives me a true object. I
    // want to access the member x within this object [ (*p).x. ] and set
    // it to 10
    (*p).x = 10;    // ❶ If p is a TRemoteFilePtr object *p would't
                    // compile!
}
```

Our class **TRemoteFilePtr** behaves like a (smart) pointer but it does not allow the dereferencing operation shown in ❶ above. It only supports the -> syntax. If **TRemoteFilePtr** behaves like a pointer, it should also support the most natural operations of a pointer. That's what operator overloading is all about—extending the accepted usage of operators to programmer defined classes. We can fix this deficiency by adding the **operator*** to the **TRemoteFilePtr** class. Here is the code:

```
class TRemoteFilePtr {
        public:
                TRemoteFilePtr(const char completeName[],
                                TRemoteFile::EOpenMode openMode);
                ~TRemoteFilePtr();
                TRemoteFile* operator->();
                TRemoteFile& operator*();
        private:
                TRemoteFile* _realFilePtr;
                char* _name;
                EOpenMode _mode;
};
```

```
inline TRemoteFile&
TRemoteFilePtr::operator*() // inlined for speed
{
      // Just reuse the implementation of ->. Dereference the returned
      // pointer.
      return *(operator->());
}
```

With this enhancement, the following code will also work:

```
main()
{
      // Open file MyTestFile which is located on machine Hercules
      TRemoteFilePtr testFile("Hercules::MyTestFile", TRemoteFile::eRead);
      char buf[256];

      // (testFile.operator*()).Read(buf, 100)
      (*testFile).Read(buf, 100); // Read 100 characters from file ❷
      cout << buf << endl; // print the contents
}
```

In ❷ above, the statement

$$(*testFile).Read(buf, 100);$$

causes the invocation of **operator*** function on **testFile**. This overloaded operator invokes our old friend, **operator->** first. Then it dereferences the return value of **operator->** (which is now **TRemoteFile** pointer). The outcome of the call to **operator*** is a reference to a **TRemoteFile** object. Finally, the **Read** member function is applied on it.

That makes our class complete. Class **TRemoteFilePtr** is a smart file pointer for **TRemoteFile** objects. It can be used with the -> syntax or the * syntax and clients do not have to bother about opening and closing files. This is one powerful application of operator overloading with the -> operator.

NOTE   In the implementation above, the **operator->** just opened the file and returned the pointer to the **TRemoteFile** object. But it need not be that simple. An implementation is free to add more functionality to the **operator->**. For example, before opening the file, the **operator->** can lock the file to prevent others from using it. It can also verify the access rights of the user trying to open the file. The important concept is that of indirection provided by the overloaded **operator->**. Also note that **operator->** function does not know which function is being invoked. The only guarantee is that the **operator->** (or **operator***) function is called first. If every operation on the **TRemoteFile** object requires some additional processing in **TRemoteFilePtr**, which depends on the specific function of **TRemoteFile** being called, then an overloaded **operator->** is not the solution. In such **CAUTION**   cases, we use surrogate objects (also called proxy objects) discussed in Chapter 11.

Objects of the class **TRemoteFilePtr** are pseudo pointers. Unlike ordinary pointers (like **char*** and **int***) they do not support increment (++), decrement (− −), comparison, etc. Attempts to use any such operations would cause a compile-time error. It may be sensible to provide such operations (particularly comparison) for some other type of smart pointer. Definitely, it does not make much sense to increment (or decrement) a TRemoteFilePtr object. A comparison operator (operator==) might be useful. Use your judgment and application domain knowledge when providing (or not providing) such operators.

NOTE   The example above is not limited to a remote file. One could very well use this scheme for any file. In fact, a general class **TFile** could be used with an associated class **TFilePtr**. Class **TFile** would determine if the file is local or remote. It is more important to understand the concept behind the **operator->**. Don't attach too much importance to the class **TRemoteFile** and **TRemoteFilePtr**, discussed above. Once you understand the mechanism and the caveats, you should be in a position to use it wherever it is appropriate.

This scheme of overloading operator-> is useful wherever a *lazy evaluation* scheme is required. In the example above, opening a remote file is an expensive and complicated operation and so it is deferred as long as possible. We open the remote file only when it is absolutely necessary. The **TRemoteFilePtr** class allows us to do that by providing another level of control over file access. Once the file is opened, the **operator->** does not have much use. This principle of delaying an operation can be used with any heavy weight object. For example, a mail message might contain an embedded audio clip. For reasons of economy of space, the audio clip might have been stored in a separate compressed file. The audio clip file need be opened and uncompressed only when it is absolutely necessary to play the sound clip. Further, it is possible that the audio clip file is located on another machine (like a remote file). In all cases where an operation is expensive, the **operator->** allows us to delay the actual operation. The other advantage is that a class like **TRemoteFilePtr** can take care of garbage collection—it knows when to open and close the file.

It is sensible to add reference counting to the **TRemoteFilePtr**. This would allow fast copying of **TRemoteFilePtr** objects, without actually copying the original file. This can be done by controlling the copy constructor and assignment operators of **TRemote-FilePtr**. The next step would be to add copy-on-write, which has been discussed earlier in Chapter 4. Making smart pointers reference counted is quite a common phenomenon in C++ programs.

☞ **Use an overloaded -> operator when an expensive operation needs to be deferred (or when additional operations need to be performed transparently). Remember that an overloaded operator -> is not a solution if you need to know exactly which member function is being called.[8]**

OPERATORS AS FRIEND FUNCTIONS

First of all, there are two rules of thumb when implementing overloaded operators. Subsequent paragraphs in this section clearly illustrate these rules. These rules are repeated again at the end of this section, just to ensure that you never forget them.

---

[8]A normal surrogate object would be able to accomplish that. More on that in chapter 12.

1. Any operator that does not require an l-value and is commutative is better implemented as a non-member function (+, − etc.). This allows the compiler to apply a conversion in case of argument mismatch for the first argument.

2. Any operator that requires an l-value is better implemented as a member function. This clearly shows that it can only be invoked on existing, modifiable objects.

An overloaded operator can be implemented as a member function or as a non-member (even a friend) function. Some operators are always implemented as member functions, where as some others are usually implemented as non-member functions. A good designer needs to understand the difference between the two. The only restriction on an operator implemented as a friend is that it should require at least one argument of the class to which it is a friend. Here is a simple example to show the difference between overloaded operators as member function v/s overloaded operators as friend functions.

```
class TRangeInt {
   public:
      enum ELimits { eLow=0, eHigh = 255 };
         // Create an TRangeInt object with these limits and value
      TRangeInt (int low, int high, int val) ;
      // Create an TRangeInt object with default limits and this value
      TRangeInt (int val=0);

      // Other details have been omitted for brevity

      TRangeInt& operator+=( const TRangeInt& addThis);
      friend TRangeInt operator+( const TRangeInt& first,
                                  const TRangeInt& second);
      // and many more not shown
};
```

Both operator + and operator += are binary operators—they require two operands. The operator+= is declared to be a member function with one argument. As with any member function, an operator that is a member function receives the implicit argument this, which is the first operand. The second operand is passed explicitly. A friend function does not receive any implicit arguments—all the operands are passed explicitly. Hence, the friend function operator+ receives two explicit arguments. The friend operator+ does receive at least one (actually two) class argument (of TRangeInt), which fulfills the language requirement mentioned earlier.

Operators that Are Member Functions

Here is a simple piece of code:

```
main()
{
    int x = 10, y, z;
    y = 100; // ❶ Works as expected
    10 = x; // ❷ Wouldn't work

}
```

In the code above, ❶ is a simple assignment of an integer constant to an integer variable. The variable y can be modified (it is an l-value) and, hence, the statement works. But in ❷, the element on the LHS is a constant—it cannot be modified. Trying to assign x to 10 wouldn't work because 10 is not an l-value. Therefore, assignment is an operation that requires a modifiable quantity on the LHS.

Continuing on the same lines, how about the code below.

```
main()
{
    int x = 10, y, z;
    y += 100;  // ① Works as expected
    10 += x;   // ② Wouldn't work

}
```

In this example, ① works because y is a variable (an l-value) that can be modified. But ② does not work because 10 is a constant—it is not an l-value.

A non-const object is an l-value. In other words, an object that is not declared as const can be modified. Now, let us use TRangeInt instead of int and see what happens.

```
main()
{
    TRangeInt x, y, z; // Initial values are provided by the default
                       // constructor
    y += z;   // ③ - Works as expected : y.operator+=(z)
    10 += x; // ④ - Wouldn't work : 10.operator+=(x)??
}
```

Here, y is an l-value—it is an object that can be modified. Hence, ③ works, but ④ does not work because 10 is not an object that can be modified. In this case, ③ worked because y is a modifiable object. Stated differently, operator+= requires an l-value. Operators such as += are called on existing objects (l-values) and they modify the l-value. In the example above, z is being added to y. The object z does not change; it is y that is modified. In order to add z to y, the object y must exist before the += operator is invoked. Someone must have created the object y. We already know that member functions can only be invoked on existing objects. If operator += is always invoked on existing objects, then it can be a member function. Operator += cannot be invoked on a non-object because it needs to modify the object on which it is called. In general, if an overloaded operator needs an l-value (it will modify the first operand) then it can be easily implemented as a member function. This implies that such operators (implemented as member functions) can only be invoked on existing objects. Once we have an object, any member function can be invoked on it. All flavors of assignment operators (+=, -=, *=, etc.) are implemented as member functions.

☞ **Any operator that requires an l-value is better implemented as a member function. This clearly shows that it can only be invoked on existing, modifiable objects.**

When implementing operators for any class, follow this rule and your class interface will be elegant and easy to understand.

Operators that Are Implemented as Non-Member Functions

Now let us look at a different scenario.

```
main()
{
    int x = 10, y, z;
    y = x + z;    // ❻ Works as expected
    y = 100 + x; // ❼ Works correctly too

}
```

In ❻, (x+z) will compute the sum but will not modify x or z. The sum of x and z is assigned to y. A temporary integer might be required to hold the sum before it is assigned to y. Compilers handle such temporary generation (if required) automatically. Similarly, in ❼, (100+x) also works correctly. The sum of 100 and x is assigned to y, but neither 100 nor x is modified. We could also write (y = x + 100) without any change in behavior. In other words, operator + is commutative; the ordering of the operand is not significant.

Let us see what happens in the following case:

```
main()
{
    TRangeInt x , y, z; // Default constructor is called for all three
                        // objects
    y = x + z;    // ❽ Works as expected
    y = 100 + x; // ❾ Works correctly too!!

}
```

In ❽, x is an object. The compiler first tries to apply x.operator+(z), but that fails because there is no member function operator+ in class TRangeInt. Once that fails, the compiler looks for a function operator+(), which can accept two TRangeInt arguments. We have declared such an operator+() function and moreover it is a **friend** of the class TRangeInt (not that it matters). So it finds the operator+ that has been declared (it only needs a matching declaration, not a definition) and the expression (x + z) works. It becomes

```
y = operator+(x, z);
```

But what happens to (100 + x) in ❾? Definitely, the member function syntax cannot be applied because 100 is not an object. Once that is ruled out, is it possible to call the operator+ that was used with (x + z)? One would assume that it is not appropriate because our operator+ expects two TRangeInt objects and 100 is not a TRangeInt object. So how will the expression work?

This is where the complexity of operator overloading in C++ becomes apparent. Once the search for an operator+ member function fails, the compiler looks for a matching non-member function operator+. But the search for a matching operator+ is done on a per operand basis. Remember that our first operand is 100 (an int) and the second operand is a TRangeInt.

1. Search for an operator+ whose <u>first</u> argument is an int.

This search might end up with more than one operator+ function. That is fine. Call this set of functions SetA.

2. Search for an operator + whose second argument is a TRangeInt.

This search results in another set. Call it SetB.

This procedure is repeated for all arguments, one argument at a time.

In our case, SetA will be empty because there is no operator+ function that expects an integer as the first argument. But SetB contains one function—the operator+ that we have already declared:

```
friend TRangeInt operator+( const TRangeInt& first,
                            const TRangeInt& second);
```

Now we have a partial match. The second operand of (100 + x) matches the operator+ that has been located, but the first formal argument for this operator+ is a TRangeInt object, and the actual argument (operand) is an integer. We can use this operator+ function if somehow we could convert 100 to a TRangeInt. Is it possible to convert 100 to TRangeInt? The answer to that question lies in the class TRangeInt. If we have a constructor in TRangeInt that can be called with an int, (or unsigned int) then we can convert 100 to a TRangeInt. Sure enough, there is a constructor in TRangeInt that accepts an int.

```
// Create an TRangeInt object with default limits and this value
TRangeInt (int val=0);
```

This constructor can be called with a single int argument. The compiler uses this constructor to create a temporary TRangeInt object (with 100 as the argument val) and passes it, along with x, to the operator+ function. This constructor, which can be called with a single argument, is called a *Converting Constructor*. One could imagine that it converts an int to a TRangeInt object.

☞ **A constructor that can be called with a single argument is a Converting Constructor. It specifies a conversion from the type of its (first) argument to the type of its class (the class to which the constructor belongs). This conversion (using the converting constructor) is applied implicitly when needed if the constructor is declared without the explicit specifier.**

In TRangeInt, the constructor requires one argument of type int. Therefore, it is possible to call this constructor with a single int parameter. It can be viewed as converting an int element to a TRangeInt object.

In the latest C++ standard, a conversion constructor can have an **explicit** specifier.

```
class X {
    public:
        explicit X(int i); // Conversion only when explicitly requested
};
```

Here, the constructor X(int) is not an implicit converting constructor. The explicit specifier indicates that it can be used for conversions only when explicitly specified by the programmer (like type casting).

```
void f(X a) { }
int i;
f(i); // Will not work because X(int) is not a converting constructor
f( X(i) ); // Works, explicit conversion requested
```

The temporary TRangeInt object created by the compiler for use with the operator+
function will be automatically destroyed (destructor called) by the compiler at the end of
the expression.

But what happens if the operator+ is a member function similar to the operator+=.
This is where the subtle difference between member functions and non-member functions
is seen with respect to operators. The conversion from 100 to TRangeInt using the conversion constructor that was applied to the first operand (100) works for non-member
functions only. If operator+ was a member function of class TRangeInt, then the compiler tries to use 100 as an object and 100.operator+(x) fails because 100 is not an object. No conversions are attempted in that case. When operator+ is a non-member function, the first operand is subject to conversion (if possible).

☞ **A single, unambiguous user defined conversion is applied to the first
argument of an expression only if the function being called is a non-
member function. No conversion is ever applied to the first argument
of a member function.**

Only one conversion is applied per value. For example. if there was no way to convert int
to TRangeInt, but a conversion from int to another class (say TFoo) is available and then
a conversion from TFoo to TRangeInt was possible, it would not be applied (because it
is more than one conversion). Moreover, conversions are applied only when they are unambiguous. If applying a conversion causes a match with more than one overloaded function. then the conversion is not applied (because the call would become ambiguous).
Please refer to the C++ language reference manual for details on these rules.

We want our expressions to look natural. For example, a+b should work the same
way as b+a. Let us see what happens in the next example.

```
main()
{
    TRangeInt x , y, z;
    y += x ;      // ❶ Works as expected
    y += 100;     // ❷ Works as expected
    y = x + 100;  // ❸ Works correctly too!!
}
```

We already know that (y += x) works because it is translated to

```
y.operator+=(x)
```

But how about ❷ above. Will that work? If we apply the same logic as ❶ it would be

```
y.operator+(100)
```

But operator+= expects an argument of type TRangeInt and 100 is not a TRangeInt. Yes, you guessed it right—a user defined conversion is applied to the second argument. There is only one operator+= function in TRangeInt and y is a TRangeInt. But the second argument (this being the implicit first argument) 100 is not a TRangeInt. The compiler needs to convert 100 to a TRangeInt for this expression to work. Such a conversion is again done by the conversion constructor of TRangeInt. A casual reader would be thoroughly confused by this scheme. Earlier, it was stated that conversions are not applied to the first argument of a member function. So how is it that 100 is being converted? Well, 100 is the second and the only explicit argument (this being the implicit first argument). Conversions are applied for second and subsequent arguments irrespective of whether it is a member function or a non-member function call.

> ☞ **A single, unambiguous user-defined conversion is applied to the second and subsequent argument(s) of member functions as well as non-member functions when there is no direct match.**

This makes

```
y += 100
```

work correctly. It becomes

```
y += TRangeInt(100);
↑ is a compiler generated temporary object
```

How about

```
y = x + 100;
```

in ❸ above? It is the same as the operator+= in ❷. The second argument for operator+ is not a direct match. Therefore, the conversion constructor is used to generate a temporary object that is passed to operator + along with the operand x. The rule about conversions for second and subsequent arguments is the same for both member functions as well as non-member functions. The difference in treatment is only for the first argument.

> ☞ **Any operator that does not require an l-value and is commutative is better implemented as a non-member function (+, – etc.). This allows the compiler to apply a conversion in case of argument mismatch for the first argument.**

All these rules might seem complicated at first. Definitely, these rules are quite hard to remember. But they have some very good applications as we shall see soon.

Why Do We Need Conversions?

One of the arguments in favor of operator overloading is the naturalness of expressions. Programmers should be able to write (a+b) and (b+a), etc. This makes our code look elegant and natural. Given that, if an expression

```
TRangeInt a, b, c;
c = a + 100;
```

works but the expression

```
c = 100 + a;
```

fails, then operator overloading hasn't helped us—it has made the scenario more complicated and unnatural. The extra rules about conversions for the first argument of a non-member function alleviates this problem. We can design classes with proper overloaded operator functions. For operators that are commutative and don't require l-values, a non member function implementation works well with conversions. A TRangeInt is a more restrictive integer and it should be compatible with the language defined type int. It is natural to compute the sum of an int and TRangeInt, but the order of arguments should not be of any consequence. Needless to state that designers and implementors should pay attention to such non-trivial details when providing operators for their classes.

For operators that do need l-values and that are not commutative (+=, −=, etc.) it makes no sense to have conversions applied to the first argument, and such operators should be implemented as member functions.

☞ **Pay attention to the different usage styles of operators. In particular, with commutative operators, order of arguments is (usually) of no consequence.**

Note that conversions are applied

- when passing arguments to functions
- when returning values from functions
- with expression operands
- with expressions controlling iteration and selection statements
- with explicit type conversions

CONVERSION FUNCTIONS

Finally, there is one more style of conversion possible in C++. These are small functions that specify a conversion to another type. Let us revisit out TRangeInt class.

```
class TRangeInt {
    public:
        enum Elimits { eLow=0, eHigh = 255 };
        // Create an TRangeInt object with these limits and value
```

```
            TRangeInt (int low, int high, int val);
            // Create an TRangeInt object with default limits and this value
            TRangeInt (int val=0);

            // Other details have been omitted for brevity

            TRangeInt& operator+=( const TRangeInt& addThis);
            friend TRangeInt operator+( const TRangeInt& first,
                const TRangeInt& second);

            operator int() { return _value; }

            // and many more not shown
    private:
            // as before
};
```

In this example. operator int() is a conversion function. It specifies a conversion from TRangeInt to type int. The advantage of such conversion functions is easily appreciated with the following example.

```
    main()
    {
            TRangeInt myInt(101); // Use the default range values
            int i = 10;
            i = myInt;
    }
```

How can we assign a TRangeInt object to myInt. Our expectation is that a TRangeInt should be compatible with myInt because it is basically an int with some restrictions. This is where the conversion function comes to our rescue. The type on the LHS is an int. Therefore, myInt must be converted to an int for this assignment to work. Is there a way to convert a TRangeInt to an int? The answer to that question can only be found in the class TRangeInt. Sure enough, there is a conversion function, operator int(). This conversion function specifies a conversion from TRangeInt to built-in type int. When looking for the conversion to int, the compiler finds this conversion function and uses it for the conversion. And this conversion happens implicitly. We can invoke this conversion function explicitly also:

```
    cout << int(myInt) << endl; // OR cout << (int) myInt<< endl;
```

Such conversion functions are very useful in many different situations. When a new class is implemented, consider if the class can be used as a built-in type in some situation. For example, a Tstring object could be used as char* (or const char*). If such conversions are needed implicitly, it is a good policy to implement conversion functions (operator char*() and operator const char*()). If both of them are present, the const char* version will be used when a const char* is needed and the char* version is used when a raw char* is needed. Such decisions are handled by the compiler. If these conversions cause any ambiguity, then it will be reported as a compile-time error.

Many programmers write code as shown below and they are sometimes surprised when it works correctly.

```
TRangeInt x(10), y;
y = (TRangeInt) 100 + x;
```

This code works because, when 100 is typecast as **TRangeInt**, the converting constructor is called to convert 100 to **TRangeInt**. This code is identical to

```
y = TRangeInt(100) + x;
```

CAUTION   Both expressions typecast 100 to a **TRangeInt** object, which ends up calling the converting constructor. This style is not preferred because forcing a variable (or constant) of one type to another type is not a very safe operation. It is always good to avoid type coercion. When conversions are required, it should happen automatically without any explicit actions by the client. We already have the necessary member functions in **TRangeInt** to make the expression (**100 + x**) work correctly. There is no need for the client to do explicit casts. Try to stay away from explicit type coercion (except when using **void** pointers). Programmers with a C background find it hard to overcome the habit of type casting variables (and constants), but your programs will be more reliable and predictable when you avoid explicit casts. Even when you really need to do type conversions, use the runtime type information (RTTI) mechanism—it is safe. RTTI mechanism is discussed in Chapter 6.

Conversion functions cannot have any return type—the name of the function is the return type. Nor do they have any arguments. They can be **virtual** and they are inherited. At most, only one user defined conversion (converting constructor or conversion function) is applied to a single value.

Conversion functions are not limited to built-in types. A conversion function can convert from class to another class also. Here is an example. Assume that we have another class **TInt** that implements very large integers (first discussed in Chapter 2).

```
class TInt {
    public:
        TInt (int value); // Create a TInt with this value
        // Implementation not shown
        // ...
};

class TRangeInt {
    public:
        // Other details as in the previous cases

        operator TInt() { return TInt(_value); }

        // and many more not shown
    private:
        // as before
};
```

This new operator, **TInt()**, specifies a conversion from **TRangeInt** to **TInt**. Where a **TInt** is expected, a **TRangeInt** can be passed as the actual argument and the conversion function will do the rest.

```
void f (TInt x) {/* some code */ }
main()
{
    TRangeInt y;
    f( y ); // Implicitly converted to TInt by operator
            // TInt of class TRangeInt
}
```

When trying to understand conversion functions, look in the object of the class being converted for the conversion functions. In the example with the **operator+**, the conversion was from 100 (type **int**) to class **TRangeInt**. One should look in the class of **TRangeInt** for the appropriate converting constructor. A built-in type can be converted to an object only by a converting constructor. It is logical to look in the target class to which the built-in type is being converted to (**TRangeInt** in our example).

The situation is a tad complicated with objects. In the example above, where a **TRangeInt** is being converted to a **TInt**, there is more than one possibility. The conversion could have come from

a) a converting constructor **TInt(TRangeInt)** in class **TInt**; or

b) a conversion function **TInt()** in class **TRangeInt** (our case).

One should look in both places for the correct answer.[9] As you get more experience with C++, you may find that it is quite easy to locate such tricky conversions.

Interactions Between Converting Constructors and Conversion Functions

Adding converting constructors and conversion functions to a class at will is not a good practice because they can lead to ambiguous situations. Here is an example, again with the class **TRangeInt**.

```
class TRangeInt {
    public:
        enum Elimits { eLow=0, eHigh = 255 };
        // Create an TRangeInt object with these limits and value
        TRangeInt (int low, int high, int val) ;
        // Create an TRangeInt object with default limits and this value
        TRangeInt (int val=0);

        // Other details have been omitted for brevity
```

---

[9]The conversion is ambiguous if both forms of conversion are present.

```
        TRangeInt& operator+=(const TRangeInt& addThis);
        friend TRangeInt operator+( const TRangeInt& first,
            const TRangeInt& second); /
        operator int() { return _value; }

        // and many more not shown
    private:
        // as before
};
```

Everything has remained the same. The conversion operator has been re-introduced into the class TRangeInt.

The corresponding test program is:

```
        main()
        {
            TRangeInt y, x, z;
            z = x + 100;
        }
```

Will this compile and run? Of course not. There are ambiguities in the expression

```
        z = x + 100;
```

For the expression (x + 100) to work, there are two possibilities

a) Convert 100 to TRangeInt and then invoke operator+(const TRangeInt&, const TRangeInt&) — [z = x + *TRangeInt(100)*]

b) Convert TRangeInt to an int and then add them together using the built-in + operator for int — [*z = int (x) + 100*]

Case (a) uses the converting constructor TRangeInt (int val = 0) to convert 100 to a temporary TRangeInt object (say temp). Then the sum of x and temp is computed using the friend function operator+ declared in the class TRangeInt.

Case (b) goes the other way. Instead of converting 100 to TRangeInt, we convert x (of type TRangeInt) to built-in type int (generating another temporary, say temp) using the operator int() of class TRangeInt. Next, the sum of temp and 100 is computed using the built-in + operator for int. Finally, the resulting int is converted to a TRangeInt using the constructor TRangeInt(int) (which generates another temporary) and assigned to z (Fig. 8-1).

Both these cases are equally good alternatives for (x + 100). The compiler should not select one over the other. And that makes the statement (x+100) ambiguous. But how did we get into this ambiguous situation? The example worked correctly with the operator+ and the converting constructor. The ambiguity was introduced by the addition of the conversion function operator int(). Without this operator, there was no way to convert TRangeInt to int. Hence, the only choice was to convert 100 to TRangeInt. But now we have more than one choice and hence the ambiguity. Adding one simple conversion function caused a simple test program to fail.

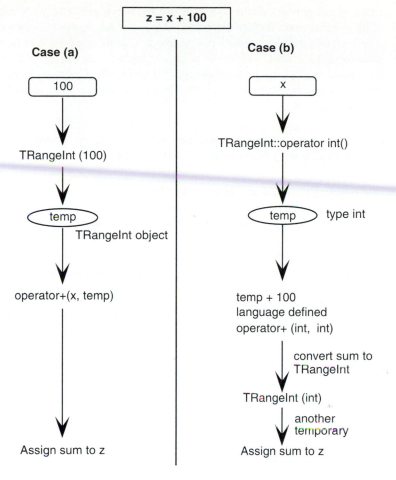

Fig. 8-1

This problem would not have been detected if we hadn't tried an expression of the form (x + 100). If both the operands are int (or TRangeInts) then no conversion is required and things would just work fine. It is the flexibility in writing expressions that sometimes leads to ambiguities. For example, if we never allowed clients to mix int and TRangeInt, then there would be no problem anywhere. But that would be too restrictive. All programming languages allow mixed mode expressions. For example, (1 + 12.2) mixes int and float. Operator overloading is intended to make expressions look more natural and convenient. This was the reason for providing the conversion function operator int().

Too many conversion paths can easily cause ambiguities in simple expressions. Class designers must exercise caution when adding conversion functions to a class. One should exercise even more caution when adding conversion functions to classes that have been already shipped to customers. For example, version 1.1 of a library (the successor to version 1.0) might add a new conversion function to a class such as TRangeInt. This can easily break existing client code that used to work perfectly with version 1.0 of the library. Clients never forgive software that breaks existing code. Backward compatibility is a very serious issue in software development. Clients might have to recompile the existing code to make it work with the new library but they should <u>never</u> be required to modify code because of a change in the library.[10] If you really need to add a new conversion function to an existing class, try using the class in different combinations to check if it breaks any existing code.

☞ **Exercise extreme caution when adding conversion functions to classes with converting constructors.**

The problem is even worse if there is more than one conversion function and/or converting constructor. For example, adding a conversion function operator long() to TRangeInt will create even more ambiguous situations.

NOTE   Types int, long, short, and double are compatible types in C++. The language can do *trivial* conversions among these types. Therefore, a function expecting a double can be called with an int, long, and short. Please refer to the language reference manual for more details.

   So how can we solve the problem that we just created (by adding the conversion function operator int()). The easiest solution is to just drop the conversion function. A better approach is to add a new set of operator+ functions that handle different combinations of int and TRangeInt.

```
class TRangeInt {
    public:
            enum Elimits { eLow=0, eHigh = 255 };
            // Create an TRangeInt object with these limits and value
            TRangeInt (int vlow, int vhigh, int val);
            // Create an TRangeInt object with default limits and this value
            TRangeInt (int val=0);

            // Other details have been omitted for brevity

            TRangeInt& operator+=( const TRangeInt& addThis);
            friend TRangeInt operator+( const TRangeInt& first,
                const TRangeInt& second); // ❸
            friend TRangeInt operator+(const TRangeInt& a, int b); // ❷
            operator int() { return _value; }

            // and many more not shown
    private:
            // as before
};

TRangeInt
operator+(int a, const TRangeInt& b) // ❶
```

---

[10]In many situations, even requiring the clients to recompile their code is considered expensive. Just requiring the clients to relink with the new library is the best approach.

```
{
      return (b + a); // Calls operator+ in ❷
}
```

Here is a small test program:

```
main()
{
    TRangeInt x(10), y;

    y = x + 100;   // Calls operator ❷ above
    y = 10 + x;            // Calls operator ❶ above
    y = y + x;     // Calls operator ❸ above

    int i;
    i = x; // Calls operator int() to convert x to an int
}
```

This solves the ambiguity problem elegantly. For (x + 100), no conversions are needed because ❷ above is a perfect match for this case. Similarly, (10 + x) will be a match with ❶ above and again no conversions are necessary. And ❸ is a perfect match for (y = y + x).

Now this is an elegant design but to arrive at this design we had to write different types of expressions to verify that none of them are ambiguous. Class designers who wish to use operators and conversion functions must go this extra mile to ensure proper behavior.

If avoiding ambiguities is almost impossible, then the restrictions on expressions must be clearly documented. Otherwise, clients will encounter ambiguities when they write simple expressions that look natural.

☞ **Perform extensive testing after implementing classes with conversion operators and converting constructors. State any known restrictions on expressions clearly.**

NOTE   In the preceding examples, the operator+ is a friend just for efficiency of implementation (faster access to private data members). There is no need to make them friend of a class if access to private data members is not required.

Eliminating the Need for Temporary Objects

There is one issue that still needs to be addressed. Conversions by constructors and conversion functions create temporary objects. When a converting constructor is used, a temporary object is created. For every object created, a constructor and the destructor (when the temporary is destroyed) needs to be called. This adds significant execution time to programs. With most conversion functions that convert from a class to a built-in type, a temporary variable (not object) is created. Creating a built-in type variable (such as int) is a lot cheaper than creating an object. It might be worthwhile to consider schemes to avoid temporary objects. Note that avoiding temporary objects is a good programming rule that pays dividends under many circumstances, not just with overloaded operators.

To understand the solution, revisit the converting constructor that was used in the expression (y = 100 + x). There was no matching operator+ function available and hence the need for the conversion. The need for the conversion will go away if we provide an operator+ that is an exact match for the operand types. The operator+ in ❶ above matches the expression (100 + x) without any user defined conversions. That eliminates the need for a temporary. For the class TRangeInt there are three possible combinations of operands for the operator+:

a) both operands are TRangeInt;

b) first operand is a TRangeInt object and second operand is an int; and

c) first operand is an int and second operand is a TRangeInt object.

If we provide three operator+ functions that correspond to these arguments, there wouldn't be any need for conversions. That is exactly what we have done in our last solution. Note that the implementation is very simple.

```
TRangeInt operator+(const TRangeInt& first,  const TRangeInt& second)
{
    // Implementation is shown in the next section.
    // In the meantime, can you write your own implementation?
}

inline TRangeInt operator+(const TRangeInt& a, int b)
{ /* Implementation code not shown here. */ }

TRangeInt operator+(int a, const TRangeInt& b)
{
    // Swap the operands and use the previous operator+
    // And this function is inline to avoid the extra function call.
    return (b + a);
}
```

That was really easy. Most problems with operator argument mismatch can be solved by implementing functions that match exactly. Most ambiguities arise because of conversion attempts. If there is no need for any conversion, then there would be no ambiguities.

NOTE   There is only one minor problem with this approach of providing exactly matching operator functions. This can cause proliferation of such operator functions. Just for operator+, we have three functions. Imagine what happens when all the other operators (−, *, /, etc.) are also overloaded. But having numerous functions is a much better solution than causing ambiguities in client's code. Furthermore, these functions eliminate the need for temporaries, which is another big win.

There is another side effect to this approach of implementing operators for all combinations of operands. Some of these new operator+ functions have a non-object as their first argument (int in the example above). Such functions cannot be implemented as member functions. They are always implemented as non-member functions. Of course, this does not cause any problems. It only minimizes the alternatives we have for implementing operator functions. Prior to this change, we could implement them as member functions or as non-member functions. But if the first operand is not a true object, then it cannot be a member function. However, the **operator+** function, shown below as a non member function

```
TRangeInt operator+(const TRangeInt& first, const TRangeInt& second) ;
```

can be implemented as a member function (with one argument)

```
TRangeInt operator+(const TRangeInt& first) const;
```

This operator only accepts true objects as its arguments. Therefore, it is suitable for a member function. Even the **operator+**, whose first argument is a **TRangeInt** and the second argument is of type **int**, can be implemented as a member function. Follow any style you like but maintain consistency among all the different operators. If you implement **operator+** as a member function (or as a non member function), then implement **operator-** and all such commutative binary operators as member functions (non member functions).

NOTE   If the implementor of the class fails to provide such simple non-member, non-friend operator functions, intelligent clients can implement them too.

RETURNING RESULTS FROM OPERATOR FUNCTIONS

Finally, we need to understand the two alternatives for returning computed results from operator functions. The **operator+=** returned the result by reference where as the **operator+** returned the computed sum by value.

```
TRangeInt operator+(const TRangeInt& first,
                        const TRangeInt& second) ;
TRangeInt& operator+=(const TRangeInt& first);
```

Why this difference, one might wonder. Why can't they both return by reference as that would eliminate the need to create another object (that is returned by value). The next few paragraphs will explain what is really happening.

Here is an implementation of the **operator+=**.

```
TRangeInt&
TRangeInt::operator+=(const TRangeInt& addThis)
{
    /*
     * The implementation is quite simple. The argument addThis is being
       added to the object in 'this'. The range limits of the resulting
       object remain the same. In fact the object denoted by 'this' already
       exists and it already has an upper and lower limits on its value.
       All we need to do is to add addThis.value to this->value ensuring
       that the result this->value is still within the existing upper
       limit. If the addition causes this->value to overshoot the upper
       limit, then we do not perform the operation.
     */
        if (addThis._value == 0) return *this; // Nothing to do
```

```
        if ( (addThis._value + this->_value) > this->_high ||
              (addThis._value + this->_value) < this-> _low) // if negative
            return *this; // Operation will cause the limit to be violated
                                    // WE SHOULD really throw an exception here

        // Ok, now we can add the number in addThis
        this-> _value += addThis._value;

        return *this; // Return a reference to the object on the LHS
}

main()
{
        TRangeInt x;
        TRangeInt y(10);

        x += y;
}
```

In the expression (x += y), the object x already exists and the **operator+=** will modify it.
Moreover, the object x is guaranteed to exist for the duration of the **operator+=** function.
In fact, x is the target of the **operator+=** member function. If an object already exists,
there is no need to create another new object. We can just return a reference to it. This is
what happens in **operator+=** above. The client invoked **operator+=** on the object x
knowing very well that x will get modified. So x becomes an l-value in the expression
(x += y). References work perfectly with l-values.

☞ **An l-value operator (operators that are invoked on existing objects)
can return a reference to the object on the LHS, the target of the operator call. This is safe, efficient and the correct way to implement an
l-value operator.**

Operator =, -=, *=, etc. belong to this category. And we already know why such operators
are implemented as member functions.

Here is the long awaited implementation of the **operator+** function.

```
TRangeInt
operator+(const TRangeInt& first, const TRangeInt& second)
{
    /*
    * We need to create another TRangeInt to hold the result. The client
      cannot create the object to hold the result. But the object that is
      created in this function (on the stack ) will be destroyed as soon as
      we leave this function. If we create a dynamic object (on the run-
      time heap), who is responsible for destroying it? Moreover the
      computed sum must be returned to the caller. So the result must exist
      beyond the scope of this function. The only way we can safely do
      that is by copying the result out of this function, i.e. return the
      result by value to the caller.

    * What should be the range limit of the new object? Should it be that
      of first or second? Or should it be something else altogether. As a
```

```
    conservative approach, we set the range limits on the result to the
    lesser of first and second. So if first has (10, 100) as its limits
    and second has (5, 50) as its limits, the result will have (10, 50)
    as its limits. One could also enforce the restriction that both first
    and second should have the same range limits. I'm providing a more
    flexible implementation. You are free to change it.
    */

int newLow, newHigh;
// Upper limit on the new number is the smaller of the two operands.
// You can also use the library function min for this operation
newHigh = (first.high > second.high) ? second.high : first.high;
// Lower limit on the new number is the bigger of the two operands.
// You can also use the library function max for this
newLow = (first._low < second._low) ? second._low : first._low;

int newValue = first._value + second._value;
if (newValue >= newLow && newValue <= newHigh) {
    // This is a valid operation. Create a local TRangeInt and return
    // it.
    return TRangeInt( newLow, newHigh, newValue);
}
// ***********************ERROR*******************************
// What should we do if the sum is beyond the upper or lower limits?
// The correct solution would be to throw an exception indicating
// failure. We aren't exception literate yet. So let's just return a
// TRangeInt with everything set to zero.

return TRangeInt(0, 0, 0);
}
```

The comments in the code are self explanatory. The **operator+** is called with two operands but none of the operands themselves are modified by the **operator+** function **operator+** needs to return a new **TRangeInt** object with the proper values in it. It cannot return a reference to any object because the expression (**x** + **y**) does not supply any extra argument to the **operator+** function to hold the return value. The **operator+** function does not have access to any other object other than the operands so **operator+** must create a new object. It can create a dynamic object (using operator new) or it can create an automatic object on the run-time stack. For a dynamic object, *someone* should assume storage responsibility. But who will that someone be in **operator+**? The caller of **operator+** (user of **x** + **y**) doesn't know anything about it.

One could try to implement the **operator+** function, as shown below, but it will leak memory.

```
TRangeInt
operator+(const TRangeInt& first, const TRangeInt& second)
{
    // WRONG IMPLEMENTATION. SHOWN HERE ONLY TO DEMONSTRATE THE PROBLEM.

        int newLow, newHigh;
        // Upper limit on the new number is the smaller of the two
        // operands. You can also use the library function min for this
        // operation
```

```
    newHigh = (first.high > second.high) ? second.high : first.high;
    // Lower limit on the new number is the bigger of the two operands.
    // You can also use the library function max for this.
    newLow = (first._low < second._low) ? second._low : first._low;

    int newValue = first._value + second._value;
    if (newValue >= newLow && newValue <= newHigh) {
    // Create a dynamic TRangeInt object to hold the result

    TRangeInt *rp = new TRangeInt (newLow, newHigh, newValue);
    return *rp; // Who will delete this dynamic memory object?
}
```

If the dynamic object is not destroyed, every time **operator+** is called there will be a memory leak. If we use an automatic object, it is going to be destructed as soon as we leave the function. So our computed sum will disappear prematurely. Somehow, we must compute the sum and move it out of the function without any chance of memory leaks. The only solution is to return the result by value. Usually a copy constructor is invoked to copy the (returned) object out of the function. A temporary object is created outside the function and the copy constructor (of **TRangeInt**) is used to copy the result object to the temporary. This is done just before returning from the **operator+** function.[11] The temporary will be destructed by the compiler at the end of the expression—we don't have to worry about it.

☞ **Commutative operators (+, -, etc.) that compute the result from their operands, cannot return a reference or a pointer. Naturally such operators return the result** *by value.*

We already know why they are usually implemented as non-member functions. They are made **friends** of the class if access to private data members is required.

    For completeness, here is the implementation of the other **operator+** functions.

```
TRangeInt
operator+(const TRangeInt& first, int second)
{
    // Same procedure as the one above. The only difference is that the
    // range limits are that of first.

    int newValue = first._value + second;
    if (newValue >= first._low && newValue <= first._high) {
        // This is a valid + operation. Create a local TRangeInt and
        // return it.
        return TRangeInt( first._low, first._high, newValue);
    }

    // ***********************ERROR********************************************
    // What should we do if the sum is beyond the upper or lower limits?
    // The correct solution would be to throw an exception indicating
```

[11]This is how it works in most compilers. There is no rule in the language that mandates this scheme. Compilers might optimize this by creating a new object (before calling **operator+**) and passing it as an additional argument to **operator+**. All this would be done transparently. No matter what, there is an extra object to be created. Some issues related to the copy constructor optimizations are discussed in Chapter 13.

```
    // failure. We aren't exception literate yet. So let's just return a
    // TRangeInt with everything set to zero.
    return TRangeInt(0, 0, 0);
}

inline
TRangeInt operator+(int first, const TRangeInt& second)
{
    // Switch the operands and use the previous operator+
    // And this function is inline to avoid the extra function call.
    return (second + first);
}
```

There is an alternate implementation for operator+ that is used quite often. In this implementation, we make use of the **operator+=** (which should be available in the class
TRangeInt for this scheme to work). Here is the code:

```
        TRangeInt
        operator+(const TRangeInt& first, const TRangeInt& second)
        {
            TRangeInt result = first; // Uses the copy constructor
            // It can also be written as: TRangeInt result(first)

            result += second; // Use TRangeInt::operator+=()

            return result; // Again return by value
        }
```

Implementing the above operators as member functions is left as a trivial exercise to the
reader.

THE ASSIGNMENT OPERATOR

The only operator that is different (in terms of language treatment) is the assignment operator, **operator=**. All other operators are inherited by a derived class automatically. But
the assignment operator is not inherited. If an assignment operator is required for a class,
it is either explicitly implemented by the programmer (which is the right thing to do for
all classes) or it is automatically generated by the compiler. This has been discussed in detail in Chapter 4.

☞ **Assignment operators are never inherited. It (they) is either provided
by the class implementor or it is generated by the compiler.**

SUMMARY

Do not provide overloaded operators just to demonstrate your prowess of the language.
Operator overloading is a powerful concept if used properly.

Designing and implementing an interface that uses overloaded operators requires a thorough understanding of the language, operators, and the class.

Operators implemented in a base class are inherited by its derived classes automatically (except assignment operators).

Most operators belong to a family of operators. If you implement one member of the family, you need to implement the others too (for a complete and coherent interface).

The behavior and outcome of using an overloaded operator must be natural. Remember that an overloaded operator only extends the existing meaning of the operator as applied to a class.

Avoid using overloaded operators in convoluted ways. Don't use overloaded operators to provide very tricky implementations that clients cannot understand.

Understand the differences between commutative and non-commutative operators. Further, understand l-value semantics with operators correctly.

Under C++, many operations can be done in more than one way using different operators. Pay attention to such operators when overloading operators.

One of the most commonly used operators is the equality **operator ==**. If you implement equality, you must implement inequality operator (**operator!=**) also for a complete interface.

Remember that operator [] can be used on both sides of the assignment operation.

Prefer non-member function implementation for commutative operators that require conversions.

Converting constructors and conversion functions can interact leading to ambiguities.

9

Generic Types

One of the most mundane tasks for a programmer is writing code to do similar tasks again and again with very few changes. This task doesn't require any intelligence or special skills. Such repeated tasks make life dull and boring. When a task is repeated many times, it is very likely that errors are introduced into the code due to the monotony of the task. Human beings are not really fit to do the same thing repeatedly. Machines can perform the repetitive task without any problems but human beings need change. So it is a good idea to let machines do repetitive tasks while we do more interesting things that are more challenging and productive.

But avoiding repetitive tasks with procedural programming is hard. With most procedural languages, we are forced to write the same type of code again and again. A simple example would clarify what I'm talking about.

THE REPEATED CODING PROBLEM

Consider the task of implementing a simple list. For the sake of completeness, let us say we want to implement a list for storing **TPerson** objects (from our University example of Chapter 5). With procedural languages such as C and Pascal, this would be declared as

```
struct TPerson {
    /* All the details about TPerson */
```

```
        TPerson* next;      /* Pointer to next TPerson on the list */
        TPerson* previous; /* Pointer to previous TPerson on the list */
};
```

This is perhaps one of the first exercises in a Pascal (or C) course (Fig. 9-1). We have written code around this implementation to add/remove new **TPerson** objects to any list, to search for specific a **TPerson** on the list, etc.

```
            void AddPerson(const TPerson* thisOne);
            void RemovePerson(const TPerson* thisOne);
```

These procedures usually access a global list and carry out the correct operation.

With the OO approach, we have refined this scheme to create two separate classes —one for the list and another for the nodes on the list. We have already discussed this in an earlier chapter (see Fig. 9-2).

```
    class TListNode; // forward declaration

    class TList {
        public:
            TList(const void* storeThisElement);
            TList(const TList& copy);
            TList& operator=(const TList& assign);
            virtual ~TList();

            // How many elements are stored on the list?
            unsigned int HowMany() const;
            // Append a new node to the list (at the tail)
            // Return true if successful
            bool Append (const void* newElementToAdd);
            // Prepend a new node to the list (at the head)
            // Return true if successful
            bool Prepend (const void* newElementToAdd);
            // Does this element exist in one of the list nodes?
            bool Exists(const void* thisElement);
            // Remove this element (if it exists) from the list
            const void* Remove(const void* elementToRemove);
            // and many more methods
        private:
            TListNode* _head;
            TListNode* _tail;
            unsigned int _count;
    };
```

A List of Person Objects—Traditional Implementation

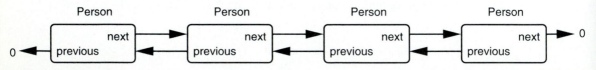

Fig. 9-1

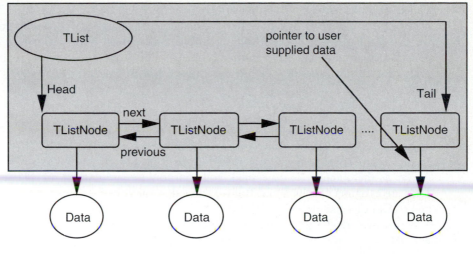

Fig. 9-2

```
class TListNode {
    public:
        // Constructor to create a new ListNode given user's data
        TListNode(const void* userDataPointer=0);
        // Copy constructor etc. not shown

        // Remove the user's data and return it and make the node empty
        const void* RemoveContent();
        // Return the pointer to data of this node (object still resides
        // on the list)
        const void* GetContent() const;
        // and others..
    private:
        TListNode* _next;
        TListNode* _previous;
        const void* _userData; // pointer to user supplied data
        friend class TList;
};
```

Using **void** pointers to store the data (**userData** above) is inherently dangerous because we lose strict type checking. Moreover, when we retrieve an object from a **TList** using **GetContent()**, we only get a **void***— we don't really know what it points to. This forces the client to perform type conversions, which brings with it its own set of problems. Furthermore, all **TList** operations are in terms of **void** pointers. If we have a **TList** object, which actually stores **TPerson** objects, there is nothing to prevent someone from adding an object that is unrelated to a **TPerson** to this list because every pointer is compatible with a **void** pointer. For example, one can write the following piece of code:

```
TList personList; // List of TPerson objects
TCar car; // Assume that class TCar is available;
personList.Prepend(&car); // Will compile but is it logically correct?
```

This code looks harmless. But it is logically incorrect because we are adding a TCar to a list of TPerson objects. When we retrieve this object later, we receive a void pointer and we assume that it is a TPerson object. So we type convert (typecast) it to a TPerson pointer leading to all kinds of run-time problems. Furthermore, one could get into really nasty problems by assigning one list object to another list object.

```
// continued from above
TList carList; // List of car object
// ... code to add objects to lists
personList = carList; // Syntactically correct but logically disastrous
```

As far as the compiler is concerned, both personList and carList are identical types. They are assignment compatible. But we know that one contains TPerson objects and the other TCar objects.

To overcome these problems with void pointers, we can replace the void pointer with the correct type when implementing a list of TPerson objects (Fig. 9-3). So here is the code.

```
class TListNode; // forward declarations
class TPerson;

class TList {
    public:
            // Objects stored on the list are not copied. Only the address of
            // the object is stored. Clients should not delete an object
            // which still resides on a TList. Before deleting an object that
```

A List of Person Objects

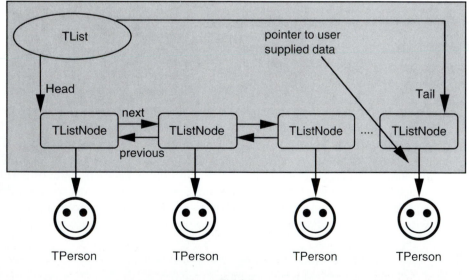

Fig. 9-3

```
        // resides on a list, remove it from the list so that everything
        // is clean. Clients still control the lifetime of an object that
        // resides on a list. The member functions of TList never destroy
        // the object belonging to a client.

        TList(const TPerson* storeThisElement);
        // When list objects are copied (or assigned) the objects on the
        // list are not copied. Only the address of the objects are
        // copied.
        TList(const TList& copy);
        TList& operator=(const TList& assign);
        virtual ~TList();

        // How many elements are stored on the list?
        unsigned int HowMany() const;
        // Append a new node to the list (at the tail)
        // Return true if successful
        bool Append (const TPerson* newElementToAdd);
        // Prepend a new node to the list (at the head)
        // Return true if successful
        bool Prepend(const TPerson* newElementToAdd);
        // Does this element exist in one of the list nodes?
        bool Exists(const Person* thisElement);
        // Remove this element (if it exists) from the list
        const TPerson* Remove(const TPerson* elementToRemove);
        // and many more methods
    private:
        TListNode* _head;
        TListNode* _tail;
        unsigned int _count;
};

class TListNode {
    public:
        // Constructor to create a new ListNode given user's data
        TListNode(const TPerson* userDataPointer=0);
        // Copy constructor etc.
        // Remove the user's data and return it and make the node empty
        const TPerson* RemoveContent();
        // Return the pointer to data of this node (object still lives on
        // the list)
        const TPerson* GetContent() const;
        // and others..
    private:
        TListNode* _next;
        TListNode* _previous;
        const TPerson* _userData; // pointer to user supplied data
        friend class TList;
};
```

This definitely makes the implementation more robust because the compiler enforces type checking. Now, if we try to **Prepend** a **TCar** object to a **personList** (code fragment shown below), it will generate a compile-time error because a **TCar** pointer is not compatible with a **TPerson** pointer.

```
TList personList; // List of TPerson objects
TCar car; // Assume that class TCar is available;
personList.Prepend(&car); // Will NOT compile!
```

Now consider a situation where we need another list to maintain the courses enrolled by a
student (or the list of courses offered by a teacher) (Fig. 9-4). The only difference between
a list of courses and a list of **TPerson** objects is the object stored on the list—**TCourse**
and **TPerson**. So we can try to create another **TList** and **TListNode** class as follows:

```
class TListNode; // forward declaration
class TCourse;

class TList {
    public:
        TList(const TCourse* storeThisElement);
        TList(const TList& copy);
        TList& operator=(const TList& assign);
        virtual ~TList();
        // Other details omitted for brevity

    private:
        TListNode* _head;
        TListNode* _tail;
        unsigned int _count;
};

class TListNode {
    public:
        // Constructor to create a new ListNode given user's data
        TListNode(const TCourse* userDataPointer=0);
        // Copy constructor etc.
```

A List of Course Objects

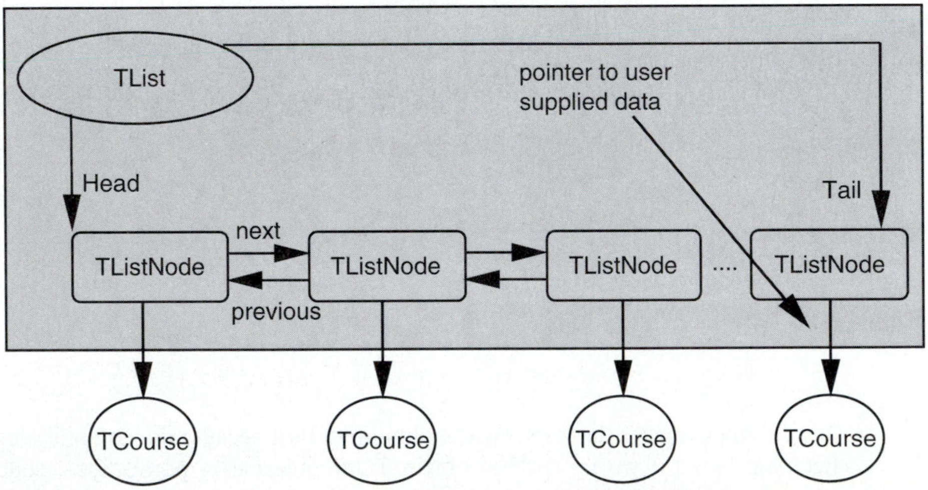

Fig. 9-4

```
            // Other details omitted for brevity
        private:
            TListNode* _next;
            TListNode* _previous;
            const TCourse* _userData; // pointer to user supplied data
            friend class TList;
    };
```

First of all, this code will not compile if this **TList** (and **TListNode**) and the previous **TList** (and **TListNode**) are in the same file because there cannot be more than one class with the same name. If these two **TList** (and **TListNode**) classes are in different files and they are linked together, the linker will generate errors complaining about the duplicate definition of the classes **TList** and **TListNode**. To overcome this problem, we can try to create two independent classes, **TPersonList** and **TCourseList**, with essentially the same interface and implementation.

```
    class TPersonListNode;
    // List for managing TPerson objects only

    class TPersonList {
        public:
            TPersonList (const TPerson* storeThisElement);

            // Other details omitted for brevity
        private:
            TPersonListNode* _head;
            TPersonListNode* _tail;
            unsigned int _count;

    };

    class TPersonListNode{
        public:
            TPersonListNode(const TPerson* userDataPointer=0);
            // Other details omitted for brevity
        private:
            TPersonListNode* _next;
            TPersonListNode* _previous;
            const TPerson* _userData; // pointer to user supplied data
            friend class TPersonList;
    };

    class TCourseListNode;
    // List for managing TCourse objects only

    class TCourseList {
        public:
            TCourseList(const TCourse* storeThisElement);
            // Other details omitted for brevity
        private:
            TCourseListNode* _head;
            TCourseListNode* _tail;
            unsigned int _count;

    };
```

```
class TCourseListNode{
    public:
        TCourseListNode(const TCourse* userDataPointer=0);

        // Other details omitted for brevity
    private:
        TCourseListNode* _next;
        TCourseListNode* _previous;
        const TCourse* _userData; // pointer to user supplied data
        friend class TCourseList;
};
```

Definitely, this scheme will work but with some major disadvantages.

1. Even though both TCourseList and TPersonList are identical classes with the same interface and implementation, clients must remember both class names and use the correct one in their code. This is a needless burden on the clients.

2. The implementation code for both TPersonList and TCourseList are mostly identical but still the code must be manually repeated in the implementation of both classes.

3. If we find a problem in the implementation of TPersonList and fix it, we must remember to patch this fix into the code of TCourseList also. We must also remember to recompile both list classes. This is highly error-prone.

4. Every time we need a list class to hold a different type of object, we need to invent another name for the new list class and duplicate the code again. Essentially, the same steps are carried out for every new list type created. Again, this is a highly boring task.

5. Any subclasses of these list classes will have to be changed if there is a change in the base class. The same change must be repeated for each and every subclass.

Steps (1) through (5) are even more daunting when there are many different list class implementations (TTeacherList, TStudentList, TClassRoomList, THolidayList, TEmployeeList, etc.). Repeating steps (1) through (5) again and again for every list class is highly unattractive and error-prone. There must be a better solution for this problem.

THE SMART SOLUTION—GENERIC PROGRAMMING

When we look closely, there is not much difference between the two TList classes (Fig. 9-3 and Fig. 9-4). Both are general list classes supporting the same interface. The only difference is the type of the objects stored on the list. The list in Fig. 9-3 manages TPerson objects where as the one in Fig. 9-4 manages TCourse objects. This is the only difference between the two list classes. In fact, even the size of these list objects is the same. The implementation code of TList will be the same no matter what it manages (TPerson or TCourse). Here is a simple implementation of the method Prepend for class TPersonList.

```
bool
TPersonList::Prepend (const TPerson* newElementToAdd)
{
    // Create a new TPersonListNode object for this element
    TPersonListNode* newNode = new TPersonListNode(newElementToAdd);

    // Now manipulate pointers to prepend this new element
    newNode->_next = this->_head; // Old head is now the second element
    this->_head->_previous = newNode; // Adjust pointers
    _head = newNode; // Our new element is the head of the list
    _ count++;

    return true;
}
```

There is nothing new or interesting in this code. We have been writing code like this for a long time. Now, here is the same method for class **TCourseList**.

```
bool
TCourseList::Prepend (const TCourse* newElementToAdd)
{
    // Create a new TCourseListNode object for this element
    TCourseListNode* newNode = new TCourseListNode(newElementToAdd);
    // Now manipulate pointers to prepend this element
    newNode->_next = this->_head; // Old head is the second element
    this->_head->_previous = newNode;
    _head = newNode; // Our new element is the head of the list
    _ count++;

    return true;
}
```

Is there any difference between the two methods? A casual reader might feel that the two methods are different. Really, the only difference in the code between the two member functions is the dependency on the type **TPersonListNode** and *TCourseListNode*. The code that manipulates the pointers is the same in both cases. Member function **Prepend** creates a new instance of list node and then manipulates the pointers. For any type **T**, we can write a general member function **Prepend** (for class **TList**) as follows:

```
// Code to Prepend an object of type T to a TList class
// Type T is a place holder which will be replaced by a real class.
bool
TList::Prepend (const T* newElementToAdd)
{
    // Create a new TListNode object for this element
    TListNode* newNode = new TListNode(newElementToAdd);

    // Now manipulate pointers to prepend this element
    newNode->_next = this->_head; // Old head is the second element
    this->_head->_previous = newNode;
    _head = newNode; // Our new element is the head of the list
    _count++;

    return true;
}
```

This method creates a TListNode object for an object of the type T being added to the list. When we want to add a TPerson object to a TList (of TPerson objects), T would be replaced by TPerson. Similarly, when a TCourse object needs to be added to a TList (of TCourse objects), T would be replaced by TCourse. Now the only dependency in Prepend is on the type T. This looks more elegant, doesn't it?

We are trying to develop a skeleton code that can be duplicated for any new type T. The code for Prepend above is just a template that needs to be converted to real code for every TList. So when we need to create a new TList class for TPerson objects, T is replaced by TPerson, and when a TList class for TCourse objects is needed, T is replaced by TCourse. That would make the programmer's life a tad easier, but still the name conflict problem remains. Each of these TList classes (for TPerson and TCourse) cannot have the same name (as discussed earlier). Somehow, we should be able to create a new name for each of these TList classes. But the programmer should not have to do that. If the programmer is again forced to pick a new name for each of these list classes, then we haven't really solved anything.

In addition, the two classes—TList of TPerson and TList of TCourse, should be treated as two distinct types. The programmer should not be able to mix objects of the two TList classes under any circumstance. But both of them should have the same interface and almost the same implementation. In other words, even though they are TList classes, in reality they are two different types of TList classes and this type distinction must be enforced.

All these operations can be done more easily by the compiler than by the programmer.

1. The generation of a new TList class for any new type just requires simple code duplication with some type checking.

2. The distinction among the different TList classes is a problem of managing type names. Each of the generated TList classes (with a different type T) should be treated as an independent class.

The preceding discussion implies that TList is a generic (or general) class. This generic class can be customized by replacing the place holder T with the appropriate type as required. When we need a TList of TPerson objects, the type T will be replaced by class TPerson. And T will be replaced by TCourse when we need a course list. In both cases, a new type of TList is generated. This facility to write *generic* classes is supported by Ada, Eiffel, and C++.

SMALLTALK   There is no concept of a generic type in Smalltalk. The entire discussion in the rest of the chapter is not applicable to Smalltalk. However, it is possible to simulate genericity with inheritance. We shall see how Smalltalk simulates genericity with inheritance in Chapter 12 (container classes).

FUNDAMENTALS OF A GENERIC TYPE (CLASS)

Any generic type depends on one or more other types. The TList above depends on the type of the object being stored in the TList. This dependency can be determined at compile time. For example, when we need a TPerson list, we know that the TList is going to contain TPerson objects and nothing else. This dependency on the type of the object stored can be stated in terms of a dummy class T, as shown earlier. The concept is very similar to that of a function (procedure or subroutine). When a function is written, the arguments it expects are stated in terms of *formal arguments*. When the function is called the *actual arguments* are supplied by the caller. Furthermore, the number and type of each and every formal argument is clearly specified. On the same lines, a generic type clearly specifies the (formal) generic arguments it requires, but there is no type attached to the formal generic arguments.[1] The generic type only specifies the need for actual arguments but it does not place any restrictions on the type. The major difference between a function and a generic type is in the way it is used. A function is called with actual arguments, but a generic type is *instantiated* at compile time to create another new type. Type checking of the actual arguments for a function is still done at compile time. Only the invocation of the function is done at run time. Type checking of a generic type is done at compile time. In C++ a generic class is called a **Template Class** (or a Parameterized type). Our TList class will now be written as follows:

```
template <class AType> class TList {
    public:
        TList(AType* storeThisElement);
        TList(const TList<AType> copy);
        TList& operator=(const TList<AType>& assign);
        virtual ~TList();

        // How many elements are stored on the list?
        unsigned int HowMany() const;
        // Append a new node to the list (at the tail)
        // Return true if successful
        bool Append(AType* newElementToAdd);
        // Prepend a new node to the list (at the head)
        // Return true if successful
        bool Prepend(AType* newElementToAdd);
        AType* Remove(AType* elementToRemove);
        bool Exists(const AType& thisObject) const;
        // and many more methods
    private:
        TListNode<AType>* _head;
        TListNode<AType>* _tail;
        unsigned int _count;
};
```

The first important feature is the introduction of the new keyword **template**. Any generic type (class or function) begins with the keyword **template**. This makes it very easy (both

---

[1] In Eiffel, the implementor can place restrictions on the formal arguments for the generic types. This is called *constrained genericity*. When there is no restriction on the formal arguments for the generic type, it is called *unconstrained genericity*. More on this later.

for the reader and the compiler) to identify generic types. The formal arguments are specified within the < > as shown above. In other words, TList is a parameterized type with AType as its parameter. Code samples in this book use the place-holder AType to identify such formal template parameters (arguments). When we need a TList of TPerson, AType will be replaced by TPerson. Here is the code that creates a TList of TPerson objects.

```
class TPerson { /* details omitted for brevity */ };

TList<TPerson> pList; // Instantiate a list of TPerson objects
```

In this example, a new class TList<TPerson> has been generated from the template class TList<AType>. The process of generating a new class (or function) from a template is commonly referred to as *template instantiation.* We have instantiated a TList<TPerson> from TList<AType>. Now we are ready to see how this template instantiation compares with function calls.

```
void g(int x);

main()
{
    int i = 10;
    g(i); // Call g() with the int argument i
}
```

In this code, the actual call to g() is made at run time with the variable i. Whatever i contains at that instance will be passed to g(). However, at compile time the compiler checks that i is an integer and that g() requires only one argument. So the type checking happens at compile time but the actual call happens at run time.

```
class TPerson { /* details omitted for brevity */ };
class TCourse { /* details omitted for brevity */ };
// Refer to TList<AType> shown above

TList<TPerson>  pList; // a list of TPerson objects
TList<TCourse>  cList; // a list of TCourse objects
```

In this code, when pList is instantiated, the compiler checks to ensure that TPerson is a known type. Further, it checks to ensure that TList requires only one actual argument. Once these checks are successful, a new class (let's call it TList_TPerson) is generated in the code.[2] In the simplest case, the compiler duplicates the entire code of TList replacing AType with TPerson. Then it compiles this generated class (TList_TPerson) to further ensure that the generated code is correct. Once these steps are completed, TList_TPerson behaves like any other programmer defined class. Note that all the work is done at compile time. There is no run-time cost associated with the use of a template class. This is the major difference between the function call with actual argument and template class instantiation with parameters.

---

[2]Compilers have their own naming schemes for generated template classes. Fortunately, we don't have to know anything about those generated class names.

What Happens When a New Template Class Is Instantiated in C++?

When we generate a new class from a template class by supplying actual arguments for the formal template arguments, the entire code of the template class (both interface and implementation code) is duplicated in the new class generated. In the new class the actual argument replaces the formal template argument (Fig. 9-5).

Once we have **TList** as a template class, we must also make **TListNode** a template class because it also depends on the *type* of the element stored on the list. Here is the new class **TListNode** (see p. 430).

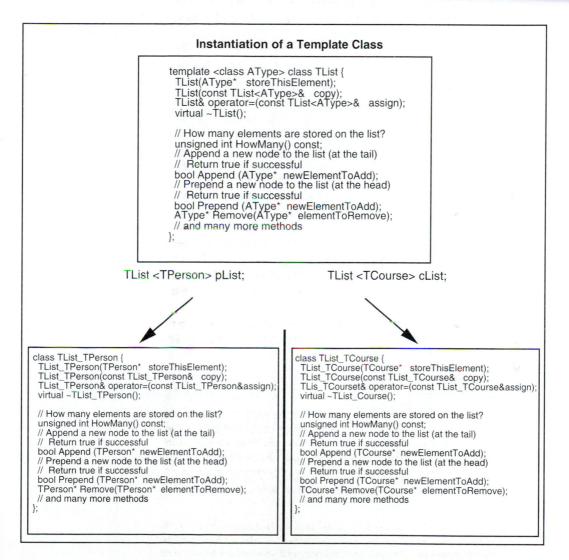

Instantiation of a Template Class

```
template <class AType> class TList {
  TList(AType*  storeThisElement);
  TList(const TList<AType>&  copy);
  TList& operator=(const TList<AType>&  assign);
  virtual ~TList();

  // How many elements are stored on the list?
  unsigned int HowMany() const;
  // Append a new node to the list (at the tail)
  //  Return true if successful
  bool Append (AType*  newElementToAdd);
  // Prepend a new node to the list (at the head)
  //  Return true if successful
  bool Prepend (AType*  newElementToAdd);
  AType* Remove(AType*  elementToRemove);
  // and many more methods
};
```

TList <TPerson> pList;   TList <TCourse> cList;

```
class TList_TPerson {
  TList_TPerson(TPerson*  storeThisElement);
  TList_TPerson(const TList_TPerson&  copy);
  TList_TPerson& operator=(const TList_TPerson&assign);
  virtual ~TList_TPerson();

  // How many elements are stored on the list?
  unsigned int HowMany() const;
  // Append a new node to the list (at the tail)
  //  Return true if successful
  bool Append (TPerson* newElementToAdd);
  // Prepend a new node to the list (at the head)
  //  Return true if successful
  bool Prepend (TPerson*  newElementToAdd);
  TPerson* Remove(TPerson*  elementToRemove);
  // and many more methods
};
```

```
class TList_TCourse {
  TList_TCourse(TCourse*  storeThisElement);
  TList_TCourse(const TList_TCourse&  copy);
  TLis_TCourset& operator=(const TList_TCourse&assign);
  virtual ~TList_Course();

  // How many elements are stored on the list?
  unsigned int HowMany() const;
  // Append a new node to the list (at the tail)
  //  Return true if successful
  bool Append (TCourse* newElementToAdd);
  // Prepend a new node to the list (at the head)
  //  Return true if successful
  bool Prepend (TCourse*  newElementToAdd);
  TCourse* Remove(TCourse*  elementToRemove);
  // and many more methods
};
```

Fig. 9-5

```
template <class AType> class TListNode {
    public:
            // Constructor to create a new ListNode given user's data
            TListNode(AType* userDataPointer=0);
            // Copy constructor etc.

            // Other details omitted for brevity
    private:
            TListNode<AType>* _next;
            TListNode<AType>* _previous;
            AType*            _userData; // pointer to user supplied data
            friend class TList <AType>; // More on this later
};
```

Shown below is the member function **Prepend** for the class **TList<AType>**. This member function needs to instantiate a new **TListNode** for an **AType** object. This is done by the statement

```
                    new TListNode<AType>;
```

Here is the complete code:

```
template <class AType>
bool TList<AType>::Prepend (AType* newElementToAdd)
{
    // Create a new TListNode object for this element
    TListNode<AType>* newNode =
        new TListNode<AType>(newElementToAdd);

    // Now manipulate pointers to prepend this new element
    newNode->_next = this->_head; // Old head is now the second element
    this->head->_previous = newNode; // Adjust pointers
    _head = newNode; // Our new element is the head of the list
    _count++;

    return true;
}
```

Note that every member function code also begins with the keyword **template**. We are implementing the **Prepend** function for the class **TList<AType>**. Wherever we need to use a class name, **TList<AType>** is used. It will be an error to use just the name **TList** because it is no longer a normal class—it is a template class. There is a **TList** of some type, but not just a **TList**. This is one of the first surprises for programmers learning the generic class concept. When the class **TList<TPerson>** is instantiated, the code for **Prepend** is also duplicated. The examples below use class names **TList_TPerson** and **TList_TCourse** to illustrate the concept. A C++ compiler would use some other mangled name for these classes.

```
bool
TList_TPerson::Prepend (TPerson* newElementToAdd)
{
```

```
        // Create a new TListNode object for this element
        TListNode_TPerson* newNode = new TListNode_TPerson(newElementToAdd);

        // Now manipulate pointers to prepend this new element
        newNode->_next = this->_head; // Old head is now the second element
        this->_head->_previous = newNode; // Adjust pointers
        _head = newNode; // Our new element is the head of the list
        ++_count;

        return true;
}
```

And the same code is again duplicated for TList<TCourse>.

```
bool
TList_TCourse::Prepend (TCourse* newElementToAdd)
{
        // Create a new TListNode object for this element
        TListNode_TCourse* newNode = new TListNode_TCourse(newElementToAdd);

        // Now manipulate pointers to prepend this new element
        newNode->_next = this->_head; // Old head is now the second element
        this->_head->_previous = newNode; // Adjust pointers
        _head = newNode; // Our new element is the head of the list
        ++_count;
        return true;
}
```

NOTE   The term *code duplication* doesn't really convey the true meaning of what happens when an object of a template class instantiated, causing the generation (specialization) of a new template class. In reality, the code in the template is replicated by substituting the actual arguments specified at the time of instantiation in place of the template arguments and the generated code is compiled. Therefore, code for a new class is being generated using the existing template code. The generated code might look very similar to the original template code but the type of the generated class is entirely different. The term *code duplication* (or *code replication*) throughout this chapter refers to the entire process of code generation, type checking of the generated code, etc.

Here are some important points to remember about generic classes.

1. A generic class represents an infinite set of classes. It can be instantiated with any actual argument in place of the formal argument. Every instantiation of a generic class creates a new class with the same interface and implementation but with the actual argument replacing every reference to the formal argument.

2. A generic class can depend on any number of formal arguments (even though it is not very common to see more than two to five).

3. Even though a generic class specifies the formal arguments as classes, actual instantiations are not restricted only to classes. A generic class can be instantiated with built-in types such as int, char, etc.

4. Because the same code contained in the generic class is used in each and every instantiation of the generic class, there is a very high degree of code reuse.

5. If a problem is fixed in the generic class implementation, each and every instantiation of the generic class automatically receives the new code with the fix in it (when the code is recompiled). This allows for single point of code control and ease of maintenance.

6. A generic class does not enjoy any special privileges with the actual generic argument(s) that it receives. It (the generic class) is just another client of the actual arguments that are passed. Any violations of the access rules (such as trying to access a private/protected member of the actual argument) by the generic class is caught by the compiler.

None of these points should be taken lightly. Each one of them has far reaching benefits and some disadvantages if not used correctly. We will discuss in detail the significance of all these issues.

EIFFEL   The concept of a generic class is the same in Eiffel, C++, and Ada but the syntax and their implications are quite different. In fact, the Eiffel syntax is less confusing and Eiffel also supports constrained genericity, which we shall discuss later. Here is the declaration of class TList in Eiffel.

```
class TLIST [G]  — G is the generic argument for the generic class TLIST
creation
    make  — how to create objects (similar to C++ constructor)
feature
    make is
       — Code to create TLIST objects
feature
HowMany : INTEGER is  — How many elements are stored on the list?
    do
       — Code for the operation
    end


— Append a new node to the list (at the tail)
Append (newElementToAdd : G) is
    do
       — Code for the operation
    end

— Prepend a new node to the list (at the head)
Prepend (newElementToAdd : G) is
    do
       — Code for the operation
    end
```

To instantiate an object of TLIST of integers we write

```
INTLIST : TLIST [INTEGER]
```

It is clear from this example that in Eiffel, a pair of [ ] following a class name signals a generic class. The generic argument(s) are contained within the [and]. Definitely, this syntax looks elegant and is easy to understand. This style of using genericity is called *Unconstrained Genericity* because there are no restrictions on the actual generic arguments. Any type can be used as the actual generic argument(s).

NOTE   The argument declaration in a generic class, such as TList above states that the argument is a class. But it does not imply that only a true class must be used as the actual argument. Any other type (including language defined types and other generic classes) can be used as the actual argument. One can create TList <int> without any problems. However, the converse is not true; if a generic class states that one of the formal arguments is a specific type, then the actual argument must be of that type—it cannot be anything else.

GENERIC TYPES AND CODE DUPLICATION

As mentioned earlier, in C++, every time a new TList object is *instantiated* with a different argument for the formal template argument AType, the entire code of the TList class is duplicated by substituting the actual argument in place of AType. Here is an example.

```
void f()
{
      TList <TPerson> pList;   // a list of TPersons
      TList <TCourse> cList;   // a list of TCourse
      TList <int>iList1;       // a list of integers
      TList <double>dList;     // list of doubles
      TList <int>      iList2; // another int list
}
```

In this example, we have *specialized* TList with four different types—TPerson, TCourse, int, and double. Under C++, the process of creating a new template class by supplying actual template arguments is called *template instantiation*. This will duplicate the code of TList four times, once for each of the types TPerson, TCourse, int, and double. If the size of the implementation code for TList is, say 4K bytes, then the actual size of the code because of these instantiations would be 16K bytes (4*4). Note that TList is instantiated twice with the int argument but the actual code for TList<int> need be generated only once.

Usually, the implementation code of a normal (non template) class is never duplicated because it is pure code (also called *text*) that is never going to change during the execution of a program. Every time a new object is created, memory is allocated for a new copy of the data required for the object. But all objects of a class share the same implementation code. In other words, the implementation code is reused for every object. So every object has its own data members but shares the implementation code with all other objects of the class. Therefore, there is no need to duplicate the implementation code.

But a generic class is not really a true class from which an object can be created. To create an object from a generic class, the programmer must supply the actual argument to replace the formal argument (the generic class argument). And every time an actual class name (or type name) is supplied as an argument for a generic class instantiation, it in effect creates a new class with the actual argument tied to the generic class name. From the example above, one could imagine that four new classes are created:

```
class TList_TPerson { /* implementation code replicated for type
                   TPerson */ };
class TList_TCourse { /* implementation code replicated for type
                   TCourse*/ };
class TList_int { /* implementation code replicated for type int */ };
class TList_double { /* implementation code replicated for type
                   double */ };
```

In reality, this is what happens in C++. But the compiler uses some other name for each of the generated classes (very similar to a *mangled* name).

One might wonder if the duplication of code is really essential. Isn't it possible for the compiler to keep the implementation code in some format such that it can be used with different types without actually duplicating the code? You are not alone if you are thinking on these lines. But until now (August '96), there isn't a C++ compiler that does not duplicate code. We could expect that this might happen in the future when C++ compiler technology evolves further (or maybe never). It is possible to minimize code replication by employing some techniques to be discussed later in this chapter.

EIFFEL   Unlike C++, in Eiffel, the generic class code is almost never replicated. The Eiffel compiler has the smarts to keep only one copy of the code that is shared among all the different instantiations of a generic class. This is one big advantage with Eiffel. Code duplication may not appear to be a big problem for most programmers but it has some adverse effects in big software systems, as we shall see later. But, along with these benefits come some disadvantages. For example, template member specialization, which is allowed in C++, is not possible in Eiffel.

CONTRACT BETWEEN A GENERIC CLASS IMPLEMENTOR AND CLIENTS

Until now there was a clear boundary between a class implementor and her clients. One could implement some class X and give it to clients who just create objects of X and use the public interface of X to do whatever they wanted to accomplish. The implementation of class X did not have any dependency on the client (programmers who create objects of X). But this principle doesn't hold good with generic classes as we are about to discover.

When a generic class is implemented, it uses a place holder (a dummy class name) in place of the actual class name that would be supplied by the client who instantiates an object of the generic class. In the examples above, clients instantiated different TList classes by supplying various actual arguments for the formal generic parameter, AType. A client of a generic class has more responsibilities compared to a non-generic class client. When a client instantiates an object of a generic class, she must provide the name of a class (or a built-in type name) for the formal argument. The generic class implementation will use the client supplied class in place of the formal generic class arguments in the generated code.

It is important to remember that in our **TList** implementation, we do not copy the client supplied object. The address of the object is stored on the list, not a copy of the original object. The client is free to modify the object even when it is on the list. Trouble arises when an object that resides on a list is silently deleted by the client without removing it from the list. In other words, it is a *reference based list* and not a *value based list*. Details on this topic can be found in Chapter 12. Let us analyze a particular member function of class **TList** to illustrate the contract between the client and **TList** implementation.

```
template <class AType> class TList {
    public:
        AType* Remove(AType* elementToRemove);
        bool Exists(const AType& thisObject) const;
        // and many more methods
};
```

Let us consider the implementation of methods **Remove** and **Exists**. The member function **Remove** is provided so that clients can remove an object placed on the list by them (or by other clients). Since we never copy client's objects when they are placed on the list, what is the correct way to search for a specified object on the list? We could search the **TList** looking for an object with the same address as the one passed as the argument to **Remove**. Here is the implementation.

```
template <class AType>
AType* TList<AType>::Remove(AType* elementToRemove)
{
    TListNode<AType>* currentNode = _head;
    AType* result = 0;
    while (currentNode != 0) {
        // Compare address of object on list with the user's object
        if (currentNode->_userData == elementToRemove) {
            result = currentNode->_userData; // save it
            // Now delink the node from the list (manipulate pointers)
            // Code not shown to keep the example simple
            // Finally delete the TListNode
            delete currentNode; // Remember that it was dynamically
                    // allocated when we added a new element to the list
        }
    }
    return result;
}
```

The scheme here is quite simple. We only store the address of objects and so removing objects from the list is also based on address comparison. As a result of this scheme, if the same object is stored on the list more than once, then only the first one (located during the search) is removed from the list. There could be another member function **RemoveAllInstances** that removes every occurrence of the object on the list. This is one simple implementation of **Remove**. Many other styles of implementation are possible.

Now let us turn our attention to the member function **Exists**. This function checks if a *specified* object exists on the list. How do we find if an object exists on the list? One simple implementation would be to follow the same scheme as **Remove**. We can look for the address of the object in the list, but the client might be looking for an object that is identical to the one passed in as the argument, but probably not one with the same address. It is possible that the list contains an object with the same data as the one passed but they may be physically different objects. In other words, the objects might be equal but not the same object. This topic came up earlier in Chapter 4 during the discussion of equality and identity of objects. For example, consider this piece of code:

```
void f()
{
    // The code for TPerson is in Chapter-5. It is not repeated here to
    // keep the example simple
    TPerson Einstein("Albert Einstein", 123456789, "3-14-1879",
                                        "Ulm, Germany");
    TList<TPerson> personList;
    personList.Append(&Einstein); // Add Einstein object to our list

    TPerson Bond("James Bond", 007, "07-24-66", "Fiction");
    personList.Append(&Bond); // Add Bond object to our list

    TPerson p3(Bond); // Make a copy of Bond object

    bool result = personList.Exists(p3); // What should be the outcome?
}
```

What should be the outcome of personList.Exists(p3) be? Should it be true or false?

There are two schemes possible here. If we search the list for a TPerson object with the same address as p3 then our search will fail because p3 was never put on the list. So the outcome of Exists will be false. On the other hand if we search the personList for a TPerson with the same state (name, address, etc.) as p3 then we shall succeed because p3 is nothing but a true copy of Bond, and Bond is already on the list. So the outcome of Exists will be true. So what is the correct approach to this problem?

Both schemes mentioned above are correct. But their implementations are entirely different. Here is one implementation using address based comparison:

```
// Check if the specified object exists on the list. Return true if it
// exists. This implementation uses address based look up. We compare the
// address of the object supplied with those on the list. If they are the
// same, then the object is on the list.

template <class AType>
bool TList<AType>::Exists(const AType& thisObject) const
{
    TListNode<AType>* currentNode = _head;
    AType* result = 0;
    while (currentNode != 0) {
        // Compare address of object on list with the address of
        // user's object
        if (currentNode->_userData == &thisObject) {
            return true; // Found it
        }
        currentNode = currentNode->_next;
    }
```

```
    return false; // Search failed
}
```

In this implementation, two pointers are being compared. This comparison is intrinsically supported by the language. No help from the programmer is required. The disadvantage is that this scheme only allows the client to search for objects that have been placed on the list. With this implementation, our search for **p3** above will return false because **p3** was never placed on the list.

Now let us look at the other implementation.

```
// Check if the specified object exists on the list. Return true if it
// exists. This implementation uses object based look up. We compare the
// the object supplied with each object on the list. If they are the same,
// then the object is on the list. This scheme does not use address
// comparison. It relies on the objects to compare themselves.

template <class AType>
bool
TList<AType>::Exists(const AType& thisObject) const
{
    TListNode<AType>* currentNode = _head;
    AType* result = 0;
    while (currentNode != 0) {
        // Compare object on list with the user's object
        if ( *currentNode->_userData == thisObject) {
            return true; // Found it
        }
        currentNode = currentNode->_next;
    }
    return false; // Search failed
}
```

What is really different about this scheme, you might wonder. The difference is between the name of an object and the contents of the object. One scheme returns true if the name **p3** is on the list and the other scheme returns true if an object with the same contents (for example **Bond**) is on the list. Suffice it to say that these two schemes are drastically different. The latter scheme puts more burden on the client.

Address comparison required no support from the objects. But how do we compare objects? For example, how can we compare one **TPerson** object with another? Only the implementor of class **TPerson** knows the issues involved in comparing **TPerson** objects. Therefore, we must rely on the **TPerson** class for comparing **TPerson** objects. The statement

```
        if ( *currentNode->_userData == thisObject)
```

invokes the comparison function on the class **AType**. The expression (*currentNode->_userData) dereferences the pointer to **AType** giving us an **AType** object. We don't have the entire object on the list but we have a pointer to it. Therefore, we must dereference the pointer to get the complete object. In a **TList<TPerson>**, **AType** is **TPerson**. So we end up comparing the object on the list with the object supplied to the member function Exists. To carry out the comparison, we are invoking the operator== on two TPerson objects. This operator== should be a member function of TPerson or an ordinary non-member function (it could be a friend function of TPerson too).

```
// Possible alternatives for operator==
// Case 1. operator== is a member function
class TPerson {
    public:
        // All other details not shown
        bool operator==(const TPerson& otherPerson) const;
};

// Case 2. operator== is a friend function
bool operator==(const TPerson& first, const TPerson& second) ;  ❶
class TPerson {
    public:
        // All other details not shown
        friend bool operator==(const TPerson& first,
                               const TPerson& second) ;
        // There is no requirement for this operator== to be a friend
        // function. It can be a free function too. Such a declaration is
        // shown in ❶ above.
};
```

But what if TPerson does not provide an operator== function of any sort? Will the implementation of Exists above compile without errors? Yes, there will be no problem in compiling the implementation code of the member function because in the implementation, AType is a dummy and not a real class. There is no error in that implementation. When a template class is implemented, nothing is known about the template arguments—AType is just a place holder. The compiler just assumes that there is a matching operator== somewhere. The real argument is known only when a template class is instantiated.

But when we try to compile the following code, there will be an error.

```
void f()
{
    // Assume that operator== is not implemented in TPerson

    TPerson p1("Marie Curie", 123456789, "11-7-1867", "Paris, France");
    TList<TPerson> personList;
    // The next statement will cause the generation of the
    // TList<TPerson>::Exists member function from the code in the
    // template class
    bool result = personList.Exist(p1); // This will not compile ❷
}
```

Assuming that TList uses the object comparison scheme for the member function Exists, if there is no operator== in TPerson (or a non-member function operator== accepting two TPerson objects), this code will not compile because when the Exists member function code is generated for TPerson, it cannot find a matching operator==.

```
// Generated code for TList<TPerson>
bool TList<TPerson>::Exists(const TPerson& thisObject) const
{
    TListNode<TPerson>* currentNode = head;
    while (currentNode != 0) {
        // Compare object on list with the user's object
        // Requires an operator== member function in TPerson
        // or a free function operator== accepting two TPerson objects
        if ( *currentNode->_userData == thisObject)
            return true; // Found it
        currentNode = currentNode->next;
    }
    return false; // Search failed
}
```

When the compiler attempts to invoke the operator== it finds that TPerson does not provide any operator==. And there is no non-member function operator== that accepts two TPerson objects either. So we are trying to invoke a non-existent function. In other words, class TList requires that its clients (like TPerson) provide an operator== if they wish to use the member function Exists. If a client (such as TPerson) does not supply a comparison operator, then it is not eligible to use the Exists member function of TList. So there is a dependency between TList and its clients. Notice that the error is detected at the point of call (such as ❷ above), and not during the implementation of the member functions of the template class TList.

Can This Be Considered *Good Design*?

- Is it correct to expect clients of generic classes to provide services to the generic class implementation?
- Is there a better way of solving this problem?

If these questions pop up in your mind, you are not alone. These are common issues faced by designers of C++ template classes.

There is nothing wrong in the design. A template class cannot carry out operations that are applied on the actual template arguments without help from the arguments themselves. Operations such as comparison cannot be implemented by the generic class where true object comparison is required. There is no way a generic class can implement such operations without help from the client.[3] There are many such situations that require help from the client. In reality, allowing the client to specify the correct behavior of the instantiated template class is the hallmark of flexible design. A generic class should not force its policies on the client. Clients must be given the choice to use whatever scheme they like. Some clients may not like to do any extra work to use a generic class (their requirements might be very simple). But other clients might want to provide their own functions to carry out critical operations. The best design is one that allows both groups of clients to coexist in harmony. We need to state any dependencies between the template class (TList) and the template arguments (such as TPerson) very clearly so that there is no room for confusion. It will be even better to provide both version of the Exists function as a pair of

---

[3]By client, I mean the class that is used as the actual argument to the generic class, such as TPerson in these examples.

overloaded functions. One of them could take a pointer to ÁType as the argument and the other one could receive a reference to ÁType.

```
// Will perform true object comparison - Calls operator== of thisObject.
bool Exists(const TPerson& thisObject) const;

// Will only perform address based comparison. Pointers in the list are
// compared with the pointer thisObject. No dependency on client class.
bool Exists(const TPerson* thisObject) const;
```

This would very clearly indicate the scheme followed by each function. It is very important that generic classes document such critical dependencies. Clients of generic classes should not receive any unanticipated errors (or unexpected behavior). Before a client uses a generic class, she must be given all the information about the class so that she is aware of any dependencies. Designing a generic class requires more forethought, responsibility, and a very clear understanding of the usage pattern of the generic class.

> ☞ **A well designed generic class should very clearly document its dependencies (if any) on the actual arguments supplied by the client.**

NOTE   The dependency on the operator== can be solved in at least two different ways.
C++ The class TPerson can provide the operator== function (member or non-member). If a client receives TPerson from some other library and is using it in a list, and TPerson does not provide operator==, there is still a chance of solving the problem. If there is enough information available from TPerson through member functions, a client of TPerson (trying to create a TList of TPerson objects) can use the member functions of TPerson to implement a simple operator== function. For example, the operator== can get the name, address, and birth date from the TPerson object and can carry out the comparison. This scheme only works when enough distinguishing information is available from TPerson to public clients.

EIFFEL   One aspect of generic classes in Eiffel is very different from C++. In C++, the template class can invoke any operations of the actual generic argument(s) that are passed in as long as those operations are available in that class. If that operation is not available in the actual generic argument (template argument) then it will be treated as a compile-time error. But in Eiffel, the generic class is not allowed to make any assumptions about the availability of operations in the formal generic arguments because it is not guaranteed that the actual generic argument supports those operations. The generic class can use the generic argument only in assignment operations (on both sides of =), as an actual argument in a function call, and in boolean comparison expressions. This is because, unlike C++, Eiffel does not duplicate the code and, hence, there is no way to type check every instantiation of a generic class to verify the validity of the operations. Therefore, a generic class can only use those operations (on a actual generic argument) that are guaranteed to be available for all types. Assignment and comparison are very general operations that can be applied to objects as well as language defined types. Hence, only such general operations are allowed on generic class arguments.

     Let's analyze the following code for a moment:

```
main()
{

    TList<int> intList; // A list of integers
    int i = 10;

    intList.Exist(i); // Use object comparison and not address comparison
}
```

Will this code compile and run correctly?

The object intList is a list of int (language type). The Exists member function for intList will generate the following code.

```
// Generated code for TList<int>
bool TList<int>::Exists(const int& thisObject) const
{
    TListNode<int>* currentNode = _head;
    while (currentNode != 0) {
        // Compare object on list with the user's object
        if ( *currentNode->_userData == thisObject)
            return true; // Found it
        currentNode = currentNode->_next;
    }
    return false; // Search failed
}
```

The important statement here is

```
if ( *currentNode->userData == thisObject)
```

The argument on the right hand side (RHS) is an int and the expression (*currentNode->userData) also results in an int. So we are comparing an int with another int. We know very well that comparison between language defined types is carried out by the language (compiler). There is no dependency on the client code in this case. Our TList class can be used for built-in types (int, double, char, etc.) without any problems. It is interesting to note what made this possible. For comparing objects we are using the == operator directly. When the compiler parses the == operation, it will try to invoke the operator== function if the operands are true objects (implemented by the programmer). But if the operands are language defined types, then it is easy for the compiler to carry out the operation without any help from the programmer. This flexibility has been achieved because we used the == operator. It is interesting to see what happens if we had used a member function, say IsEqual instead of operator== for comparison.

Operators vs Member Functions in Generic Class Implementations

Consider this new implementation of Exists for TList.

```
// Check if the specified object exists on the list. Return true if it
// exists. This implementation uses object based look up. We compare the
// object supplied with each object on the list. If they are the same, then
```

```
// the object is on the list. This scheme does not use address comparison.
// It relies on the objects to compare themselves. Clients must implement
// the method IsEqual in their class to use this method on TList objects
// For example, class TPerson must implement the method as follows.
//       bool IsEqual (const TPerson& other) const
//          { compare other with this and return true if they are equal }

template <class AType>
bool TList<AType>::Exists(const AType& thisObject) const
{
    TListNode<AType>* currentNode = _head;
    while (currentNode != 0) {
        // Compare object on list with the user's object
        if ( currentNode->_userData->IsEqual ( thisObject) )
        // OR if ( *(currentNode->userData).IsEqual (thisObject) )
            return true; // Found it
        currentNode = currentNode->_next;
    }
    return false; // Search failed
}
```

In this code, (currentNode->userData) gives us a pointer to the user object whose address is on the list. The expression

```
(currentNode->userData->IsEqual(thisObject))
```

invokes the member function IsEqual on that user object passing thisObject as the other argument. We are using pointers to objects in this statement. The other style (shown in comments) uses objects instead of pointers by using dereferenced pointers. No matter what style you use, the intent is to invoke the IsEqual member function on an object on the list passing it the thisObject argument.

In this implementation, we have to state clearly that TList::Exists depends on the IsEqual member function in the client's class. If the client's class (such as TPerson) provides this IsEqual member function then no problem is encountered while compiling and running programs that use TList objects. If the client of TList does not implement the IsEqual method, then generation of the TList::Exists member function will fail resulting in a compile-time error.

Now consider creating a TList of integers with this new implementation of TList::Exists.

```
main()
{
    TList<int> intList; // A list of integers
    int i = 10;

    intList.Exist(i); // Will this compile?
}
```

The generated code for TList<int>::Exists is shown below.

```
bool
TList<int>::Exists(const int& thisObject) const
```

```
{
        TListNode<int>* currentNode = _head;
        while (currentNode != 0) {
            // Compare object on list with the user's object
            if ( currentNode->_userData->IsEqual ( thisObject ) ) {
            // OR  if ( *(currentNode->_userData).IsEqual ( thisObject ) )
                    return true; // Found it
            currentNode = currentNode->_next;
        }
        return false; // Search failed
}
```

The statement

```
        if ( currentNode->userData->IsEqual ( thisObject ) )
```

tries to invoke the member function IsEqual on userData, which is an int. But we know very well that int is not an object. How can we possibly invoke a member function on a non-object? Definitely, this generated code will not compile. We have painted ourselves into a corner by using a member function (IsEqual) of the client's class in the implementation of the generic class TList. We did not encounter any problem while using == because operator== is directly supported for built-in types by the language. This is one advantage of using operators as opposed to member functions in the implementation of a generic class. Operators such as ==, !=, etc. are provided by the language for all the built-in types. Therefore, a generic class generated for built-in types that uses any of the language defined operators will compile without errors. Therefore, it is beneficial to use operators rather than member functions in the implementation of generic classes.

☞ **Use operators (==, !=, +, -, etc.) on client objects in the implementation of generic classes. Try to avoid member functions (such as IsEqual above). This will allow for the generation of the generic class for language defined types without any help from the client.**

This is one more benefit of operator overloading. Many frequently used operators have a well defined implementation in the language. Hence, generic class instantiations for built-in types will work correctly.

NOTE   There are other solutions to this problem. Instead of using ordinary member functions we can use non-member, global functions to do the comparison. Such functions can be implemented for language defined types also. Later in this chapter, we shall see even more sophisticated solutions involving comparator objects. Designers should know all the alternatives and pick the right one based on their (and client's) needs.

The Alternative Solution—Specialization of Generic Classes

There is another solution to the problem discussed above. It involves specialization of classes and functions. Assume that a team has already implemented a TList class that uses the IsEqual member function call in the implementation.[4] Further, assume that we don't

---

[4]This discussion holds good in cases where a library implements TList using IsEqual member function calls.

have the flexibility or the time to change the entire implementation to use operator== in-stead of IsEqual. Such situations are very common in commercial software development. Sometimes, we have to learn to live with software that we know is not really flexible. We invent schemes to work around them. This is one such situation.

A client wants to use TList<int>, but the generation of TList<int>::Exists will not compile because type int is not a class. We know that the problem is with the generation of the Exists method. Our problem will disappear if we can prevent the generation of TList<int>::Exists from the generic code of TList. But, can we implement a special TList<int>::Exists member function? The answer is a resounding yes. This is called *explicit template specialization*.

TEMPLATE SPECIALIZATIONS

As we already know, a generic class represents an infinite set of classes. It can be gener-ated for any type. But for a specific type, we may not like the generated code. This might be due to a couple of reasons.

1. The generated code does not work for some specific type(s).

2. The generated code is inefficient for specific type(s).

We still want to use the generic class for other types but not with those types that cause problems when compiled (or executed, i.e., not fast enough). We are only interested in changing the implementation of the generic class for a specific type without changing the interface or behavior of the generic class. For example, many clients might be using TList with different types. A modified implementation for TList<int> must still retain the look, feel, and behavior of any other TList. Only the internal implementation of TList<int> must be changed. The solution here is to *specialize* the template code. We can specialize the entire template class or just a member function that does not compile for a specific type. Implementing code for a specific instantiation of a template class is called *explicit template specialization*.

Specialization of a Template Member Function

In the TList example above, the offending (generated) member function is Exists (for class TList<int>). What if we prevent the compiler from generating this member function. The only way to do that is to provide a special implementation of TList<int>::Exists. If the compiler encounters this specialized member function before it generates the default implementation from the generic code of the class, then it will not proceed with the gener-ation of TList<int>::Exists.

Here is a specialization of TList<int>::Exists.

```
// Specialization of TList::Exists for type int
// This implementation does not depend on the IsEqual method. Instead
// it lets the language do the comparison.

bool TList<int>::Exists(const int& otherInt) const
```

```
{
        TListNode<int>* currentNode = _head;
        while (currentNode != 0) {
            // Compare int on list with the user supplied otherInt
            if ( *currentNode->_userData == otherInt ) return true;
                // Found it
            currentNode = currentNode->_next;
        }
        return false; // Search failed
}
```

There is nothing magical about this. All we have done is to rewrite the implementation of the Exists member function, which does not use the IsEqual member function for the TList<int> class. Other than that, the code is identical to the previous implementation. Here (*currentNode->_userData) gives us the value of the integer and we are comparing that with the other integer otherInt, the user supplied integer variable. Now the code below will compile without any errors.

```
main()
{
    TList<int> intList; // A list of integers
    int i = 10;

    bool result = intList.Exist(i);
    // Will compile because of the specialized implementation above
}
```

Note that it is not necessary to provide the entire implementation of the specialized member function before the call to it in main() above. We can keep this implementation anywhere we like. All we have to do is to provide the signature of the specialized member function before the call.

```
bool TList<int>::Exists(const int& otherInt) const; // Just declare it
main()
{
    TList<int> intList; // A list of integers
    int i = 10;

    intList.Exist(i);
    // Will compile because of the specialized member function declaration
    // above
}
```

We just need to prevent the compiler from generating the default TList<int>::Exists from the generic class TList. The prototype of Exists above tells the compiler that such a function already exists. Once the compiler recognizes the existence of the function, it does not (and should not) generate the function using the generic implementation in TList. As far as the linker is concerned, it could care less as to who implemented the function. The advantage of just providing the function declaration is that we can keep all such special implementations in one place, giving us more control over the source code.

CAUTION   There is only one caveat here. The implementation of TList<int>::Exists assumes
that we know how the generic class TList works. We are using the private data members
in this implementation. This is all fine if you (or your team) is also the implementor of the
generic class TList. If you don't have access to the source code of TList (for whatever
reason), then even if you know about the private data members, you will not be able to
implement the code above because you wouldn't know how the data members are used in
the implementation of TList (don't forget encapsulation!). If you are in such a situation,
then your implementation of Exists above must use member functions of TList to navigate the list (or use an iterator if one is available). This problem doesn't arise in most
cases because when generic classes are used, every new generic class instantiation causes
generation of a new class that requires access to the source code of the generic class in
C++. If that is the case, all we have to do is to copy the code of TList<AType>::Exists
and modify it for TList<int>. In fact, that is what we did for the example above. But just
having access to the source code is not enough to solve this problem under all circumstances. In order to modify and implement the specialized code, one must clearly understand the existing implementation, which is a nontrivial task. Modifying the existing code
of a generic class is a very complex task, not to be taken lightly. Moreover, if the TList
class depends on many other classes, then TList<int>::Exists needs to understand the dependencies clearly to provide the correct implementation. Having the facility to specialize
a specific member function of a template class is not very useful if you don't understand
the existing implementation clearly.

Another Alternative: Separating Comparison of Objects

Another way to solve the List.Exists() problem would be to factor out the dependency on
comparison of objects in the member function Exists(), in anticipation that clients might
want to customize the comparison operation. So, instead of directly comparing objects,
member function Exists() calls another function, Compare() supplying it the arguments
to be compared. This way clients only have to rewrite the function Compare() without
having to know about TList internals. The skeleton code is shown below.

```
template <class AType>
bool
TList<AType>::Exists(const AType& thisObject) const
{
    TListNode<AType>* currentNode = _head;
    while (currentNode != 0) {
        // Compare object on list with the user's object using the non-
        // member function Compare() Compare should return:
        // 0 - if objects are equal, 1 if not equal
        if ( Compare(*currentNode->_userData, thisObject) == 0 )
            return true; // Found it
        currentNode = currentNode->_next;
    }
    return false; // Search failed
}
```

With this scheme, a client can write a Compare() function for any type and supply their
own comparison schemes without worrying about the TList internals. Note that we do not

make Compare() a member function because we want this scheme to work even for primitive types.

The general scheme for Compare() is:

```
template <class AType>
int Compare(const AType& first, const AType& second)
  {
      return (first == second) ? 0:1;
  }
```

When TList<int> is created, a Compare() function accepting two integers is also instantiated, as shown below:

```
int Compare(const int& first, const int& second)
  {
      return (first == second) ? 0:1;
  }
```

Now, when a specific TList is instantiated and the client calls Exists() on it, the Compare() function gets called. The Compare() function that is called might have come from the general template above or it could be a specialized function supplied by the client.

NOTE   As of this writing (August '96) many compilers still don't support specialization of template class member functions. But it is very much part of the ANSI C++ draft standard.

The example above brings out another nuance of generic classes. Not all types work with generic classes. Definitely, TList<TPerson> and such worked correctly (at least it compiled correctly), but there is no guarantee that a generic class will work with *all* types. The TList<int> above proves the point. Designers of generic classes must document such limitations. Imagine what happens if there is no such documentation. We start using the generic class TList in our project extensively and everything seems to be going smoothly until one fine day (very close to the project deadline date) someone tries to use TList<int> and hell breaks loose. The whole team starts to panic because the new code does not even compile. It is a good design practice to clearly state such limitations more than once (in different parts of the implementation and interface).

☞ **Very clearly, document all limitations/restrictions/assumptions made within generic classes. Without such documentation, clients might face difficulties when using the generic class.**

The problem here is that a generic class is quite different from a non-generic class. Once a non-generic class implementation code compiles and links without errors, it is guaranteed to work correctly no matter how the clients use it. In fact, the implementation code of a non-generic class is not compiled every time an object of the class is instantiated. But it is an entirely different story with generic classes. When a generic class object is instantiated with a new type (which has not been used before), new code is generated with the actual argument supplied and the generated code is compiled. There is every chance that this generated code will not compile. And remember that the code is generated as part of the client's program. So the errors are reported in the client's program.

Generic classes require more exhaustive testing than normal classes. They must be tested with a wide variety of actual class arguments, including language defined types, normal classes, other template classes, constant values, etc. Only such testing will bring to fore any deficiencies and limitations of generic classes.

☞ **Generic classes must be tested very thoroughly before giving them to clients. Testing a generic class is more tedious and time consuming than testing a non-generic class.**

This is because a generic class really represents an infinite set of classes. Every new type argument passed to a generic class results in the creation of a new class with the same interface as the original class but with a slightly different implementation. There is no guarantee that the implementation will work as documented for every new class generated. Hence the need for more testing.

What if One Can't Specialize a Specific Template Member Function?

Due to the problems discussed above (complex code, inaccessible source code, too many dependencies on other classes, compiler doesn't allow it, etc.), we may not be able to specialize a specific member function of a generic class for some type for which the generic class code does not work. Should that stop us from using the generic class for that type? The simple answer to that question is NO, we must continue to use the generic class. This is because of interface compatibility. Remember that many functions/classes might already be using the TList generic class in their interface. Consider the example below.

```
template <class AType>
void DisplayList(const TList<AType> theList)
{
    // Code to display a list in a decorated window
}
```

There could be many such useful functions (and classes) that are built around the interface of the generic classes. If we stop using the generic class TList<int> because it doesn't work for the type int, then we will not be able to use the different facilities offered by these functions that use the generic class in their interface. This is not a trivial problem because, as we already know, a class depends on many other classes for its implementation. One must adhere to the published interface of all those classes that we depend on. The rest of the project team might already be using the published interface and every TList is expected to honor that usage. Now, if we stop using the TList<int>, we will be violating the accepted behavior and we will be forced to implement too many functions to support a new list type that might be implemented. Furthermore, consider clients of TList. They (clients) might be using TList in different situations in many different ways and they might have written many classes and functions that use TList in their interface. It would be expected of all TList instantiations to use those classes and functions for a well defined, uniform interface. Just because TList<int> does not compile, we should not stop using TList<int> and implement another class (say TIntList). We would then be violating the accepted usage and none of the functions that work with TList<AType> as the argument would be able to accept TIntList because there is no relationship between TList and TIntList. Therefore, we will be unable to pass a TIntList object where a TList object is expected. All the code that is already implemented to support TList<AType> will not support TIntList. All the advantages of reusable code is completely lost when TIntList is used. If TIntList has a completely different interface and behavior when compared with TList<AType>, then anyone wishing to use TIntList will be forced to understand a new class (TIntList) and clients cannot use their existing knowledge of TList with TIntList. Because of these serious shortcomings, we definitely don't want to stop using TList<int> completely.

TEMPLATE CLASS SPECIALIZATION

We cannot use the generic class TList<AType> to generate TList<int> because of the problems stated earlier. In other words, we need a TList<int> but not the one generated from generic class TList<AType>. This is where template class specialization helps. We can provide a specialized implementation of a template for specific template arguments. For example, we can write a specialized implementation of TList<int> as follows:

```
// THIS IS THE TEMPLATE CLASS DECLARATION
template <class AType>
class TList {
    public:
            TList(AType* storeThisElement);
            TList(const TList<AType>& copy);
            TList& operator=(const TList<AType>& assign);
            virtual ~TList();

            // How many elements are stored on the list?
            unsigned int HowMany() const;
            // Append a new node to the list (at the tail)
            // Return true if successful
            bool Append (AType* newElementToAdd);
            // Prepend a new node to the list (at the head)
            // Return true if successful
            bool Prepend (AType* newElementToAdd);
            AType* Remove(AType* elementToRemove);
            bool Exists(const AType& thisObject) const;
            // and many more methods
};

// THIS IS A SPECIALIZATION OF THE ENTIRE TEMPLATE CLASS TList FOR type
// int

class TList<int> {
    public:
            TList(int*  storeThisElement);
            TList(const TList<int>&  copy);
            TList& operator=(const TList<int>&  assign);
            virtual ~TList();

            // How many elements are stored on the list?
```

```
        unsigned int HowMany() const;
        // Append a new node to the list (at the tail)
        // Return true if successful
        bool Append (int* newElementToAdd);
        // Prepend a new node to the list (at the head)
        // Return true if successful
        bool Prepend (int* newElementToAdd);
        int* Remove(int* elementToRemove);
        bool Exists(const int& thisObject) const;
        // and many more methods
    private:
        // Can be anything that this class needs. Need not be the same as
        // the general template class.
};
```

The specialization provides a new implementation for class **TList** where the template argument type is **int**. This is called *Specialization of a Template class*. Here is the definition of the **Exists** member function:

```
// Specialization of TList for type int
// This implementation does not depend on the IsEqual method. Instead it
// lets the language do the comparison.

bool
TList<int>::Exists(const int& otherInt) const
{
    TListNode<int>* currentNode = _head;
    while (currentNode != 0) {
        // Compare int on list with the user supplied otherInt
        if ( *currentNode->_userData == otherInt))
            return true; // Found it
        currentNode = currentNode->_next;
    }
    return false; // Search failed
}
```

Note that a specialization of a template class need not have the same set of member functions as the general template, but it is a good practice to have the same interface. That way, a client can just use the specialized implementation just like the general template class (nothing new to learn about the specialized class).

☞ **Try to keep the interface of specialized template class the same as the general template class.**

The code below will now use the **TList<int>** class declared above.

```
main()
{
    TList<int> intList; // Automatically uses the Specialization above
    int i = 10;

    intList.Exist(i); // Will compile because of the specialized
                        // implementation above
}
```

This is a very common practice when using templates. When a general template class fails to work with specific types (or isn't good enough), a specialized implementation is the way to go. Many template libraries provide specialized implementations of template class for built-in types along with the general template implementation. This makes it easy for the clients to use the template class for all types.

☞ **When implementing a template class (library), if your implementation does not work for specific types, consider providing a specialized implementation for such types along with the general implementation. You will save your clients a lot of time and trouble.**

Any client can provide a specialized implementation of a template class even if she is not knowledgeable about the implementation of it. All the specialization is doing is implementing a new class for a known type. This implementation needs to work with only one type.

THE CONCEPT OF GENERIC FUNCTIONS

Just like generic classes, we can also create generic functions. A generic class can be instantiated with any template argument(s). On the same lines, a generic function can be called with any argument(s), and each call (with arguments of a new type) causes the generation of a new function. A simple example will clarify the concept.

Consider a general Sort function that can sort an array of integers. Here is a simple implementation using shell sort.

```
void Exchange(int& x, int& y)
{
    int temp = x;
    x = y;
    y = temp;
}


// intarray is a pointer to an array of integers to be sorted.
// nitems is the number of integers to be sorted (the size of the array)
void
Sort(int intarray[], int nitems)
{
    // The Shell Sort algorithm for sorting
    // From Kernighan and Ritchie: The C Programming Language
    for(int gap = nitems/2; gap > 0; gap/=2)
        for(int i=gap; i < nitems; i++)
            for(int j=i - gap;
                    j >= 0 && intarray[j] > intarray[j+gap];
                        j -= gap)
            Exchange(intarray[j], intarray[j+gap]);
}
```

This is a simple function carrying out a simple sort operation for integers. What if we want to sort an array of TCar objects in a garage and an array of TPerson objects in a university? We would have to duplicate the code and replace int with TCar for the garage and repeat the same steps for TPerson. This is repetitive work that is uninteresting, which is best left to a machine. We should be able to write a general Sort function that can be used with any type. That leads us to a template function. We would rewrite Sort as follows in C++:

```
template <class AType>
void
Exchange(AType & x, AType & y)
{
    AType temp = x;
    x = y;
    y = temp;
}

template <class AType>
void
Sort(AType array[], int nitems)
{
    // The Shell Sort algorithm for sorting
    // From Kernighan and Ritchie: C Programming
    // Sort in ascending order
    for(int gap = nitems/2; gap > 0; gap/=2) {
        for(int i=gap; i < nitems; i++) {
            for(int j=i - gap;
                    j >= 0 && array[j] > array[j+gap];
                    j -= gap)
                Exchange(array[j], array[j+gap]);
        }
    }
}
```

The concept here is very similar to the class template concept. Now Sort is a general global function that can be instantiated for any type.[5] Note that Sort is not a member function of any class. The only requirement is that any type to be sorted (AType) support the operator > (greater than), which is used inside the function. This will automatically work for language defined types because operator> is provided by the language. If we want to sort an array of TPerson objects, then class TPerson must have operator> implemented in it (or a non-member function operator> capable of comparing TPerson objects must be available). It is interesting to see how the correct function is generated. Here is a typical usage:

```
main()
{
        int ia[] = {22, 1, 3 ,9, 4, 0, 11 };
        Sort(ia, 7); // Try to sort the array ia
        for (int i =0; i < 7; i++)
        cout << ia[i] << "\t"; // Print the array
}
```

---

[5] Actually, it is global within the namespace where it is declared.

When we call Sort with the array ia, the compiler looks for a matching Sort function but doesn't find one. Next, it looks for a template Sort function that accepts two arguments from which the exact Sort function can be generated. It finds the template Sort implementation above and replaces AType with int and generates a new Sort function. Whenever a call is made to Sort with a new type argument, the compiler generates a new version of Sort from the template function. Also note that Sort internally calls Exchange when it needs to exchange elements in the array. Since Exchange is also a template function, it is generated automatically when needed.

☞ **An appropriate function is automatically generated from a template function based on the arguments used in the call. All such functions generated from a template functions form a set of overloaded functions.**

Again, code is duplicated. It is as though the programmer wrote a number of overloaded Sort functions. These generated functions are nothing but a bunch of overloaded functions. Note that we don't have to provide the implementation of Sort for the code to compile: A declaration is good enough.

```
template <class AType>
void Sort(AType array[], int nItems); // Just declare the template function

main()
{
    int ia[] = {22, 1, 3 ,9, 4, 0, 11 };
    Sort(ia, 7); // Try to sort the array ia
    for (int i =0; i < 7; i++)
            cout << ia[i] << "\t";

    int ib[] = {11, 1, 3 ,9, 6, 0, 101, 2 };
    Sort(ib, 8); // Try to sort the array ib

}
```

Now the compiler generates a call to

```
                    Sort<int> (int* array, int nitems);
```

All that is required is that the code for Sort(int[], int) be available at link time. Note that the second call to Sort with the array ib does not require the generation of another Sort function because the required Sort function has been already generated when the array ia was sorted. Compilers (and linkers) should take care of that.[6]

Just like template classes, a template function can also be specialized. Consider sorting an array of character strings (type char*). This is a bit tricky because comparing strings involves the lexical comparison of each and every character in the strings being compared.[7] Our template Sort wouldn't work because it does not have the intelligence to take care of strings. So we implement a specialized Sort function as follows:

---

[6]Compilers have their own way of keeping track of generated functions and classes. Usually programmers need not have to worry about such details.

[7]This generated Sort function wouldn't work for international character strings (multi-byte character) either.

```
void
Sort<char*> (char* stringArray[], int nItems)
{
     // Special implementation to Sort array of pointers
     // Bubble sort algorithm is used here
     for(int i = 0; i < nItems -1; i++) {
          for(int j=i+1; j < nItems; j++) {
               // strcmp is a library function that lexically compares
               // two strings. It returns 0 if the strings are equal, 1
               // if first string is bigger and -1 if the second one is
               // bigger. The comparison is based on ASCII values of
               // characters.
               if ( strcmp(stringArray[i], stringArray[j]) > 0) {
                    // Swap them
                    char* p = stringArray[i];
                    stringArray[i] = stringArray[j];
                    stringArray[j] = p;
               }
          }
     }
}
```

Here **stringArray** is a pointer to an array of pointers. The array size is again indicated by
the argument **nItems**. Here is an example of usage.

```
int
main()
{
     // Create an array of char pointers
     char* sa[] = { "bbbbbb", "AAAAAA", "111111", "ZZZZZZ" };
     Sort (sa, 4); // Try to sort the array of strings - Uses the
                    // specialized function
     for (int i = 0; i < 4; i++)
          cout << sa[i] << "\t";

     cout << "\n Done\n";

     return 0;
}
```

The output produced is:

```
                         111111 AAAAAA ZZZZZZ bbbbbb
                         Done
```

Again, there is nothing unusual about this **Sort** function. Once the compiler sees the declaration of **Sort** for an array of char pointers, it does not attempt to generate another **Sort**
function from the template—it just uses the one provided by us. Note that there is no call
to **Exchange** in our special **Sort**.

Every member function of a template class is automatically a template function.
Therefore, generation of a new class from a template class causes the generation of a
number of member functions from the template class member functions, very similar to

the generation of Sort above with different arguments. Each of the generated member functions is specialized for the actual type supplied with the instantiation of the template class. For example, when an object of TList<TPerson> is created, every member function of the class TList<AType> is specialized and replicated for the type TPerson.

☞ **Member functions of a template class are automatically template functions.**

INSTANTIATION OF TEMPLATE CLASSES AND MEMBER FUNCTIONS IN C++

When a user of a template class instantiates an object of the class with a specific template argument, don't assume that *all* member functions of the template class for the specific template argument are instantiated; they are not. As per the C++ language specification, a compiler should not instantiate a function or class unless it is required. This only implies that a new class for that template argument is generated from the template class. But the member functions of the template class are not generated unless they are required. If a user instantiates a new object from a template class but never invokes any member functions on the new object, then none of the member functions (except the constructor that was used in the creation of the object and the destructor) of the template class are generated for the new type. This is a compile time decision.

Consider this example.

```
main()
{
    TList<double> dList; // A list of doubles
    double d = 10;
    char c = 'A';

    bool result =- dList.Prepend( &d );
    // The code for TList<double>::Prepend must be generated

    TList<char> charList; // A list of characters
    charList.Append(&c);
    // The code for TList<int>::Append is generated

    TList<int>* pIntList; // Pointer to a list of integers - Generation of
                          // TList<int> not required
}
```

In this example, to create the dList object, the class TList<double> must be generated from the template class TList. As we already know, a constructor is required to create an object of any class. So the appropriate constructor of TList<double> is generated when dList is declared. Every object created must be subject to destruction sometime later using the class destructor. So the destructor of TList<double> is also generated. No other member function of TList<double> should be generated at this point in the code. A couple of statements later, we invoke the member function Prepend on dList. Now the compiler must generate the code for the member function TList<double>::Prepend from the template class TList.[8] Following the same logic, only a constructor and destructor must be generated when charList is created. The member function TList<char>::Append must be generated when Append is invoked on charList. In other words, only those member functions of a template class that are actually called are instantiated for every object created from a template class. All member functions should not be generated. A compiler should not generate a specialized function(s) from a template function unless the definition of the specialized function(s) is required. However, virtual functions may have to be generated even if they are not called explicitly because any virtual function might get invoked polymorphically through a base class interface.[9] In the example above, generation of TList<int> is not required because we have only declared a pointer to it. The pointer is not used with an object of the class inside the function. Therefore, generation of the class TList<int> is not required.

There are a number of major and minor advantages resulting from this *need based code generation*. First of all, unused code is never added to the final executable image making the executables smaller. A smaller program requires less memory to run and it will probably run faster (fewer page faults in a virtual memory system). Second, the program will compile and link faster because there is less code to compile and link (minor advantage).

INSTANTIATION CONTROL SCHEMES AND C++ COMPILERS

When template classes and functions are used (by creating objects and calling template functions with specific arguments), generation of a specialization of the template code is necessary. For example, assume that class TList<AType> is provided along with its implementation source code. Now, when we create an object of TList<int> and invoke the member function Prepend on the object, the compiler must generate the specialized version of the member function—TList<int>::Prepend(). The first time a function is called (template member function or normal template function), the code for the specialized function must be generated from the source code of the function. With most compilers, automatic generation of the actual class/function from the template code is the default. We already know that generation of the specialization definitely requires the source code of the template function/class. But what if (for some reason) the source code is not available for the function being called? How can we still call the function and defer the generation of the specialized function code? We want to tell the compiler to place a call to the function but not to try generating the actual code of the specialized function.

---

[8]Code is really generated only if automatic template code generation option (which is usually the default) has been turned on during compilation. If automatic template code generation has been turned *off*, the compiler inserts a call to the function (TList<double>::Prepend) in the code being compiled. At link time, the code for this function must come from one of the modules being linked. Otherwise, it will result in a link error (unresolved external).

[9]It is not absolutely necessary that a compiler generate *all* virtual functions. It is up to the implementation of the compiler to decide what virtual functions to instantiate.

Let us analyze another scenario where generation of specialization causes problems. First, remember that generation of the same function specialization (by the compiler or the user) more than once in a compilation unit is an error. This is identical to defining a normal function twice in a compilation unit, which causes a *redefinition error*. Now consider the case where we have a C++ file **a.cpp**, which uses the template class **TList** as follows:

```
// File a.cpp
#include "List.h"    // Contains the declaration of TList<AType.
#include "List.cpp" // Contains TList implementation code.
void f()
{
    TList<double> dList; // A list of doubles
    double d = 10;

    bool result = dList.Prepend(&d);
    // The code for TList<double>::Prepend is generated
}
```

The code for **TList<double>::Prepend** is generated in this file. The compiled file **a.obj** contains the object code.

Now consider another file **b.cpp**, which contains the following code:

```
// File b.cpp
#include "List.h" // Contains the declaration of TList<AType.
#include "List.cpp" // Contains TList implementation code.
void g()
{
    TList<double> myList; // A list of doubles
    double dx = 10;

    bool result = dList.Prepend(&dx);
    // The code for TList<double>::Prepend is generated
}
```

The code for **TList<double>::Prepend** is generated in this file also. The compiled file **b.obj** contains the object code.

There is no relation between the files **a.cpp** and **b.cpp**. It might very well have been written by two different programmers who aren't even aware of what the other is doing with **TList**. The usage of **TList** by both of them is perfectly legal and correct. Now consider another program that needs to call both functions **g()** and **f()**. Let us say it resides in file **main.cpp**.

```
void f(); // Prototype of the function
void g();
main()
{
    // Some code here
    g(); // Call g
    //..
    f(); // call f
}
```

We need to link main.obj with a.obj and b.obj to resolve the calls to f() and g(). There is nothing unusual about that either (Fig. 9-6).

But this causes problems. The specialized function TList<double>::Prepend (and possibly other functions of TList) exists in both a.obj and b.obj. As soon as the linker encounters the second definition of TList<double>::Prepend, it will generate an error message (or warning) about the multiple definitions and an executable module will not be generated. This is where the trouble starts. When compiled independently, both a.cpp and b.cpp compile without any errors but the linker isn't happy with the situation. If we did not include the source code of TList in a.cpp or b.cpp they will not compile because generation of TList<double>::Prepend is needed in both files. There is no way we can overcome this problem without some help from the compiler and/or linker.

If we somehow generate the code for Prepend in only one of the files (a.obj or b.obj), then our problem will go away. Still, we need to let the compiler know that we are calling TList<double>::Prepend in each of the files so we can overcome the problem by generating the specialized code in one of the files (a.cpp or b.cpp) and just using the code (generated in the other file) in the other. Let's assume that we are going to generate the code only in b.cpp. When compiling a.cpp, we don't want to generate the code for the class TList<double>. We achieve this by not including the TList implementation code in a.cpp.

```
// Modified File a.cpp
#include "List.h" // Contains the definition of TList<AType>.
// TList implementation code intentionally not included
void f()
{
    TList<double> dList; // A list of doubles
    double d = 10;

    bool result = dList.Prepend( &d );
    // The code for TList<double>::Prepend is NOT generated
}
```

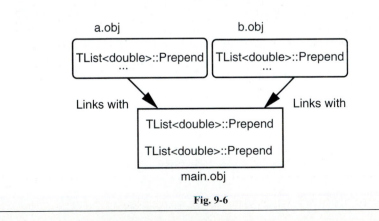

Fig. 9-6

Now the compiler is unable to generate the code for class **TList<double>** because it does not see the implementation code of **TList**. A call to **TList<double>::Prepend** is still generated in **a.obj** but it is unresolved. File **b.cpp** remains the same. When **main.obj**, **a.obj**, and **b.obj** are linked together, there are no multiple definitions of any functions and the final executable is generated. This is one possible solution. Note that class **TList** must be completely defined to create an object of type **TList<double>**, but the source code of the implementation should not be included.

There is another solution to this problem, which is more elegant and powerful. In the example above, what if we cannot separate the implementation code from the class definition code for the template class **TList**? Both the class definition and implementation might be in the same file **List.h**. It is also possible that one of the *included* files includes (directly or indirectly) the implementation code of **TList**, causing the generation of the specialized function code. When we are dealing with a large number of files (created by a team of programmers) it is very hard to control template instantiations. It is even harder for the programmer to determine exactly what to (and what not to) instantiate in her code. This is a very cumbersome task in cases where the code is constantly being modified. Moreover, consider the case where we don't want to generate specialized functions in each and every file. Instead, every template specialization that is required is generated in one separate file and linked with the other modules in the final link phase. This gives us more control over template instantiations because all instantiations are in one file. *No other file in the project should generate any specialized function code even if the source code is available when the file is compiled.* We should be able to tell the compiler not to generate template specialization code (on a per compilation unit basis). Most compilers automatically generate the specialization code as soon as an object is created.[10] This is the default mode. For our scheme to work correctly, we do not want automatic code generation in all but one compilation unit (file). The compiler must provide an option to disable automatic template code generation. Some compilers (that I have used) don't provide an option to disable automatic template code generation. If you need this facility but your compiler doesn't provide such an option, you can either get a better compiler or force the compiler vendor to fix the problem (provided you can wait until they fix it). Or, you could use a set of #ifdef directives and disable the inclusion of the implementation code. This is done by placing an #ifdef directive just before the implementation code starts in a file. For example, we can put the interface and implementation of **TList** in **List.h** and control code generation as follows.

```
// File List.h for manual control of template code generation
template <class AType> class TList {
  // The declaration of member functions not shown for brevity
  //...
};

// Implementation code begins here
#ifdef EXPOSE_LIST_IMPLEMENTATION
```

---

[10]This is usually called *Automatic code generation for template classes (functions)*.

```
    // All the implementation code for TList goes here
    // Or the file List.cpp can be included here

  #endif // EXPOSE_LIST_IMPLEMENTATION
```

With this change, anyone who needs the generation of template code for a **TList** specialization, can just define the identifier **EXPOSE_LIST_IMPLEMENTATION** to make the implementation code available to the compiler, which causes the generation of the template specialization code.[11] This needs to be done for each template class (or file) and can get quite ugly. If your compiler doesn't provide you some decent options, you have no other choice.

With this mechanism, if you want to expose the implementation code of **TList** in a program, the code would look like this:

```
      #define EXPOSE_LIST_IMPLEMENTATION
      // Now TList implementation code is visible
      #include "List.h"
      int main()
      {
          TList<int> il; // code is generated for TList<int>
      }
```

If you have a decent, industrial strength compiler, you wouldn't have to go through all this jugglery —you can just turn off template instantiations. So the solution is to turn off automatic template code generation in all files except the one that instantiates the templates. This file should include all the implementation code for all the templates that need to be instantiated and should explicitly instantiate the required classes and functions. This task is not as complex as it appears. All one has to do is to gather the unresolved symbols reported by the linker and add the corresponding classes (that require instantiation) to the instantiations file. Repeat this step until there are no more linker errors. This process can even be automated by using some scripting language (like awk or tcl).

C++ defines a clear syntax for *explicit instantiation* of template classes. For example, if file **main.cpp** wants to explicitly instantiate **TList<double>**, the code will be as follows.

```
void f(); // Prototypes of the function
void g();
// Explicit instantiation of TList<double>.
// The entire class along with all the member functions is instantiated
// for type double. Complete definition of TList must be available
template class TList<double>;
```

---

[11]If you need to ensure that source code is included only once in any file, then you need one more set of tokens to check if the source code is already included by some other file. This is what is done by header files (.h files) to ensure that a class is declared only once in any compilation unit (the #ifndef construct at the top of header files).

```
main()
{
    // Some code here
    g(); // Call g
    //..
    f(); // call f

}
```

The statement

```
template class TList<double>;
```

directs the compiler to explicitly instantiate TList<double> from the class template. All member functions of TList<double> (which are not already generated) are instantiated. This is called the *explicit instantiation* of TList from its template. Even functions can be explicitly instantiated as follows.

```
        // Prototype of the template functions
        template <class AType>
        void Sort(AType array[], int sizeOfArray);

        // Explicitly instantiate Sort for type double
        template void Sort<double>(double[], int);
```

With this declaration, the function Sort<double> is generated in the compilation unit that contains this declaration.

There is another inelegant scheme that can be used to eliminate multiple instantiations. In this scheme, the linker is directed to ignore all but the first definition of a function. If a function is instantiated more than once, the linker accepts the first definition and ignores all subsequent definitions. This is not the best way to control instantiations because we don't have any clue about the instantiation points and we wouldn't know why there are duplicate instantiations. Furthermore, duplicate definitions of a function is an error in C++. This scheme might be useful in cases where the compiler doesn't allow turning off template instantiations on a per file basis. Note that, here we do not prevent multiple instantiations but we eliminate them later (not prevention but cure).

Some compilers provide options that a programmer can use to determine template instantiations. When this option is turned on, the compiler lists all the templates that are being instantiated in a file. This gives us the necessary information to control instantiations.

These schemes for controlling template instantiations are very useful and quite powerful. It is essential when dealing with shared libraries (also called dynamically linked libraries). We shall revisit this topic later when discussing dynamic libraries in this chapter.

GENERIC TYPES AND TYPE CHECKING

One of the big advantages of using generic types is strict type checking.[12] Consider the following example.

```
class X {
     // A Dummy class just for this example
};

void f()
{
     TList<int> il;      // A list of integers
     TList<char> cl;     // A list of characters
     TList<X> xl;        // A list of X objects

     int i = 10;
     char c = '?';
     X a;

     il.Append(&i);      // Valid operation
     il.Append(&c);      // Illegal - not the same type

     cl.Append(&c);      // Fine. c is a character and cl is char list
     cl.Prepend(&a);     // Illegal, a is not a character

     il = cl; // Illegal - incompatible types
}
```

In this example, we try to perform different operations on TList objects. The statement

$$il.Append(\&i)$$

is correct because il is a TList<int> and i is an element of type int. A TList<int> accepts int elements only. But the operation

$$il.Append(\&c)$$

will not compile because il is a TList<int> (read it as *TList of int* and it makes more sense) and no member function of TList<int> will accept a char argument. In other words, the types char and int are not the same. This is something we ought to remember. It might appear that type char and int are compatible but that's not so with generic classes. TList<int> will only accept elements of type int and nothing else. Along the same lines,

$$xl.Append(\&a)$$

is perfectly correct because a is of type X.

This makes generic class objects really robust. They maintain their type integrity very well. Note that an expression of the form

---

[12]In other words, generic types are useful only in statically typed languages.

```
il = cl;
```

is invalid because the object on the RHS is not the same type as the object on the LHS. All such errors are caught at compile time. One can appreciate these benefits by comparing the template implementation of TList with another TList implementation that uses void pointers.

One way to view this type system is to understand that TList is a homogeneous list. It only accepts elements of one type (int, char, X, etc.). It is not possible to mix elements of different types on the same list. This is one very common aspect of most generic classes.[13]

Even though TList is one generic class, every instantiation of TList with a different actual generic argument (template argument) creates a new class. It is this instantiated class that determines the type of elements that can live on the list. This is true of all generic classes. As mentioned earlier, a generic class is an unbounded set of classes. Every generic function also represents an infinite set of overloaded functions. Every instantiation of a generic class (or function) uniquely determines the type of that class. It is easy to understand generic functions because, in most cases, the required function is instantiated based on the arguments passed in the call. But with classes, the situation is a bit more complicated because we create objects and try to use the objects in different situations. In doing so, objects might get assigned to one another. This is where the type system restrictions are felt. But, don't panic—as you gain more experience with generic classes, these type system rules seem natural and logical.

CONSTRAINED AND UNCONSTRAINED GENERICITY

From the discussions so far, one thing is very clear. A generic class can be instantiated with any type we like—there is absolutely no restriction on what can be used as the actual argument in a generic class instantiation. In other words, the actual generic argument is not constrained to a specific type. This is called **Unconstrained Genericity.**

C++   Mostly, all generic classes in C++ are unconstrained. There is absolutely no restriction enforced by the language on the actual template arguments. The implementor of the generic class might impose explicit restrictions (through documentation) on the template arguments, but the language itself doesn't impose any rules. It is also possible that the template implementation depends on some functions that must be provided by the template arguments, imposing some restrictions on the template arguments, but that's again a programmer enforced rule.

But let us consider a case where unconstrained genericity is not a good thing. Consider a specialized list class TOrderedList that keeps the elements on the list always sorted (ascending or descending). We are not too much concerned about all the details of this class but some features are important. Here is a skeleton of this class.

---

[13]A TList<void*> would also be homogeneous—it only accepts pointers to void. One can store the address of any object on such a list because any pointer is implicitly convertible to a void pointer.

```
const unsigned int defaultSize = 256;

template <class AType>
class TOrderedList {
    public:
        enum EOrderType { eAscending, eDescending };
        TOrderedList(unsigned int size = defaultSize , EOrderType
                                    ascendOrdescend= eAscending );
        // Other methods not shown

        // Return true if thisElement was put on the list
        // - return false otherwise. The element is stored in order.
        bool Put(AType* newElementToAdd);
    private:
        TListNode<AType>* _head;
        TListNode<AType>* _tail;
        unsigned int _count;
        EOrderType _sortOrder;
};
```

Now let us attempt an implementation of the member function Put.

```
// Storing an element involves finding its place on the list by comparison
// with other elements. Remember that elements are always ordered. We have
// to start at the head of the list and compare each element on the list in
// sequence with the new element until we can find the correct slot. In a
// commercial implementation, this code would use iterator objects to
// traverse the list to locate the correct object.

template <class AType>
bool TOrderedList <AType>::Put(AType* newElementToAdd)
{
    if (_head == 0) {
        // This is the first element. Store it and get out
        _head = new TListNode<AType>(newElementToAdd);
        _head->_next = 0;
        _head->_previous = 0;
         _count++;
        return true;
    }

    if (_sortOrder == eAscending) {
        // Start at the head and compare elements
        TListNode<AType>* current = this->_head;
        while (current && ( *current->_userElement < *newElementToAdd) )
            current = current->_next; // Go to next node
    if (current == 0) { // Reached end of list
        // Code to put newElementToAdd at the end of list - Not shown
        _count++;
        return true;
    }
    else {
        // Found slot - Now manipulate pointers to store element
        // Create a new TListNode to add to list
        TListNode<AType>* newElement =
```

```
                    new TListNode<AType> (newElementToAdd);
          TListNode<AType>* addAt = current->_previous;
          if (addAt != 0) {
                    // Manipulate pointers — code that you might have written
                    // too many times in your programmer lifetime :-)
                    addAt->_next = newElement ;
                    newElement->_previous = addAt;
                    newElement->_next = current;
                    current->_previous = newElement;
                    _count++;
                    return true;
            }
        }
    }
    else { // It is a descending order sort
        // Start at the head and compare elements. Identical code as above
        // not shown
        TListNode<AType>* current = this->_head;
        while (current && ( *current->_userElement > *newElementToAdd) )
            current = current->_next; // Go to next node
    }
    return true;
}
```

The most important part of this member function is

```
    while (current && ( *current->userElement < *newElementToAdd) )
```

To find the correct place for the element, we keep searching the list, comparing each element with the element to be added, until we find the right slot (or we run out of elements). If the list is an ascending order list, then we use the less than (<) operator; otherwise we use the greater than (>) operator. We are comparing a user supplied object with an object on the list. The only way to determine the relation between two objects is by comparison. For this to work, we must use some kind of comparison operation. The objects on the list are user supplied objects. The class **TOrderedList** does not have any knowledge about them. Given that, the only logical way to determine the relationship between two user objects is by invoking a function < (less than) or > (greater than) on the objects itself. The statement

```
            *current->userElement < *newElementToAdd
```

dereferences the pointer **userElement** and invokes the **operator<** on it with the other object *newElementToAdd. Therefore, **TOrderedList** is invoking a member function (or even a non-member function) on the objects in question. This is absolutely correct. As we know, objects have their own behavior and they should be able to determine relationships between them. Class **TOrderedList** cannot (and should not) make any decisions about their relationships. Moreover, there is no default scheme for determining the relationship (such as less than or greater than) between two objects. For example, comparing two **TPerson** objects might involve comparing their ages (or their last names) and comparing two TCourse objects might be based on the courseID number. Each class that cares to be on the list must provide a comparison mechanism.

So we need an operator< (or a member function LessThan) for any class that wishes to use the TOrderedList class. But how do we enforce this rule and convey this information to the clients? This can be done in Eiffel by *Constrained Genericity*. The formal generic argument would be another class and only objects of that class (or classes derived from it) can be used as the actual generic argument. Using a specific class as the formal generic argument enforces some restrictions on the actual generic argument and allows the generic class to rely on features provided by the actual generic argument. For example, if we use a formal generic argument TCOMPARABLE as the formal generic argument with some deferred operations (pure virtual functions of C++), then class TORDEREDLIST can use the interface of TCOMPARABLE to carry out the operations. The actual derived class of TCOMPARABLE would provide the implementation. Inheritance takes care of the rest. Here is the code in Eiffel.

```
deferred class TCOMPARABLE
feature
        LessThan( otherObject : TCOMPARABE) : BOOLEAN is
           - Code to compare otherObject with Current
           deferred - Needs to be implemented in the derived class
           end
        GreaterThan(otherObject : TCOMPARABLE) : BOOLEAN
           - Code to compare otherObject with Current
           deferred - Needs to be implemented in the derived class
           end
        Equal(otherObject : TCOMPARABLE) : BOOLEAN
           - Code to compare otherObject with Current
           deferred - Needs to be implemented in the derived class
           end
        NotEqual(otherObject : TCOMPARABLE) : BOOLEAN
           - Code to compare otherObject with Current
           deferred - Needs to be implemented in the derived class
           end
end - class TCOMPARABLE

class TORDEREDLIST [ T -> TCOMPARABLE ]
        - The generic argument must be of type TCOMPARABLE
        - Other class Details omitted
end - class TORDEREDLIST
```

The expression

```
TORDEREDLIST [T->TCOMPARABLE]
```

states that any actual generic argument for TORDEREDLIST must be of type TCOMPARABLE. For any class to be of type TCOMPARABLE, it must inherit from it directly or indirectly, which guarantees that all the operations of TCOMPARABLE are available in the actual generic argument. In other words, the generic argument is constrained to classes that support the interface of TCOMPARABLE. If class TPERSON is implemented as follows, then we can easily create a person list.

```
class TPERSON
inherit
     TCOMPARABLE
feature
     LessThan( otherObject : TCOMPARABE) : BOOLEAN is
     do
         - implementation of deferred operation LessThan
     end
     - other inherited deferred methods not shown
end - TPERSON
```

Now we can create a person list as follows.

```
personList : TORDEREDLIST [ TPERSON ];
```

This constrained genericity mechanism ensures that a generic class can rely on operations implemented by the actual generic argument. Note that Eiffel does not relax type checking rules just because constrained generic arguments are used. In fact, generic classes with constraints are even more restrictive than unconstrained generic classes because the actual generic argument(s) is restricted to a specific type.

Constrained genericity uses inheritance to enforce constraints. With inheritance, we can specify interface requirements and implementation responsibilities for derived classes. With generic classes, we provide the same interface and implementation for all instantiations of the generic class. The inheritance mechanism here enforces the interface of the actual generic argument and the generic class still functions like any other generic class.

Constraints on Template Arguments in C++

It is not possible to enforce any direct constraints on template arguments in C++. Any type can be used as the template argument when a generic class is instantiated. There is no way to specify constraints on the template arguments. But that should not make you feel that C++ template classes are inferior to Eiffel generic classes. Because of code replication in C++, the need for specific member functions in template arguments can be verified and enforced when a template class is instantiated with an actual argument. In our example of **TOrderedList** above, if some programmer instantiates **TOrderedList** with a class that does not implement the **operator<** and **operator>**, the compiler generates errors about the missing operators. One can only use classes that support **operator>** and **operator<** as the actual argument with **TOrderedList**. Isn't that a constraint on **TOrderedList** generic arguments? Even though there is no syntactic equivalent of constrained genericity in C++, we can still achieve the same effect by using specific member functions from the template argument classes in the template class implementation. For example, in the **TOrderedList** example, the member function **operator<** of the template argument was used in the template class implementation for determining the ordering among the elements on the list. This enforces the constraint that any template argument used with the **TOrderedList** class implement the **operator<** member function.

Specific Types as Template Arguments in C++

Using specific types (such as int, char, etc.) as template arguments also enforces some constraints. A client cannot instantiate a template class with a different type of argument, other than the one specified, if the formal template argument is a language defined type. For example, a template array class can be declared as

```
// Size is the size of the array that will be created
template <class AType, unsigned int Size> class TSafeArray {
    // Details not shown
};

// Create an array of 1024 double elements
TSafeArray<double, 1024> dArray;
TSafeArray<TPerson, TCourse> cArray;   // invalid - Compile time error
```

But when such constraints are implicit in template classes, there should be clear documentation of what is expected from the template arguments. As mentioned earlier, there should not be unexpected surprises when a client uses such template classes.

NOTE   One might wonder about the advantage of specifying the size of the array as a template argument as opposed to a constructor argument (as is done with non-template classes). When a template class requires an argument, it must be specified when the template is instantiated. We already know that template instantiation is a compile-time operation. Therefore, the size of the array is known at compile time. Once we know the size at compile-time, there is no need for dynamic memory allocation in the implementation. That would make the array creation and destruction faster and more efficient.[14] This is even more useful when creating small arrays (such as character strings), which are allocated on the stack. In summary, just remember that there is a definite advantage in not using dynamic memory (*heap allocation*) in the implementation of classes. Here is a code snippet that uses statically allocated memory.

```
template <class AType, unsigned int Size> class TSafeArray {
    public:
        enum ESortOrder { eAscending, eDescending };
        TSafeArray();
        TSafeArray(const TSafeArray<AType, Size>& copy);
        TSafeArray<AType, Size>&
            operator=(const TSafeArray<AType, Size>& assign);
        virtual ~TSafeArray() { }
        unsigned int GetSize() const { return arraySize; }
        virtual AType& operator[](int index);
        void Sort(ESortOrder = eAscending);
        //...
    protected:
        int _arraySize;
        AType    _ip[Size]; // static array - size fixed at compile time
};
```

---

[14]Remember that every piece of dynamic memory allocated must be deallocated sooner or later.

```
// The implementation of some member functions
// Other member functions left as an exercise to the reader

template <class AType, unsigned int Size>
TSafeArray<AType, Size>::TSafeArray() : _arraySize(Size) {}

template <class AType, unsigned int Size>
AType& TSafeArray<AType, Size>::operator[](int index)
{
    if (index >= 0 && index < _arraySize) return _ip[index];
    else { /* Throw an exception! */ }
}

main()
{
    TSafeArray<int, 10> x, y; // An array of 10 elements
    x[3] = 10;   // Uses operator[]
    x[4] = x[3];
    for(int i=0; i < 10; i++)
        x[i] = i;
}
```

THINK   This **TSafeArray** class is not really a very elegant generic class because it really creates as many objects as the size of the array. Furthermore, it invokes the default constructor for each element of the array (not very flexible). A better implementation would only create the specified number of slots for the objects but not the objects. In other words, it would be an empty array of pointers. The client would have the freedom to store whatever object (subject to type checking) they like in the available slots of the array; the array just holds the object as long as the client leaves them in the array. Can you implement such an array class? An implementation will be shown in a subsequent chapter.

CAUTION   Note that *hard-wiring* calls to member functions of template arguments (as was done in **TOrderedList** above) is neither elegant nor flexible but it helps in exemplifying the problems of template class design. The general problem here is that of providing operations in template classes that depend on the template arguments. Better schemes are discussed elsewhere.[15]

Default Values for Template Arguments

C++ allows a template class interface to specify default values for template arguments just as with normal functions. For example, the **TSafeArray** class shown above can be written as

```
template <class T, unsigned int Size = 256> class TSafeArray {
    public: // Other details omitted
};
```

[15]In brief, a better scheme is to have another template argument (say **TComparator**) that is supplied by the client when a template is instantiated. **TComparator** would be responsible for the necessary comparison operations.

This declaration indicates that, if the client doesn't specify the size of the array, the size of the array would be 256 elements. The same restrictions, such as only trailing arguments can have default values, etc., also applies to template default values. Given this declaration, one can create an object as follows.

```
TSafeArray<TPerson> employeeArray; // 256 element array
TSafeArray<int, 1024>  intArray;     // 1K array of int
```

The object **employeeArray** now contains 256 elements, but **intArray** contains 1024 because the size has been explicitly specified.

The default values are not limited to just integers and constants. It can be any known class too. For example, in an electronic mail system, class **TMailBox** represents distinct mail boxes used to store messages addressed to different users. Clients might prefer to sort the messages based on different criteria. To facilitate this, the **TMailBox** class allows the client to supply a **MailSorter** argument (another class with a specific interface) for every **TMailBox** object. By default, it provides the **TGeneralMailSorter** class. Here is the declaration:

```
class TGeneralMailSorter { /* declarations */ };

template <class MailSorter=TGeneralMailSorter>
class TMailBox { /* Declarations */ };
```

This specifies that if the template argument **MailSorter** is not specified, then the **TGeneralMailSorter** class will be used for sorting messages. Many compilers still don't support this enhancement.

ENFORCING CONSTRAINTS ON TEMPLATE ARGUMENTS IN C++

It is possible to enforce some constraints for template arguments even in C++. Revisiting the **TorderedList** class, let's consider an interface that enforces some constraints.

```
template <class AType> class TComparator; // discussed below

const unsigned int defaultSize = 256;
template <class AType> class TOrderedList {
    public:
        enum EOrderType { eAscending, eDescending };

        TOrderedList(TComparator<AType>& comparator,
            unsigned int size = defaultSize ,
                    EOrderType ascendOrdescend= eAscending ); // ❶
        // Other methods not shown

        // Return true if thisElement was put on the list
        // - return false otherwise. The element is stored in order.
        bool Put(AType* newElementToAdd);
    private:
        TListNode<AType>* _head;
```

```
            TListNode<AType>* _tail;
            unsigned int _count;
            EOrderType _sortOrder;
            TComparator<AType>& _comparator; // ❷
};

// This comparator class acts as a boiler plate for comparing objects. Any
// class requiring comparison operations must inherit and override the pure
// virtual member functions.

template <class AType> class TComparator {
    public:
            virtual bool IsEqual(const AType& first, const AType& second)
                const = 0;
            virtual bool NotEqual(const AType& first, const AType& second)
                const = 0;
            virtual bool LessThan(const AType& first, const AType& second)
                const = 0;
            virtual bool GreaterThan(const AType& first, const AType& second)
                const = 0;
            // and probably more
};


class TPerson {
    public:
            TString GetName() const;
            unsigned long GetIdentification() const;

    // Other details as shown in previous chapters
};
```

Class **TComparator** is an abstract base class. It defines a set of comparison functions that are all pure virtual. A client of **TOrderedList** must inherit from this class and implement all the pure virtual functions. Let's say we create a derived class **MyComparator** shown below:

```
class MyComparator : public TComparator<TPerson> {
    public:
            bool IsEqual(const TPersonX& first, const TPerson& second) const
            {
                return (first.GetName() == second.GetName()
                        && first.GetIdentification() ==
                        second.GetIdentification() );
            }
            bool NotEqual(const TPerson& first, const TPerson& second) const
            { return !(IsEqual(first, second) ); }
            bool LessThan(const TPerson& first, const TPerson& second) const
            {   return (first.GetIdentification() <
                second.GetIdentification() ); }
            bool GreaterThan(const TPerson& first, const TPerson& second)
                const
            {   return (first.GetIdentification() >
                second.GetIdentification() ); }
};
```

This class provides comparison functionality for TPerson objects. It is a derived class of TComparator<TPerson>. It can be substituted anywhere a TComparator<TPerson> is required. This class uses a person's name and persons social security number (some identification number) to determine equality (and other relationships) between TPerson objects. How MyComparator carries out its operations is of no interest to TComparator.

Returning to the TOrderedList class, in ❶ the constructor specifies that it needs a TComparator object (of the appropriate type). This must be supplied by the client. In ❷, the comparator object supplied by the user is stored and is used internally as shown below.

Now consider the member function Put again. When the need arises to compare objects on the list with a client supplied object, the appropriate member function of the _comparator object is invoked and it is given both the objects that are being compared. For example, in ❸ below, the member function LessThan is being called with *current and _userElement, the two objects that are to be compared. Decisions are made based on the outcome of the function call.

```
template <class AType>
bool TOrderedList <AType>::Put(AType* newElementToAdd)
{
    if (_sortOrder == eAscending) {
         // Start at the head and compare elements
         TListNode<AType>* current = this->_head;
         // Invoke the member function of the comparator supplied
         while (current &&
             _comparator.LessThan(*current->_userElement,
                              *newElementToAdd) ) // ❸
         current = current->_next; // Go to next node
         if (current == 0) { // Reached end of list
             // Code to put newElementToAdd at the end of list - Not shown
             _count++;
         }
         // Rest of the code not important
}
```

Here is typical test program:

```
                   main()
                   {
                       MyComparator mc;
                       TOrderedList<TPerson> personList(mc);
                   }
```

When creating the list object personList, we supply the comparator object mc. This is the comparator we like to use with our list object.

This enforces a constraint on the users of TOrderedList. A client who needs to create an object of TOrderedList must be prepared to supply an appropriate TComparator object. Without a comparator, an object of TOrderedList cannot be created. So we have successfully imposed a constraint on the users of TOrderedList class.

For classes (and primitive types) that already have operators such as <, > , ==, and != defined, we can make it easier for clients to use the TComparator class as below:

```
// This comparator class can be used for classes (and types) which support
// operator based comparison functions. And it works directly for language
// defined types.

template <class AType> class TOperatorComparator :  public
    TComparator<AType>{
    public:
        virtual bool IsEqual(const AType& first, const AType& second)
            const
        { return first == second; }
        virtual bool NotEqual(const AType& first, const AType& second)
            const
        { return first != second; }
        virtual bool LessThan(const AType& first, const AType& second)
            const
        { return first < second; }
        virtual bool GreaterThan(const AType& first, const AType& second)
            const
        { return first > second; }
        // and probably more
};
```

Now we create an ordered list of **double** numbers as follows:

```
TOperatorComparator<    double> doubleComparator;
TOrderedList<double>        doubleList(doubleComparator);
```

If the use of virtual functions in **TComparator** seems like overkill, one can also switch to **static** member functions in **TComparator**, giving up a little flexibility.

Using a comparator has the additional benefit that the same class (such as **TOrderedList**) can be used with different comparison criteria, by supplying appropriate **TComparator** objects. For example, one comparator might compare **TPerson** objects on a list based on their age and another might compare them using their postal zip code. Essentially, the comparison operation has been delegated to a different class making it possible to use different comparator objects without changing anything in the objects that need to be compared.

With such a scheme, it is also possible to enforce constraints on template classes in C++. Note that it still allows the clients to define the appropriate behavior for the operations.

GENERIC CLASSES AND SELECTIVE EXPORTS

Without any doubt, beginners need time (and a lot of programming) to clearly understand the generic class concept. Until this chapter, our attention was focused on single classes and relationships among individual classes. But generic classes are not really individual classes—they represent an infinite set of classes. It will be interesting to understand selective exports (Chapter 7) as applied to generic classes.

Let's revisit the **TListNode** declaration that we have been using all through this chapter.

```
template <class AType> class TListNode {
    public:
        // Constructor to create a new TListNode given user's data
        TListNode(AType* userDataPointer=0);
        // Other details omitted for brevity
    private:
        TListNode<AType>*  _next;
        TListNode<AType>*  _previous;
        AType*             _userData; // pointer to user supplied data
        friend class TList<AType>;
};
```

What is the relationship between TList and TListNode? That's easy, you say—TList is a friend of TListNode. But is any TList a friend of every TListNode? Or is some TList a friend of every TListNode? Or is a specific TList a friend of a corresponding TList-Node?

All these questions pop up because we are no longer dealing with just simple classes. TList and TListNode represent an unbounded set of classes. We should focus our attention on individual instantiations of TList and TListNode. Here is an example.

```
main()
{
    TList<int> il;
    int myInt;
    il.Prepend(&myInt);

    TList<TPerson> pl;
    TPerson mySelf; // Constructor arguments not shown
    pl.Prepend(&mySelf);

    TList<TCar> cl;
    TCar myCar;  // TCar is just another class (details not shown)
    cl.Append(&myCar);
    //..
}
```

As soon as an object is added to any TList, a TListNode object is created. So in this example, we have created TListNode<int>, TListNode<TPerson>, and TListNode <TCar>.

Class TListNode should grant friendship to TList but not to *all* TList classes. TListNode<int> should grant friendship to TList<int> and not to TList<TPerson> or any other TList<?>. This is clearly depicted in the Fig. 9-7.

The friendship exists only between the classes connected by lines. The declaration in the class TListNode

```
friend class TList <AType>;
```

states that TListNode<AType> is granting friendship to TList<AType> and not to other TList classes. This is what is usually required. Why should TListNode<TPerson> grant friendship to TList<int>? So the friendship among template classes is usually a one-to-one relationship. This is enforced by the template argument AType. Class TListNode uses the same template argument name in the friend declaration above. So when AType is

Friendship among Template Classes

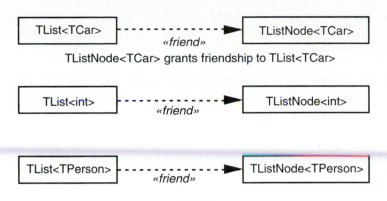

Fig. 9-7

TPerson, we have a TListNode<TPerson>, which grants friendship to a TList<TPerson>.

Consider another declaration.

```
template <class AType> class TListNode {
    public:
        // Constructor to create a new TListNode given user's data
        TListNode(AType* userDataPointer=0);
        // Other details omitted for brevity
    private:
        TListNode<AType>* _next;
        TListNode<AType>* _previous;
        AType*            _userData; // pointer to user supplied data
        friend class TList <AType>;
        friend class TFoo; // Dangerous! See below
};
```

Here, the class **TListNode** is granting friendship to another class **TFoo**. But note that **TFoo** is not a template class. So class **TFoo** is a friend of every **TListNode** class instantiated anywhere. Class **TFoo** is a friend of every **TListNode** that is already instantiated and those that will be instantiated in the future. It is a truly open ended *no holds barred* friendship. Is this something we really need? Mostly not. But there are some rare situations where such a friendship might be useful. But use it with extreme caution. Class **TFoo** can now access any instantiation of **TListNode**. A programmer instantiating a specific type of **TListNode** has no control over this friendship.

Another rarely used friend relation is between a non-template class and a specific instantiation of a template class. Consider this example:

```
class TBar {
    public:
        //...
        friend class TList<int>;
};
```

Here, class **TBar** grants friendship to another class **TList<int>**. Only **TList<int>** is granted friendship; no other instantiation of **TList** can access anything inside **TBar**. As mentioned in a previous chapter, friend relationships are confusing and some even feel that it is a violation of true OO principles. Use any friend relation with caution and be extremely wary of friendship among template classes.

☞ **Do not use friend relations between template classes and/or non-template classes unless you clearly understand the implications and consequences.**

EIFFEL   The export control mechanism works exactly like a normal class. For example, in Eiffel, class **TLISTNODE** can export the fields next, previous, etc. to the class **TLIST** as follows:

```
class TLISTNODE [T] — it is a generic class
export
    next {TLIST}, previous {TLIST}, userData {TLIST}
— other details
end — class TLISTNODE
```

This declaration selectively exports the fields next, previous, and userData to class **TLIST**. Needless to point out that the exports are between correspondingly typed classes. **TLISTNODE[INTEGER]** exports to **TLIST[INTEGER]** and so on.

INHERITANCE AND GENERIC CLASSES

Inheritance is a very powerful OO technique useful in many different situations. Inheritance can also be used with generic classes to achieve even more code/interface reuse. Moreover, with C++, public and private derivation with template classes can be used very effectively to solve some tricky problems.

As far as inheritance relationships are concerned, a generic class is no different from a non-generic class. The only thing that complicates the picture is the unbounded nature of a template class.

Inheritance can be used between one generic class and another generic and also between a generic class and a non-generic class. The base class can be a non-generic class with the derived class being a generic class or both the derived class and the base class can be generic classes. The former is a very powerful facility for code reuse and the latter is a very common inheritance relationship for interface reuse. Both styles are demonstrated with examples in the rest of this chapter.

To illustrate simple inheritance between generic classes, consider a simple **TDictionary** class. A dictionary is also called a map or an associative array. In its simplest form, a dictionary is a collection of key-value pairs.[16] Every key has a value associated with it and the dictionary can be queried for the value of a specific key. As a simple ex-

---

[16]The C preprocessor is nothing but a dictionary that remembers tokens and their values. Once a token is defined, the preprocessor replaces every instance of the token by its corresponding value in the program.

TABLE 9-1

Country Name	Country Code
Albania	355
Algeria	213
. . .	. . .
United Kingdom	44
Zimbabwe	263

ample, consider the following dictionary (Table 9-1) of telephone codes and country names used in a telephone lookup system.

Now one can query the dictionary for the country code of any country by name. The dictionary would store the name of the country as the *key* and its telephone code as the corresponding *value*. When asked for a country by name (a string), it will lookup the corresponding country name in the list and returns the telephone code found in the dictionary. The <country name, telephone code> forms a *tuple*. So a dictionary is a collection of tuples. The tuples can be a combination of whatever the user wants. For example, we could have a dictionary of elements on the periodic table along with their atomic weights. An astronomer could keep a dictionary of planet names and the number of moons they have. Therefore, a dictionary is very useful class in a variety of applications.

The preceding examples clarify certain aspects of a dictionary. First of all, there are no restrictions on what keys and values can be used. In our example, country name, planet name, etc. are keys. And telephone code, number of moons, etc. are values. The exact type of key and value is specified by the clients (just like the type of elements in an array or list). Therefore, a dictionary is a prime candidate for a generic class with the key and value as the formal generic arguments. Here is a first version of our dictionary class.

```cpp
// An abstract dictionary class. No objects of this class can be created.
// Derived classes must override all the pure virtual methods. This class
// provides an interface only — it can only be used as a base class.

template <class AKey, class AValue> class TDictionary {
    public:
        // Stores the specified key (with the value )into the dictionary
        // if the key doesn't already exist in the dictionary. If the key
        // already exists in the dictionary, it returns false.
        virtual bool AddKeyValuePair (const AKey& thisKey,
                                const AValue& withThisValue) = 0;
        // Returns the value of the (key, value) pair for the specified
        // key An exception should be thrown if thisKey does not exist in
        // the dictionary.

        virtual AValue GetValueAt (const AKey& thisKey) = 0;
        // Returns the count of the number of <key, value> pairs in the
        // dictionary
        virtual size_t HowMany() const = 0;
        // Returns true if thisKey is defined in the dictionary
        virtual bool KeyExists(const AKey& thisKey) const = 0;
        // If thisKey is defined in the dictionary, erase it from
        // the dictionary and return true. Otherwise false is returned.
        virtual bool RemoveKey(const AKey& thisKey) = 0;
```

```
// Removes all <key, value> pairs from the dictionary
virtual void ClearDictionary() = 0;
// Returns true if both dictionaries have identical <key, value>
// pairs
virtual bool operator==(const TDictionary& other) const= 0;
// Returns ! of operator== - Intentionally not virtual
bool operator!=(const TDictionary& other) const
          { return ! (*this == other); }

// Default constructor
TDictionary();
virtual ~TDictionary(); // Destructor
// Copy constructor
TDictionary(const TDictionary<AKey, AValue>& copy);
// Assignment operator
TDictionary<AKey, AValue>& operator=(const TDictionary<AKey,
                                        AValue>& assign);
};
```

NOTE   The type size_t is a pre-defined typedef found in the file stddef.h. This is a portable type guaranteed to work correctly on all platforms. Usually it is an unsigned long or unsigned int.

Our class TDictionary is an abstract class. The only clients of this class are derived classes. The comments in the interface are almost self explanatory. The important operations are AddKeyValuePair and GetValueAt. The method AddKeyValuePair adds a new (key, value) pair to the dictionary. Method GetValueAt returns the value of the specified key.

A dictionary can be implemented in many different ways. A simple implementation can use a doubly linked list (such as our TList class). A more efficient implementation can be provided with hash tables where the key is used to hash into a table to look up its value. Class TDictionary does not specify any implementation requirements—it only stipulates an interface. Implementation issues are left to the derived classes (see Fig. 9-8).

Clients can use the TDictionary interface without worrying too much about the different implementation issues of the derived classes. Any dictionary can be used polymorphically by understanding the interface of the abstract class TDictionary. Since TDictionary is generic, is it necessary that the derived classes be generic too? A client must be able to cre-

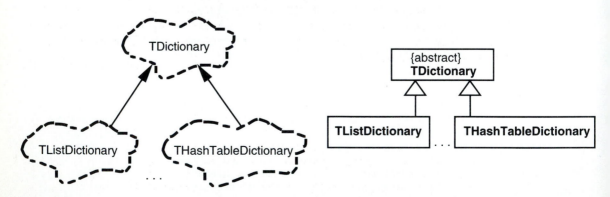

Fig. 9-8

ate dictionaries to handle any (key, value) pairs they wish. Class **TDictionary** should not impose any restrictions on the domain of (key, value) pairs. This is exactly the same situation as with our **TList** class earlier. To allow the flexibility to handle any (key, value) pairs, we need to make **TDictionary** a generic class. When we create an object of **TListDictionary**, the same rules apply. It should also handle any (key, value) types. Needless to state that **TListDictionary** must be a generic class. Here is the declaration of **TListDictionary**.

```
template <class AKey, class AValue> class TListDictionary : public
    TDictionary<AKey, AValue> {
    public:
        // Implements all the pure virtual methods inherited
        virtual bool AddKeyValuePair (const AKey& thisKey,
                                        const AValue& withThisValue);
        virtual AValue GetValueAt (const AKey& thisKey) ;
        virtual size_t HowMany() const;
        virtual bool KeyExists(const AKey& thisKey) const;
        virtual bool RemoveKey(const AKey& thisKey);
        virtual void ClearDictionary();
        virtual bool operator==(const TListDictionary<AKey, AValue>&
                                        other);
        // Default constructor
        TListDictionary();
        virtual ~TListDictionary(); // Destructor
        // Copy constructor
        TListDictionary(const TListDictionary<AKey, AValue>& copy);
        // Assignment operator
        TListDictionary<AKey, AValue>& operator=(
                    const TListDictionary<AKey, AValue>& assign);
    private:
        // whatever data members needed
};
```

NOTE   The implementation details of dictionary classes aren't shown here just to keep the example simple and easy to understand. In fact, there are some design refinements that can be applied to this hierarchy, which will be discussed in Chapter 12. The focus here is on the concept of inheritance with generic classes.

There are some interesting features here. We are stating that **TListDictionary** is a derived class of the abstract class **TDictionary**. Both **TListDictionary** and **TDictionary** have the same formal generic parameters (template arguments), **AKey** and **AValue**. When a **TListDictionary** object is created using the constructor, an object of **TDictionary** is also instantiated. Here is an example:

```
void f()
{
    // Let's assume that we have a class TString (shown in Chapter-4)
    // which stores character strings. And every country code is an
    // unsigned integer. Create a new dictionary object
    TListDictionary<TString, unsigned int> phoneDictionary;
    TString norway("Norway");      // Country name, the Key
    unsigned int norwayCode = 47; // Country code, the Value
    phoneDictionary.AddKeyValuePair(norway, norwayCode);
}
```

When we create the phoneDictionary object above, an object of the base class of TListDictionary, TDictionary is also created. Our phoneDictionary has two template arguments of type <TString, unsigned int> and TDictionary is also of type <TString, unsigned int>. In effect, we have caused the instantiation of two classes by instantiating an object of TListDictionary<TString, unsigned int>. There is nothing unusual about it. With non-generic classes, whenever an object of the derived class is instantiated, an object of the base class is also instantiated. The same rule applies with generic classes. The difference is the template argument(s). When an object of a derived template class object is created, it causes the instantiation of the corresponding template base class (if the base class is also a template class). The template arguments for both the derived class and the base class are usually the same. The template base class may not need all the template arguments that the derived class needs. There isn't any rule that requires the base class to use all the template arguments of the derived class (see Fig. 9-9).

So every instantiation of the TListDictionary class with proper template arguments causes the instantiation of two new classes. Class TDictionary <TString, unsigned int> is a new class instantiated from TDictionary <AKey , AValue>. All the code of class TDictionary<AType, AValue> is replicated in TDictionary<TString, unsigned int>. The same thing happens with TListDictionary <TString unsigned int>. This is an important issue to keep in mind when using generic classes with C++. This class generation doesn't exist in Eiffel. It is very specific to C++.

Instantiation of a Generic Class Object

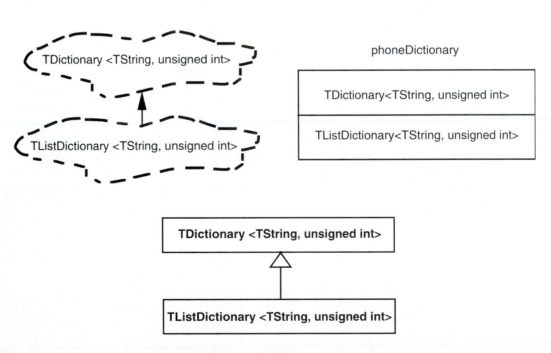

Fig. 9-9

Polymorphism and Generic Classes

All the rules and restrictions of inheritance are still valid with generic classes. In particular, *polymorphic substitution principle* (discussed in Chapter 5) still applies between a base class and derived class. But polymorphism may not be as easy to understand with generic classes. An example should clarify the nuances.

Consider a simple template function that accepts TDictionary objects polymorphically. Let us use another dictionary object that maintains countries and their capitol cities. Both country name and city name are TString types.

```
// A simple function that accepts a TDictionary polymorphically
template <class AKey, AValue>
void Foo(TDictionary<AKey, AValue>& theDictionary)
{
     // Do something with the dictionary object
}

main()
{
     TListDictionary<TString, unsigned int> phoneDictionary;
     TListDictionary<TString, TString>      capitolDictionary;
     Foo(phoneDictionary);    // ❶
     Foo(capitolDictionary); // ❷
}
```

When we invoke Foo() with the phoneDictionary object (in ❶), the compiler must find a matching function. There is no function Foo() that directly accepts a TListDictionary <TString, unsigned int> type. However, there is a template function Foo() from which a new function which accepts our phoneDictionary object can be generated. But this generated function will accept a TDictionary object and not a TListDictionary object.

```
// Generated function Foo()
void Foo(TDictionary<TString, unsigned int> theDictionary) { /* ... */ }
```

TListDictionary *is-a* TDictionary because of inheritance but not every TListDictionary of some type can be polymorphically substituted for a TDictionary of an unrelated type. A TListDictionary<TString, unsigned int> is a valid substitute only for TDictionary<TString, unsigned int> and nothing else. It should be remembered that every generated template class is a new type, which is only compatible with a base class with identical template arguments. Even a small difference in the types of the template arguments (such as int and unsigned int) is not acceptable when looking for a matching function.

Next, in ❷ above, when we attempt to call Foo() with the capitolDictionary object, another function Foo(), which accepts TDictionary<TString, TString>, is generated. This is an entirely different function from the one generated earlier.

This example works fine because the function Foo() is itself a generic function. So every call to Foo() causes the generation of the appropriate function. But what if there aren't any template functions but only functions with specific arguments? Here is an example:

```
    void Bar(TDictionary<TCourse, float>* aDictionary) { /* ... */ }

    void Fun(TDictionary<TPerson, float>* aDictionary)
        { /* ... */ }

    main()
    {
        // Dictionary of courses with their fee. Assume TCourse exists
        TListDictionary<TCourse, float> courseFeeDictionary;
        TListDictionary<TTeacher, float> teacherSalaryDictionary;
        Bar (&courseFeeDictionary);
        Fun (&teacherSalaryDictionary);
    }
```

This example uses the TPerson-TStudent-TTeacher hierarchy from our university example of previous chapters.

The call to Bar() with courseFeeDictionary succeeds because a TListDictionary
<TCourse, float> is a TDictionary<TCourse, float> because of inheritance between
TListDictionary and TDictionary. But how about the call to Fun() with the teacher-
SalaryDictionary object? The second template argument is the same type (float) in both
objects. The first template argument in Fun() for TDictionary is of type TPerson but in
teacherSalaryDictionary it is TTeacher. However, TTeacher is also a TPerson. Would-
n't that make teacherSalaryDictionary compatible with TDictionary<TPerson, float>? If
you are thinking on these lines, you are not alone. This is a classic inheritance trap with
generic classes. Inheritance between their template arguments does not make two generated template classes compatible. That is easy to verify because TDictionary <TPerson,
float> is an entirely different class, compatible with TListDictionary<TPerson, float>.
But TListDictionary<TTeacher, float> is not compatible with TDictionary<TPerson,
float> because there isn't any inheritance between TDictionary<TPerson, float> and
TListDictionary <TTeacher, float>. Because of this reasoning the call to Fun() with
teacherSalaryDictionary   fails   with   a   compile   time   error.   Note   that
TListDictionary<TTeacher, float> is compatible with TDictionary <TTeacher, float>.
See Fig. 9-10.

☞ **Inheritance between template class arguments does not imply inheritance between their template classes. Two generated template classes
differing in their template arguments (which are themselves related by
inheritance) are not compatible.**

It might be easier to understand this behavior if you imagine that TDictionary<TPerson,
float> is a new class with a different name, say TDictionary_TPerson_float, and
TListDictionary<TTeacher, float> is another class with a completely different name,
TListDictionary_TTeacher_float. Clearly, there is no relationship between these two
classes.

NOTE   Any member function of the TDictionary<TPerson, float> class accepting a
TPerson argument can be invoked with a TTeacher argument because of inheritance between TTeacher and TPerson. This is syntactically correct but there is no guarantee that
it will be logically correct. Logical correctness depends on how the argument is used
within the function. If the argument is a reference or a pointer, it might work correctly.
Double check the behavior of the class before relying on this scheme.

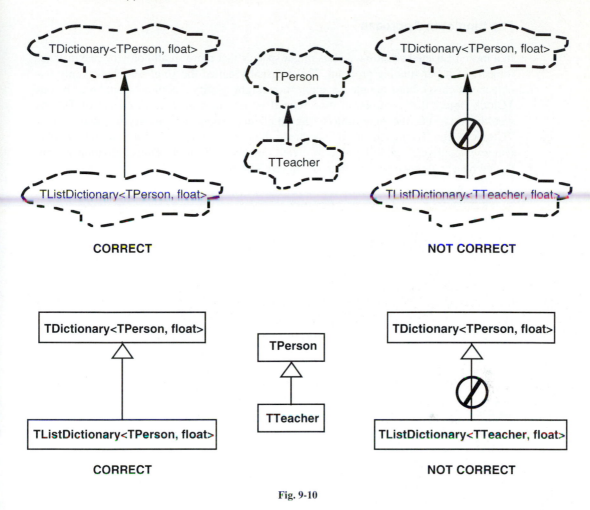

Fig. 9-10

USEFUL APPLICATIONS OF INHERITANCE
WITH GENERIC CLASSES

Inheritance can be put to use in a variety of different ways with generic classes. Some of the examples from previous chapters can be made more powerful and elegant by combining inheritance with generic classes.

In Chapter 6 (under Multiple Inheritance) we created a class **MReferenceCounter**, which provided reference counting semantics to any class deriving from it. Sometimes we don't need reference counting but instance counting and instance limiting. For example, an application might want to control the number of instances of **TPlotter** objects that might be created (limited to the number of physical plotters available). Moreover, the client must be able to specify the maximum number of instances that can be created for every such resource that needs counting. We will discuss a special case of instance counting first and then generalize the problem.

The Singleton Approach

In a more restricted situation, a class might specify that there should only be one instance (object) of it per running program. This is usually called the *singleton* object (only one object of a class). For example, an application might specify that there should only be one TClock object that controls all time related issues. In such a case, clients of TClock would always get the same object (the singleton) whenever they try to create a new TClock object. To implement such controls, the constructor of TClock cannot be public. Otherwise, anyone would be able to create objects of TClock. Object creation is controlled by a static member function, say MakeObject.

```
class TClock {
    private:
        TClock();
        static TClock* _cp;
    public:
        static TClock* MakeObject()
        {
            if (_cp != 0) _cp = new TClock(); // Call appropriate ctor
            return _cp;
        }
        // other details not important
};

TClock* TClock::_cp = 0; // initialize the static data member
```

Here is test program:

```
main()
{
    TClock* cp = TClock::MakeObject(); // ❶
    // ...
    TClock* cp2 = TClock::MakeObject(); // ❷
}
```

When MakeObject is called in ❶, the static data member _cp is 0 and, hence, a new TClock object is created. Next time, when MakeObject is called in ❷, the pointer value is checked and, since it has been already created, _cp is returned as it is and no new TClock object is created. This way, there is always only one TClock object in a process. In other words, class TClock is a singleton.

There are some problems with this approach:

1. The static data member must be initialized before use. This can be tricky across modules.

2. Some other code must be responsible for the deletion of the singleton object.

Definitely, it is better than using global objects or pointers and creation of TClock is fully controlled. See [Gamma94] for more information on this technique.

SMALLTALK   This technique is applicable to Smalltalk also. It can be implemented using class methods and class variables.

EIFFEL   Here we can use once functions to create the sole object achieving the same effect.

A GENERAL TECHNIQUE FOR CONTROLLING OBJECT CREATION

Creating a single object is a special case of the more general problem of controlling object creation. In some cases, we don't want to restrict instances to just one but a pre-defined limit (one being the singleton case).

Class MBoundedCounter is a generalized version of the singleton approach. It allows a class to restrict itself to not just once instance but any pre-defined number of instances (a singleton being a special case where there is only one instance). This can be achieved through the class MBoundedCounter shown below:

```
template <class AType> class MBoundedCounter {
protected: // Must be subclassed - not for direct instantiation
    MBoundedCounter() {
        if (_numInstances < _maxInstancesAllowed) {
            // Limit has not been exceeded
            ++_numInstances++; // One more instance
        }
        else {
            // No more instances allowed.
            // Throw an exception to indicate failure
        }
    }
        ~MBoundedCounter() { -numInstances--; }
        // Copy constructor
        MBoundedCounter(const MBoundedCounter<AType>& copy)
        {
            if (_numInstances < _maxInstancesAllowed))
                    ++_numInstances;
            else {
                // No more instances of this object allowed. throw an
                   exception
            }
        }
    public:
        // Helper function
        static unsigned int Count() { return _numInstances; }
    private:
        // count of the number of objects in existence
        static unsigned int _numInstances;
        // Maximum number of objects allowed
        const static unsigned int _maxInstancesAllowed;
};
```

This MBoundedCounter should be usable by different classes that need instance counting in the same application. Hence, the need for a template class. For example, what if

TPlotter and another class TNetworkFax (discussed below) need instance counting (independent of each other) and are in the same application. If MBoundedCounter is not a template class, there would be a single copy of all static data members that will be shared between TPlotter and TNetworkFax, causing all kinds of problems. Class TPlotter must inherit from a specific type of MBoundedCounter. We would like to inherit from an MBoundedCounter for objects of TPlotter. So the correct derived class is as follows:

```
class TPlotter : private MBoundedCounter<TPlotter> {
    public:
        static TPlotter* MakePlotter();
        Plot(const char* fileToPlot);
        ~TPlotter(); // destructor
        // other necessary methods
        // Re-export Count method of the base class
        MBoundedCounter<TPlotter>::Count;
    private:
        TPlotter(); // simple default constructor
        TPlotter(const TPlotter&); // copy constructor
        TPlotter& operator=(const TPlotter&); // assignment operator
};

TPlotter* TPlotter::MakePlotter() { return new TPlotter(); }

TPlotter::TPlotter() // Constructor
        { /* Do whatever is necessary to create and initialize the object
            */ }

TPlotter::~TPlotter() // Destructor
    { /* Do whatever clean-up is required */ }

// Definitions for the static data members
unsigned int MBoundedCounter<TPlotter>::_numInstances = 0;
const unsigned int MBoundedCounter<TPlotter>::_maxInstancesAllowed= 10;
                    // 10 is just an arbitrary limit
```

This scheme also works correctly. When MakePlotter calls the constructor for TPlotter, the default constructor for MBoundedCounter<TPlotter> is called first (by the compiler). If the number of instances of TPlotter already exceeds the limit specified in _maxInstances, then an exception will be thrown (or a 0 pointer could be returned). If not, the MBoundedCounter<TPlotter> constructor just increments the numInstances member and returns to the TPlotter constructor, which proceeds normally. When a TPlotter object is deleted, the destructor of TPlotter executes and the MBoundedCounter<TPlotter> destructor is also called. The destructor just decrements the number of instances and everything works correctly. So, TPlotter needs to know nothing about instance counting—it is done by the general base class MBoundedCounter<TPlotter>. Every instantiation of MBoundedCounter with a new type gets its own copy of the static data members numInstances and _maxInstancesAllowed. When TPlotter derives from MBoundedCounter<TPlotter>, it is specifying that MBoundedCounter be instantiated for TPlotter. Every new instantiation of MBoundedCounter with a new type (such as TPlotter) is a new class. We already know that static data members are shared by all objects of the class. This is a very neat way of solving static data member problems.

☞ **Every new instantiation of a template class has its own static data member. This is useful in solving tricky problems involving static data members.**

The advantage with this scheme is that the derived class doesn't need to know anything about instance counting (other than initializing the count limits). The derived class that wishes to be counted (TPlotter) has remained the same. There is no conflict between the static data members in MBoundedCounter<TPlotter> and the static data members in any other instantiation of MBoundedCounter. For example, if we also want to control the instantiations of a networked fax machine TNetworkFax, we can instantiate MBoundedCounter for TNetworkFax as follows:

```
class TNetworkFax : private MBoundedCounter<TNetworkFax> {
    // other details not important
};
```

The static data member

```
MBoundedCounter<TNetworkFax>::_maxInstancesAllowed
```

is completely distinct from the static data member

```
MBoundedCounter<TPlotter>::_maxInstancesAllowed
```

There is absolutely no conflict between them. Every time MBoundedCounter is instantiated with a new type, the new instantiation creates another set of static data members.

NOTE   If you ever implement a useful technique that uses static data members inside non-template classes, consider if the technique is useful with other classes as well. If so, you will not be able to use a non-template class with static data members. Try to move the static data members to a template class and use specific instantiations of the template class wherever the new technique is useful. This solves the problem of static data members in non-template classes.

IMPLEMENTING COUNTED POINTERS

Another very useful application of template classes and operator overloading is in the implementation of counted pointers. C and C++ programmers are quite familiar with ordinary pointers. But the trouble with ordinary pointers is that when they are copied (or assigned) the programmer needs to remember to use the multiples copies of the pointers correctly. Otherwise, memory leaks and dangling references are possible. Even worse, programs can crash when pointers reference memory that has been deallocated (the *double delete* problem). Also, when a programmer no longer needs the resource pointed by the pointer, she must remember to deallocate (delete) the pointer to recover the resource. It would be very useful if the pointers are smart enough to reference count themselves when they are copied. As long as the reference count is positive, the resource should not be deallocated (usual reference counting semantics). In other words, the pointer should count itself. The counted pointer should deallocate the resource when the reference count drops to zero. This would be easy if the counted pointer is an object.[17] Needless to state that the counted pointer must still retain pointer semantics—it should support the usual operators -> and *, otherwise, the counted pointer class would be useless.

We would like to use such (reference) counted pointers with any user-defined type. Just as we can create normal pointers to int, char, TPlotter, etc., we must be able to instantiate counted pointers for any of these types. However, the reference counting mechanism is the same no matter what the type of pointer is. So we must implement the counted pointer class as a template class. Here is the class TCountedPointer.

```
#include <iostream.h>

// A Reference Counted Pointer using overloaded operator-> and operator*.
// This implementation is NOT multi-thread safe. In order to make it multi-
// thread safe, the typedef ReferenceCount should be a separate class.
// CAUTION: This class must be used with heap allocated objects only.
// It should not be used with objects created on the stack.

// Change this to a class if thread safety is needed
typedef unsigned long ReferenceCount;

template <class AType>
class TCountedPointer
{
    public:
        TCountedPointer(); // ❶ Default constructor
        // adoptTarget must point to a resource allocated using new.
        // It will be deleted when the pointer object goes away.
        TCountedPointer(AType* adoptTarget); // ❷
        TCountedPointer(const TCountedPointer<AType>& copy); // ❸
        virtual ~TCountedPointer(); // ❹
        TCountedPointer<AType>&
                operator=(const TCountedPointer<AType>& assign) ; // ❺

        // Return true if the object is a pointer to a non-zero target
        bool IsValid() const; // ❻

        bool operator==(const TCountedPointer<AType>& other) const; // ❼
        bool operator!=(const TCountedPointer<AType>& other) const;

        AType& operator*() const; // ❽

        AType* operator->() const; // ❾
        // This is used for testing purposes only
        int GetReferenceCount() const; // ❿

    protected:
        void AddReference(); // ⓫
        void RemoveReference(); // ⓬

    private:
```

[17]This is a general trick used in C++. When some housekeeping must be done when a resource goes away, convert the resource into a true C++ object. Objects are subject to automatic destruction and the destructor takes care of the housekeeping chore.

```
        ReferenceCount _*refCount;
        AType* _targetPointer;
};
```

Definitely, we need to carefully analyze this class to understand the details.

❶ This is the default constructor. The internal pointer (**targetPointer**) is not attached to any resource. The reference count is zero because it is not bound to any target.

```
template <class AType>
TCountedPointer<AType>::TCountedPointer() : _refCount(0), _targetPointer(0)
    { }
```

❷ This next one is also a constructor but here, while creating the pointer object, we specify the target (**adoptTarget**) to which this pointer is attached. Our data member is setup to point to this target and we set the reference count to 1 by incrementing the existing value of the reference count. Incrementing and decrementing reference counts is done by the methods **AddReference** and **RemoveReference**. More on these methods later. Once a **TCountedPointer** object is given control of an object (target), the user should not delete the target or destroy it in any way. The **TCountedPointer** takes over the responsibility of managing the target. Hence, the name **adoptTarget** for the argument. The **TCountedPointer** object *adopts* the target object.

```
template <class AType>
TCountedPointer<AType>::TCountedPointer(AType* adoptTarget) : _refCount(0),
    _targetPointer(adoptTarget)
    { AddReference(); // Increment the reference count }
```

❸ This is the copy constructor. When a counted pointer is copied, the target object is not copied. Only the pointer needs to be copied. At the same time, we need to remember that because of the copy operation, one more pointer will point to the same target. In other words, one more reference is being added. Therefore, we copy the target pointer and then add one more reference to the existing reference count. Now, both the original pointer and the new pointer refer to the same target.

```
        template <class AType>
        TCountedPointer<AType>::TCountedPointer(const
              TCountedPointer<AType>& copy) :
            _refCount(copy._refCount), _targetPointer(copy._targetPointer)
            { AddReference();} // Add one more reference }
```

❹ Next is the destructor. When a **TCountedPointer** object is destroyed, the target is not destroyed immediately. First of all, the reference count is decremented by 1. If now the reference count drops to zero, there are no more pointers referencing this target. So it is deleted by calling the **delete** operator. If the reference count is positive, there are some more **TCountedPointer** objects still using the target. Therefore, the target is not destroyed. All this is done by **RemoveReference** (discussed later).

```
        template <class AType>
        TCountedPointer<AType>::~TCountedPointer() { RemoveReference(); }
```

❺ In the assignment operator, the object on the LHS loses a reference and the object on the RHS gains a new reference. We decrement the reference count for the **TCountedPointer** on the LHS (**this**) and copy the target pointer, then we add a reference to the object on the RHS (**that**).

```
template <class AType>
TCountedPointer<AType>&
TCountedPointer<AType>::operator=(const TCountedPointer<AType>& that)
{
    if (this != &that) {
            RemoveReference(); // LHS loses a reference
            this-> _targetPointer = that._targetPointer;
            this-> _refCount = that._refCount;
            AddReference(); // RHS gains a reference
    }

    return *this;
}
```

❻ This is just a helper function that tells the client if the pointer is attached to a target. If **targetPointer** is not zero, then the **TCountedPointer** is a pointer to a valid object.

```
template <class AType>
bool
TCountedPointer<AType>::IsValid() const { return (_targetPointer != 0); }
```

❼ This is the comparison operator. Two **TCountedPointer** objects compare equal if they point to the same target. Ordinary language defined pointers can be compared in restricted circumstances but **TCountedPointer** objects are always comparable.

```
template <class AType>
bool
TCountedPointer<AType>::operator==(const TCountedPointer<AType>& other)
      const
{ return (_targetPointer == other._targetPointer); }
```

For completeness, we also provide the counterpart of the equality operator.

```
template <class AType>
bool
TCountedPointer<AType>::operator!=(const TCountedPointer<AType>& other)
      const
    { return !operator==(other); }
```

❽ This is a very crucial and powerful operator for the **TCountedPointer** class. When pointers are used, programmers can get to the object by dereferencing the pointer using the * operator. For example,

```
int i;
int *ip = &i; // ip points to i
*ip = 10; // Store 10 in whatever ip points to
```

is a simple usage of a pointer. Since our **TCountedPointer** is nothing but a glorified pointer, we must be able to dereference it to get to the target object. Unfortunately, **TCountedPointer** is an object and not really a pointer. But, our clients should not feel any difference. When a **TCountedPointer** object is dereferenced using the operator *, our overloaded **operator*** gets called. This operator returns the dereferenced target object. This is correct because a **TCountedPointer** is nothing but an alias to the target object.

```
template <class AType>
AType&
TCountedPointer<AType>::operator*() const { return *_targetPointer; }
```

❾ This is the counter part of the **operator***. Pointers are usually used with the -> notation to access members. We have already seen this in many examples. The same operation must be possible with **TCountedPointer** objects also. So when the -> is applied to a **TCountedPointer** object, the overloaded **operator->** is invoked. This operator returns the target pointer. Next, the compiler applies whatever operation the client is attempting on the returned pointer (for details on the workings of the overloaded **operator->** refer to the chapter on overloaded operators Chapter 8). This is clarified further in the example shown later. Both **operator*** and **operator->** are constant member functions because they do not modify the state of the **TCountedPointer** object.

```
template <class AType>
AType*
TCountedPointer<AType>::operator->() const { return _targetPointer; }
```

❿ This is a helper function that is useful when debugging this class. Put this under #ifdef control so that it is not part of the regular code. It just returns the reference count of the **TCountedPointer** object.

```
// This is a debug support function
template <class AType>
int
TCountedPointer<AType>::GetReferenceCount() const
{
    if (_refCount) return *_refCount;
    else return -1;
}
```

⓫ This member function adds one more reference to the **TCountedPointer** object. In this example, the reference count is an integer but it need not be so. The reference count could be another class that maintains a thread safe reference count. One can always replace our simple integer with an object. The reference count lives outside the **TCountedPointer** object. Each **TCountedPointer** object maintains a pointer to it. If the reference count pointer is zero, we create a new reference count object (**int**).

```
template <class AType>
void
TCountedPointer<AType>::AddReference()
{
```

```
                     if (_refCount) (*_refCount)++;
                     else {
                         _refCount = new ReferenceCount;
                         *_refCount = 1;
                     }
                 }
```

⓬ This is a crucial function. Whenever the reference count needs to be decremented, this member function must be called. It takes care of the rest. First, it decrements the reference count. If it drops to zero after the decrement, then there are no more TCountedPointer objects referring to the target contained in the TCountedPointer. So the targetPointer is deleted (remember that the target was adopted by the TCountedPointer in the constructor). Next, we set the refCount pointer and the targetPointer to zero just to ensure that nothing bad can happen under any circumstance.

```
template <class AType>
void
TCountedPointer<AType>::RemoveReference()
{
    if (_refCount) {   // Decrement the reference count and delete the master
         (*_refCount)-;
         if (*_refCount == 0) { // delete the target object
              delete _refCount;
              delete _targetPointer;
              _refCount = 0;
              _targetPointer = 0;
         }
    }
}
```

THREAD   Incrementing and decrementing the reference counts under multi-threaded environ-
SAFETY   ments must be protected with some type of mutual exclusion lock. This can be done in a number of ways and a separate class (very similar to MReferenceCounter described in Chapter 6) can be created for this purpose. A plain integer has been used here just to keep the example simple.

CAUTION   There is one extreme precaution needed when this class TCountedPointer is used. When the reference count drops to zero in RemoveReference, the pointer to the target is deleted. Only pointers to heap allocated objects (i.e. objects created using operator new) can be deleted. If one passes the address of a static (stack) object to the TCounted-Pointer constructor, it is an invitation for trouble.

          Here is a test program to verify the correctness of the implementation. Class TExample is a test class created just to test the implementation. Every object of this class contains an identification number specified when it is created. This identification number helps in recognizing objects. The member function Print displays the identification number of the object that was specified at the time of creation.

```
// A Test program
#include <iostream.h>
class TExample {
```

```cpp
    public:
        ~TExample() { cout << "Destructor for TExample("
                          <<  _id << ")\n"; }
        TExample(int i) _id(i) {}
        void Print() const
                { cout << "Print TExample(" << _id << ")" << endl; }
    private:
        int _id;
};

main()
{
    // Create a dynamic object of TExample with id = 1
    TExample * px = new TExample (1);
    // Create a TCountedPointer object for px
    TCountedPointer<TExample> ap(px);
    // Create a copy of TCountedPointer object ap. Copy constructor is
    // used.
    TCountedPointer<TExample> bp = ap;
    // Create an unattached TCountedPointer object
    TCountedPointer<TExample> cp;
    // See Figure 9-11 below
    // The next line doesn't compile!  See below
    // TCountedPointer<const TExample > constp;

    cout << "Number of references to ap (must be 2): " <<
    ap.GetReferenceCount() << endl;

    cout << "Assign ap to cp...\n";
    cp = ap;
    // See Figure 9-12 below
    cout << "Number of references to ap (must be 3): " <<
    ap.GetReferenceCount() << endl;

    TExample * qx = new TExample (100);
    TCountedPointer<TExample> dp(qx);

    ap = dp; // Decreases the reference through ap

    cout << "References to px (should be 2): " <<
    bp.GetReferenceCount() << endl;

    cout << "References to qx (should be 2): " <<
    dp.GetReferenceCount() << endl;

    dp->Print();
    (*cp).Print();

    // This causes a compile time error - See below
    // constp = cp;
}
```

Here is the output of this program:

```
        Number of references to ap (must be 2): 2
        Assign ap to cp...
```

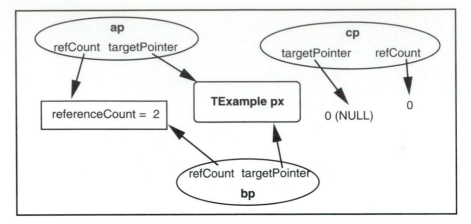

Fig. 9-11

```
Number of references to ap (must be 3): 3
References to px (should be 2): 2
References to qx (should be 2): 2
Print TExample(100)
Print TExample(1)
Destructor for TExample(1)
Destructor for TExample(100)
```

In Fig. 9-11 above, both **ap** and **bp** point to the same resource **px**. Hence, the reference count is 2. On the other hand, **cp** is an independent TCountedPointer object and does not point to anything yet.

Here in Fig. 9-12 **ap** has been assigned to **cp**. Therefore, both **cp** and **ap** point to the same resource. But from the figure above, we know that ap already shared resource **px** with **bp**. Therefore, now three objects are sharing **px**. Hence, the reference count is 3.

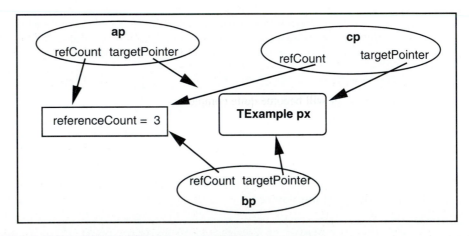

Fig. 9-12

The statement

```
dp->Print();
```

causes the **operator->** to be applied on **dp** as follows.

```
( dp.operator->() )->Print();
```

Since class **TCountedPointer** implements the overloaded **operator->**, this works correctly. The **Print()** member function is invoked on the return value of (**dp.operator->(())**), which in our example returns a pointer to **TExample** object, which does implement the method **Print()**.

On the same lines

```
(*cp).Print();
```

causes

```
(cp.operator*()).Print();
```

to be executed.

Finally, the statement

```
TCountedPointer<const TExample > constp;
```

will not compile because the type of the template argument in **TCountedPointer** (**AType**) now becomes **<const TExample>**. Therefore, _targetPointer is now (**const TExample***)—a pointer to a **const** object. But when the destructor for the class **TCountedPointer** is instantiated for this case, the **delete** call on _targetPointer tries to delete a pointer to a const object, which is not allowed. Hence, the compiler will flag this as an error. This error manifests at the point of instantiation.

This is a very useful class that can be used with any user defined type without any reservations. The only disadvantage is that, unlike ordinary pointers, **TCountedPointer** objects cannot be incremented or decremented. One might contemplate the implementation of operators ++ and − − (that increment/decrement _targetPointer) for this class but that causes more trouble because _targetPointer is shared among a number of **TCountedPointer** objects. If one were to implement the ++ and − − correctly, class **TCountedPointer** will become quite complex.

NOTE   One might consider adding some other useful member functions to the **TCountedPointer** class. One can add a member function (say **SetTarget**) to modify the _targetPointer. Another method might be added to get the current value of _targetPointer (**GetTarget**). Yet another method might give the ownership of the _targetPointer (**ReleaseTarget**) back to the client, internally setting _targetPointer to zero. Providing such utility functions is only limited by your imagination and need. Also note that **TCountedPointer** cannot be instantiated for language defined types (**int**, **char**, etc.) because the member access operator (**operator->**) has special semantics (as discussed in the chapter on overloaded operators). The operator-> should return a pointer to some other object on which the expression on the RHS of the -> can be applied. This wouldn't work with language defined types.

MINIMIZING CODE DUPLICATION WITH TEMPLATE OBJECTS

One of the problems with template classes in C++ is the replication of code for every instantiation of the template class with a new type. This causes *code bloat*. A casual programmer may not find any disadvantages with such code duplication but any professional software developer is aware of the many problems of increased code size. In the ensuing paragraphs we will discuss the disadvantages of code replication and some possible solutions. We will then discuss problems and solutions for template classes in shared libraries.

Consider the class TCountedPointer above. For every new type of pointer we create, the entire implementation code of TCountedPointer is duplicated. Here is a simple example:

```
main()
{
    // Create a number of different counted pointer objects
    TCountedPointer<TPerson>              tpp;
    TCountedPointer<TStudent>             tsp;
    TCountedPointer<TGraduateStudent>     tgp;
    TCountedPointer<TCourse>              tcp;
    //...
}
```

This causes the code of TCountedPointer to be duplicated four times, one each for TPerson, TStudent, TGraduateStudent, and TCourse (see Fig. 9-13).

Code Replication with Template Objects

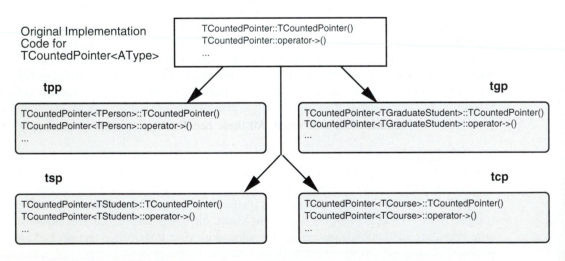

Fig. 9-13

For every instance of **TCountedPointer** with a different argument for **AType**, the code is replicated by substituting **AType** with the actual template argument. Since we use pointers very frequently in C++, we can end up with quite a large number of **TCountedPointer** objects of different types, causing increased code duplication.

When code is duplicated, the size of the final executable image of the program (or the size of the library that contains the instantiations) increases. As the executable image size increases, memory requirement also increases correspondingly. In other words, a smaller program requires less memory to run where as a bigger program requires more memory. With the modern operating systems (OS) that use *demand paging* schemes, each executable program image is divided into *pages* of memory. Typical page sizes is 4K (4096) bytes. If the size of the executable image is 3000 bytes, then it requires one page (the size is rounded to the nearest integral page size). If the size is 64768 bytes it will be rounded to 16 pages (assuming 4K byte pages). We all know that computers have limited physical memory and a huge virtual memory address space. An operating system can only load and run programs that fit in the limited physical memory. So when a program is run, not all pages required by it are loaded into physical memory. Only the first few pages needed are loaded into physical memory. During execution, if an instruction (in a page) not yet loaded into physical memory is referenced by the program, the program suffers a *page fault*. At this time, it is the responsibility of the OS to load the required page into physical memory. This might cause the swapping out of a different page of memory. This demand paging is quite expensive in terms of execution time. The running program that caused the page fault cannot execute until the required page is loaded into memory. If the available physical memory on a machine is not too big (say 16 Mega bytes), then there is more paging activity. If the available physical memory is quite big (say 128 Mega bytes), then it is possible that all the pages of a program fit into memory and, hence, there would be no paging activity at all. A bigger executable image requires more pages and could cause more paging activity and a degradation in performance. As more and more programs start running simultaneously, there is an increase in the paging activity. It is a very good practice to minimize the size of a program for a number of reasons. First of all, a smaller program can be loaded more quickly compared to a large program. Hence, it starts executing quickly. In other words, the start-up time is shorter. With limited physical memory, many small programs can fit into memory requiring less paging and more throughput. Smaller programs benefit from the instruction caches because of more hits than misses, resulting in faster execution times. A large program tends to invalidate the cache more often (more misses), causing slower execution. A smaller program has a smaller *locality of reference* and runs faster. But a large program needs a bigger locality of reference, which may not fit in the cache, causing the program to run slower. A smaller program requires less disk space. All these benefits of smaller programs imply that we should try to avoid (or at least minimize) code duplication as much as possible.

The language helps to some extent in minimizing code size. When a template class is replicated for a new type, not all member functions are duplicated. Only those member functions that are actually called (or are required) are duplicated. Member functions that are not called need not be duplicated, but this rule cannot be applied to virtual functions. They must be duplicated even if they are not directly invoked. Moreover, if a class is explicitly instantiated by the programmer for a specific type, then all member functions must be duplicated.

Memory Footprint of a Program

The minimum size of memory required to run a program efficiently is usually called the *memory footprint* of the program. A large program usually has a bigger footprint than a smaller program. As the size of the executable image increases, so does the memory footprint. System developers try to reduce the memory footprint of a program as much as possible by employing various tricks. But template code replication hampers this effort very much.

Schemes for Reducing Template Code Size

There are certain schemes we can employ to reduce the executable image size. Since we know that template code is replicated, we might consider code sharing. With normal non-template classes there is only one copy of the implementation code in a running program, no matter how many objects of the class are created. If we somehow reduce the implementation code of a template class, less code is replicated for every template object instantiation. Therefore, instead of keeping all the implementation code of a template class inside the template implementation, it would be better if we could divide the code into shared and non-shared (duplicated) code. Not all of the code in a template class needs to reside in the template implementation. Some of the member functions do not depend on the type of the template argument. Such member functions need not be duplicated at all. As the first cut, we should identify member functions that do not depend on the type of the template argument and move them out of the template class. Once we achieve this separation, we can move this code to a separate non-template class and use it (by containment or inheritance) in the template class. Usually, this is done by using private derivation. Here is a trivial example.

The member function **AddReference** of the class **TCountedPointer** does not depend on the type of the template argument. It only uses the **_refCount** data member. The code in this member function will be the same irrespective of the type of the template argument. So why should this be part of the template implementation? Let us create a new base class **TCountedPointerBase** and move the implementation of **AddReference** into this new class. **AddReference** uses the data member **_refCount** so we must also move **_refCount** into the base class **TCountedPointerBase**. To make it easy for member functions of **TCountedPointer** to access the **refCount** data member of the base class, we shall make it a protected member of **TCountedPointerBase**.

```
#include <iostream.h>

// A Reference Counted Pointer using overloaded operator->
// This class is NOT multi-thread safe. In order to make it multi-thread
// safe, the typedef ReferenceCount should be a separate class,
// that is capable of providing thread-safety.

typedef unsigned long ReferenceCount;

// This class is used only by TCountedPointer as a private base.
// This class exists solely to minimize code replication.

class TCountedPointerBase {
```

```
    protected:
        TCountedPointerBase();
        TCountedPointerBase(const TCountedPointerBase& copy);
        TCountedPointerBase&
            operator=(const TCountedPointerBase& assign);
        ~TCountedPointerBase();
        void AddReference();
        ReferenceCount* _refCount;
};

TCountedPointerBase::TCountedPointerBase() : _refCount(0) {}

TCountedPointerBase::TCountedPointerBase(const TCountedPointerBase& copy)
    : _refCount(copy._refCount) {}

TCountedPointerBase&
TCountedPointerBase::operator=(const TCountedPointerBase& assign)
    { _refCount = assign._refCount; return *this;}

TCountedPointerBase::~TCountedPointerBase() { }

void
TCountedPointerBase ::AddReference()
{
    if (_refCount)(*_refCount)++;
    else {
        _refCount = new ReferenceCount;
        *_refCount = 1;
    }
}
```

This reduces the code size of **TCountedPointer** a little bit. But remember that every in-struction that we eliminate from the template class goes a long way in reducing the size of the final executable (or library). The new **TCountedPointer** class is shown below.

```
template <class AType>
class TCountedPointer : private TCountedPointerBase
{
    public:
        TCountedPointer();
        TCountedPointer(AType* adoptTarget);
        TCountedPointer(const TCountedPointer<AType>& copy);
        virtual ~CountedPointer();
        TCountedPointer<AType>&
            operator=(const TCountedPointer<AType>& assign) ;
        // TRUE if the object is a pointer to a non-0 master
        bool IsValid() const;
        bool operator==(const TCountedPointer<AType>& other) const;
        bool operator!=(const TCountedPointer<AType>& other) const;
        AType& operator*() const;
        AType* operator->() const;
        // This is used for testing purposes only
        int GetReferenceCount() const;

    protected:
```

```
            void RemoveReference();
    private:
            AType* targetPointer;
};

template <class AType>
TCountedPointer<AType>::TCountedPointer() : _targetPointer(0) {}
```

The default constructor sets the reference count to zero because there is no pointer attached to it. The reference count gets incremented when it adopts an existing object.

```
        template <class AType>
        TCountedPointer<AType>::TCountedPointer(AType* adoptTarget) :
            _targetPointer(adoptTarget)
            { AddReference(); /* Calls the base class function */ }
```

This constructor creates a new **TCountedPointer** object with a reference count of 1. No one else is sharing this object and, hence, the reference count is set to 1.

```
    template <class AType>
    TCountedPointer<AType>::TCountedPointer
            (const TCountedPointer<AType>& copy) :
            _targetPointer(copy._targetPointer), TCountedPointerBase(copy)
        { AddReference(); }
```

The copy constructor invokes the base class copy constructor and then invokes the **AddReference** method to add one more reference. Since a new object is created from an existing object, the existing object gains a reference.

```
        template <class AType>
        TCountedPointer<AType>::~CountedPointer() { RemoveReference(); }
```

The destructor relies on the **RemoveReference** method to do the needful. It should take care of decrementing the reference count and deleting the object if necessary.

```
    template <class AType>
    TCountedPointer<AType>&
    TCountedPointer<AType>::operator=(const TCountedPointer<AType>& that)
    {
      if (this != &that) {
            RemoveReference();
            this-> TCountedPointerBase::operator=(that);
            this-> _targetPointer = that._targetPointer;
            AddReference();
      }
      return *this;
    }
```

The assignment operator first invokes the base class assignment operator. First it removes one reference from the object on the LHS and then it adds one more reference to the object on the RHS of the assignment operation. Next, it copies the target pointer and returns a reference to the object on the RHS.

```
template <class AType>
bool
TCountedPointer<AType>::IsValid() const { return (_targetPointer != 0); }

template <class AType>
bool
TCountedPointer<AType>::operator==(const TCountedPointer<AType>& other)
     const
{ return (_targetPointer == other._targetPointer); }
```

The equality operator just compares the embedded target pointers and returns the result.

```
template <class AType>
bool
TCountedPointer<AType>::operator!=(const TCountedPointer<AType>& other)
     const
{
    // Just use the operator== and return the negation of the value
    return ! operator==(other);
}

template <class AType>
AType&
TCountedPointer<AType>::operator*() const { return *_targetPointer; }
```

The **operator*** returns the dereferenced target pointer where as the **operator->** just returns the target pointer.

```
template <class AType>
AType*
TCountedPointer<AType>::operator->() const { return _targetPointer; }

// This is a debug support function
template <class AType>
int
TCountedPointer<AType>::GetReferenceCount() const
{
    if (_refCount) return *_refCount;
    else return -1;
}

template <class AType>
void
TCountedPointer<AType>::RemoveReference()
{
    if (_refCount) {
        // Decrement the reference count and delete the master
        (*_refCount)-;
        if (*_refCount == 0) {
            delete _refCount;
```

```
                        delete _targetPointer;
                        _refCount = 0;
                        _targetPointer = 0;
                }
        }
}
```

Nothing much has changed but the generated code is smaller. Note that we don't have to worry too much about the size of **TCountedPointerBase**. This class is never duplicated no matter how many different types of **TCountedPointer** objects are created. This is a very good example of a template class deriving from a non-template base class.

If you look carefully at the new implementation, the only difference between any two types of **TCountedPointer** objects is the type of the data member _targetPointer. Everything else remains the same. The only value added by the template is the type checking, which ensures that two **TCountedPointer** objects of different types cannot be mixed together. This is a very important benefit. Another benefit is that it takes care of deleting the pointer when no one is using it (the proper destructor is called on _targetPointer). This ensures that all the memory pointed by _targetPointer is deleted correctly. If we could move the complete implementation of **TCountedPointer** to a different class, while keeping the required type checking interface in **TCountedPointer**, we can achieve even more code size savings. What I'm contemplating is a counted pointer base class using **void** pointers and a template **TCountedPointer** class that ensures type checking. We can create a new class **TCountedPointerImplementation**, which contains all the code. Our **TCountedPointer** class acts as a front end, providing type checking. The clients get all the benefits of counted pointers, including type checking. But the code explosion problem is almost completely eliminated. The template class **TCounted-Pointer** ensures that every new type of counted pointer is different as far as the type mechanism is concerned. But internal implementation for all the different instantiations will be the same. This way, we retain all the advantages of template classes and also eliminate code bloat. Here is the class **TCountedPointerImplementation**. Notice that in this class, there are no constructs that cause code bloat.

```
// A Reference Counted Pointer using overloaded operator->
// This class is NOT multi-thread safe. In order to make it multi-thread
// safe, the typedef ReferenceCount should be a separate class.

typedef unsigned long ReferenceCount;

// This class is used only by TCountedPointer as a private base.
// This class exists solely to minimize code replication.

class TCountedPointerImplementation {
    public:
        TCountedPointerImplementation();
        TCountedPointerImplementation(void* adoptTarget);
        TCountedPointerImplementation(const
            TCountedPointerImplementation& copy);
        virtual ~TCountedPointerImplementation();

        TCountedPointerImplementation& operator=(const
            TCountedPointerImplementation&  assign);
```

```
        // Returns true if the object is a pointer to a non-0 master
        bool IsValid() const;
        bool operator==(const TCountedPointerImplementation& other)
            const;
        bool operator!=(const TCountedPointerImplementation& other)
            const;

    protected:
        void AddReference();
        void RemoveReference();
        // Must be implemented by the derived class
        virtual void DeleteTarget() = 0;
        ReferenceCount* _refCount;
        void*    _targetPointer; // THIS IS A BIG CHANGE
};
```

The implementation of this class is quite trivial.

```
TCountedPointerImplementation::TCountedPointerImplementation() :
    _targetPointer(0), _refCount(0) {}

TCountedPointerImplementation::TCountedPointerImplementation(void*
        adoptTarget) :
    _targetPointer(adoptTarget), _refCount(0)
    { AddReference(); }

TCountedPointerImplementation::TCountedPointerImplementation(const
        TCountedPointerImplementation& copy) :
    _targetPointer(copy._targetPointer), _refCount(copy._refCount)
    { AddReference(); }

TCountedPointerImplementation::~TCountedPointerImplementation()
    { /* All the work is done by the derived class. */ }

TCountedPointerImplementation&
TCountedPointerImplementation::operator=(const
        TCountedPointerImplementation& that)
{
    RemoveReference();
    this-> _targetPointer = that._targetPointer;
    this-> _refCount = that.refCount;
    AddReference();
    return *this;
}

bool
TCountedPointerImplementation::operator==(const
        TCountedPointerImplementation& other) const
    { return (_targetPointer == other._targetPointer); }

bool
TCountedPointerImplementation::operator!=(const
        TCountedPointerImplementation& other) const
{
    // Just use the operator== and return the negation of the value
```

```
        return ! operator==(other);
    }

    // This is a debug support function
    int
    TCountedPointerImplementation::GetReferenceCount() const
    {
        if (_refCount) return *_refCount;
        else return -1;
    }

    bool
    TCountedPointerImplementation::IsValid() const
        { return (_targetPointer != 0); }

    void
    TCountedPointerImplementation::AddReference()
    {
        if (_refCount) (*_refCount)++;
        else {
            _refCount = new ReferenceCount;
            *_refCount = 1;
        }
    }

    void
    TCountedPointerImplementation::RemoveReference()
    {
        if (refCount) {
            // Decrement the reference count and delete the master
            (*_refCount)—;
            if (*_refCount == 0) {
                this->DestroyObject(); // Call derived class function
                _refCount = 0;
                _targetPointer = 0;
            }
        }
    }
```

As in the previous implementation, class **TCountedPointer** again derives privately from **TCountedPointerImplementation**. Here is the class interface.

```
template <class AType>
class TCountedPointer : private TCountedPointerImplementation
{
    public:
        TCountedPointer();
        TCountedPointer(AType* adoptTarget);
        TCountedPointer(const TCountedPointer<AType>& copy);
        virtual ~TCountedPointer();
        TCountedPointer<AType>& operator=(const TCountedPointer<AType>&
                                                            assign) ;

        // Re-exported members of the base class
        TCountedPointerImplementation::IsValid;
```

```
        TCountedPointerImplementation::operator==;
        TCountedPointerImplementation::operator!=;

        AType& operator*() const;
        AType* operator->() const;
        // This is used for testing purposes only
        int GetReferenceCount() const;
    protected:
        // Override the base class pure virtual member function
        virtual void DeleteTarget();
};
```

There is hardly any implementation in this class. All the work is done in TCountedPointerImplementation class. The interesting methods are operator->, operator*, and of
course DeleteTarget. Both operator-> and operator* must return the correct type of
pointer. For example, if we create a counted pointer object for TPerson class (TCount-
edPointer<TPerson>), operator-> must return a TPerson* for this object. But the base
class stores the pointer as a pointer to void. We already know that void pointers can be
converted to any other pointer type by explicit type conversion (use extreme caution). The
pointer in the base class TCountedPointerImplementation is modified and set only by
the TCountedPointer member functions. Therefore, when a counted pointer object is
created for TPerson, the void pointer (_targetPointer) in TCountedPointerImplementation is really a pointer to TPerson. So the operator-> casts _targetPointer to a
TPerson pointer and returns it. Same thing happens in operator*. We can confidently
perform the casts because we know that inside a TCountedPointer<TPerson>,
_targetPointer must be a TPerson pointer and nothing else. Here is the implementation.
In this code, notice the type conversion of the void pointer to an AType pointer.

```
template <class AType>
AType&
TCountedPointer<AType>::operator*() const
{
    // We have to use an explicit cast here because targetPointer
    // is a void*. But this function returns AType&. This cast is safe
    // because targetPointer was set up by us and it is guaranteed to be
    // an AType*. See Chapter-6 for RTTI and reinterpret_cast
    return * ( reinterpret_cast<AType*>(_targetPointer) );
}

template <class AType>
AType*
TCountedPointer<AType>::operator->() const
{
    // See operator* above. Same rules apply here.
    return reinterpret_cast<AType*>(_targetPointer);
}
```

The other interesting piece of code is in DeleteTarget, which is pure virtual in the base
class. Why am I introducing a new virtual function in the base class? There was no such
function in the earlier implementations!

```
template <class AType>
void
TCountedPointer<AType>::DeleteTarget()
{
    delete _refCount;
    delete ( (AType* )_targetPointer);
}
```

When it is time to delete the _targetPointer, in order to ensure correct behavior, we must keep in mind the original type of _targetPointer. Even though _targetPointer is maintained as a void pointer in the base class, it is really a pointer to some other type, such as TPerson. So when we invoke operator delete on _targetPointer, the destructor of TPerson is called only when the compiler knows that _targetPointer is of type TPerson. We cannot just delete a void pointer because nothing is known about the memory pointed by it. To correctly delete a pointer, the compiler must know the static type of the pointer. Then it will know how much memory to reclaim. A void pointer can point to anything at any time and the compiler knows nothing about what it points to. Therefore, it doesn't know anything about the type of the address stored in the void pointer. This is why void pointers cannot be deleted directly. By casting it to a known type (such as AType), we provide the compiler the necessary information that the it needs. But TCountedPointerImplementation knows nothing about the actual type of _targetPointer. We should not delete _targetPointer in the base class.[18] Class TCountedPointer knows the actual type of _targetPointer. Therefore, TCountedPointer must take responsibility for deleting the pointer. Everything else happens in the base class. When it is time to delete the _targetPointer in member function RemoveReference, the virtual function DeleteTarget is invoked. The dynamic binding mechanism binds the call to the actual implementation in the derived class TCountedPointer, which casts _targetPointer to the correct type (AType) and then deletes it. The code in the member function DeleteTarget is definitely duplicated for every instantiation but it is a very small function.

Here is the rest of the implementation. Notice the simplicity of the code.

```
template <class AType>
TCountedPointer<AType>::TCountedPointer()
    { } // Nothing to do. Automatic invocation of base class ctor

template <class AType>
TCountedPointer<AType>::TCountedPointer(AType* adoptTarget)
    : TCountedPointerImplementation(adoptTarget)
    { } // Nothing else to do.

template <class AType>
TCountedPointer<AType>::TCountedPointer(const
        TCountedPointer<AType>& copy) :
    TCountedPointerImplementation(copy)
    { } // Nothing else to do.

template <class AType>
TCountedPointer<AType>::~TCountedPointer()
```

---

[18]If we don't do this correctly, it will cause horrendous memory leaks.

```
{
    RemoveReference();
}

template <class AType>
TCountedPointer<AType>&
TCountedPointer<AType>::operator=(const
        TCountedPointer<AType>& that)
{
    if (this != &that)
        TCountedPointerImplementation::operator=(that);
    // Invoke the base class function

    return *this;
}

// This is a debug support function
template <class AType>
int
TCountedPointer<AType>::GetReferenceCount() const
{
    if (_refCount) return *_refCount;
    else return -1;
}

template <class AType>
void
TCountedPointer<AType>::DeleteTarget()
{
    delete    _refCount;
    if (_targetPointer != 0)
        delete (reinterpret_cast<AType*> (_targetPointer);
}
```

Here is a simple test program along with the output. Notice the usage style of the reference counted pointer objects.

```
// A Test program

#include <iostream.h>
class X {
    public:
        ~X() { cout << "Destructor for X(" << _id << ")\n"; }
        X(int i) {_id = i; }
        void Print() const { cout << "Print X(" << _id << ")
            " <<endl; }
    private:
        int _id;
};

int main()
{
    X* px = new X (1);
    TCountedPointer<X> ap(px);
    TCountedPointer<X> bp = ap;
```

```
TCountedPointer<X> cp;
cout << "Number of references to ap (must be 2): " <<
     ap.GetReferenceCount() << endl;

cout << "Assign ap to cp...\n";
cp = ap;

cout << "Number of references to ap (must be 3): " <<
     ap.GetReferenceCount() << endl;

X* qx = new X(100);
TCountedPointer<X> dp(qx);

ap = dp; // Decreases the reference through ap

cout << "References to px (should be be 2): " <<
     bp.GetReferenceCount() << endl;

cout << "References to qx (should be be 2): " <<
     dp.GetReferenceCount() << endl;
cout << "ap.IsValid() returned " << ap.IsValid() << endl;
cout << "ap == bp returned " <<(int) (ap == bp) << endl;
cout << "cp == bp returned " << (int) (cp == bp) << endl;

dp->Print();
(*cp).Print();

return 0;
}
```

The output is:

```
Number of references to ap (must be 2): 2
Assign ap to cp...
Number of references to ap (must be 3): 3
References to px (should be 2): 2
References to qx (should be 2): 2
ap.IsValid() returned 1
ap == bp returned 0
cp == bp returned 1
Print X(100)
Print X(1)
Destructor for X(1)
Destructor for X(100)
```

NOTE   The member function **RemoveReference** is invoked from TCountedPointer destructor and not **TCountedPointerImplementation** destructor for a good reason. When a **TCountedPointer** object goes out of scope, the destructor of **TCountedPointer** is called first. When it completes execution, the destructor of **TCountedPointerImplementation** is called. When we get to the destructor of **TCountedPointerImplementation**, the object is no longer a **TCountedPointer** object but really a **TCountedPointerImplementation** object. If we invoke **RemoveReference** from within **TCountedPointerImplementation** then if it (RemoveReference) needs to delete the target, **DeleteTarget** is called. But in class **TCountedPointerImplementation**, **DeleteTarget** is a pure virtual function without an implementation. So we end up invoking a pure virtual method. This is definitely asking for trouble. With most compilers, it will crash your program. This is the reason for making the call to **RemoveReference** from the destructor of **TCountedPointer** and not **TCountedPointerImplementation**. See Fig. 9-14 below.

With this implementation, the template class contains very little code. Most of the implementation code is in the base class, which is not duplicated. The *per instantiation cost* for **TCountedPointer** class is now minimal. This is one very powerful technique for minimizing the code replication side effect of template classes while still retaining all the benefits (*tastes great and less filling*). Are there any extra overheads in this implementa-

GOOD	**VERY BAD**
1. TCountedPointer destructor is called. It completes and calls base class destructor	1. TCountedPointer destructor is called. It completes and calls base class destructor

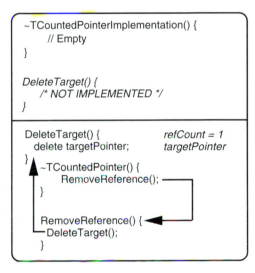

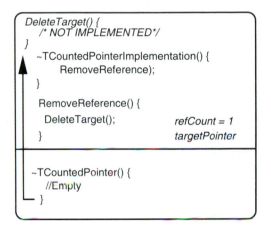

2. TCountedPointerImplementation destructor completes.

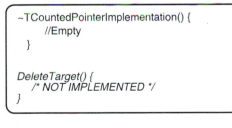

3. Object is destroyed

2. TCountedPointerImplementation destructor runs. It calls a pure virtual function which is not implemented

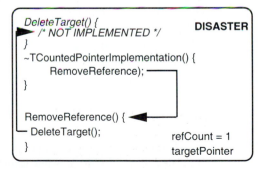

3. Crash and burn

Fig. 9-14

tion that might affect performance? We have added a new virtual function that will cost us a little bit when targetPointer must be deleted. We also have an extra constructor and destructor call per object. The calls to TCountedPointerImplementation class constructor and destructor did not exist in the original implementation. This is almost negligible because there is hardly any code in TCountedPointer constructor. In terms of object size, the virtual function will add one pointer (the virtual function table pointer) to every object.

THINK   A careful reader might have already noticed the unnecessary extra work done in TCountedPointer in managing reference counts. Didn't we already create a class MReferenceCounter in Chapter 6 for this purpose? And shouldn't we reuse that class here (*we are doing object-oriented programming, aren't we*)? Yes, it can be reused here and it is a trivial exercise left to the reader.

TEMPLATE CLASSES AND SOURCE CODE PROTECTION

When a client uses a template class, invariably she is going to instantiate a new class (such as TList<TPerson> from TList<AType>) by supplying the template arguments. As we already know, instantiating a new template class requires the class implementation source code. Traditionally, in the software industry, a client only receives object code (a library) and not the source code. This protects trade secrets and proprietary algorithms of the implementor and also allows the implementor the freedom to change the code in the future. But when template classes are shipped, the implementor must ship source code (of the template class implementation) if the client must instantiate new template classes. So how can vendors of template classes protect their trade secrets and proprietary algorithms? This is a very delicate problem with template classes.

The technique of using a non-template private base class (or even a public base class) discussed above is very helpful in solving this problem. All the proprietary code can be pushed into the non-template base class. Clients never need the source code of this base class. All trivial, non-proprietary code should be in the template derived class. The implementor must restructure the code with great care to take advantage of this scheme. If any part of the code in the base class needs to know the actual type of the template argument, it must be in the derived class. Partitioning code this way requires a thorough understanding of the code and C++ language. Using void pointers to achieve this separation is a well known technique in the C++ development community. See the previous section for more details on the implementation.

TEMPLATE CLASSES IN SHARED (DYNAMIC) LIBRARIES

Nowadays, it is very common to use shared libraries in systems. They are also called dynamic-link libraries (DLL). A few sentences about them is in order.

Traditionally, when a program is compiled and linked, all the code it needs, including those functions that exist in other libraries, are pulled into the final executable. So the executable program contains one copy of all functions that the program will ever need.

This is also called *static linking*. This creates a monolithic application. There is nothing wrong with this approach and it has been in use for a long time and is still in use.

Building programs this way is inefficient with modern multi-tasking operating systems and multi-processor machines. Consider a situation in which three application programs, App1, App2, and App3, use three different libraries, Lib1, Lib2, and Lib3. For the sake of this discussion, let us just assume that App1, App2, and App3 use many functions from Lib1, Lib2, and Lib3. With the traditional approach, each of App1, App2, and App3 will contain a copy of Lib1, Lib2, and Lib3 in their executable image. In other words, App1, App2, and App3 are statically linked with Lib1, Lib2, and Lib3 (see Fig. 9-15).

Consider a multi-tasking system in which App1, App2, and App3 can execute simultaneously. When the OS loads App1, it also loads (into virtual memory) all the li-

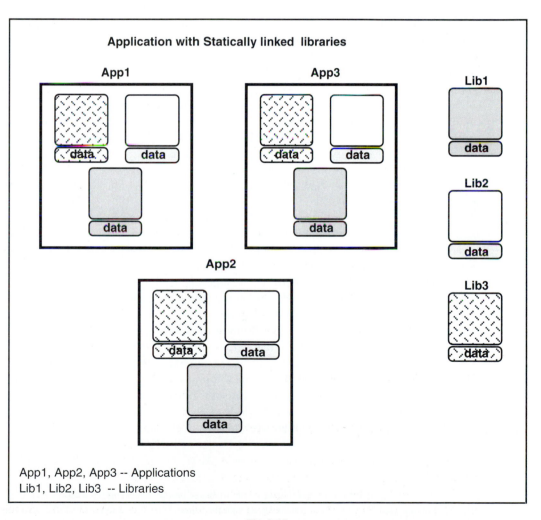

App1, App2, App3 -- Applications
Lib1, Lib2, Lib3 -- Libraries

Fig. 9-15

braries it needs. So Lib1, Lib2 and Lib3 are all loaded into the application's memory. When a user starts App2 while App1 is already running, the OS will again load all the libraries needed by App2. Once again, Lib1, Lib2, and Lib3 are loaded into the application's memory by the OS. In effect, now there are two copies of Lib1, Lib2, and Lib3 loaded into the computer's memory (but in different applications and different address spaces). If some user runs another copy of App1, App2, or App3, one more copy of the libraries Lib1, Lib2, and Lib3 will be loaded into the computer's memory. Because of static linking of libraries, whenever an application is run, all the libraries that it needs are loaded into the computer's memory, even if the library is already loaded into memory as part of some other application. This really eats up the memory in the machine. Wouldn't it be better if there is only one copy of the library loaded into memory that is shared by all applications? This is the concept behind shared libraries.

When Lib1, Lib2, and Lib3 are *shared libraries*, the first time an application makes a call to a function in one of the libraries, say Lib1, the library is loaded into memory. When some other application makes a call to a function in Lib1, another copy of the library is not loaded into memory. Instead, the OS sets up a link between the new application and Lib1, which is already loaded into memory.[19] The only copy of Lib1 in the computer's memory is now shared by two (or more) applications.[20] Shared libraries are also called dynamic link libraries (DLL) because when an application makes a call to a function in the library, the link between the library and the application is set up *dynamically* by the OS. In other words, *dynamic linking* of the application with the library is carried out at run time. A shared library is shared among all the applications that need to use the library. Note that the code (or text) in the library is shared. Any data (variables, objects, etc.) contained in the library may or may not be shared depending on the implementation (see Fig. 9-16). (Usually the OS gives the programmers the freedom to specify whether a piece of global data must be shared among all applications or they must be duplicated per application.)

Using shared libraries instead of statically linked libraries saves a lot of memory because, no matter how many applications need the library, there is only one copy of it in the entire system. Shared libraries facilitate a much higher degree of code sharing compared with static libraries. Because of the savings in memory, more applications can simultaneously run in a machine. Furthermore, the applications will run faster because there is less paging activity involved. Modern operating systems provide extensive support for creating and manipulating shared libraries.

On most operating systems, a shared library has two parts—an *export list* and an *import list*. The export list contains all the entities (functions and data) exported from the shared library. Applications use this export list when linking. The import list contains all the entities needed by this shared library, which it probably imports from other shared libraries or applications. The compiler/linker (or some other tool) might generate these import and export lists automatically or it might have to be done manually by the programmer. The exact details of these steps are very specific to each OS.

---

[19]The shared library Lib1 is mapped into the address space of the new application by the OS.

[20]In reality, the library is reference counted and now there are two references to the library because two different applications are using it.

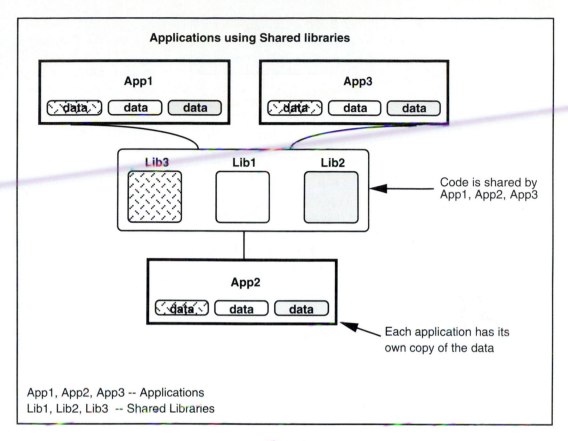

Applications using Shared libraries

App1, App2, App3 -- Applications
Lib1, Lib2, Lib3 -- Shared Libraries

Fig. 9-16

Template Classes in Shared Libraries—Multiple Instantiations Problems

The code sharing and memory savings benefits will all become useless if we don't understand the side effects of using template classes in shared libraries. The next few paragraphs shed some light on the problems.

Consider application **AppX**, which uses our template list class **TList**. In particular, assume that **AppX** needs **TList<TPerson>**. The functions needed by **AppX** can be in a shared library **SLibX**. So class **TList<TPerson>** is completely instantiated in **SLibX** (see Fig. 9-17).

Some other programmer writes another application **AppY**. Application **AppY**'s code is contained in the shared library **SLibY**. Application **AppY** also needs **TList<TPerson>**. So **TList<TPerson>** is completely instantiated in the shared library **SLibY** (see Fig. 9-18).

When applications **AppX** and **AppY** are running simultaneously, both **SLibX** and **SLibY** are resident in RAM (Random Access Memory) (see Fig. 9-19).

Now two copies of **TList<TPerson>** are kept in memory unnecessarily. The code for **TList<TPerson>** in **SLibX** is exactly the same as the code for **TList<TPerson>** in

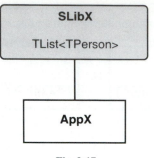

Fig. 9-17

SLibY. We have wasted memory (RAM). Application AppX knows nothing about AppY or the shared library SLibY. On the same lines, AppY knows nothing about AppX or SLibX. Both AppX and AppY need to use the template TList class and it is correct to instantiate TList<TPerson> in SLibX and SLibY. But memory is wasted when both AppX and AppY are running on the same system.

    Note that code duplication in shared libraries is not a trivial problem that can be solved easily. With multiple shared libraries and many different applications, it is very easy for the same code to exist in many different shared libraries, causing wastage of memory. If many template classes with many different instantiations are used, this can be a very serious problem.

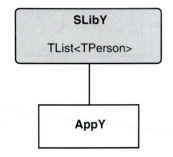

Fig. 9-18

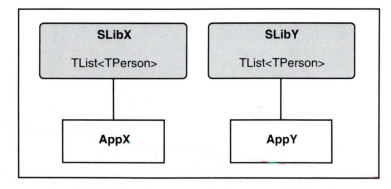

Fig. 9-19

Eliminating Multiple Instantiations in Shared Libraries

We can probably avoid this unnecessary waste of memory by simple restructuring of our code. If AppX and AppY are developed by the same team, then common functions (member functions and others) needed by both the applications can be moved into another shared library—SLibXandY. Since both AppX and AppY need TList<TPerson>, it can be moved into SLibXandY. Code specific to application AppX is kept in SLibX. Similarly, code specific to AppY is kept in SLibY. Now when AppX is started, both SLibX and SLibXandY are paged into memory by the OS. When AppY is started, only SLibY needs to be loaded because SLibXandY is already loaded into memory (see Fig. 9-20).

For this scheme to work, automatic instantiation of TList<TPerson> must be suppressed when SLibX and SLibY are compiled (or the programmer should explicitly instantiate all required classes). Automatic instantiation for TList<TPerson> must be enabled when SLibXandY is compiled. The linker must know where the code for TList<TPerson> will come from. Otherwise, references to functions in TList<TPerson> would be unresolved in the final executable. Therefore, AppX and AppY must use (link with) the export list of SLibXandY.

This scheme requires that developers of AppX and AppY coordinate with each other to eliminate the duplicates. It would not work if AppX and AppY have been developed by teams that do not have any relation to each other (they might be two different companies altogether). Moreover, source code for the template class (TList<AType>) must be available when SLibXandY is compiled to instantiate TList<TPerson>.

Developers of applications AppX and AppY must determine the common template instantiations between them and suppress automatic code generation for all of them. This

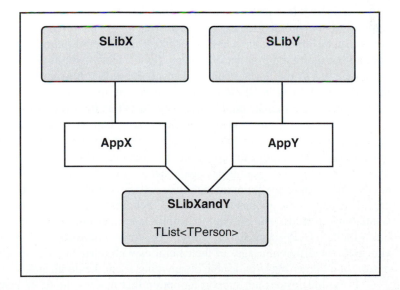

Fig. 9-20

is not a trivial task. One easy way to do that would be to turn off automatic template code generation for all classes and analyze the linker errors. The linker errors indicate which of the needed functions are missing. Repeat this step for both AppX and AppY. Next, find out what is common between AppX and AppY link errors. These belong in the shared library SLibXandY. It is easier to manage instantiations if all instantiations are kept in a separate file. The process of finding common template instantiations is more tedious as more and more applications start sharing code. Instantiating one class to eliminate a final link error can cause more link errors because the new class being instantiated may depend on other classes that must also be instantiated. This process can be really frustrating. Also remember that the code in SLibXandY might depend on other shared libraries. In such cases, those other shared libraries must be loaded when SLibXandY is loaded. This chain of dependencies can get very complicated in big projects involving many shared libraries. Factoring out common code across multiple shared libraries is a very difficult task because of intricate code dependencies among classes.

Suppressing automatic template code generation for specific classes is not easy. Some possible solutions were discussed earlier. When compilers implement the complete C++ language specifications for template classes, one would be able to instantiate specific classes and functions easily.

Linking with Existing Shared Libraries

Imagine another situation where you receive two shared libraries, SLibA and SLibB, from two different vendors. Further, assume that both SLibA and SLibB internally use a common library from some other vendor. It is very likely that both SLibA and SLibB contain some common template instantiations. If application AppZ depends on both SLibA and SLibB, then it must link with both of them. But wouldn't we run into problems of duplicate definitions while linking because both SLibA and SLibB contains some common template instantiations (or even ordinary classes with the same name)?

This is another problem faced by template library users. There are some possible solutions to this problem. Many linkers provide an option to ignore duplicate names. This option can be turned on when linking AppZ. With this option turned on, the linker will ignore all but the first definition of a name. So if SLibA is the first library in the list of libraries passed to the linker, then the second definition of a name in SLibB (which has been already defined in SLibA) will be ignored by the compiler. This has been used in many projects to eliminate duplicates easily. Note that this approach is a godsend in cases where we don't have any control over the libraries that we link with but it should not be used in cases where two (or more) libraries that you created contain duplicate instantiations. In such cases, move the common instantiations to one of the libraries and eliminate them from the others. There is not much that a user can do about the duplicates in SLibA and SLibB because any program that links with SLibA but not SLibB must execute properly. The same logic applies to SLibB. So each library must contain all the template instantiations it needs. The problem of duplicates arises only when an application tries to link with both SLibA and SLibB. It would be almost impossible for creators of libraries to anticipate the different usages of their libraries with other libraries by clients. Hence, the creator of a library may not be able do anything about the duplicates.

If the linker does not support an option that ignores duplicate names, then there is no way an application can successfully link with both SLibA and SLibB. Eliminating

SLibA or SLibB is not an option because the application needs functions from both libraries. Names (functions and variables) that are duplicated in both libraries are the source of the problem here.

NOTE   If the shared libraries use different namespaces, this problem will go away because the application can specify the namespace from which the functions must be imported, it eliminates the linking problem. When the application is executed, both SLibA and SLibB are still loaded and there is definitely memory being wasted. However, the elimination of duplicates to satisfy the linker would not be a problem. Please refer to the ANSI C++ reference manual for details about the namespaces facility.

Using shared libraries has other benefits too. If many of the shared libraries used by an application have been already loaded by the OS at the request of other applications, a new application started by a user will come up faster because very little time is spent in loading shared libraries.

☞ **The problem of eliminating duplicates when linking with multiple shared libraries and the consequent waste of memory is not unique to template classes. It is possible with any class/function that exists in more than one shared library. It is a more common phenomenon with template classes because of template code generation for specific template arguments. With non-template classes there isn't any issue of generating specific instantiations. All we have to worry about is the inclusion or exclusion of the object code of the class.**

Container Classes

Classes such as TList, TOrderedList, TSafeArray, etc. are very similar classes. In general, they provide a storage mechanism for user objects such as TPerson, TCourse, etc. When we create TList<TPerson>, TSafeArray<TCourse>, etc. and store our objects in them, these template classes are acting as containers for our objects. Each type of container enforces some storage and retrieval policy on the objects it contains. Such classes are usually called *Container Classes* or *collection classes*. In this book they are called container classes.

Designing and implementing container class hierarchies is a challenging and interesting task. There are many good lessons and tricks that one can learn from their design and implementation. Generic classes are highly suited for implementing container classes. Languages that do not support generic classes (for example, Smalltalk) implement container classes by using inheritance.

More details about container classes can be found in the second part of the book (Chapter 12).

COMPARING GENERIC TYPES AND INHERITANCE

We have studied Inheritance in Chapter 5 and Chapter 6. In this chapter we have analyzed generic types. Looking at these two concepts, one might wonder about their similarities and differences.

Inheritance is a neat technique to use when you would like to provide some default implementation for operations (all or some) that derived classes might override. This provides a lot of flexibility. But inheritance is a compile time (static) decision. Inheritance also has the benefit of providing uniform interface to an entire hierarchy. Inheritance also has the benefit of polymorphism, allowing us to substitute derived class instances in place of a base class instance. This is a very powerful tool in building extensible software.

First of all, generic types are useful only in statically typed languages. Languages that use run-time type checking wouldn't need generic types. Generic types allow the user to change the types that a class can use. In other words, the dependency on a particular type is eliminated by making the type an argument to the template class (which must be specified at compile time). This is again a compile time binding. Like inheritance, every instance of a generic type has the same interface. Therefore, TList<TCar> has the same interface as a TList<TRangeInt>. But, generic type instances are not compatible with each other, i.e., a TList<TCar> cannot be used in place of a TList<TRangeInt>, even though they are instances of the same generic type TList. But, this can also be seen as a benefit because it enforces very strict type checking.

Both inheritance and generic types are powerful tools. They can be combined to solve many complex problems. One such example was seen in the TDictionary class. We used the strict type checking and type independence benefit of generic types and combined it with inheritance to achieve uniform interface and dynamic binding.

CAUTION   Both inheritance and generic types by themselves are powerful concepts, and every OO designer and programmer must understand them clearly. Ensure that you are comfortable with them independently before trying to use them together in any solution. If you have difficulty understanding the concept of inheritance and generic types by themselves, then you will have a tough time using them together.

This discussion might lead you think that it might be possible to simulate inheritance with generic types or vice-versa. In short, generic types can be simulated with inheritance but not the other way around. A more detailed discussion can be found in Chapter 12.

PORTABILITY   Multiple inheritance, Templates and Exceptions are problematic areas for compiler
CAUTION   implementors. There are numerous differences among compiler implementations, more so on UNIX platforms. What works on one platform may not even compile on another. This has caused a lot of grief to system implementors developing cross-platform applications. Over the years, compilers have improved but still there isn't a compiler that is fully conformant with the latest definition of the language. Of course, the numerous additions/enhancements to the language over the years haven't made the life of the compiler developers any easier. If you are developing cross-platform software, refrain from using the very latest and greatest features of the language—your code may not even compile on all platforms. Some of these problematic areas are default value arguments in templates, template code generation, template specialization, static data members in template classes, covariant return types in inheritance hierarchies, operator-> in template classes, inheritance between template classes, exceptions with template objects, partial completion of constructors with exceptions, etc. Don't try to use a language enhancement that was introduced a month ago and expect your compiler to support it.

SUMMARY

Generic classes and functions maximize code and design reuse and reduce programmer fatigue and boredom.

Every generic class depends on user supplied types (or built-in types).

There can be infinite instantiations of a generic class. Each instantiation behaves like a new class (but with the same interface).

Designing a generic class is a lot harder than designing a normal class because of the interactions between the generic class and its generic argument.

C++ template classes cause code replication and a corresponding increase in the executable image size, if not controlled by the implementor.

Client of a generic class does not just create and use objects of the class. She must also supply an actual generic argument when creating objects. This establishes a special relationship between the client of the generic class and the implementator of the generic class.

A generic class may not work with all types. Any special requirements and restrictions of generic classes must be clearly documented.

Combining genericity with inheritance results in a very powerful design tool that can solve complex problems and it also reduces code bloat.

Using C++ template classes inside shared libraries can cause unnecessary code bloat. Exercise caution when instantiating templates in shared libraries.

10

Expecting the Unexpected

One of the major problems in software development is that of managing error conditions. No matter how good our software is, errors are still bound to happen due to a number of reasons (programming errors, unexpected operating system errors, resource exhaustion, etc.). A well designed software should anticipate and manage such abnormal situations gracefully. This chapter deals with the schemes employed by different object-oriented languages for error handling and shows the C++ scheme in detail.

WHY SHOULD WE HANDLE ERROR CONDITIONS?

When we write code, it is natural to assume that certain conditions are valid before attempting an operation. If one of those conditions is not true, then the attempted operation would probably fail. For example, accessing an element beyond the end of the array is an invalid operation, and opening a non-existent file is another invalid operation. But when such invalid operations are attempted, it will be very helpful if our software checks the necessary pre-requisite conditions before attempting the operation. In the case of accessing beyond the end of an array, we can check the index before accessing the specified element. This will at least prevent more serious damage that can be caused by accessing invalid memory addresses.

If we attempt to open a file that doesn't exist, it is not going to cause any problems as such. Usually, the operating system returns an error code indicating the cause of failure. The program that attempted to open the file must remember to check the error code returned by the operating system and do whatever is necessary to recover from that situation. But what happens if the program just ignores the error code and continues? Any subsequent operations on the file will cause more errors. In this case, the program that attempted to open a non-existent file should not be allowed to ignore the error code—it must be forced to examine the error code or it should be stopped immediately. This will prevent more serious errors down the road.

What's Wrong with Error Codes?

Software developers have been using codes to indicate error conditions for a long time. Usually procedures return a code to indicate their outcome. For example, a procedure OpenFile might return 0 (zero) to indicate failure. Some other procedure might return (−1) to indicate failure and 0 to indicate success. Operating systems and software libraries document all possible error codes that might be returned by a procedure. Programmers using such procedures should carefully check the returned code and do the right thing there after. But a programmer might forget to check the returned error code from a procedure call. This can cause more serious problems in subsequent code. For example, if a procedure returns a pointer (an address) and if this address happens to be 0, the calling procedure should not use the returned pointer. But if the code fails to check for a nil pointer, subsequent code might encounter a more serious problem (nil pointer dereferencing) causing the application to terminate abnormally.[1] When the application terminates abnormally, no house keeping code is executed to ensure that things are in order. For example, files that were open are not closed, network connections are not closed, data is not written to disk, etc. A well designed (and implemented) application should not allow this to happen.

Errors should not be allowed to propagate unnecessarily. If errors are detected and handled as soon as they happen, more serious damage (in subsequent code) is prevented. When errors propagate to different parts of the code, it will be much harder to trace the real cause of the problem because the symptoms of the problem may not indicate the real cause. In many situations, a very innocent looking piece of code might run into rough weather because an earlier piece of code did not check an error condition.

When an error is detected by an application, it may be able to fix the cause of the problem and retry the operation that caused the error. For example, the index that caused access beyond the end of an array can be fixed easily. In other situations, the application may not be able to do anything to fix the error condition. A graceful exit might be the only solution in such situations. The programmer must be given the freedom to make the correct decision.

When a procedure encounters an error condition and returns to the caller, it would be expected that the procedure perform necessary clean-up before returning to the caller. The code that detects and handles the error condition must incorporate extra code for this clean-up chore. In other words, the procedure should not *leak* any resources. This is not an easy task by any means. And it is harder when there are multiple exit points from the

---

[1]This usually causes a *segment violation* on UNIX systems. On most operating systems, trying to access some element using a NIL pointer causes abnormal program termination.

procedure. If there are multiple locations in the code where errors conditions must be checked, then all such locations must have proper code for clean-up (this is like guarding a house that has multiple doors). This can really make the procedure complicated and ugly.

In certain cases, a procedure may not have the necessary information to handle an error condition. But there might be some other procedure calling chain that might have the necessary information to manage the error condition. It should be possible to safely (and cleanly) propagate the error condition to the outer procedure where it can be handled. Procedures returning simple error codes would not be able to meet this challenge easily.

Error codes returned from procedures do not convey much information to the calling procedure. It is usually a number that indicates the cause of failure. But in many situations, it would be very helpful if more information about the cause of failure is available to the caller. This would help in fixing the error condition (if possible). A simple error code cannot fulfill this goal.

WHAT IS THE ALTERNATIVE?

The shortcomings of returning error codes discussed above can be overcome by employing other schemes. One of the most popular schemes that has been time tested and supported by many languages is the principle of *raising exceptions*. An exception is raised in case of an error. An exception indicates an abnormal condition that should not be encountered during normal code execution. An exception indicates an urgent need for remedial action.

NOTE   The word *exception* here indicates a software exception. This should not be confused with hardware exceptions. A software exception is caused by a piece of code written by a programmer. It has nothing to do with hardware exceptions. A software exception is initiated by some piece of code encountering an abnormal condition.

An exception might be raised when the contract between the caller and the callee is violated. For example, trying to access an element beyond the end of an array is violation of the contract between the subscripting function (the **operator[]** in C++) and the caller using the array. The subscript function guarantees to return the element at the specified location if the index passed to it is valid. But if the index is invalid, the subscript function must indicate the error condition. Whenever such violation of contract occurs, an exception condition should be raised.

Once an exception is raised, it does not disappear if the programmer just ignores it—an exception cannot be ignored or suppressed. An exception condition will go away only when someone recognizes and *handles* the exception. An unhandled exception keeps propagating up the dynamic calling chain until it reaches the top level function. If the top level function (**main** in C++) also fails to handle the exception, the application is terminated without mercy.

Any error detection and correction scheme should not unduly affect the performance and efficiency of the normal code that is executed when there is no error. Any error handling mechanism, no matter how good, is useless if it degrades the performance of the normal code. Languages that support the exception mechanism tend to keep the exception code quite separate from the normal code.

CAUTION   Error handling using exceptions does not prevent errors—it only allows for cleanup and possible recovery in case of errors. Preventing errors might be done by using assertions (discussed in chapter 2).

In general, the exception mechanism (in most languages) allows

    1. forceful error detection and possible recovery;

    2. cleanup and graceful exit in case of unhandled errors; and

    3. systematic propagation of errors in the dynamic call chain.

Adding exception management to normal code to handle errors doesn't come for free. New code must be added to procedures to manage exceptions. The exception management code interspersed with normal code obscures the logic of the original procedure. Adding exceptions to an application also increases the executable image size.

THE C++ EXCEPTION HANDLING MODEL

The C++ exception model introduces three new keywords **try**, **throw**, and **catch**. These keywords are very appropriate for what they do. First of all, a programmer will *try* an operation anticipating errors. When a procedure encounters an error, it *throws* an exception. Throwing an exception is the act of raising an exception. Finally, someone interested in an error condition (for cleanup and/or recovery) should anticipate the error and *catch* the exception that is thrown. Here is a simple example to illustrate the model.

```
void f()
{
        // Some code that will cause an exception to be thrown
        //...
        throw 1;
        //...
}

main()
{
        try {
            f(); // Call f - Be prepared for any errors
            // More normal code here
        }
        catch(...)
        {
            // Catch any exceptions thrown by f()
            // Do whatever is necessary
        }
        // Normal code of main() continued
}
```

f() is a simple procedure. When it encounters an error condition, it throws an exception. This is done by the statement

```
throw 1;
```

The operand of a **throw** expression is an object. Usually objects with information about the error are thrown.

In the **main**() program, the call to f() is enclosed in a **try** block. The code

```
try {
     //...
}
```

is a **try** block. In other words, it is a block of code enclosed within a **try** statement. A **try** block indicates to the compiler the possibility of an exception.

A **catch**() block catches an exception of the indicated type. In the example above

```
catch(...)
```

indicates that it will catch exceptions of all types. The ... (ellipses) matches any argument. A catch expression is comparable to a procedure with an argument. It gets called when an actual argument of a matching type is passed (thrown).

How the C++ Exception Mechanism Works?

When an exception of some type is thrown, control is transferred to the *nearest* handler of the *appropriate* type. The run-time exception system immediately starts looking for a **catch** block that matches the argument passed to the **throw** statement. Within a procedure, a **catch** block should follow a **try** block. When f() throws an exception, there is no way to handle the exception within f() because there isn't any **catch** block in f(). Now an abnormal return from f() will happen. None of the statements following the **throw** statement are executed. Control returns to the caller of f(), the **main**() function. This return from f() is no different from a normal return from f(). Destructors for all local objects are invoked before leaving f() due to an exception. In other words, whatever clean-up that happens with a normal return from f(), will also happen when returning due to an exception.

Now control has been returned to **main**() but the exception condition still exists. The run-time system looks for an appropriate handler (a matching **catch** block) for the pending exception. There is a **catch** block that immediately follows the **try** block in **main**(). This **catch** block matches any exception because of the (...) argument. The ellipses mean *match with anything*. So now a matching handler has been found. The **catch** block is entered and the code within the **catch** block is executed. Thereafter, execution is sequential and continues as if nothing abnormal happened (see Fig. 10-1).

An exception propagates until a matching handler is found. Exceptions can be handled only by **catch** blocks (also called **catch** handlers). To be considered for a match, a **catch** block must always follow a **try** block. A **try** block is a hint to the compiler to look for a **catch** block(s). That is, a **try** block creates a dynamic call chain. An exception is

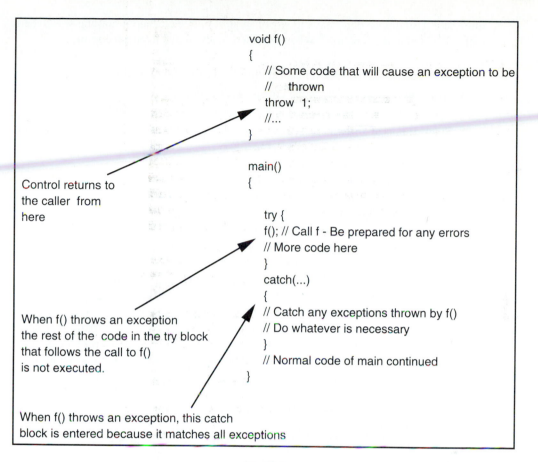

```
                                    void f()
                                    {
                                        // Some code that will cause an exception to be
                                        //   thrown
                                        throw 1;
                                        //...
                                    }

                                    main()
                                    {

Control returns to
the caller  from
here                                    try {
                                        f(); // Call f - Be prepared for any errors
                                        // More code here
                                        }
                                    catch(...)
                                    {
                                        // Catch any exceptions thrown by f()
When f() throws an exception         // Do whatever is necessary
the rest of the  code in the try block   }
that follows the call to f()            // Normal code of main continued
is not executed.
                                    }

When f() throws an exception, this catch
block is entered because it matches all exceptions
```

Fig. 10-1

considered handled as soon as a **catch** block is entered. An exception is considered finished (the exception condition no longer exists) when the corresponding **catch** block exits.

If main() did not have a matching **catch** block, the exception remains unhandled, and the pre-defined function **terminate()** is called as soon as control is returned to main() from f(). Note that, in such a situation, the rest of the code in the try block that follows the call to f() in main() is never executed. As soon as control returns to main() because of the exception thrown by f(), we are in the exception processing mode. The function terminate() will cause abnormal termination of the application.

☞ **If an exception is not handled even by main(), the predefined function terminate is called, which causes the termination of the program.**

Throwing an exception is very similar to returning from a function during normal execution. Cleanup that happens when we return from a function is also done when we leave a function due to an exception. Viewed this way, exiting a function due to an exception is

quite safe. Usually we don't have to worry about resource cleanup if nothing was dynamically allocated in the function.[2] When we exit a function due to an exception:

- Destructor is called for every local object created in the function.
- All arguments passed by value are also destroyed.
- Any temporary objects created in the function are also destroyed.
- Stack frame of the function is removed from the stack and control returns to the
  caller.

The above steps are repeated for all functions exited (in the dynamic call chain) during the
search for a matching handler. The process of calling destructors for automatic objects is
called *stack unwinding*.

Significance of the try **Block**

The try block is a hint to the compiler to look for catch blocks in case of an exception. A
catch block(s) that does not follow a try block is useless.[3] When an exception is thrown,
the search for a matching handler starts with the try block that was most recently entered
by the thread of control but which has not yet been exited. It is very likely that one try
block was entered as part of another try block. The dynamic nesting of try blocks reflects
the nature of nested function calls. In the example above, the call to f() is within the try
block of main(). The search for a matching handler starts in main() because it was the
most recent try block that was entered and not yet exited.

There is usually no significant run-time cost due to the try block when no exceptions are thrown. The search for a matching catch handler only happens when an exception is thrown. Therefore, the run-time cost of adding try blocks is not very high.[4] But definitely, there is an increase in code size (adding exceptions to any program increases the
code size). Also remember that the cost of exceptions depends on the compiler.

Significance of the throw **Expression**

When an exception is raised, what is thrown is an object. The compiler initializes a temporary object of the static type of the operand of throw. This temporary object is used to
initialize the appropriately typed variable in the matching catch handler. The memory for
the temporary object is allocated in an implementation dependent way. It is up to the compiler writer to decide how this memory is allocated. The temporary object will persist as
long as the exception persists. In other words, the temporary is guaranteed to exist until
the handler completes execution.

---

[2]Resources that require special treatment must be handled by the programmer. More on this later.

[3]A series of catch blocks that follow one another after a try block. are all considered to be following the
same try block.

[4]Some compilers even claim *zero cost* exceptions.

A **throw** expression can throw any object. Here are some examples:

```
throw("Hell broke loose");
```

throws a **char***. It Can be caught by

```
catch (const char* message);
```

Similarly

```
throw (2.11);
```

throws a floating point (or **double**) number. This can be caught by

```
catch (double x);
```

Of course

```
catch (...)
```

will catch any type of exception. In fact, finding a matching catch block is very similar to resolving an overloaded function call. The same argument matching and conversion rules hold good. The difference is, the compiler can resolve overloaded functions statically but when an exception is thrown, the search for a matching catch handler is dynamic.

A **throw** expression without any operand rethrows the exception being handled.

```
try {
    //...
}
catch(...)
{
    // Perform necessary clean up and rethrow the exception
    throw; // Pass the exception up the dynamic chain to some other handler
}
```

When an exception is rethrown this way, a copy of the original object thrown is not made. The same exception (object) is thrown again. This re-throw facility is very useful when a **catch** handler does not possess the necessary information to handle an exception but needs to perform cleanup.

CAUTION   If no exception is currently being handled, executing a **throw** without an operand calls **terminate()**, which causes premature termination of the program.

The Dynamic Call Chain

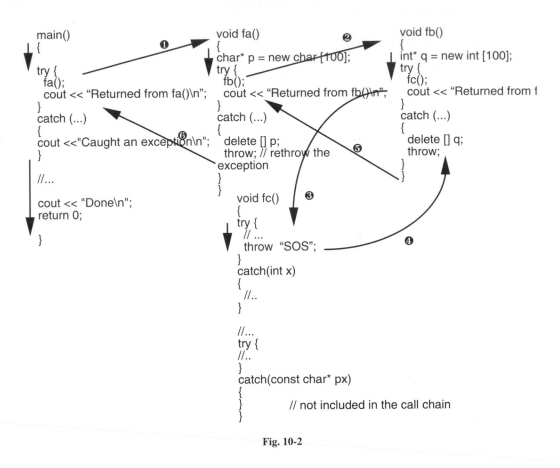

```
main()                          void fa()                    void fb()
{                               {                            {
                                char* p = new char [100];    int* q = new int [100];
try {                           try {                        try {
   fa();                           fb();                        fc();
   cout << "Returned from fa()\n";  cout << "Returned from fb()\n";  cout << "Returned from f
}                               }                            }
catch (...)                     catch (...)                  catch (...)
{                               {                            {
cout <<"Caught an exception\n";    delete [] p;                 delete [] q;
}                                  throw; // rethrow the        throw;
                                exception                    }
//...                           }                            }
                                }
cout << "Done\n";               void fc()
return 0;                       {
                                try {
}                                  // ...
                                   throw "SOS";
                                }
                                catch(int x)
                                {
                                   //..
                                }

                                //...
                                try {
                                //..
                                }
                                catch(const char* px)
                                {
                                }                    // not included in the call chain
                                }
```

Fig. 10-2

Understanding the Dynamic Call Chain

When understanding the C++ exception mechanism, it is very important to understand the significance of the dynamic call chain. Here is an example that brings out the nuances (Fig. 10-2).

❶ When main() calls function fa() from within a try block, the starting point of the call chain is established. There is a catch block that will catch any exception for this try block in main(). Now control is transferred to function fa().

❷ From fa(), a call is made to function fb(). This call to fb() is also within a try block in fa(), which also has a catch handler that will catch any exception. Now the dynamic call chain has two try blocks in it—the first one from main() and the second one from fa(). The try block of fa() is within the dynamic chain of main's try block.

❸ From fb() a call is made to fc() from within another try block. This try block also has a catch handler that can catch any exception. This try block in fb() is also within the dynamic call chain of fa()'s try block, which is within the dynamic call chain of main()'s try block.

Function fc() has two **try** blocks with matching **catch** handlers. The first **try** block has a **catch** handler that can catch exceptions of type int only. The second **try** block has a **catch** handler of type const char*. Note that the first **try** block in fc() is now in the dynamic call chain but not the second **try** block.

❹ When fc() throws an exception with the statement

```
throw "SOS";
```

the search for a matching **catch** handler within the call chain starts. The existing **catch** handler in fc() of type int can only catch exceptions of type int. Therefore, this **catch** handler doesn't match the current exception (of type const char*). The second **catch** handler in fc() handles exceptions of type (const char*) but this catch handler is not available now because it is not in the dynamic call chain. Remember that only catch handlers that are in the dynamic call chain are included in the search.

☞ **Only the catch handlers that are part of the dynamic call chain are included in the search for a matching catch handler.**

At this point, there aren't any matching catch handlers in fc() for the exception thrown, so the unwinding of the call stack begins. After all the automatic objects (if any) in fc() are destructed, control returns to fb(). The search for a matching catch handler begins in fb(). The try block in fb() has a **catch** handler that can handle any exception. The search for a matching **catch** handler ends and control is given to the **catch** block in fb(). The cleanup code in the catch block deletes the dynamic memory that was allocated before the call to fc(), preventing any memory leaks. Next, it rethrows the original exception. There are no matching **catch** handlers to handle this rethrown exception (of type const char*) within fb() at this point, so the search for a matching **catch** handler continues within the dynamic call chain.

❺ The **try** and the matching **catch** handler in fb() are within the dynamic call chain of the **try** block in fa() so the search for a matching **catch** handler now continues in fa(). The **try** block in fa() has a catch handler that will handle any exception. Control enters the only **catch** block fa(). Here again, a piece of dynamic memory that was allocated before the call to fb() is freed and the exception is rethrown.

❻ The search for a matching **catch** handler now continues in the dynamic call chain. The **try** and **catch** handler in fa() are within the dynamic call chain of main()'s try block, where everything started. So control returns to main() where the search for a matching **catch** handler is initiated. The **try** block in main() does have a matching catch handler capable of handling any exception. This is a matching handler for the exception on hand. So control enters the catch block in main(). This catch block just prints a message. The exception is finished as soon as we leave the catch block. Execution continues further in main(). Ultimately, main() prints a message and exits normally.

There are a number of important aspects that are very clear from this example:

- Only the catch blocks within the current dynamic call chain are included in the search for a match.

- The code in a catch handler is executed only when an exception is thrown and the exception matches the catch handler argument. A catch handler is never entered without an exception. In the example above, if main() hadn't received an exception (by propagation) from fa(), it would have skipped the code in the catch block and continued normal execution. In other words, the code in a catch handler exists only to handle error conditions and for resource cleanup.

- After an exception has been handled, execution continues as if nothing happened. An exception does not always imply that the application will exit abnormally.

- A procedure can contain any number of catch and try blocks. There is no language limit on the number of try/catch blocks that a piece of code can contain.

CAUTION   A library you developed might contain a large number of try/catch blocks that handle almost all kinds of errors that can be generated, but it is possible that your testing isn't exhaustive and all the catch blocks are not executed (i.e., code coverage is not complete). This can cause errors in the client's code that your tests never encountered while testing. If your test code never throws all possible exceptions, one or more of the catch handlers may never be visited. If there is any problem in any of these untested catch blocks, the client's code will experience problems even though it is your (the library implementor) fault. It is possible that while handling an exception (probably due to some error in the client's code), one of the untested catch blocks is entered and the code in the catch block does something wrong (such as dereferencing a NIL pointer, writing to non-existent memory, etc.) that causes the program to crash. The client will have a very frustrating experience detecting and fixing such a problem. It is difficult for the client to detect and fix such problems because they usually don't have the source code. Ensure that every catch block that you write is thoroughly tested before giving it to clients.

NOTE   try and catch blocks can be nested. There can be try within a catch block with its own catch handler. The language does not place any limits on the levels of nesting but programmers would have a hard time understanding deeply nested combinations.

Handling Multiple Exceptions

For any try block, there isn't any restriction as to the number of catch blocks that can be provided. A try block can have more than one catch block, with each catch block handling a different error condition. Here is a pedagogic example:

```
//These are all classes related to errors in a floating point computations
//library
class Overflow {
        // Details of the cause of an Overflow error in a math computation
};

class Underflow {
        // Details of the cause of an Underflow error in a computation
};

class DivideByZero {
        // Details of the cause of a divide by zero situation
};
```

```
void fx()
{
        try {
              // Some floating point operation code that might
              // cause one of the above errors
        }
        catch (const Underflow& u)
        {
              // Code to fix the problem (if possible)
        }
        catch (const Overflow& o)
        {
              // Code to fix the problem (if possible)
        }
        catch (const DivideByZero& z)
        {
              // Code to fix the problem (if possible)
        }
        // more code for normal processing
        ❶

        //...
}
```

In this example, function fx() is attempting some operations (within a try block) that might cause one of the exceptions, Overflow, Underflow, or DivideByZero. If one of the functions called from the try block causes an exception, the search for a matching catch handler is first attempted within fx(). If the exception is one of Overflow, Underflow, or DivideByZero, then an immediate match is found. In searching for a matching catch handler, the available catch handlers are evaluated sequentially in the order they appear. In this example, the catch handler for Underflow is evaluated first for a match followed by Overflow and then DivideByZero. Note that once a matching catch handler is found, there is no need to evaluate the remaining catch handlers for a match. If the exception thrown is an Overflow object, then the matching catch handler for Overflow is entered (after evaluating the Underflow catch handler that fails to match). If this catch handler takes care of the exception, then execution continues with the code that appears after all the catch blocks (at ❶ above). If the try block never encounters any exception, then all the catch handlers are skipped and execution continues at ❶ above.

Responsibilities of a catch **Block**

A catch block catches exceptions of an indicated type. Once the exception mechanism enters a catch block, what happens next is determined by the code in the catch block. We haven't paid much attention to what needs to be done inside a catch handler until now. So here it goes:

1. If the code has sufficient intelligence/information to fix the problem and continue, then it should to do so. Fixing the problem doesn't necessarily mean that the same code that caused the exception is executed again after fixing the cause. It is quite likely that, based on the error condition, some alternate code path is followed. For example, an application trying to connect to a stock quotes server, might receive an exception indicating that the designated server is not available. Based on this information, the catch handler might try to connect with other alternate servers and may succeed in connecting to one of them. A client should not see the effects of such exceptions. This is the ideal situation.

2. If the function doesn't understand the cause of the exception condition, it should not silently suppress the exception condition and continue. It is possible that some other function up in the dynamic call chain has the necessary knowledge to understand and fix the exception condition. In such situations, the exception must be propagated up the dynamic calling chain to the parent. But before propagating the exception, the function that originally received the exception must free any resources it has acquired. This might involve closing files, deleting memory, closing network connections, etc.[5] The function might also want to add more information to the exception object that might be useful to the caller before rethrowing the exception. Finally, the exception must be rethrown. These operations are usually done in a catch(...) handler.

3. In some cases, a function might intentionally cause an exception. This usually happens while testing code. Here, the exception condition is part of the normal code and the catch block might just print a message and continue further. For example, a test program might be verifying that a library really throws the correct exception as documented under the specified condition.

4. The C++ language itself throws some pre-defined exceptions. For example, when using the dynamic cast operation (when using RTTI—Run-Time Type Identification) with references, the exception bad_cast is thrown by the language. Programmers attempting dynamic cast operation must be prepared to handle such cases. RTTI has been discussed in Chapter 6.

NOTE   If you haven't already noticed, when an exception is thrown, it is an indication of some unexpected problem. But there is no automatic way to fix the problem and retry the failed operation. It is up to the programmer to decide what to do in case of an exception. The language does not automatically restart the offending operation after the exception has been handled. Programmers can fix the error, restore the state of the application to that which existed before the exception, and then retry the operation hoping that it would not fail again. Any such recovery effort is left to the programmer; the language doesn't do anything to help you.

THE EXCEPTIONS MODEL IN EIFFEL

Eiffel follows a different approach to managing the unexpected. Unlike C++, in Eiffel, automatic retry of a failed operation is possible. But before going into more details, we must understand the concept of preconditions and postconditions in Eiffel that ensure software reliability and fault tolerance.

When a routine (a general term for procedure or function) attempts an operation, it assumes that certain conditions are valid. For example, the Pop operation in a Stack class

---

[5]Any one of these operations itself might cause another exception. Don't panic.

might assume that the **Stack** is not empty. Such requirements can be documented but it doesn't help in ensuring the reliability of the class. It should be possible to check this condition before the body of the **Pop** function is executed. This is where preconditions are useful.

A precondition is an assertion that stipulates certain conditions prior to the execution of the body of the routine. A precondition is stated with the keyword **require**. Here is a skeleton of the class **Stack**.

```
— For simplicity, assume a stack of integers
class Stack
    export
        Push, Pop, HowMany, IsEmpty, IsFull, Size
    feature
        HowMany : INTEGER;
        Size    : INTEGER;
        IsEmpty : BOOLEAN is — Is the stack empty?
           do
                Result := HowMany > 0;
                   — Result is the return value of the function
                        (predefined)
           end;


        IsFull : BOOLEAN is — is this stack already full?
        do
           Result := HowMany = Size;
        end;


        Pop : INTEGER is — remove the top element of the stack
        require — This is the precondition
           not IsEmpty — Ensure that the Stack is not empty
        do
           — code to remove the top element and return it
        ensure — This is the post condition
           not IsFull — after popping an element the Stack should not be
                             full
        end;


        Push (element : INTEGER) is
        require
                not IsFull
        do
           — code to add another element to Stack
        ensure
           not IsEmpty — if Push succeeded the stack cannot be empty
        end;
end — class Stack
```

The operation **Pop** enforces the precondition that before the **Pop** operation is attempted, the **Stack** should not be empty. Trying to **Pop** an element from an empty **Stack** is clearly an invalid operation that might crash the program. If and only if the precondition is true, the body of the routine is executed. This precondition (**not IsEmpty**) expresses a constraint under which the routine functions correctly. If the precondition fails, the Eiffel runtime system prints a message identifying the precondition clause that caused the failure and the application terminates. Preconditions are boolean expression that evaluate to true or false. Such preconditions are not limited to simple expressions—they can be a concatenation of a series of expressions that evaluate to true or false.

After Popping an element from a Stack, the Stack can no longer be full (even if it was full before the Pop operation was invoked). This constraint is expressed in a postcondition. The postcondition specifies the constraints for the Stack after the successful completion of an operation. If the postcondition fails for some reason, again the Eiffel runtime system terminates the program with a message identifying the postcondition clause that caused the failure.

In the operation Push, a new element can be stored in the Stack only if the Stack is not already full. Trying to add an element to a Stack that is already full is definitely an invitation for trouble. This constraint is expressed in the precondition (not IsFull). The postcondition (not IsEmpty) ensures that the stack is not empty after a successful Push operation.

Preconditions and postconditions are crucial parts of any routine that are essential for robust, reliable software. They avoid trouble by checking conditions before an operation is attempted. Remember that prevention is better than cure. But terminating a program because of an assertion failure may not be an ideal solution in many cases. Developers might want to fix the cause of the problem and continue. Or at least they (developers) might want to know when an assertion failure occurs so that necessary cleanup and proper state restoration can happen.

Every routine (and class) can have a rescue clause, which is very similar to a catch clause. When a precondition or postcondition fails (i.e., evaluates to false), then the rescue clause (if the routine has one) is entered automatically. There can be only one rescue clause in each routine.[6] The responsibilities of the rescue clause are quite simple. The rescue clause can fix the cause of the exception and retry the operation, which might now succeed. In the absence of a retry instruction, the rescue clause can just try to restore the state of the object to whatever it was before the start of the routine and return to the caller. In the latter case, the exception propagates to the caller and the same process is repeated again. The rescue clause itself should not cause any new exceptions. In fact, assertion checking is turned off during the execution of the rescue clause. Therefore, the rescue clause should only contain a simple sequence of statements that should never fail.

When the rescue clause fixes the cause of the exception and executes the retry instruction, the execution of the routine is restarted. Now the routine might succeed without any exceptions. In this case, the routine has executed successfully, doing whatever it was supposed to do, and execution of the program proceeds normally thereafter. Therefore, the caller of the routine will not experience any exceptions.

Eiffel supports both the *organized panic* and the *resumption* models of exception handling. In cases where there is only a rescue clause, the routine fails (organized panic). But if there is a retry clause, the operation resumes again (resumption strategy).

In the case where there is no retry instruction, the instructions in the rescue clause are executed sequentially. At the end of the clause control returns to the caller but with the same exception condition. Now the search for a rescue/retry starts all over again in the caller and the process is repeated. If the exception ultimately propagates to the top level,

---

[6]A class can have a rescue clause, which is applicable to the entire class. If any routine that does not have its own rescue clause receives an exception, then the rescue clause of the class is entered.

then the program terminates and a message is printed, informing the client about the exception. The rescue clause should try to restore the environment to a stable state. The rescue clause is not required to satisfy the precondition or the postcondition of the routine—that is the duty of the body of the routine.

Here is a part of the stack class shown with the rescue clause.

```
— For simplicity, assume a stack of integers
class Stack
        export
            Push, Pop, HowMany, IsEmpty, IsFull, Size
feature
        — Other operations not shown
            Pop : INTEGER is — remove the top element of the stack
            require — This is the precondition
               not IsEmpty
            do
               — code to remove the top element and return it
            ensure — This is the post condition
               not IsFull — after popping an element the Stack should not be
                            full
            rescue
               — Code to restore state of the stack (if possible)
               — Might also print a message
            end;

end — class Stack
```

The retry instruction is not useful in all situations. If the routine cannot fix the cause of the exception, there is no point in having a retry clause. In the Stack class, the Push operation might provide a retry clause. If the Stack is already full when the Push operation is invoked, the implementation might be able to grow the Stack and retry the operation. Here is the code:

```
— For simplicity, assume a stack of integers
class Stack
        export
        Push, Pop, HowMany, IsEmpty, IsFull, Size
feature
        Push (element : INTEGER) is
        require
              not IsFull
        do
          — code to add another element to Stack
        ensure
              not IsEmpty — if Push succeeded the stack cannot be empty
        rescue
           — Check if the exception was cause because the stack is full
           — If so grow the stack and retry the operation
           if IsFull then
                 — Code to grow the stack
              retry
           end
        end;
end — class Stack
```

When the retry instruction is executed, the operation is restarted. Before retrying, the rescue clause should fix the state of the object so that retry can succeed. It is possible that an exception (a new one or the one being retried) is encountered again when the operation is retried. The operation should take into consideration all these issues when implementing the rescue clause with a retry operation. If the operation keeps retrying without any success, there should be some limiting condition that will stop the retry operations. For example, the operation could keep a count of the number of retries, aborting the retry after a predetermined number of failures. Only the class implementor has control over all such details.

In Eiffel, an exception can occur in a routine f() due to the following conditions:

1. A precondition is violated in the routine.

2. A postcondition is violated in the routine.

3. The class invariant is invalidated on entry or exit from the routine.

4. A routine called by f() fails.

5. f() attempts an operation on a void reference.

6. An operation attempted in f() results in a hardware or operating system error.

MERITS AND DRAWBACKS OF THE EIFFEL AND C++ EXCEPTIONS MODELS

The Eiffel model of exception handling is somewhat different from the C++ model, particularly in case of retry. The Eiffel model allows a routine to fail or to succeed—there is no other alternative. The implementor has the freedom to decide between failure and retrying an operation. Unlike C++, an Eiffel routine can only have one rescue clause. Any exception causes the execution of the only rescue clause (if one is provided). All error handling code is in one place. The rescue clause must determine the cause of failure by using the information available in the object (class) or routine. This can be a demanding task in routines that have multiple points of failure.

In C++, the code in a procedure can be cluttered with normal code and exceptions code making the logic of the procedure fuzzy. Programmers might find it very hard to follow the logic of the code if the exception management code is complex. The Eiffel model is very elegant in this aspect. All exception management code is in one place at the end of the routine. The code logic remains unaffected by the exception handling code.

The retry instruction is really powerful when used correctly. In many situations, it is quite easy to fix the problem and restart the operation without any help from the client. To harness the power of the retry instruction, the implementor of the class must use the facility judiciously. Otherwise, it is easy to get into an endless loop of rescue and retry operations.

Unlike the C++ model, where exceptions must be raised (thrown) explicitly by the programmer, the Eiffel model causes exceptions to be raised automatically. Preconditions and postconditions are part of the code, which must always be true for an operation to be successful. Any violation of these preconditions and postconditions is an indication of a serious problem. The system automatically raises an exception in all such cases. In C++, it is the responsibility of the programmer to detect failures and throw exceptions. The language does not detect errors automatically. Detecting errors and converting those errors into meaningful exceptions is no easy task. It is easy to incorporate assertions into C++ code. It is also possible to implement assertions such that a well known, predefined exception is thrown in case of an assertion failure. But catching such exceptions still requires **try** and **catch** blocks around the code that might cause an assertion failure. There is no easy way of catching all assertion failures in one place within a procedure. In Eiffel, dereferencing a **void** reference causes an exception to be raised automatically. But in C++, dereferencing a NIL pointer might cause a run-time failure (depending on the compiler implementation), but no exceptions are thrown. It is very expensive and tedious to check for NIL pointers in each and every procedure. The Eiffel model is better in this regard.

Retrying a failed operation is supported directly by Eiffel. Programmers can rely on the language to restart a failed operation by using the **retry** instruction. There is no such automatic way of restarting an operation in C++. Any such mechanism must be implemented by the programmer without much help from the language.

In Eiffel, there are only two outcomes possible when an exception is raised. The routine can either fail or it can retry the failed operation, causing it to succeed. If there is no retry instruction, the exception propagates. There is no other possible choice. This might seem overly restrictive. C++ does not have any restrictions on what a procedure can do in the event of an exception. An implementation can catch an exception and select an alternate path of code to overcome the cause of the exception. In other words, the programmer decides the outcome of an exception—it could cause termination of the program (if not caught) or it can be an indication of a simple error that requires programmer intervention. As far as the languages is concerned, an exception condition no longer exists at the end of a **catch** block. The Eiffel model of exceptions supports the organized panic or resumption strategy only (the routine fails or it succeeds). There is no other outcome possible. The C++ model is more generous in this regard. An exception in C++ is just an indication of an error in some operation. The strategy of handling the error is entirely up to the programmer. The language doesn't enforce any rules about what the programmer should do.

In C++, an exception can be handled at the point of occurrence. The **try-catch** blocks support this model. Exceptions propagate when there is no localized handling of the exception. In other words, the code to handle an error is usually close to the point of cause of the error. It is easy to associate the exception code with the code that caused the exception. In Eiffel, all the exception handling code is in one **rescue** clause. This can make the **rescue** clause quite complex. Moreover, the cause of the exception and the code that attempts the repair are not in close proximity. It is not easy to correlate the code that caused the error with the code that fixes it (Eiffel advocates small routines).

Both Eiffel and C++ allow easy and automatic propagation of exceptions. In C++, if there is no **catch** handler that matches the exception thrown, then the exception automatically propagates to the caller. In Eiffel, if there is no **retry** instruction in the **rescue** clause or if there is no **rescue** clause, the exception is propagated to the caller.

In C++, there is always a type associated with an exception. Any client can catch only those exceptions that she is interested in while ignoring others. This allows for filtering of errors and ease of exception management. Moreover, in C++, when an exception is thrown, an object is passed from the throw point to the catch handler. This exception object can be used to pass any information about the cause of the exception. The catch handler can use the information contained in the exception object to determine the correct action. Eiffel doesn't allow the programmer to catch specific exceptions. In fact, there is no type associated with an exception. Any kind of failure (preconditions, postconditions, etc.) causes an exception condition that transfers control to the **rescue** clause (if one exists). It is hard to determine the cause of the exception. Also, there is no way to pass important information about the error from the point of the exception to the rescue clause. The **rescue** clause must deduce the cause based on the local variables and state information contained in the object. The C++ scheme is superior to that of Eiffel in this regard.

NOTE   The preceding paragraphs just indicate the differences (and similarities) between the models—it is just a summary of the features. The intent is not to praise one language while chiding the other. Every language has its own way of handling things and programmers can become better designers by understanding these nuances.

USING C++ EXCEPTIONS EFFECTIVELY

Exceptions facility is a powerful tool that can be used very effectively by a skilled craftsman. Just understanding the syntax is not good enough to use exceptions effectively.

One of the problems in managing exceptions in any system is the problem of handling too many different exceptions. Any procedure called by a client might raise a wide variety of exceptions. It would be very difficult to deal with each one of those individual exceptions separately. Imagine writing a catch handler for every exception thrown by a procedure. To deal with this complexity, it would be helpful if we can group exceptions.

CREATING EXCEPTION HIERARCHIES

If exceptions are grouped into hierarchies, then instead of dealing with the exceptions individually, we can deal with them as a group. This is where inheritance comes to the rescue. We have already seen in earlier chapters that a base class of a hierarchy is a polymorphic representative of all the derived classes. In other words, a function expecting a base class object (reference or pointer) can polymorphically deal with any object of a derived class. This polymorphic behavior is also very useful in dealing with exceptions .

Let us consider the case of a client using a remote file access library, RFLIB. This library allows clients to locate, open, and operate on files on remote systems. The library manages all the issues involved in the communication between the local machine and the remote machine. A client would specify the name of the file (with full pathname), name of the remote machine on which the file is located, and the type of access desired (read, write, execute, etc.). Some of the possible errors when locating a remote file are

1. remote machine not found on the network;

2. specified file not found on the remote machine;

3. remote machine does not grant access at this time;

4. specified file does not allow access by the client; and

5. file does not allow specified access permissions.

The implementor of RFLIB can map these errors into individual exception classes. The exception classes could be (TRemoteMachineNotFound, TRemoteFileNotFound, TNoAccessToMachine, TNoClientAccessToFile, and TBadPermissions). Functions in RFLIB can throw any of these exceptions. A client programming with this library must deal with all these exceptions individually. There should be one catch handler for each of the five exceptions in the client's code. The client writing an application might be programming with many such libraries at the same time. If all these libraries throw many different exceptions, writing a catch handler for every one of them would be a programming nightmare. The client is probably more interested in knowing which library caused the exception rather than what exception it was. Writing a catch handler that catches all exceptions (catch(...)) is not a solution because the client wants to know exactly which library caused the exception. The client should be able to treat all exceptions coming out a library as one. This is where exception hierarchies are indispensable.

The implementor of RFLIB must definitely throw all the exceptions mentioned above. But there should be some relationship among them. Since all these exceptions are related to the remote file access library, it would be convenient to group them under a single class, TRemoteFileLibraryException. This would be the base class for all the exceptions originating from RFLIB (see Fig. 10-3).

```
class TRemoteFileLibraryException {
    // Fundamental details of any remote file access exception
};

class TRemoteFileNotFound : public TRemoteFileLibraryException {
    // Specific details of "file not found" exception
};
// and so on for other exception classes shown above
```

The hierarchy shown above is usually called an *Exception Hierarchy*. It exists to support efficient and easy exception management. These classes are useful only when exceptions are generated. They don't add any value to normal code that manages remote file systems. A well designed library must provide its own exception hierarchy that allows clients to deal with exceptions easily. A client programming with multiple libraries must be prepared to deal with exception hierarchies exported by all those libraries.

Any client not interested in the details of a specific exception thrown from RFLIB needs to deal with the class TRemoteFileLibraryException only. But that does not prevent the client from catching any of the more specific exceptions. Here is an example.

```
void Fx()
{
    try {
        // some code to invoke functions from the remote file access
        // library
        // Let's say a function
        // TRemoeFile::OpenFile(const char* fileName, const char*
```

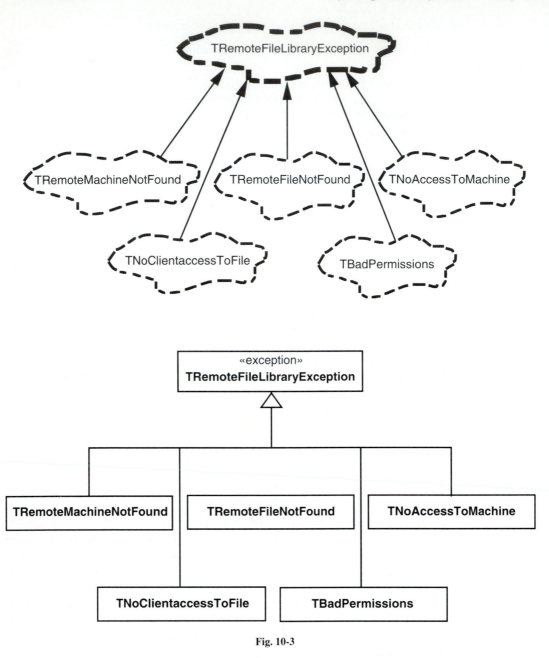

Fig. 10-3

```
        // machineName) is being called here. MyDataFile.Dat is the file
        // name and Sphinx is the name of the remote machine
        TRemoteFile           myFile;
        myFile.OpenFile("MyDataFile.Dat", "Sphinx");
}
catch (const TRemoteFileLibraryException& exc)
{
        cout << "Some exception from remote file access library caught\n";
```

```
        // code to perform any housekeeping operations
        throw; // rethrow the exception
    }
        // More normal code
}
```

Here is a skeleton code for the OpenFile function.

```
class TRemoteFile {
    TRemoteFile(); // Simple Constructor
    bool OpenFile(const char* file, const char* machine);
    //other details not important
};

bool
TRemoteFile::OpenFile(const char* filename, const char* machineName)
{
    // Let's say it throws the exception TRemoteFileNotFound
    throw TRemoteFileNotFound(fileName);
}
```

Remember that a throw with an argument is very similar to a function call with the specified argument. When OpenFile() throws the exception TRemoteFileNotFound, it is very similar to making a call to a function (with the name catch) that accepts a TRemoteFileNotFound argument. We know that any function that accepts a TRemoteFileLibraryException argument can also be called with a TRemoteFileNotFound argument because TRemoteFileNotFound is a derived class of TRemoteFileLibraryException. This is an implicit conversion from derived class to base class. It is the essence of polymorphism. Polymorphism is also applicable catch to handlers. Therefore, any catch handler that accepts a TRemoteFileLibraryException is also capable of catching a TRemoteFileNotFound exception. In resolving the search for a catch handler, a catch handler that accepts a base class argument is compatible with a throw that uses a derived class object. Therefore, the catch handler in Fx() will catch the TRemoteFileNotFound exception also. In fact, the catch handler in Fx() will catch a TRemoteFileLibraryException exception as well as any of its derived classes.

Creating such exception hierarchies is very useful for the clients of the library. It satisfies the needs of a wide variety of clients. Not all clients are interested in each and every exception thrown from a library. Some client might only be interested in knowing that an exception was thrown from the library where as a more sophisticated client capable of initiating recovery might need to know the exact exception thrown. The exception hierarchy satisfies the needs of both types of clients. The simple client will just catch the base class of the exception hierarchy and a more sophisticated client will catch specific exceptions in addition to the base class exception.

Ordering of Catch Handlers

This approach to handling exceptions uses the power of inheritance very well. But some precaution is required here. If a client is specifically interested in catching the TRemoteMachineNotFound exception in addition to TRemoteFileLibraryException, then two catch handlers are required, as shown below.

```
void Fx()
{
    try {
        // some code to invoke functions from the remote file access
        // library. Let's say the function
        // TRemoteFile::OpenFile(const char* fileName, const char*
        // machineName) is being called here.
        TRemoteFile myFile;
        myFile.OpenFile("MyDataFile.Dat", "Sphinx");
    }
    catch (const TRemoteMachineNotFound& fexc)
    {
        cout << "The remote machine was not found on the network\n";
        // code to perform any housekeeping operations
        throw; // rethrow the exception
    }
    catch (const TRemoteFileLibraryException & exc)
    {
        // Code to handle any other exception from RFLIB
        cout << "Some exception from remote file access library caught\n";
        // code to perform any housekeeping operations
        throw; // rethrow the exception
    }
        // More normal code
} // end function
```

This ordering of catch handlers is very important. When an exception is thrown, the **catch** handlers are searched sequentially in the order they are declared in the code. If the exception thrown is a **TBadPermissions** exception, the first catch handler accepting **TRemoteMachineNotFound** is not a match for this exception. But the next handler that accepts a **TRemoteFileLibraryException** is compatible with **TBadPermissions** exception because **TBadPermissions** is a derived class of **TRemoteFileLibraryException**.

NOTE   The details of how a compiler might search for a catch handler is compiler specific and might even be proprietary. Here we are more interested in knowing what happens when an exception is thrown. We are not interested in the details of how the compiler locates the **catch** handler.

If the exception thrown was really a **TRemoteMachineNotFound** exception, then the catch handler for **TRemoteMachineNotFound** is encountered first in the search and it matches the exception perfectly. There is no need to search any further. But on the other hand, if the code is modified as below, things don't work as before.

```
// Warning: WRONG CODE — Shown here to demonstrate the problem
void Fx()
{
    try {
        // some code to invoke functions from the remote file access
        // library
        // Let's say a function
        // TRemoteFile::OpenFile(const char* fileName, const char*
        // machineName) is being called here.
        TRemoteFile myFile;
```

```
        myFile.OpenFile("MyDataFile.Dat", "Sphinx");
    }
    catch (const TRemoteFileLibraryException & exc)
    {
        // Code to handle any other exception from RFLIB
        cout << "Some exception from remote file access library caught\n";
        // code to perform any housekeeping operations
        throw; // rethrow the exception
    }
    // **** Oops, this catch handler is never executed even if the
    // exception is a TRemoteMachineNotFound exception!
    catch (const TRemoteMachineNotFound& fexc)
    {
        cout << "The remote machine was not found on the network\n";
        // code to perform any housekeeping operations
        throw; // rethrow the exception
    }
    // More normal code
}
```

The catch handler for TRemoteFileLibraryException not only matches with an exception of type TRemoteFileLibraryException but also with any of its derived classes (TRemoteFileNotFound, TBadPermissions, etc.). Once a matching catch handler is found, there is no need to look for any other catch handler. Therefore, the more specialized catch handler for TRemoteMachineNotFound exception is never executed because the catch handler for TRemoteFileLibraryException is found first during the search and it matches with any TRemoteFileLibraryException thrown.

☞ **A catch handler for a base class must follow the more specific catch handlers for its derived classes.**

Writing Exception Safe Functions

Any function that you write must not leak any resources no matter what happens. In particular, the function must behave correctly no matter what exception is thrown. When a function is exited due to an exception, it must ensure that any resource it acquired has been freed properly or the ownership of the resource has been successfully transferred to some other code.

In general, a well designed program should handle exceptions in the following order:

1. Provide catch handlers for specific exceptions that you want to catch.

2. Next, provide catch handlers for the base classes of the exception hierarchies.

3. Finally, to handle any other exception that you are not interested in, provide the generic catch handler catch(...).

Here is an example of such a scheme.

```
void Fy()
{
    // This function handles exceptions in a disciplined manner. It handles
    // the more specific exceptions first. Then it handles base class
    // exceptions. Finally it handles any other exception that might be
    // thrown.

    try {
        // some code to invoke functions from the remote file access
        // library. Let's say the function TRemoteFile::OpenFile(const
        // char* fileName, const char* machineName) is being called here.
        TRemoteFile myFile;
        myFile.OpenFile("MyDataFile.Dat", "Sphinx");
    }
    // Handle more specific exceptions first. Here I'm only interested in
    // catching TRemoteMachineNotFound exception. This catch handler might
    // try to connect with a different machine and try again.
    catch (const TRemoteMachineNotFound& fexc)
    {
        cout << "The remote machine was not found on the network\n";
        // code to handle the exception
    }

    // Next handle all other exceptions of type
    // TRemoteFileLibraryException
    catch (const TRemoteFileLibraryException& exc)
    {
        // Code to handle any other exception from RFLIB
        cout << "Some exception from remote file access library caught\n";
        // code to perform any housekeeping operations
        throw; // rethrow the exception
    }

    // Finally, handle any other exception that might be thrown
    // This is the catchall handler which will catch all exceptions not
    // handled by the earlier catch handlers.
    catch (...)
    {
        // Perform necessary clean up and rethrow the exception to parent
        throw;
    }
}
```

This scheme ensures that function Fy() is safe no matter what exception is thrown, and it is quite easy to understand. The catch handler, such as the one for TRemoteMachine NotFound above, takes care of specific exceptions that you might be able to recover from. These are exceptions that you are capable of managing without causing program failure. For example, if the file is not found on one machine, you could try to find the file on an alternate machine (or you might create that file). You might be able to initiate such recovery for some specific set of exceptions. Provide handlers for such exceptions first. This ensures that all such exceptions are handled correctly.

Next, you might consider dealing with base classes of the exception hierarchies. You may not be able to do much with these exceptions in terms of recovery, but catching such base class exceptions is quite useful. If you at least know which library (or subsystem) caused the exception, you might be able to report the problem to the implementors of the library who might provide more insight into the problem.[7] This at least narrows down the search for the cause of the exception.

Finally, there are some general exceptions that any program might encounter. These include timeouts, out of memory, disk space exhaustion, etc. If you are interested in handling such individual exceptions (provided you know the names of such exceptions), provide catch handlers for them. If not consider a catchall handler (catch(...)) that catches any exception. This catchall handler ensures that no exception will ever escape out of your functions unhandled. There isn't much you can do in this catch handler. This handler should release any resources that are not yet freed in the function, close any files that are open, relinquish network connections that are still active, etc. Finally, rethrow the exception because your caller might be able to handle this exception and initiate recovery. This handler might also log the error in a central error logging system (or perform any such standard actions).

ARCHITECTING EXCEPTION HANDLING INTO PROJECTS

When to Throw an Exception

So far this discussion concentrated on handling exceptions in programs. But when should a program throw an exception? Should a function convert all errors into an exception object and throw them? Or is it sufficient if the function just throws one exception for all kinds of errors? The next few paragraphs shed some light on these issues.

In C++, exceptions can be used as an alternative to all the error codes that programmers use to indicate different failure modes. That doesn't mean that every error code becomes an exception class. The prime purpose of an exception is to indicate failure of some operation (preventing the operation from proceeding any further) that requires immediate attention. Not all errors are catastrophic, and definitely a client is not interested in each and every error that could happen in a function. At the same time, a function should provide enough information to the client about errors.

Any error that requires a client's attention must be thrown as an exception. The error must be converted to an object with more meaningful information than just an error number. For example, the exception thrown might include useful details such as the name of the library, name of function, line number inside the function, etc. In case of distributed systems, this information should include the name of the machine (and/or the address of the machine) that encountered the error.

Converting each and every error code into an exception object is an overkill, as mentioned earlier. This usually happens in cases where a procedural code is converted into an object-oriented implementation. Mapping every error code into an exception causes an explosion of exception classes. Remember that these exception classes are used only for error handling. Imagine a library that generates 100 different error codes. Mapping them directly into classes would create 100 exception management classes. The li-

---

[7]At the least, you can call the customer service department of the library vendor and report the problem.

brary already contains many classes for normal processing. Such designs don't make it any easier for the client to deal with errors. On the contrary, it will complicate the client's view of the system.

First of all, create an exception base class for the entire library (framework or subsystem). This base class should be used by all exception classes in the library. General information that is common to all exceptions in the library goes into this base class. This allows simple clients to ignore all other exceptions and just focus on the base class.

A derived class is created for every exception that is important from the client's perspective. If an error condition is important for a client, it must be converted to an exception class. A derived class might represent a group of errors. For example, the **TRemoteMachineNotFound** exception might be thrown in a number of situations. The failure to find the remote machine may be due to an error in the name of the machine, it might be due to an error in the network that connects the machines, or it might be because the remote machine is temporarily down. All such errors would throw the same exception. However, a client might be interested in knowing the exact cause of the failure. For example, if the error is because the remote machine is temporarily down, the client can retry the operation sometime later. The client should be able to retrieve such precise details from the exception thrown. One easy way to do that would be to include an error code (in the form of an enumerated set of error codes) in the exception object. The exception object must provide member functions to extract the exact error code from the exception object. Here is an example:

```
// Specific reasons for TRemoteFileNotFound error
enum EReason { eMachineTemporarilyDown, eNetworkError, eInvalidName,
                                                       eUnknown };

class TRemoteFileLibraryException {
    public:
        // Fundamental details of any remote file access exception
        EReason GetReason() const { return errorCode; }
    private:
        EReason errorCode;
};

class TRemoteFileNotFound : public TRemoteFileLibraryException {
    public:
        // Specific details of "file not found" exception
        // Constructor passes the error code to the base class
        TRemoteFileNotFound (EReason code)
            : TRemoteFileLibraryException(code) {}
    //...
    private:

};
```

If a function in RFLIB throws the **TRemoteFileNotFound** exception because the remote machine is temporarily down, the code would be

```
void Fz()
{
```

```
        // some code in RFLIB
        throw TRemoteFileNotFound (eMachineTemporarilyDown);
}
```

A client catching the **TRemoteFileNotFound** exception can examine the error code using the **GetReason()** member function, which is supported by the base class **TRemoteFileLibraryException**. In cases where the exact cause of the exception is unknown, the error code should be set to **eUnknown**. The enumeration **EReason** should contain all possible error codes used in the remote file library.

This scheme divides error codes into groups and uses one exception class to represent the error codes in a group. The scheme minimizes the number of exception classes while still providing the necessary information to the clients.

When dealing with error codes coming out of the operating system, this scheme is even more powerful. Almost all of the modern operating systems return error codes to the caller. Usually, any code other than zero indicates an error. There are hundreds of such error codes possible. Imagine the complexity of an exception management system that translates each error code into a separate class. To make the life of the client easier, software that deals with the operating system should map the error codes returned by the operating system into a set of meaningful exception classes. The actual error code can be made available through a member function (such as **GetReason**) of the exception class.

The task of designing an effective, powerful, and efficient (yet easy to use) exception management system is not easy. It requires a thorough knowledge of the entire system (or library) and the client's needs.

STRATEGIES FOR SUCCESSFUL ERROR MANAGEMENT IN PROJECTS

Error handling cannot be an afterthought while designing and implementing software systems. Any non-trivial software development project must deal with error handling, right from the beginning. It will be disastrous trying to add error handling after the project has been in development for a considerable amount of time. When the error handling scheme uses exceptions, the importance of proper design is even more important. An exception hierarchy is developed in parallel with other parts of the project. Anyone writing code should know what exception to throw in case of failures.

In traditional procedural programming, an error is indicated by an error code (a number). There isn't much meaning attached to them. In fact, it is common for programmers to use a sequence of numbers, giving them meaningful names later. When a new piece of code that could generate a new error is added, all that must be done is to define a new error code with a number that has not been already used anywhere else in the system. This approach is disastrous when dealing with object-oriented software using exceptions. Every exception is an object of a class. The details of the class being used in a throw statement must be known to the programmer and the compiler. If each and every programmer ends up creating a new class for every new exception on the fly, there will be a huge set of unrelated classes just for exception handling. There could even be duplication of functionality among these classes. Such a system will fail to project a clear, coherent picture (to the client) of the exception management scheme followed in the system. This is even worse than arbitrary error codes.

If possible, the complete interface of the major exception handling classes that are going to be used in the project must be designed along with the rest of the project (or at least before any major development starts). At the minimum, the interface of the base class of the exception hierarchy must be well defined. Developers must adhere to the published exception architecture of the system in their code. This benefits both the clients and the developers. Before the entire system is ready, clients can study the exception hierarchy of the system and develop their code accordingly. It will help the clients even if only the base class of the exception hierarchy is published before the system is ready. Developers in the project will benefit from the well defined exception hierarchy because functions in the system definitely call each other.

It is very difficult to add exception management to a system that is already implemented. Adding code to throw and catch exceptions requires modification of the existing code (new try blocks and catch handlers must be added). Moreover, resource management must be taken care of in each function that might receive or throw exceptions. This is not a trivial task. Modifying any working code is always dangerous because it can introduce new defects.

The purpose of exception handling mechanism is to provide a means for one part of a system to indicate some sort of failure to another part of the system. The assumption is that the part of the system that actually handles the exception can do something sensible about the cause of failure and can probably recover from it.

To use exception handling mechanisms effectively in a project, an overall strategy is required. Different parts of the system should agree on a simple, reliable scheme to manage errors. When an exception is generated, the function that receives the exception may not have access to the necessary information to do anything useful with it; so it must propagate the exception to upper layers of the system where more information is available. This implies that exception handling is really non-local. An error in one part of the system might be handled in a completely different part of the system. This is the fundamental reason why error handling strategies must be considered right from the start of the design cycle. Everyone involved in the project must adhere to the accepted strategy. Needless to state, any error handling mechanism planned must be simple (easy to understand, implement, and manage). If the error handling scheme is as complex as the system, rest assured that no one is going to follow the guidelines and the behavior of the final system will be unpredictable. The need for a *simple* yet useful error handling scheme cannot be stressed enough. Error handling is a tricky issue and not all types of errors can be handled in the same way. But devising an error management scheme that is as complex as the system itself is fool hardy. The prime focus of the project is not on error handling. Errors do happen but that is not the normal behavior of any system.

Any successful error handling strategy cannot use a single technique or mechanism to cope with all types of errors. Trying to achieve that will lead to unnecessary complexity and increases the burden on the implementors and clients. Instead, successful fault tolerant, reliable, and efficient systems employ multi-level approaches to error handling. Each level (or layer) copes with as many errors as possible without making the implementation too complex and propagates other errors to higher levels. Every level handles errors that it understands and can cope with. This makes the overall error handling strategy simple while avoiding complexity at every level.

A Function Is Not a Firewall

All this discussion about error handling should not lead you to believe that every function that you ever write should be a firewall. Trying to write functions that either succeed or fail in a well defined manner, no matter what happens, is a sure recipe for disaster, especially in large projects. If a function tries to be reliable under all circumstances, the cost involved in achieving that is too high due to the following reasons:

1. The function must protect against each and every possible path of failure. This can lead to very complex code.

2. The run-time cost (both in time and space) of ensuring such reliability is very high and performance is highly degraded. This is because the same argument must be tested for validity every time it is used (and in every function that uses it), every pointer must be checked every time (not just once in the function) it is used, the result of every computation must be checked, etc.

3. Functions written in other languages (including C) cannot be trusted anymore because they may not have the same level of error checking and moreover, there is no way of preventing run-time failures in them.

4. Some operations just cannot be protected. For example, in spite of checking for validity of memory addresses at every level, what if accessing the address causes a hardware exception? The software exception scheme just cannot do anything about such errors.

Trying to achieve such reliability will make the system very complex and hard to understand. It will be a nightmare trying to enhance/modify/maintain such systems. In addition, the system will be so slow, no one will want to use it, hence, the stress on multi-level approach to error handling.

The overall error handling mechanism should try to recover from errors wherever possible. But if recovery is impossible (or too expensive), a graceful shutdown is the best solution. If nothing else, the exception handling mechanism should guarantee graceful shutdown, and not an unexpected crash.

NOTE   In any project involving many exception classes, it will be very helpful if every exception class contains a member fucntion that provides a simple textual description of the error. The textual description of the error would be very useful for reporting errors to the implementors of the software. Such a member function can be made part of the base class of the exception hierarchy.

Designing Exception Hierarchies

Managing exceptions in big projects with many subsystems (or frameworks) is even more difficult than managing exceptions in small libraries. One needs to worry about the exception management needs of each and every subsystem. Each subsystem might throw a completely different set of exceptions not related to exceptions in other subsystems. Unifying such diverse exception classes under a single hierarchy is a challenging task requiring the cooperation of the entire team involved in the project.

For example, a big project might have subsystems that deal with file system, user interface, security, operating system, etc. Each of these subsystems need very different exception classes. But if these subsystems are allowed to throw arbitrary exceptions, clients of the project (who develop software using the services provided by the different subsystems) would have a tough time ensuring predictable behavior of their applications. Clients need a coherent model of the exception management scheme employed by the entire system. In such cases, it might be beneficial to define a single base class that is common to every exception class in the entire project. Subsystems can add their own sub-hierarchies under the common base class. Let us call the common base class TBasic Exception.

The file system can define another sub-hierarchy rooted in the class TFileSystem Exception. Any exception class used by the file system will be a derived class of TFileSystemException. The same principle is applied to each and every subsystem (see Fig. 10-4).

The file system can add subclasses to indicate exceptions thrown by member functions in file system classes (see Fig. 10-5).

The security subsystem can define a similar hierarchy for exceptions used in its classes (see Fig. 10-6).

Now a client can catch exceptions at any level desired. For example, a client interested in exceptions due to security breach will only catch TSecurityException and its subclasses. Another client not interested in any specific exception but only interested in

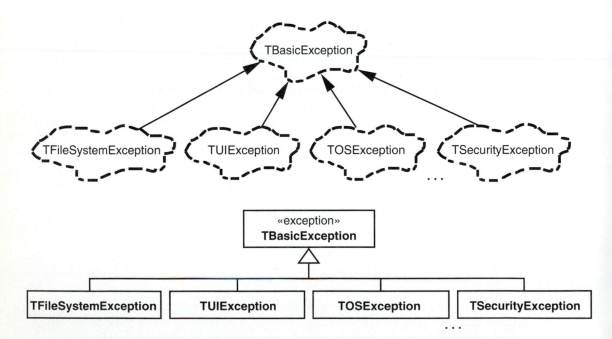

Fig. 10-4

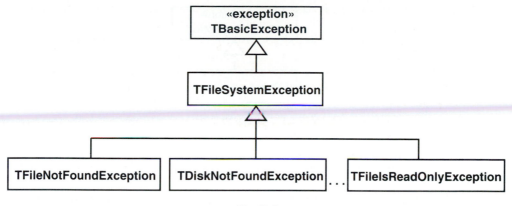

Fig. 10-5

catching exceptions from any of the subsystems can do so by just catching TBasicException.

For exceptions that are common to all subsystems (for example, timeout), an independent class can be added to the exception hierarchy (see Fig. 10-7).

Once again, inheritance has proved to be an invaluable tool in solving a complex problem. This scheme builds on the principle of multi-level approach to error handling. Inheritance is used to manage the complexity in different layers. Lower levels of the hierarchy worry about specific errors known to them while propagating other errors to upper levels of the system.

NOTE   One very useful facility that can be invaluable when debugging exceptions is a stack trace. When an application terminates due to an unhandled exception, it will be very helpful if the stack trace that caused the exception (from the point of throw to the termination routine) is provided. Some compilers provide this information without any effort from the programmer. If your compiler does not, you can do this with little effort. A catch

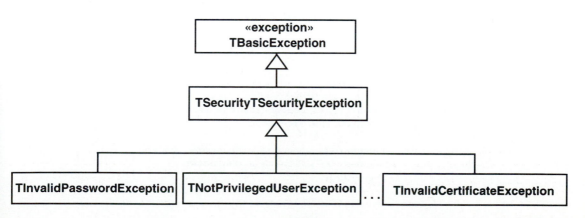

Fig. 10-6

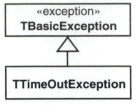

Fig. 10-7

handler, before rethrowing the exception just caught, can append the name of the class and member function to the exception object. If every member function that rethrows an exception follows this policy, then the entire stack trace is available in the exception object. Finally, when the exception object is destroyed, the destructor of the class can just print the stack trace on the display. This information gives the developers a starting point for debugging the software that caused the exception.

RESOURCE MANAGEMENT IN AN EXCEPTIONS ENVIRONMENT

One major problem when writing software that throws exception is that of resource management. A function that catches an exception and returns to the caller should deallocate any resources that it has acquired before leaving the function. This is easier said than done. Remember that there could be many catch handlers in many different parts of the function. Ensuring correct behavior in all code paths is no easy task, particularly in an environment where exceptions are possible. Consider this simple function **Gx**.

```
// Resource management problem in an exception environment
void Gx()
{
    char* namePtr = new char[100]; // Allocate an array of 100 characters
    strcpy(namePtr, "THIS IS A TEST STRING"); // Write something into it

    try {
        // some operations that might cause an exception
    }
    catch (...)
    {
        delete [] namePtr; // Deallocate the resource ❶
        throw; // rethrow the exception
    }
    // No exception occurred, continue with normal code
    char* cPtr = new char; // Allocate a character

    try {
        // Some other operation that might cause exceptions
    }
```

```
    catch(...)
    {
        delete [] namePtr;  // ❷
        delete cPtr;
        throw; // rethrow exception
    }
    // We are lucky, No exceptions ever occurred. Clean up and return
    delete [] namePtr; // ❸
    delete cPtr;
}
```

This is a very simple function that allocated an array of characters and later a single character. While performing normal operations, it is prepared to catch exceptions. When an exception is caught, the function promptly deallocates resources and rethrows the exception.

❶ When an exception is caught, the only resource that has been allocated is the array of characters. It is freed and the exception is rethrown.

❷ Again, an exception is caught and both resources (array of characters allocated at the top and the single character allocated recently) are freed and the exception is rethrown.

❸ Execution gets here only when there are no exceptions. Just before leaving the function, all resources allocated along the way must be freed. We promptly free the array of characters and the single character and return to the caller.

But even a casual reader will notice the repetition of code. Every time an exception is anticipated and a catch block is implemented, the programmer must remember to free all resources allocated until that point. This is repeated in every catch block. Finally, when the function is about finish execution without any exceptions (a successful completion), it must again free all resources allocated during the execution of the function. Doing the same operation over and over again is really boring and error prone. Remember that freeing a resource requires knowledge of how the resource was allocated. In the code above, the syntax for deleting cPtr is different from that of deleting namePtr. We must remember to do this correctly in every catch block and also at the end of the function. If any one of the catch handlers or the final code of the function forgets to release all the resources allocated, then we have introduced memory leaks. Remembering to do the same steps over and over again is not really safe. This gets even more complicated as more and more resources are allocated and as we go further into the function. It would be really nice if this whole process can somehow be automated.

Automating Resource Management

There are two events guaranteed in the life cycle of a C++ object. A constructor must be called to create it and a destructor is (mostly automatically) called when it is about be destroyed. This guarantee can be used very effectively in managing resources even under exceptions. If we somehow convert a simple character pointer into an object of a class, then we don't have to remember to delete the memory pointed by the pointer—that can be done by the destructor. Here is a simple implementation:

```
#include <stddef.h>

class TCharResource {
    public:
        // Create a character array of the specified size. Default is an
        // array of 1 character.
        TCharResource(size_t size=1) {
            if (size > 0)
                    _resource = new char[size];
            else
                    _resource = 0; // invalid size, pointer set to nil
        }

        // It is safe to delete a pointer which is nil (0) in C++
        ~TCharResource() { delete [] _resource; }
        char* GetResource() { return _resource; }
    private:
        char* _resource;
}; // end class TCharResource
```

This simple class can help us immensely in managing character resources. Instead of allocating unprotected character arrays, we create **TCharResource** objects. The constructor allocates memory for an array of characters. Even a single character is treated as an array of 1 element. The destructor deletes the pointer to the array of characters allocated in the constructor. The member function, **GetResource**, returns the internal pointer to the array of characters.

The function **Gx()** can now be modified to use this new class.

```
// Automatic Resource management in an exception environment
void Gx()
{
    TCharResource namePtr(100); // ❹ Create a resource object for 100
                                // characters

    try {
        // some operations that might cause an exception
    }
    catch (...)
    {
        // No need to deallocate the resource, it is automatic ❺
        throw; // rethrow the exception
    }
    // No exception occurred, continue with normal code
    TCharResource cPtr; // Create a resource object for 1 character

    try {
        // Some other operation that might cause exceptions
    }
    catch(...)
    {
        // No need to deallocate resources explicitly ❻
        throw; // rethrow exception
    }
    // We are lucky, No exceptions ever occurred. Clean up and return
    // Again no need to deallocate resources explicitly ❼
```

```
    // Destructor for namePtr object and cPtr objects are called on exit
    // from this function, which deletes the memory.
}
```

❹ Instead of explicitly allocating a dynamic array of characters, an object of **TCharResource** is created. The size of the array (100) is passed to the constructor. The constructor (shown earlier) creates the array of characters dynamically.

❺ In the first catch handler, we do nothing special to get rid of the character resource object **namePtr**. Because **namePtr** is a C++ object, on exit from **Gx** (either due to an exception or on normal exit), the destructor for **namePtr** is automatically invoked. The destructor deletes the pointer to the resource, ensuring a clean state.

❻ In the second catch handler no extra code exists to delete the resource object. Just as in the first catch handler, resource clean up is automatic. If **Gx** is exited from this second catch handler, destructor is invoked for the **namePtr** object and also for the **cPtr** object.

❼ At the end of the function, the scenario is no different. The destructors for the local objects are invoked on exit from the function. Both **namePtr** and **cPtr** are automatically destroyed (destructor is called) which takes care of deleting the arrays inside the objects.

In fact, if there was nothing else to be done in the catch blocks (other than freeing up the resources in **namePtr** and **cPtr**), then we don't even have to write the **try** and **catch** blocks. Clean-up would be automatic.

The problem of resource management has been taken care of elegantly. But how does one use the resource in their programs. For example, how can we write into the character array inside **namePtr**. As the first cut, class **TCharResource** has a member function **GetResource**, which returns a pointer to the internal array. This member function can be used directly to access the array. Here is a simple example.

```
void Gx()
{
    TCharResource namePtr(100); // Create a resource object for 100
                                // characters

    char* p = namePtr.GetResource(); // ❽ Get a pointer to the char array
    strcpy(p, "THIS IS A TEST STRING"); //

    try {
        // some operations that might cause an exception
    }
    catch (...)
    {
        // No need to deallocate the resource, it is automatic
        throw; // rethrow the exception
    }
}
```

❽ We get a pointer to the array of characters inside the resource **namePtr** using the member function **GetResource**. Next, we copy a test string into the memory pointed by the pointer **p**. As with any other resource, the programmers are responsible to ensure that they do not overshoot the limits of the resource.

This method of explicitly calling a member function to get access to the array is not very elegant. We shall see better solutions soon.

Generalizing the Resource Management Solution

This solution seems to work for character arrays. But what about the case where one wants to create an array of **TPerson** objects or an array of int and would like to use this automated scheme? It is not good enough if the above scheme works only for the type char. We must be able to extend the solution to any type that a client likes to use. Is it possible to generalize this solution?

Yes, you guessed it; all we need to do is to make the **TCharResource** a generic (template) class. The template argument should specify the type of the resource is to be allocated. We also need a better name for this class. Since we are trying to make any resource safe to use, why not call the class **TSafeResource**? So here is the new class:

```
#include <stddef.h> // For size_t definition
#include <string.h> // For strcpy prototype, file to include depends on the
                    // compiler

template <class AType> class TSafeResource {
    public:
        TSafeResource (size_t size=1) {
            if (size > 0)
                _rp = new AType[size];
            // If the user did not provide a positive size, set pointer to
            // nil
            else _rp = 0; // Or even throw an exception
        }
        ~TSafeResource () { // deallocate resource
                delete [] _rp;
        }
        operator AType*() { return _rp; } // ❾

    private:
        AType* _rp;
};
```

There is nothing magical about this class. We have only changed the type of resource; it is now a template argument. Everything else has remained the same. With this new implementation, our function **Gx** can be modified as follows:

```
#include <iostream.h>

void Gx()
{
    // Create a resource object for 100 characters
    TSafeResource<char> namePtr(100);

    strcpy(namePtr, "THIS IS A TEST STRING"); // ❿
    cout << "Contents of namePtr: " << namePtr << endl; // Works!
    try {
        // some operations that might cause an exception
    }
```

```
     catch (...)
     {
          // No need to deallocate the resource, it is automatic
          throw; // rethrow the exception
     }
}
```

⓾ In the earlier implementation, we had to retrieve the pointer to the array using the GetResource member function. That function no longer exists, so how will this code access the array contained in the resource object? This is where some magic happens.

❾ We have added a special operator to the **TSafeResource** class. This is a conversion operator that converts a **TSafeResource** (of **AType**) to an **AType*** (pointer to **AType**). What is more interesting is the fact that this conversion operator is invoked by the compiler automatically when needed. A client uses a **TSafeResource** object as a substitute for a raw resource. Instead of using array of **char**, we are using a **TSafeResource<char>**. In doing so, the user should not have to do anything extra with **TSafeResource <char>** objects to use them as **char** pointers. This job is done by the conversion operator. When **namePtr** needs to be converted to a **char*** (in the call to **strcpy**), the compiler looks in the class **TSafeResource** for help and finds the conversion operator that fits in perfectly.

NOTE　　This is what we mean by *designing for the client*. It is not good enough to provide a class that mitigates some problem. If using such a class causes the clients to change the way they write code, then the designers haven't fulfilled their responsibility. An elegant design should solve a problem while retaining the simplicity of the original code (it should not require the client to do something extra). This is what **TSafeResource** has done. A client uses it in place of an unprotected resource but still uses it as if it was a raw pointer.

THINK　　Is there anything missing from the **TSafeResource?** What if you don't want the destructor to delete the resource at the end of the function? One can add another member function (**Release**) to tell the object not to delete the resource. This member function just sets the internal pointer to 0 and returns the existing address to the user. Add this member function. Another helper function could replace the existing pointer with a new pointer passed in by the user. It should return the existing pointer to the caller. Add this function (**ReplaceResource**). It is easy to combine these two functions into a single function with a default argument of 0.

NOTE　　Is this resource safety required in all programs? This is a reasonable question to ask. Should every piece of software worry about fault tolerance and reliability under all circumstances? If you are writing some test code that is never going to be shipped to any client, then there is absolutely no need to worry about such resource management issues. If the program leaks some resource, it will be recovered when the process (task) that runs the program is killed by the OS at the end of the program. But designers of libraries and commercial frameworks cannot make any such assumptions. There is no way to tell how a client would use a library/framework. Such software should ensure reliability even under worst case scenarios. Maintaining resource control under all circumstances is very important. In general, this principle applies to the entire issue of exception handling. A simple program should terminate with a diagnostic message in case of a run-time failure.

There is no point in providing elaborate exception handling schemes for all possible exceptions, but commercial software should be reliable even under the worst case scenario and exceptions of all types must be handled properly.[8]

EXCEPTIONS AND CONSTRUCTORS

Until now, we really didn't have a safe way of indicating failure of a constructor (and destructor) to the client. The possible solutions were

1. To leave the object in a bad state, probably with a flag set inside the object to indicate failure. A member function may be provided to check this state.

2. Force the clients to pass in an extra reference argument (probably an int) to the constructor. This argument would be set by the constructor (0 if successful, 1 if failed). The client should check the value of this argument after the constructor completes execution.

But none of these methods are fool proof. It requires explicit action by the client to ensure the correctness of their code and it will be disastrous if the client forgets to check for success or failure after every constructor call.

We now have a better solution. A constructor should throw an exception when it fails. This forces the client to notice the failure and take immediate action, making the software more reliable.

Returning Safe Resources from Functions

We are familiar with functions returning pointers to different resources (pointer to char, TPerson, etc.). The caller of a function that returns a pointer to a new piece of resource must remember to delete it when she no longer needs it. If she forgets to delete it, then there is a resource leak (garbage is generated). Here is an example:

```
// This function reads characters typed in and stores them in a dynamic
// array. A pointer to this dynamic array is returned. Caller must delete
// the returned pointer when it is no longer required.

#include <iostream.h>

char* GetUserName()
{
    char* ptr = new char[100]; // Assume that user knows the limit
    char *savedPtr = ptr;
    int userInput;

    cout << "Enter your name followed by <ENTER>: " << flush;
    // get the name from the user. Code is not important
```

---

[8]Just imagine what happens when a satellite control system, implemented in C++, receives an uncaught exception.

```
    while ( (userInput=cin.get()) != '\n')
        *ptr++ = (char) userInput;
    *ptr = '\0';

    return savedPtr;
}

void hx()
{
    char* userName;
    userName = GetUserName();
    // do something with the name
    //...
    delete[] userName; // ❶Don't forget this step
}
```

In this code, if the function **hx()** forgets to delete the pointer ❶, then a memory leak is caused. Remembering to delete all such pointers with the correct format of **delete** is an error prone task. Wouldn't it be nice if this task was automatic? We can definitely do that using template classes.

Consider the class **TAutoPtr**, shown below. This class handles character arrays.

```
class TAutoPtr {
    public:
        TAutoPtr(char* adoptResource)  // ❶
            : _resourcePtr (adoptResource) {}
        ~TAutoPtr() { delete [] _resourcePtr; }  // ❷
        operator char*() { return _resourcePtr; } // ❸
    private:
        char* _resourcePtr;
};
```

There is no change in **GetUserName**. The modified calling function is shown below.

```
void hx()
{

    TAutoPtr nameReclaimer( GetUserName() ); // ❹
    char* userName = nameReclaimer; // ❺ automatic conversion
    //do something with the name
    //...
    cout << "User name is " << userName << endl;
    // No need to delete worry about garbage collection
    // ❻
}
```

In this implementation, there is no need for explicit garbage collection. We have delegated that responsibility to the class **TAutoPtr**.

❶ We create a local **TAutoPtr** object. The constructor for **nameReclaimer** accepts a pointer to a character and stores it in the data member **resourcePtr**.

❷ The destructor of this class just deletes whatever **_resourcePtr** points to. It assumes that **_resourcePtr** points to an array.

❸ This is a convenience function that returns the value of _resourcePtr.

❹ In function hx(), we call GetUserName and pass the return value to TAutoPtr constructor. This creates a local TAutoPtr object (nameReclaimer) that holds the address of whatever GetUserName returned.

❺ We then extract the address in the TAutoPtr object and store it in a local pointer and use it in the function (automatic conversion by operator char*).

❻ When we exit hx(), destructor is called for all local objects. This includes our nameReclaimer object. The destructor just deallocates the memory pointed by _resourcePtr, which is what we wanted to do. Now garbage collection is automatic.

By using a helper class, we have automated garbage collection. No modifications were done to the function GetUserName to achieve this goal.

As you would expect, TAutoPtr needs to be a template class to accommodate all types. Not only that, we need two different flavors of TAutoPtr—one for reclaiming memory used by single objects and another to reclaim arrays of object. So we create two template classes as shown below:

```
// This class reclaims memory (using the delete[] operator).
// *** Use this class to delete arrays of objects only. ***
// Pass in the pointer that you need to delete to the constructor. Use this
// class to automate garbage collection of return values from functions.
// There is no storage allocated in the class — it just deletes
// whatever you pass in when the destructor is called. All functions are
// inline to minimize the cost of using these objects
// *** Objects of this class must be created on the Stack only. Do not use
// them with the new() operator.

template <class AType> class TAutoArrayPtr {
    public:
        // Constructor
        TAutoArrayPtr(AType* adoptResource = 0) :
            _resourcePtr (adoptResource) { }
        // Destructor
        ~TAutoArrayPtr() { delete [] _resourcePtr ; }
        operator AType*() const { return _resourcePtr ; }
        // A convenient subscripting operator for arrays
        AType& operator[](size_t index)
            { return _resourcePtr[index]; } // ❼
        void operator= (AType* adoptNewResource) { // ❾
            if (adoptNewResource != _resourcePtr ) {
            // Check if same address
                // Get rid of existing resource
                delete [] _resourcePtr ;
                // And adopt the new resource
                _resourcePtr = adoptNewResource;
            }
        }

    private:
        // See discussion below about copying and assignment
        TAutoArrayPtr& operator=( TAutoArrayPtr<AType>& assign);
        TAutoArrayPtr( TAutoArrayPtr<AType>& copy);
        AType* _resourcePtr ;
};
```

```
// This class reclaims memory (using the delete operator).
// *** Use this class to delete single objects only. ***
// Pass in the pointer that you need to delete to the constructor. Use this
// class to automate garbage collection of return values from functions.
// There is no storage allocated in the class — it just deletes whatever
// you pass in when the destructor is called. All functions are inline to
// minimize the cost of using these objects
// *** Objects of this class must be created on the Stack only. Do not use
// them with the new() operator.

template <class AType> class TAutoPtr {
    public:
        // Simple constructor
        TAutoPtr (AType* adoptResource = 0) : _resourcePtr (adoptResource)
            { }
        // Destructor
        ~TAutoPtr () { delete _resourcePtr ; }
        operator AType*() const { return _resourcePtr ; }
        // Convenience function for using -> (member access)
        AType* operator->() const { return _resourcePtr; } // ❽
        // Assign a new resource pointer to this object
        void operator= (AType* adoptNewResource) { // ❿
            if (adoptNewResource != _resourcePtr ) {
                // Check if sameaddress
                // Get rid of existing resource
                delete _resourcePtr ;
                // And adopt the new resource
                _resourcePtr = adoptNewResource;
            }
        }

    private:
        // See discussion below about copying and assignment
        TAutoPtr& operator=( TAutoPtr<AType>& assign);
        TAutoPtr( TAutoPtr<AType>& copy);
        AType* _resourcePtr ;
};
```

It is that easy. Our function **hx()** would be modified as follows:

```
void hx()
{
    // Create a reclaimer object that deletes the memory allocated in
    // GetUserName function.
    TAutoArrayPtr<char> nameReclaimer( GetUserName() );

    char* userName = nameReclaimer; // automatic conversion
    cout << "In hx: username=" << userName << endl;
    //do something with the name
    //...
    // No need to worry about garbage collection
}
```

❼ The subscript operator (operator[]) is provided for the TAutoArrayPtr class to allow for subscripting of an array of objects. Just as with any other array, it returns a reference to the object at the specified index. Note that no subscript bounds checking is performed (p. 560).

❽ The operator-> for class TAutoPtr (and not TAutoArrayPtr) is provided for ease of operation. Pointers are usually used with the -> operator to access members. This member function makes that possible. See the chapter on operator overloading for more details on the subtleties of this operator. This operator is not applicable to the TAutoArrayPtr because it encapsulates an array and not a single object (p. 561).

❾ ❿ The assignment operator with the AType* argument is another helper function that makes it easy to assign a new resource to the reclaimer objects. It deletes the existing resource and takes over responsibility for the new resource passed in.

Here is an example of how the -> operator could be used.

The example here deals with a simple parking garage management. A garage class is responsible for storing automobiles belonging to customers. When an automobile is parked, the garage returns a number identifying the slot where the automobile was parked. Customers later retrieve their automobile by using this slot number.

NOTE   The primary goal of this garage-automobile example is to understand the usefulness of automatic resource management. Don't worry too much about the logic of parking and releasing cars and ownership issues.

```
class TAutomobile;
typedef unsigned int SlotNumber;
TAutomobile* FREE_SLOT=0;
class TGarage {
    public:
        // Creates a new garage with the specified _capacity
        TGarage (unsigned int howMany_slots);
        // Park the automobile thisOne and return the slot number where
        // it was parked
        SlotNumber Park(TAutomobile* adoptVehicle);
        // Release the vehicle parked at the slot "which"
        // Return a pointer to the released automobile. If the slot number
        // is invalid, a nil pointer is returned.
        TAutomobile* ReleaseVehicle(SlotNumber which);
        // Show identity of all automobiles parked
        void ListVehiclesParked() const;
        ~TGarage ();
    private:
        TGarage(const TGarage &);
        TGarage& operator=(const TGarage &);
        TAutomobile**      _slots;
        unsigned int    _capacity;
        unsigned int    _freeSlots;
};

class TAutomobile{
    public:
        TAutomobile(const char type[], const char licensePlate[]);
        void PrintIdentity() const;
        virtual ~TAutomobile();
    private:
        char* _name;
```

```
            char* _licensePlate;
};

TGarage::TGarage(unsigned int howManySlots)
{
    // We create an array of pointers to automobiles Each pointer can hold
    // the address of one TAutomobile object
    if (howManySlots > 0)
          _slots= new TAutomobile* [howManySlots];
    _freeSlots = _capacity = howManySlots;
    for(int i=0; i < _capacity; i++)
          _slots[i] = FREE_SLOT;
}

TGarage::~TGarage() {delete [] _slots; /* not the vehicles in the slot */ }

// Park an automobile and return the slot number where it was parked
SlotNumber
TGarage::Park(TAutomobile* adoptVehicle)
{
    if (free_slots <= 0)     return -1; // full - thrown an exception

    if (adoptVehicle != 0) {
          for(int i=0; i < _capacity; i++)
                if (_slots[i] == FREE_SLOT) {
                      _slots[i] = adoptVehicle;
                      _freeSlots—;
                      return i;
                }
    }
    // Should really throw an exception
    else
          return -1;
}

// Return the automobile parked in this slot
TAutomobile*
TGarage::ReleaseVehicle(SlotNumber which)
{
    TAutomobile* released = 0;

    if (_slots[which] != 0) {
          released = _slots[which];
          _slots[which] = FREE_SLOT; // mark as free
          ++_freeSlots;
    }

    return released;
}

void
TGarage::ListVehiclesParked() const
{
    for (int i = 0; i < _capacity; i++) {
          if (_slots[i] != FREE_SLOT) {
                cout << "Vehicle at:" << i << " is: ";
                _slots[i]->PrintIdentity();
```

```
                        cout << endl;
                }
        }

}
```

The implementation of the automobile hierarchy is shown below in Fig. 10-8.

```
TAutomobile::TAutomobile(const char type[], const char lp[])
{
    if (type != 0) {
            _name = new char[strlen(type) + 1];
            strcpy(_name, type);
    }
    else name = 0;

    if (_licensePlate != 0) {
            _licensePlate = new char[strlen(lp) + 1];
            strcpy(_licensePlate, lp);
    }
    else _licensePlate = 0;
}

TAutomobile::~TAutomobile() { delete [] _name; delete [] _licensePlate; }

void
TAutomobile::PrintIdentity() const
{
    char* lp = _licensePlate ? _licensePlate : "none";
    char* nm = _name ? _name : "none";

    cout << nm << " " << lp;
}

class TCar : public TAutomobile {
    public:
        TCar(const char* licensePlate = 0)
            : TAutomobile("Car ", licensePlate) {}
};

class TVan : public TAutomobile {
    public:
        TVan(const char* licensePlate = 0)
```

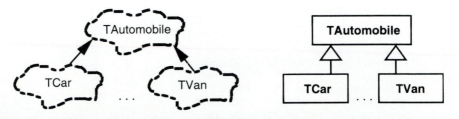

Fig. 10-8

```
                    : TAutomobile("Van ", licensePlate) {}

};
```

Here is a test program. When **ReleaseVehicle** returns a pointer to a **TAutomobile**, we don't want to worry about deleting it before exit from this function. We can use a **TAutoPtr** object to do that.

```
void TestGarage()
{
    TCar*           aCar = new TCar("2MEB410");
    unsigned int aCarSlot;
    TVan*           aVan = new TVan("3EML110");
    unsigned int aVanSlot;

    // Create a garage to hold 400 automobiles
    TGarage*        theGarage = new TGarage(400);

    // Park some automobiles
    aCarSlot = theGarage->Park(aCar);
    aVanSlot = theGarage->Park(aVan);
    theGarage->ListVehiclesParked();

    // Try to retrieve an automobile with an invalid slot number
    TAutoPtr<TAutomobile> ap =
        theGarage->ReleaseVehicle(10); // What happens here?
    cout << "ReleaseVehicle(10) returned: " << static_cast<TAutomobile*> (ap)
                                                        << endl; // ❶

    ap = theGarage->ReleaseVehicle(aVanSlot); // ❷
    // Verify if the garage released the correct vehicle
    if (ap != 0) { // ❸
        cout << "ReleaseVehicle(aVanSlot) returned: ";
        ap->PrintIdentity(); // ❹
        cout << endl;
    }
    else
      cout << "ReleaseVehicle(aVanSlot) returned: " <<
          static_cast<TAutomobile*> (ap) << endl;
    // Finally, remove the other automobile from the garage

    TAutoPtr<TAutomobile> bp = theGarage->ReleaseVehicle(aCarSlot);
    // I can also say, ap = theGarage->ReleaseVehicle(aCarSlot);
    // It works correctly too because the assignment operator
    // of TAutoPtr deletes the existing resource

    if (bp != 0) {
        cout << "ReleaseVehicle(aCarSlot) returned: ";
        bp->PrintIdentity();
        cout << endl;
    }
    // No need to worry about garbage collection
    delete theGarage;
}
```

We create a garage and park some vehicles. Next, we try to retrieve the parked automobiles.

❶ Here we try to retrieve an automobile from a slot that doesn't exist. Definitely, the ExitGarage method should return 0. We need to check the returned pointer but our pointer is safely tucked away in a TAutoPtr object. So how can we check an object for 0 (nil)? This is where the operator AType*() comes in handy. When we cast the object ap to a TAutomobile*, the conversion operator (operator AType*()) is automatically invoked and it returns a TAutomobile pointer (because AType is now TAutomobile).

❷ Here we try to retrieve an automobile that was parked by us in the garage. Now the ExitGarage member function must return a valid pointer to TAutomobile. The returned pointer is being assigned to ap. But ap is not a TAutomobile pointer. There is an assignment operator in TAutoPtr that accepts an AType* argument (which in this case is a TAutomobile*). This assignment operator is invoked because the argument on the RHS is an AType* and the argument on the LHS is a TAutoPtr object. This happens implicitly. This assignment operator takes care deleting the existing pointer (which is nil in this example).

❸ When we compare ap to 0, the object ap needs to be converted to some type that is compatible with 0. Here again, the conversion operator (operator AType*()), used earlier, helps us. The object ap is converted to a TAutomobile* and compared with 0.

❹ Finally, we would like to print the identity of the automobile retrieved from the garage but we don't have a pointer to a TAutomobile object anymore. All we have is a TAutoPtr object. When the statement (ap->PrintIdentity()) is invoked, we are first using the -> operator on ap. This operator has been overloaded in class TAutoPtr and it returns a pointer to AType (TAutomobile, in this case). Once this happens, we have a pointer to TAutomobile and the member function PrintIdentity can be invoked on it. Without this operator->, clients would have a very difficult time using a TAutoPtr object just like a pointer. After all, a TAutoPtr is nothing but a glorified pointer with a little intelligence; it should be usable just like an ordinary pointer. The operator-> makes it very easy.

Cost of Automatic Garbage Collection

The only extra cost for this automatic garbage collection scheme is the constructor and destructor calls for TAutoPtr. But since all the member functions of TAutoPtr are inline, there are no function calls when these reclaimer objects are created. Moreover, since TAutoPtr (and TAutoArrayPtr) objects are always created on the stack (automatic objects), there is no dynamic memory allocation cost. The reclaimer objects themselves do not allocate any dynamic memory in their implementation. There are no virtual functions in either of these classes and hence there is no dynamic binding cost. The only other cost is the minimal code duplication because of templates.

Considering all these advantages, it is very beneficial to use these reclaimer objects where one must remember to deallocate resources returned from functions.

Copying Reclaimer Objects

There is one thing that is missing from these classes: the copy constructor and the assignment operator. If more than one TAutoPtr object holds a pointer to the same object, it will cause double (or even multiple) deletes of the same memory causing major problems. We must avoid such problems. One way to do that is to set the value of the pointer in the source (RHS) TAutoPtr object to 0 (zero) after copying the address to the destination

(LHS) object (❶ below). This is done in the copy constructor. But in case of the assignment operator, before copying the address, we must delete the pointer in the **TAutoPtr** object on the LHS (❷ below). Here is an implementation:

```
// Shown here to exemplify the implementation issues. May not be
// appropriate to have public copy constructor
// *** Note that we need to modify the source object, copy. Hence the
// argument is a non-const
template <class AType>
TAutoArrayPtr<AType>::TAutoArrayPtr(TAutoArrayPtr<AType>& copy)
{
    // Copy the pointer first
    this->_resourcePtr = copy._resourcePtr;
    // Clear the pointer in the source to avoid double deletes
    copy._resourcePtr = 0; // ❶
}

// Shown here to exemplify the implementation issues. May not be
// appropriate to have public assignment operator
// *** Note that we need to modify the source object, assign. Hence the
// argument is a non-const
template <class AType>
TAutoArrayPtr<AType>&
TAutoArrayPtr<AType>::operator=(TAutoArrayPtr<AType>& assign)
{
    if (this == &assign)
        return *this;
    // First get rid of whatever the destination object points to
    delete [] this->_resourcePtr; // ❷
    // Then copy the pointer from source
    this->_resourcePtr = assign._resourcePtr;
    assign._resourcePtr = 0; // Clear the pointer in the object on the RHS
    return *this;
}
```

Identical implementation is required in the **TAutoArrayPtr** class.

CAUTION   Copying (and assigning) these reclaimer objects may not be correct. The whole purpose of these classes is to automate garbage collection. If copying of such objects is allowed, it might defeat the original intent and also makes them less efficient. Besides, these are supposed to be very low cost objects. Adding copying and assignment operations with the proper semantics does not preserve the low cost of these objects. After considering all these issues, I feel that copying and assignment of these reclaimer objects should not be allowed. Hence, I have made the copy constructor and assignment operator private. I have discussed and provided the implementation just so that you are aware of the issues and consequences.

THINK   Is there anything missing from the **TAutoArrayPtr** (and **TAutoPtr**)? What if you don't want the destructor to delete the resource at the end of the function? One can add another member function (**Release**) to tell the object not to delete the resource (which can also be accomplished by assigning 0 to a **TAutoPtr** object). This member function just sets the internal pointer to nil and returns the existing address to the user. Add this member function. Replacing the existing resource with a new one is done by the assignment operator.

NOTE   The standard C++ library now contains a class auto_ptr, which has similar functionality as our TAutoPtr class. But, some compilers still don't provide it with their libraries. If you are one of those unlucky programmers, just use the class TAutoPtr shown here.

PARTIAL COMPLETION OF CONSTRUCTORS

When a constructor is called for an object allocated on the heap (using the new operator), one might suspect that a destructor would be called for an object that was not completely created because the new operator failed. Consider this simple example:

```
#include <iostream.h>

void Gx()
{
    // Create a resource object for 100 characters
    TSafeResource<char> namePtr(100);
    // Rest of the code not important
}
```

When constructing the namePtr object, if the new operator fails to allocate memory (inside the TSafeResource constructor) and throws an exception, then the pointer _rp inside namePtr doesn't point to a valid address. So if the destructor is called for namePtr at the end of the function, wouldn't try to delete a piece of memory that was never allocated?

This is not allowed to happen in C++. Destructors are automatically called only for fully constructed objects. If an object contains other sub-objects and the constructor fails after constructing some sub-objects, then the destructors are only called for fully constructed sub-objects. If the constructor of namePtr receives an exception which is not caught and exits the function prematurely, then it implies that the constructor did not complete, and so the object namePtr does not exist. Consequently, the destructor is never invoked on namePtr, ensuring proper behavior.

☞ **The constructor (and destructor) is never called for an object if the operator new() fails to allocate memory.**

CREATING A SAFE ARRAY USING EXCEPTIONS

In an earlier chapter, we implemented an array class just for integers and then modified it to be template class. The implementation here is more elegant and also robust.

This new array TSafeArray is different from our earlier implementations. The array no longer creates objects. Instead, it accepts objects supplied by the user and holds them. Clients can remove their objects whenever they like. In other words, it is not a *value* array, but a *reference* array. The elements of the array are not values (objects); instead, they are pointers to client supplied objects.

We already know that a **void** pointer can hold the address of any type. We shall use this property of **void** pointers to avoid code duplication in template classes.

```cpp
#include <stddef.h>
#include <iostream.h>

enum ESortOrder { eAscending, eDescending };

class TArrayImplementation {
    protected:
        TArrayImplementation(size_t sz);
        TArrayImplementation(const TArrayImplementation& copy);
        // the famous Copy Constructor
        ~TArrayImplementation() { delete [] _vp; }
        // Assignment operator
        TArrayImplementation& operator=(const TArrayImplementation&
                                                          assign);

        void* Get(size_t index);
        void* Put(size_t index, const void* what);
        // and many more functions
        void Print() const;
        size_t _size;
        void** _vp;
};

// The implementation of member functions

#include <stdlib.h> // all C library functions
TArrayImplementation::TArrayImplementation(size_t sz)
{
    if (sz > 0) {
        _size = sz;
        _vp = new void* [_size]; // ❶
        for(int i=0; i < _size; i++)
            _vp[i] = 0;
        }
    else {
        _vp = 0;
        _size = 0;
    }
}
// This is the copy constructor
// Called (mostly) by the system for copying objects
// (for temporaries etc.)
TArrayImplementation::TArrayImplementation(const TArrayImplementation&
                                                          other)
{
    if ( other.size > 0) {
        _size = other._size;
        _vp = new void* [_size];
        for(int i=0; i < _size; i++)
            _vp[i] = other._vp[i];
    }
```

```
        else {
                _size = 0;
                _vp = 0;
        }
}
TArrayImplementation&
TArrayImplementation::operator=(const TArrayImplementation& other)
{
    if (_size >= other._size) {
            // The easy case - Just copy elements
            for (int i=0; i < other._size; i++)
                    _vp[i] = other._vp[i];
                    _size = other._size;
            }
    else {
            if (_vp != 0)
                    delete [] _vp; // discard existing memory
            _vp = new void* [other._size];
            _size = other._size;
            // Copy elements
            for(int i=0; i < _size; i++)
            _vp[i] = other._vp[i];
    }
    return *this;
}

void* TArrayImplementation::Put(size_t index, const void* what) // ❷
{
    void* oldValue = _vp[index]; // Save the address of the object already
                                 // stored here
    _vp[index] = const_cast<void*> (what); // Put the object in the array
    return oldValue;   // return the saved value
}

void* TArrayImplementation::Get(size_t index) { return _vp[index]; }
                            // ❸ No error checks

void TArrayImplementation::Print() const        // ❹
{
    cout << endl;
    for (int i =0; i < _size; i++)
            cout << _vp[i] << " " ;
    cout << endl;
}
```

This is a simple class that maintains an array of void pointers. The data member _vp points to an array of pointers.

❶ The constructor allocates enough storage for an array of void pointers. Actually, _vp is a pointer to an array of pointers. The constructor also stores the size of the array. Finally, all the slots in the array are set to 0.

❷ Put: This is another important function. To store objects into the array, the address of the object and the index of the slot in the array are passed in. The address of the object already stored at the specified index (if any) is returned from the function.

❸ Get: This is a key function in the class. When the client needs to extract an object from the array, she needs to pass the index of the slot she is interested in. The address contained at the specified index is returned. It is up to the derived class to take care of error checking. No error checking of any sort is done here.

❹ This is just a helper function. When debugging a derived class implementation, it might help to look at the addresses stored in the array. The addresses are just printed in sequence.

Next, we look at the implementation of the safe array class. This class provides all the error checking needed by clients. It uses the implementation of the TArrayImplementation class from above. Needless to state, we are using private derivation because we just want implementation reuse.

```cpp
// This exception indicates that there is no object at the specified index
class TNoObjectException {
    public:
        TNoObjectException(size_t whichIndex) : _index(whichIndex) {}
        size_t GetFailingIndex() const { return _index; }
        // Returns a textual description of the error
        const char* GetDescription() const
            { return "There is no object at the specified index"; }
    private:
        size_t _index; // that caused the exception
};

class TRangeErrorException {
    public:
        TRangeErrorException(size_t whichIndex, size_t arraySize)
            : _index(whichIndex), _size(arraySize) {}
        size_t GetFailingIndex() const { return _index; }
        size_t GetArraySize() const { return _size; }
        const char* GetDescription() const
            { return "The specified index is out of range"; }
    private:
        size_t _index; // that caused the exception
        size_t _size; // actual size of the array
};

const size_t ARRAY_SIZE = 256;

template<class AType> class TSafeArray : private TArrayImplementation {
    public:
        TSafeArray(int sz = ARRAY_SIZE);
        TSafeArray(const TSafeArray<AType>& copy);
        TSafeArray<AType>& operator=(const TSafeArray<AType>& assign);
        ~TSafeArray() { /* nothing to delete */ }

        int GetSize() const { return _size; }
        AType& Get(size_t fromWhere);
        AType& Put(size_t where, const AType& what);
        AType& operator[](size_t index);
        void Print() const;
};

// The implementation of member functions

#include <stdlib.h> // all C library function prototypes
```

```
template<class AType>
TSafeArray<AType>::TSafeArray(int theSize)
    : TArrayImplementation(theSize)
{ /* All the work is done in TArrayImplementation class */ }

template<class AType>
TSafeArray<AType>::TSafeArray(const TSafeArray<AType>& copy)
    : TArrayImplementation(copy)
{ /* All the work is done in TArrayImplementation class */ }

template<class AType>
TSafeArray<AType>&
TSafeArray<AType>::operator=(const TSafeArray<AType>& assign)
{
    if (this == &assign) {
        cout << "Warning: Trying to assign object to itself\n";
        return *this;
    }
    TArrayImplementation::operator=(assign); // call base class function
    return *this;
}

template<class AType>
AType& TSafeArray<AType>::Get(size_t fromWhere)
{
    if (fromWhere >= 0 && fromWhere < _size) {
        void* p = TArrayImplementation::Get(fromWhere);
        if (p != 0) // cast the void pointer to AType
            return *( reinterpret_cast<AType*> (p) );
        else throw TNoObjectException(fromWhere);
    }
    else throw TRangeErrorException(fromWhere, _size); // throw an exception
}

AType& TSafeArray<AType>::Put(size_t where, const AType& what)
{
    if (where >= 0 && where < _size) {
        void* p = TArrayImplementation::Put(where, &what);
        return *(reinterpret_cast<AType*> (p)); // cast the void pointer to
                                               // AType
    }
    else     throw TRangeErrorException(where, _size); // throw an exception
}

template<class AType>
AType& TSafeArray<AType>::operator[](size_t index) { return Get(index); }

template<class AType>
void TSafeArray<AType>::Print() const
{
    cout << endl;
    for (int i =0; i < _size; i++)
        if (_vp[i] != 0) // cast the void pointer to AType
        // This works only if class AType has an overloaded operator<<
            cout << *(reinterpret_cast<AType*> (_vp[i]) ) << " " ;
    cout << endl;
}
```

Most of the work is done in the **TArrayImplementation** class. Member functions **Get()** and **Put()** perform necessary subscript bounds checking and then invoke the base class functions. Otherwise, an appropriate exception is thrown.

The method **Get()** receives a void pointer from the base class, but the client is interested in the original object. Therefore, **Get()** performs the necessary type conversion and returns a reference to the object. If the client had not stored any object at this location, then an exception is thrown because a 0 pointer should not be converted to a valid reference to an object.

NOTE   This may not be the best implementation for an array of integers. It is better to specialize this array implementation for basic types (**char**, **int**, **long**, etc.). It should not be very difficult to do so.

THINK   Can you add a member function **Sort()** to the **TSafeArray** implementation? Use an **enum** to indicate the sorting order (ascending, descending). Next, add another utility function **Find(AType& what)** which searches the array for the specified object and returns the index (or a pointer to the object) where it is found (or throws an exception if not found). Then, add an **operator+=**, which appends one array to another. This exercise is not that trivial.

Here is trivial test program that exercises the implementation.

```
// Test the templateTSafeArray
main()
{
    TSafeArray<int> x(10), y(10); // An array of 10 elements
    int a = 10;
    int b = -100;
    x.Put(0, a);
    x.Put(1, b);
    x.Print();
    x[1] = x[0];
    x = x;// Will print a warning
    y = x;
    // Check if assignment was done!
    y.Print();

    try {
        x[11] = x[3]; // Should cause a TNoObjectException
    }
    catch(const TNoObjectException& exp)
    {
        cout << "Caught TNoObjectException exception\n";
        cout << "Index in error= " << exp.GetFailingIndex() << endl;
    }
    catch(...) { cout << "Caught an exception\n"; }

    cout << "Try access beyond end of array\n";
    try {
        x[11] = x[12];// Should generate illegal index error
    }
    catch(const TRangeErrorException& exp)
    {
```

```
        cout << "Caught TRangeErrorException exception\n";
        cout << "Index in error= " << exp.GetFailingIndex() << endl;
    }
    catch(...) { cout << "Caught an exception\n"; }

    return 0;
}
```

REMEMBER   When exceptions are enabled in a C++ compiler, the size of executables increase considerably because of the extra code needed to manage exceptions at run-time. Don't be surprised if you see huge executables. Compilers need to generate quite a bit of code to support efficient exception management. With some compilers, code that is compiled without exceptions enabled is not compatible with one in which exceptions are enabled. Check your compiler.

SUMMARY

Exceptions allow applications to shutdown gracefully when errors are detected

Exceptions force programmers to handle errors as soon as they happen. This eliminates unhandled errors from causing more problems in other parts of the system.

Exceptions can be used to implement the organized panic (shutdown) model or the resumption model (recovery).

C++ exceptions code can make the logic of the code in a function fuzzy (because of the interspersed exception handling code).

Programmers must anticipate errors in order to recover (or gracefully shutdown) from them.

Eiffel causes automatic exception generation when any assertion fails.

In Eiffel, all exceptions in a function are handled in a single **rescue** clause with an optional retry instruction.

Designing a simple, efficient exception management scheme in a project is no easy task. It requires careful design right from the early phases of the project.

Exception hierarchies are very useful in managing exceptions in large projects.

Finally, there is considerable cost (both in time and space) when exceptions are used in a program. However, the time cost is not very significant when no exceptions are thrown.

11

Mastering Data Abstraction

In Part I, we have learned the essential principles of data abstraction. Moreover, we have used data abstraction in many of the examples. Now it is time to focus on the finer techniques of data abstraction. The techniques described here are powerful tools when used properly. One needs to understand the advantages and disadvantages of each of the techniques described here before using them.

HIDING IMPLEMENTATION DETAILS OF AN ABSTRACTION

C++ In C++, programmers are required to declare all the private and protected data members inside the class header even though they are not accessible by normal clients. Clients can see all the private data members of a class but they cannot access them (they are visible but are not accessible). It is logical to think that something that clients cannot access should not be shown.

Private (and protected) data members are essential for the implementation of a class but they are useless for normal clients. But a C++ compiler needs to know the details of all the members (private, protected, public) of a class before it allows a programmer to create objects of the class. This is because the compiler must allocate enough memory for the object. Objects are usually created by clients and the compiler needs to know the size of the class when the client's programs are compiled. But clients only use the class interface file. Therefore, the compiler must be able determine the size of an object of any class just by using the class header file. This is the only reason why private and protected members of the class must be shown in the class header file.

Another disadvantage of declaring all the data members of a class in a header file is related to the cost of compiling programs. When the size of class changes, all clients of that class must recompile their programs using the new class header file. The size of a class can change when a data member is added or removed from the class.[1] Here is a simple example. We revisit the **TString** class used in Part I for this example.

```
/*
 * A TString class implementation. It is based on the ASCII character set.
 * TString objects can be copied and assigned. Class implements deep copy.
 */
class TString {
    public:
        // Constructors
        // Create an empty string object
        TString();
        // Create a new string object which contains the characters pointed
        // by s. s must be NULL terminated. Characters are copied from s.
        TString(const char* s);
        // Create a string containing the single character in aChar
        TString(char aChar);
        // Other details of the class are not relevant here.
    private:
        // _length is the number of characters stored in the object.
        // But the memory pointed by _str is at least _length+1 long.
        unsigned _length;
        char* _str; // pointer to characters stored
};
```

In this example, there are two private data members. On a 32 bit system (where the size of a machine word is 32 bits), the total size of the data members would be 8 bytes (4 bytes for **_length** and 4 bytes for _str). Clients can use this class as they like and create as many objects as they want. After this implementation of **TString** is shipped, we might decide to change the implementation of the class to make it more efficient. As we already know, changing the implementation of a class does not have any effect on the interface of the class and, hence, there should be no effect on the clients because of a change in the implementation.

In the next implementation, we would like to allocate memory in chunks. Initially, we might allocate an array of characters a little bigger than required. Then, when the string object needs more memory, we grow the memory (actually allocate a new piece of memory) in chunks of, say 128 bytes. This way, we reduce the number of (expensive) memory allocation calls and, hence, improve the execution speed of the class in situations where the string size changes frequently. In order to remember the size of the allocated array of characters, we need one more data member so we add a new data member **_strCapacity** to the **TString** class.

---

[1]Adding and/or removing member functions can also affect clients.

```
// A TString class implementation. It is based on the ASCII character set.
// TString objects can be copied and assigned. Class implements deep copy.

class TString {
    public:
        // Constructors
        // Create an empty string object
        TString();
        // Create a new string object which contains the characters pointed
        // by s. s must be NULL terminated. Characters are copied from s .
        TString(const char* s);
        // Create a string containing the single character in aChar
        TString(char aChar);
        // Other details of the class are not relevant here.
    private:
        // _strCapacity is the maximum number of characters that the buffer
        // pointed by _str can hold.
        unsigned _strCapacity ;
        // _length is the actual number of characters stored in the object.
        // But the memory pointed by _str is at least _length+1 long.
        unsigned _length;
        char* _str; // pointer to characters
};
```

The implementation of this class is trivial and not shown here. It is very easy to modify the implementation shown in Part I to accommodate the new feature.

Now the size of an object of class **TString** is bigger than the first implementation (by 4 bytes). Every client of **TString** must now recompile their code. But forcing clients to recompile their code is not a good thing to do. As far as possible, a change in the class implementation should not force the clients to recompile their code. Compiling code is a time consuming task. In many projects, compiling all the code can take many hours to many days (or even weeks). Furthermore, in many cases, there is a strict requirement that object sizes never change. This is usually the case, where binary compatibility must be maintained across releases. More on this later.

One of the benefits of data abstraction is the freedom to change the implementation. If we lose the freedom to change the implementation just because it might cause a change in the size of an object, then we have lost one of the major advantages of data abstraction. We need a solution to this problem.

The answer is to use a separate implementation class. Instead of keeping all the data members of a class inside the header file, we just keep a pointer to an implementation object in the class. This pointer is also referred to as a *handle*. The details of the implementation are kept inside the other class. Usually, the name of the implementation class has the suffix **Impl** (or even **Implementation**). Here is the modified **TString** class that uses a separate implementation class.

```
// This version uses a separate implementation class

class TStringImpl; // ❶ Forward declaration - this is the implementation
                   // class
```

```
class TString {
    public:
        // Constructors
        // Create an empty string object
        TString();
        // Create a new string object which contains the characters pointed
        // by s. s must be NULL terminated. Characters are copied from s .
        TString(const char* s);
        // Other details of the class are not relevant here.
    private:
        TStringImpl* _handle;
};
```

Class **TStringImpl** is *not* exported to clients. Any client of **TString** knows about the use of **TStringImpl** inside **TString**, but the details of **TStringImpl** are not exposed. The class **TStringImpl** is shown below.

```
class TStringImpl {
    public:
        // _strCapacity is the number of characters that the buffer pointed
        // by _str can hold.
        unsigned _strCapacity ;
        // _length is the actual number of characters stored in the object.
        // But the memory pointed by _str is at least _length+1 long.
        unsigned _length;
        char* _str; // pointer to characters
};
```

The constructor of class **TString** would create an object of the class **TStringImpl** and make **_handle** point to it. Here is a skeleton implementation.

```
// Details of TStringImpl are required here.
#include     "StringImpl.h"

TString::TString(const char* arg)
{
    _handle= new TStringImpl; // Create a new object of the implementation
                             // class
    if (arg && *arg) { // pointer is not 0 and also points to non-zero
                     // characters
        _handle->_length = strlen(arg);
        _handle->_str = new char[_handle-> _length + 1];
        _handle->_strCapacity = _length;
        strcpy(_handle->_str, arg);
    }
    else {
        _handle->_str = 0;
        _handle->_length = 0;
        _handle->_strCapacity = 0;
    }
}
```

With this implementation, the size of the main class **TString** is not affected by any changes to the **TStringImpl** class. Class **TString** always contains a single pointer to a

TStringImpl object. Therefore, the size of an object of TString will always be the same. We are free to change the size of TStringImpl as often as we like. Moreover, clients of TString know nothing about TStringImpl. The details of TStringImpl are required in the implementation of TString and not in the interface of TString. A compiler just needs to know that TStringImpl is a separate class. This is taken care of by the forward declaration at ❶ above.

We can also make TStringImpl a simple struct. When TStringImpl is a very simple collection of data, it would be logical to make it a simple struct. But if TStringImpl is a powerful abstraction providing many services, then it should be a class with a separate interface and implementation.

Advantages of Using Handles

1. The main class, TString is not affected by changes in the implementation class, TStringImpl. Clients of TString will not have to recompile (but they must re-link) their code when the implementation of TStringImpl changes.

2. Clients of TString cannot see any details about the data members of the class. This prevents them from *hacking* into the class using a debugger (or some such tool).

3. Clients unnecessarily don't waste any time compiling the implementation code. This speeds up the compilation process, which is not a benefit that can be ignored.

4. As we shall see later, handles can be used to implement other powerful strategies also.

Disadvantages of Using Handles

1. None of the member functions of TString can be inline. This is because any member function of TString must access information stored inside TStringImpl. But the details of TStringImpl are not known when the client's code is compiled. Therefore, an inline function of TString cannot be expanded inline. For example, if we try to inline the Size function, as below, it causes a compile time error.

```
class TStringImpl;

class TString {
    public:
        // Constructors
        // Create an empty string object
        TString();
        // Create a new string object which contains the characters pointed
        // by s.
        // s must be NULL terminated. Characters are copied from s .
        TString(const char* s);
        // Other details of the class are not relevant here.

        // Test if Size can be an inline member function
        int Size() const
        {           return _handle->_length;
```

RELEASE-TO-RELEASE BINARY COMPATIBILITY (RRBC)

Release-to-Release Binary compatibility is the ability to continue to use old executable files (i.e., applications and shared libraries) when parts of the system (other shared libraries) have been upgraded to newer, but otherwise compatible versions. It would be helpful to your clients if you could modify classes without requiring your clients to recompile their code. If you somehow achieve this goal, then you can confidently state that your system provides RRBC. One of the touted benefits of OO software development is the ability to change the implementation of an abstraction without affecting the interface. But in C++, this is not easy to achieve. To maintain RRBC, developers must follow certain guidelines and the compiler must also provide certain implementation guarantees.

It should be possible (or at least desirable) to maintain RRBC even when the following changes to a class are made:

1. Adding new member functions to classes should not cause the clients to recompile their code.

2. The ability to add new data members to existing classes without causing the recompilation of the client's code. This is a valuable capability, but its absence can be worked around, albeit with some difficulty.

In the list above, (1) is the most important feature that must be supported by compilers to allow RRBC. We can overcome the lack of support for (2) by using handles described earlier.

Most compilers require that clients follow the rules mentioned below for RRBC.

- The existing class hierarchy must remain unchanged.
- Declarations for new virtual functions must appear after the declarations for all pre-existing virtual functions.
- All old virtual functions must remain and be declared in the same order.
- Non-virtual and static member functions can be added without restriction.
- Previously existing public or protected functions must continue to exist.
- The total size of an instance of a class must remain unchanged, and all public or protected data members must continue to exist and must remain at the same offset within the class. Private data that is referenced from public or protected inline member functions count as public data.

By adding new member functions at the end of the class, the offsets within the vtbl (pronounced v-table) of the existing functions will not change. Maintaining the same order among the virtual functions ensures that functions remain at the same offset within the vtbl (see Chapter 13 for Vtbl details).

To keep the size of an object of a class unchanged from release to release, handles as described earlier are essential. One can add new data members and remove existing data members of the handle class (TStringImpl above) without affecting the size of the original class.

```
                // Wouldn't compile because details of class TStringImpl is
                // not known
        }
    private:
        TStringImpl* _handle;
};
```

When this code is compiled, the compiler does not know the details of TStringImpl. Therefore, it does not know that _length is a member of TStringImpl. Hence, the code will not compile. But if the class TStringImpl is completely defined, inline functions would be allowed. If the intention of using handles is just to keep the class size constant, it would be correct to fully define TStringImpl before TString is defined, which would allow inline member functions in TString. For example, the following code will compile:

```
class TStringImpl {
    public:
        // _strCapacity is the number of characters that the buffer pointed
        // by _str can hold.
        unsigned _strCapacity ;
        // _length is the actual number of characters stored in the object.
        // But the memory pointed by _str is at least _length+1 long.
        unsigned _length;
        char* _str; // pointer to characters
};

class TString {

    public:
        // Constructors
        // Create an empty string object
        TString();
        // Create a new string object which contains the characters pointed
        // by s.
        // s must be NULL terminated. Characters are copied from s .
        TString(const char* s);
        // Other details of the class are not relevant here.

        // Test if Size can be an inline member function
        int Size() const
        {
            return _handle->_length;
            // This will compile because TStringImpl is fully defined
            // above.
        }
    private:
        TStringImpl* _handle;
};
```

   2. With handles, every access to a data member is through a pointer to another class. There is an extra pointer (_handle above) in every object of class TString. This pointer is in addition to all the data members that were present in TString (which are now in TStringImpl). This causes the size of every object of TString to increase by one pointer (4 bytes on a 32 bit system).

3. Access to data members of TStringImpl is through the handle in TString. This causes one more level of indirection. In other words, to get to a data member of TStringImpl direct access is not possible; we must use the handle in TString. This could result in the execution one or two extra assembly language instructions.

4. There is also the cost of creating (and destructing) the object that the handle points to. In the TString class, we must create the TStringImpl object dynamically (using operator new) and finally it (the TStringImpl object) must be deleted. Calls to operator new() and operator delete() don't come for free.

We could also make _handle a reference to TStringImpl instead of a pointer. We again have the same advantages of using a pointer but for one difference. When _handle is a reference, as soon as a TString object is created, a TStringImpl object must be bound to the reference _handle. But when _handle is pointer, there is no need to create a TStringImpl object immediately. We can set _handle to 0 in the constructor of TString. The TStringImpl object need be created only when required. This concept is discussed in more detail in the next strategy.

THE COST OF RECOMPILING V/S RELINKING

To convert source code to an executable program, there are two steps involved. First step is compiling and the second step is linking.

When a program is compiled, the compiler checks for syntax and semantic errors and then generates an object file. In the generated object file, there are calls to many functions. Some of these functions might exist in the object module and other might yet be unresolved. Calls to library functions will definitely remain unresolved. The compilation process can take a long time to complete. If many files need to be compiled, then the compilation time is even longer. If the interface (header file) of a class X changes, then any other class that uses X must recompile its code. In other words, any class (or function) that depends on X must recompile. In many commercial systems, recompiling the entire project can take many days. In other words, the *cost* (the time required) of recompiling a large project is quite high. We try to avoid changes that would cause the recompilation of the entire system. Also remember that to compile code, source code must be available.

When the object module and libraries are given to the linker to produce an executable program, it tries to resolve all the unresolved function calls. All the object modules and libraries are searched to find unresolved functions. It also checks to ensure that variables and functions are defined only once in the final executable module. Once everything is resolved, an executable program is generated. The main task in linking is address mapping. The unresolved function calls are mapped to the correct address of the function. Linking takes very little time compared to recompilation. If the interface (header file) of a class X remains the same, but the implementation of the member functions is modified, then any client that depends on X must re-link with the object module that contains the new implementation. There is no need to recompile the source code of clients of X. In the example above using handles, if the implementation of class TString is modified, then clients of TString would just re-link their code with the new implementation of TString. But if the class interface of TString is modified, then every client of TString must recompile their code. If we add a new data member to TStringImpl, clients of TString do not have to recompile their code because there is no change in class TString. When the implementation is changed and the interface remains the same, clients of the modified class must re-link with the new implementation. Relinking only requires the compiled object modules (libraries).

The cost of recompilation is high but the cost of relinking is very small. This is the reason why we strive to avoid recompilation.

In many modern development systems, one may not be able to see the separation of compiling and linking as separate steps. But it still happens internally. There are also systems that employ incremental compilation and incremental linking strategies to avoid recompilation and relinking of the entire project.

What changes can cause recompilation?

Any of the following changes in a class interface causes the clients to recompile their code.

1. Adding a new data member

2. Adding a new member function

3. Changing the size (or type) of a data member

4. Changing the prototype of a member function declaration[2]

5. Changing the order of data members

6. Changing the order of member functions

7. Changing any of the declarations (enum, struct, etc.) inside the class interface

8. Removing a member function

9. Removing a data member

10. Any changes to the inline member functions declared inside the class

If only the implementation of a member function changes, then it only causes relinking of code and not recompilation. The logic here is quite straight forward. When the implementation of a function changes, one should link with the address of the new function. If there is no change in the code that calls the function, then there is no need to recompile the code in the calling program.

---

[2]Changing a non-const member function to a const member function (or vice-versa) is also a change in the prototype of the function declaration.

USING POINTERS AS DATA MEMBERS (LAZY EVALUATION)

C++ When picking data members for a class, we have to select from the following three choices:

1. Use a pointer

2. Use a reference

3. Use a value

Consider the following example. In a vehicle simulation system, a car is represented by the class TCar. A car contains internal objects like engine, transmission, fuel injector, etc. Here is a skeleton of class TCar and related classes.

```
class TEngine {/* details not important for this example */ };
class TTransmission {/* details not important for this example */ };
class TFuelInjector {/* details not important for this example */ };

class TCar {
    public:
        // Some member function to operate the car
        void StartEngine();
        void Stop();
        void Drive();
        void ShiftToHigherGear();
        size_t GetOdodmeterReading() const;
        void ShiftToLowerGear();
    private:
        // an object, reference, or pointer to TEngine
        // an object, reference, or pointer to TTransmission
        // an object, reference, or pointer to TFuelInjector
        // and many more data members
};
```

Let's say we use an embedded object for TEngine, a reference for TTransmission, and a pointer for TFuelInjector.

```
class TCar {
    public:
        // Some member function to operate the car—details as before
    private:
        TEngine _engine;
        TTransmission& _transmissionRef;
        TFuelInjector* _pInjector;
        // and many more data members
};
```

When a TCar object is instantiated, the constructor of TCar must perform the following steps.

1. Create the _engine object by calling a constructor of TEngine.

2. Create (or receive a TTransmission object and bind the reference _transmissionRef to it.

3. Create a TFuelInjector object and make _pInjector point to it or initialize _pInjector to 0 .

In (1) there is no choice. The _engine object must be constructed and it will remain inside TCar for the lifetime of a TCar object. If the interface of TEngine changes, then TCar (and clients of TCar) must recompile. But what if a user creates a TCar object and never uses the _engine (i.e., doesn't start the engine)? Then the creation (and destruction) of the _engine object is a waste. When creating objects, it is a good practice to create an object only when it is required. But with embedded objects, such as _engine above, there is no choice. As soon as a TCar object is created, the _engine sub object must be created. Furthermore, once a TCar object is created and its embedded _engine object is also created, there is no way to replace the _engine object with another object of class TEngine, easily. Objects of TCar get an object of TEngine (called _engine) when they are created and they must use that _engine object in their entire lifetime.

In (2), instead of an object of TTransmission, we have used a reference to TTransmission. Once again, as soon as a TCar object is created, the constructor of TCar must bind the _transmissionRef to a valid TTransmission object. Once this is done, we have the same situation as in (1). The implementor cannot separate the binding between _transmissionRef and the associated TTransmission object. The only advantage of using a reference is that class TCar does not depend on the size of class TTransmission. If class TTransmission is changed, class TCar need not be recompiled. In reality, it is not possible to create a TTransmission object and bind it to _tranmissionRef when TCar is constructed. If a new TTransmission is created (using a new() operator) who is going to delete it? This implies that _transmissionRef must be bound to a TTransmission object that already exists. The user who creates a TCar object might supply the TTransmission object.

In (3), as in (2), class TCar does not depend on the size of class TFuelInjector (this has been discussed earlier with handles). When a TCar object is created, it is not required to bind _pInjector to a valid TFuelInjector object. The pointer _pInjector can be set to 0 to indicate that a TFuelInjector object is not attached to the pointer. When the need arises for a TFuelInjector object (for example, when the _engine is started), the pointer can be checked to see if it is 0 and if so a new TFuelInjector object can be created and attached to _pInjector. Moreover, we can also use different fuel injector objects with the same car object. The _pInjector pointer can also be made to point to different TFuelInjector objects during the lifetime of a TCar object. In both (2) and (3), a single object can be shared by different TCar objects if the constructor of TCar accepts user provided TTransmission and TFuelInjector objects. In (3), if a TCar object is never driven, there is no need to create a TFuelInjector object. This makes programs run faster because objects that are not used are not created. This is the concept of *creation on demand*. An object is not created until it is required. It is also called lazy evaluation.

The benefits of using a pointer to an object as a data member are:

1. The pointer need not be bound to an object as soon as the object that contains the pointer is created. This makes the object creation faster (less work in the constructor).

2. During the lifetime of a TCar object, different TFuelInjector objects can be attached to the pointer (_pInjector).[3] This provides more flexibility.

3. If the client of the enclosing object never invokes a member function that requires the services of the object pointed by the pointer (_pInjector), creation (and later destruction) of an unused object is eliminated.

4. One TTransmission object can be shared among multiple TCar objects. This is also possible with a reference but it is more convenient with pointers.

There are some disadvantages also.

1. Every member function of TCar must be careful not to use _pInjector without checking to make sure that it is not 0. If _pInjector is 0, then it must be attached (by some means) to a TFuelInjector object.

2. If the object pointed by _pInjector is created dynamically using a new() operator in one of the member functions, then the destructor of TCar must remember to delete whatever _pInjector points to. Otherwise, serious memory leaks are caused.

Using a pointer as a data member is useful only if flexibility is required. If TCar requires that one of its components be available as soon as TCar is created, then a reference or an embedded object is easier to use than pointer. When a reference (or an embedded object) is used, class TCar is not responsible for deleting the object bound to the reference. In case of an embedded object (_engine above) the compiler takes care of invoking the destructor for TEngine.

When a pointer or a reference is used polymorphic behavior is enabled. But when an embedded object is used, polymorphism is not possible. This is discussed in more detail later.

☞ **If possible, do not create something that may never be used.**

CONTROLLING OBJECT CREATION

C++ When public constructors and destructors are supplied in a class, any user can create objects of that class. But in some situations, such uncontrolled object creation may cause problems. If required, class designers should be able to restrict object creation. Some possible solutions are discussed below.

Allowing Object Creation Using the new() Operator Only

Here, users are allowed to create objects only using the new() operator. Clients should not be able to directly instantiate objects on the run-time stack. This could lead one to think that making constructors private would be the solution. But that wouldn't work because the new() operator needs access to the constructor too. For example,

---

[3]Remember to take care of memory leaks when doing so.

```
class X {
        public:
            X();
            ~X(); // Destructor
        private:
            X(int); // another constructor
        // ...
};
void f()
{
    X* p = new X; // This calls the default constructor of class X
                    // if it is accessible in the scope of f()
    X* p1 = new X(10); // Does not compile because X(int) is not accessible
                    // from f()
}
```

We would like a solution that works as follows.

```
X globalObject; // Should not compile
void h()
{
    X objectA;      // ❶ This should not compile either
    X* ptr = new X;  // ❷ This should compile without any errors!
}
```

When the user tries to create **objectA** (❶ above), the compiler should flag it as an error. But when the user attempts to create an object of **X** dynamically using the **new()** operator (❷ above), it should work fine. However, remember that in ❷ operator **new()** calls the default constructor. Here it works because the default constructor of **X** is a public member function. Therefore, function **h()** can access it. But if the default constructor of **X** were to be protected or private, the call to **new()** above will be a compile-time error because of the inaccessible constructor. In other words, we need a solution in which the constructor(s) would be public but still object creation on the stack (automatic objects) should not be possible.

In C++, when a user attempts to create an object on the stack (❶ above), the compiler looks for a matching, accessible constructor, and also an accessible destructor. The constructor is used in the creation of the object and the destructor is used to destroy the object when it goes out of scope. If one of them (constructor and/or destructor) is not accessible at the point of call, then it would be a compile-time error. We have already seen that we need public constructor(s) because even the **new()** operator needs to call a matching constructor. Therefore, we still provide public constructors. The trick is to make the destructor private. Here is the code.

```
class X {
        public:
            X();
        private:
            ~X(); // private destructor
        // ...
};
```

With this interface, the following test program would compile without errors.

```
void ff() {X* ptr = new X; /* ❸ This will compile! */ }
```

But still there is one final problem. How are we going to get rid of the object pointed by ptr (❸ above)? If we say

```
delete ptr;
```

it will cause a compile-time error because **delete** attempts to call the destructor of the class X. But our destructor is private, so we need some other mechanism to get rid of the object. A simple solution is to provide another member function for that purpose. Let's add another public member function **Delete** for this purpose.

```
class X {
        public:
            X();
            void Delete() { delete this; } // calls the destructor
        private:
            ~X(); // private destructor
        // ...
};
void gg()
{
    X objectA; // This will not compile
    X* ptr = new X;
    //...
    ptr->Delete(); // The statement "delete ptr" will not compile
}
```

That's all there is to it. In the **Delete** member function, we just need to call the **delete** operator. The pointer to the object is **this** and we just delete it. This in turn calls the destructor. This is fine because **Delete()** is a member function of X and, hence, it has access to private member functions also.

CAUTION   Don't use the **this** pointer after invoking **Delete** on it. This technique must be used with extreme caution. Deleting the **this** pointer is always dangerous and should be undertaken only under very special circumstances by programmers who know what they are doing. Invoking the **Delete** member function on an object looks to be a very simple operation. But, it has the side effect of deleting the object. The object pointed by **ptr** is no longer available. Deleting the **this** pointer is almost suicidal but it is required in some extreme situations. Use it with caution.

☞ Use a private destructor to prevent object creation on stack (automatic objects)

NOTE   This technique is not just a C++ trick. It has very practical applications. Certain specialized classes require that objects of the class be created at special locations using specialized **new()** operators. Such objects cannot live anywhere else. In such cases, the technique described above is very useful.

Preventing Object Creation Using the new() **Operator**

This is the converse of the previous situation. Here we should disable object creation using the new() operator but allow object creation on the stack. This is very easy to accomplish. All that is required is an inaccessible new() operator(s). Here is the skeleton code.

```
class Y {
        public:
            Y();
        private:
            void* operator new(size_t size);
            void operator delete(void* address);
        // ...
};

void hh()
{
    Y stackObject; // Fine. Calls the public constructor
    Y* ptr = new Y; // Will not compile. operator new is private
}
```

Code in function hh() fails because the compiler will try to invoke the class specific new() operator but it is private. The same thing happens with the operator delete().

NOTE   Again, this technique has specific applications. Classes that represent synchronization locks on resources are implemented this way. The intention is to make the lock acquisition and release automatic. The constructor would acquire the lock and the destructor relinquishes the lock. Allowing such lock objects to be created using new() can lead to deadlocks if some lock is never released. To overcome such problems, objects of such classes disallow dynamic creation.

USING POINTERS AND REFERENCES INSTEAD OF EMBEDDED OBJECTS

The issues surrounding the use of pointers, references, and embedded objects has been already discussed in our discussion of pointers as data members. But here we look at the consequences from a different angle.

When a data member must behave polymorphically, using embedded objects is not possible. We must use a pointer (preferred) or a reference. Take a look at this simplified example, which is based on the University-Teacher-Student hierarchy discussed earlier in Chapters 5 and 6.

```
class TMyClass {
    public:
        // some member functions, not relevant
    private:
        TPerson* _personPointer;
        TPerson& _personRef;
        TPerson _personObj;
```

```
};
// TPerson is a base class. TTeacher, TStudent are direct derived classes
// of TPerson.
// TGraduateStudent, and TGradTeachingAsst are indirect derived classes of
// TPerson.
```

Here the data member _personPointer can initialized with the address of a TPerson object or an object of any derived class of TPerson. Similarly, the reference _personRef can be initialized with a TPerson object or an object of one of the derived classes of TPerson (TStudent, TTeacher, etc.). But the embedded object _personObj can only be a true TPerson object. It cannot become a TStudent or a TTeacher. In other words, _personObj is a *monomorphic* object. On the other hand, _personRef and _personPointer are polymorphic objects.

There is a subtle difference between _personPointer and _personRef. When a TMyClass object is created, _personRef must be initialized with a TPerson (or a derived class of TPerson) object. Once _personRef is initialized, it becomes a monomorphic object. For example, if _personRef is initialized with a TStudent object, then _personRef remains a TStudent object during the lifetime of _personRef. Even if a TTeacher object is assigned to _personRef later, _personRef still exhibits the behavior of TStudent. In other words, the type of _personRef is set when it is initialized.

But with the _personPointer, there is polymorphism during the entire lifetime of the object. When a TMyClass object is created, _personPointer can be set to point to a TTeacher object. Later, it can be set to point to a TStudent object. In other words, the pointer _personPointer can be made to point to any TPerson object polymorphically. This flexibility of changing the binding is not possible with a reference.

☞ **If polymorphic behavior of a data member is essential, use a reference or a pointer as a data member. If polymorphism is not an issue, then using an embedded object is also an equally good choice.**

AVOID USING LARGE ARRAYS AS AUTOMATIC VARIABLES (OR DATA MEMBERS)

There is nothing wrong in using arrays of primitive types or arrays of objects. But how an array comes into existence is important. When an array is created as a local variable in a function, it is allocated on the run-time stack. Creating large arrays on the run-time stack is dangerous. Run-time stacks usually have some preset size and are platform dependent. Creating large arrays on the stack can cause a run-time crash. This problem is even more serious if the function where the large arrays is created is recursive.

Along the same lines, using a large array as a data member may not be safe. When an object containing a large array is created on the stack, we might face the same set of problems as discussed above. Creating large objects on the stack is not a good practice.

When creating large arrays or large objects, consider using the heap. But, using the heap is expensive. Consider alternatives that will minimize the cost of creating objects on the heap (such as reusing large objects without deleting them, lazy evaluation, etc.).

When using arrays as data members, consider using a pointer instead of an array.

```
class X {
        X() { _parray = new int[1024]; }
        //...
    private:
        int * _parray; // pointer to an array of integers
        int _arraySize;
        // int _array[1024]; This is not recommended
};
```

Here, objects of **X** would be small. But when an object of **X** is created, it allocates memory on the heap (not stack). Moreover, the constructor of **X** can determine the size of the array at run time. An array of 1024 may not be required in all objects of **X**. Furthermore, it is possible to increase or decrease the size of the dynamic array (by allocating a bigger/smaller array and copying elements). In other words, dynamic arrays are more flexible.

USING ARRAYS OF OBJECTS AND ARRAYS OF POINTERS TO OBJECTS

Traditionally, when we need an array, we just declare an array and use it. But when dealing with objects in C++, we usually avoid creating object arrays. There are some drawbacks to using an array of objects. Here is a simple example. Class **TRangeInt** comes from Part I.

```
class TRangeInt {
    public:
        enum ELimits { eLow=0, eHigh = 255 };
        // Create an TRangeInt object with these limits and value
        TRangeInt (int vlow, int vhigh, int val);
        // Create a TRangeInt object with default limits and this
        // value - val
        TRangeInt (int val=0);
        // What is the value contained?
        int GetValue() const;
        // Methods to get limits
        int Low() const { return _low; }
        int High() const { return _high;}
        // and many more methods not shown
    private:
        int _value; // actual integer value
        int _low, _high; // range limits
};
    TRangeInt intArray[10];
```

With this declaration, we are creating an array of ten **TRangeInt** objects. We already know that to create an object we must call a constructor. Here, the default constructor of **TRangeInt** is called ten times, once per element of the array. Similarly, when the **intArray** goes out of scope, the destructor of **TRangeInt** is invoked, again ten times. We are not allowed to call any other constructor of **TRangeInt** in this declaration. But if we wish to initialize the first two elements of the array with a different constructor, we can use the following style.

```
TRangeInt intArray[10] = { 101,              // calls TRangeInt(int)
                    TRangeInt(5, 50, 25) // Calls TRangeInt(int, int, int)
                    };
```

Constructor calls for the first two elements of **intArray** are taken care of. For the remaining eight elements (2 to 9), the default constructor is called. This style of explicitly initializing arrays with specific constructor calls is only feasible with small arrays. Imagine explicitly initializing an array of 100 **TRangeInt** objects!

Even though we have created an array of ten **TRangeInt** objects, it is quite possible that not all the ten objects are going to be used in the program. If all the objects in the array are not used, then we would have unnecessarily wasted CPU time (and memory) creating those unused objects. Moreover, we don't have much flexibility in using specific constructors when creating the elements of the array.

A better solution might be to use an array of pointers to objects. With an array of pointers to objects, the user has complete freedom in creating objects with specific constructors. Furthermore, not all the elements of the array are required to contain objects. We can create objects as and when needed and place them in the array. Here is the declaration and associated usage.

```
// pIntArray is an array of 10 pointers to TRangeInt objects
    TRangeInt *pIntArray[10];
```

Usually, we would like to initialize all the pointers to 0 before using any element of the array. This way we can check if a particular slot in the array contains a valid address or not.

```
for (int i =0; i < 10; i++)
        pIntArray[i] = 0; // initialize each address to 0
```

Each element of this array can hold the address of a **TRangeInt** object. We can put addresses of dynamic as well as static objects into this array. Here is an example:

```
TRangeInt ri(100); // a TRangeInt object on the stack
pIntArray[0] = new TRangeInt(10, 100, 55); // Store a dynamic object at
                                           // index 0
pIntArray[1] = &ri;
```

The lifetime of the objects whose addresses are stored in the array are controlled by the programmer or the compiler, not by the array. We also have the flexibility of replacing the address in a particular index of the array with a new address.

An array of pointers is more flexible but one must be cautious when using it. For example, when a member function must be invoked on an element in the array, we must first ensure that the element is not 0.

```
int value;
if (pIntArray[3] != 0)
     value = pIntArray[3]->GetValue(); // Invoke a member function
```

This is an extra step needed while accessing elements. But if it is guaranteed that every element always points to a valid object, then such checks are not necessary.

The array of pointers itself can be created dynamically. What we need is a pointer to an array of pointers. In other words, we want a pointer to a pointer. Here is the declaration:

```
TRangeInt   **ppArray; // pointer to a pointer of TRangeInt
int         size = 100;

ppArray = new TRangeInt*[size]; // create an array of pointers to TRangeInt
ppArray[0] = new TRangeInt(10, 100, 25); // Store a new TRangeInt object in
                                          // slot 0
```

This provides more flexibility.

In summary, using an array of pointers instead of an array of objects is more flexible. But it also requires more caution because the slots in the array of pointers may not point to objects.

PREFER OBJECTS INSTEAD OF PRIMITIVE TYPE POINTERS FOR DATA MEMBERS AND RETURN VALUES OF MEMBER FUNCTIONS

Consider a simple class TEmployee, which is an abstraction for any employee.

```
class TEmployee {
    public:
        enum EDepartment { eFinance, eHR, eEngineering /* and more */ };
        TEmployee(const char name[], const char address[],
            EDepartment dept);
        virtual ~TEmployee();
        const char* GetName() const;
        void SetName(const char* newname);
        const char* GetAddress() const;
        void SetAddress(const char* newAddress);
        // and many more that are not relevant in this example
    private:
        char* _name;
        char* _address;
        EDepartment _dept;
};
```

Here is a typical implementation of some member functions.

```
char* Strdup(const char* src) // This is helper function
{
    char* ptr = new char[strlen(src)+1];
    strcpy(ptr, src);
    return ptr;
}
```

```
TEmployee::TEmployee(const char name[], const char address[],
                EDepartment dept)
   : _dept(dept)
{
    _name = name ? Strdup(name) : 0;
    _address = address ? Strdup(address) : 0;
    // more implementation code
}

void
TEmployee::SetName(const char newname[])
{
    unsigned oldLength = _name ? strlen(_name) : 0;
    unsigned newLength = newName ? strlen(newName) : 0;

    if (oldLength < newLength) { // Not enough space in _name
       delete [] _name;  // Garbage Collection
       // Use Strdup function defined above
       _name = (newName ? Strdup(newName) : 0);
    }
    else {
       if (newName) strcpy(_name, newName);
       else {
          delete [] _name;
          _name = 0;
       }
    }
}

void f()
{
    TEmployee mickey("Mickey Mouse", "Disney World", TEmployee::eHR);
    //..
    cout << mickey.GetName() << endl;
}
```

In class **TEmployee**, the constructor must allocate memory for the name and address of the employee (data members **_name** and **_address**). The destructor must remember to deallocate the memory. Also, any member function that needs to modify the name (such as **SetName**) must remember to deallocate the memory in **_name** and allocate a new piece of memory, if necessary. This is unnecessary burden for the implementor of **TEmployee**.

Clients of **TEmployee** receive a **const char*** when they use the member function **GetName** and **GetAddress**. It doesn't prevent them from casting the pointer to a normal **char*** and modifying them directly.[4] This would modify the private data members of an **TEmployee** object. It would be nice if we could prevent such problems.

In such situations, it is better to use an abstraction instead of **char*** to hold the characters. Managing memory using **char*** is always prone to errors. We might as well leave that to a different class. We implemented a class **TString**, which does exactly this. The

---

[4]However, doing so is not really correct or safe, but it is possible.

standard C++ library also has a set of classes that support strings. The most commonly used class is class **string**.[5] When objects are used as data members, we don't have to worry about destructor calls. Similarly, when objects are returned from functions, there is no problem of exposing the private data members of the class. So instead of using **char*** data members, let's use our **TString** class from Part I. You could also use the **string** class from the C++ library.

```cpp
// Modified version
#include "String.h"
class TEmployee {
    public:
        enum EDepartment { eFinance, eHR, eEngineering /* and more */ };
        TEmployee(const char* name, const char* address, EDepartment dept);
        virtual ~TEmployee();
        TString GetName() const;
        void SetName(const char* newname);
        TString GetAddress() const;
        void SetAddress(const char* newAddress);
        // and many more that are not relevant in this example
    private:
        TString _name;
        TString _address;
        EDepartment _dept;
};
```

Here is a typical implementation of some member functions.

```cpp
TEmployee::TEmployee(const char* name, const char* address,
                  EDepartment dept)
  : _name(name), _address(address), _dept(dept)
// Initialize the data members
      {}

void
TEmployee::SetName(const char* newname)
{  _name = newname; /* TString assignment operator can handle this */ }

void f()
{
    TEmployee mickey("Mickey Mouse", "Disney World", TEmployee::eHR);
    //..
    cout << mickey.GetName() << endl;
}
```

With this change, the **TEmployee** class is easier to implement and manage. Objects of class **TString** know how to manage their memory, so we don't have to worry about checking lengths, deleting memory, etc.

In general, when a raw type (such as **char***) is used, the implementor is responsible for managing them correctly. But objects manage themselves, reducing the burden on the implementor and in many situations, also the client.

---

[5]This is a typedef which refers to a template class, basic_string.

There is also some cost associated with this approach. We have to incur the cost of constructor and destructor calls for the TString objects and the size of TEmployee objects will be bigger than our earlier implementation because now it includes two TString objects as opposed to simple character pointers.

Using objects internally also has some other advantages. For example, comparing TString objects is easier than comparing plain character pointers. Class TString would provide operator== (and operator !=) for comparing objects. If class TEmployee wishes to provide a comparison operator, it can be implemented using the comparison operator of class TString.

☞ **Wherever possible, use objects instead of raw pointer types.**

NOTE   The decision to use classes, such as TString should not be taken lightly. Using such a class adds additional dependencies to the interface (and implementation) of class TEmployee, consequences of which much be carefully considered before taking the plunge.

COMPATIBILITY WITH C

Some classes need to work with programs written in C also, but we cannot pass objects directly to C programs. For example, consider an abstraction for manipulating dates, class TDate. This class allows users to manage dates easily.

```
class TDate {
    public:
        enum EMonth { eJan-1, eFeb, eMar, eApr, eMay, eJun, eJul, eAug,
            eSep, eOct, eNov, eDec };

        TDate( short day, EMonth month, short year); // Simple constructor
        TDate(const char date[]); // date passed in as a string
        TDate(); // sets date from the operating system date

        short GetYear() const;
        EMonth GetMonth() const;
        short GetDay() const;

        // Convenience function.
        void AdddToYear(int increment); // Increment can be negative
        void AddToMonth(int increment); // Increment can be negative
        void AddToDay(int increment);   // Increment can be negative

        TString GetDate() const; // Returns a character representation of
                                 // the date
    private:
        // some implementation data
};

// A set of helper functions for TDate class

// Increments the day (same as AddToDate)
TDate& operator++(TDate& oldDate); // Prefix version
```

```
TDate& operator++(TDate& oldDate, int notUsed); // Postfix version

TDate& operator-(TDate& oldDate); // Decrements the day - Prefix version
TDate& operator-(TDate& oldDate, int notUsed); // Postfix version

// Add n days to this date object
TDate& operator+=(TDate& toThis, int n);

// Comparison functions
bool operator==(const TDate& first, const TDate& second);
bool operator !=(const TDate& first, const TDate& second);
// and probably operator<, operator>, etc.

// Returns the difference (in days) between the two TDate objects
size_t operator-(const TDate& first, const TDate& second);

ostream& operator<<(ostream& stream, const TDate& date); // print date
istream& operator>>(istream& i, TDate& date); // read into date
```

The implementation of these helper functions do not require access to the private data members of the class **TDate**. For example, here is **operator++** and **operator==**.

```
TDate& operator++(TDate& oldDate)        // Prefix version
{
    oldDate.AddToDay(1);
    return oldDate;
}

bool operator==(const TDate& first, const TDate& second)
{
    return (first.GetYear == second.GetYear()
            && first.GetMonth() == second.GetMonth()
            && first.GetDay() == second.GetDay() );
}
```

The implementation of this class is not very difficult and it is not important for this discussion. Non-member functions **operator–**, **operator+**, etc. are convenience functions to compute difference between two dates, sum of two dates respectively. But if someone wants to get a C-style array representation of **TDate**, it is not easy to do so. It would be more helpful if class **TDate** could provide a function that supports C-style representation of **TDate**. To accomplish this, it is better to add a member function **GetDateAsCString()** that provides a C-style array representation of **TDate**.

```
class TDate {
    public:
        // Other details as above, not repeated here.
        // Returns a character representation of date. Caller owns the
        // memory pointer by the returned pointer.
        void GetDateAsCString(char outputArray[]) const;
};
```

This makes it easy to use the date representation in C programs also. Member function GetDateAsCString fills in the character string that is passed to the function. Caller of this function must ensure that outputArray points to enough storage.

NOTE   Member functions operator++ and operator– – are provided for convenience. With operator++ (and operator– –) it is easy to write programs that are elegant. For example, here is a typical usage:

```
void foo(TDate& from, const TDate& to)
{
    // It is assumed that from is less than to
    for (; from != to; ++from) { // Uses operator++ of TDate
        // do something
    }
}
```

PAY ATTENTION TO IMPLEMENTATION ALTERNATIVES:
OBJECT SIZE V/S CODE EFFICIENCY

Revisiting the TDate class, let's analyze the various implementation schemes possible. For the purpose of validating different dates, it is quite normal to use Julian day numbers. For any date after September 14, 1752, the Julian day number can be generated. Julian day numbers are sequential. For example, the Julian day number for January 1, 1996 is 2450084 and the Julian day number for January 2, 1996 is 2450085. With the Julian day algorithm, it is easy to compare dates, add and subtract dates, etc. The algorithm for computing Julian day numbers (and converting Julian day numbers back into month, year, and date) was first published in the *Communications of the ACM*, Volume 6, No. 8, (Aug., 1963). The code for this algorithm is shown later. Human beings are accustomed to the Gregorian calendar (the month, date, year scheme). A Julian day number can be converted to the Gregorian format. This algorithm is also shown later.

To implement the TDate class, let's use Julian day numbers. As soon as a TDate object is constructed, we compute the Julian day number for the specified date and store it in the object. We have two implementation choices at this point:

a. We can just store the Julian day number in a TDate object and nothing else. With this scheme, every time we need to find the day, month, or year of the TDate object, we use the Julian day conversion algorithm to parse the Julian day number into its parts (day, month, year). In this scheme, the size of a TDate object is very small (one unsigned long int to hold the Julian day number). But, the disadvantage in this scheme is that every time we need some part of the date, the Julian day number must be parsed into its parts. This is not cheap because we must execute some code to parse a Julian day number into a (day, month, year) format. This can be expensive if such parsing is done very often. Here is part of the header file for TDate using this approach:

```
class TDate {
    public:
        // Other details as before, not shown
    private:
```

```
        unsigned long _julianDayNum;          // Only the julian day number
                                              // is stored
        void JulianToGregorian(unsigned& month, unsigned& day, unsigned&
                               year) const;
};
```

This ordinary function computes the Julian day number given the month, date, and year.

```
unsigned long
ComputeJulianDay(unsigned month, unsigned date, unsigned year)
{
    if( y <= 99 ) y += 1900; // For dates like 7/2/95
    unsigned long c, ya, julian;
    if( ! (::IsDayInMonth(d, m, y)) ) return 0L;
    if (m > 2)       m -= 3;  // remove the the leap day
    else             m += 9; y--;
    c = y / 100;
    ya = y - 100*c;
    julian = ((146097*c)>>2) + ((1461*ya)>>2) + (153*m + 2)/5 + d + 1721119;
    return julian;
}
```

This next member function converts a Julian day number into a Gregorian date.

```
    void JulianToGregorian(unsigned& month, unsigned& day, unsigned& year);
```

To understand the cost of execution, consider the member function **GetYear** of class **TDate**.

```
                    unsigned short
                    TDate::GetYear() const
                    {
                        unsigned m, d, y;

                        JulianToGregorian(m, d, y);
                        return (y);
                    }
```

This function must convert the Julian day number into a Gregorian format and then return the year. This is not cheap. For example, here is the code for the function **JulianToGregorian**.

```
// Convert a Julian day number to its corresponding Gregorian calendar
// date. Algorithm from Communications of the ACM, Volume 6, No. 8, (Aug.
// 1963). Gregorian calendar started on Sep. 14, 1752. This function not
// valid before that date.

void
TDate::JulianToGregorian(unsigned& month, unsigned& day, unsigned& year)
    const
{
```

```
    unsigned long d;
    unsigned long j = _julianDayNum - 1721119;

    year = (unsigned) (((j<<2) - 1) / 146097);
    j = (j<<2) - 1 - 146097*year;
    d = (j>>2);
    j = ((d<<2) + 3) / 1461;
    d = (d<<2) + 3 - 1461*j;
    d = (d + 4)>>2;
    month = (unsigned)(5*d - 3)/153;
    d = 5*d - 3 - 153*month;
    day = (unsigned)((d + 5)/5);
    year = (unsigned)(100*year + j);
    if (month < 10) month += 3;
    else { month -= 9; year++; }
}
```

As can be seen, this is not a very trivial operation.

Member functions have another advantage with this scheme. For example, if the **operator==** is a member function (or a friend of **TDate**), then comparing two **TDate** objects reduces to a trivial comparison of two Julian day numbers. This will be a blazingly fast operation. The **operator!=** derives the same benefit.

b. In the second alternative, we store the date, month, year inside the **TDate** object. When needed, the Julian day number is computed from these values. Now definitely, the size of a **TDate** object is bigger than that in scheme (a). Also, the Julian day number must be computed whenever needed. In (a), we never had to compute the Julian day number more than once. However, the advantage here is that extracting different components of a date is very simple operation because the components (day, month, year) are already stored inside every **TDate** object. Moreover, the data members must be changed only when some part of the date changes. With this implementation, most member functions would be faster because they do not have to compute the Gregorian date (components are already available). Here is a part of the header file with this scheme:

```
    class TDate {
        public:
            // Other details as before, not shown
        private:
            unsigned short _year;
            unsigned short _month;
            unsigned short _date;
    };
```

Now the **GetYear** function is very simple:

```
    unsigned short TDate::GetYear() const {return (this->_year); }
```

Here comparing two **TDate** objects involves comparing the corresponding elements (date, month, year). An implementor might also choose to store the Julian day number inside **TDate** for faster operations.

Given these two schemes, naturally an implementor must pick an appropriate implementation. If TDate object size must be kept as small as possible, then (a) is a better implementation. However, if the speed of execution is more critical, then definitely (b) is better. An implementor might want to provide both implementation to her clients, leaving the choice to the client. But, both classes cannot be called TDate—one of them must be given a different name (say TFastDate).

☞ **Decide on an implementation scheme based on the requirements of the clients who will use the class. If possible, provide more than one implementation, allowing the clients the freedom to pick the right one.**

AVOID TEMPORARY OBJECTS

Every object must be created by a constructor and execution of a constructor, like any other function, takes time. If an object is being used as a constant, it is better to create it once and use it repeatedly. Programmers are sometimes not aware of the fact that they are creating objects repeatedly. Here is an example:

```
void f(const TString& x); // some function accepting a TString reference
```

Here is call to f():

```
void g()
{
    f( TString("Hello There") ); // Can be Expensive
}
```

Every time g() is called, a temporary TString object is created and then destroyed on exit from g(). But notice that the contents of this temporary object is not going to change. It would be better to create this object once and use it repeatedly.

```
TString HelloObject("Hello There"); // ❶

void g() {f( HelloObject );}
```

This is very good. The other advantage here is that we don't have to worry about concurrency issues. In other words, because HelloObject is not contained within any function, we don't have to worry about two threads entering the function and trying to use HelloObject concurrently. But HelloObject will be created even if it is never used.

Another alternative is to create HelloObject as a static object inside a function.

```
void g()
{
    static TString HelloObject("Hello There"); // ❷
    f( HelloObject );
}
```

In this case, one must worry about concurrency problems because two threads can enter g() concurrently.

A similar situation arises in cases where conversions take place. For example, consider a call to f(), which uses the following syntax.

```
void g(){ f( "Hello There" ); /* Expensive */ }
```

Here the compiler must generate a temporary object to convert "Hello There" to a TString object. The constructor of TString that accepts a const char* argument would be used to create the temporary object. And the generated temporary object must be destroyed before exiting g(). Use ❶ or ❷ here also to avoid the creation of a temporary object.

☞ **Avoid creating temporary objects—pay attention to trivial statements.**

USE THE COPY CONSTRUCTOR TO INITIALIZE OBJECTS

In many situations, we would like to create new objects using existing objects. The copy constructor is ideal for such situations. Here is an example.

```
class TComplex {
    public:
        TComplex(double real_part = 0, double imag_part = 0);
        TComplex(const TComplex& copy);
        TComplex& operator=(const TComplex& assign);
        ~TComplex();

        double GetRealPart() const;
        double GetImaginaryPart() const;
        void SetRealPart(double r);
        void SetImaginaryPart(double i);

        // Add a complex number to this complex number
        TComplex& operator+=(const TComplex& other);
        // and other member functions
    private:
        double _real;
        double _imaginary;
};
```

The operator+ function for computing the sum of two TComplex objects is shown below.

```
// Helper function - Computer sum of two TComplex numbers
TComplex operator+(const TComplex& first, const TComplex& second);

// An efficient implementation of operator+
TComplex operator+(const TComplex& second, const TComplex& second)
```

```
{
    // Create a new TComplex object to hold the sum and initialize
    // it with the first operand. Uses copy constructor
    TComplex result = first;      // ❶
    // Append the second operand. Use the += member function
    result += second;
    return result;                // by value
}
```

This is a good implementation. But, it is easy to write the following code.

```
// A not so efficient implementation
TComplex operator+(const TComplex& second, const TComplex& second)
{
    TComplex result ;       // ❷ Create a new TComplex object
    result =  first;        // ❸ Assign the first operand
    result += second;       // Append the second operand
    return result;          // return by value
}
```

In this implementation, we create a new **TComplex** object **result** using the class constructor. Then we assign the first operand (the object **first**) to it. The rest of the code is the same as the original implementation. When **result** object is created, the real part and the imaginary part are set to zero. Immediately following that, we assign **first** to it and overwrite the values stored by the constructor. Wouldn't it be better to put the values from **first** into **result** when it is created? For the purpose of this analysis, the cost of the copy constructor is almost the same as the cost of the default constructor in **TComplex**. So the cost of ❶ and ❷ is almost the same. Both implementations are identical in all respects except for ❸. The cost of assignment is extra in the second implementation and this cost is significant. Therefore, the first implementation is superior to the second. The cost of the extra assignment operation would have been negligible if **TComplex** were an ordinary integer. But for objects with significant state information the cost of assignment is not trivial.

☞ **Assignment operation between objects is expensive. Try to avoid it if possible.**

USING PROXY (OR SURROGATE) OBJECTS EFFECTIVELY

An object that act as a stand-in for another object is a proxy object. Proxy objects are also called surrogate objects because the object being is used is a surrogate for the original object. The real object to be used might exist in a different address space (different process or even a different machine). In such a situation, we must use a proxy object to represent the original object. We can also use proxy objects to defer the cost of creating/copying expensive objects. Proxy objects are useful in many different situations as shown below.

Proxy Objects to Facilitate Safe Sharing of Objects

When expensive resources are copied, making a real copy of the original object might be too expensive, both in terms of memory and CPU time. It would be better if we could share the original (master) object among the different copies. Each copy would act as a proxy for the master object. But if one of the clients tries to modify the master through a proxy object, a new copy of the master object is created. This is the popular scheme of *copy on write*, which has been discussed in Part I. This scheme is used heavily in operating systems to minimize copying of memory pages.

As an example, consider sharing memory among processes. It would be nice to share regions of memory without really making copies of it as long as possible. In this example, class **TMemory** represents real memory. Each **TMemory** object represents a distinct piece of memory not shared among processes. Instead of using **TMemory** objects directly, let's use a class **TMemoryProxy** that acts as a proxy to **TMemory**. Objects of **TMemoryProxy** ensure sharing as long as possible. But when the memory represented by a **TMemoryProxy** object (actually the **TMemory** object) is modified by a client of a **TMemoryProxy** object, a new **TMemory** object is created and the **TMemoryProxy** object is now a proxy for this new **TMemory** object (see Fig. 11-1).

When one of mp1, mp2, mp3, or mp4 tries to modify the memory in mmaster, a new **TMemory** object is created. Fig. 11-2 shows the scenario.

There are two alternatives when implementing this scheme. Class **TMemory** can be an ordinary class or a hidden class. When **TMemory** is an ordinary class, clients can use it just like any other class. But when **TMemory** is not available for general consumption, clients must use **TMemoryProxy** objects to access memory. Note that the use of **TMemory** within **TMemoryProxy** is transparent to the users of **TMemoryProxy**.

When the last **TMemoryProxy** object goes away, the hidden **TMemory** object must be destroyed. Class **TMemoryProxy** can use some reference counting scheme to implement this.

TMemoryProxy objects share TMemory object

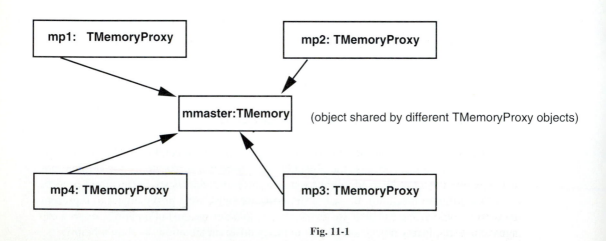

Fig. 11-1

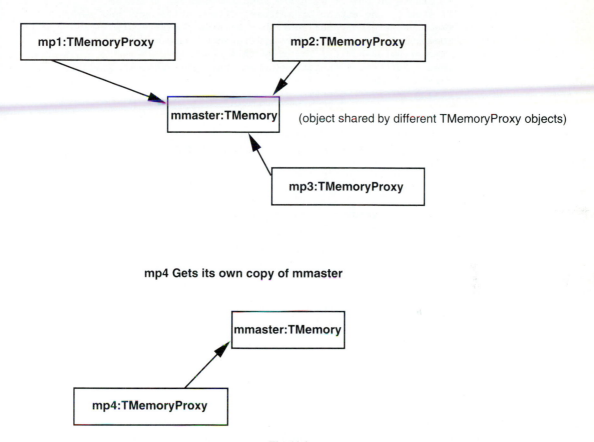

Client of mp4 tries to modify memory in mmaster

mp1:TMemoryProxy

mp2:TMemoryProxy

mmaster:TMemory   (object shared by different TMemoryProxy objects)

mp3:TMemoryProxy

mp4 Gets its own copy of mmaster

mmaster:TMemory

mp4:TMemoryProxy

Fig. 11-2

Class **TMemoryProxy** must implement almost all methods supported by **TMemory**. In most cases, methods in **TMemoryProxy** just turn around and call appropriate (or even identical) **TMemory** methods.

A variation of this scheme requires the client to supply the original **TMemory** object when a **TMemoryProxy** object is created. It is also possible to implement **TMemoryProxy** such that **TMemory** isn't created until it is actually required (*lazy evaluation*).

Proxy Objects for Ease of Use

Here, the proxy object just adds useful features and makes the underlying entity more user friendly. Consider a class **TMemoryReference**, which is a proxy for real memory managed by a user. Class **TMemoryReference** itself does not allocate memory but it manages client supplied memory. Here is a skeleton of that class.

```
class TMemoryReference {
    public:
        // Create an object with the supplied address and size
        // size is the extent of address. Client still owns the memory
        TMemoryReference(void* address = 0, size_t size = 0);
        TMemoryReference(const TMemoryReference& copy);
        ~TMemoryReference() { /* empty */ }
        TMemoryReference& operator=(const TMemoryReference& assign);
        void* GetAddress() const;
        size_t GetSize() const;

        // Convenience functions
        // Populate the memory with the pattern. Takes care of address
        // boundary limits and alignment requirements
        void FillWith(char pattern);
        void FillWith(short pattern);
        void FillWith(long pattern);

        // Sets all words to zero
        void Clear();

        bool operator==(const TMemoryReference& other) const;
        bool operator !=(const TMemoryReference& other) const;

        // Setters
        // Store in a new address - Returns the old address
        void* SetAddress(void* newAddress);
        size_t SetSize(size_t newSize);
    private:
        size_t _size;
        void* _address;
};
```

Class **TMemoryReference** just adds useful operations to a piece of memory. Clients do not have to write the simple yet essential functions time and again. The responsibility of creating and managing the lifetime of the memory is still left to the client. It is also convenient to use this class wherever a memory address and a size must be passed. Instead of passing an address and a size, it is real convenient to pass a **TMemoryReference** object. Filling memory with characters and integers is also a common operation that we wouldn't want to write over and over again. Class **TMemoryReference** takes care of such mundane operations. This class is also very useful where a function must return a memory address and a size. A client would just pass in a **TMemoryReference** object and the function can just store the address and the size. The constructor with default values comes in handy in such situations. Such classes should be fast and should not incur any extra overheads. Hence, most of the functions would be inline and the destructor would not be virtual either.

Proxy Objects that are Stand-ins for Remote Objects

This is common in distributed systems. A local proxy object might be created to represent a resource that exists in a different address space. For example, class **TRemoteThread** represents a thread on a different machine (or process). Operations carried out on **TRemoteThread** objects are translated into operations on the actual thread that exists in another address space. Users of **TRemoteThread** would use objects just like any other object. Class **TRemoteThread** member functions can perform optimizations to minimize the cost of using the remote thread. The interface of **TRemoteThread** might be identical to the interface of class, say **TThread**, which represents a local thread. Taking this one step further, we could create a hierarchy with **TThread** as the base class and **TLocalThread**, **TRemoteThread**, etc. as the derived classes.

A similar example would be a class **TTask**, which represents a task in the operating system. The operating system itself may not provide a real **TTask class. It might be con-venient to implement the proxy TTask** to make the operating system task look like a real object. Member functions of **TTask** would use the operating system API to provide the necessary interface (move like a *wrapper* class).

Smart Proxy Objects that Provide Additional Functionality

A smart pointer (or a smart reference) is a typical example of a proxy. Raw pointers are convenient but programmers must always remember to keep track of their allocation, copying, and deallocation. Otherwise, it is very easy to generate garbage, or even worse, dangling references. A pointer disguised as an object is a better solution to overcome these problems. The object acts as a proxy for the raw pointer. One such class, **TCountedPointer** was discussed in Chapter 9, Part I and is reproduced below.

```
typedef unsigned long ReferenceCount;

template <class AType>
class TCountedPointer
{
    public:
        TCountedPointer(); // Default constructor
        // adoptTarget must point to a resource allocated using new.
        // It will be deleted when the pointer object goes away.
        TCountedPointer(AType* adoptTarget);
        TCountedPointer(const TCountedPointer<AType>& copy);

        // Copy ctor, destructor, assignment not shown
        // Return true if the object is a pointer to a non-zero target
        bool IsValid() const;

        bool operator==(const TCountedPointer<AType>& other) const;
        bool operator!=(const TCountedPointer<AType>& other) const;

        AType& operator*() const;
        AType* operator->() const;
        // This is used for testing purposes only
        int GetReferenceCount() const;

    protected:
        void AddReference();
        void RemoveReference();

    private:
        ReferenceCount* _refCount;
        AType* _targetPointer;
};
```

This is a very simple class that provides reference counted pointers. It makes use of the overloaded **operator->** for convenience. Objects of **TCountedPointer** act as proxies for the real pointer. See Chapter 9 for details of implementation.

Another example is the C++ standard library class **auto_ptr**, which takes care of deleting a pointer when it is no longer needed. A similar class, **TAutoPtr** was shown in Part I.

Using an overloaded **operator->**, it is possible to implement powerful proxy classes. Another such example is the class **TRemoteFilePtr** that was discussed in Chapter 8. This class was a proxy for objects of the class **TRemoteFile**. Class **TRemoteFilePtr** used **operator->** to create **TRemoteFile** objects, only on demand. Proxy classes can be used implement such additional functionality.

Proxies for Solving Syntactic/Semantic Problems

When implementing certain classes that contain overloaded operator [], it is easy to get into tricky situations. Operator [] can be used both on the left hand side as well as on the right hand side of assignment, and even in the same statement. A classic example of this situation arises with the class **TFileArray**, which treats a file as an array of characters.[6] This class should overload the operator[] because subscripting is one of the basic operations on an array. But how can one return a reference to a character that resides in a file on the disk? References are only valid for things in memory. Here is an example:

```
void foo()
{
    TFileArray myFile("MyFile.txt"); // opens the file read/write
    char c = 'M';
    myFile[2] = c; // Should work correctly
    c = myFile[3]; // This must work too!
    myFile[10] = myFile[12]; // ❶ copy a character from one location to
                             // another
}
```

This can be easily solved with a simple class implementation shown below.

```
class TFileArray {
    public:
        TFileArray(const char* fileName);
        TFileArray& operator[](unsigned index);
        TFileArray& operator=(char c);
        operator char();
    private:
        fstream _fs; // the file
        streampos _location; // offset in the file
};
```

---

[6]Why one should bother implementing a **TFileArray** class is a different issue.

When the statement

```
myFile[2] = c;
```

is executed, a couple of things happen. The subscript operator is invoked first, which returns a reference to a **TFileArray** object. We end up with an assignment operation involving a character on the RHS and a **TFileArray** object on the LHS. This is handled by the member function

```
TFileArray& operator=(char c);
```

Similarly, in the operation

```
c = myFile[3];
```

myFile[3] returns a **TFileArray&**. We end up with an assignment operation between a **TFileArray** object on the RHS and a character on the LHS. This is directly not possible. It will only work if **TFileArray** object can be converted to a char. This is made possible by the conversion operator

```
operator char();
```

of the class **TFileArray**. So, everything works correctly. Every object of **TFileArray** has a private data member _location that contains the location in the file being accessed by the operator [].

How can we make

```
myFile[10] = myFile[12]; // copy a character from one location to another
```

work correctly? Here the subscript operator is being used both on the RHS and LHS in the same expression. When the **operator[]** is invoked on the LHS, it stores the value 10 in the data member _location. This is the position for writing into the file. Next the **operator[]** is invoked with the value 11 on the RHS. This stores the value 12 in _location overwriting the existing value 10 because the operation is being carried out on the same object myFile, which has only one data member _location. Therefore, the copy operation fails. The problem here is that the location in the file is getting overwritten. In other words, the state of the object is getting clobbered. Once state integrity is lost, the behavior (which depends on state) is incorrect. We must prevent state corruption to make the class work correctly. This can be achieved by using a proxy object to represent the location used by the operator[] in every operation.

We need a proxy to represent a character at a particular offset inside a file. Here is the declaration of a new class **TFileIndex**, which represents the position within a file. Class **TFileIndex** should not be used directly by other clients. This is achieved by making the constructor private.

```
class TFileIndex {
    public:
        TFileIndex& operator= (char c); // used when writing a character
                                        // into the file
        TFileIndex& operator=(const TFileIndex& src);
    private:
        friend class TFileArray;
        TFileArray* _fp;
        streampos _location;
        TFileIndex(TFileArray* fa, streampos  x);
        operator char(); // used when reading a character from the file
        // compiler generated destructor is good enough
};
```

Our old class **TFileArray** uses the **TFileIndex** class in the subscript operation (See Fig 11-3).

```
class TFileArray {
        friend class TFileIndex;
        TFileArray& operator=(const TFileArray&);
        fstream _fs;
    public:
        TFileArray(const char* filename);
        TFileIndex operator[](streampos where);
};
```

Every **operator[]** returns a **TFileIndex** object by value, which has a data member **_location** that holds the location in the file. When the operation

```
myFile[10] = myFile[12]; // copy a character from one location to another
```

is attempted, the subscript operation on the LHS returns a temporary **TFileIndex** object t1 (with the value 10 in **_location**). Similarly, the operator[] on the RHS returns another temporary **TFileIndex** object t2 with the value 12 in **_location**. So the assignment operation between **TFileArray** objects is transformed into an assignment between two TFileIn-

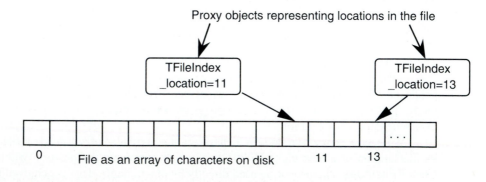

Fig. 11-3

dex objects, t1 and t2. The TFileIndex object on the RHS represents the read side and the TFileIndex object on the RHS represents the write side.

An object of TFileIndex is a proxy for a character at some offset within a file. Implementation of the classes is trivial.[7]

A General Subscript Proxy Technique

Based on the preceding discussion, we can generalize a proxy scheme for differentiating l-values from r-values in our implementations of operator[]. This was the problem that we encountered in the TFileArray class. For any object of a class that supports operator[], the statement

$$x[4] = x[5];$$

causes a read operation for x[5] and a write operation for x[4]. In other words, x[5] is a get() operation and x[4] is a set() operation. These two operations definitely require very different implementations in many classes. But, with a simple operator[], we will not be in a position to distinguish between a read and write because it is the same operator[] function that gets called. To overcome this problem, we can use general proxy objects.

Let's create a new class TSubscriptProxy, which is a proxy for the object returned from operator[]. Since this class must be usable by any class, it must be a template.

```cpp
template <class AType> class TSubscriptProxy {
    public:
        TSubscriptProxy(AType& target) : _master(target) {}
        TSubscriptProxy(const TSubscriptProxy<AType>& copy) :
            _master(copy._master) {}
        TSubscriptProxy<AType>& operator=(const TSubscriptProxy<AType> rhs)
        {
            // Do whatever is necessary to get the values from rhs and then
            // set the values in *this. Assume that the class AType provides
            // two member functions GetValue and SetValue
            if (this != &rhs)
                    this->_master.SetValue( rhs._master.GetValue() );
            return *this;
        }
        // Helper for ease of use
        operator AType&() { return _master; }
    private:
        AType& _master; // the true object for which this object is a proxy
};
```

Just as an example, consider a class TArray, which implements an array.

```cpp
template <class AType> class TArray {
    public:
        TArray (int size) : _size(size) { _ip = new AType[_size]; }
```

<hr>

[7]Complete details of this example can be found in *C++ Programming Style* by Tom Cargill, a very good book worth reading for anyone attemtping serious C++ programming and design.

```
        TSubscriptProxy<AType> operator[](int index)
        { return TSubscriptProxy<AType>(_ip[index]); }
    private:
        AType* _ip; // pointer to elements
        unsigned long _size;
};
```

Class **TFoo** is just a test class. We could have also used our **TFileArray** here. The member function **GetValue** would be the equivalent of a read operation and **SetValue** is the write operation.

```
class TFoo {
    public:
        TFoo(int i = 0) : _data(c) {}
        int GetValue() const {cout << "GetValue " << endl; return _data; }
        void SetValue(int newValue) { cout << "SetValue " << endl;
                                      _data= newValue; }
    private:
        int _data;
};
```

And here is the test program (see also Fig. 11-4).

```
        main()
        {
            TArray<TFoo> array(10); // An array of TFoo objects
            array[4] = array[5];
        }
```

From this example, it is clear that **TSubscriptProxy** can be used with all classes that support **GetValue** and **SetValue** operations. Also note that subscript operator in **TArray** now returns a **TSubscriptProxy** object and not a reference to **AType**. Of course this doesn't come for free. Every subscript operation causes the creation of a temporary **TSubscriptProxy** object.

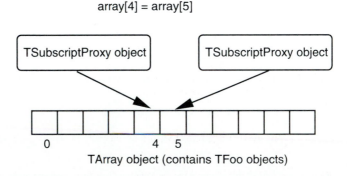

array[4] = array[5]

TArray object (contains TFoo objects)

Fig. 11-4

USE SIMPLE ABSTRACTIONS TO BUILD MORE COMPLEX ABSTRACTIONS

Abstractions need not be complex and hard to implement. A majority of the abstractions that are heavily used are very simple, easy to understand, and easy to extend. For example, given a TDate (discussed above) and a TTime class (shown below), it is easy to implement a TDateAndTime abstraction.

```cpp
class TTime {
    public:
        TTime(size_t hour, size_t minutes, size_t seconds);
        TTime(); // use system time for the values
        TTime(const TTime& copy);
        TTime& operator=(const TTime& assign);

        size_t GetHour() const;
        size_t GetMinutes() const;
        size_t GetSeconds() const;

        void SetHour(size_t hour);
        void SetMinutes(size_t minutes);
        void SetSeconds(size_t seconds);

        //Set the time in the object to the current system time
        void SetToSystemTime();
    private:
        size_t _hour;
        size_t _minutes;
        size_t _seconds;

};

// Helper functions
// Return difference between two TTime values
TTime operator-(const TTime& first, const TTime& second);
// Return the sum of two TTime values
TTime operator+(const TTime& first, const TTime& second);

TTime operator==(const TTime& first, const TTime& second);
TTime operator !=(const TTime& first, const TTime& second);
// and many others

class TDateAndTime {
    public:
        TDateAndTime(TDate date, TTime time);
        TDateAndTime(); // set time and date from system clock
        // provide useful methods...
};
```

It is also easy to build a TStopWatch clock from TTime.

```cpp
class TStopWatch {
    public:
        TStopWatch (bool startCounting=false);
```

```
        // Start the stop watch
        void Start();
        // Stop it and return the time elapsed
        TTime Stop();
        TTime GetElapsedTime() const;
    private:
        TTime _startTime;
        TTime _stopTime;
        bool _isActive;
};
```

Here are the methods TTime ::Stop and TTime ::Start.

```
void    TTime::Start()
{
    _isActive = true;
    _startTime.SetToSystemTime();
}


TTime TTime::Stop()
{
    if (_isActive ) {
        _stopTime.SetToSystemTime();
        return (_stopTime - _startTime);
    }
    else {
        // thrown an exception indicating that stop watch was not activated
    }
}
```

And here is the constructor.

```
TStopWatch::TStopWatch(bool startCounting /* false */)
{
    if (startCounting == true) {
        _isActive = true;
        _startTime.SetToSystemTime();
    }
    else_isActive = false;
}
```

ABSTRACTIONS MUST ALLOW CLIENTS TO USE A CLASS
IN MANY DIFFERENT WAYS

Let's look at a simple modification to the class TTime that looks very trivial but causes major problems.

```
// A modified interface. Makes it very difficult to use.
class TTime {
    public:
            TTime(size_t hour, size_t minutes, size_t seconds);
            TTime(); // use system time
```

```
        TTime(const TTime& copy);
        TTime& operator=(const TTime & assign);
    // other details as before, not shown here again
};
```

The **SetToSystemTime** member function has been eliminated. When the default constructor is used, the internal time is set to the system clock so it doesn't seem like any functionality has been lost by eliminating the **SetToSystemTime** function.

But with this change, implementing **TStopWatch** becomes very difficult and expensive. Class **TStopWatch** uses two **TTime** objects internally in the implementation. In the earlier implementation, when the **Start** method is invoked, the stop watch starts running by setting the internal **TTime** object to the system time. But now we cannot do that because **SetToSystemTime** is missing. Creating **TStopWatch** objects causes it to start running immediately. The **TStopWatch** constructor automatically invokes the default constructor of **TTime** objects and causes them to be set to the system clock. But how do we get the time elapsed when the **Stop** method is invoked? Here is an implementation:

```
class TStopWatch {
    public:
        TStopWatch(bool startCounting=false);
        // Start the stop watch
        void Start();
        // Stop it and return the time elapsed
        TTime Stop();
        TTime GetElapsedTime() const;
    private:
        TTime _startTime;
};

void
TTime::Start()
{
    _isActive = true;
    TTime timeNow; // a local object to get the current time
    _startTime = timeNow; // assign it to _startTime to store the starting
                          // time
}

TTime
TTime::Stop()
{
    if (_isActive) {
        TTime stopTime; // create a local TTime object getting the
                        // current time
        return (stopTime - _startTime);
    }
    else {/* throw an exception */}
}
```

Now every time a **TStopWatch** is started and stopped we create and destroy two temporary **TTime** objects—one in the **Start** member function and another in the **Stop** member function. We also pay the cost of assignment between two **TTime** objects in the **Start**

member function. We have to resort to all these tricks to overcome the lack of the
SetToSystemTime member function in TTime. The assumption in TTime was that the
constructor would set the internal time to the system time and everything would be fine
after that. But as this example shows, the lack of **SetToSystemTime** is really inconvenient. Every time we need a TTime object containing the system clock value, we must
create a new TTime object using the default constructor. There is no way to reset a
TTime object to the system clock value. Note that we would have had the same set of
problems if **SetToSystemTime** was a private member function. We got into this problem because of a lack of understanding of how clients might use a class.

These (TDate, TTime, etc.) are all simple abstractions but very useful in many different domains. The power of data abstraction and object-oriented programming lies in
creating simple classes and extending them in many ways to create more powerful and
useful abstractions. Such classes are the building blocks of software development. More
powerful software is built using many such simple abstractions. Making these building
blocks faster and more efficient benefits everyone. Usually, many such classes are provided by compiler and library vendors.

☞ **Concentrate on simple abstractions and make them very efficient and
small. This benefits the entire system.**

SUMMARY

Always focus on the purpose of the abstraction. Don't try to provide too much in one
class.

Try to build simple, elegant abstractions that can be used in building more powerful abstractions.

Pay attention to the cost associated with each and every data member used in a class.
Clearly understand the time/space consequences of using a pointer/object as a data
member.

Be wary of using (object) arrays as data members.

Try to eliminate temporary objects.

Design classes that can be used in many different scenarios without undue effort from the
client.

Try not to create a sub-object until it is absolutely required (usually in default constructors).

12

Using Inheritance Effectively

As you already know, inheritance is one of the powerful paradigms in object-oriented programming. But inheritance is just an elegant tool. You need to use this tool effectively and judiciously to achieve good results. This chapter focuses on powerful inheritance techniques that have been very widely used in the industry.

USING INHERITANCE TO IMPLEMENT ELEGANT MENUS AND COMMANDS

Whenever we develop an application, we provide a set of commands to interact with the application. For example, an internet browser would provide commands to move backwards and forwards among web pages, to open a new web page, to print the current page, etc. Usually, such commands are all available in a (pull-down) menu. A user selects a menu item (which is a command) from the menu and the application executes it. But the menu itself should be a general abstraction that can be used in different applications. It should be possible to use the menu to control different sets of commands. Moreover, it would be even better if commands in the menu can be activated and deactivated selectively (context sensitive menu).

Each command is unique and is very specific to the application. And every command does something useful in the application. But a general menu cannot implement any of the commands because it doesn't know anything about the application that uses the commands. The menu class should be able to control the selection and execution of commands without really knowing anything about the commands. In other words, the menu abstraction should interact with the commands in some well defined manner.

Every command is very tightly coupled with the application. There would be quite a bit of state management in different commands. We should allow every command to behave independently and still provide a common interface to control them through menus. This is where an inheritance hierarchy becomes very handy (see Fig. 12-1).

When a menu item (which is a command) is selected from a menu, the user is directing the application to execute that command. Therefore, executing the command is one of the fundamental operations on a command abstraction. We start with a base class **TCommand** that captures the essential interface of any command. Here is the skeleton of the class **TCommand**:

```
class TCommand {
    public:
        TCommand();
        virtual ~TCommand();
        TCommand(const TCommand& copy);
        virtual void Execute() = 0;
    private:
        TCommand& operator=(const TCommand& assign);
};
```

This is an abstract base class. The crucial member function is **Execute()**, which causes the execution of the command. The base class cannot decide what needs to be done as part of the command execution and hence it is left to derived classes, which implement specific commands. Here is a skeleton of the **TOpenCommand** class.

```
class TOpenCommand : public TCommand {
    public:
        TOpenCommand();
```

A Simple Menu with Menu Items

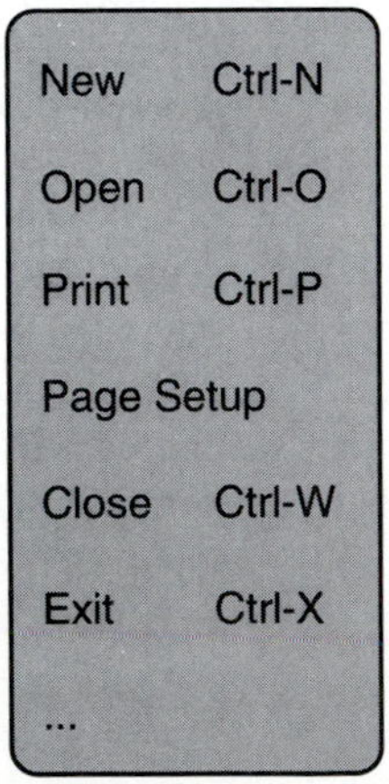

New	Ctrl-N
Open	Ctrl-O
Print	Ctrl-P
Page Setup	
Close	Ctrl-W
Exit	Ctrl-X
...	

Fig. 12-1

```
        ~TOpenCommand();
        TOpenCommand(const TOpenCommand& copy);
        virtual void Execute();
    private:
        TOpenCommand& operator=(const TOpenCommand& assign);
        //...
};
```

All other classes are implemented in a similar fashion. The **Execute()** member function implements the command by storing the necessary state information related to the application. Without knowing anything about a particular command, we can polymorphically execute it.

```
void foo(TCommand& cmd) // Polymorphically accepts any TCommand object
{
    cmd.Execute(); // virtual function call
}

TOpenCommand openCmd;
foo(openCmd);
```

Each item in the menu is a command that can be executed. A menu is a list of menu items. So we create two other classes, **TMenu** and **TMenuItem** (see Fig. 12-2).

```
class TMenuItem; // forward declaration
class TMenu {
    public:
        TMenu(size_t maxItems);

        // Add a new menu item to the menu
        virtual void AddMenuItem(MenuItem* newItem);
```

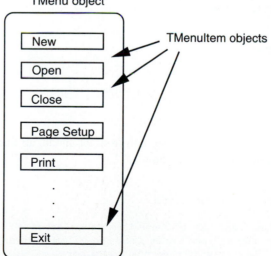

TMenu object

New

Open

Close

Page Setup

Print

.
.
.

Exit

TMenuItem objects

Fig. 12-2

```
            // Remove an existing menu item from the menu
            virtual void RemoveMenuItem(MenuItem* thisOne);
            // Disable the specified item in the menu (greyed out items)
            virtual bool DisableMenuItem(MenuItem* thisOne);
            // Enables the menu item which was previously disabled
            virtual bool EnableMenuItem(MenuItem* thisOne);

            virtual void Display() const;
            virtual void ExecuteSelection();
            // Returns the number of menu items in the menu
            size_t HowManyItems() const;
     private:
            size_t _count; // of menu items in the menu
            size_t _size; // max. menu items this menu can accommodate
            TList<TMenuItem> _items; //  list of items in the menu
};

class TMenuItem {
     public:
            // Create a menu item containing this command
            TMenuItem(TCommand* cmd);
            virtual void DoSelection() { _command->Execute(); }
            //...
     private:
            TCommand* _command;
};
```

When a **TMenu** object is created, it allocates space for the specified number of **TMenuItem** objects. New **TMenuItem** objects are added as needed to the menu.

```
            TMenu myMenu(10); // allow up to ten menu items in this menu
            // Create a menu item for TOpenCommand
            TMenuItem   *open = new TMenuItem(new TOpenCommand());
            myMenu.AddMenuItem(open);  // Add the menu item to the Menu

            TMenuItem   *close = new TMenuItem(new TCloseCommand());
            myMenu.AddMenuItem(close);

            //...
            TMenuItem    *exit = new TMenuItem(new TExitCommand());
            myMenu.AddMenuItem(exit);
```

When a user selects the ith menu item from the menu, all that the menu does is to invoke **DoSelection()** on the menu item.

```
void TMenu::ExecuteSelection()
{
    // Assume that the i^{th} menu item is selected
    //  Get the i^{th} menu item from the _item list and invoke DoSelection on
    // it. This trivial code not shown here
    // ...
}
```

A **TMenu** object is only aware of **TMenuItem** objects, which in turn contain **TCommand** objects. **TMenuItem** objects know nothing about specific **TCommand** derived classes. Class **TMenuItem** deals with all **TCommand** derived classes polymorphically. Clients of **TMenu** are free to add a **TMenuItem** containing a **TCommand** object of their choice. This allows clients to build menus dynamically. Furthermore, clients can selectively enable and disable menu items. This makes it possible to disallow certain selections from the menu, which are usually displayed as grayed out items.

Class **TMenu** only depends on **TMenuItem**, which in turn is only dependent on **TCommand**. Clients can create any number of **TCommand** subclasses without affecting the operation of the menu. New items can be added (or removed) from menus dynamically. The navigation, screen management, and selection of the menu items is managed by **TMenu** class (see Fig. 12-3).

There are a number of advantages gained by creating the **TCommand** hierarchy.

1. New commands can be added without affecting the menu operations. Class **TMenu** (and **TMenuItem**) needs to know nothing about **TCommand** objects.

2. A uniform interface is provided to the **TMenu** class by the **TCommand** hierarchy. This allows application developers to add new capabilities to their application without worrying about modifying the menus provided by their applications.

3. More complex commands can be built using simple commands. For example, we can build a macro command, which is a sequence of simple commands, by creating a new class—**TMacroCommand**.

```
class TMacroCommand : public TCommand {
    public:
        virtual void Execute();
    private:
        // a list to hold the commands
        TList<TCommand> _commands;
};
```

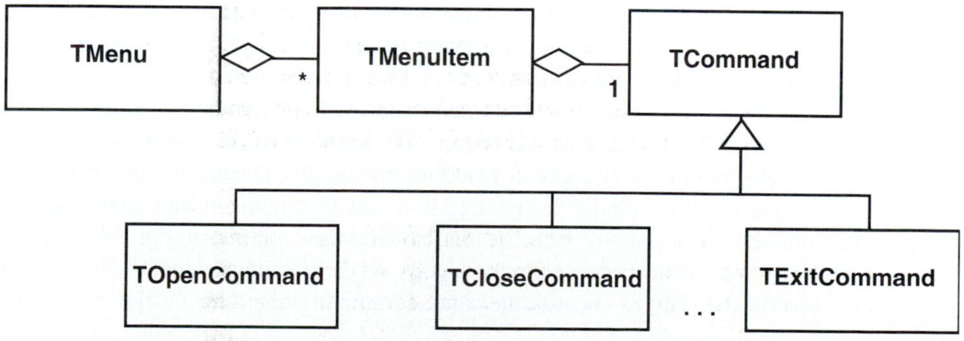

Fig. 12-3

```
TMacroCommand ::Execute()
{
    // Walk the list of commands and invoke Execute on every one of them.
    // Ordering is important.
}
```

The **TMacroCommand** class should provide member functions to manage its constituent commands.[1]

4. Another important feature of commands is the ability to *undo* them. The command system described above should enable us to implement undoable commands easily. When a command is executed as part of an application, some state of the application might get modified. There are commands that cannot be undone. For example, undoing a **Print** command doesn't make any sense. Let's focus only on commands that are undoable. When a command is executed, the corresponding **TCommand** object carries out the necessary operations within the application to satisfy the request. To support the undo operation, we must save the state of the application before the command executes. This can be achieved if the commands support an **Undo** operation. When **Undo** is invoked, the command object (magically) restores the state of the application to what it was before the command executed.

```
class TCommand {
    public:
        virtual void Undo() = 0;
        //...
};
```

Note that the support for undoing (and also redoing) a command must come from the command objects themselves because only they know how to restore the state back to what it was before it executed. The menu can only provide the necessary hooks to make the undo mechanism work but it cannot itself implement the undo operation.

Supporting a single level of undo operation is easy. The application must remember the most recently executed command object every time a command is executed. When the user wishes to undo the previous operation, the **Undo** member function is invoked on the remembered command object. This would restore the application state to what it was before the command executed. For this to function correctly, all undoable commands, before executing, must store enough state information that can be later used in the **Undo** member function. Only implementors of command objects are capable of doing this.

Implementing multi-level Undo is a bit more complicated. Here, a history list of all commands executed by the user is maintained. After an undoable command is executed, it (or a copy of it) is placed on the history list. In other words, the history list contains the sequence of commands executed. Undoing just involves traversing this list backwards, invoking the **Undo** method at every step. It is easy to support infinite undo capability—limited only by the amount of memory available on the system (see Fig. 12-4).

It might be necessary to make a copy of the command object before it is placed on the history list. This is because the same command object that carries out the original re-

[1] An excellent discussion of this pattern can be found in *Design Patterns*, Gamma, et al.

Sequence of Commands Executed

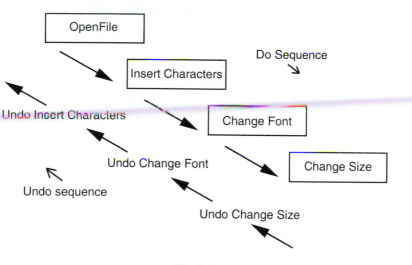

Fig. 12-4

quest, will perform other requests at later times. Remembering that a menu is a collection of command objects (menu items), the same set of command objects are used every time an item in the menu is selected. If there is a possibility of the state of the command object getting changed during execution, a copy of the command object must be saved on the history list to distinguish among the different invocations of the command object. This can be expensive. For example, a ChangeFont command that changes the size of characters in a selection must work with different selections at different invocations. So it must save different sets of information every time it executes in order to support undo capability. Therefore, the ChangeFont command must be copied after an execution and the copy must be placed on the history list. Commands that are not undoable would not be placed on the history list.

Supporting Different Types of Menus

The example above focussed more on the command classes and not on the menu side of things. Most of us would think of a menu as a set of choices displayed on a video screen from which a user can select (using mouse, keyboard, light pen, joystick, etc.) their choice.[2] But this is not the only type of menu. Most of us have also used some other types of menu. For example, a telephone voice mail system does support a menu that is navigated using the push buttons on the telephone. For example, you might have voice mail system that tells you to push 7 to play the current message, 3 to delete the current message, etc. This is another type of menu. Here the selection is done by using the push buttons on the telephone (or even voice commands). Let's call these menus as telephone menus. Yet another type of menu is becoming popular with the advancement of voice recognition technology. There are gadgets that respond to human voice commands. This

[2]Restaruant menus are excluded from this discussion for obvious reasons.

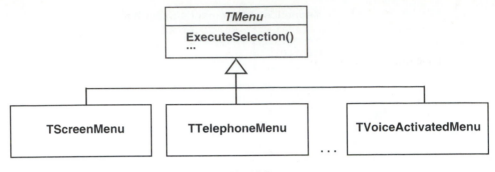

Fig. 12-5

is a boon to the visually handicapped. Even computers that can be operated by voice commands are in use. Here the menu is played through a speaker and user makes a selection by speaking out her choice.[3] This is definitely another type of menu where selections are made using voice commands. Let's call these as voice activated menus. How can we incorporate the menu-command technique to these types of menus. The example above assumed displayable menus. The steps involved in presenting and selecting a choice from a voice mail menu is completely different from the steps involved in doing the same with a computer screen based menu. But the ultimate goal of the menu abstraction is the same—present choices and accept a selection. In other words, the semantics of the operations on the menu are the same but their implementations are entirely different.

Well, inheritance comes to the rescue again. Instead of treating the TMenu abstractions as a normal class, let's make it an abstract base class. Different menu types would be derived classes of TMenu (see Fig. 12-5).

Here, TScreenMenu is the traditional menu displayed on computer screens and selections are made using some input device. Class TTelephoneMenu represents a typical menu in a telephone voice mail system and class TVoiceActivatedMenu is a menu that responds to voice commands. Now the implementors of these derived classes have full freedom to do what they want. Class TMenu just defines an interface for all menu types. An application managing different types of menus would just focus on TMenu and polymorphism takes care of the rest. For example, a computer that supports a voice activated menu as well as traditional screen based menu does not have to worry about the differences among the different menus. The user interface part of the computer operating system will be written to deal with TMenu objects polymorphically.

ENCAPSULATING OBJECT CREATION DETAILS

Revisiting the TMenu hierarchy, let's analyze another situation that might cause problems. Consider a gadget (for example, a VCR) that can be operated by voice commands, a telephone, or by ordinary text menus operated using the remote control.[4] The software in-

---

[3]Video cassette recorders that respond to human voice commands are available.

[4]This is not fiction. Telephone programmable VCRs have been available at least since 1989.

side the VCR must respond to commands entered using any method. Depending on the device used by the user (telephone, remote control, or voice), the software in the VCR must create the appropriate type of menu to interact with the user. So a typical piece of code might look like this:

```
void f()
{
    // Pseudo code
    if (user connected by telephone)          Create TTelephoneMenu;
    if (user operating using remote control)      Create TScreenMenu;
    if (user is using voice commands)         Create TVoiceActivatedMenu;
}
```

There is nothing interesting or unusual here, but it is easy to recognize one problem: whenever the software in the VCR needs to create a menu to interact with the user, it must go through these steps. If a new type of menu is added (for example, VCRs that can be remotely controlled through the internet), then every piece of code that creates a menu must be changed to account for the new type of menu. In other words, any piece of code that needs to create a menu must know about all available types of menu. Further, it must know what type of menu to create. This is definitely tedious and error prone. It will be really helpful if the knowledge of menu creation (of the appropriate type) is encapsulated in some function (or class), say **CreateMenu()**. Then any part of the system needing a menu would ask the function **CreateMenu** to create a new menu object. The return value of this function would be a (polymorphic) pointer to a new **TMenu** object. Only the function **CreateMenu()** needs to know what type of menu to create and the available types of menus.

```
TMenu* // Pseudo Code CreateMenu(); // Function that creates an appropriate
                                  // menu
{
    // Code to create the appropriate type of menu
    if (user connected by telephone)      return new TTelephoneMenu;
    if (user operating remote control)    return new TScreenMenu;
    if (user is using voice)              return new TVoiceActivatedMenu;
}

void f()
{
    TMenu*  myMenu = CreateMenu();
    // Add menu items to the menu and show it
    //...
};
```

When new types of menus are added, only the **CreateMenu()** function needs to be changed. No other part of the system need worry about different types of menu. This is possible because the interface of different types of **TMenu** objects (voice, screen, telephone, etc.) is defined by the abstract base class **TMenu**. To create and manage a menu object, one needs to understand the interface of class **TMenu** only. This scheme really simplifies the rest of the system, restricting the knowledge of different menu types to one function.

This scheme can be employed in situations where specific derived class objects must be created based on some criteria, but clients only interact with the object using the base class interface. The object creation knowledge can be encapsulated in a separate class that knows about all the different classes and also has the information necessary to create the correct type of object. In other words, the class *manufactures* the appropriate type of object. In the menu example, the CreateMenu() function can determine the type of menu required based on some conditions; no other part of the system needs to know about it. This scheme has been employed in many commercial systems successfully. This pattern technique is called a *Factory* [Gamma 94].

THE CONCEPT OF VIRTUAL CONSTRUCTORS

C++ Continuing with the menu-command technique, we will now learn a new technique for making copies of objects. In supporting undo/redo, the application (or the menu class) might have to store a copy of the command object on the history list. That seems like a simple operation, but we are ignoring a crucial issue. In order to make a copy of any command object, we must know the exact type of the command object so that the copy constructor of the class can be invoked. Here is a function that tries to implement the history mechanism.

```
void SaveForUndo(TCommand& lastCommand)
{
    // lastCommand was executed and a copy of this command
    // must be saved on the history list for undo operation.

    // Invoke the copy constructor on the lastCommandobject
    TCommand* copy = new TCommand(lastCommand);  // Will not compile
    // Next put copy on the history list
}
```

But there is a flaw in this approach. In the function SaveForUndo, the argument lastCommand is polymorphic—it can be any one of the derived classes of TCommand. But in the statement

```
    TCommand* copy = new TCommand(lastCommand);
```

we are invoking the copy constructor of TCommand. Therefore, regardless of what lastCommand happens to be, we always treat it as a TCommand object and try to copy it. Instead of copying the true command object, we are copying only the base class. There are two flaws here:

a. Since TCommand is an abstract class, we cannot create TCommand object directly. The the code above wouldn't even compile.

b. Even if TCommand were not an abstract class, it is logically incorrect because we end up copying only the TCommand part of the command object. The derived class will normally have additional state that needs to be copied as well.

What is copied must be the true command object itself, not just the base class part. We know for sure that **lastCommand** is an object of some derived class of **TCommand**, but we don't know which derived class it is. We need the dynamic binding mechanism to bind the copy operation to the correct derived class based on the object type. In the code above, we are invoking the copy constructor but copy constructors cannot be virtual (i.e., cannot be bound dynamically). So we cannot have a virtual constructor even though virtual destructors are allowed. The logic is that when you want to create an object, you must clearly specify which class to use. But here we are trying to duplicate an object from an existing object. But since the copy constructor is also another constructor, it cannot be virtual. The solution is to use a virtual member function to achieve the same effect.

There are two ways of making copies of an object. In some situations we just want to create a new object that is of the same type (class) as the original object. The contents of the original object are not copied into the new object. In the second case, we would like to create an exact duplicate of the original object (using the copy constructor in C++). We can easily support both these operations. Let's use a member function **Copy()** to create an object of the same type as the original, and another member function **CloneObject()** to make an exact duplicate of the original object (also called *cloning* the object). These two functions would be added to **TCommand**.

```
class TCommand {
    public:
        TCommand();
        virtual ~TCommand();
        TCommand(const TCommand& copy);
        // Make a new object of the same type as  "this" and return a
        // pointer to it
        virtual TCommand*  Copy() = 0;
        // Make a new object that is a true  clone of "this" and return a
        // pointer to it
        virtual TCommand*  CloneObject() = 0;
        virtual void Execute() = 0;
    private:
        TCommand& operator=(const TCommand& assign);
        //...
};
```

Derived classes must implement these member functions. The implementation is trivial.

```
class TOpenCommand : public TCommand {
    public:
        TOpenCommand();
        ~TOpenCommand();
        TOpenCommand(const TOpenCommand& copy);
        TOpenCommand& operator=(const TOpenCommand& assign);
        // Make a new object of the same type as  "this" and return a
        // pointer to it
        virtual TOpenCommand*  Copy();
        // Make a new object that is a true  clone of "this" and return a
        // pointer to it
        virtual TOpenCommand*  CloneObject();
```

```
         virtual void Execute();
         // ...
    private:
         //...
};

TOpenCommand* TOpenCommand::Copy()
{
   // Return a new object of this class (TOpenCommand )
   return new TOpenCommand; // ❶ Call the default constructor
}


TOpenCommand* TOpenCommand::CloneObject()
{
   // Return a copy of *this
   return new TOpenCommand(*this); // ❷ Call the copy constructor
}
```

If we enter ❶, then we know that we are in the Copy() member function of class TOpenCommand. So we must be trying to copy an object of class TOpenCommand. We create a new object of TOpenCommand and return it.

Similarly, if we enter ❷, the same logic applies but now we must create an exact duplicate of an object of class TOpenCommand (pointed by the this pointer). We know that a copy constructor makes a new object from an existing object so we use the copy constructor to make a copy and return it.

Every derived class of TCommand implements CloneObject and Copy identically. For example, a class TCloseCommand would look like this:

```
TCloseCommand* TCloseCommand::Copy()
{
    // Return a new object of this class (TCloseCommand )
    return new TOpenCommand; // Call the default constructor
}

TCloseCommand* TCloseCommand::CloneObject() /
{
    // Return a copy of *this
    return new TOpenCommand(*this); // Call the copy constructor
}
```

With these Copy() and CloneObject() member functions in place, it easy to implement SaveForUndo:

```
void SaveForUndo(TCommand& lastCommand)
{
    // lastCommand was executed and a copy of this command must be saved
    // on the history list for undo operation. Invoke the CloneObject
    // operation on the lastCommandobject. Since CloneObject() is
    // dynamically bound, the function called will be correct.
    TCommand* copy = lastCommand.CloneObject();  // Make a duplicate
    // Next put this copy on the history list
}
```

```
main()
{
    TOpenCommand cmdOpen;
    TCloseCommand cmdClose;
    //...
    SaveForUndo(cmdOpen);   // ❸
    SaveForUndo(cmdClose);  // ❹
}
```

In ❸, when SaveForOpen is entered, lastCommand is a an object of TOpen-Command. So when the statement

$$lastCommand.CloneObject();$$

is executed, the CloneObject() method from class TOpenCommand is called because CloneObject() is a virtual function. We know for sure that the CloneObject() in TOpenCommand makes a true clone of the original object so everything works correctly. Same thing happens in ❹ but now the object is of class TCloseCommand and so the CloneObject() member function from TCloseCommand is called.

So we have successfully cloned objects even when we didn't know their class. This is the concept of a *virtual constructor*. We have simulated the effect of a virtual constructor by using virtual member functions.

This technique is not unique to C++. It is useful in other object-oriented languages also.

EIFFEL   In Eiffel, a predefined routine Clone is available for all classes. This routine clones the object on which it is invoked, exactly as we did above.

SMALLTALK   Here, every class receives three standard methods copy, shallowCopy, and deepCopy. These have almost the same functionality as our Clone and Copy functions. As described in Chapter 4 (Part I), copy returns a new object of the same type as the original object (identical to our Copy() method above). The method shallowCopy creates a copy of the original object but instance members are shared between the original object and the new copy. On the other hand, deepCopy makes true clone of the original object—nothing is shared between the original object and the new object.

COMBINING VIRTUAL AND NON-VIRTUAL FUNCTIONS FOR PROTOCOL CONTROL

Virtual functions (i.e., dynamic binding) are very useful in many different situations, but there are some drawbacks associated with virtual functions that professional programmers must be aware of.

When a function is made virtual, the base class loses control over that function. Meaning, when a client uses a derived class object polymorphically (using a base class pointer or reference) and invokes a virtual function, it is the derived class member function that is called and not the base class function. The base class function doesn't know anything about the call to the derived class function. Here is a simple example:

```
class A {
    public:
        virtual void f() { cout << "In A::f()\n"; }
        void h() { cout << "In A::h()\n"; }
};

class B : public A {
    public:
        virtual void f()  { cout << "In B::f()\n"; }
        void h() { cout<< "In B::h()\n"; }
};

void g()
{
    A* pa = new B;
    pa->f(); // Calls B::f() because object is of type B and function is
             // virtual
    pa->h(); // A::h() is called!
}
```

When pointer **pa** is associated with an object of class **B**, everything is quite as usual. Class **A** is the base class for class **B** and, hence, a pointer to **A** can point to an object of the derived class. When the statement

pa->f()

is executed, because of dynamic binding it is the f() in class **A** that is invoked. If class **A** counted on its f() being called first, no matter which derived class object is used, it will never succeed. The dynamic binding mechanism decides which f() gets called.

On other hand, when the statement

pa->h()

is executed, no matter what object is used, it is always **A::h()** that is called. This is because h() is not a virtual function. Here, derived classes cannot do anything to overcome the static binding of **A::h()**.

In summary, when a base class member function is virtual, the base class cannot control the dynamic binding of the function call. The run-time mechanism decides the binding based on the type of the object. When the base class member function is non-virtual, under polymorphic usage, it is always the base class function that is invoked no matter what object is used. Both of these are extremes.

In some design scenarios, the base class needs to carry out certain parts of a protocol before a derived class member function executes. The derived class member function implements most of the operations but the base class enforces the sequence of operations. The base class would like to have its member function called first no matter what derived class object is used (which implies a non-virtual function). But most of the code to implement the specific operation is in the derived class. To execute the derived class specific code we need a virtual function. But the problem is that all this needs to be part of one base class member function. We need the behavior of a non-virtual function to enforce protocol and we need dynamic binding to implement the protocol. In other words, we are looking for a function that is non-virtual when invoked but behaves like a virtual function during its execution. The problem gets a bit more complicated because clients do not know anything about the relation between the base class and the derived class (it is an implementation issue). The solution is to use a pair of functions, one of which is non-virtual and the other is virtual.

To illustrate this concept, let's revisit our **TDictionary** class from Part I. The class interface is shown below.

```
// An abstract dictionary class. No objects of this class can be created.
// Derived classes must override all the pure virtual methods. This class
// provides an interface only— it can only be used as a base class. The
// type of each member function (virtual or non-virtual) is not known yet.
// This decision will be made soon. Read on.

template <class AKey, class AValue> class TDictionary {
    public:
            // Stores the specified key (with the value )into the dictionary
            // if the key doesn't already exist in the dictionary. If the key
            // already exists in the dictionary, it returns false.
            virtual bool AddKeyValuePair (const AKey&  thisKey,
                const AValue& withThisValue) = 0;

            // Returns the value of the (key, value) pair for the specified
            // key. An exception should be thrown if thisKey does not exist
            // in the  dictionary.
            virtual AValue& GetValueAt(const AKey& thisKey) const = 0;
            // Returns the count of the number of <key, value> pairs in the
            // dictionary
            size_t HowMany() const { return _count; }

            // Returns true if thisKey is defined in the dictionary
            bool KeyExists(const AKey& thisKey) const;

            // If thisKey is defined in the dictionary, erase it from
            // the dictionary and return true. Otherwise false is returned.
            bool RemoveKey(const AKey& thisKey);
            // Removes all <key, value> pairs from the dictionary
            void  ClearDictionary();

            // Returns true if both dictionaries have identical <key, value>
            // pairs
            virtual bool operator==(const TDictionary& other) const;
            // Returns ! of operator== — Intentionally not virtual
            bool operator!=(const TDictionary& other) const
                { return ! (*this == other); }

            // Default constructor
            TDictionary();
            virtual ~TDictionary();   // Destructor
            // Copy constructor
            TDictionary(const TDictionary<AKey, AValue>& copy);
            // Assignment operator
            TDictionary<AKey, AValue>&
            operator=(const TDictionary<AKey, AValue>& assign);
```

```
private:
    int_count; // number of elements in the dictionary
};
```

Our class TDictionary is an abstract class. The only clients of this class are derived classes. The comments in the interface are almost self explanatory. The important operations are AddKeyValuePair and GetValueAt. The method AddKeyValuePair adds a new (key, value) pair to the dictionary. Method GetValueAt returns the value of the specified key.

A dictionary can be implemented in many different ways. A simple implementation can use a doubly linked list (such as our TList class). A more efficient implementation can be provided with hash tables where the key is used to hash into a table to look up its value. Class TDictionary does not specify any implementation requirements—it only stipulates an interface. Implementation issues are left to the derived classes (see Fig. 12-6).

Clients can use the TDictionary interface without worrying too much about the different implementation issues of the derived classes. Any dictionary can be used polymorphically by just understanding the interface of the abstract class TDictionary.

The base class TDictionary provides a simple interface. The base class implementor would also like to minimize the burden on the derived classes. In the member function AddKeyValuePair, the following operations must be carried out.

a. Ensure that the specified key doesn't already exist in the dictionary.

b. If (a) is true, then try to add the key-value pair to the dictionary.

c. If (b) succeeds, then increment the count of the number of key-value pairs in the dictionary.

These are simple steps. But there is a problem. The base class TDictionary does not know how to add a key-value pair to the dictionary because the implementation for that depends on the type of the dictionary. The derived classes TListDictionary and THashTableDictionary know how to add a new key-value pair to the dictionary. The base class TDictionary is definitely capable of maintaining the count of the number of elements. But before (c) can be carried out, step (b) must be completed successfully. And

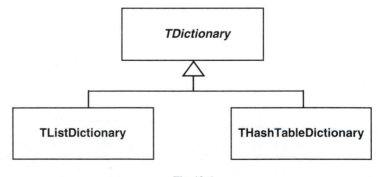

Fig. 12-6

implementation of step (b) is done by the derived classes and TDictionary doesn't know anything about it. So part of TDictionary::AddKeyValuePair's implementation can be done by the base class TDictionary but the rest of the implementation must be done by the derived classes. But TDictionary would like to carry out the operation in this exact sequence (a), (b), followed by (c).

If AddKeyValuePair is made virtual, then every derived class must follow steps (a), (b), and (c) in the exact sequence. This is because, dynamic binding always invokes the derived class function. But maintaining the count of the number of elements is a trivial operation that can be done in the base class. However, AddKeyValuePair and such operations affect the count. This implies that the derived class would need access to the count of the number elements. Requiring every derived class to follow this protocol is risky and expensive. For example, consider what happens if there are additional steps to be carried out when a new key-value pair is added to a dictionary. Let's say we would like the TDictionary to be thread safe. We can do this by using some kind of a thread synchronization object (semaphore, mutex, critical section, etc.) inside a TDictionary object. Now when AddKeyValuePair is invoked on an object of TDictionary, the implementation must first acquire the synchronization object (acquire the lock on the object) and then perform steps (a), (b), (c). If AddKeyValuePair is virtual, every derived class must modify the implementation of almost all member functions to incorporate this change. Whenever there is a modification to existing code, new bugs can be introduced easily. Moreover, all derived classes must be tested individually to ensure that they work as published. This process can be quite expensive. It would be nice if the derived classes didn't know anything about the steps involved in adding an element to the dictionary. It would be beneficial if the derived classes are insulated from the protocol. It would be even better if the derived class implementation does not have to be modified even when the protocol changes. That way the base class implementor has the freedom to change the protocol (or sequence of operations) without worrying about their effect on the derived classes.

If AddKeyValuePair is not virtual, and derived class objects of TDictionary are manipulated polymorphically using a base class pointer or reference, then TDictionary::AddKeyValuePair is called even when derived class objects override AddKeyValuePair. Now TDictionary can enforce the protocol. But there is only one problem: TDictionary does not know how to add a key-value pair to a dictionary because that depends on the implementation details of the dictionary, and the implementation is only known to the derived classes.

To solve this problem, we use a pair of functions. The AddKeyValuePair in TDictionary enforces the correct protocol. But TDictionary depends on the implementation support from the derived class. The member function AddKeyValuePair in TDictionary will be non-virtual. This ensures that the entry point for adding a key-value pair to a dictionary is always in TDictionary. But within TDictionary::AddKeyValuePair() we invoke some virtual functions that are implemented in the derived classes. Here is the new interface of TDictionary.

```
// An abstract dictionary class. No objects of this class can be created.
// Derived classes must override all the pure virtual methods. This class
// provides an interface only— it can only be used as a base class.

template <class AKey, class AValue> class TDictionary {
```

```
      public:
            bool AddKeyValuePair (const AKey&  key, const AValue& val);
            AValue GetValueAt (const AKey& thisKey) const;
            bool KeyExists(const AKey& thisKey) const;

            // Other member functions not shown for brevity of example
            // Default constructor
            TDictionary();
            virtual ~TDictionary();  // Destructor
            // Copy constructor
            TDictionary(const TDictionary<AKey, AValue>& copy);
            // Assignment operator
            TDictionary<AKey, AValue>&
            operator=(const TDictionary<AKey, AValue>& assign);

      protected:
            virtual    bool DoAddKeyValuePair(const AKey&  thisKey,
                const AValue& withThisValue) = 0;
            virtual bool DoKeyExists(const AKey& thisKey) const = 0;
            virtual AValue DoGetValueAt(const AKey& thisKey) const = 0;
      private:
            int _count; // number of elements in the dictionary
};

template <class AKey, class AValue>
bool TDictionary <AKey, AValue>::AddKeyValuePair(const AKey& thisKey,
      const AValue&  thisValue)
{
      // Check if this key is already in the dictionary
      if ( this->KeyExists(thisKey) ) { // ❶
            // This key already exists in the dictionary. Cannot satisfy
            // request
            return false;
      }

      // OK. Key doesn't exist in the dictionary. Invoke derived class
      // function to add it to the dictionary
      bool result = this->DoAddKeyValuePair(thisKey, thisValue); // ❷
      // Now check the outcome
      if (result == true) // Key-Value pair of was successfully added
            _count++; // ❸
      return result;
}

template <class AKey, class AValue>
bool TDictionary <AKey, AValue>::KeyExists(const AKey& thisKey) const
{
      if (_count == 0)      return false; // ❹ No elements in the dictionary
      bool result = this->DoKeyExists(thisKey); // ❺ Invoke derived class
                                                // method

      return result;
}
```

No matter what derived class of TDictionary is used, invoking AddKeyValuePair always ends up in TDictionary::AddKeyValuePair because it is not a virtual function. Inside AddKeyValuePair of TDictionary, in ❶ it is first checked if a key-value pair with the key (thisKey) being added already exists in the dictionary. For this the member function KeyExists() is used. This ends up calling TDictionary::KeyExists(). In KeyExists() above, we first check if the count of elements is greater than zero (❹). If that test fails, we must search the dictionary for the specified key—thisKey. This can only be done by the derived classes. So we invoke the pure virtual method DoKeyExists() from within TDictionary::KeyExists. Since DoKeyExists is a pure virtual function, it must be implemented by the derived class. So the call to DoKeyExists transfers control to a derived class function. In other words, KeyExists() depends on DoKeyExists to complete its work. After KeyExists() returns to AddKeyValuePair, we invoke DoAddKeyValuePair() (❷ above). This is another pure virtual function that must be implemented by the derived classes. So now we end up calling a derived class implementation of DoAddKeyValuePair. Finally, when DoAddKeyValuePair is successful, the count of elements is incremented (❸).

```
void f()
{
    TListDictionary<TString, int> ld; // just an ordinary object
    TString zimbabwe("Zimbabwe");

    ld.AddKeyValuePair(zimbabwe, 263);  // The country-name, telephone
                                        // code
    /*
      This will also work
          TDictionary* pd = &ld;
          pd->AddKeyValuePair(zimbabwe, 263);
    */
}
```

For every member function in TDictionary that depends on some implementation in the derived class, we create a pair of member functions. The implementation function that must be provided by the derived class is a pure virtual function, which has a similar name as the member function that is provided by the TDictionary class, but it has an added prefix or suffix. I prefer to use DoXXX() just to indicate that the function will just *Do* that operation. This pure virtual function should not be visible to the normal client because it is not part of the public interface. The DoXXX() functions are part of the protocol between the base class and its derived class(es). Therefore, the DoXXX() function is usually a protected member function. It can also be a private member function. A protected member of a base class can be accessed by a derived class but a private member cannot be accessed by the derived class. If derived classes of TDictionary need access to the DoXXX() functions in their implementation, then it is sensible to make the DoXXX() functions protected member functions (see box on next page for more details). If this is not a requirement, then they can be private member functions.

Here is the declaration of TListDictionary.

```
template <class AKey, class AValue> class TListDictionary : public
    TDictionary<AKey, AValue> {
  public:
            TListDictionary();              // default constructor
            virtual ~TListDictionary();   // Destructor
        // Other details not important for this example
  protected:
        virtual bool DoAddKeyValuePair(const AKey&  thisKey,
                          const AValue& withThisValue) ;
        virtual bool DoKeyExists(const AKey& thisKey) const;
        virtual AValue DoGetValueAt(const AKey& thisKey) const;
};
```

This technique uses inheritance effectively to overcome problems encountered when using plain virtual functions. The protocol is enforced by the base class and the derived class does its part by providing the crucial parts of the implementation. The base class defines the end points of the protocol that must be provided by the derived class implementors. This way, none of the derived classes need to worry about changes in the protocol of the base class. The derived classes just do what they do best when requested by the base class.

PRIVATE VIRTUAL FUNCTIONS

In C++, it is possible to have virtual functions in derived classes that are private, That does not prevent a base class client from invoking those functions. Here is an example:

```
class B {
    public:
        virtual void f() { cout << "B::f()\n"; }
};

class D : public B {
    private:
        virtual void f() { cout << "D::f()\n"; } // Override B::f()
};

main()
{
    B objB;
    D objD;

    objB.f();   // ❶ Fine, B::f() is public
    objD.f();   // ❷ Error, D::f() is not public

    B*  pb = &objD;
    pb->f();        // ❸
    // Calls D::f() but that is fine because access is through B's
    // interface
}
```

Here in ❶, we are using a B object and the access is based on the interface in B. f() is public in B. In ❷, we are using a D object. But, in D, f() is private member function. When an object of D is used, the access is based on the declarations in D. In ❸, we are using a pointer to B, which points to a D object. When the call **pb->f()** is checked, the access rights of f() in B are used because **pb** is of type B. In B, the member function f() is public. Hence, there is no access violation but because of dynamic binding, we end up executing D::f().

This scheme is useful if you want to inform your clients that a derived class must be used polymorphically through the base class interface only (❸). In the example above, the correct way to use D is by using a reference or pointer to B.

The situation is a bit different when the base class member function is private.

```
class B {
    private:
        virtual void f() { cout << "B::f()\n"; }
    public:
        void g() { this->f(); } // This is fine
};

class D : public B {
    public:
        virtual void f() { cout << "D::f()\n"; }
};

main()
{
    B objB;
    D objD;
    objB.f(); // Error, f() is not public
    objD.f(); // Fine. D::f() is public
    objB.g();  // Calls B::g() which calls D::f()  internally
}
```

Here, the base class function is private. It cannot be accessed by clients directly. However, other base class member functions can invoke the private member function. The base class uses a private member function in its implementation. This can be overridden by the derived classes if needed (or it might be pure virtual as discussed in the TDictionary example earlier). Such private member functions are for the use of the base class only, (i.e., the base class member functions invoke the private virtual function and dynamic binding may cause the execution of a derived class function). Even though normal clients and derived classes cannot directly invoke the private virtual function, it can still be used by the base class member functions just like any other virtual function.

EIFFEL   This scheme is also applicable to Eiffel and Smalltalk. The only difference is that
SMALLTALK Smalltalk and Eiffel do not have the notion of a protected region. Therefore, in Eiffel and
Smalltalk the DoXXX() methods would be private methods in the base class. In Eiffel,
the non-virtual operations become frozen in the base class.

CAUTION   The base class must clearly document what it expects from the derived classes in
the DoXXX() implementations. If there is any miscommunication between the base class
and the derived class, clients will suffer and the entire hierarchy loses its usefulness.

THE DOUBLE DISPATCHING CONCEPT

C++   Dynamic binding is a very powerful feature that is extremely useful but it comes with a
EIFFEL   limitation. When a virtual function is invoked, the actual function invoked is determined
SMALLTALK based on the type of one object. This is called *single-dispatch*. The call to the appropriate
function is dispatched based on the run-time type of a single object. In essence, the function executed is based on the actual type of the object receiving the operation (or message). But in some solutions, we would like to invoke a virtual function based on the type
of two objects. That is, the function to be called is based on the actual type of not one, but
two different objects. This is called *double-dispatch*. In fact, this can be generalized to
any number of objects (*multi-dispatch*). Some languages have direct support for double-
dispatch (e.g., CLOS). It is possible to achieve the effect of double-dispatch using single-
dispatch quite easily.

          To illustrate the concept of double-dispatch, let's use a simple example. Consider a
video editing/multiplexing system that can handle video images of different formats
(NTSC, PAL, SECAM, MSECAM, etc.).[5] The system can convert from one recording
format to another. It can accept a PAL video clip and display it on an NTSC monitor. In
designing such a system, we could start of with a base class TVideoClip that represents a
video clip in any format (Fig. 12-7).

          All the different video formats are unified under a single class—TVideoClip. Class
TVideoDevice handles output of video clips.

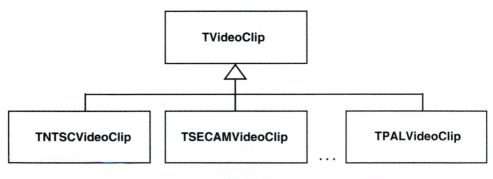

Fig. 12-7

---

[5]A system of color television developed in France as an alternative to PAL and NTSC.

```
class TVideoDevice;

class TVideoClip {
    public:
        TVideoClip();
        virtual ~TVideoClip();

        // Returns the number of frames in the clip
        virtual size_t HowManyFrames() const;
        //...
        // Display produces an output on a video device
        virtual void DisplayTo(TVideoDevice& device) const = 0;
    private:
};
```

A skeleton of the derived classes of **TVideoClip** is shown below.

```
class TNTSCVideoClip : public TVideoClip {
    public:
        TNTSCVideoClip ();
        // Display produces an output on a video device
        virtual void DisplayTo(TVideoDevice& device) const;
        //...
    private:
        //...
};

class TPALVideoClip : public TVideoClip {
    public:
        TPALVideoClip ();
        // Display produces an output on a video device
        virtual void DisplayTo(TVideoDevice& device) const;
    private:
        //...
};
```

Other derived classes of **TVideoClip** would be implemented in a similar fashion.

On the same lines, we must have a set of video devices that can display video images of a specific format(s). It is also possible that some video devices can convert an input image from one format to another before displaying. Not all devices would have the capability to convert. If a **TVideoDevice** is not capable of doing a conversion from one format to another, then it probably throws an exception.

We can represent the video devices in a similar hierarchy as the video clips (see Fig. 12-8).

Here is a skeleton of the classes for **TVideoDevice** hierarchy.

```
class TVideoDevice {
    public:
        TVideoDevice ();
        virtual ~TVideoDevice ();
        //...
        // Display video clip on this device
        virtual void Display(const TVideoClip& clip) = 0;
```

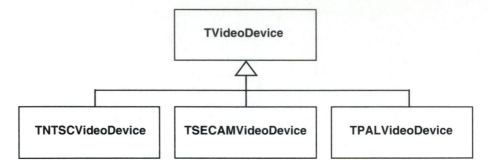

Fig. 12-8

```
        private:
    };
    // other details not important

    class TNTSCVideoDevice : public TVideoDevice {
        public:
            virtual  ~TNTSCVideoDevice();
            TNTSCVideoDevice();
            //...
            // Display clip on this video device
            virtual void Display(const TVideoClip&  clip);
        private:
            // ...
    };
```

Any **TVideoDevice** object must somehow determine the type of the video clip that is being passed to **Display()** function before it can display it.

Now consider a function **DisplayVideo()** that displays a video clip of some format on a **TVideoDevice**.

```
void DisplayVideo(const TVideoClip&  inputClip, TVideoDevice&
                                           outputDevice)
{
    /*
        Here we must determine the recording format of the inputClip and
        also the format acceptable  to the outputDevice. If the video
        device is a PAL device and the input clip is in NTSC format, the
        output device must perform a conversion from NTSC to PAL. The
        behavior is dependent on  the format of the input clip and also
        the type of the video device.
        We first determine the true type of the video format by using the
        virtual  function DisplayTo on the video clip.
    */

    inputClip.DisplayTo(outputDevice);
            // ❷ This will dispatch to the correct class of inputClip.
}
```

Here **DisplayVideo** must know the actual type of both the video clip object and the output device object. To display a PAL video clip on an NTSC video device requires the ability to convert a PAL clip to NTSC format. A virtual function depends on the true type of one object. But here we are dependent on the true type of two objects, the **inputClip** and the **outputDevice**. Calling a virtual function is referred to as *dispatching*. Here we need to be dispatched based on two objects. Hence, it is double-dispatch. In other words, the exact operation that needs to be done depends on the true types of two different objects that are passed in polymorphically.

```
void f()
{
    TNTSCVideoClip ntscVideo; // Create an NTSC video clip
    // Record some information in NTSC format in ntscVideo

    TPALVideoDevice  palDevice;// Just a video device object
    // Now display the NTSC video on PAL device
    DisplayVideo(ntscVideo, palDevice);// ❶
}
```

To determine the format of the input clip, we use the virtual function mechanism. The implementation of the **DisplayTo()** member functions would have the following format. In the example above, ❶ will make a call to **DisplayVideo**() with two objects. In ❷, we determine the true type of the **inputClip** by using the virtual function **DisplayTo**().

```
void TNTSCVideoClip::DisplayTo(TVideoDevice& outputDevice) const
{
    // Now we know that the video being displayed is of NTSC format.
    // But, we still don't know the output device format. We could use RTTI
    // in C++ to determine the true type of outputDevice and carry out
    // the conversion.

    // Get the type of outputDevice
    const type_info& outputType= typeid(outputDevice);

    if (outputType == typeid(TNTSCVideoClip) ) {
        // There is no conversion required. The input format is the same
        // as the output format. A direct transfer of information is all
        // that is required. This is the easy case.
        // Just call the Display() function of TVideoDevice.
        outputDevice.Display(*this);
        return;;
    }

    if (outputType == typeid(TSECAMVideoClip) ) {
        // Code to handle conversion of a NTSC video to SECAM video
        //...
        // Then call the Display() function of TVideoDevice.
        return;
    }

    if (outputType == typeid(TPALVideoClip) ) {
        // Code to handle conversion of a NTSC format video to PAL
        //...
```

```
        // Then call the Display() function of TVideoDevice.
        return;
    }


    // and so on for other possible video formats
    // If the conversion is not possible, throw an exception.
}
```

The class **TVideoDevice** still receives the **TVideoClip** object polymorphically. But **TVideoDevice** objects don't have to worry about the conversion because they always receive the video clips of the right format (because of the conversion done in **DisplayTo** member function shown above). Another alternative is to move the conversion code to **TVideoDevice** itself. In that scenario, a **TVideoClip** is just passed polymorphically to **TVideoDevice**, which determines the true type of the **TVideoClip** object (using RTTI) and performs the conversion (if it is capable of doing the conversion) and displays it. In the example above, the RTTI code and conversion happens in **TVideoClip**.

This doesn't look too elegant because:

a. Encapsulation is being broken. Every **DisplayTo()** function must know about all the derived classes (sibling classes).

b. If a new derived class is added to **TVideoClip** (such as **TMSECAMVideoClip**), then every **DisplayTo()** function must be updated. This is dangerous.

c. Using RTTI always makes the code highly type dependent and, hence, brittle.

It is always a good practice not to write code that depends on the type information of an object. Virtual functions are provided for the purpose of writing type independent code. Moreover, this solution is very specific to C++ because of the use of RTTI. We may not have this luxury of type determination in other OO languages.

We are trying to solve two problems here:

1. Given a **TVideoClip** object and a **TVideoDevice** object, we must be capable of displaying the clip on the device, performing conversions if necessary. This requires that somehow we determine the true type of the video clip and the video device.

2. We don't want to use RTTI to determine the actual type of the **TVideoClip** or the **TVideoDevice**.

We can solve this type dependency problem by using a set of overloaded functions in **TVideoDevice** class. Where necessary, the conversion of video clips from one format to another would be done by the **TVideoDevice** derived classes.

```
class TVideoDevice {
    public:
        TVideoDevice();
        virtual  ~TVideoDevice();
        //...
        // Display clip on this video device
        virtual void Display(const TVideoClip&     clip) = 0; // Optional
        virtual void Display(const TNTSCVideoClip& clip) = 0;
```

```
            virtual void Display(const TPALVideoClip& clip) = 0;
            virtual void Display(const TSECAMVideoClip& clip) = 0;
    private:
            // ...
};

class TNTSCVideoDevice {
    public:
            virtual  ~TNTSCVideoDevice();
            TNTSCVideoDevice();
            //...
            // Display clip on this video device
            virtual void Display(const TVideoClip& clip);
            virtual void Display(const TNTSCVideoClip& clip);
            virtual void Display(const TPALVideoClip& clip);
            virtual void Display(const TSECAMVideoClip& clip);
    private:
            // ...
};

class TPALVideoDevice {
    public:
            TPALVideoDevice();
            virtual  ~TPALVideoDevice();
            //...
            // Display clip on this video device
            virtual void Display(const TVideoClip& clip); // Optional
            virtual void Display(const TNTSCVideoClip& clip);
            virtual void Display(const TPALVideoClip& clip);
            virtual void Display(const TSECAMVideoClip& clip);
    private:
            // ...
};

void TPALVideoDevice::Display(const TNTSCVideoClip& inputClip)
{
    // Perform necessary conversion from NTSC to PAL and display the clip
    // Otherwise throw an exception
}

void TPALVideoDevice::Display(const TVideoClip& inputClip)
{
    // If this member function is entered, it implies that a video clip of
    // some (yet) unknown format has been sent to the video device. Reject
    // it and throw an exception. It is possible that some new video
    // format has been added in the TVideoClip hierarchy but TVideoDevice
    // hasn't been updated to process this new video clip type.
}
```

With this modification, **DisplayVideo** looks as follows:

```
void DisplayVideo(const TVideoClip&  inputClip, TVideoDevice&
                              outputDevice)
{
    //  Here we must determine the recording format of the inputClip and
```

```
// also the correct format of outputDevice  to determine the
// conversion process. We can determine the true type of the input
// video clip by using the DisplayTo() virtual function.

inputClip.DisplayTo(outputDevice); // ❸  This will dispatch to the
                                   // correct class of inputClip.
}
```

The **DisplayTo()** function in all **TVideoClip** classes would have the following code:

```
void TNTSCVideoClip::DisplayTo(TVideoDevice&  outputDevice) const
{
    // When in this function, the input clip (object *this) must be a
    // TNTSCVideoClip. So our input video format is NTSC. The output device
    // format is determined by the next call to Display(*this);

    outputDevice.Display(*this); // ❹ Call Display with an TNTSCVideoClip
        // object the type of *this is TNTSCVideoClip
}
```

In the new scheme of things, ❸ determines the real type of the video clip object. When the virtual function **DisplayTo()** is invoked on a **TVideoClip** object, it automatically transfers the execution to the correct derived class of the object (**inputClip**) being used. This solves the first hurdle. But we still don't know the real type of the video device object, **outputDevice**. Not only that, we must somehow tell the output device the true format of the video clip.

In ❹, we overcome the remaining obstacle. We have added a set of overloaded **Display()** functions to **TVideoDevice**, one for each type of **TVideoClip** derived class. Once we enter the **DisplayTo()** function of a **TVideoClip** derived class, we know the real type of the video clip object being processed. Next we use dynamic binding on the **TVideoDevice** object to execute the **Display()** function of the correct **TVideoDevice** derived class. In the statement

```
outputDevice.Display(*this);
```

the type of (***this**) is whatever derived class we are in. In other words, the type of (***this**) is the actual type of the **TVideoClip** object (**inputClip**) passed to **DisplayVideo**. So now we know the exact type of video clip being displayed, without using RTTI. We should somehow pass this information to the **Display()** function in **TVideoDevice**. For this we use the set of overloaded virtual functions in **TVideoDevice**. There is one virtual function for each derived class of **TVideoClip**. So the call ends up in the correct derived class of the **outputDevice** object. Here is the test function again:

```
void f()
{
    TNTSCVideoClip ntscVideo; // Create an NTSC video clip
    // Record some information in NTSC format in ntscVideo
    // ...
    TPALVideoDevice palDevice;// Just a video device object
```

```
              // Now display the NTSC video on PAL device
              DisplayVideo(ntscVideo, palDevice);
      }
```

In DisplayVideo(), inputClip is an object of TNTSCVideoClip and outputDevice is an object TPALVideoDevice. In ❸, we enter TNTSCVideoClip::DisplayTo because inputClip is an object of TNTSCVideoClip. Next, in ❹ we are dispatched to TPALVideoDevice::Display(TNTSCVideoClip&) because outputDevice is an object of TPALVideoDevice. So when we are in TPALVideoDevice::Display(TNTSCVideo-Clip&), we have all the information needed to display the clip. If TPALVideoDevice is capable of performing the conversion, then the video clip would be displayed correctly. Otherwise, an exception should be thrown.

This scheme no longer uses RTTI and is portable. This can be implemented in all OO languages because every OO language must support dynamic binding. But, there is also a drawback in this scheme. If we create a new derived class of TVideoClip (say TM-SECAMVideoClip), then the TVideoDevice hierarchy must be updated by adding a new overloaded Display() function that accepts the new video clip format. Otherwise, the default member function Display(TVideoClip&) would be selected by the dynamic binding mechanism and it would throw an exception. If this member function is not declared in TVideoDevice, then it will cause a compile-time error when the DisplayTo() member function of the new derived class of TVideoClip is compiled (matching Display() function not found). In other words, changing the TVideoClip hierarchy causes a change in the TVideoDevice hierarchy and a complete recompilation of the TVideoDevice hierarchy (not very good).

☞ **Double dispatching is expensive and not very easy to understand. Use it when absolutely necessary.**

DESIGNING AND IMPLEMENTING CONTAINER CLASSES

One of the most tedious task for a programmer is the repetitive job of implementing traditional data structure classes such as List, Queue, HashTable, Dictionary, etc. This is even more troublesome in languages that do not support generic programming (C++ templates). Fortunately, C++ and Eiffel do not have this problem.

Classes such as those mentioned above are in general referred to as *Container Classes* because they usually contain other objects. For example, an array of films in a camera is a container of films. Similarly, a list of video frames in a video tape is a container of video frames. A paragraph in a book is a container of sentences. In general, when focusing on high level design, we don't think of specific types of classes such as List, Array, etc., but in general we show the presence of some container.

Efficient container classes are not easy to design or implement. It requires a thorough knowledge of each and every type of container to implement them efficiently. But, a normal programmer shouldn't have to implement container classes in every software project. Life would be too dull and boring if we had to implement container classes over and over again.

There are two views of a container class. First of all, they store other objects in them. For example, a List in a parking garage contains Automobile objects. Similarly, a Directory object in a file system contains File objects. A simple String object contains characters. In general, a container is used wherever we need to store some other objects. We need different types of containers depending on the problem on hand. A directory in a file system needs a container that can dynamically grow efficiently as and when new files are added to the directory. A container of words in a language dictionary must be fast in locating words in the dictionary. Here, dynamic growth is not a very important issue. A container that holds cells in a spread sheet must allow insertion and deletion of cells efficiently. Secondly, general container classes must satisfy different requirements. To satisfy such demands, different types of container classes are implemented.

1. An array is a simple (usually fixed size) container, which can be indexed very easily but it is not very efficient when dynamic size changes of the container is needed.

2. A hash table is another container that is fast in locating objects stored in it (by using a hash value). Again, hash tables are not very efficient when dynamic growth is needed.

3. A simple list (single, double, or multi-way linked) is a very flexible container, which is quite easy to grow or shrink. Even insertions and deletions are easy. But lists are not very efficient in look-up (locating a specific object) capabilities.

HETEROGENEOUS AND HOMOGENEOUS CONTAINERS

A Heterogeneous Container can hold objects of different types without any problem. For example, a heterogeneous array can hold a Telephone object, a Book object, and a Floppy disk object, all within the same container object. In other words, a heterogeneous container allows mixing of different types. Languages that do not support

Heterogeneous Container	**Homogeneous Container**
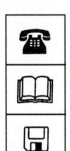	

Fig. 12-9

generic classes usually support heterogeneous containers only. For example, Smalltalk container classes are all heterogeneous. We shall see the design of such container classes soon (see Fig. 12-9).

On the other hand, a Homogeneous Container can only hold objects of one type. A List container of Book objects will only allow storage of Book objects in it and nothing else. This would be enforced by the language type system. So all the objects in a homogeneous container are of the same type.[6] These are the easiest to implement.

Most of us have been through an elementary data structures and algorithms course and we are quite familiar with the advantages and disadvantages of these containers.

DESIGNING TO DEAL WITH DIFFERENT CONTAINERS

Without worrying too much about the differences between heterogeneous and homogeneous containers, let's look at some scenarios where we must design software to deal with different types of containers.

Visualize a simple electronic mail system implementation where every mail system user is given a mail box. Assume that class **TMailBox** holds the messages addressed to a user. Users can extract messages from their mail boxes whenever they want. So class **TMailBox** must allow a user to retrieve messages stored in the mail box. Assume that there is class **TMailMessage** that represents messages received/sent by the mail system users. Here is a skeleton of the class **TMailBox**.

```
class TMailMessage;

class TMailBox {
    public:
        TMailBox();
        size_t HowManyMessages() const;
        void RetrieveUserMessages(/* an object passed by reference to
            hold the messages */);
        // and many more methods
};
```

When a user wishes to retrieve messages from her mailbox, she might want it stored in a **TArray** object (assuming that class **TArray** has been already implemented). To support this requirement, class **TMailBox** must have a member function **RetrieveUserMessages()** as follows:

```
class TArray;

class TMailBox {
    public:
        TMailBox();
        size_t HowManyMessages() const;
```

[6]In a pointer based implementation, these objects can be polymorphic, (i.e., a container of base class objects can contain derived class objects).

```
            // Mail messages in the mailbox are copied into the array
            // storeHere
            void RetrieveUserMessages(TArray&  storeHere);
            // and many more methods
    };
```

Implementor of **TMailBox** must understand the interface and behavior of **TArray** in order to store **TMailMessage** objects in the array object supplied by the user. That seems simple enough until we come across another user who likes her messages to be stored in a **TList** object. Then we must add another overloaded member function **RetrieveUserMessages()** to **TMailBox** that accepts a **TList** argument.

```
    class TList;
    class TArray;

    class TMailBox {
        public:
            // Mail messages in the mailbox are copied into the array
            // (or list) storeHere
            void RetrieveUserMessages(TArray&  storeHere);
            void RetrieveUserMessages(TList&  storeHere);
    };
```

So every time a user brings in a new type of container object, our **TMailBox** class must be modified to accept the new class. Needless to state this is not the best way of designing interfaces. There is no end to this problem. Furthermore, class **TMailBox** implementor must understand the interface and behavior of each and every type of container so that **TMailMessage** objects can be stored in the container correctly. There is no way in the world the implementor of **TMailBox** can understand all the different container classes and their idiosyncrasies. If we were to go with this approach, class **TMailBox** would have to be modified almost daily. Now, there is a good way of ensuring perpetual employment!

Definitely, this approach isn't acceptable. If we could somehow abstract the behavior of all the different container classes into a common base class, we wouldn't have to worry about specific types of container classes.

Recognizing the fact that a container stores other objects, it must support member functions to store objects into it and also to retrieve objects from it, in addition to other member functions. If we call this base class, **TContainer** we have achieved some degree of success. Let's just assume for the time being that a container only stores **TItem** objects.

```
class TItem;

class TContainer {
    public:
        TContainer();
        virtual ~TContainer();

        // Add a new item to the container
        virtual void Add(TItem* anItem) =  0;

        // Looks for thisItem in the container and if found removes it
        // from the container and returns it. Only the first instance of
        // thisItem in the  container is removed. Uses the comparison
```

```
                // operator == to determine equality of objects.
                virtual TItem* Remove(const TItem& thisItem) =  0;

                // Similar to Remove, but removes all instances of thisItem
                // Returns a pointer to the last occurrence
                virtual TItem* RemoveAllOccurrences(const TItem& thisItem) =  0;

                // Removes every object from the container. Nothing happens to
                // objects that were stored. They are not deleted but they no
                // longer exist in the container
                void MakeEmpty() = 0;

                // Deletes every object stored in the container. Careful, objects
                // are removed from the container and then delete operator is
                // invoked on them.
                void DeleteAll() =  0;

                // Is thisItem in the container? Again operator== is used to
                // determine equality of objects
                virtual bool IsMember(const TItem& thisItem) const =  0;

                // How many Item objects in the container?
                virtual size_t HowMany() const =  0;

                // Append the contents of the otherContainer to this
                // container
                void Add(const TContainer&  otherContainer);

                // and definitely many more member functions
};
```

This looks reasonable. Now we need to ensure that this interface can be applied (and implemented) by TArray, TList, etc. If the interface is not general enough, then class TContainer cannot be used as a base class.

Let's analyze the requirements of a container object:

a. It must be able to store objects supplied by the user.

b. It must be able to find (membership in the container) objects in the container.

c. It should be possible to remove selected objects from a container.

d. It would be convenient if we could add one container to another.

Our base class easily meets these requirements. But, that's not good enough. It should be possible to implement various types of container classes (i.e., derived classes) using this class as the base class and all such derived classes should be able to support the operations exported by TContainer. Let's look at some general purpose containers and see if they can meet these requirements.

1. Array container: Normal operations like adding a new object and removing an object are easily implemented. The array object should maintain the index of free and oc-cupied slots in the array and the array can grow when needed by allocating a new array object and copying existing contents. Note that, TContainer does not support direct subscripting using operator [].

2. Set container: This will easily support Add and Remove operations. The RemoveAllOccurrences function wouldn't be useful because a set doesn't allow duplicates in it. Other member functions are implemented easily.

3. A Queue container: Here again Add and Remove are easy. Objects are added at the back and removed from the front. Membership checks are also easily implemented.

4. A Dictionary container: This is a bit tricky. A dictionary stores (Key, Value) pairs. So when we add an item to a dictionary, it is not a single object but a pair of objects. So, at first sight it looks like a dictionary cannot be a normal container. But, that's easy to solve. We define an auxiliary class TPair which holds a key and a value. Now the TDictionary class is defined in terms TPair objects and not just keys and values.

5. A Bag container: As the name indicates, a bag will store objects (even duplicates) without any problem. All member functions of TContainer can be implemented easily.

So, it appears as though our TContainer is general enough to suit most common types of containers. But, remember that each of these containers have their own schemes to add and remove objects. This freedom is available to them because most of the member functions of TContainer are (pure) virtual and, hence, can be overridden.

The member functions like Add() and Remove() are pure virtual because, adding and removing elements from a container requires intimate knowledge of the implementation. The algorithm to add an element to a set is completely different from that of adding an element to a dictionary or an array. The derived classes of container must implement them but it should be possible to add an element to any container, no matter what type it is. The member function Add(TContainer&) need not be virtual because it can be implemented using the other member functions. Adding one container to another just involves the task of navigating the entire container, adding elements from the source to the destination. No other implementation knowledge about the specific type of container is required.

NOTE   This is only the first cut. We shall make more refinements and organize the hierarchy in a better way soon. For now, I'm trying to bring out the general philosophy of containers (see Fig. 12-10).

But, there is still one problem. What we have is a container of TItem objects. That was the original assumption when we designed the TContainer class. In other words, these container classes will only store objects of type TItem, including derived classes of TItem (see Fig. 12-11).

This implies that all of our objects that need to be stored in a container must inherit from class TItem, the common base class. We may not like it, but that's the way it is now. This isn't very bad, but we shall soon have better solutions for this problem.

Class TItem must be a general class that provides a very generic interface that can be applied to any class. Here is a simple interface:

```
class TItem {
    public:
```

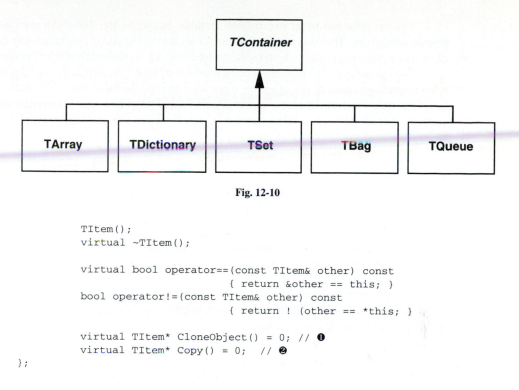

Fig. 12-10

```
        TItem();
        virtual ~TItem();

        virtual bool operator==(const TItem& other) const
                        { return &other == this; }
        bool operator!=(const TItem& other) const
                        { return ! (other == *this; }

        virtual TItem* CloneObject() = 0; // ❶
        virtual TItem* Copy() = 0;   // ❷
};
```

❶ This is the member function that returns a clone of the original object. This was discussed earlier under virtual constructors.

❷ This is the counterpart of the **CloneObject** function. It creates a new object that is a copy (not a clone) of the original object. Again, refer to the virtual constructor discussion earlier in this chapter.

A Container with TItem Objects

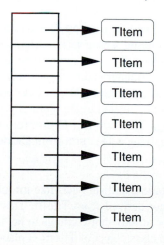

Fig. 12-11

The operator == is an overridable member function. By default, it uses address based comparison. This may not be suitable for all derived classes. Therefore, any derived class that wishes to provide a better scheme for comparison should override this function.

The intent here is to provide enough protocol in TItem so that any class that derives from it can implement it. For example, if we want the capability to store TPerson objects in a TContainer, then TPerson would inherit from TItem and should override the pure virtual methods.

```
class TPerson : public TItem {
    public:
        //...
        virtual TPerson* CloneObject();
        virtual TPerson* Copy();

        virtual bool operator==(const TItem& other) const;
        // and all the other member functions
    };
```

Returning to the class TMailBox, if we decide to use TContainer in the interface for the member function RetrieveUserMessages, then the class TMailMessage and TMailBox would be declared as follows:

```
class TMailMessage : public TItem {
    // Details not important
};

class TMailBox {
    public:
        TMailBox();
        size_t HowManyMessages() const;
        // TMailMessage objects would be added to container
        void RetrieveUserMessages(TContainer& container);
        // and many more methods
    };
```

C++   Note that the return value type for Copy() and CloneObject() in TPerson is different from that in TItem. Nothing wrong here. Originally, in C++, derived class virtual functions were required to have the same return type as the base class function. This restriction has been relaxed for pointer and reference return type. If the base class returns a B* (or B&) the derived class can return a D* (or D&) provided D is a derived class of B. Note that B and D need not be related to the hierarchy in which the virtual functions are being delcared. Even though TPerson is a TItem, for clients who directly create objects of TPerson and use it, receiving a TPerson from CloneObject() and Copy() is the preferred solution.

NOTE   With this implementation, built-in types like int, char, etc. cannot be stored in containers because they are not derived from TItem. This is one serious drawback of this scheme. But there are more serious shortcomings to be discovered soon.

a. When any derived class object of TItem is placed in a container, our assumption is that the address of the object (the pointer passed to Add) would be stored in the container and not the entire object. That is perfectly sensible. So every object inside a container looks identical—they are all pointers to TItem objects. When the Remove() member function is called on a container of TPerson objects, it returns a pointer to a TItem object and not a TPerson object. It is true that a TPerson is a TItem but you wouldn't know that by looking at the return value of Remove(). So, Remove() returns pointers to TItem objects polymorphically. When we need to use the returned TItem as a TPerson, it must be safely tested and converted to a TPerson. In C++, this would be possible using RTTI but it doesn't come for free. Adding TItem objects to containers is easy because any derived class of TItem is a TItem object because of inheritance but that doesn't help the client when objects are removed from the container.

b. The class TContainer is a heterogeneous container. It is a container of TItem objects. As stated in (a), every derived class of TItem is also a TItem. Therefore, when a container object holds pointers to TItem objects, it is most probably holding pointers to different derived class objects of TItem. For example, if TTelephone, TPerson, and TBook are all derived from TItem we could end up with a container as shown below.

```
class TTelephone : public TItem { /* details omitted */ };
class TBook : public TItem { /* details omitted */ };
```

If objects of these classes are added to some container, then we have a heterogeneous container (Fig. 12-12).

Since any derived class of TItem can be placed in the container, very strict type checking cannot be enforced. Anyone expecting a container of TBook objects as an argument to a function might receive a container that contains TBook objects, TTelephone objects, etc. This would force the users to resort to RTTI (in C++, and similar mechanisms in other languages) to determine the real type of every object in the container.

Heterogeneous Container

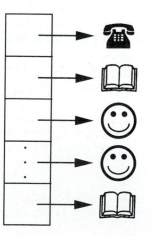

Fig. 12-12

```
void f(TContainer&  container)
{
    // This function expects a container of TBook objects but
    // there is no guarantee of that.

    TBook *tolstoy  = new TBook; // some book object
    container.Add(tolstoy);  // Just put this book on the container

    // Remove the book object from the container
    TItem* removedItem = container.Remove(*tolstoy);

    /*
        Here we know that the object that was removed must be a TBook
        object. Otherwise, Remove() would not have been able to locate it
        in the container. As we already know, Remove() compares each
        object in the container with the supplied argument and when they
        are equal (based on the result of operator==), it removes it and
        returns a pointer to it. But, the return type of Remove() is still
        TItem*. So we must cast the pointer returned to a TBook pointer.
        We don't need a dynamic cast because we know  for sure that it is
        a TBook object.
    */

    TBook*  pBook = static_cast<TBook*>(removedItem);
    // You can compare the *pBook with *tolstoy and they should be equal

    delete tolstoy;
}
```

But this is a simple example. The type of the object added is known to us. But what about a case where you want to carry out a specific operation on all **TBook** objects in a container. For example, we might be interested in all **TBook** objects with the word *Philosophy* in their title. Assuming that we have a an iterator object available for the container, the iterator can be used to sequentially traverse the container. On every object in the container, we must determine the real type of the object and then if it is a **TBook** object, the operation can be carried out.

NOTE   The details of creating and managing iterators with containers are not shown yet (even though it was mentioned in Part I). For now, just assume that there is a class **TIterator**, whose basic interface is shown below. We shall see all the details of iterators soon.

```
// Just a simple iterator class, Details to be discussed soon.

class TIterator  {
        public:
        // Create an iterator for this container
          TIterator(TContainer& c);
          ~TIterator();

        // Moves to the next TItem in the container and returns
        // a pointer to that TItem (if possible). Otherwise 0 is returned
          virtual TIterator* Next() = 0;

        // Moves to the first TItem in the container and returns
```

```
                // a pointer to that TItem (if possible). Otherwise 0 is returned
                  virtual TIterator* First()  = 0;

                // Remove the current element from the container
                virtual void Remove() = 0;
                // and many others
        };

        void ff(TContainer& container, TIterator& iterator)
        {
                // The argument iterator is associated with the argument container
                // If the item in the container is a TBook do something.

                // Move the iterator to the first item in the container
                TItem* element = iterator.First();

                const type_info&  bookType = typeid(TBook); // ❶

                while (element != 0) {
                        // Check the type of the element in the container
                        if (typeid(*element) == bookType) // ❷ Yes, it is a TBook object
                                // Perform a static cast and  do something with the TBook
                                // object
                        }
                        else {                   /*  It is not a book; skip it */ }
                        // Move to the next element
                        element = iterator.Next();
                }
        }
```

In this example, the iterator enables easy navigation of the container. The code in ❶ returns the internal type information (compiler generated) for objects of class **TBook**. We don't want to do this operation for every object. Therefore, we do it once and save the result. Then we move through the items in the container. At every step we will be looking at a **TItem** object because **TContainer** only stores **TItem** objects. Then in ❷ we compare the **typeid** of the object in the container with the **typeid** of **TBook** that we got in ❶. This isn't a zero cost operation. For every object in the container, we must determine the **typeid** and then compare them. Even though it is not as expensive as a dynamic cast, it does have some run-time cost. We need to do this because of the heterogeneous nature of the **TContainer**. If it was guaranteed that the **TContainer** passed in was really a container of **TBook** objects, we wouldn't have to go through these hoops.

Given this discussion, it is clear that these heterogeneous containers are useful to store different types of objects in them but they are not useful when homogeneous containers are needed. In reality, there isn't a frequent need for heterogeneous containers.

SMALLTALK   This style of containers was first implemented in Smalltalk. Since then it has been implemented by programmers in many other OO languages. In Smalltalk, every instance (i.e., object of a class) of every class is derived from the common base class **Object**. Therefore, our **TItem** is equivalent the class **Object** in Smalltalk. The root of the container hierarchy is the class **Collection**. In C++, we use RTTI to determine the real type of an instance of a class. This is not a big problem in Smalltalk. Every class supports some common messages to determine the type of the object (see Table 12-1 below).

❶ This is the equivalent of getting the **typeid** of an object in C++.

❷ This can be done in C++ by using dynamic casting. In C++, we try to cast to (using **dynamic_cast**) the target class. If the operation is possible then it succeeds; otherwise a 0 pointer is returned.

❸ This can be done in C++ using **typeid**. Just get the **typeid** of the object and the class and then compare them.

❹ This cannot be done in standard C++ because the C++ model does not support invoking arbitrary member functions on an object. Therefore, if the class does not support a member function, then the code does not compile.

The Smalltalk collection hierarchy is quite elaborate. It has different classes that support various kinds of data structures. The hierarchy is shown in Fig. 12-13. If you are interested, please refer to the Smalltalk reference manual for more information.

NOTE   Some newer Smalltalk implementations provide a collection class hierarchy that is somewhat different from the one shown here. The one above is the traditional Smalltalk collection class hierarchy.

In the Smalltalk system, **Integer**, **Float**, etc. are classes derived from class **Object**. Hence, the **Collection** hierarchy that uses **Object** as the common base is appropriate. In fact, class **Collection** is also derived from class **Object**. The advantage of the common root class **Object**, is that we get heterogeneous containers without any extra effort. Depending on your viewpoint this can be an advantage or a disadvantage (the cup is half empty or it is half full).

Returning to our **TMailBox** example, as we have already seen, **TMailMessage** is now a derived class of **TItem**.

```
class TMailMessage : public TItem {
    // Details not important
};

class TMailBox {
    public:
        TMailBox();
        size_t HowManyMessages() const;

        // TMailMessage objects would be added to container
        void RetrieveUserMessages(TContainer& container);
        // and many more methods
};
```

TABLE 12-1

Message	Functionality
❶ class	Returns an object which represents the real class of the object receiving the message
❷ isKindOf : someClass	Returns true if the object receiving the message is a superclass (or the real class) of the argument someClass passed.
❸ isMemberOf : someClass	Returns true if the object receiving this message is an object of someClass
❹ respondsTo :someSymbol	Returns true if the object (or one of its superclasses) can respond to the message someSymbol.

Smalltalk Container Classes

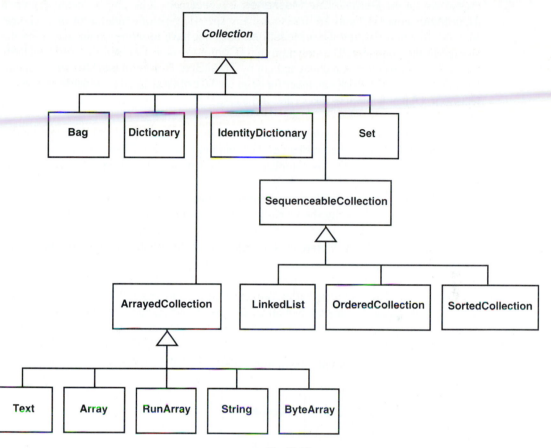

Fig. 12-13

In general, any class that needs to store its objects in a container (any object that can be *contained* in a container), must be a derived class of **TItem**. This is not really a very flexible design as far as C++ and Eiffel are concerned. We should be able to construct class hierarchies without the restriction of being a derived class of some root class.

But the advantages of a container class are still evident from this example.

1. With this modified design, class **TMailBox** does not have to know anything about specific types of containers. The member function **RetrieveUserMessages** is now written to use the interface of **TContainer**. This member function must be changed only when the interface of **TContainer** is modified. That eliminates the problem of dealing with different types of containers.

2. Looking at the other side of the coin, clients of **TMailBox** still have all the flexibility they need. A client can pass in any derived class of **TContainer** as the actual argument to the RetrieveUserMessages member function and everything still works correctly. As far as RetrieveUserMessages is concerned, it is always dealing with a TContainer object. Clients are free to use any specific type of container of their choice. Member function RetrieveUserMessages does not have to worry about managing the storage in the container. The polymorphic TContainer object passed to RetrieveUser-Messages is owned by the client and not by TMailBox. RetrieveUserMessages member function uses the Add() member function on TContainer to add TMailMessage objects to it. Dynamic binding takes care of the rest.

So we have again used inheritance successfully to solve type dependency problems. But we are still left with the problem of the common base class TItem. If we could eliminate this root class, our task is complete. And the solution should be obvious—**generic classes**.

Hereafter, we shall focus on a simplified container class hierarchy very similar to the Smalltalk class hierarchy shown earlier. This new hierarchy is shown below (see Fig. 12-14).

As you can see, this hierarchy is modeled on the Smalltalk hierarchy but the names are somewhat different.

NOTE   This hierarchy is modeled after Taligent's container classes (which is modeled after the Smalltalk container classes). Not all classes are shown and definitely we are not going

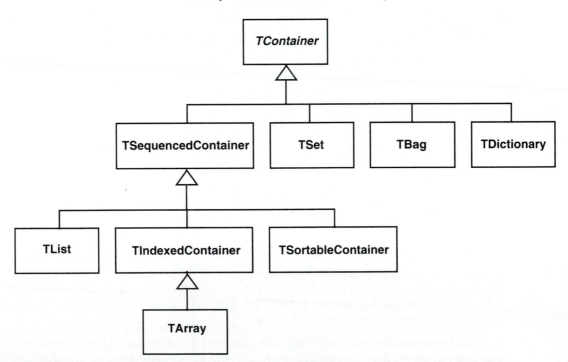

A Simple Container Class Hierarchy

Fig. 12-14

to implement any part of this hierarchy. Thanks to all the wonderful people at Taligent, who designed, implemented, and maintained these classes.

TSequencedContainer: Containers of this type maintain an ordering among the elements. Operations like insert before an element, insert after an element, etc. are supported.

```
template <class AType>
class TSequencedContainer : public TContainer<AType> {
     public:
          TSequencedContainer();
          TSequencedContainer(const TSequencedContainer<AType>& that);
          virtual ~TSequencedContainer();

          // Return a pointer to the element (if any) before obj
          virtual AType*      ElementAfter(const AType& obj) const  = 0;
          // Return a pointer to the element (if any) after obj
          virtual AType*      ElementBefore(const AType& obj) const = 0;
          virtual AType*      LastElement() const = 0;
          virtual AType*      FirstElement() const = 0;

          virtual size_tHowManyOccurrences(const AType& obj) const = 0;
     };
```

TIndexedContainer: Containers of this type are indexable using an external integer. A simple array is an example of this type. Here elements can be put into the container at specified indices.

```
template <class AType>
class      TIndexedContainer : public TSequencedContainer<AType> {
       public:
          virtual AType*      ElementAt(size_t index) const = 0;
          // Insert a new element at the specified index. Every element
          // after this element is moved one place to the right.
          virtual AType* InsertAt(size_t index,  AType* element) = 0;
          // Replace the element at specified index with this new element
          // Return the element already contained there.
          virtual AType* ReplaceAt(size_t index,  AType* element) = 0;

          // Return the index of this obj in the container. If obj is not
          // found, return -1
          virtual size_t IndexOfElement(const AType& obj) = 0;
          //...
     };
```

IMPLEMENTING HOMOGENEOUS CONTAINER CLASSES USING GENERIC PROGRAMMING

For the ensuing discussion, refer the container class hierarchy in Figure 12-14 above. We would like our container classes to store objects of any class. But, it would be much more safe and convenient if every container object holds objects of one class only. A container of **TBook** objects only allows **TBook** objects to be stored in it. Similarly, a container of

TPerson objects does not allow any other type of object to be stored in it. As we already know, such containers are homogeneous containers.

Design Goals

a. The container class must not allow mixing of different types of objects in a container object.

b. Clients must be able to create container class objects for any type of object without any requirement of a common base class (like TItem).

c. It should be possible to implement different types of container classes to suit the needs of different applications.

d. It would be an added bonus if heterogeneous containers can also be implemented in this design.

The goals (a–d) might seem daunting, but don't panic. We can easily achieve all these goals by using C++ template classes (or generic classes in Eiffel but without goal (d)).

As we already know, the real type associated with a generic class is specified when the class is instantiated, so we can create a generic TContainer class. The type of the object stored in the container would be the template argument.

```
//An abstract templatized container class

template <class AType>
class TContainer {
    public:
        TContainer();
        virtual ~TContainer();

        // Add a new item to the container
        virtual void Add(AType* anItem) =  0;

        // Looks for thisItem in the container and if found removes it
        // from the container and returns it. Only the first instance of
        // thisItem in the container is removed. Uses the comparison
        // operator == to determine equality of objects.
        virtual AType* Remove(const AType& thisItem) =  0;

        // Similar to Remove, but removes all instances of thisItem
        // Returns a pointer to the last occurrence
        virtual AType* RemoveAllOccurrences(const AType& thisItem) =  0;

        // Removes every object from the container. Nothing happens to
        // objects that were stored. They are not deleted but they no
        // longer exist in the container
        virtual void MakeEmpty() = 0;

        // Deletes every object stored in the container. Careful, object
        // are remove from the container and then delete operator is
        // invoked on them.
```

```
        virtual void DeleteAll() = 0;

        // Is thisItem in the container? Again operator== is used to
        // determine equality of objects
        virtual bool IsMember(const AType& thisItem) const =  0;

        // How many Item objects in the container?
        virtual size_t HowMany() const =  0;

        // Append the contents of the argument container to this
        // container
        void Add(const TContainer<AType>&  otherContainer);

        // and definitely many more member functions
};
```

Now **AType** is the type of the object that would be placed in the container. When **Add()** is called, it will be called with an object of **AType**. Similarly, **Remove()** returns an object of **AType**. Given this interface, we can easily implement derived classes that provide different styles of containers like lists, dictionaries, etc.

Here is a **TSet** container.

```
template <class AType>
class TSet:  public TContainer<AType> {
   public:
      TSet();
      TSet(const TSet<AType>&  copy);
      // Other usual member functions not shown

      virtual void  Add(AType* obj);
      virtual AType* Remove(const AType& obj);
      virtual AType* RemoveAllOccurrences(const AType& thisItem);
      virtual void  RemoveAll();
      virtual void  MakeEmpty();
      virtual bool IsMember(const AType& obj) const;
      virtual size_t HowMany() const;

      virtual void Difference(const TSet<AType>& set2); // ❶
      virtual TSet<AType> operator-(const TSet<AType>&
                                    set2) const ; // difference  ❷

      virtual void Intersection(const TSet<AType>& set2); // ❸
      virtual TSet<AType> operator&(const TSet<AType>&
                                    set2); const // intersection  ❹

      virtual void  Union(const TSet<AType>& set2); // ❺
      virtual TSet<AType>  operator|(const TSet<AType>&
                                    set2); const // union  ❻

      virtual void  Xor(const TSet<AType>& set1);   //❼
      virtual TSet<AType> operator^(const TSet<AType>&
                                    set2); const // xor     ❽
};
```

It is quite simple. Some extra operations that are specific to a set are added.

❶   This member function computes difference between two sets. The first set is the object itself. The second set is passed explicitly as the argument to the function. The result is stored in the original object. Therefore object *this is modified.

❷ This is an operator function that computes the difference between two sets. But unlike the first one, it does not modify the original object. It computes the difference and returns the result in a new object.

❸   This is a member function that computes the Intersection of two sets. The object in *this holds the result.

❹   This is an operator function that also computes the intersection of two sets but it returns the result of the computation in a new object.

❺ ❼   These member functions compute the Union and Xor of two sets. They modify the original set (*this).

❻ ❽ These are operator functions that also compute the Union (|) and Xor (^) of two sets. They return the resulting set object without modifying the original object.

The implementation is left as an exercise to the reader.

```
class TMailMessage  {
      // Details not important
};

class TMailBox {
      public:
            TMailBox();
            size_t HowManyMessages() const;

            // TMailMessage objects would be added to container
            void RetrieveUserMessages(TContainer<TMailMessage>& container);
                  // ①
            // and many more methods
};
```

Some important things to notice here:

①   The member function **RetrieveUserMessages** accepts not just any container, but only a container that holds **TMailMessage** objects. Instead of just a container, it requires a **TContainer<TMailMessage>**. This is the important thing about template classes. Usually functions (member functions and non-member functions) accept a container of some specific type. Here, the class **TMailBox** is going to store the **TMailMessage** objects it holds in the container passed in by the user. Naturally, the container supplied must be of the appropriate type.

```
void TMailBox::RetrieveUserMessages(TContainer<TMailMessage>&
                                         mailContainer)
{
```

```
        // Just as an example, create some TMailMessage objects and
        // add them to the container
        TMailMessage* msg = new TMailMessage;
        mailContainer.Add(msg); // ②

        msg = new TMailMessage; // Another message
        mailContainer.Add(msg);
    }
```

② Here, the member function RetrieveUserMessages is just adding a new TMailMessage object to the container of TMailMessage objects.

```
        class TFoo { }; // Just a dummy class

        void ff(TMailBox& mailbox)
        {
            TSet<TMailMessage> myMailSet; // ③
            mailbox.RetrieveUserMessages(myMailSet); // ④
            TSet<TFoo> fooSet; // ⑤
            mailbox.RetrieveUserMessages(fooSet); // ⑥
            //...
        }
```

③ Here, a TSet object is being instantiated. But TSet is a template class. Therefore, the required template argument must be supplied (we must specify what the TSet object is going to contain). We want to store TMailMessage objects in the set. Therefore, we create a TSet<TMailMessage>. Now the AType in the TSet (and TContainer) will be replaced by TMailMessage.

④ The TSet<TMailMessage> is polymorphically passed to RetrieveUserMessages member function; type matching is perfect.

To understand the type system and implications of strict type checking, consider the dummy class TFoo.

⑤ Here, a TSet of TFoo objects is created. This set will only accept TFoo objects.

⑥ Here, we try to pass the fooSet object to RetrieveUserMessages member function. This will not compile because a TSet of TFoo objects is not compatible with a TSet of TMailMessage objects. Even though both are TSet objects, they are not compatible because what they contain is also part of the type system. For a detailed discussion of this topic see Chapter 9.

Because of the template class type checking mechanism, the container classes discussed above are automatically homogeneous containers because they do not allow mixing of different types of objects in them. The only exception is in case of derived classes. A container of TPerson objects can accept a TStudent object if TStudent is derived from TPerson.

As another example, here is a TDictionary container. A dictionary is a table of <key, value> pairs. It can be considered to be a table of pairs (or tuples). When adding an element to a dictionary, the element must represent a pair—a key and a value. But our Add() member function in TContainer only accepts an AType object. So how can we pass two objects to Add() when it expects just one? Well, it's easy. Just make a new class that combines a key and value together. Call this a TPair.

```cpp
template <class AKey, class AValue>
class TPair {
    public:
        TPair(AKey k, AValue v);
        //... Other details not important
};


template <class AKey, class AValue>
class TDictionary : public TContainer<TPair<AKey, AValue> > {
    public:
        TDictionary();
        TDictionary(const TDictionary<AKey, AValue>& other);
        virtual ~TDictionary();
        TDictionary<AKey,AValue>&
                operator=(const TDictionary<AKey,AValue>& other);

        virtual void   Add(TPair<AKey, AValue>* pair);
        virtual TPair<AKey, AValue>*
                    IsMember(const TPair<AKey, AValue>& pair) const;
        virtual TPair<AKey, AValue>*
                    Remove(const TPair<AKey,AValue>& pair);
        virtual TPair<AKey, AValue>*
                    RemoveAllOccurences(const TPair<AKey,
                                            AValue>& thisItem);

        // Removes all TPairs in the dictionary
        virtual void   MakeEmpty();
        // Removes all TPairs in the dictionary and invokes delete on them
        virtual void   DeleteAll() ;
        virtual size_t HowMany() const;

        // Return true if this key exists in the dictionary
        virtual bool KeyExists(const AKey& key) const;
        // Return the key of this value if it exists. Return 0 otheriwse
        virtual AValue* ValueOfKey(const AKey& key) const;
        // Return the value of this key if it exists. Return 0 otheriwse
        virtual AKey* KeyAtValue(const AValue& val) const;
        // delete key and return value, return 0 if key not found
        virtual AValue* DeleteKey(AKey* key);
        virtual void AddKeyValuePair(const AKey& key, const AValue& val);
        // and many other member functions
};

class TPhoneNumber { /* Details not important */};
class TString { /*...*/ };

// This is a telephone book that maps names of people to their phone
// numbers
TDictionary<TString, TPhoneNumber> telephoneBook;

// This one maps the ticker (symbol used for a stock of a company, a
// string) with the current stock price (a float)
TDictionary<TString, float> stockQuoteTable;
```

A dictionary is just another useful container. The only difference here is that a dictionary accepts tuples. But our container required exactly one template argument. The mismatch has been overcome by creating a pair from key and value.[7] Implementation of a dictionary is not trivial. One could implement a simple dictionary using a linked list. A faster, more efficient implementation would use hash tables. In any case, this book is not about data structures and suffice it to say that container classes bring out many interesting design issues.

Advantages of Template-Based Homogeneous Containers

1. Very strict type checking is enforced. Elements of the container can be of only one type (homogeneity). Clients do not have to resort to RTTI to determine the type of an object retrieved from a container. This will enable faster and safer programs.

2. Implementors writing code to the interface of the **TContainer** class need not have to worry about the differences among different container types. This advantage results from inheritance and it is no different from the Smalltalk style (**TItem** based) container discussed earlier.

3. The Smalltalk style containers do not work with built-in types. But, the template based container can be made to work with built-in types by careful design. Even if the template containers don't work with built-in types directly, template specialization (discussed in Chapter 9) can be used to create specific template container classes for the built-in types. In general, if a template based container doesn't work for a specific type, it is not too difficult to write a specialized implementation for that type. Even though this is not a very easy task, experienced professionals can do it. There is no way it can be made to work with the Smalltalk style containers without substantial run-time cost.

4. With the Smalltalk style of containers, every object must derive from a common base class (**TItem** in our example, class **Object** in Smalltalk). This implies that container class implementors must only use the interface supported by the common base class in their implementation. Otherwise, the code will not compile. This can cause difficulties in implementation. With template-based containers, the container class implementors can use specific member functions from the template arguments.[8] This way, the template argument can be forced to provide services to the container class. Otherwise, an error would be generated at compile time. Another related difficult is that every class that wishes to be placed in a container must override all the pure virtual member functions of **TItem**, irrespective of whether they are used by the client or not. With template based containers, only those member functions of the container that are actually used by the client are generated (at compile time), and, hence, unused functions need not be implemented by clients.

5. If a general template container implementation fails to offer satisfactory performance, you can always implement a specialized version of the container for specific tem-

---

[7]A dictionary is also called a Map. Key and Value are also called Domain and Range respectively. A Map is a mapping from a set of Domain values to a set of Range values.

[8]This does not imply that an implementor can arbitrarily depend on functions from the template arguments. Extreme care is required to achieve good design (see Chapter 9 for details).

plate arguments to match your performance needs. No such flexibility with any non-template container. Sure, you can implement a special non-template container class that is ten times faster than the general (non-template) container but it cannot have the same name as the existing container class. For example, if you are unhappy with the general TArray class, you can implement your own special container TTurboArray but it cannot be used in place of TArray (unless it derives from TArray, but doing so brings in a host of other problems). Sure, TTurboArray can be used in place of TContainer (if it is derived from TContainer) but not in place of TArray. This is not a very serious drawback but it can be an irritant in some special circumstances.

DISADVANTAGES OF TEMPLATE-BASED CONTAINERS

1. As with any C++ template class, code replication is a major problem. But, to some extent, it can be overcome by using non-template-base classes. Even with this type of code sharing, the code size of a template container is almost always bigger than an non-template container.

2. If clients really need a heterogeneous container, implementing them may not be easy with a template based container. More on this soon.

3. With the TItem base class for all objects, implementors of containers can depend on the common interface of TItem to carry out their operations. This advantage is not easily available with template based containers. It is possible to state such requirements explicitly in the template based container classes but it is not easily visible in the interface. However, this does not cause any run-time errors because even with template based containers, the compiler detects missing functions when code is generated (at compile/link time).

POINTER-BASED CONTAINERS V/S VALUE-BASED CONTAINERS

A careful reader might have already noticed that all the containers (both template and non-template) discussed so far are *pointer based* containers. These containers store the address of (pointers to) the client supplied objects. They do not make copies of the client supplied objects. Every object in a container is still owned by the client who created it. In other words, there is no transfer of ownership. Not only are they very common, they are fast, flexible, and easy to implement. I only focus on pointer based containers. But, if the client is not careful, it can lead to dangling reference problems. To be safe, a client should not delete an object whose address has been placed in a container without first removing it from the container. If the client deletes an object that is still resident in a container, and then the client asks the container to delete all the objects in the container, disaster is just waiting to happen. It requires discipline and a thorough understanding of the storage ownership responsibilities to use a pointer based container.

The other style of containers are *value based* containers. They do not store point-ers to client supplied objects but a copy of them. Every time an object is added to the container, a copy of the object is created (usually using the new() operator) and the copy is placed in the container. Such containers are definitely more safe but can be very expensive, especially when large objects are placed in the container.

INTRUSIVE AND NON-INTRUSIVE CONTAINERS

The Smalltalk style containers that require a common base class are also called *intru-sive containers* because the containers require that objects that are placed in the con-tainer provide some services to the container.

The template based containers do not require any services from the client's ob-jects. Such containers are called *non-intrusive* containers.

Implementing Heterogeneous Containers Using Pointer-Based Homogeneous Containers

It is possible to implement a heterogeneous container using void pointers. We are now going to try that with a template container.

We already know that a void pointer is capable of retaining the address of any type. Therefore, if we could build a container of void pointers, it should be a heterogeneous container. So TContainer<void*> becomes a heterogeneous container. For example, a TArray<void*> is an array of void pointers. Therefore, every slot in the array can hold the address of any type of object (see Fig. 12-15).

Here is a small code fragment that illustrates the concept:

```
void f()
{
    int i;
    int j;
    TArray<void*> voidArray;
    voidArray.Add( &i); // Add the address of an int to the container
    vs.IsMember(&j); // Check if some other address is a member of the
                     // container
    void *vp = voidArray.Remove(&i);
}
```

This looks convenient, but the situation is not that simple. Some of the member functions may not compile and work with void pointers. Such member functions that do not compile have to be specialized. If there are too many such problems, then you are bet-ter off implementing specialized containers for void pointers. The problem arises because in the declaration

```
TArray<void*> voidArray;
```

Heterogeneous Container using a
Homogeneous Container of void pointers

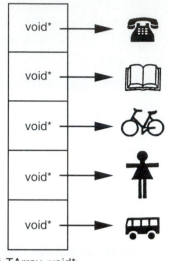

A TArray<void*>

Fig. 12-15

AType is **void***. So when the member function **Add()** is instantiated, it looks as follows:

```
TArray::Add(void** thisObject);
```

It was not our intention to add the address of a **void** pointer to the array, was it? But the template class instantiation causes this to happen. Similarly, the **Remove()** member function expands as follows:

```
void** TArray::Remove();
```

Same problem as before. The solution here is to implement a specialized set of template classes for **void** pointers. You do not have to implement all of the container classes that are available. Not everyone needs a heterogeneous container. Moreover, most of the clients would not need the entire container hierarchy for **void** pointers. Select the easy ones (such as **TArray** and **TSet**) and implement a specialization for **void** pointers.

```
class TArray<void*> {
    //...
};
```

If you do not wish to provide heterogeneous containers, that is fine too. Clients who need such classes would have to implement it themselves.

NOTE   In this section on container classes (and in the next section on iterators), the focus is on the design concepts and implementation strategies. The interface of the different container classes are only shown to illustrate the differentiating features of different types of containers. However, the interface shown is in no way complete. We are not trying to design a complete set of container classes here. Most of us would never have to go through the daunting task of implementing container classes. But, understanding their design and usage helps us all in becoming better software developers.

REMEMBER   Note that heterogeneous containers can be implemented even in languages that do not support generic types by using a common unifying base class. This has been discussed earlier in this chapter with containers that used a TItem base class. The only disadvantage with a common base class is that even primitive types must be wrapped in a class (say Int, Float, etc.).

NAVIGATING CONTAINERS

So far, we have conveniently ignored the problem of traversing a container object. What good is it if you can place objects in a container without the capability to iterate over them as needed? But, navigating a container is no easy task. The code and knowledge required to navigate a simple array is completely different from that required to navigate a set. The navigation philosophy is specific to each and every container. There is no easy answer to the navigation problem. Also, clients would like to have different styles of navigation support and satisfying all their needs is no easy task.

Any iteration scheme, irrespective of the implementation, must allow some basic operations:

1. Go to the next logical element in the container.

2. Go to the first element in the container.

3. Go to the previous element (if the container permits) in the container.

4. Get the current element in the container.

5. Remove the current element from the container.

In general, there are two styles of iterators commonly available with container classes—*Passive Iterators* and *Active Iterators* [Booch94]. They are also called *external iterators* and *internal iterators,* respectively [Gamma94]. A fundamental issue with iteration is deciding who controls the iteration—the client who uses the iterator or the iterator itself. If the client who uses the iterator controls the iteration (advancing to the next element, requesting the current element, etc.) then the iterator is considered an active (or external) iterator. Here, the client *actively* controls the iteration. When the iteration is controlled by the iterator itself, then the iterator is a passive iterator, (i.e. the client plays a *passive* role in the iteration process).

Passive Iterators

Passive iterators are implemented through functions. The container usually provides a function(s) that iterates over the container. This function accepts a pointer to another function supplied by the client. At every step in the iteration (i.e., for every item in the container), the client supplied function is called. This function returns a value that determines when the iteration is terminated. Here is an example of this scheme. Class **TContainer** provides a member function **Navigate()**, which accepts a pointer to a member function.

```
template <class AType>
class TContainer {
    public:
        // Pointer to function accepting AType and returning bool
        typedef bool (*FunctionPointer)(AType& item);

        TContainer();
        virtual ~TContainer();

        // Other details as before

        // clientFunction is called at each step in the iteration
        // This function returns true if the iteration went till the end
        // of the container. Otherwise it returns false
        virtual bool Navigate(FunctionPointer clientFunction) = 0;
};
```

Here, the client wishes to *apply* some operation (a function, **clientFunction**) to all (or a select group) of items in the container. Every derived class of container must implement **Navigate()**. The **clientFunction** returns a boolean value indicating continuation or termination of the iteration. If the client function returns true, then the iteration continues. Otherwise, the iteration stops. Note that iteration will automatically stop if the end of the container is reached. Here is a typical usage:

```
class TBook {
    public:
        TBook(const char* title, float price);
        float Price() const; // What's the price?
        TString Title() const;
        //...
    };

bool ShowPriceInfo(TBook& aBook)
{
    float price = aBook.Price();
    if (price < 25.5) {
        cout << "Book: " << aBook.Title() << " Price: " << price << endl;
        return true; // continue iteration
    }

    return false;
```

```
}

void ff(const TContainer<TBook>& bookList)
{
    bookList.Navigate(ShowPriceInfo);
    // Apply the ShowPriceInfo function to each book in the container
}
```

A **TArray** class can implement **Navigate()** as follows:

```
// This is pseudo code only

template <class AType>
TArray<AType>::Navigate(FunctionPointer clientFunction)
{
    AType* currentItem;

    // Go to the first element in the list and start
    while (clientFunction(currentItem))
        // go to the next item in the container

    if (all items in the container exhausted)
        return true;
    else return false;
}
```

Now the **Navigate()** function iterates over the container and for every **TBook** object in the container it calls the **ShowPriceInfo()** function. This continues until the end of the container is reached or **ShowPriceInfo()** (actually the function pointed by **clientFunction**) returns false, whichever happens first. The container is responsible for advancing from one item to another inside the container and maintaining the correct state.

This is quite easy to implement and is also easy to use and understand. However, it is not very powerful. Usually, clients would like to accumulate some state information during iteration and make decisions based on the accumulated state. In the passive iteration scheme, clients only supply a function and there isn't much scope for accumulating state information. Clients would have to resort to static/global variables for state accumulation. Another problem is that multiple clients cannot iterate at the same time, (i.e., only one iterator can iterate over a container at a time). This is because the container must maintain some kind of cursor inside to provide iteration. Naturally, a second call to **Navigate()** while the first one is still not complete, would overwrite the iteration state inside the container (some solutions to this problem are possible).

A somewhat better scheme of passive iteration can be implemented using objects instead of functions. Here, **Navigate()** accepts an object of a class.

```
template <class AType>
class TNavigationHelper {
    public:
        virtual bool Apply(AType& item) = 0;
        //...
};
```

```
template <class AType>
class TContainer {
    public:

        TContainer();
        virtual ~TContainer();

        // ... Other details as before

        // useThis.Apply()  is called at each step in the iteration
        // This function returns true if the iteration went till the end
        // of the container. Otherwise it returns false
        virtual bool Navigate(TNavigationHelper<AType>&  useThis) = 0;
};
```

With this scheme, a client can accumulate state in a derived class object of TNavigationHelper. Here is an example that computes the total price of all books in a container.

```
class TBookNavigationHelper : public TNavigationHelper<TBook> {
    public:
        TBookNavigationHelper() : _totalCost(0) {}
        virtual bool Apply(TBook& book);
        double TotalPrice() const { return _totalCost; }
        //...
    private:
        double _totalCost;
};

bool TBookNavigationHelper::Apply(TBook& book)
{
    _totalCost += book.Price();
    return true;
}

void ff(TContainer<TBook>& bookList)
{
    TBookNavigationHelper priceComputer;

    bookList.Navigate(priceComputer);
    cout << "Total: " << priceComputer.TotalPrice() << endl;
}
```

A client can now derive from the TNavigationHelper class and override the Apply() function to do whatever they want. This derived class can have anything it needs, making state accumulation easier.

THREAD-SAFETY   Passive iterators can be made thread-safe by using some thread synchronization mechanism. The container would maintain some internal locks to ensure iteration by a single thread. When one thread is iterating over the container, all other threads wanting to use the same container object will have to wait. This wait can be quite long if the thread currently holding the iterator performs complex operations during the iteration.

ACTIVE ITERATORS

The solution to many of the problems of passive iterators is to use an *active iterator*. As already seen, the problem is with iteration state management. To allow iteration control by client, we could try adding a set of member functions to the container class. The other problem with this approach of mixing storage philosophy and navigation into one abstraction is the lack of clear separation between the two abstractions. A container is an abstraction that provides storage where as an iterator is an abstraction that provides navigation control. It would be easier to understand the system when the two abstractions are separate. One of the first rules in data abstraction is to keep each abstraction simple and well focussed. Even though the scheme shown below is not preferred (and is very rare), it is discussed here for completeness.

```cpp
// NOT THE RIGHT APPROACH. SHOWN HERE TO ILLUSTRATE THE PROBLEMS
template <class AType>
class TContainer {
    public:
        TContainer();
        virtual ~TContainer();

        // Add a new item to the container
        virtual void Add(AType* anItem) =  0;
        // other member functions as before

        // Iteration related functions
        // Move (the imaginary iterator) to the first object in the
        // container and return a pointer to the object there
        virtual AType* First() = 0;

        // Iteration related functions
        // Move (the imaginary iterator) to the last object in the
        // container and return a pointer to the object there
        virtual AType* Last() = 0;

        // Move ( the imaginary iterator) to the next object in the
        // container and return a pointer to the object there. Return 0
        // if there is no next object.
        virtual AType* Next() = 0;

        // Return a pointer to the current object in the container  (that
        // the imaginary iterator is looking at)
        virtual AType* Current() = 0;

        // Remove current element (as indicated by the iterator) from the
        // container
        virtual void Remove() = 0;
};
```

The iteration related member functions are pure virtual because their implementation requires knowledge of the exact type of container (the code required to move to the next element in a list is entirely different from that required in a array). But definitely, these are functions that any container can support. Here is an example usage of the iterators:

```
void ff(TMailBox& mailbox)
{
    // This is an array container for TMailMessage objects only
    TArray<TMailMessage>          myMailSet;

    // Ask the mailBox to put messages in myMailSet
    mailbox.RetrieveUserMessages(myMailSet);

    // Get a pointer to the first message in the container myMailSet
    TMailMessage*         messagePtr = myMailSet.First();

    while (messagePtr ) {
        // do something with each message
        // Then move to the next message
        messagePtr = myMailSet.Next();
    }
    //...
}
```

This looks quite simple. Every derived class of **TContainer** must implement the iteration support functions. Therefore, **TArray** must implement them too. We create a **TArray** object and use the iterator functions on it.

Because these iteration support functions are embedded in the container itself, they probably use some kind of a cursor to move around in the container (see Fig. 12-16).

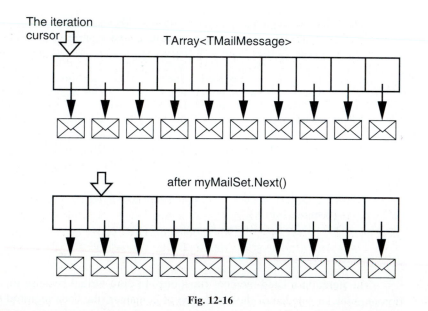

Fig. 12-16

This cursor would just be a pointer to the current element in the container. Every time some iteration function is applied on a container, the pointer would be moved to the next element in the container. Implementing these iteration functions is quite easy.

A TSequencedContainer would also add a member function to move to the previous element in the container and a TIndexedContainer would also allow you to move to any element in the container.

Consider a situation where you are looking at a container of char elements, searching for palindromes. One easy way of doing that is to scan from both ends of the container matching characters. While scanning the container, once we reach the middle of the container, our search is complete and the set of characters in the container represents a palindrome. How can this be accomplished with the iterator functions? The function Search-ForPalindrome() shown below only accepts containers of type TSequencedContainer because it uses two iterators, one from the beginning and another from the end.

```
bool SearchForPalindrome(TSequencedContainer<char>& charContainer)
{
    char* begin = charContainer.First(); // ❶ Get the first character
    char* end = charContainer.Last();    // ❷ Get the last character
    // #o f character in container/2
    unsigned count = charContainer.HowMany()/2;

    while (count-- && (*begin == *end) ) { // characters match
        begin = charContainer.Next(); // Advance one step
        end = charContainer.Previous(); // Move back a step from tail
    }
    if (count <= 0) return true;  // all characters matched
    return false;                 // not a palindrome
}
```

This looks ridiculously simple. But, you would be surprised to find that it never works correctly. Further scrutiny reveals the flaw. The container provides functions for iterating and these functions maintain an internal cursor to keep track of the current state of iteration.

❶ When the iterator function First() is called, the cursor moves to the first element in the container.

❷ This is immediately followed by a call to Last() to place another cursor at the end of the container. That also succeeds but not without damaging the previous operation. Since there is only one cursor per container, you can only have one iterator active in the container at any time. When a user invokes one of the iteration functions on a container, the internal cursor is modified. So our call to Last() moved the cursor (which was at the first element because of the previous call to First()) to the last element. This is where everything went wrong. There is no way to save the position of a cursor. Therefore, multiple iterators for the same container are not possible. At any time the iteration scheme only remembers one position within the container. Each of the iteration functions move the same cursor. This scheme is again fraught with the same problems of passive iterators.

THREAD-SAFETY   This problem is even more serious in multi-threaded environments. If two threads (or processes) want to iterate over the same container concurrently, they are out of luck.

The iteration state is encapsulated within the container and the threads will interfere with the iteration steps of each other. Moreover, it is not possible to save the iteration information outside the container so that the iteration can be restarted later; the container does not provide any information about the state of iteration to the client.

Furthermore, clients do not have much control over the style of iteration. We must just accept whatever the iteration functions provide. Not all clients have the same needs when iterating over a container. Some clients would want an iteration that follows some order (ascending or descending). Such needs cannot be met easily in this scheme.

Iterators as Objects

Looking back, even though each container is different, we abstracted the general interface of a container in a common base class **TContainer**. The interface of **TContainer** is general enough to be adaptable by any specific derived class. The same technique can be used here with iterators.

Every iterator must allow some basic operations:

1. Associate the iterator with a container.

2. Go to the next logical element in the container.

3. Go to the previous element (if supported by the iterator) in the container.

4. Go to the first element in the container.

5. Compare one iterator with another.

These are common operations for any container and can be implemented for almost all types of containers. But their implementation is very specific to the type of the container. So, why can't we just create an abstract base class for iterators?

We still have one more issue to deal with. A templatized container is instantiated with a specific argument. So we can create a **TArray** for **TMailMessage** objects or a **TList** for **TStudent** objects. How can we use the same iterator object to iterate over a container of **TMailMessage** objects and a container of **TStudent** objects. We solved this problem in containers by making the container a template class. The type of the objects in the container is determined by the template argument supplied by the client instantiating a container object. Along the same lines, we can create templatized iterator classes. An iterator for a **TList** of **TStudent** objects can only iterate over a **TList<TStudent>** but not over a **TArray** of **TMailMessage** objects. This is the same restriction we had in containers (no mixing of types). With this knowledge, we are ready to create our abstract iterator class.

```
// Only a skeleton of the class is shown—it is not complete.
// See discussion below for more additions to this class

template <class AType>
class TIterator {
    public:
        virtual ~TIterator();
```

```
        // Move the iterator to the first object in the container and
        // return a pointer to the object there
        virtual AType* First() = 0;

        // Move the iterator to the last object in the container and
        // return a pointer to the object there
        virtual AType* Last() = 0;

        // Move the iterator to the next object in the container and
        // return a pointer to the object there. Return 0 if there is no
        // next object.
        virtual AType* Next() = 0;

        // Return a pointer to the current object in the container  that
        // the iterator is looking at.
        virtual AType* Current() = 0;
    private:
        // Implementation data
};
```

This is a simple class whose interface is very easy to understand and use. However, we cannot instantiate this class. Every specific type of container requires custom implementation of this class. Class **TSet** must implement a separate iterator class, **TSetIterator**, and class **TDictionary** must implement a **TDictionaryIterator**. Each of these iterators only know how to iterate over their corresponding containers. Therefore, **TSetIterator** would know how to iterate over a **TSet** and **TDictionaryIterator** knows how to iterate over a **TDictionary**. Therefore, there will be a derived class of **TIterator** corresponding to each derived class of **TContainer**. Here is the parallel iterator hierarchy (Fig. 12-17) for our container classes shown earlier in Fig. 12-14.

```
template <class AType>
class TSetIterator : public TIterator {
    public:
        TSetIterator(TSet<AType>* forThisContainer);
        TSetIterator(); // not attached to any container

        // Move the iterator to the first object in the container and
        // return a pointer to the object there
        virtual AType* First();

        // Move the iterator to the last object in the container and
        // return a pointer to the object there
        virtual AType* Last();

        // Move the iterator to the next object in the container and
        // return a pointer to the object there. Return 0 if there is no
        // next object.
        virtual AType* Next();

        // Return a pointer to the current object in the container that
        // the iterator is looking at.
        virtual AType* Current();
    private:
        // Implementation data
};
```

Iterator Hierarchy for the Container Classes

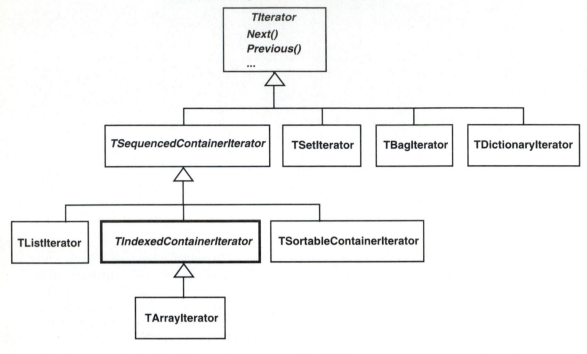

Fig. 12-17

An iterator for a **TSequencedContainerIterator** would have the following interface:

```
template <class AType>
class TSequencedContainerIterator : public TIterator<AType> {
    public:

        // All other pure virtual member functions are inherited as it is
        // from TIterator.

        // Move the iterator to the previous  object in the container and
        // return a pointer to the object there. Return 0 if there  is no
        // previous object.
        virtual AType* Previous() = 0;

    private:
        // Implementation data
};
```

Clients can now create any number of iterators for a container because every iterator is an independent object. Our palindrome example will work correctly with this iterator hierarchy. Now it is also possible to copy and assign iterator objects. Since each iterator is a separate object, it maintains its own state independent of the container (and other iterator objects). This scheme is also perfect for multi-threaded environments. Each thread can create its own iterator object without affecting any other thread (but some coordination and control among the multiple iterators is required).

We are still not done! Let's revisit the palindrome example again. The function SearchForPalindrome() receives a TSequencedContainer object polymorphically. It can be a TSet, TArray, or any other container. Inside SearchForPalindrome we must create two distinct iterator objects to take care of proper iteration from both ends. But, what type of iterator should we create? If we know the exact type of the container that has been passed as the actual argument, then we can create the appropriate container. How do we create an iterator without knowing the true type of the container?

We have already solved a similar problem earlier in this chapter. Remember the problem of creating the appropriate TMenu object. We are in a similar situation here. Why don't we just let the container deal with the problem of creating the appropriate iterator object? The container should know what iterator is needed to iterate on it. So, let's add a new member function CreateIterator() to the TContainer class. This will be a pure virtual function.

```
template <class AType>
class TContainer {
    public:
        // ...
        // Add a new item to the container
        virtual void Add(AType* anItem) =  0;
        // other member functions as earlier
        // The returned iterator is owned by the caller. It should be
        // deleted after use.
        virtual TIterator<AType>* CreateIterator() = 0;
        friend class TIterator; // See discussion below
};
```

It is that simple. Derived classes of TContainer implement this member function correctly.

```
template <class AType>
class TSet : public TContainer<AType> {
    public:
        // Add a new item to the container
        virtual void Add(AType* anItem);
        // other member functions as earlier
        virtual TSetIterator<AType>*  CreateIterator()  {
            return new TSetIterator<AType>(this);
        }
        friend class TSetIterator; // See discussion below
};
```

A TSet container must create a TSetIterator and a TArray must create a TArrayIterator. Dynamic binding does the trick here.

NOTE   This scheme does not come for free. The iterator returned by **CreateIterator** is a dynamically created object. So, to start with, we are paying for the cost of creating a dynamic object. Since the iterator returned is a polymorphic object, all operations on it would be done through virtual functions. That's another added cost. If the type of the iterator was known statically, even calls to virtual functions can be bound at compile time. Finally, when the iterator is no longer needed, it must be disposed off. A call to **delete** (again dynamically bound) is required.

Now we are ready to solve the palindrome problem correctly. As mentioned earlier, **SearchForPalindrome()** only accepts containers that maintain a sequence because it iterates from both ends simultaneously.

NOTE   You can test this example by using the **TArray** and **TArrayIterator** class implementations provided at the end of this chapter. The code is not shown here because the implementation code is too big and breaks the continuity of the discussion.

```
void SearchForPalindrome(TSequencedContainer<char>& charContainer)
{
    bool result = false;
    TSequencedContainerIterator<char>* begin =
                        charContainer.CreateIterator(); // ❶
    TSequencedContainerIterator<char>* end    =
                        charContainer.CreateIterator();  // ❷

    char* first = begin->First(); // ❸ Move iterator to first character
    char* last  = end->Last();    // ❹ Move iterator to last character
    unsigned count = charContainer.HowMany()/2;

    while (count— && (*first == *last) ) { // characters match
        first = begin->Next(); // ❺ Advance iterator one step forward
        last = end->Previous(); // ❻ Move iterator one step back
    }
    if (count <= 0) result = true;

    delete     begin; // Dispose off the dynamically allocated iterator
    delete     end;

    return result;
}
```

❶ Here we get the first iterator from the container.

❷ This returns another iterator for the same container. If it was possible, we could have *Cloned* the first iterator to get the second one. See the discussion about virtual constructors earlier in this chapter.

❸ We move the iterator to the first character in the container. This operation returns a pointer to the current element in the container, which is stored in **first**.

❹ The other iterator is moved to the last element in the container and the pointer returned is stored in **last**.

❺ If the characters compare equal, we move the first iterator to the next element.

❻ We move the second iterator to the previous element in the container and continue the comparison operation. If we compare one half of the string with the other half, and they are equal it is a palindrome.

It is easy to create more than one iterator for the same container (see Fig 12-18).

```
void ff(TMailBox& mailbox)
{
    TArray<TMailMessage> myMailSet;

    mailbox.RetrieveUserMessages(myMailSet); // Get message into myMailSet
    TArrayIterator<TMailMessage> first(myMailSet); // An iterator
    TArrayIterator<TMailMessage> second(myMailSet); // Another one
    second.Last(); // Move it to the end
    //...
}
```

Finally, how can we implement fast, efficient iterators? The speed of iteration is stressed because none of us want to spend considerable CPU cycles just doing iteration on containers. In particular, when built-in arrays are used, simple pointers (and integers) are used as iterators and they are blazingly fast. These active iterators must be comparable in speed.

The iterator implementation requires access to the internal implementation details of the container. Every iterator class must have a thorough understanding of the container class for which it is implemented. In other words, there is a tight coupling between the iterator and the corresponding container. Therefore, it makes perfect sense to establish a friend relationship between the container and iterator. The container class grants friendship to the iterator.

Implementing an active iterator is no trivial task. It requires a very good understanding of the container class and much more. The container and the iterators must cooperate to ensure that no damage is done to the container no matter how many iterators are created. It is even more difficult in cases where the container is being modified when iterators are present. Imagine what happens if an element currently being visited by an iterator is deleted by some other iterator. Multi-threaded environments add to the complexity. When the container can be modified while there are iterators outstanding, some kind of communication between the container and the iterators is required. Most implementations require the iterators to register with the container. When items are added or removed from

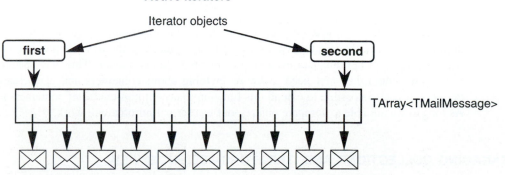

Fig. 12-18

Table 12-2 Comparison of Passive Iterators and Active Iterators

Passive Iterator	Active Iterator
The iterator is a <u>function</u> that traverses the structure of the container calls client supplied function at each step of the iteration provides traversal control through parameters to the function	The iterator is an <u>object</u> that traverses the structure of a container and exports operations to control the traversal maintains its own state
Advantages Easy to understand and implement Iterators cannot be copied - safe	*Advantages* Can be stored (saved) by clients Any number of iterators per container Can provide direction control
Disadvantages Cannot save the iterator Cannot have multiple iterators per container	*Disadvantages* Very complex; hence hard to implement Slower because more function calls Copying semantics have to be clearly defined Storage management responsibilities must be clearly defined

the container, the container itself can update the internal state of the iterators to reflect the changes in the container. Most of us would not have to implement container classes, but it is good to know the difficulty involved and the techniques used.

NOTE   The SearchForPalindrome() function can also ask the caller to provide two iterators, instead of it (the function) creating iterators explicitly. This makes it easy for clients to pass only parts of containers for palindrome test rather than whole containers. And the function need not know anything about the container. The prototype of SearchForPalindrome with this modification would be

```
bool SearchForPalindrome(TSequencedContainerIterator<char>& begin,
                         TSequencedContainerIterator<char>& end)
{
    // Now begin points to the beginning of the string where the sequence
    // starts and end points to the end of the sequence. Use the supplied
    // iterators to access elements in the container. Most of the code as
    // shown earlier
}
```

This design also makes it easy to even pass non-contiguous sequences for palindrome test because the iterator always knows how to move to the next (or previous) element. Specialized iterators can even skip elements in the container. This way, SearchForPalindrome() does not need to know anything about containers and also creating iterators. It is also possible to extend this function to accept non-character containers too. As long as we are able to compare objects, our test for palindrome will work.

MANAGING COLLECTIONS AND ITERATORS—CLIENT'S VIEW

When using containers and iterators, designers have a choice as to how they would like to provide access to a container. Let us use the example of the TMailBox class again.

Style 1. Create and Return an Iterator from the Container for the User to Use

Here, the TMailBox implementor provides an iterator to navigate the list of TMailMessage objects in the mail box (which would be some container). The client receiving the iterator can access any element in the container by using the iterator. If the container is modified while the client is iterating (e.g., a new TMailMessage is placed in the mail box), the changes are immediately seen by the client, which is an advantage. However, this scheme can be dangerous if the iterator allows unrestricted access to the container. A naive client can do severe damage to the container. It might be better to return a controlled iterator. For example, a read-only iterator that allows the client to read the contents of the container but does not allow modifications to the container through the iterator is safer. But, implementing such iterators is not easy.

Style 2. Return a Container by Value that the User Can Manipulate by Using Iterators

Here, the TMailBox implementor returns a container (or copies the messages to a container) to the client. The client receiving the container has complete freedom to operate on the returned container. This protects the mail box from any damage caused by the client. But, copying messages (i.e., an entire container) is an expensive operation both in terms of memory and speed.

The client must create and manage an iterator to navigate the container. The advantage is that the clients can use containers of their choice. The mail box doesn't care about the true type of the container passed in by the client. An alternative is to have the TMailBox class return a dynamically created container. This would be useful to clients that are not very familiar with different types of containers. The client must remember to dispose off the returned container when they are done with it. This scheme suffers from the *stale* data problem. As soon as the TMailBox object returns a container, the data in the container is stale because a new message might have been added to the mailbox after the copying of messages from the container. So the user only receives a snap shot of the state of the mailbox. This could be useless in highly dynamic situations. Imagine returning a container of threads in an operating system. Because threads come and go frequently, the container of threads would be out of sync with the current state of the operating system almost immediately. However, if the objects in the container cannot be copied, then there is no other choice than returning an iterator. Both styles are shown below:

```
class TMailBox {

    public:
            // Style 1:  Return an iterator into the container
        TIterator<TMailMessage>* CreateMessageIterator() const;

            // Style 2 - Return a copy of the container
        // Return the list of messages for this user  in the container
        // "storeInThis". Caller is free to pick the exact container type

        void RetrieveUserMessages(TContainer<TMailMessage>&
                                        storeInThis);
```

```
                // Also Style 2 - Return a copy of the container
                // In this case, the MailBox returns a dynamically allocated
                // Container of messages. The caller is responsible for
                // deallocating the storage in the  returned container.

                TContainer<TMailMessage>* RetrieveUserMessages() const;
};

void Foo(TMailBox& m)
{
        // Style 1
        TIterator<TMailMessage>* messageIterator = m.CreateMessageIterator();
        // ... Use the iterator
        delete messageIterator1;

        // Style 2
        TIterator<TMailMessage>* itr; // An iterator pointer
        TContainer<TMailMessage>* cm = m.RetrieveUserMessages();
        // Create an iterator for the container returned
        itr = cm->CreateIterator();
        //... Use the iterator to navigate the container
        delete itr; // dispose it off

        // Also Style 2
        TArray<TMailMessage> messageArray;
        m.RetrieveUserMessages(messageArray);
        // Mailbox writes the messages to container,  messageArray
        TArrayIterator<TMailMessage> iterator(&messageArray);
        // use the iterator object
}
```

It might be better to support both styles, as shown above in the **TMailBox** class. This way, the clients are free to pick their choice—the class does not force upon them what it feels is correct. But, you may not have this freedom in all classes.

SMALLTALK   Iterators don't have to be defined explicitly in Smalltalk. The standard collection classes (discussed earlier) define an internal iterator method do: which takes a block as an argument. Each element in the collection is bound to the local variable in the block, and then the block is executed.

Table 12-3 Two styles of Managing Containers and Iterators

Returning Container by Value (Style 2)	Returning an Iterator into a Container (Style 1)
Advantages	*Advantages*
The original container is safe.	No storage management problems for the user.
The client can choose the container type.	Fast, because nothing is copied.
(by passing it in by reference/pointer)	Users are free to follow their style of navigation.
	The contents of the container reflects the actual state.
Disadvantages	*Disadvantages*
The client is responsible for storage management and how/what iterator to use	Client has direct access to the container, it is not very safe
The container is only a snap shot of the state. With containers that are constantly updated, the information in the container is *stale*.	Client must remember to dispose of the iterator once done with it.

This is equivalent to applying a function to each element in the container. For example, here is a Smalltalk code fragment that uses the **Bag** container. Here class **BeerBustItem** represents an item which is essential for a drinks party. A new **BeerBustItem** is created by using the message **name: description price: number**. Furthermore, each BeerBustItem's price can be had by sending the message **cost:** to it.

```
shoppingBag <- Bag new.
shoppingBag add: (BeerBustItem name: #PepsiSixPack  price:3.00).
shoppingBag add: (BeerBustItem name: #ChivasRegalScotch  price: 4.50).
shoppingBag add: (BeerBustItem name: #LowFatChips price: 2.50).
shoppingBag add: (BeerBustItem name: #CubanCigar  price: 12.00)
                                       withOccurrences: 6.
```

This code adds items essential for a beer bust into a shopping bag (a **Bag** container). The message **withOccurrences** is a standard message for a **Bag** container which replicates the item a specified number of times. Now, to compute the total bill, we write a **do:** block as follows:

```
totalBill <- 0.
shoppingBag do: [:eachPartyItem | totalBill <- totalBill +
    eachPartyItem cost]
```

Here **do:** indicates the beginning of the block and **eachPartyItem** is the block argument. The expressions following the | are the expressions that make up the block. When this **do:** block is applied to an object, the block is evaluated once for each element contained in the data structure (container). One could imagine that a **do:** block is like a **for** loop. Each element in the container is set to be the value of the block argument (**eachPartyItem**) and the **do:** block is evaluated. The expressions in the **do:** block can be anything desired. This is very identical to our iterators discussed above. By the way, let me know if you ever find Chivas Regal scotch whiskey for $4.50!

Smalltalk container classes also support many other enumeration (iteration) messages. Some of them are shown below in Table 12-4.

THE C++ STANDARD TEMPLATE LIBRARY (STL)

A discussion of container classes wouldn't be complete without at least a cursory look at the standard template library, usually referred to as STL. This (STL) is perhaps one of the major additions into the standard C++ library. STL is a templatized library of **containers**,

Table 12-4 Iterators for Smalltalk Collections

do: aBlock	Evaluate the block once for every item in the container
select: aBlock	Evaluate the argument (aBlock) once for each element in the container and collect into a new container all those elements for which aBlock evaluates to true.
reject: aBlock	Almost same as select but collects those elements for which aBlock evaluates to false (used for conditional selections)
collect: aBlock	Return a new collection that contains the value returned by the block on each evaluation of aBlock (used for transformations).
detect: aBlock	Evaluate aBlock for each element and return the first element for which the evaluation is true (like finding the first item matching a criterion).

algorithms, and **iterators**. It uses operator overloading heavily in its implementation. A copy of STL implementation is shipped with most C++ compilers. The STL does not use any virtual functions. Its primary focus is on generic programming and efficiency. STL allows straightforward implementation of software components in economic and expressive ways. But, unless you are highly comfortable with templates, you shouldn't even take a look at it. STL also enables significant levels of source code reuse. At the same time STL promotes new and powerful programming techniques.

All the STL classes are very generic. They are designed and implemented so as to work with many different kinds of containers and algorithms. In essence, STL algorithms pretend to be ignorant of the implementation details. For example, the **search** and **sort** algorithms never assume anything about the size of containers. Instead they work on ranges which are delineated by iterators supplied by the user.

STL Containers

STL provides a basic selection of sequenceable container classes. These containers organize their objects into a strict linear arrangement (like an array). The major sequenceable containers are:

```
deque
list
vector
```

It also provides classes **priority_que**, **queue**, and **stack** which are built using the basic sequences. In addition, class **bitset**, which is another sequenceable container capable of manipulating fixed-size sequence of bits, is also provided.

Here is a synopsis of class **vector**:

```
template <class T, class Allocator = allocator>
class vector {
    // Various typedef statements are included
    explicit vector(Allocator& = Allocator()); // a basic constructor
    // Iterators
    const_iterator       begin();
    iterator             begin();
    iterator             end();
    const_iteratorend();
    reverse_iterator     rbegin();
    reverse_iterator     rend();

    size_type size();       // size_type is a typedef for size_t
    size_type max_size();

    T& operator[](size_type n);
    void push_back(const T& x);
};
```

STL allows users to provide their own specialized memory allocators. And a default memory allocator is provided for users who don't want to bother with special memory allocators.

STL also provides associative containers (like our **TDictionary** classes discussed earlier).

```
set
multiset
map
multimap
```

Class **multiset** allows duplication of elements (like a bag). On the same lines, multimap allows multiple copies of the same key and value.

Iterators

Most operations on vectors require some notion of a position within the vector. Traditionally in C and C++ this is represented by a pointer. Pointers are very fast but they can be dangerous if the programmer is not careful. STL supports iterators instead of ordinary pointers but tries to provide the same degree of efficiency as ordinary pointers. With arrays and pointers, we usually write:

```
int intArray[100];
//... fill it
for (int i=0; i < 100; i++) intArray[i] = i;

int* ip = intArray;
while (ip != (intArray + 100)) cout << *ip++; // print the values stored
```

The STL code for the same operation is surprisingly similar:

```
vector<int> intVector;
//... fill intVector
for (int i=0; i < 100; i++) intVector[i] = i;

// Create an iterator and make it point to the beginning
vector<int>::iterator  itr = intVector.begin();
while (itr != intVector.end())          //  Go until the end of the vector
     cout << *itr++;                    // print the element there
```

These iterators can be used to move through containers. Different classes of iterators (input, output, forward, bidirectional, random, etc.) are provided. A container's start and end (in fact, 'one past the end') are given by **begin()** and **end()** member functions of every container. These member functions return iterator objects. Using these iterators one can navigate all the elements in a container. Iterators support convenient overloaded operators like **operator++**. This makes them look just like pointers.

Algorithms in STL

Container classes provide member functions and iterators for fundamental operations. But, we also need more powerful and flexible algorithms. Many basic algorithms are provided in the STL algorithms library. These algorithms are template functions parameterized on iterators and often also on functions.

Algorithms that do not modify containers include:

```
// Apply function F to each element between first and last
template <class InputIterator, class Function>
Function for_each(InputIterator first, InputIterator last, Function F);

// Find a specified "value" in the container
InputIterator find(InputIterator first, InputIterator last, const T&
                    value);

// find an element i  for which predicate(*i)==true
InputIterator find_if(InputIterator first, InputIterator last, Predicate
                    pred);
// and many others
```

Algorithms that modify the container include:

```
// Copy elements between (first, last) to result
OutputIterator copy(InputIterator first, InputIterator last, OutputIterator
                    result);

// transform elements between (first, last) with op and put in result
OutputIterator transform(InputIterator first, InputIterator last,
                    OutputIterator result, UnaryOperation op);
// and many others
```

Sorting algorithms include:

```
// Sort elements between (first, last)
void sort(RandomAccessIterator first, RandomAccessIterator last);

// Relative order among equal elements is preserved
void stable_sort(RandomAccessIterator first, RandomAccessIterator last);
// and many others
```

There are also algorithms for merge, binary search, partial sort, copy, etc.

Here is a simple example that uses the vector to perform some operations using the STL algorithms.

```
int intArray[100];
//
for (int i=(10-1); i >= 0 ; i—) intArray[i] = i;
// Now let's sort it
sort(v.begin(), v.end());

// square each element of in the vector of integers
void Square (int i) {cout <<  (i*i) << " " ; }
for_each(v.begin(), v.end(), Square );

// Replace all even elements by -1
int  IsEven(int i) { return i/2 == 0; }
replace_if(intArray.begin(), intArray.end(), IsEven, -1};
```

The key feature here is the use of iterators to specify ranges. When operations are applied to containers, one must specify the bounds of the operation. Typically, this is done by specifying indexes for arrays. But, that approach wouldn't work for non-array containers. To make it really flexible, STL uses iterators to specify the bounds. Every operation accepts two iterators (begin and end), that denote a range in the container to which the operation must be applied. For example, the sort operation shown below uses two client supplied iterators to navigate the container.

```
sort(RandomAccessIterator first, RandomAccessIterator last);
```

This way, the operation (**sort** here) need not know how to navigate the container. That responsibility is left to the iterators supplied. Moreover, the client can call this function to sort only parts of a container by using different iterators. This is a major benefit of using iterators. One could imagine that these iterators are like pointers. A client provides two pointers that are set at some locations in the container. The operation uses these pointers to navigate the container. Unlike primitive pointers, increment and decrement operations for these pointers is implemented in the iterator class itself.

With this approach, an operation that deals with containers need not know anything about the layout and navigation of the container. The navigation responsibility (and the associated complexity) is left to the iterators.

Our earlier **SearchForPalindrome** function can be implemented using STL iterators very easily. Here is the code for the function.

```
template <class ForwardIterator, class BackwardIterator>
bool SearchForPalindrome(ForwardIterator first, BackwardIterator last)
{
    int n = 0;
    // The distance function increments n by the number of times it takes
    // to get to last from first
    distance(first, last, n);
    n /= 2;
    while (n--)
        if (*first++ != *last--)  // search for palindrome failed
                return false;

    return true;// Yes, it is a palindrome
}
```

Here is a test program.

```
main()
{
    vector<int> intVector(10); // Create a vector
    //... fill intVector
    for (int i=0; i < 5; i++) // Populate it with integers
            intVector[i] = i;

    for (int i=5; i < 10; i++) // Repeat the steps
            intVector[i] = 9-i;
```

```
    vector<int>::iterator  itr1 = intVector.begin();    // Get iterator to
                                                        // first element
    vector<int>::iterator  itr2 = intVector.end();      // Get iterator to
                                                        // last element

    if (SearchForPalindrome(itr1, —itr2)) // This one should succeed
        cout << "YES, IT IS A PALINDROME" << endl;
    else cout << "NOT A PALINDROME" << endl;

    —itr2;  // move back by one element
    if (SearchForPalindrome(++itr1, —itr2)) // This one should fail
        cout << "YES, IT IS A PALINDROME"" << endl;
    else cout << "NOT A PALINDROME" << endl;
}
```

STL is widely becoming the library of choice for containers and iterators. Most compilers ship with an implementation of STL. The preceding paragraphs just provide a very brief overview of what STL supports. Serious C++ programmers should understand and try to use STL when containers and iterators are needed.

SUMMARY

Inheritance is a very powerful concept that can be very useful in solving a myriad of problems.

Understand the cost of inheritance before using it in any problem solution.

Double dispatching is not required in most situations. It is expensive and is not easy to understand.

Container classes bring out many design and implementation issues. Most of us will never implement our own containers, especially after the widespread support for standard template library, but it is worth understanding the issues.

IMPLEMENTATION CODE FOR TARRAY CONTAINER

The code below is presented just as an example implementation to test some of the code samples presented in this chapter. It is in no way perfect and is not the most efficient either. In particular, there are no optimizations to eliminate code replication. It just shows a simple implementation of a specific container class and its associated iterator.

```cpp
const unsigned INITIAL_SIZE = 256;
const unsigned CHUNK_SIZE = 32;

/*
 * Some disclaimers: This array is a dynamically growing array
 * If initial size is not specified, a default size is assumed.
 * When the array is full, it grows automatically
 */

template <class AType>
class TArray : public TIndexedContainer<AType> {
    public:
        TArray(size_t initialSize = INITIAL_SIZE, size_t growthRate =
            CHUNK_SIZE );
        virtual ~TArray();

        // Add a new item to the container
        virtual void Add(AType* anItem);

        // Looks for thisItem in the container and if found removes it
        // from the container and returns it. Only the first instance of
        // thisItem in the container is removed. Uses the comparison
        // operator == to determine equality of objects.
        virtual AType* Remove(const AType& thisItem);

        // Similar to Remove, but removes all instances of thisItem
        // Returns a pointer to the last occurrence
        virtual AType* RemoveAllOccurrences(const AType& thisItem);

        // Removes every object from the container. Nothing happens to
        // objects that were stored. They are not deleted but they no
        // longer exist in the container
        void MakeEmpty();

        // Deletes every object stored in the container. Careful, object
        // are remove from the container and then delete operator is
        // invoked on them.
        void DeleteAll();

        // Is thisItem in the container? Again operator== is used to
        // determine equality of objects
        virtual bool IsMember(const AType& thisItem) const;

        // How many Item objects in the container?
        virtual size_t HowMany() const;

        // Append the contents of the argument container to this
```

```cpp
            // container
            void Add(const TContainer<AType>&  otherContainer);

            // Return a pointer to the element (if any) before obj
            virtual AType* ElementAfter(const AType& obj) const;
            // Return a pointer to the element (if any) after obj
            virtual AType* ElementBefore(const AType& obj) const;
            virtual AType* LastElement() const;
            virtual AType* FirstElement() const;

        virtual size_t HowManyOccurrences(const AType& obj) const;
        virtual AType* ElementAt(size_t index) const;
        // Insert a new element at the specified index. Every element
        // after this element is moved one place to the right.
        virtual AType* InsertAt(size_t index,  AType* item);
        // Replace the element at specified index with this new element
        // Return the element already contained there.
        virtual AType* ReplaceAt(size_t index,  AType* item);
        // Return the index of this obj in the container. If obj
        // is not found, return -1
        size_t IndexOfElement(const AType& obj) const;

        // Grow the size of the array by howMuch
        void Extend(size_t howMuch);
        virtual TArrayIterator<AType>* CreateIterator();
        //...

        private:
            size_t PrivateIsMember(const AType& element, size_t fromWhere =
                                                                 0) const;
            AType **_elements;
            size_t _chunkSize;
            size_t _size; // allocated array size
            size_t  _count; // # of element stored
            size_t _index;// index where next element is stored
            friend class TArrayIterator<AType>;
};

template <class AType>
class TIterator {
     public:
         TIterator(TContainer<AType>* forThisContainer);
         TIterator(); // not attached to any container
         virtual ~TIterator() {}

         // Move the iterator to the first object in the container
         // and return a pointer to the object there
         virtual AType* First() = 0;

         // Move the iterator to the last object in the container
         // and return a pointer to the object there
         virtual AType* Last() = 0;

         // Move the iterator to the next object in the container
         // and return a pointer to the object there. Return 0 if there
         // is no next object.
         virtual AType* Next() = 0;
```

```cpp
        // Return a pointer to the current object in the container
        // that the iterator is looking at.
        virtual AType* Current() = 0;
    private:
        // Implementation data
};


template <class AType>
class TSequencedContainerIterator : public TIterator<AType> {
    public:
        TSequencedContainerIterator();
        virtual ~TSequencedContainerIterator();

        // Move the iterator to the first object in the container
        // and return a pointer to the object there
        AType* First() = 0;

        // Move the iterator to the last object in the container
        // and return a pointer to the object there
        AType* Last() = 0;

        // Move the iterator to the next object in the container
        // and return a pointer to the object there. Return 0 if there
        // is no next object.
        AType* Next() = 0;

        // Return a pointer to the current object in the container
        // that the iterator is looking at.
        AType* Current() = 0;

        // Move the iterator to the previous  object in the container
        // and return a pointer to the object there. Return 0 if there
        // is no previous object.
        virtual AType* Previous() = 0;
    private:
        // Implementation data
};

template <class AType>
class TIndexedContainerIterator : public TSequencedContainerIterator<AType> {
    public:
        TIndexedContainerIterator(TIndexedContainer<AType>* thisOne);
        TIndexedContainerIterator();
        virtual ~TIndexedContainerIterator();

        // Move the iterator to the first object in the container
        // and return a pointer to the object there
        AType* First() = 0;

        // Move the iterator to the last object in the container
        // and return a pointer to the object there
        AType* Last() = 0;

        // Move the iterator to the next object in the container
        // and return a pointer to the object there. Return 0 if there
```

```
                // is no next object.
                AType* Next() = 0;

                // Return a pointer to the current object in the container
                // that the iterator is looking at.
                AType* Current() = 0;

                // Move the iterator to the previous  object in the container
                // and return a pointer to the object there. Return 0 if there
                // is no previous object.
                AType* Previous() = 0;
};

template <class AType>
class TArrayIterator : public TIndexedContainerIterator<AType> {
     public:
                TArrayIterator(TArray<AType>* thisOne);
                TArrayIterator();
                virtual ~TArrayIterator() {}

                // Move the iterator to the first object in the container
                // and return a pointer to the object there
                AType* First() ;

                // Move the iterator to the last object in the container
                // and return a pointer to the object there
                AType* Last();

                // Move the iterator to the next object in the container
                // and return a pointer to the object there. Return 0 if there
                // is no next object.
                AType* Next();

                // Return a pointer to the current object in the container
                // that the iterator is looking at.
                AType* Current();

                // Move the iterator to the previous  object in the container
                // and return a pointer to the object there. Return 0 if there
                // is no previous object.
                AType* Previous();
     private:
                AType** _pointer;
                size_t _current;
                TArray<AType>* _container;
                // Implementation data
};

template <class AType>
TArray<AType>::TArray(size_t initialSize, size_t chunkSize)
{
     if (initialSize < 0)
           initialSize = INITIAL_SIZE;

     _elements = new AType*[initialSize]; // Allocate an array of pointers
     for(int i = 0; i < initialSize; ++i)
           _elements[i] = 0;
```

```cpp
    _size = initialSize;
    _count = 0;
    _index = 0;
    _chunkSize = chunkSize;
}


template <class AType>
size_t TArray<AType>::PrivateIsMember(const AType& obj, size_t where) const
{
    for(int i = where; i < _index; i++)
        if (*_elements[i] == obj)
                return i;
    return -1;
}

template <class AType>
TArray<AType>::~TArray()
{
    delete [] _elements;
}

template <class AType>
void TArray<AType>::Extend(size_t howmuch)
{
    _size += howmuch;
    AType** ptr = new AType*[_size];
    // Now copy elements
    int i;
    for (i = 0; i < _index; i++)
        ptr[i] = elements[i]; // Copy elements
    for( ; i < _size; i++)     // zero the rest
        ptr[i] = 0;

    delete [] _elements;
    _elements = ptr;
}

template <class AType>
void TArray<AType>::Add(AType* item)
{
    if (item) {
        _elements[_index++] = item; // append item
        _count++;
    }
}

template <class AType>
AType* TArray<AType>::Remove(const AType& thisItem)
{
    AType* rv = 0;

    size_t where = PrivateIsMember(thisItem);
    if (where >= 0) { // element exists in the array
        AType* rv = _elements[where];
        _elements[where] = 0;
        _count-;
```

```
        }

        return rv;
}

template <class AType>
AType* TArray<AType>::RemoveAllOccurrences(const AType& thisItem)
{
        AType* rv = 0;
        size_t where = 0;

        while ( (where = PrivateIsMember(thisItem, where)) >= 0 ) {
                AType* rv = _elements[where];
                _elements[where] = 0;
                where++;
                _count--;
        }

        return rv;
}

template <class AType>
void TArray<AType>::MakeEmpty()
{
        for(int i=0; i < _index; i++) {
                _elements[i] = 0;
        }
        _count = 0;
}

template <class AType>
void TArray<AType>::DeleteAll()
{
        for(int i=0; i < _size; i++) {
                if (_elements[i])
                        delete _elements[i];
        }
        _count = 0;
        _index = 0;
}

template <class AType>
bool TArray<AType>::IsMember(const AType& thisItem) const
{
        if (PrivateIsMember(thisItem))
                return true;

        return false;
}

template <class AType>
size_t TArray<AType>::HowMany() const
{
        return _count;
}
```

```
template <class AType>
void TArray<AType>:: Add(const TContainer<AType>&  otherContainer)
{
     size_t nItems = otherContainer.HowMany();

     if (nItems > 0) {
          TIterator* iter = otherContainer.CreateIterator();
          AType* element = iter.First();
          while (nItems— && element) {
               this->Add(element);
               element = iter.Next();
          }
          delete iter;
     }
}


template <class AType>
AType* TArray<AType>::ElementAfter(const AType& obj) const
{
     size_t where = PrivateIsMember(obj);

     if (where >= 0 && where < (_size -1) )
          return _elements[where+1];

     return 0;

}


template <class AType>
AType* TArray<AType>::ElementBefore(const AType& obj) const
{
     size_t where = PrivateIsMember(obj);

     if (where >= 0 )
          return _elements[where - 1];

     return 0;

}


template <class AType>
AType* TArray<AType>::InsertAt(size_t where,  AType* item)
{
     if ( (_index + 1) >= _size) // Need to grow array
          Extend(_chunkSize);


     // Now shift elements to the right from the insertion point
     for (int i=_index-1; i >= where; i—)
          _elements[i+1] = _elements[i];

     _elements[where] = item;
     _count++;
     _index++;

     return _elements[where+1]; // the old object
```

```
}

template <class AType>
AType* TArray<AType>::ReplaceAt(size_t where,  AType* newitem)
{
    AType* olditem = _elements[where];
    _elements[where] = newitem;

    return olditem;
}

template <class AType>
AType* TArray<AType>::LastElement() const
{
    if (_index > 0)
        return _elements[_index-1];
    else
        return 0;
}

template <class AType>
AType* TArray<AType>::FirstElement() const
{
    return _elements[0];
}

template <class AType>
size_t TArray<AType>::HowManyOccurrences(const AType& obj) const
{
    size_t total = 0;

    for (int i=0; i < _index; i++)
        if ( *_elements[i] == obj)
            ++total;

    return total;

}

template <class AType>
AType* TArray<AType>::ElementAt(size_t where) const
{
    if (where < _index)
        return _elements[where];

    return 0;
}

template <class AType>
size_t TArray<AType>::IndexOfElement(const AType& obj) const
{

    for (int i=0; i < _index; i++)
        if ( *_elements[i] == obj)
            return i;
```

```
        return -1;
}

template <class AType>
TIterator<AType>* TArray<AType>::CreateIterator()
{

        return new TArrayIterator<AType> (this);
}

//================================= Iterator implementation

template <class AType>
TArrayIterator<AType>::TArrayIterator(TArray<AType>* container)
{
        _pointer = container->_elements;
        _container = container;
        _current = 0;
}

template <class AType>
TArrayIterator<AType>::TArrayIterator()
{
        _pointer = 0;
        _container = 0;
        _current = -1;
}

template <class AType>
AType* TArrayIterator<AType>::First()
{
        if (_pointer)
              return _pointer[0];

        return 0;
}

template <class AType>
AType* TArrayIterator<AType>::Last()
{
        if (_pointer) {
              _current = _container->_index - 1;
              return _pointer[_current];
        }
        return 0;
}

template <class AType>
AType* TArrayIterator<AType>::Next()
{
        if ( (_current != -1) && ( (_current+1) < _container->_size) ) {
              _current++;
              return _pointer[_current];
        }
        return 0;
}
```

```
template <class AType>
AType* TArrayIterator<AType>::Previous()
{
    if ( (_current != -1) && ( (_current - 1) >= 0) ) {
        _current—;
        return _pointer[_current];
    }
    return 0;
}

template <class AType>
AType* TArrayIterator<AType>::Current()
{
    if (_current != -1)
        return _pointer[_current];

    return 0;
}

template <class AType>
void TArrayIterator<AType>::Remove()
{
    if (_current != -1)
        _pointer[_current] = 0;

}
```

13

Understanding the C++ Object Model

The preceding chapters focused on the object-oriented paradigm, its benefits, drawbacks, C++ issues, etc. But, we haven't paid much attention to the internal object model of C++. A professional programmer benefits from understanding the cost, efficiency, advantages, and tradeoffs of the object implementation model. This final chapter is an under the hood look at the internals of the C++ object model. Even though it does not cover all aspects of the C++ model, most important topics are explored.

EFFICIENT IMPLEMENTATION

One of the primary goals of C++ is implementation efficiency. Bjarne Stroustrup has strived to minimize the cost of objects and has still maintained compatibility with C. Even though the language does not specify a particular implementation model, most compiler writers follow his suggested strategies.

HOW OBJECTS ARE REPRESENTED IN C++

An object is no different from a C struct in most situations. However, we must distinguish among normal objects, object of classes with virtual functions, and objects of classes with static data members and/or static member functions. The following paragraphs are devoted to this topic.

Classes Without Any Virtual Functions

A class without any virtual functions is a simple C struct. The representation is no different than C.

```
class TTime  {
    public:
        TTime(size_t  hour, size_t minutes, size_t seconds);
        TTime(); // use system time for the values
        TTime(const TTime& copy);
        TTime& operator=(const TTime& assign);
        ~TTime();
        size_t GetSeconds() const;
        static unsigned long TimeNow() const;
            // Details not important for this discussion
    private:
        size_t _hour;
        size_t _minutes;
        size_t _seconds;
};
```

This is represented in memory as shown in Fig. 13-1.

A struct in C is also represented exactly like this. The size of an object of **TTime** is the sum of the sizes of its data members. There is no other overhead. Of course, there is no requirement in the language that the data members be stored in this exact sequence (the declaration order in the class), but most compilers follow this scheme. An implementation might also store them in the reverse order of their declaration.

Given this representation, a C++ object is compatible with a C struct and can be passed to a C program without any complications.

Member Functions

Every member function of a class is represented by a simple function with a mangled name. The name mangling scheme is not standardized and compilers can follow their own scheme. Invocation of a member function on an object is translated into a call to a function with an argument.

Object representation in memory

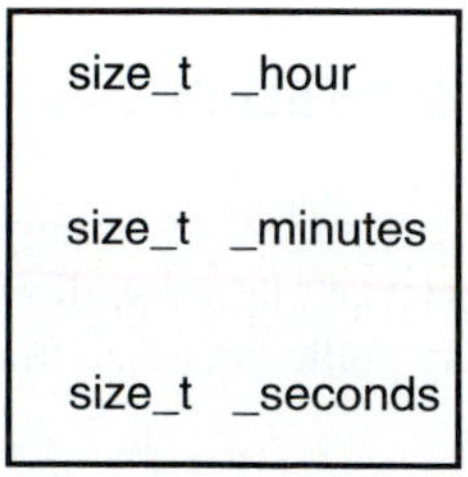

size_t _hour

size_t _minutes

size_t _seconds

Fig. 13-1

Our implementation of **GetSeconds** is

```
TTime::GetSeconds() const { return _seconds; }

TTime time(11, 33, 22); // a TTime object
size_t seconds = time.GetSeconds();
```

is translated as

```
GetSeconds__5TTimeFi(&time); // the mangled name depends on the compiler
```

where the function **GetSeconds__5TTimeFi** is the mangled function name of the member function **TTime::GetSeconds**. Therefore, the real declaration of the mangled function is:[1]

```
GetSeconds__5TTimeFi(const TTime * const this)
{
    return this->_seconds;
}
```

The **this** pointer is usually the first argument to a member function. Again, this is true with most compilers, but there is no requirement to do so.

The address of the object on which the member function is invoked is passed as the **this** argument. Every unqualified reference to any data member inside a member function is qualified using the **this** pointer.

With this scheme, there is no extra run-time cost for calling member functions. It is as inexpensive as any C function call and there is no extra cost in terms of space for a normal object. This is true even for operator functions. This is one of the design goals of C++; programmers who use C++ as a better C should not incur any extra cost just because of the language.

☞ **An object of a class without any virtual functions is as efficient as an instance of a C struct. Accessing a member of an object is exactly identical to accessing a member of a C struct.**

If a class contains an embedded object of another class, then unrolling of the data members of the embedded object is done. This is carried out recursively for embedded objects of embedded objects.

Static Data Members

A static data member in a class is almost equivalent to a global variable. Accessing a global variable does not incur any extra cost. The same rule applies to a static data mem-

---

[1]The mangled name is shown here just as an example. This may not be exactly what your compiler generates. It is important to know that mangling takes place but not what the mangled name looks like.

ber. Reference to a static data member is translated into a reference to a global variable (usually maintained in the data segment of the process) with a mangled name.

```
class X {
    public:
            static int static_member;
            void f();
        //...
};

void X::f() { this->static_member = 0; /* Or static_member = 0; */ }
```

is translated as

```
void X::f()
{
   ::static_member__1X = 0; // Some mangled name for the static data member
}
```

Here again, there is no extra cost for accessing a static data member. Along the same lines, call to a static member function is translated as a call to a global function with a mangled name, but the address of the object used in the class (the this pointer) is not passed.

```
void f()
{

    TTime t;
    unsigned long now = t.TimeNow(); // or TTime::TimeNow()
    // translates to unsigned long now = TimeNow__5TTime_Fi();
    // Here TimeNow__5TTime_Fi() is the mangled name of the static
    // member function TimeNow.
}
```

Constructor Functions

Names of constructors and destructors are also mangled. Continuing with the TTime example, here is what the constructor might look like:

```
            TTime::TTime(size_t h, size_t m, size_t s))
            {
                _hour = h;
                _minutes = m;
                _seconds = s;
            }
```

This would probably become:

```
__ct__5TTimeFvi(TTime* const this, size_t h, size_t m, size_t s)
{
    this->_hour = h;
```

```
        this->_minutes = m;
        this->_seconds = s;
    }
```

and **TTime::TTime()** would become

```
            __ct__5TTimeFv(TTime* const this); // ①
```

Objects can be constructed using the **new()** operator. The language guarantees that a constructor for an object will not be called if the **new()** operator fails to allocate memory.

```
            TTime* pTime = new TTime;
```

is translated as

```
    TTime* pTime = 0;

    if ( pTime = __new (sizeof(TTime)) )
    {
        pTime = __ct__5TTimeFv(pTime); // Call constructor function ①
    }
```

NOTE   If there is no default constructor function declared for a class without any virtual functions, there is no real need to generate the default constructor because nothing needs to be done inside this constructor, even if there are data members. Most compilers don't generate such constructors. Users are led to believe that a default constructor has been generated, but in reality it is not there. With classes that do contain virtual functions, this is not true, as we shall see soon.

CLASSES WITH VIRTUAL FUNCTIONS

In reality, the representation of a class with one or more virtual functions is no different from a class without any virtual functions. But, every object incurs an extra storage cost and most calls to virtual functions will incur a fixed run-time cost.

Virtual functions are implemented through a table of pointers to functions, the vtbl. Every object (that contains at least one virtual function) contains a pointer to this table of pointers to functions. Calling a virtual function is reduced to indexing into the vtbl and calling a function through a pointer to the function.

```
            class B {
                public:
                    virtual void f();
                    virtual void g();
                    virtual void h();
                private:
                    int x;
            };
```

```
class D1 : public B {                    class D2 : public D1 {
    public:                                  public:
        virtual void g();                        virtual void f();
    private:                                  private:
        int y;                                   int z;
};                                       };
```

Placement of the vtbl Pointer

In the original cfront implementation, the vtbl pointer (vptr) was stored at the bottom of an object (see Fig. 13-2). This preserved compatibility with a C struct layout. But, once multiple inheritance and virtual base classes were added to C++, many implementations started placing the vptr at the top of an object. This scheme is more efficient in supporting some virtual function calls through pointer to members under MI, but it breaks interoperability of a C++ object with a C struct. Currently, many implementations place the vptr at the top of an object. Figures in this chapter show the vptr at the bottom of an object. The vptr placement issue is a topic of debate within the C++ compiler community.

Continuing with the original object layout, objects of class D1 and D2 are implemented as in Fig. 13-3.

The RTTI info shown in Fig. 13-4 will be discussed soon. The pointer to the virtual function table is shown as vptr. Also, the position of the vtbl pointer vptr is fixed in B and is at the same offset in all the derived classes.

If an object of D2 is created, its address is the same as the address of D1 and the address of B. A call of the following type

```
B* pb = new D2;
pb->g();
```

is a call to a virtual function. This is translated as

a. Retrieve the vtbl pointer

b. Get the address of the function by indexing into the vtbl.

c. Jump to the function whose address is stored there.

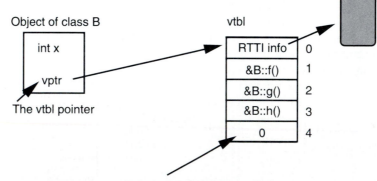

marks the end of the virtual function table

Fig. 13-2

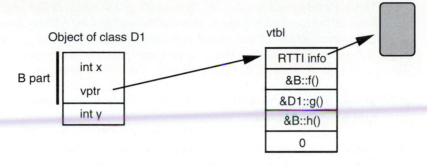

Fig. 13-3

This (**pb->g()**) can be written as

```
( * (pb->vptr[2]) ) ();
```

Matching the steps from above

a. pb->vptr (retrieve the vtbl pointer)

b. pb->vptr[2] (go to the index where the address of **g()** is stored)

c. (*(pb->vptr[2]))() (jump to the function whose address in stored there)

This can be implemented with three assembly language instructions on most processors.

```
;Note: function_offset and vptr_offset known at compile time
load [object_address + vptr_offset], reg1 ;get the vptr into reg1
load [reg1 + function_offset], reg2 ;get the address of the function
                                    ;from vtbl into reg2
call reg2 ;invoke the function found there
```

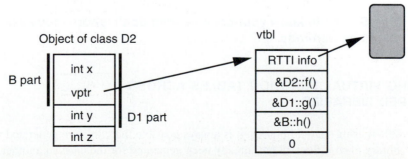

Fig. 13-4

This is exactly three instructions. When calling a virtual function everything except the address of the function is known. This mechanism gets the address from the vtbl and calls it. However, when MI and virtual base classes are involved, two more instructions might be required to locate the address of the virtual function (and to get to the correct address of the object). More on this later.

☞ **Single inheritance with virtual functions is easily taken care of by virtual function tables.**

These instructions for calling a virtual function are usually expanded inline at the call site. But, in applications where there are too many calls to virtual functions from different places, this inlined code can cause a significant increase in code side. Some compilers use *call thunks* to overcome this increase in code size (i.e. the code to handle virtual function calls is out-of-line).

Note that the offset of g() (the function called in the above example) is known at compile time. The ordering of functions in the vtbl is usually based on their declaration order in the base class(es). The same vtbl is shared by all objects of a class within a process.

As can be seen, the vtbl scheme makes it fast and very efficient but, it is not flexible. It is not possible to add more functions to the table at run time.

When compiling different modules that go into one executable, a naive compiler might generate the vtbl in all the modules where the header file(s) are included. This might be done because the compiler doesn't know whether the vtbls have already been generated in some other module(s). But, in the final application, there can only be one vtbl because the linker would complain about duplicates otherwise. To overcome this problem, the compiler can include the name of the source file where the vtbl was generated (another kind of name mangling). So, in the final executable (or library), you end up with multiple copies of the vtbl containing the same information. This causes an unnecessary increase in code size and waste of memory. A smart compiler does not generate vtbls in all separately compiled modules. Some heuristics are applied to determine the appropriate module for the vtbl generation. This is usually done by generating vtbl in the module where the first non-inline member function is defined. This is a reasonable approach. But, in cases where a class does not contain any non-inline virtual member functions, this scheme still causes generation of duplicate vtbls. To overcome this problem, some compilers require that at least one member function be non-inline to generate vtbls properly (in only one module). This can be easily achieved by making the destructor a non-inline member function.

☞ **So, get to know your compiler and don't ignore those seemingly harmless warnings.**

SHARING VIRTUAL FUNCTION TABLES ACROSS SHARED LIBRARIES

When using shared libraries, it is always possible that vtbls are generated in every shared library even if the vtbl has already been generated for the class in another shared library. The vtbl might be generated in more than one shared library because there is no guarantee that the shared libraries are loaded together. This again causes memory wastage. When more than one shared library containing the same vtbls is loaded in memory, it is definitely a waste of memory. Your linker (or compiler), with some help from the operating system, can come to your rescue here.

Class vtbls are never modified at run time—they are read-only. Operating systems usually share memory pages containing read-only data among different processes. This is easily done by mapping the same physical memory page to different virtual memory pages. In fact, this is the normal mechanism employed by virtual memory systems to share code (text) and read-only data. If the compiler/linker marks the pages (or segments) containing vtbls as read-only, then it makes it easier for the operating system to share them among different processes. To achieve this goal, all vtbls in a library are grouped into one or more pages that are then marked read-only. Some compilers/linkers do this automatically. However, your mileage may vary. Check your compiler manual.

VIRTUAL FUNCTIONS AND MULTIPLE INHERITANCE (NO VIRTUAL BASE CLASSES)

Things are a bit more complicated with the vtbl under multiple inheritance. Here is an example:

```
class B {
    public:
        virtual void f();
        virtual void g();
        virtual void h();
    private:
        int x;
};

class D1 {
    public:
        void ff(); // non-virtual function
        virtual void f();
    private:
        int y;
};

class D3 : public B, public D1 {
    public:
        virtual void f();
        void hh();
    private:
        int w;
};
```

As with single inheritance, the layout of the final object can be represented by unrolling the base class objects (see Fig. 13-5).

There are two different situations to consider under MI. When an object of D3 is used as a D1 object or as a B object, or when a non-virtual member function call is made,

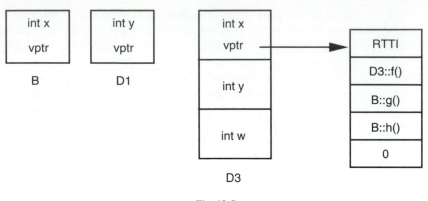

Fig. 13-5

only some compile-time offset adjustments need be done. But, when a virtual function call is made, things are somewhat more complicated.

With the layout above, consider the following examples:

```
B* pb = new B;
pb->x = 0;
```

Here the pointer is of type **B** and the object is also a **B**. This is no different from the single inheritance case.

```
B* pb = new D1;
pb-> x = 0; // Again, no different from single inheritance

D3* pd3 = new D3;
pd3->ff(); // ff is in D1
```

This is a valid call. But, there is one problem. Member function **D1::ff()** expects a (**this**) pointer to **D1** and not **D3**. The address of a **D3** object is the same as the address of a **B** object—they start at the same address. But, the address of a **D1** within a **D3** is at an offset from the beginning of **D3** (or **B**). The member function **D1::ff()** should receive the correct **this** pointer that points to a **D1** object. The offset of **D1** in **B** is known at compile time. So, we can easily take care of it at compile time without any run-time cost. Let's call the offset of **D1** within **D3** as **offset_D1** (see Fig. 13-6).

Therefore, **pd3->ff()** becomes

```
pd3->ff() is    (  (D1*)  (  ((char*) pd3) + offset_D1 )  ) ->ff();
```

All the compiler is doing is adding **offset_D1** to the address in **pd3** and casting it to a **D1***. But, before adding **offset_D1** to **pd3**, **pd3** must be treated as a **char** pointer and not a **D3** pointer, to ensure that the pointer arithmetic is correct. Hence, the cast of **pd3** to **char***. Finally, the resulting address is cast to a **D1*** (what we want) and the call is made to ff(). Now, **D1::ff()** receives the correct **this** pointer. All this is done at compile time.

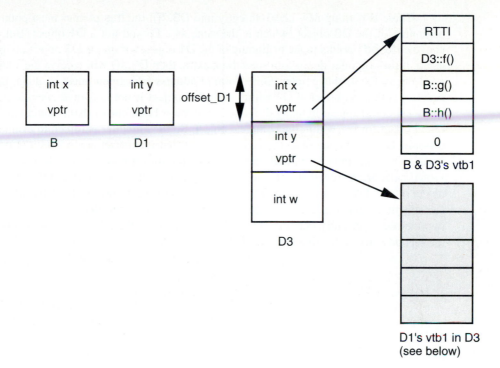

Fig. 13-6

There is no run-time overhead. This holds good for any other situation where a D1 is needed but a D3 is passed.

```
void foo(D1* d1) { /* ... */ }

D3 d3;
foo(&d3); // Do the same offset adjustment and call foo
// foo ( (D1*) ( ((char*) &d3) + offset_D1) )
```

So far so good!

Now, let's turn our attention to virtual functions. Here is a simple code fragment:

```
D3* pd3 = new D3;
D1* pd1 = new D3;// pd1 must point to the D1 part in D3
B*  pb = new D3;
```

All three pointers point to a D3 object. This is correct because D3 derives from both B and D1.

```
pd3->f(); // Calls D3::f() because of dynamic binding
pd1->f(); // Again D3::f(), but pd1 points to the beginning of D1 in a D3
          // object
pb->f(); // D3::f()
```

There is nothing new here. On entry into D3::f(), the this pointer must point to the beginning of the D3 object (which is the same as a B) and not a D1 object. But, in the above code, pd1 points to the beginning of the D1 object within the D3 object assigned to it. So, if the compiler doesn't do something extra, then D3::f() will receive the address of a D1 object for its this pointer. Some form of address adjustment must be done. But, the problem is that the offset of D1 within any other object is not known at compile time because D1 could appear in many different hierarchies. Each one of them would have a different offset for D1 within the complete object. So the compiler is forced to evaluate this offset of D1 within any object at run time. Note that this offset computation at run time needs to be done only for virtual function calls and not for non-virtual calls because non-virtual calls are resolved at compile time. Again, let's call the offset of D1 within a D3 object offset_D1. This offset of D1 within any other object must be available when a virtual function call is made. So, a logical place for it is in the vtbl. Here is the new vtbl, with two members per entry (see Fig. 13-7). The first entry is the address of the function and the second entry is the offset for the object.

```
struct vtbl_entry {
    void (*function)(); // address of the function to be called
    int offset;         // offset to apply for address of object
};
```

Virtual functions in MI with dual entry vtbl

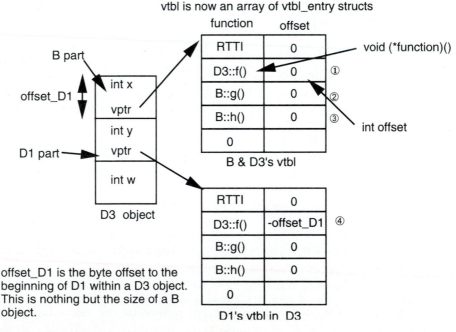

offset_D1 is the byte offset to the beginning of D1 within a D3 object. This is nothing but the size of a B object.

Fig. 13-7

① This is the actual function that will be called within a D3 object because D3 overrides B::f() (Fig. 13-7). Hence D3's vtbl contains the address of D3::f(). The address of B and D3 are the same. Therefore, there is no offset needed to be added before the call to D3::f(). Hence, the offset entry is 0.

② In a D3 object, B::g() has not been overridden. Hence, the vtbl entry for g() within D3 is the address of B::g(). Since B and D3 have the same address, no adjustment to the this pointer is necessary. Hence, the stored offset is 0.

③ This is the same as ② because B::h() has not been overridden in D3.

④ But when a call is made to f() using a pointer (or reference) of type D1 which points to a D3 object, the function called is still D3::f() because D3 overrides B::f(). But, a pointer of type D1 will point to the D1 object (see pd1 above) wihtin a D3. But, when we are in D3::f(), the this pointer must point to the beginning of a D3 and not D1. To make this happen, the offset of D1 from the beginning of a D3 object must be algebraically added to the address of a D3 object. This offset is offset_D1, the offset to the beginning of the D1 part within a D3 object. To get to the beginning of D3, we just need to add -offset_D1. This is what is stored in the second slot of the table.

The offset stored in the new vtbl is added to the address of the object and this address is used as the this pointer. In this example, offset_D1 must be subtracted from the address of D1 within D3 (or B) to get to a D3 object. So, -offset_D1 is placed in the vtbl. With this modification, the call is:

```
pd1->f();
 ( *(pd1->vptr[1].function) ( (D1*) ((char*) pd1 + pd1->vptr[1].offset)) );
```

Here (pd1->vptr[1].function) gives the address of the function in the vtbl and the rest is the address manipulation to get to the beginning of the object. In this example, the offset would be negative. One might feel that an int offset might be limiting but on most platforms this is good enough.

This scheme increases the size of the vtbl and also requires that every call to a virtual function go through the offset computation mechanism, even when the address is already correct (i.e., the offset stored in the table is zero). Unnecessary memory (and also CPU time) is being wasted. The offset adjustment is not needed in most cases. But still the offset is stored in every slot of the vtbl. It would be better if we could avoid this waste.

Some compilers follow an alternative scheme to overcome these problems. Here, the *thunk* model is used. Instead of increasing the size of the vtbl, the old vtbl with a function address (only one slot per function) is used. When there is no adjustment required for the this pointer the address stored in the vtbl is a pointer to the function to be executed (as before). When an offset adjustment is needed, the address points to a piece of code (the thunk) that makes the adjustment and calls the appropriate function. The execution of the actual function is now a two step process. The advantage here is that only those virtual function calls that require an offset adjustment of the this pointer incur the extra cost. This also keeps the size of the vtbl small. The cost of computing the offset is the same in both schemes (see Fig. 13-8).

When executing pd1->f(), the compiler just does what it normally does for any virtual function: It picks up the address in the vtbl and calls the function. However, now instead of jumping to the actual function, the address in the vtbl transfers execution to the offset adjustment thunk. This is another small function that performs the adjustment to the

Virtual functions in MI using thunks

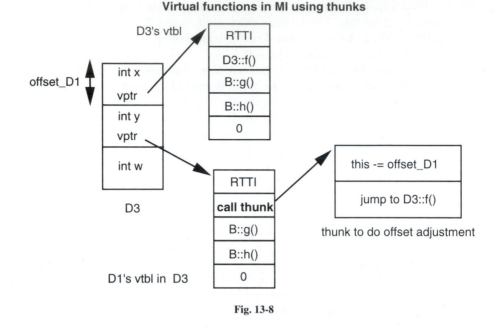

Fig. 13-8

this pointer and then invokes the actual function. This way, all calls to virtual functions are treated uniformly. The offset adjustment code is maintained elsewhere.

It is clear from this example that in MI hierarchies

a. access to non-virtual member functions and data members is straightforward. No extra run-time cost is incurred.

b. But, when calling a virtual function, depending on the compiler implementation, all calls might incur an extra cost with increased vtbl size, or only those calls that require an adjustment of the this pointer incur extra run-time cost without any increase in vtbl size.

None of these issues should be taken as an argument against MI. Yes, there are costs involved, but the cost is justified in cases where MI reduces the coding burden and also makes the problem solution more elegant.

In summary,

☞ **There are n-1 additional virtual function tables associated with a multiple inheritance hierarchy of (n) base classes. The derived class and the left-most non-virtual base class shared the same virtual function table.**

Therefore, an MI hierarchy with two base classes has (2-1=1) virtual function tables for the base classes and one for the derived class, which is shared with the left most base class. In total, there will be two virtual function tables.

VIRTUAL BASE CLASSES

If you think that understanding of the virtual base concept is difficult, wait until you see its implementation. It opens up a whole new set of problems. First, let's analyze the implementation of the object and then the virtual function mechanism.

Let's use the hierarchy shown below for this example. All data members are made public just for convenience.

```
class V {                          class D1 : virtual public V {
    public:                            public:
        virtual void f();                  virtual void g();
        virtual void g();              public:
        virtual void h();                  int y;
    public:                        };
        int x;
};


class D2 : virtual public V {      class MD : public D1, public D2 {
    public:                            public:
        virtual void f();                  virtual void h();
    public:                            public:
        int w;                             int z;
};                                 };
```

As you already know, each D1 object and D2 object contains a V object, but an MD object contains only one V object. It is evident that the virtual base V cannot be at the same position relative to both D1 and D2 in all objects. Therefore, in order to get to the virtual base object, a pointer must be maintained in all objects that have V as a virtual base.

In most implementations, the virtual base object is at the bottom of the completed object (see Fig. 13-9).

The pointer pVbase is the extra pointer stored in every sub-object that uses V as a virtual base class. Note that these extra pointers are needed because V is being used as a virtual base class—it is not a property of V itself. Given this layout, here is what their declarations would refer to in an MD object (see Fig. 13-10).

```
MD  md;
V*  vp  = &MD;
D1* dp1 = &MD;
D2* dp2 = &MD;
MD* mdp = &MD;
```

Member Access with Virtual Base Classes

Definitely, the complexity of the object implementation and the size of an object is increased. The vtbl for the MD object is shared with the V object. Given a D1 object or a D2 object, the virtual base pointer pVbase is used to get to the virtual base class object. Depending on the usage, there might be a run-time cost involved in the evaluation of access to members of virtual base class objects.

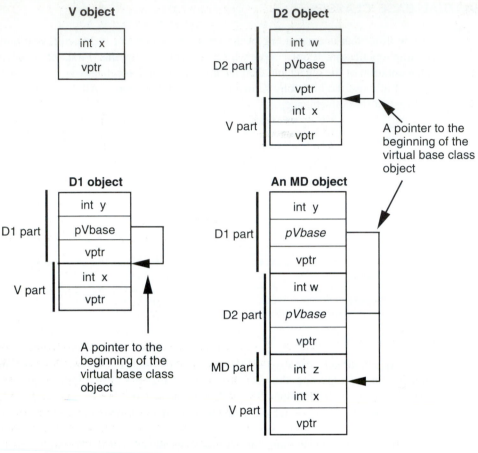

Fig. 13-9

Continuing with the declarations of dp1, dp2, mdp, & vp:

```
D1 d1;
dp1 = &d1; // No problem, compile time initialization

vp = &d1; // Again, compile time evaluation because offset is
          // known at compile time

V* vp1 = dp1;// Requires run-time evaluation because we don't know
          // what dp1 points to
```

Access of a member of an inherited virtual base class through a reference or a pointer requires run-time evaluation as the following example illustrates.

```
dp1 = &d1; // d1 is a D1 object, declared above
dp1->x = 0; // becomes dp1->pVbase->x = 0
```

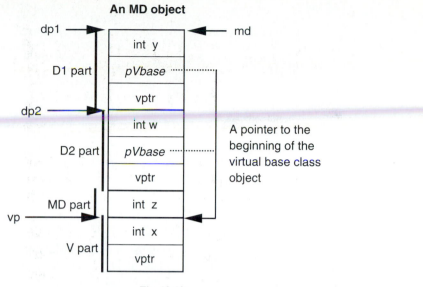

Fig. 13-10

In this case, **dp1** is a pointer to a **D1** object. When it is initialized with the address of a **D1** object, it is a straight forward initialization. But, when we try to access a member of the virtual base class **V** through this pointer, it is not exactly known where the virtual base object is located with respect to the **D1** object. In order to get to the virtual base object, the pointer to the virtual base **pVbase** is used.

However, access of a virtual base class member through an object of a derived class (not a pointer or reference), is no different from normal single inheritance. The offsets are known at compile time and hence the expression can be evaluated at compile time.

```
D1 d1;
d1.x = 0; // access a virtual base member
          // *((V*) ( (char* )&d1) + (sizeof(D1) - sizeof (V)))).x = 0;
```

Here, the offset of the virtual base **V** within **D1** is known at compile time (see Fig. 13-9). All that needs to be done is to adjust the access to **x** within **D1**. This is no different from ordinary inheritance without virtual base classes.

☞ **There is a run-time cost while accessing virtual base class members through derived class pointers and references (but not with objects)**

Now, let's look at the even more complicated case of virtual base classes with virtual functions.

Virtual Base Classes with Virtual Functions

Let's continue with the same hierarchy using B, D1, D2 and MD. The hierarchy is reproduced below for your reference.

```
class V {                          class D1 : virtual public V {
    public:                            public:
        virtual void f();              virtual void g();
        virtual void g();          public:
        virtual void h();                  int y;
    public:                        };
        int x;
};


class D2 : virtual public V {      class MD : public D1, public D2 {
    public:                            public:
        virtual void f();              virtual void h();
    public:                            public:
        int w;                             int z;
};                                 };
```

In this layout (Fig. 13-11), the beginning of an MD object is the same as the offset of a D1 in an MD object. The offset of D2 from the beginning of an MD object is offset_D2. Similarly, the offset of the virtual base class object within an MD object is offset_V. In total, there are three virtual function tables, one for each base class and one for the virtual base class. The derived class object shares the vtbl with the left most base class.

As usual, when a virtual function is entered, the this pointer must point to the correct address. Here are some cases where offset adjustment is needed.

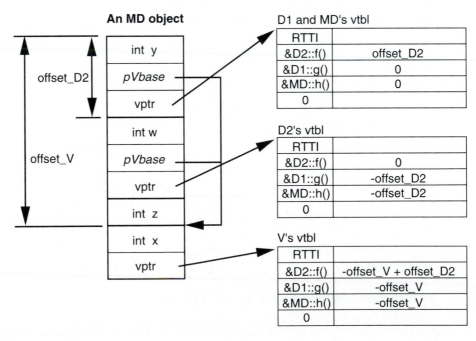

Fig. 13-11

```
MD* pmd = new MD;
pmd->f(); // Should call D2::f()
```

Here, the pointer **pmd** points to an **MD** object. But the virtual function f() is implemented by **D2**. Hence, the call must be dispatched to **D2::f()**. When D2::f() is entered, the **this** pointer must point to the **D2** part with in the **MD** object. To get to the **D2** part from the beginning of an **MD** object, we must add the **offset_D2** (shown in Fig. 13-11 above) to the **this** pointer. Assuming the following structure for the vtbl entry,

```
struct vtbl_entry {
    void (*function)(); // address of the function to be called
    int offset; // offset to apply for address of object
};
```

the call is transformed as

```
( *(pmd->vptr[1].function) ( (D2*) ((char*) pmd + pmd->vptr[1].offset)) );
```

This should come as no surprise because, we have already seen the same adjustment with normal MI virtual function calls.

IMPLEMENTATION SUPPORT FOR RTTI (RUN-TIME TYPE IDENTIFICATION)

Support for RTTI also comes from the virtual function tables. Slot zero in the vtbl holds a pointer to a **type_info** object. Class **type_info** is as shown below and in Fig. 13-12.

```
class type_info {
public:
    virtual ~type_info();
    bool operator==(const type_info&) const;
    bool operator!=(const type_info& other) const;
```

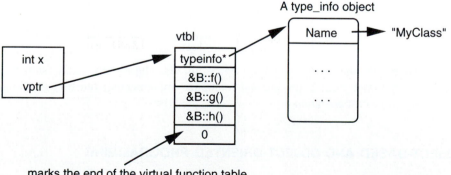

Fig. 13-12

```
    bool before(const type_info&) const;
    const char *name() const;
private:
    const char * Name;
    // some type encoding information – compiler specific
    // this information is used for comparing types and also for collating
    // order. It encodes the actual type information and also the publicly
    // accessible base classes, etc.
    Typedescriptor  Desc;

    type_info(const type_info&);
    type_info& operator=(const type_info&);
};

class MyClass {
    public:
        virtual void f();
        virtual void g();
        virtual void h();
    private:
        int x;
};
```

As you already know, vtbl is generated only for classes with virtual function(s). Therefore, dynamic type casting is only possible for polymorphic types because they contain vtbls. For any RTTI related operation, the compiler uses the vtbl to get to the **type_info** object and then carries out the operation. For example, a **dynamic _cast** operation might be implemented as follows:

```
void foo(TPerson* p)
{
    TStudent* sp;
    if ( sp = dynamic_cast<TStudent*>(p) ) {
        // Internal implementation
        // if ( sp = __dynamic_cast("TPerson", p->vptr[0].type.Desc))
    }
}
```

Here **type** is

```
        type_info* type; // the name of the element in vtbl[0]
```

Desc is the type encoding entry in the **type_info** class shown above and **__dynamic_cast** is the internal (compiler implemented) function that implements the dynamic cast operation.

OBJECT-BASED AND OBJECT-ORIENTED PROGRAMMING

Given all the complexity and cost of virtual functions, many programmers who like the benefits of using objects but still love the efficiency and compactness of C, can entirely avoid the cost associated with dynamic binding by using only non-virtual functions in classes. As seen earlier, there is no extra cost for objects of classes that do not have any virtual functions. In such cases, C++ is as efficient as C. This is usually called *Object-Based programming*. It gives you the full power of data abstraction and encapsulation but none of the cost of dynamic binding. You can also use inheritance for code reuse but not virtual functions. It also makes a C++ class completely compatible with a C struct.

Using virtual functions and polymorphism leads to *Object-Oriented Programming*. This makes use of the advantages of dynamic binding while accepting the cost involved. In large projects, it makes sense to have a mixed mode where some subsystems (usually those that need to interface with C code) are truly object-based and others are object-oriented.

REFERENCES, POINTERS, AND VALUES

Assignment of References and Pointers

Internally, a reference and a pointer are implemented the same way. What is different about them is the usage and their implications. We shall see some nuances of this kind in this section. For this section, let's reuse the **TPerson/TStudent** example.

```
class TPerson {
    public:
        TPerson(/* details not important*/);
        virtual ~TPerson();
        virtual void Print() const;
};

class TStudent : public TPerson {
    public:
        TStudent(/* details not important*/);
        ~TStudent();
        virtual void Print() const;
};
```

What's important is the object's behavior, so let's ignore the constructor arguments, etc. Consider the following function, which accepts two pointers to **TPerson**:

```
void foo(TPerson* p1, TPerson* p2)
{
    p1->Print(); // Uses dynamic binding to invoke the correct Print
                 // function TStudent::Print
    p1 = p2;     // What happens?
    p1->Print(); // No change. Still uses dynamic binding to invoke the
                 // correct Print function, TStudent::Print

}

int main()
{
    TStudent s1, s2;
    foo(&s1, &s2);
}
```

In the assignment of p2 to p1, nothing happens to the objects pointed by p1 and p2. All that is happening is simple address assignment, so p1 is an alias for p2. In other words, it is reference semantics. You could also see this as a *shallow copy* operation. After this assignment, if a virtual function (such as Print above) is invoked on p1, then it really takes on the behavior of whatever p1 (or p2) points to. Here the address stored in p2 is being assigned to p1 (i.e., p1 is an alias for p2).

Switching gears, let's see what happens with references:

```
void foo(TPerson& rp1, TPerson& rp2)
{
   rp1.Print(); // Uses dynamic binding to invoke TStudent::Print()
   rp1 = rp2;   // What happens now?
   rp1.Print(); // No change. Still uses dynamic binding to invoke the
                // correct Print function, TStudent::Print
}

main()
{
   TStudent s1, s2;
   foo(s1, s2);
}
```

Would you expect that the behavior is similar to the pointer case above? Is rp1 now an alias for rp2? This is where the most important difference between pointers and references is felt. In this case, references behave like true objects and the assignment operator for TPerson is invoked because rp1 and rp2 are references to TPerson. Therefore, assignment between two TPerson objects is taking place, even though the references rp1 and rp2 are actually bound to TStudent objects. So here the references have value semantics. This can be dangerous if you are not careful. But, if you invoke a virtual function on rp1 or rp2 the behavior is that of a TStudent object because when the assignment was done, the virtual function tables were not affected. The TStudent objects s1 and s2 still have the same vtbls in them. So rp1 and rp2 are still aliases to TStudent objects and, hence, they behave like TStudent objects. However, the assignment of rp2 to rp1 only assigned (or copied) the TPerson part. This can easily cause data inconsistencies leading to strange behavior and unexpected results.

Copy Constructor

Now let's see an example where the vtbl is affected when copy constructors are used. Let's use the same TPerson and TStudent classes from above:

```
void foo()
{
   TStudent s1;
   TPerson      p1 = s1; // ❶
   // Same as TPerson p1(s1) — calls the copy constructor of TPerson

   p1.Print(); // Invokes TPerson::Print!
}
```

In ❶ above, we are creating a TPerson object and then initializing it with a TStudent object. The TStudent object s1 already exists. At this point, the copy constructor for TPerson is used to create the p1 object. The type of p1 cannot be anything other than a TPerson.

When the virtual function is invoked, you might be surprised to find that TPerson::Print is invoked and not TStudent::Print. How come the vtbl of TStudent was not copied into p1? Here the compiler intercedes and ensures that the vtbl is not affected. First, the compiler allocates enough memory for a TPerson object and builds the vtbl of TPerson in that memory. Next, it invokes the copy constructor of TPerson (which is another function) on this new object supplying the TStudent object. The copy constructor (implemented by the programmer or the compiler) cannot affect the vtbl in p1. Hence, p1 really behaves like a TPerson object.

☞ **Once an object is constructed, the virtual function table is built for the object and it will not be modified during the lifetime of the object.**

Note that the creation of the vtbl in an object is based on the compile-time (static) type of the object.

Responsibility of a Constructor

So far we haven't seen the guts of a constructor in any detail. This section looks at the implementation of a constructor. Here is a simple example:

```
class TTransmission {
    public:
        TTransmission(char c = 'A') { type = c;}
        // default is automatic transmission
    private:
        char type; // A -auto, M - manual
        // Other data members
};

class TTruck {
    public:
        //...
    private:
        TTransmission _superTranny;
        int _driveType;   // 4 wheel, 2 wheel
};
```

If we try to create an object of TTruck as follows

```
TTruck  myTruck;
```

the default constructor of TTruck must be generated by the compiler. What should this constructor do? In this case, the *synthesized* default constructor must have some code because it must initialize the _superTranny object. So there is some work that needs to be done in the constructor.

```
inline      TTruck* TTruck::TTruck(TTruck* const this)
{
    // driveType is uninitialized
    // Call the constructor for _superTranny object
    __ctor__13TTransmission(&this->_superTranny);
    return *this;
}
```

You might wonder why this is an inline function. That's because the header file of **TTruck** can be included in many different modules and the constructor must be generated in each module (because the compiler cannot assume that some other module will generate it). If it is not an inline function, then it will cause linker errors (multiple definitions). This can also be seen as a problem with compiler generated functions.

As another example, how about implementing a constructor taking two arguments, one for the transmission type and another one for the drive type. A programmer can implement it as follows:

```
TTruck::TTruck(char transmission, int drive)
    :    _driveType(drive), _superTranny(transmission) {}
```

There is nothing wrong here, but the compiler needs to do some extra work. The initialization of data members must be changed to follow the declaration order. The initialization of the embedded transmission object must be moved into the body of the constructor. So here is the internal implementation:

```
TTruck* TTruck::TTruck(TTruck* const this, char transmission, int drive)
{
    // First, call the ctor for the transmission object, _superTranny
    __ctor__13TTransmission(&this->_superTranny, transmission);
    // Next, initialize the drive type data member
    _driveType = drive;

    return *this;
}
```

☞ **If there are no embedded objects or base classes (including virtual base classes) requiring initialization, then there is probably no need to do anything in the generated default constructor. So, the constructor function is not required. But, if the class contains a virtual function, then the constructor must take care of initializing the vptr (the vtbl pointer).**

For a class without base class(es) and virtual functions, and no embedded objects, there is no need to synthesize the default constructor function.

Let's modify the **TTruck** class and add a virtual destructor:

```
class TTruck {
    public:
        virtual ~TTruck();
    private:
```

```
        TTransmission _superTranny;
        int _driveType;  // 4 wheel, 2 wheel
  };
```

Now, the generated default constructor looks like this:

```
inline
TTruck* TTruck::TTruck(TTruck* const this)
{
    this->__vptr = __vtbl__6TTruck; // ❶
    // driveType is uninitialized
    __ctor__13TTransmission(&this->_superTranny);
    return *this;
}
```

❶ Here **__vtbl__6TTruck** is the virtual function table that is shared by all objects of class **TTruck** and __vptr is the virtual function table pointer.

If **TTruck** is a derived class of **TVehicle**, then we need to do even more in the constructor of **TTruck**:

```
class TVehicle {
public:
    TVehicle();
    virtual ~TVehicle();
};

class TTruck : public TVehicle {
        public:
            virtual ~TTruck();
        private:
            TTransmission _superTranny;
            int _driveType;  // 4 wheel, 2 wheel
};
```

And here is the new constructor:

```
inline TTruck* TTruck::TTruck(TTruck* const this)
{
  // Call base class constructor first
  __ctor__8TVehicle(this);

  this->__vptr = __vtbl__6TTruck; // Setup vtbl pointer
  // driveType is uninitialized
  __ctor__13TTransmission(&this->_superTranny);
  return *this;
}

TVehicle::TVehilce(TVehicle *this const)
{
  this->__vptr = __vtbl__8TVehicle;
  return *this;
}
```

The generated constructor being inline increases code size. These inline functions can be complex when multiple base classes and virtual functions are involved. This is another very good argument for implementing non-inline constructors, even when they are empty.

RESPONSIBILITY OF A COPY CONSTRUCTOR

Now let's turn our attention to copy constructors. If a class does not provide a copy constructor, then the compiler will generate a default copy constructor *where needed*. What is meant by *where needed*?

Consider the class TTransmission shown above. Should the compiler generate a copy constructor for this class when objects of TTransmission are copied?

```
class TTransmission {
    public:
        TTransmission(char c = 'A') { type = c;}
        // default is automatic transmission
    private:
        char type; // A -auto, M - manual
        // Other data members
};

void foo()
{
    TTransmission    t1;
    TTransmission    t2(t1); // ❷
}
```

In ❷ above, should the compiler generate the default copy constructor function and call it? Not in this case because the TTransmission exhibits bitwise copy semantics. All that needs to happen is the copying of bits in t1 into t2. There is no need to invoke a copy constructor function for this purpose. Therefore, the compiler does not have to synthesize a copy constructor. In this example, the compiler just makes a bitwise copy of t1 into t2 because t1 and t2 are no different from a C struct (just a collection of bits). This can be done with a single memory move instruction on most processors.

```
class TTruck {
    public:
        //...
    private:
        TTransmission _superTranny;
        int _driveType;  // 4 wheel, 2 wheel
        //...
};
```

But, this argument does not hold good for TTruck because TTruck's copy constructor must have code to invoke the copy constructor of TTransmission. Whether the copy constructor in TTransmission is compiler generated or programmer defined does not matter here.

In general, the bitwise copy semantics mentioned above does not hold good when

a. Class contains an embedded object (i.e., object of another classes as a data member) for which a copy constructor exists (compiler generated or programmer defined).

b. Class is derived from one or more base classes for which a copy constructor exists (programmer defined or compiler generated).

c. Class declares virtual functions.

d. When the class inherits from a virtual base class (independent of whether a copy constructor exists for the virtual base class).

In (a) and (b), the class must insert code in its copy constructor to invoke the copy constructor of the embedded objects or base classes. This is evident in the **TTruck** example above.

In (c) and (d), the new object must have its **vptr** set properly. If the compiler were to follow the bitwise copy semantics, it would be disastrous. An example to this effect shown above is repeated below:

```
void foo()
{
    TStudent s1;
    TStudent s2 = s1; // ❶ Can be done correctly even with bitwise copy
    TPerson    p1 = s1; // ❷ But this will fail with bitwise copy
    // Same as TPerson p1(s1) — calls the copy constructor of TPerson

    p1.Print(); // Invokes TPerson::Print correctly
}
```

Here in ❶, even if bitwise copy semantics are followed, nothing would go wrong. Since both are **TStudent** objects, the vtbl in **s2** would be correct.

But in ❷, bitwise copy will not be correct. Definitely, the vtbl in **p1** should be that of **TPerson** even though the source **s1** is a **TStudent** object. Therefore, the compiler must generate the copy constructor to ensure that **vptr** is set properly in each **TPerson** object.

Virtual base classes impose even more complications when initializing objects. Suffice it to say that the run-time offsets needed to access the virtual base class object must be setup in every new object by the compiler. Such operations are not trivial.

OPTIMIZATIONS FOR PASS BY VALUE AND RETURN BY VALUE OF OBJECTS

Pass By Value

When objects are passed by value (and returned by value), it is generally assumed that a copy constructor is invoked to make a copy of the object to be passed by value (or returned by value). This can be very expensive. Compilers usually employ some well known optimizations here. We shall see such optimizations in this section.

```
class TTruck {
    public:
        virtual ~TTruck();
    private:
        TTransmission _superTranny;
        int _driveType;   // 4 wheel, 2 wheel
        //...
};
void Register(TTruck argTruck) // ❷
{
    // register the truck with the department of motor vehicles
}

void gg()
{
    TTruck myTruck;
    Register(myTruck); // ❶
}
```

When function **Register()** is called at ❶ with the **myTruck** argument, the formal argument **argTruck** in **Register()** must be initialized with the **myTruck** argument. Therefore, **argTruck** must be copy constructed from the **myTruck** argument. As per the C++ language standard, this is equivalent to

$$\text{Ttruck} \quad \text{argTruck} = \text{myTruck};$$

A compiler can easily do this by adding a temporary object in **gg()**. Here are the modified functions **gg()** and **Register()**.

```
void Register(TTruck&  argTruck) // ❸
{/* register the truck with the department of motor vehicles */ }

void gg()
{
    TTruck  myTruck;

    TTruck __temp; // ❹ This is the compiler generated temporary object
    TTruck(&__temp, myTruck); // ❺ Copy constructor invocation to copy
                             // myTruck into __temp
    Register(__temp); // This is the new call to Register
    // Destructor is invoked on __temp here
}
```

❹ Here, the compiler creates a temporary object of type **TTruck**. Note that this is not a call to the default constructor (or any other constructor) of **TTruck**.

❺ The temporary object must be initialized with the actual argument, **myTruck**. So, the copy constructor function is invoked with the temporary object as the destination. This temporary object must be passed as a reference object to **Register()**. To make this work (prototype matching), the argument mode for **Register()** must be changed.

❸ This is the modified **Register()** function declared to accept the argument **argTruck** as a reference to **TTruck**.

As we already know, the class destructor must be invoked on all objects passed by value. With this implementation, that object is the temporary __temp. The destructor is invoked on __temp after returning from Register().

Note that this is just an implementation scheme and it does not cause any reduction in the cost of pass by value.

Return by Value

Next, consider returning objects by value from functions. This can be expensive without compiler optimizations.

```
TTruck foo()
{
    TTruck      monsterTruck;
    //...
    return      monsterTruck;
}

void bar() { foo(); }
```

Here, function foo() returns a truck object by value. As you are already aware, the monsterTruck object will be destructed on exit from foo(). Therefore, the compiler must somehow copy the monsterTruck object out of foo(). This can also be implemented by passing an additional reference argument.

```
void foo(TTruck&      __result )
{
    TTruck monsterTruck; // ❶ default constructor of TTruck is invoked
                    // ...
    TTruck(&__result, monsterTruck); // ❷ Compiler invokes copy constructor
                        // to copy monsterTruck into __result
    return; // ❸ function returns nothing
    // destructor invoked on monsterTruck here
}

void bar()
{
    TTruck __temp;
    foo(__temp); // ❹
}
```

❶ The creation of the local monsterTruck object remains the same. This is created by the programmer.

❷ At the end of the function, the compiler invokes the copy constructor on __result to copy the monsterTruck object into __result.

❸ The function returns nothing because the result of the function is in the argument __result passed to it. The prototype of foo() is changed to return nothing. The destructor of __result is invoked at the end of foo().

❹ Note that even though __temp is being created in bar(), what is created is a raw object. A real constructor is not invoked. The object is copy constructed in foo().

With this simple implementation, everything works as expected. But, this approach is beneficial when you consider how **foo()** might be invoked.

```
TTruck foo();

void bar() {TTruck resultTruck = foo(); }
```

If this were to be transformed by the compiler directly without any optimizations, this is how it would look:

```
TTruck foo();

void bar()
{
    TTruck __temp; // Construct a temporary object.

    foo (__temp); // Call foo passing __temp by reference

    TTruck resultTruck; // Construct the return value object
    TTruck (&resultTruck, __temp); // Copy return value into resultTruck
                                   // using the copy constructor
}
```

Here, an extra **TTruck** object is being constructed (and destroyed) unnecessarily. All that is required by the user is that the return value of **foo()** be in **resultTruck**. This can achieved easily without the additional **__temp** object.

```
Truck foo();

void bar()
{
    // Code transformed by the compiler
    TTruck resultTruck;
    foo( resultTruck); // result of foo is built into resultTruck by foo
}
```

This makes it much more efficient because it avoids the unnecessary creation of **__temp**. This is a standard optimization that is almost mandatory in all compilers.

In certain cases, even more optimization is possible. Consider the following code fragment:

```
TTruck ff()
{
    TTruck localTruck;

    // do something with localTruck
    if (/*...*/) {
        return localTruck;
    }

    return localTruck;
}
```

With the optimization described above, this would become:

```
void ff(TTruck& __result)
{
    TTruck localTruck; // ❼

    // do something with localTruck
    TTruck (&__result, localTruck); // ❽ copy construct into __result
    return;
    // ❾ localTruck destructed here
}
```

It might seem unnecessary to copy construct __result from localTruck. Why not just create __result in ff() and use it directly, avoiding the copy construction completely?

```
void ff(TTruck& __result)
{
    TTruck (&__result); // default constructor for __result is invoked

    // do something with __result directly
    return; // no need to copy construct anything
}

void bar()
{
    TTruck resultTruck;
    foo(resultTruck); // result of ff is built into resultTruck by foo
}
```

This eliminates the constructor and destructor calls to localTruck in ❼ and ❽ above, making it a more efficient optimization. This is possible only if the function ff() returns the same named object from every path in the function. This scenario is quite common in operators +, −, etc. This is another optimization seen in some compiler implementations. However, your compiler might not perform this optimization. Most compilers still use the optimization ❼ ❽ ❾ described above (default constructor-copy construction-destructor). But, there are some aggressively optimizing compilers that do implement this scheme.

CAUTION   You might suspect that this type of optimization violates the program correctness. If a user relied on the fact that the copy constructor is called to copy the result out of ff(), it never happens here. But, the program behavior has not changed. However, if there are some side effects in a copy constructor of TTruck, you would never see it here because the copy constructor is not called. Compiler implementors are given sufficient freedom to optimize code and the language does not make any guarantees about the copy constructor being called in ff(). Note that the overall behavior of the program hasn't changed at all.

RUN-TIME INITIALIZATION

All initializations cannot be done at load time in C++. In particular, initializations involving non-constant expressions must be done at run time using extra code. Here is an example:

```
int j = 100; // ❶ This is done at load time
int k = j;   // ❷ This cannot be done until run-time
```

Here, ❶ is a trivial expression. The initialization value is known at compile time and, hence, when the program containing this fragment is loaded, the value of j is set 100.

But in ❷, k cannot be initialized at load time because the value of j is not known at compile time. After all, j is just another variable. The fact that j has already been initialized is not known to the compiler. Hence, the initialization of k must be done through some run-time code. The compiler can create a tiny function for this purpose:

```
__init_k__j() { k = j; }
```

The name of the function is dependent on the compiler. Definitely, there is a small cost involved in the initialization of k. By itself, this cost is trivial but, if many such initializations need to be done, the cost can definitely add up. But, we don't have any alternatives to avoid this cost.

SUMMARY

Understanding the implementation model of the language helps programmers in writing better code.

Try to be aware of the cost of every feature that you use. In particular, understand the speed/size tradeoffs.

Always remember that implementation details vary widely across compilers.

Don't ever write code that depends on some implementation feature of the compiler—program to the language standard, not the compiler.

Finally, remember that C++ compiler technology is evolving and compilers are catching up with the ANSI draft standard. Sooner or later, almost all compilers can be expected to be conformant with the language standard.

Bibliographical References and Recommended Reading

(Books marked with * are a *must have*).

*1. [Gamma94] Gamma, Erich, Helm, Richard, Johnson, Ralph, and Vlissides, John. *Design Patterns: Elements of Reusable Object-Oriented Software.* Addison-Wesley, 1995.

If you ever undertake any kind of OO design, you should read this book. The patterns detailed here will save you a lot of time.

*2. [Booch94] Booch, Grady. *Object Oriented Analysis and Design with Applications;* Benjamin Cummings, 1994.

Don't even think of doing any OO development without reading this book, at least once. It is an invaluable companion for any OO professional.

*3. Stroustrup, Bjarne. *The C++ Programming Langauge*, 2d. ed. Addison Wesley, 1991.

A *must have*. Get the details of the language from the master himself. It also contains some invaluable information on system/library development.

4. Jacobson, Ivar. *Object Oriented Software Engineering; A Use Case Driven Approach.* Addison Wesley, 1992.

This book gives you another approach to OO system development.

*5. Meyer, Bertrand. *Object Oriented Software Construction.* Prentice Hall, 1988.

(Check for second edition in 1997). One of my all-time favorites. It has some solid advice for anyone developing OO software. No matter what language you use, this book will help you immensely.

6. Dijkstra, Dahl, Hoare. *Structured Programming.* Academic Press, 1972.

If you write software, you should have already read this at least once.

7. Rumbaugh, et al.. *Object Oriented Modeling and Design.* Prentice Hall, 1991.

This book is the ultimate guide to the OMT methodology. It contains highly useful information for system designers. Another must read. (Note: as of this writing, James Rumbaugh, Grady Booch and Ivar Jacobson are all part of Rational Software Corporation. The "amigos" (as the triumvirates are known) are the people behind Unified Modeling Language [UML].)

8. Wirfs-Brock, Rebecca, et al. *Designing Object Oriented Software.* Prentice Hall, 1990.

9. Meyer, Bertrand. *Object Success: A Manager's Guide to Object Orientation, Its Impact on the Corporation, and Its Use for Reengineering the Software Process (Object O).* Prentice Hall, 1995.

*10. Benteley, Jon. *Programming Pearls.* Addison Wesley, 1989.

*11. Benteley, Jon. *More Programming Pearls.* Addison Wesley, 1988.

Whether you follow OOP or procedural programming, you should read these books.

12. Budd, Timothy. *An Introduction to Object-Oriented Programming.* Addison-Wesley, 1990.

13. Champeaux, Dennis, et al. *Object-Oriented System Development.* Addison Wesley, 1993.

14. Rist, Robert, Terwilliger, Robert. *Object-Oriented Programming in Eiffel.* Prentice-Hall, 1995.

*15. Cargill, Tom. *C++ Programming Style.* Addison Wesley, 1992.

This book tells you what not to do when developing software in C++. The information in this book is very useful to anyone writing C++ code.

16. Meyers, Scott. *Effective C++.* Addison Wesley, 1992.

A useful collection of 50 steps that any C++ programmer must remember. A good companion to have.

17. Murray, Robert. *C++ Strategies and Tactics.* Addison Wesley, 1992.

Contains some powerful strategies that C++ programmers can employ to improve their design/implementations.

*18. *Taligent's Guide to Designing Programs*: *Well-Mannered Object-Oriented Design in C++*. Addison Wesley, 1994.

Anyone contemplating serious software development in C++ should read this book. It contains invaluable information gathered from experiences in a large project.

19. Ellis and Stroustrup. *The Annotated C++ Reference Manual.* Addison Wesley, 1990.

The ultimate C++ dictionary. Some of the material here is now out-of-date due to changes in the language, but it is still very useful.

20. *The ANSI C++ Draft Standard.*

This is the ultimate and the most up-to-date C++ reference manual.

21. Stroustrup, Bjarne. *The Design and Evolution of C++.* Addison Wesley, 1994.

22. *The Usenix C++ Conference Proceedings*, 1987, USENIX Association, Berkeley, CA.

23. *The Usenix C++ Conference Proceedings*, 1988, USENIX Association, Berkeley, CA.

24. *The Usenix C++ Conference Proceedings*, 1989, USENIX Association, Berkeley, CA.

25. *The Usenix C++ Conference Proceedings*, 1990, USENIX Association, Berkeley, CA.

26. *The Usenix C++ Conference Proceedings*, 1991, USENIX Association, Berkeley, CA.

27. *The Usenix C++ Conference Proceedings*, 1992, USENIX Association, Berkeley, CA.

These proceedings contain a wealth of information about C++ and its usage in the industry.

28. Goldberg and Robson. *Smalltalk-80, The Language and Its Implementation.* Addison Wesley, 1989.

The only book you ever need to learn about Smalltalk.

29. Shlaer, S. *Object-Oriented Systems Analysis: Modeling the World in Data.* Yourdon Press, 1989.

30. Grimes, Jack D. *Objects 101—An Implementation View.* Digest of Papers, Compcon'94, 39th IEEE Computer Society International Conference, February 28, 1994, San Francisco, CA, IEEE Catalog N. 94CH3414-0, pp. 106–111.

31. Andert, Glenn. *Object Frameworks in the Taligent OS.* Digest of Papers, Compcon'94, 39th IEEE Computer Society International Conference, February 28, 1994, San Francisco, CA, IEEE Catalog N. 94CH3414-0, pp. 112–121.

32. Gamma, Erich and Helm, Richard. *Designing Objects for Extensions.* In Dr. Dobbs Sourcebook, #236, pages 56–59, May/June 95.

Index